Self-Deception and the Common Life

American University Studies

Series VII
Theology and Religion

Vol. 11

PETER LANG
New York · Berne · Frankfurt am Main

Lloyd H. Steffen

Self-Deception and the Common Life

PETER LANG
New York · Berne · Frankfurt am Main

Library of Congress Cataloging in Publication Data

Steffen, Lloyd H.
Self-Deception and the Common Life.

(American University Studies. Series VII, Theology
and Religion; Vol. 11)
  Bibliography: p.
  Includes index.
  1. Self-Deception – Moral and Ethical Aspects.
  2. Self-Deception – Religious Aspects. I. Title.
  II. Series: American University Studies. Series VII,
  Theology and Religion; v. 11.
  BF697.S754   1986   121   85-19812
  ISBN 0-8204-0243-5
  ISSN 0740-0446

CIP-Kurztitelaufnahme der Deutschen Bibliothek

Steffen, Lloyd H.:
Self-Deception and the Common Life / Lloyd H.
Steffen. – New York; Berne; Frankfurt am Main:
Lang, 1986.
  (American University Studies: Ser. 7,
  Theology and Religion; Vol. 11)
  ISBN 0-8204-0243-5

NE: American University Studies / 07

© Peter Lang Publishing, Inc., New York 1986

All rights reserved.
Reprint or reproduction, even partially, in all forms such as
microfilm, xerography, microfiche, microcard, offset prohibited.

Printed by Lang Druck, Inc., Liebefeld/Berne (Switzerland)

To my Father

Howard C. Steffen

in loving memory

TABLE OF CONTENTS

PREFACE ix

INTRODUCTION 1

    A. The Problem of Self-Deception 1
    B. Methodological Considerations 5
    C. Outline of the Essay 13

CHAPTER ONE
AN ORDINARY LANGUAGE ANALYSIS OF PROBLEMS 21

    A. The Deceptive Self-Relation 23
        1. Deception: The Initial Analysis 23
            a. An Ordinary Language Analysis 24
            b. The Moral Dimension 26
            c. The Religious Qualification 29
            d. Exceptions and Conceptual Complexity 30
            e. The Epistemic Deficit 32
            f. A Restatement of Problems 35
            g. Intention, Error and Deception 35
            h. Deception: Conscious and Unconscious Intention . . . 41
            i. Review of Intention Issues 44
            j. Self-Deception: Unconscious Intentions, Beliefs
               and Neurosis 45
            k. Cognition and Action: A Summing Up 48
            l. The "Doing" of Self-Deception and the Wishful Thinker 49
            m. The Problem of the Epistemic Object 52
            n. Action and Cognition: What the Ordinary Language
               Analysis Reveals 53
            o. From 'Deception' to 'Self': Restating the Problem . . 55
        2. Self: Holistically Conceived Self-Relatedness 56
            a. Analysis 56
            b. Toward Solution 63
            c. The Paradox Restated and Resolved 67
    B. Paradox 78
    C. Facts 90
    D. Conclusion 100

CHAPTER TWO
SELF-DECEPTION: THE PERSPECTIVE OF PHILOSOPHICAL PSYCHOLOGY 119

    A. Three Examples of Self-Deception 120

	B.	In Search of A Model	137
		1. The Cognitive Model	137
		2. The Translation Model	147
		3. The Action Model	153
		4. Freud and Sartre: Two Other Models	163
		a. The "Different Selves" or "Multiple-Agent" Model	163
		b. Sartre's Dialectical Model	177
		c. Conclusion	194
	C.	Synthesis: The Emotional Perception Account	195

CHAPTER THREE
SELF-DECEPTION: THE ETHICAL AND RELIGIOUS PERSPECTIVES 229

	A.	The Moral Perspective	233
		1. Self-Deception and Akrasia	233
		a. Akrasia: Voluntary Wrongdoing	234
		b. Self-Deception and Akrasia: Distinct Concepts	237
		c. Self-Deception and Akrasia: Related Concepts	242
		d. Voluntary Wrongdoing and Voluntary Ignorance	246
		e. Conclusion	260
		2. The Ethics of Self-Deception	262
		a. The Moral Issues	264
		b. Analysis of an Example: The Akrates as Self-Deceiver	265
		c. Three Conclusions	274
		d. The "Immorality" of Self-Deception	277
		1. Misconception: Moral Means Prudential	281
		2. Misconception: Self-Deception is Mendacity	292
		3. The Imprudence of Self-Deception	293
		e. Conclusion: The Benefit of the Moral/Prudential Distinction	296
	B.	The Religious Perspective	301
		1. Self-Deception and Sin: The Sin of Pride	303
		a. The Religious Perspective on Self-Relatedness and Sin	305
		b. The God-Relation	311
		c. Sin and Pride	314
		d. Pride and Self-Deception	320
		e. Theological Self-Deception: Some Descriptions	329
		f. Conclusion	339
		2. Self-Deception and Sin: Kierkegaard and "Despair is Sin"	340

CONCLUSION 375
BIBLIOGRAPHY 387
INDEX 403

PREFACE

In undertaking a study of self-deception, my primary objective was to restore 'self-deception' to its status as a problem so real that it affects--and threatens to affect--all of us in the common life. After surveying the vast and methodologically diverse literature on the topic, I found that so much confusion, so many unquestioned assumptions, and so many blind spots permeated that literature that a new study was in order. This recognition did little, however, to calm my disquiet or ease the frustration of sorting out the contradictory accounts. As I say in the text, everything that could be said on this topic has, in fact, been said. The problem is that little of it has been said in a way that renders the concept coherent and non-paradoxical.

Accounts of self-deception are launched at the point where certain relations governing the concept are accepted as givens; and I have entered the debate at these various points. Those relations--the self-relations of psychology, the self-other relations of ethics, the God-relation of theology-- guided my inquiry by framing issues, posing questions and establishing relevant theoretical assumptions. My "meta-perspective" is inspired by what today we might call the "inter-disciplinary" inquiry into questions about existence that was illustrated in the literature of Søren Kierkegaard. I accept Kierkegaard as one whose still relevant contribution to philosophy is a certain methodological stance. For all the irony involved in this project to make myself an expert in self-deception, I do not imitate Kierkegaard, for this is certainly not a poetic study. It is, however, dialectical, and it does concern itself, ultimately, with philosophical tangles only because they impinge on questions about how we live. This intellectual undertaking has had practical benefit for me, but the practical implications will have to be spelled out elsewhere.

For the reader who wants the benefit of this study without following me through the work of conceptual elucidation; and for the reader who wants to know if I recommend ways to avoid self-deception, I can say two things. First, those writers who think self-deception "cannot happen" are deceiving themselves about self-deception. In fact, the more I took this issue on, the more I began to appreciate the Kierkegaard who flashed on a simple but devastating critique of Hegel. That critique amounted to only one charge, namely, that issues of logic were being confused with questions about existence. Such confusion persists to this day in the literature on self-deception. Secondly, I can only urge readers curious to know if self-deception can be avoided to reflect on their own lives, to cultivate habits of self-confrontation, and to seek honesty in their self-relations no matter how painful the process. Inadequate though that be, that will have to suffice.

I am indebted to several people for helping me bring this study to a conclusion. First and foremost, I must thank the faculty of the Department of Religious Studies at Brown University to whom this study was originally submitted as a doctoral dissertation. The criticisms which I received from the Western Religious Thought faculty have made this a better, more readable work than would have otherwise been the case.

I am indebted to Sumner B. Twiss, who directed this work as a dissertation, stimulated the original inquiry and took me to task in the ethics section; to John Giles Milhaven, for his encouragement and cogent evaluations; and to Wendell S. Dietrich, who has set a standard of excellence that is a benefit, as well as a burden, for all privileged to study with him. Thanks also to John P. Reeder, who started me thinking about the implications of the moral/prudential distinction in Kantian ethics, a distinction I modify but make use of in Chapter Three. The critical eye of former teachers was looking over my shoulder throughout this work, and I express a debt of gratitude to D. Marshall Barry, Roger Hazelton, and Paul L. Holmer, all of whom, in one way or another, have affected what goes on in these pages. I have benefited from the criticisms of Dr. Robert Gibbs and Dr. Michael Fitzgerald; and I thank Dr. James M. Cahalan for discussing with me the implications of this study for literary analysis. Three other persons deserve a heartfelt "thank you:" Dr. Paul Lauritzen, who arranged for me to present my initial run at the ethics of self-deception issue at a 1981 New England Ethics Colloquium; Dr. Thomas P. Kasulis, my teaching colleague, for discussing this work as a dissertation and encouraging my efforts; and Ms. Cathy Steffen for various labors on my behalf, including the typing of the original dissertation.

I am particularly indebted to the National Endowment for the Humanities for a Summer Stipend that made it possible for me to prepare this study for publication.

Finally, for all of her support and tolerance, I thank Emmajane S. Finney, with whom I have shared a life of sorts on the the beautiful but bizarre Madeline Island.

July, 1985
Madeline Island
La Pointe, Wisconsin

INTRODUCTION

A. The Problem of Self-Deception

Self-deception is a feature of the common life.
    This is not to say that self-deception is simple or easily understood. Few features of the common life are. We can say, however, that what is identified by the concept 'self-deception' is within the reach of our linguistic resources and that the expression provides a conduit of intelligibility and serves to convey meaning. Persons employing the concept can be assumed to mean something by it when they use it, so there is significance in the fact, which is here noted, that they do actually use it.
    We put the linguistic expression 'self-deception' to work to perform various kinds of meaning tasks. In our linguistic community, we use the concept to identify, describe or otherwise demarcate a phenomenon with which we claim familiarity. Ideally, we who use the expression ought to be able to explain why we used it the way we did; but even if we find ourselves unable to give a strict definition, we can assume that because it was used, this expression was deemed preferable to others, that it, in fact, said what was meant. We expect our language to work on our behalf to say what we mean, and this expectation holds for any concept that would claim to be a part of our common life, the life we share as members of a common linguistic community.
    The language of 'self-deception' may not appear particularly difficult, and the assertion that self-deception is a feature of the common life may not appear controversial. We do, after all, use the language of self-deception in the common life, agreeing that that self-deception is not to be cultivated as a good of life; and if asked to say something about self-deception, most of us would remark that we would avoid self-deception if we could.[1] Despite this consensus about the meaning of the concept, even casual reflection on the idea of persons deceiving themselves raises the specter of misunderstanding, even unintelligibility. We would avoid self-deception, we say, but it is not immediately apparent that we can. Why? With that question we ask a question requiring deeper reflection, for now it looks as if self-deception is complex and that understanding it will require sustained attention and further thought.
    Although the concept 'self-deception' is a feature of our common linguistic life and the phenomenon itself is all too familiar in our experience, deep, sometimes dark, uncertainty surrounds this topic. Various disputes have arisen about the meaning of self-deception; and since even the most casual reflection on the meaning of the concept can occasion a furrowed brow, let us ask: Why the perplexity? What might the problem of self-deception be?
    We want to say, first of all, that self-deception poses a problem about description. If we hold to a certain model of deception, where one person, (a deceiver), who knows or believes something to be true, acts to mislead another

person's beliefs (the deceived), it follows by analogy that a self-deceiver is one who believes and yet somehow does not-believe. In self-deception, the deceiver would be identical to the deceived: the deceiver who believes is one and the same person with the deceived whose belief has been mislead. But how can a person both believe something to be true and also not believe it to be true?

To reflect on the meaning of self-deception this ways leads one to the conclusion that self-deception involves a paradox, for it suggests that one person or consciousness can play two incompatible roles simultaneously. How can that be? To ask that question is to acknowledge that self-deception is difficult to describe without contradiction, which is to say that self-deception raises a philosophical problem. On first glance, it appears that if self-deception does in fact refer us to such a contradictory state of affairs, it is an unintelligible and incoherent notion, a concept that cannot withstand the most superficial kind of philosophical scrutiny.

Yet the fact is that 'self-deception' is a meaningful linguistic feature of the common life. The fact is that persons who are linguistically endowed and initiated into the common life do have occasion to remark that "so-and-so is self-deceived." Rather than assuming that such a remark is itself incoherent or unintelligible, our assumption ought to be that this remark represents a meaningful communication that others, too, can and do understand. Furthermore, we can assume that using 'self-deception' this way identifies, describes or otherwise demarcates some feature of the common life--here a <u>psychological</u> feature, for 'self-deception' refers us to mental and behavioral characteristics of persons. How are we to reconcile the fact that 'self-deception' is employed as a meaningful cipher of communication with the prospect that the concept may be unintelligible? I do not propose to answer that question at this point. I only wish to suggest that this preliminary line of inquiry into the meaning of self-deception establishes that there is a <u>philosophical</u> problem here that needs to be addressed.

We could not proceed to further questions about self-deception if we did not first resolve the coherence and intelligibility problem. For a moment, however, let us assume that 'self-deception' is intelligible, our grounds being that persons actually use the concept to perform a variety of meaning tasks. Then we must consider another difficulty. Since self-deception is obviously related to deception, and 'deception' is subject to moral analysis and evaluation, as most of us would readily concede, should we not expect a moral issue to arise over 'self-deception'? Clearly, another kind of inquiry or philosophical task awaits one who would inquire into the meaning of self-deception. If a self-deceiver is the agent of a deception, does the self-deceiver <u>qua</u> agent warrant moral censure for that deceptive act? This, too, is a potentially complex issue, especially in light of the fact that there are cases of deception where no morally relevant consequences obtain, as in the misleading of belief occasioned by the magician or actor. And there is the not insignificant aspect of self-deception that makes the self-deceiver a "self-deceived" victim of deception, further complicating moral matters.

It is reasonable to assume that because a self-deceiver is, or can be understood to be, the agent of a deception, there is at least the possibility of a moral problematic pressing itself into a discussion of the meaning of self-deception. For the moment, moral accountability, not the degree of it, is the issue. Does self-deception lend itself to inquiry aimed at ascertaining moral accountability?

Other questions arise beyond this. If self-deception be a feature of the common life, could there be yet other contexts of meaning, other realms of discourse beyond the philosophical and the ethical, where 'self-deception' has actually been put to use and accorded status as an authorized cipher of meaning? I would answer this question in the affirmative, noting that religious thinkers have often used 'self-deception' for theological purposes. Perhaps, then, we should be open to the possibility that religious discourse is another context that requires our attention. Would an employment of 'self-deception' within such a context further our understanding of self-deception?

In order to respond positively to this last question, a case must be made that the concept of self-deception does lend itself to employment in other meaning contexts and that a religious context is indeed relevant. If 'self-deception' has been used to perform meaning tasks in a religious or theological context, then the particularities of this employment must be examined since the religious setting could significantly affect our ability to understand the full extent of the concept's meaning.

I shall argue in these pages that the concept 'self-deception' does lend itself to use in various contexts of meaning and that the religious context is relevant to any thorough inquiry into the meaning of self-deception.

In these pages I shall hold to the position that "To understand a concept is not simply to be able to define it but to be able to do the proper things with it."[2] One of the proper things to do with the concept 'self-deception' might be to investigate its use in a religious context. Such an investigation would, as I just suggested, further our understanding of self-deception in general, although it would enable us to see how self-deception has been used to illuminate certain religious ideas (e.g., "sin") in particular. Although a religious employment may appear vague at the moment, I reiterate the fact that religious thinkers have actually used 'self-deception' to elucidate features of faith and human being. That use would suggest that those who employed the concept in a religious context intended to communicate thought that was meaningful and capable of being understood.

The problem of self-deception, then, is not one problem, or if we say that there is a general problem of intelligibility, we should say that it is not a one-dimensional problem. It is potentially several problems; and thinkers from diverse perspectives--philosophical, ethical and religious--have contributed to the debate about the meaning of a concept by bringing the resources of their perspectives to bear on this problem of the common life, the problem of self-deception. As we shall see, self-deception is not only a topic of concern to philosophers and psychologists; but moralists and religious thinkers, as well as poets, novelists and playwrights, have found in self-deception a topic worthy of their attention and consideration.

The philosophical problems of coherence and intelligibility require immediate attention. After all, if self-deception cannot withstand the coherence test and is shown to be a piece of conceptual non-sense, employment of the expression in other contexts of meaning can be expected to do nothing save compound the non-sense. On a fundamental level, 'self-deception' must be shown to be a meaningful cipher of communication, an expression that has rules for correct employment, a concept that identifies or expresses a "meaning complex" that we as members of a linguistic community can use and understand.[3]

How are we to understand self-deception? What is it? How does it function? What are the conceptual issues involved? What are the empirical issues that might be raised if our employment of the concept implies that some actual behavioral phenomenon is described whenever we press 'self-deception' into service?

Self-deception requires conceptual clarification, but conceptual issues are not the only issues involved. There is an empirical issue at stake here, one related to a coherent description of the concept. After all, a concept that is shown to be unintelligible because it is self-contradictory can not be expected to provide empirical evidence to support the unintelligibility. On the contrary: If the concept 'self-deception' refers us to some fact about human behavior we should inquire into that issue to determine what evidence might support such a claim. In the end, we must resolve whether 'self-deception' is an appropriate use of language. Does this linguistic expression perform its function well? Does it identify a particular behavioral phenomenon without distortion? Or is it a misleading linguistic indicator? Does our use of the expression 'self-deception' represent a mistake in our use of language?

All of these questions pose significant problems for one who would seek to understand the meaning of self-deception. These problems are essentially philosophical, but we must understand that philosophical investigation need not necessarily confine us to problems of contradiction and coherence. Philosophical investigation will lead us to consider the meaning of 'self-deception' as it is authorized in other realms of discourse and contexts of meaning, to meaning "beyond" analytic claims or reductionist commitments.

The purpose of this extended essay is to investigate and elucidate the concept 'self-deception.' The aim here is not only to address the philosophical issues that concern an apparent contradictoriness and the necessary requirements for intelligibility, but to sort out the moral complexities that attend the concept and to urge consideration of a religious perspective as a fitting and proper move warranted by actual use. At the outset, I must state that the overriding interest of this essay is to advance an understanding of self-deception that will permit us to see the sense of a theological employment. It is already clear, however, that a concept that does not make sense when we scrutinize its claim to meaning in the context of everyday discourse is not going to be of much use elsewhere, in other, more specialized contexts, like the moral or religious. Having expressed a commitment to philosophical clarity, let me add that for the purposes of this essay, religious discourse will be assumed to be meaningful (contra A. J. Ayer). I mean by that remark that religious discourse is rule-governed discourse and that it stakes a claim on intelligibility. Therefore, if 'self-deception' is to play a role in religious thought, it can only do so on the basis of a prior determination that the concept is, indeed, intelligible. Religious language is language before it is religious.

Providing a justification for a religious employment is not my immediate concern. The first priority is to get at the meaning of the concept 'self-deception' as it is used by persons who intend by their use to share an understanding and to communicate that understanding in a meaningful way. To achieve this requires that we first attend to the philosophical problems that not only threaten the concept's claim to intelligibility, but render its value in a linguistic community suspect.

It is my intention to undertake a philosophical investigation of the concept 'self-deception' so that we might come to understand more thoroughly how the concept is and can be employed meaningfully. Therefore, I shall further outline my proposal, the next order of business being to consider the methodological underpinnings that will restrict the scope of this inquiry while shaping its advance.

B. Methodological Considerations

'Self-deception' is a philosophical perplexity. Various descriptions of the concept have been proposed to resolve specific difficulties, but like bad pennies certain fundamental problems keep surfacing, raising as many questions as they have answered. Taken separately, those questions represent specific obstacles to intelligibility, and, as I have noted, a failure to surmount those obstacles satisfactorily will result in our being faced with a contradictory notion. I reiterate my assumption that such a result ought not to obtain, for the fact that 'self-deception' has been authorized for use within our linguistic community indicates that on any actual occasion of its use, the tasks that are to be performed in virtue of having this concept (describing, referring, evaluating, judging) are intended to be meaningful rather than nonsensical. Beginning with this "natural language" assumption, I shall proceed to elucidate the concept 'self-deception,' addressing my inquiry to those obstacles that some claim challenge the conceptual integrity--and intelligibility--of the concept. My interest is in the meaning of the concept, and the several preliminary questions asked in the previous section can be distilled to precipitate an essential problematic: What is self-deception and how are we to understand it? This question will introduce the methodological considerations that will underwrite and guide this investigation.

The question "What is self-deception and how are we to understand it?" indicates that two issues are at stake, that they are interdependent and ultimately inseparable aspects of a single interrogative, which is inquiry into the meaning of self-deception. This is to say two things. First, "what self-deception is" can be understood to be a function of the actual use to which the linguistic expression is put by human subjects. Secondly, if our claim is that "what it is" cannot be considered apart from "how it is used,"[4] an inquiry into the meaning of 'self-deception' promises to be a complicated affair, for the task we are assigning ourselves is not to search for the <u>definition</u> of a word but to inquire into the meaning of a <u>concept</u>. This distinction calls for clarification.

If our interest were simply to define 'self-deception' such that the resulting definition reflected current standards of usage, we could ascertain the meaning of self-deception by consulting a recognized linguistic authority, say, the <u>Oxford English Dictionary</u>. We read in the <u>OED</u> that 'self-deception' is a noun that stipulates "the action or fact of deceiving oneself." As a definition, that is not only authoritative in that it comes from an authoritative source, but it describes essential, non-accidental features of the expression in terms that can be clearly understood. It is non-ambiguous, intelligible, neither too simple nor too complex; and in accordance with certain well-established rules for defining,[5] this definition meets the requirements for defining a word or expression. If we can further assume that the meanings of 'deception,' 'oneself,' 'act' and 'fact' are accessible in ordinary parlance, we can appreciate the fact that 'self-deception' is not only capable of being used, but that it is actually used in this linguistic community, and that people who use it intend by their use to communicate in a meaningful way. It should not come as a surprise to learn that everyone who has written on the topic of self-deception knows "what self-deception is" in this definitional sense. What this means is that questions about the meaning of self-deception arise as a consequence of having understood an ordinary, commonly accepted meaning for the expression found, for example, in the <u>OED</u>.

What happens, however, when we say about the <u>OED</u> definition that in spite of knowing <u>what</u> it says, or <u>that</u> it says such-and-such, the <u>definiens</u> stipulated by the <u>OED</u> is in some fundamental way uninformative? Would it be paradoxical to suggest that we can <u>define</u> self-deception yet claim in the same breath that we are unclear about the meaning of 'self-deception'? We can resolve this apparent paradox by distinguishing the sense it makes to say, on the one hand, that we have the definition of a word at our fingertips, from the sense it makes to say, on the other, that we have acquired an ability to use a concept. This way of speaking highlights the fact that meaning is not synonymous with definition, that meaning is broader and deeper than definition, that meaning does not hang only on linguistic form, but involves the interests and purposes of the linguistic subject, the person who speaks.

Definitions are concerned with the meaning of words in a sentence (formally: definitional meaning). Concepts, however, are concerned with the meaning implicit in linguistic activity, the meaning that issues from considering how people use words and sentences to help themselves comprehend things (formally: meaning as use).[6] A concept is by definition "what is meant (or imagined) by the term used to designate it."[7] A definition is restrictive with respect to meaning--it is word-centered. A concept is complex and empowers the person using it in linguistic and non-linguistic ways. A concept is subject-centered[8] and activity-related.

The definition of a word, which one can have at one's fingertips, functions more or less to overcome informational deficits that arise because, for some reason, one does not know the commonly accepted meaning of a word, or the meaning stipulated by the user. A definition serves a purpose, a linguistically necessary purpose, which is to inform us about the meaning of a word when that meaning is not clear from the word's position in a context of words that are understood. The kind of knowledge deficit specified here is like that facing a person who does not know particular vocabulary items. One may think of a person studying word lists while learning a foreign language, or a person who checks the answers to a Reader's Digest quiz, or the person who does not recognize the force of a word like "corrigibility" in a technical philosophical discussion. Each of these persons has need of definitions, and by consulting authoritative reference sources of one sort or another, the person can act to overcome the knowledge deficit in a way that is quite literally "at one's fingertips." With respect to 'self-deception,' a definition like that found in the OED can remedy such a deficiency. The "act or fact of deceiving oneself" stipulates an exact meaning for 'self-deception,' circumscribing that meaning in accordance with strict rules of usage; and this, as I have said, serves a purpose.

In light of these remarks about definition, it is necessary to note that the concepts we use do not, for the most part, meet the standards of exactness stipulated by a definition: "For remember that in general we don't use language according to strict rules; it hasn't been taught us by strict rules either."[9] Furthermore,

> For not only do we not think of the rules of usage--of definitions, etc.--while using language, but when asked to give such rules, in most cases we aren't able to do so. We are unable clearly to circumscribe the concepts we use; not because we don't know their real definition, but because there is no real 'definition' to them. To suppose that there must be would be like supposing that whenever children play with a ball they play a game according to strict rules.[10]

Concepts do not function to remedy knowledge deficits or to provide a calculus of strict rules. Neither is a concept a circumscribed essence of meaning. A concept presents a more complicated picture, a "meaning complex" if you will. Concepts express what we can do rather than what we ought to know. Because concepts are subject-centered and activity-related, "having acquired a concept," as opposed to "having a definition," indicates the extent to which we are disposed to do certain things in virtue of having a concept at our disposal. A concept expresses a kind of achievement level for the person putting it to work. Its employment in actual situations will indicate an individual's capacity for use and reflect his or her competence as a user.

The picture of concepts being sponsored here can be illumined with an example. In his attempt to explain how the concept 'religion' is to be understood, William James made use of an analogy to 'government.' He was concerned, first of all, to show how the concept 'government' differs from its definition, and, secondly, to show how 'government' expresses a "meaning complex" rich in possibilities for meaning and use:

> If we should inquire for the essence of "government," for example, one man might tell us it was authority, another submission, another police, another an army, another an assembly, another a system of laws; yet all the while it would be true that no concrete government can exist without all these things, one of which is more important at one moment and others at another. The man who knows governments most completely is he who troubles himself least about a definition which shall give their essence. Enjoying an intimate acquaintance with all their particularities in turn, he would naturally regard an abstract conception in which these things were unified as a thing more misleading than enlightening.[11]

The meaning of 'government,' then, is not to be had by abstracting an essence or simply defining a word. Meaning is to be had, rather, by acquiring an intimate acquaintance with the concept in the complexity of its particulars. An actual employment of the concept 'government' will therefore express some aspect of this intimate knowledge--it will mean what the person using it authorizes it mean for some intended purpose. Its use will reflect a personal ability to target meaning and elicit understanding. Its use will speak from a context to a situation, connecting through imagination a person's interest and picture of things to an acquired linguistic skill. If 'government' requires an intimate acquaintance, a "knowing how" (Ryle), in order to be understood; if 'government' can serve a wide variety of linguistic purposes and reflect a great many personal capacities; if 'government' can be meaningful at the very moment 'government' defies capture by a strictly-ruled definition, isn't James right to ask, as he did, "And why may not religion be a conception equally complex?"[12] James' question shall be ours: Why may not self-deception be a concept as complex as others which are familiar features of our common linguistic life?

If the kind of particularities associated with the concept 'government' were to be included in a definition, the result would be a very long and complicated definition indeed. It would be so long and so complicated, in fact, that it would no longer serve the purpose of a definition, or serve as one. Yet the fact remains that those particulars mentioned in James' statement are all important aspects of the concept. By examining those particulars, we discern the "meaning complex" that is the concept; and our interest in understanding the meaning of the concept will press us to consider more and more of those particularities so that, in the end, investigating "how the concept is used" to perform specified meaning tasks reveals to us the meaning complex itself. The result is a more complete picture of the concept and "what it is."

We, too, are interested in a complex concept, and just as James prepared to investigate the meaning of religion via the 'government' analogy, we are preparing to investigate the concept 'self-deception.' Our interest is not in defining a word but in coming to understand the meaning of a concept, doing so by acquiring what James called an "intimate acquaintance" with our topic--in its buzzing hub-bub of particularity.

Consider some ways 'self-deception' is used: A philosopher uses self-deception to illustrate a logical contradiction. A psychologist describes the dynamics of neurosis and repression by invoking 'self-deception.' A person who denies that his or her behavior amounts to anything more than friendship toward another's spouse is said by friends to be "protesting too much" and gripped by self-deception. A person who dreads the dentist "conveniently" forgets a dental appointment. A person suffering a serious, perhaps terminal illness talks about going back to school and getting a law degree. Reflecting on past action, a person says that he did not do what he knew "deep down" was the right thing to do. A theist, having discerned a form of despair wherein a person exhibits a lack of self-understanding as well as understanding of the God-relation, offers a theological remark that characterizes such disrelationship as self-deception.

About all these uses one may say that the concept 'self-deception' has been used to perform certain meaning tasks: describing, evaluating, interpreting, judging, explaining. By employing the concept 'self-deception,' the employer is able to understand and communicate to others some aspect of the world, here, a specific feature of human behavior. The concept, however, is not used in an exact way, as if one precise and circumscribed appeal to the meaning of the concept fits the psychological, philosophical, moral or religious contexts in the same respects. Rather, each context is said to authorize an employment for certain purposes, and consistent with those purposes the concept is put to work and works meaningfully.

These various employments share a formal structure, though the particulars of meaning are hardly collapsible. A philosopher shows that the concept 'self-deception' is incoherent and contradictory, thus an existential impossibility. Another philosopher presents self-deception as a feature of existence part and parcel of the moral life (e.g. Sartre's "bad faith"). Yet another kind of thinker offers the view that self-deception pertains to issues of ultimate concern, issues about the meaning of life, as one finds in the works of Tolstoy.[13] Yet another employs 'self-deception' to explain how certain kinds of exclusivistic attitudes arise and become dominant on a broad cultural level,[14] while another explains that 'self-deception' is implicated in such invidious social phenomena as racism or sexism.[15]

As James' government analogy showed, concepts can be used to emphasize certain features on given occasions or under certain circumstances. We can therefore talk about 'government' in terms of all kinds of particulars--assembly, army, budgets, etc.--none of which is government, each of which is necessary if we are to become intimately acquainted with 'government.' Generally speaking, the ability to discern the complexity of a concept develops over time and emerges with the gradual increase in linguistic power. The meaning of a concept is built up as we expand our linguistic horizon through training and practice, as questions are pressed consistent with particular interests, as society and culture make demands on linguistic ability and personal capacity. As our linguistic horizon broadens, we become increasingly familiar with the subtlety and complexity of a concept, and that increased ability expresses an increased power to discriminate with the language. Acquiring a concept enables us to do many things that express competence and control. In a more reflective mood, let me say that acquiring a concept enables us to grasp the "fullness of being" which is our true desire; for, as linguistically endowed creatures, we understand ourselves in relation to speech, and speech is understood to be integral to and expressive of our true humanity. And acquiring a concept allows us to become intimately acquainted with the world and ourselves through the awesome and mysterious power of speech.

In order to understand how a concept is acquired, we must attend to the dialectic in which the linguistic community authorizes a concept, which it creates, to become an objective cipher of communication that all can meaningfully share. Actual employments of 'self-deception' express the fact that our community has conferred on 'self-deception' conceptual status, which is to say that this meaning complex has been authorized for use in the common life of this linguistic community. As such, many things can be said about self-deception and many things inquired into, not least of which are the problematic particulars of the OED definition--'deception,' 'oneself,' 'act' and 'fact.' As James' example of 'government' showed, a concept is actually used in a variety of ways to perform a variety of meaning tasks, and just as 'government' expresses a complexity beyond the range of strict definition, so, too, 'self-deception' must be investigated so that we can, amid the complexity, come to "comprehend things" as Wittgenstein said.

These remarks on concepts clear the way for the methodological concerns that will advance--and restrict--this inquiry into 'self-deception.'

1. My purpose is to conduct an investigation of 'self-deception.' By that I mean that I shall conduct a conceptual analysis. It is by now clear that in seeking the meaning of a concept I am not simply seeking the meaning of a word or definitional meaning,[16] for a definition, like the OED, begs the very questions with which a conceptual analysis is concerned, namely: "Is self-deception a fact?" "Is it an act?" "How is it related to 'deception'?" "What restrictions and conceptual adjustments are imposed by the 'self-' prefix?" These are questions that pertain to the ostensive meaning of the concept. They are the problems, not--as might be inferred from the definition--resolutions of problems.

In order to address these issues and thereby elucidate the meaning of the concept, I shall take a methodological cue from the "analytic tradition" of modern philosophy. While this can mean many things, one contemporary meaning of "analytic" philosophy is that it is philosophy concerned with the actual workings of language. "Analyzing a concept," then, constitutes a philosophical task that requires the philosopher to attend to the distinctions and everyday examples that are embedded in ordinary discourse. Language can be likened to a toolbox,[17] and the distinctions and examples provide the "tools" that enable us to examine the problems, subtleties and ambiguities associated with linguistic relationships, hence with the meaning of concepts themselves. Since 'self-deception' is actually employed in different kinds of statements, the task of the philosopher is clear: "We are to ask what is done by the use of the statement. . . . We shall find out by finding out what the utterance of that statement enables us to do."[18] By finding out *that* 'self-deception' can be used to do many different things, we find out how these uses authorize the concept to be meaningful in different meaning contexts. 'Self-deception' is featured in discussions involving behavior, cognition, emotion, volition, logic, empirical data, ethics, even religion; and none of these contexts can single-handedly define the concept, though each contributes necessarily to the meaning complex that is the concept. By investigating these featured uses, we come to understand the concept in the complexity of its particularities, and this is the purpose of a conceptual analysis.

As another slant on this presentation, let me say that for the purposes of this essay, a point of view sympathetic with "ordinary language" philosophy will be adopted. That is, I shall view everyday discourse as adequate for philosophical use, assuming by that view that ordinary language itself presupposes a structure or view of reality that is correct.[19] I am thereby refusing to approach 'self-deception' as a technical term. With "meaning as use" functioning as a kind of heuristic principle, the idea of context dependence generated by that theory of meaning will enable us to shift from one kind of employment to another, from, say, a philosophical-logical to a religious employment. These moves may appear disruptive or discontinuous, and, in a sense, they are. But the different types of employers will assume different premises and philosophical commitments, thereby generating different problematics. It is only by respecting the apparent discontinuity of employments that we can build up the concept in its complexity. This approach, which is edifying in that it "builds up" the concept in its richness and subtlety, will enable us to acquire the form of understanding--the intimate acquaintance--we seek.

2. As a systematic inquiry into self-deception, this essay will rely on the resource opportunities and restrictions provided by the analytic-linguistic tradition. As a complement to that general methodological position, and because of my stated interest in examining a religious employment, I shall take further cues, both methodological and substantive, from the literature of Søren Kierkegaard. Kierkegaard has often been used as such a complement,[20] and despite obvious problems that arise because of the pseudonymity issue, the Kierkegaard corpus can be viewed as contributing in a unique way to our understanding of self-deception. It could even be argued--though it is not my purpose to do so, for this is not to be a study about Kierkegaard--that the entire corpus can be read as having a discernible preoccupation, both implicitly and dialectically, with self-deception.[21]

Kierkegaard's pseudonymous authors, even Kierkegaard himself (i.e., non-pseudonymously), attend to the problem and phenomenon of self-deception. The authors scrutinize it, or scrutinize characters experiencing it, or inadvertently illustrate and exemplify it. A particular author's interest in self-deception will always appear through a point of view that is consistent with a deeper existential stance. I wish to suggest that our contemporary literature on the topic of self-deception reflects a similar situation and that critics of that literature can profit by heeding Kierkegaard's diagnostic procedure. It is perhaps trivial to say that the way 'self-deception' is investigated reveals the interests and commitments of the perspective involved in the investigation, but even so, it is of the utmost significance to recognize this very fact. Without attending to this "subjective" aspect, we shall not appreciate a particular author's problematic, the kinds of questions being asked or the kinds of solutions being offered. Disparate interests explain the wide variety of accounts, the incompatibility of accounts, and the confusion that results from saying about self-deception everything that can be said, from: "Self-deception cannot happen" to "Self-deception is an empirically verifiable fact."[22]

I shall follow Kierkegaard in one unconventional methodological tack. I shall assume the problematic, the question at issue, as it has already been formulated within a particular context of philosophical interest and commitment. My aim, like Kierkegaard's, is to exhaust the "givens," not simply to refute them. They will collapse as they run their course--and I seek to show that, not simply critique a misstep here or a logical problem there. Kierkegaard's corpus-wide attention to self-deception reveals an approach to the concept, a method if you will, that not only presages the contemporary discussion in overt ways, but that also enables us to comprehend how a particular point of view addresses itself to 'self-deception' such that certain conclusions necessarily follow.

Kierkegaard's approach permits us to sort out particular issues as they arise, in context, with respect to the perspective whence they issue. Like Kierkegaard, I shall let others set the agenda of issues (e.g., the paradox of self-deception, akrasia, etc.) for I accept the fact that certain issues provide a savory chew for one kind of thinker while others feed at different troughs. My analysis will respect the philosophical commitments and interests of these many voices, for it is only by such a show of respect that I can exhaust what they have to offer, thereby pushing the analysis on to other kinds of considerations. In the end, this approach permits us to understand self-deception in its relational complexity, as a "meaning complex," without also finding ourselves constrained to say that self-deception is just one thing, or that we have now defined it, or that we have acquired the strictest rules that allow us to employ it in a similar way on all occasions. By showing us how to respect relational contexts (psychological, ethical, religious), Kierkegaard provides a methodological complement to what was written above concerning the "analytic tradition." Although it should not be apparent to the reader once we get underway, Kierkegaard's methodological innovations will continue to direct the argument, for Kierkegaard has, in a provocative though unconventional way, inspired this study.

C. Outline of the Essay

Having taken care of these methodological chores, let me outline for the reader the actual course of this study.

In the first chapter, I shall expose certain problems that threaten to undermine fundamental intelligibility, drawing these problems from what are essentially well-established and accessible aspects of the term's definiens. I shall examine via an "ordinary language" analysis how self-deception is related to 'self' and 'deception,' for we must know if the language works and if it can be trusted. Then shall the problem of paradox be discussed, followed by a separate treatment of the empirical issue: Is self-deception a fact of human behavior as stipulated by ordinary usage?

In the second chapter, I shall examine 'self-deception' from the point of view of philosophical psychology, looking at the various models that have been proposed to elucidate the meaning of the concept and render it intelligible. My aim here is to see if we can develop an adequate description of the concept philosophically. In putting forth my own "emotional perception" theory and in taking an integrative approach, I shall argue that 'self-deception' can be shown to be intelligible and meaningful in the face of challenges to that claim.[23]

My third chapter will concentrate on the moral issues that attend 'self-deception.' In addition to examining the issue of <u>akrasia</u>, which certain philosophers have associated with self-deception, this chapter will also present examples that will help us to ascertain under what--if any--circumstances self-deception can be said to represent a moral failure. The issue here is this: Does conceptual analysis reveal that 'self-deception' is <u>always</u> a moral failure? If it can be shown that 'self-deception' need not entail as a necessary part of its description an actual moral failure, we not only further expose the richness and complexity--and ambiguity--of the concept, but also make the point that a moral employment represents a specific conceptual rendering. I shall argue that to use 'self-deception' as a term of unmitigated moral censure is not warranted by the facts of use, nor by the relational context of the moral domain itself. An absolutist "always immoral" position will be shown to misrepresent relevant facts and ignore conceptual particularities, the result being, ironically, a moralizing that reveals a deeper moral insensitivity.

My third chapter will also seek to connect 'self-deception' to religious concern and theological discourse. The most obvious connection to be made will be the applicability of the concept 'self-deception' to the religious awareness associated with the concept 'sin.' The family resemblance between the two will be described, and I shall show how this resemblance cuts across Catholic, Reformed and Lutheran lines. Self-deception, I shall argue, is a theme in Christian thought, both ancient and modern, and I shall examine a variety of viewpoints to show a consistency of usage and meaning, paying particular attention to Kierkegaard's exposition of 'double-mindedness.'

Finally, having elucidated the meaning of the concept by describing its employments, I shall suggest certain strategies for overcoming self-deception. To be included here are general remarks about the role of reflection and its cultivation and how reliance upon certain virtues that give rise to habits of confrontation may prevent self-deception from obtaining. There will also be an investigation of the idea that religious faith can be considered a strategy for avoiding self-deception, even if religious truths are ultimately illusory (i.e., eschatologically falsified). The backdrop for these remarks will have been provided in previous description and analysis, so the remarks at the end are intended to be suggestive rather than comprehensive.

As a final methodological qualification, let me add that this is a study in Western Religious Thought, one specifically focused on the existential strain of Christian reflection. Self-deception is, finally, a concept that has been put to work by Christian theologians who have, perhaps surprisingly, used the language of 'self-deception' correctly while arguing that self-deception can infect the spiritual life and cast out happiness. In other words, Christian thinkers have long understood that self-deception is a feature of the common life, and they have performed the hard work of elucidating the concept 'self-deception' amid other theological labors.

This study is intended to demonstrate to a theological community that has been in the woodshed for a long time now sharpening its methodological tools that we must at some point put those tools to work to build something. We must, that is, don an apron and clutter the workbench. The work will be basic, for it will be nothing less than elucidating concepts that express our complexity as persons. The workshop may become a very busy place, with lots of curious heads peeping in to see what's going on; but the door will be open so that other perspectives and possibilities may contribute to the conversation about the world around us and within us, the conversation that will consider all that pertains to our humanness. This study is meant to illustrate how theology can be done today, and my purpose is to construct one concept relevant to that discussion, the concept 'self-deception.' Although some will consider this study nothing more than prolegomena, and its method so indirect as to be irrelevant, my hope is that it will locate a topic that is vital to theological reflection. Doing theology today requires conversation with other voices. In this particular study, the voice of the the psychologist, the linguistic and analytic philosopher, the ethicist, the literary artist, and the theologian will be heard. The theological voice is one among many, yet without the theologian to speak on behalf of the possibility of transcendence, we shall neither grasp the deeper significance of the common life we share, nor acquire an understanding shaped by the intimate acquaintance we seek. The theologian has much to learn from conversation with other disciplines and perspectives, but also much to contribute.

This study will not read like theology: I hope that will not obscure my point, but make it.

INTRODUCTION

[1] Guy Durandin conducted a survey that queried typical linguistic users about their understanding of 'self-deception.' The results confirmed that people do use the linguistic expression to describe or explain some aspect of human behavior. They hesitate, however, to ascribe the concept to themselves, even as a past event. Durandin concluded that his survey had provided an actual occasion for eliciting self-deceptive behavior. See Guy Durandin, Les Fondements du Mensonge (Paris: Flammarion, 1972), pp. 195-398.

[2] Paul L. Holmer, The Grammar of Faith (San Francisco: Harper & Row, 1978), p. 140.

[3] For a more complete discussion of concepts as "meaning complexes" see Holmer, ibid., pp. 136-158.

[4] This is a claim widely advanced in the literature of modern linguistic philosophy. For a review of major statements of a "meaning as use" position, see William Alston, "Meaning and Use," The Philosophical Quarterly 13 (1963), pp. 107-24; reprinted in The Theory of Meaning, ed. G.H.R. Parkinson (Oxford: Oxford University Press, 1968, 1978), pp. 141-165. My aim is not to present a defense of this position, but to use it, believing it to be defensible. For more on the idea of "knowing how" see Gilbert Ryle, The Concept of Mind (New York: Barnes and Noble, 1949, 1970), p. 60.

[5] See Peter A. Angeles on "Rules for Defining" in Dictionary of Philosophy (New York: Barnes & Noble, 1981), pp. 55-56. A more thorough discussion of definition is Raziel Abelson, "Definition" in Encyclopedia of Philosophy, II, (New York: Macmillan Publishing Co. & The Free Press, 1967), ed. Paul Edwards, pp. 314-24.

[6] Ludwig Wittgenstein, Remarks on the Foundations of Mathematics, trans. G.E.M. Anscombe (Cambridge: MIT Press, 1967, 1975), p. 194: "And concepts held us to comprehend things. They correspond to a particular way of dealing with situations."

[7] Angeles, Dictionary of Philosophy, p. 42.

[8] This "subject-centered" theory of concepts is prominent in those modern philosophers of language who consider concepts to be fundamentally "subjective." See, for example, Peter Geach, Mental Acts (New York: Humanities Press, 1957), p. 13: "A concept, as I am using the term, is subjective--it is a mental capacity belonging to a particular person;" ". . . no concept at all is acquired by the supposed process of abstraction" (p. 18). I prefer using "subject-centered" because "subjective" is a red flag for so many. In a formal sense, this theory of concepts is associated with what is known as the dispositional account. This view holds that concepts dispose one to act in virtue of having acquired them, that they are subjective, but because of 1.) common environment and 2.) social training and education, we share concepts and there develops a "standard repertory of concepts held in common by virtually all members of a given cultural or linguistic group." (See P.L. Heath, "Concept," Encyclopedia of Philosophy, II, p. 179.)

[9] Ludwig Wittgenstein, The Blue and the Brown Books (New York: Harper & Row, Harper Torchbook, 1965), p. 25.

[10]Ibid.

[11]William James, The Varieties of Religious Experience (New York: Modern Library, n.d.), pp. 28-29.

[12]Ibid., p. 29.

[13]Authors interested in psychological presentation often illustrate self-deception through characterization. Shakespeare, Melville, Hawthorne, George Eliot, Henry James, Eugene O'Neill, Gide constitute a representative sample. For a discussion of self-deception and "meaning of life" issues as dealt with by Tolstoy, see Ilham Dilman & D. Z. Phillips, Sense and Delusion (New York: Humanities Press, 1971), esp. the chapter by Dilman, "Self-Deception."

[14]Michael Foucault has argued that Western social attitudes toward sexuality are essentially self-deceptive. See his History of Sexuality, I: An Introduction, trans. Robert Hurley (New York: Random House, Vintage Books, 1980), p. 33.

[15]See Sara Ann Ketchum, "Moral Redescription and Political Self-Deception" in Sexist Language: A Modern Philosophical Analysis, ed. Mary Vetterling-Braggin (Totowa, NJ: Rowman & Littlefield, 1981), pp. 279-289.

[16]I note that the very idea of talking about the meaning of a word this way has been challenged, but further pursuit would cause us to stray from our inquiry. For reasons behind the conclusion that "The phrase 'meaning of a word' is a spurious phrase," see J. L. Austin, "The Meaning of a Word" in Philosophical Papers, 2nd ed., eds. J. O. Urmson & G. J. Warnock (Oxford: Oxford University Press, 1970), p. 78.

[17]The picture of language being pressed into service here is derived from the later Wittgenstein. See his Philosophical Investigations, 3rd. ed., trans. G. E. M. Anscombe (New York: Macmillan Co., 1958, 1969), esp. p. 12, no. 23: ". . .the multiplicity of tools in language."

[18]J. O. Urmson, Philosophical Analysis: Its Development Between the Two World Wars (New York: Oxford University Press, Galaxy Book, 1967), p. 179.

[19]For more on this matter, one may consult Wittgenstein's Philosophical Investigations, The Blue and the Brown Books. For more detail, see Lloyd H. Steffen, "Self-Deception: A Conceptual Analysis in Three Relational Contexts" (Ann Arbor: University Microfilms, Brown University dissertation), pp. 32-33.

[20]See for example D. Z. Phillips, Faith and Philosophical Inquiry (New York: Schocken Books, 1971); Norman Malcolm, "Anselm's Ontological Arguments" in The Existence of God, ed. John Hick (New York: Macmillan, 1964), pp. 66-68. For further discussion of this point, see Andrew J. Burgess, Passion, 'Knowing How' and Understanding: An Essay on the Concept of Faith (Missoula: Scholars Press, 1975); Essays on Kierkegaard and Wittgenstein, eds. Richard H. Bell and Ronald E. Hustwit (Wooster: College of Wooster, 1978).

[21]This point has served as the organizing principle for a recent introduction to Kierkegaard's thought, John Douglas Mullen, Kierkegaard's Philosophy: Self-Deception and Cowardice in the Present Age (New York: New American Library, Mentor Book, 1981). This is a book about Kierkegaard, not about

self-deception. Self-deception is presented as a major theme of the literature, which it is, as other scholars too have noted.

[22]Consider for example the conclusion of M.R. Haight, <u>A Study of Self-Deception</u> (Atlantic Highlands, NJ: Humanities Press, 1980), p. 73: "I have argued that self-deception is literally a paradox. Therefore it cannot happen." This is to be contrasted with the studies of Sackeim & Gur (see Bibliography), which are discussed in the next chapter.

[23]I would note that this philosophical-psychology approach is <u>one</u> way to analyze the topic at hand. Certain of its proponents see it as the only way. I warn my reader that this analysis should not be read--for the purposes of this essay--as if it were my own point of view. It is not. The point of my analysis is to show that the philosophical psychology perspective generates conclusions about self-deception based on commitments, both philosophical and existential. Ironically, many spokespersons of this perspective would refuse to concede that their approach is in some fashion "subject-centered." That is, of course, a small illusion, but one not without consequence.

CHAPTER ONE

SELF-DECEPTION: AN ORDINARY LANGUAGE ANALYSIS OF PROBLEMS

The philosophical literature that has been proliferating for two decades around the topic of self-deception would suggest to even a casual peruser that 'self-deception' is a philosopher's find. A great many prospectors have staked out a claim on this promising philosophical territory. A few have even claimed to have discovered in the murky waters of conceptual confusion a description that glitters with promise. There is no fever here, but the topic has attracted attention, and philosophical assayers have worked hard to establish clarity and separate the dross. An ever-increasing body of literature about self-deception has emerged.

Interestingly enough, the problems that first provided the focus of attention persist to this day. An important epistemological controversy continues to unsettle: how is self-deception to be conceived, its structure described and its dynamics explained, non-paradoxically? Beyond that, self-deception has taken on increasing stature as a moral issue. It is now generally admitted that self-deception plays a role of some importance in the ethical theories of such diverse thinkers as Plato,[1] Bishop Butler,[2] Hegel,[3] and Sartre.[4] Every new account of self-deception proceeds having determined that preceding work has begged questions or otherwise left crucial issues unresolved. It is not unusual to find a new claim being staked out on already prospected land: ". . .the problem still awaits convincing theoretical treatment"[5]; ". . .all attempts by other philosophers to provide an analysis of self-deception are, sad to say, not adequate."[6]

Our ability to understand the concept 'self-deception' is significantly affected by the fact that after twenty-five years of focused attention, genuine interest and competent treatment by philosophers of standing and ability, self-deception has not yet met with "convincing theoretical treatment." In one sense this is not itself surprising. With due respect: philosophers do not often agree about things, and we do not expect them to. If there is no broad philosophical consensus about self-deception--what it is and how we are to understand it--neither is there any such consensus about other fundamental conceptual issues, including language theory, knowledge and its foundations, the nature of the self or God, and so on. The disagreements about 'self-deception,' however, go deep enough to challenge the very coherence of the concept. Were that challenge to prove successful, 'self-deception' would be precluded from playing a role in our common linguistic life.

With certain exceptions,[7] the controversy surrounding the topic of self-deception in philosophical circles can be said to represent neither a fruitless debate within an enervated discipline, nor, in a more technical sense, specific failures by individual philosophers to bring their projects of elucidation to successful conclusions. The debate, rather, concerns <u>what it</u>

_is_ that makes itself available to investigation.

For some, there is nothing there but a word. David Kipp has written, and it is certainly true that, ". . .neither the mere existence of the word 'self-deception' nor frequent use of that word in common language suffices to guarantee the existence of what the word literally means."[8] Accordingly, there are some philosophers who have argued that there can be no such thing as literal 'self-deception,' a position that implies that our common use of the term is a kind of culture-wide mistake, as if 'self-deception' were functioning in our language akin to 'unicorn:' a word we are familiar with, but a word without a corresponding reality. How 'self-deception' does function in our language is an issue of paramount importance. It is therefore the first issue I shall tackle.

My concern in this chapter is to clarify the problems that arise in light of ordinary language features. By that I mean: How do we understand 'self-deception' if we understand _deception_ to be such and such, or _self_ to be a relational qualifier that can significantly alter conceptual structure and linguistic dynamics?

'Deception' and 'self' constitute two obvious targets for an investigation into the meaning of 'self-deception.' Since our aim is to elucidate meaning and expose problems on the basis of ordinary language features of the concept, we shall begin here, with the language itself our resource. Following this linguistic analysis, I shall address the paradox issue. Then, in a separate but related exposition, I shall examine the facticity issue: Is there an actual phenomenon of self-deception to which our use of the expression meaningfully points? Strictly speaking, this is an empirical rather than a conceptual issue. But it is appropriate to address it here because our ordinary language analysis--even the OED definition itself--reveals that we intend by our use of this linguistic expression to refer to something phenomenally actual and empirically factual: the _fact_ of deceiving oneself. The question is: What evidence can be marshalled to support this claim? Is there any such evidence? If there is, how is it to be interpreted? I shall examine these issues and discuss the relevance of empirical investigation to the kind of conceptual analysis being undertaken in these pages.

A. The Deceptive Self-Relation

'Self-deception' obviously entails a deception. The nature of that entailment is not, however, self-evident, so we ask: In what respect and with what assurance can we properly speak of 'self-deception' as a deception? Secondly, how is one person able to assume the dual, and apparently contradictory, roles of deceiver and deceived required for a deception? These are the problems that confront us at the outset of our investigation. Analysis of 'self-deception' in light of these questions reveals that there is reason to hold that a deception perpetrated by one person (deceiver) on another (deceived) is phenomenally distinct from a deception that occurs intrapsychically and that the phenomenal distinction is embedded in a linguistic distinction. This in turn reflects the fact that 'deception' and 'self-deception' are distinct concepts--separate, though related.

1. Deception: The Initial Analysis

A person, let us call her Nora, is seeking a job. Having just dropped out of college because she did not complete her final graduation requirement, a senior thesis, she moves to a new city to be near friends. She is short on experience, but very bright and capable. She knows that she would like to work in the mental health profession on a practical level, perhaps as a psychiatric aide. This is an entry level position that would give her experience, and because she is capable and could advance on merit, she decides to seek such a position. While preparing her resume and filling out standard job applications, she discovers, much to her chagrin, that a college degree is required for even the entry level position of psychiatric aide. She therefore doctors her resume to state that she did in fact receive a bachelor's degree. The application she submits at a hospital requires that she sign a statement declaring that all information on the application is true to the best of her knowledge. A hospital personnel officer reviews her application and checks out her references, though he does not ask about her academic credentials or otherwise require proof of graduation from college. Nora is offered a job as a psychiatric aide, which she accepts. We can say about Nora that she deceived her new employer about her credentials.

This is a quite common example of deception.[9] In describing this deception we will note that first of all, Nora wants something--a job. Although she is technically unqualified for the position, she is perfectly capable of handling it. This is not only her belief but the belief of the personnel officer who hires her. On one point of her application, Nora misrepresents herself, leading the personnel officer to believe by her explicit misstatement of fact that she has a college degree when she does not. Nora knows that she has not met the requirement that all psychiatric aides have bachelor's degrees, but in order to be considered for the position, in order to prevent herself from being disqualified solely on the basis of this academic requirement, Nora falsely states that she has met the requirement. If the personnel officer knew that Nora were not a college graduate, he would not approve her application. Nora also knows this. She therefore lies to him. It is her intention to misrepresent herself, she enacts that intention, and she achieves her desired result by so doing. By leading the personnel officer to accept as true what is not true, she deceives the personnel officer into approving her hiring, thereby accomplishing the intended purpose of this project to mislead another's belief.

a. An Ordinary Language Analysis

This deception can be analyzed by pointing out relevant conceptual features.
    1.) Nora <u>intended</u> to deceive someone for a certain reason.
    2.) Nora <u>knows</u> what is and what is not the case with respect to her credentials.
    3.) She <u>acts</u> to create an epistemic deficit between herself and her potential employer, effecting this by making an explicitly false statement that is presented as true.
    4.) By her deceptive activity, another person (the personnel officer) comes to believe or assume something to be true that is not true, which is the <u>result</u> consistent with Nora's intention.
    5.) The deception is occurrent when Nora's original intention is actually achieved, which is when the personnel officer finds no obstacle to her employment on the basis of credentials.

Intention, knowledge and successful results are generally recognized features of an occurrent deception.[10] A more minimalistic description might simply hold that Nora knows p and misleads another into believing <u>not-p</u>.[11] I shall hold to the prior analysis, however, for it provides a more adequate account of the commissive deception perpetrated by Nora on the personnel officer. Our description is not complete at this point; more needs to be said.

    Certain <u>relations</u> are involved in this deception. There is a primary interpersonal relation involving the participants themselves. That is, Nora's deceptive act involves two persons and a relation to the truth. By this I mean that Nora, as <u>deceiver</u>, knows the truth about p. If p is taken to be a proposition that states "Nora has earned a bachelor's degree," Nora knows p is a false statement and knows it to be false at the very moment she asserts that p is true. In the occurrent deception, Nora maintains epistemic access to the truth of p. She knows that the claim that p is true is a false claim, and she knows that p is being asserted as true in order to mislead the other person into thinking that p is true--again, for specific reasons.

    The other person in this relation, the <u>deceived</u> (personnel officer), believes he knows the truth about p. His belief is justified because an assertion "that p" on a resume or job application is equivalent to saying "p is true," and Nora assumes that her statement about credentials will be believed. Nora's deception, however, has prevented him from acquiring full or actual access to the truth about p. The result of the deception is that he knows that p is being asserted as true and he believes it to be true, but he does not know that it is actually false.

An epistemic deficit appears in the gap between what Nora and the personnel officer believe to be true about p. Nora knows p is false, the personnel officer does not. The personnel officer is in error about p, but through no fault of his own. He is in error because he has been deceived. Nora has deceived him about the truth of p, and an epistemic imbalance exists. Nora knows that the personnel officer does not know the truth about p, for the personnel officer is unaware that p is false, and, furthermore, he has good reason for believing p to be true. Should the personnel officer discover that p is false, the epistemic imbalance will be restored to equilibrium and the deficit will be eliminated.

In speaking about a relation to the truth about p, it is of course necessary to point out that our example does not cover all features of every type of deception. Deception is a complex concept, and this example, as given, illustrates only one type of deception, deception by commission, a readily accessible form to be sure, a deception simpliciter: a deception in which one person misleads another person into acquiring a (false) belief.[12]

This example has the virtue of presenting certain features of deception in a straightforward way. Nora's epistemic awareness vis-a-vis the truth about p has not been challenged in this example. Nora knows that p is false, for she knows that she did not graduate from college. In another situation, however, it could be that a deceiver is mistaken about the truth of p: intending to deceive another, the deceiver could inadvertently deceive the other into believing not-p, which, as it happens is true. The result of this belief-misleading project would be that the deceived holds a true belief. Is this still a deception? Since a formal falsehood is tied to the intention of the deceiver (Aquinas), we could say that a formal deception still obtains even though there is no material deception. Inasmuch as the intention is to enact a belief-misleading project, it is appropriate to identify this case as a deception, for "falseness is beside the intention of the speaker."[13] By this qualification we further intensify the notion that 'deception' is an intention-related concept, which reinforces the position that in ordinary discourse, when we say that Smith deceives Jones, we mean by that that Smith deceives Jones intentionally.

As a meaning complex, as a concept that authorizes many rule-guided employments, 'deception' is sometimes used in such a way that the intention feature is relaxed. We can sometimes speak of an unintentional deception, though I hasten to add that such a use is generally so qualified that using 'deception' to refer to a particular unintentioned act is like resorting to "second-string verbiage"--a qualified, modified, and not totally inappropriate use, but a use that is not, so to speak, "normal."[14]

A bare-boned example of an "unintentional deception" might look like this: Smith believes p to be true and convinces Jones that p is true. However, p is not true, so Jones has been unintentionally but materially deceived. Or, for example, if I cross over into another time zone and forget to reset my watch, I would deceive anyone who, in asking me for the time, believed my inaccurate response to be a true report of the time. We could say that I deceived the person inquiring about the time, but normally, other first-order remarks would suggest themselves prior to ascribing this error to deceit on my part. The "deception" I would have perpetrated on another individual as a result of failing to adjust my watch would represent something more akin to an extended error than to a normal, first-order employment of 'deceit.' That is, having realized my mistake, I would not, let us say, avoid acknowledging that I was responsible for misleading another's belief. By accepting responsibility for initiating another into a false belief, however, I make it clear that I wish to attribute the cause of the error to an unintentioned blunder on my part. So I would say "I was mistaken" or "I forgot to reset my watch" or even "I was stupid." These are explanations that are also "excuses," excuses in the sense that I seek to assure others about my intentions. By accepting responsibility for an error that I have inadvertently extended to another, I accept responsibility as the actual agent of another's false belief. Yet I do this so that I can mitigate another kind of responsibility, namely, that which falls to the person who intends to mislead another into believing what is not the case. But why is confessing stupidity preferable to admitting that I intended to deceive another? This brings us to another feature of our description of deception, the moral dimension.

b. The Moral Dimension

Because the realm of morals is concerned with values and human action and because moral reasoning occurs with reference to the duties and responsibilities that fall on each member of a human community, it is clear that the concept 'deception' invites moral scrutiny. Rational persons desire protection from deception, "for to be deceived generally increases one's chances of suffering evil or lessens one's chances of obtaining those things which one is seeking."[15] With this remark, we can say that there are self-interested or prudential reasons for the rule or action guide "Don't deceive," reasons which may be associated with a "duty of prudence;"[16] but beyond this, it is clear that a rational person would censure deception for moral reasons. A rational person could argue, for instance, that a moral principle that states "one ought not to deceive others" is a universal moral requirement expressing the right of persons to be free from deception in their relations with others and that, ideally, a universal agreement or contract exists between persons on this point. Moreover, an ordinary, first-order employment of 'deception' can be said to specify an intention-related concept that is appropriately employed with reference to any of a number of particular actions (overt or covert) that have the effect of tearing at the fabric of moral obligation, violating moral norms, or otherwise subverting interpersonal contract. By the act of deception, a deceiver infringes on the rights of others, so that deception qualifies as a justice issue. Deception disrupts interpersonal relationships,[17] and, more fundamentally, violates a person's own moral integrity (Kant).[18] Deceitful conduct, from a moral perspective, sets one "in opposition to the conditions and means through which any society is possible"[19] and, as our example of Nora and the personnel officer illustrates, undermines a basic trust.[20]

For all these reasons, a deceiver is generally denounced by society and deemed worthy of moral censure. The deceiver acts in such a way that he or she subverts the conditions of trust and undermines the requirements of truthfulness deemed essential to the harmonious functioning of society (to be Hobbesian about it), not to mention the more fundamental moral evaluation that attends the deceitful act, which is this: deceivers abase themselves and thereby renders themselves unworthy of happiness. Deceitful action demonstrates a lack of good faith in community; and it violates the requirement that our speech acts and interpersonal conduct reflect a basic respect for persons by being well-intentioned and supportive of moral principles of truthfulness. It must be reiterated that it is <u>intention</u> that comes under the scrutiny of moral reasoning. As Kant said, "If all men were well-intentioned it would not only be a duty not to lie, but no one would do so because there would be no point to it."[21]

The fact, however, is that persons are not always well-intentioned. Not all persons seek to promote the flourishing of others, especially at their own expense. As a means to an end, prudence may dictate that deceit is a permissible expedient in realizing certain desired ends, and these ends may themselves be well-intentioned (e.g., Nora's desire to "help people") or involve real moral dilemmas (e.g., lying to protect innocent refugees from their Nazi pursuers). What is certain is that 'deception' does factor into the moral life as an intention-related concept. It is a concept related to freedom and responsibility and it involves the interests of the moral community. 'Deception' is a moral problem for it is action that abuses of freedom. It is a form of self-abasement or self-mutilation that deprives persons of certain valued goods of life, for deceivers impede their own efforts to achieve fullness of being and constitution as moral persons. Motives of self-aggrandizement can be attributed to the deceiver, motives which dispose the person to act such that moral requirements and moral agreements are overridden.

A moral analysis of deception will note that a deceiver can expect to receive censure not only from external moral authority, but from conscience as well. The deceiver is intimately acquainted with his or her own act. The deception is self-abasing and (potentially) harmful to others, and the deceiver is privileged to know his or her own purpose in undertaking to mislead another's belief. A deceiver is therefore likely to experience guilt or regret as a result. Guilt is the subjective concomitant to the deceptive act. It is experienced through related affective states, such as remorse or anxiety, and the weight of those affective awarenesses may prove so burdensome that relief is to be found only in acting to restore the epistemic imbalance with the deceived. Acknowledging the deception through confession would accomplish this end. The person who forgets to reset the watch and unintentionally misleads another person into believing it is two o'clock when it is not may feel badly, even stupid, for being the author of such an extended error. But this calls forth a qualitatively distinct self-evaluation and affective response from that which would attend the intentional deceiver either during an occurrent deception or after its exposure. I would mention parenthetically that the fear of moral censure may be so great that the exposed deceiver may feign 'self-deception' in order to blunt the force of moral condemnation or reprisal: better to be thought stupid, even self-deceived than to be thought a person either willing to act unjustly by deceitfulness, or disposed to ". . .carve out his own egotistical way to his own, and if necessary at the expense of other, ends."[22] Having subjected 'deception' to a preliminary moral analysis, having described an intentional deception and taken into account its subjective moral accompaniment (guilt), let us return to the example of Nora and the personnel officer to get the moral picture.

Nora is a liar. Her intentional misrepresentation of her credentials to the personnel officer constitutes an act that violates a duty on Nora's part to act in accordance with a prescription not to lie or deceive for reasons of personal advantage. Her act is self-aggrandizing. She breaks moral rules in order to achieve a clearly defined purpose. By subverting other-regarding ends for self-regarding reasons, she adopts a strategy of action whereby the personnel officer is treated as a means to an end. As a result, Nora can be said to have acted in a manner that is non-other-regarding, morally disrespectful, and fundamentally unfair. She violates the personnel officer's trust in her truthfulness, for the personnel officer has taken Nora's application to be an accurate self-report worthy of his trust beyond any formal statement Nora may have signed to that effect.

This too is morally relevant: Were the personnel officer to discover later that Nora lied on her application, policy would dictate that Nora be fired. The officer would do so regardless of the quality of Nora's work, even if it had been exceptional from the moment she went to work as an employee of the hospital. We can assume that the hospital would sanction this move, but, even more importantly, a socio-ethical norm would sanction the reprisal. "Society" might even urge legal action beyond the firing. Moral reasoning would consider the facts and urge that Nora be fired for having broken a moral agreement about which Nora's consent can be reasonably assumed through some version of the universalizability principle. Nora, it would be argued, acknowledged an obligation to be truthful when she actually signed a statement and affixed her name to what is essentially a promise to represent herself and her credentials in a trustworthy manner. When Nora lied, she compromised her moral integrity by violating the moral conventions of her community and by acting contrary to those principles and prescriptions which Nora herself could be expected to hold about right action, namely, principles concerning what she ought to do regardless of inclination or the prospect of personal advantage.

By her deliberate and explicit deception, Nora has diminished her worth as a moral being. By taking a position under false pretenses, she has made herself doubly contemptible in a moral sense: first, in the eyes of her community, which would adjudge her action a violation of the basic norms governing social harmony and just interpersonal relationships; and secondly, in her own eyes. She has abased herself and could be expected to feel guilty, even remorseful, about what she has done. Does Nora actually feel remorse? We can assume it, but our example does not establish that. The example as presented has not probed Nora's mental states except to say that she did have a purpose in deceiving the personnel officer and that without deceiving him her purpose would not have been realized.

c. The Religious Qualification

Can we say more about deception? Our description can be extended to include concerns raised from the religious point of view. We can justify including this voice in our discussion because it is commonplace that religion has something evaluative to say about deception. Religion will say that deception is sinful. In a religious context, 'deception' is understood to be an act that has a depth of meaning not captured in a moral evaluation. "The meaning of 'sin,'" writes Rudolf Otto, "is not understood by the 'natural,' or even by the merely moral, man;" for sin carries a specifically religious surplus of meaning, is to say that sin indicates a sense of "numinous unworthiness or disvalue [that has been] transferred to and centered in moral delinquency."[23]

The religious perspective looks beyond natural limitation to see in any deceptive act a more profound disruption in the human heart. The sinful act points to a disrelationship between finite and infinite, expressing a deeper violation, a willful abuse of freedom that constitutes ". . .the denial, negation, and conscious and deliberate destruction of the reality which is created by God and which consists in God. . . ."[24] The deceiver, like any sinner, acts such that his or her sin can be taken as rebellion against goodness, rebellion against God. It is, in one view, a self-divinizing pretense to being God, a prideful protest against finitude: ". . .egoism is the driving force of sin, dishonesty its final expression.[25] Moreover, sin expresses despair, for it manifests itself in the absence of "faith, hope, and charity." The guilt associated with sin is not equivalent to moral guilt, since what is at issue is a specifically religious sense of unworthiness. Here the context of evaluation and judgment is governed by the "numinous" realm of meaning and value, by a God-relationship. Moral inquiry can proceed quite independently of such considerations.

'Deception,' then, is wrong from both a moral and a religious point of view, but the reasons for condemning the deceiver differ dramatically. Different relations are involved in each context, and those relations determine the nature of the analysis and affect how evaluations will be made.

d. Exceptions and Conceptual Complexity

The example of Nora and the personnel officer is only one of several kinds of deception. Yet, as a result of this explicit deception by commission, we have advanced our understanding of the concept 'deception' by, first of all, clarifying that a first-order employment entails intention, knowledge, results, purposeful action, moral reference and religious evaluation; and by, secondly, highlighting the complexity of the concept. That complexity is made manifest when one considers the fact that the grammar of 'deception' governs exceptions to some of the first-order uses (an unintended belief-misleading action).

In light of our moral analysis of deception, and in tandem with the reference to exceptions, lets us clarify the issue by asking: Are all deceptions moral violations?

The answer to this question is "Decidedly not." Deception is a multi-faceted concept; its status as a moral concept is contingent. Nora's deception of the personnel officer is morally objectionable; but the person whose belief-misleading action deceived another person about the time, as in the other kind of example, would not come under a moral description in any overt way. Nora invites moral censure, but the unintentional deceiver in the other case does not. There are, after all, honest mistakes. There are unintended errors that mislead others' beliefs but do not, on that account, invite moral censure. Even Kant was able to say that "not every untruth is a lie,"[26] and I would add: not every belief-misleading action, even if intended, provokes moral censure. This last qualification invites us to consider one other exception to our ordinary understanding of deception.

We can think of certain kinds of deceptions that are intentional, yet seem exempt from moral accountability.

As the result of his acting ability, an actor who plays Hamlet may deceive us into believing he is Hamlet for the time he is on stage. A magician may deceive us into thinking he pulled a pigeon out of thin air or a rabbit out of a hat. A teacher may deceive students into thinking that he or she personally believes p is true in order to force the students into questioning the truth of p, which they would not normally question because of the teacher's authority. These kinds of deceptions evade strict moral accounting.

These examples of non-moral but intentional deceptions must, however, be qualified. When a person decides to attend the theater, or witness a magic performance, or attend a class in which the teacher uses a Socratic teaching method, the <u>intention</u> to deceive is either made clear explicitly or can be inferred from the context. That is, if Mr. Geelgood who plays Hamlet fails by the quality of his performance to make me believe that the person I see on stage as Hamlet is a real person with real problems, then his <u>failure</u> to deceive me is also a remark on his performance. In a sense I go to see Hamlet in order to be deceived. It is Mr. Geelgood's intention to deceive me, mine to be deceived. It is clear that no epistemic deficit exists, though one might be "created" temporarily in the context of a dramatic performance. Since, strictly speaking, no actual epistemic deficit exists, one of the necessary conditions that permits a deception to come under moral scrutiny does not obtain, hence no moral censure, only aesthetic criticism. Yet it is still possible to talk about the performance as a belief-misleading project that achieves its intended purpose, so one can argue, with qualification of course, that the use of 'deception' in this instance is justified.

'Deception' may be authorized for use in these cases as suggested, but, again, as a matter of first-order preference, we do not use the language of 'deception' when the language of 'performance' is so readily available for unqualified use. The aesthetic language of 'performance' appropriately suspends the rules of moral appraisal. To use 'deception' here is to use it loosely. That is because as a matter of the first-order, 'deception' plays a role compatible with moral appraisal. A remark about the performance of Hamlet in terms of 'deception' may make sense and even be appropriate given sufficient qualification, but it constitutes a <u>satellite</u> meaning, a use of second-order verbiage.

The use of 'deception' in aesthetic rather than moral contexts, or in referring to unintended but extended errors, or as a term that connotes error by misjudgment--all of which may be said to issue in belief-misleading projects--are exceptions to a first-order use. When we employ 'deception' in a first-order way, we usually mean to make a moral evaluation, and we are usually bent on evaluating the person's intention. To call a person a deceiver is to evaluate his or her intentions as unworthy of the person <u>qua</u> moral agent. By considering these exceptions to first-order use, we further expose the complexity of the 'deception' concept, and this may prove relevant to our examination of 'self-deception,' a concept at least as complex. Because we can reasonably assume that 'self-deception' is analogous to 'deception,' we must consider two possibilities: one, that there are satellite meanings for 'self-deception' as well as 'deception'; and secondly, that those satellite meanings may provide the point of contact between the two concepts. In other words, our justification for saying that 'self-deception' is a 'deception'-related term may depend on an analogy to some second-order meaning of 'deception.' Let us consider further how 'deception' and 'self-deception' are related.

e. The Epistemic Deficit

By considering the analogy of 'self-deception' to 'deception,' we resort to the most ordinary kind of linguistic evidence as the most obvious clue to meaning. The OED definition discussed previously made exactly this move, and while that definition did make sense, I also suggested that it was inadequate and uninformative with respect to conceptual meaning: How does one deceive oneself? How does one deceive oneself?

In order to answer these questions, we must keep in mind the concept 'deception' and the guidelines that govern its use. Literally speaking, the concept 'self-deception' refers to a belief-misleading project directed by the self against the self. Analyzing 'self-deception' from the 'deception' pole leads one to this conclusion: if a deceiver is one for whom an epistemic deficit obtains interpersonally, a self-deceiver is one for whom an epistemic deficit obtains intrapsychically. The epistemic state of affairs in an instance of self-deception would compare neatly to a first-order self-other deception, for in both cases an intentional project to create an epistemic deficit between p and not-p is successfully enacted. 'Self-deception' literally refers to this epistemic state of affairs in an intrapsychic context. Analogy to a first-order 'deception' gives rise to this description, though how the intrapsychic epistemic deficit referred to by the expression 'self-deception' is possible, either logically or existentially, is neither obvious nor, at this point, clear.

Adherence to the first-order model of deception permits us to preserve an essential harmony between 'deception' and 'self-deception.' The difference lies in the fact that the parties involved in a deception, the deceiver and the deceived, have been transferred from an interpersonal to an intrapersonal context. Making this move raises troublesome issues, for it appears that a single individual must hold two contradictory beliefs (p and not-p) simultaneously, a description that is on first glance hard to swallow. Furthermore, the end result of the belief-misleading project appears to require that the self-deceiver not believe the very thing he or she does believe. This is a puzzling notion that commits one either to the idea that the self-deceiver is unaware of one of the held beliefs, or that the very idea is paradoxical, even logically contradictory: we can't both believe p and not believe p at the same time.

In a deception we can establish the fact of an epistemic deficit between deceiver and deceived by either getting the deceiver to admit his or her true position with respect to p, an admission at odds with his or her deceptive claim about p; or by establishing the fact of that deficit through independent evidential corroboration. A friend of Nora's could, after all, find out about Nora's lie and come forward with evidence to discredit Nora's claim about the truth of p. In self-deception, however, we must ask: what would count as evidence for the assertion that the self-deceived person both believes, and intended to believe p and not-p? What would count as evidence that an eventual disavowal of p is the result of an intentional self-directed maneuver?[27] In short, what evidence could establish that a person is, in fact, self-deceived, meaning by that that the person has directed a project aimed at the misleading of his or her own beliefs--and succeeded? If we are going to claim that self-deception, like deception, yields an epistemic deficit, we must marshall such evidence and defend this way of describing the state of affairs constitutive of self-deception.

A picture of 'self-deception' that strictly conforms to the first-order deception requires the following kind of description: a self-deceiver is one who believes p is true, but because he or she has reasons for wanting not-p also to be true, the person engages in certain maneuvers that are intentional with respect to this desired end, and, consistent with that intention, actually becomes able to believe that p is false while also being aware that p is, in fact, true. This is not only complicated, but it presents a picture that looks existentially unfeasible and logically untenable. That is because it pictures a contradiction: the deceiver believes p to be true when he or she either knows that p is false or has good reason to suspect p is not-true.

This contradictory result stands in the way of declaring 'self-deception' a coherent and intelligible concept. From a philosophical point of view, it is this paradox that must be eliminated or resolved. As it stands, the idea that a person can believe to be true what he or she knows to be false defies the conventions of logic and the conditions of coherence that any meaningful statement must satisfy. A person cannot both know and not know p in the same respect at the same time. This is the paradox of self-deception that has badgered the philosophical community, and it is this apparent contradiction to which I, too, shall refer when invoking the "epistemological paradox" of self-deception.

Evidence must be found to support a meaningful use for the expression 'self-deception.' If a strict analogy to a first-order 'deception' should prove inadequate, then another description must be offered. Support for using 'self-deception' as a deception-related term must be enlisted from other quarters. Let us remember that 'deception' can be used to mean an honest mistake or an unintended error. Will 'self-deception' be rendered intelligible by invoking one of the satellite meanings of 'deception' and using that satellite meaning as our clue to the meaning of 'self-deception'?

If so, a self-deceiver could be said to be one who has misled his or her own belief, which is to say the person holds a false belief p but does so unintentionally. On this description, the person in question is still responsible for the 'deception' directed toward the person's own self, for clearly the self-as-agent is the author of mistaken belief about p. Furthermore, holding the person responsible for the mistaken belief about p is not equivalent to holding the person morally accountable. The problem, however, is that if we describe such a 'deception' without intent and view the 'deceiving' action as lacking purposefulness, we not only take such a deception out of the domain of moral scrutiny, but, on this view of things, we render the meaning of 'self-deception' indistinguishable from the concept 'error,' whether innocently or through misjudgment. The question, of course, is whether this will suffice. Clearly it will not. The ordinary language features that could make 'self-deception' a near relative of 'deception' proper, complete with action, intention, and an epistemic deficit, are entirely severed. Making 'self-deception' a synonym for 'error'--and on this view of things any error would be equivalent to 'self-deception'--violates our sense of family resemblance between 'deception' and 'self-deception.' In the common life, we do not employ 'self-deception' to describe or refer to every or any conceivable error.

The case has also been made that the meaning of 'self-deception' is to be associated with a pretense on the part of a "self-other" deceiver, who, having been "discovered," feigns a case of self-deception in order to mitigate culpability and moral censure. Here 'self-deception' is meant to be a peculiar form of interpersonal deception. This position has been advanced,[28] but it is question-begging. A deceiver could only pretend to be self-deceived--and succeed--if there already existed a common consensus within the linguistic community about the meaning of self-deception, a meaning that was not equivalent to 'pretense.' The pretender would have to rely upon a reasonable assumption that what he or she did in the process of feigning self-deception could, in fact, be mistaken for the real thing. Furthermore, the victim of the pretense would mitigate moral accountability only to the extent that he or she understood "mitigation of responsibility" to be a consequence of ascribing 'self-deception.' In order for Smith to deceive Jones into believing that Smith is self-deceived, both Smith and Jones must be able to recognize 'self-deception' as a feature of the common life, one that can be identified according to behavioral evidence and certain easily accessible conceptual criteria. Curiously enough, this "pretense" argument has been advanced by at least one philosopher (M. R. Haight) who has found 'pretense' to be a meaningful use for the expression while claiming that 'self-deception' itself is conceptually unintelligible and the phenomenon identified by the literal expression cannot happen. A person can indeed feign self-deception, but to argue that this is the normative meaning of the concept seems to me thoroughly confused.

f. A Restatement of Problems

It is clear that on the basis of an ordinary language analysis, certain features of 'deception' beg questions when applied analogously to 'self-deception.' My purpose here is to formulate those questions as problems. The following issues are raised when considering the relation of 'deception' to 'self-deception':

First of all, does self-deception involve an epistemic deficit as a necessary feature of its description, meaning by that a cognitive conflict involving beliefs or knowledge? My response is that on the basis of ordinary language features, the belief-misleading project that is 'deception' does describe an epistemic deficit; but then the question is, "Can this deficit be transferred to 'self-deception' or does 'self-deception' come under another kind of description?" The problem: On the one hand, it is clear that the paradox of self-deception can be traced to the contradiction that results when an interpersonal epistemic deficit is transferred to an intrapsychic context. On the other hand, were we to avoid using the language of cognition so important to 'deception' would we not run the risk of escaping the orbit of even a "satellite" meaning of deception, thereby rendering the linguistic expression thoroughly idiosyncratic with respect to 'deception'?

Secondly, I have suggested that intention is a contingent feature of 'deception.' It is not readily apparent, however, that the same thing can be said about 'self-deception.' The question is this: Is there a use of 'self-deception' analogous to this contingent employment of 'deception,' i.e., a non-intentional or unintentional meaning? The problem: If non-intentional or unintentional deception can be considered of a piece with error or mistaken judgment or even forgetting, then what would be the meaning of an unintentional 'self-deception'? What is the meaning of 'self-deception' if it is authorized for an employment analogous to the "extended error" form of 'deception' (e.g., the person who unintentionally misleads another into believing it is two o'clock when it is really only one o'clock)?

g. Intention, Error, and Deception

One could argue that 'self-deception' is analogous to the unintended form of 'deception.' The evidence of ordinary linguistic usage will not support this position, however, for we do not use 'self-deception' to mean an unintended self-directed belief-misleading project. And even though the grammar of 'error' assumes someone to be responsible ("self"), our everyday use of 'error' does not refer to an intended act whereby one creates an intrapsychic epistemic deficit for which the person is morally accountable. 'Self-deception' then, is not equivalent to the redundant idea of an "unintended error" for which someone is responsible: that is what 'error' means.

Even if we grant that a self-deceived person seems to be mistaken or in error about the truth of p, our ordinary use of 'self-deception' suggests that when this expression, rather than some other, is employed for some referential or descriptive purpose, we mean that the person has some forward-looking reason for action (intention), some desire acting on the will to cause it to act (motive) such that an error results. In other words, a self-deceived individual is one whose "mistake" or "error" is willed, intended and motivated. To state this idea simply: As a linguistic community, we, typical linguistic users, have not authorized 'self-deception' to include in its description a contingent notion of intention. In this, 'self-deception' is not like 'deception.' There are, as we showed above, authorized uses for the idea of an unintended deception, for it is proper to speak about persons who unintentionally mislead the beliefs of other persons. And even though this is not, as we also indicated, a first-order meaning for 'deception,' we must say that on this point there is no equivalent use for 'self-deception.' Put positively, every instance of 'self-deception' is intentional. While intention is a contingent feature of the concept 'deception,' it is a necessary feature of the concept 'self-deception.' An "unintentional self-deception" is either to be regarded as 1.) meaningless or 2.) a misleading euphemism for 'mistake' or 'error.'

Some far-reaching consequences follow from this analysis, and these consequences pose further difficulties. Thus far, I have said that if intention serves a contingent role in 'deception,' then there are intended deceptions (Nora's lie) and unintended deceptions (misleading a person inquiring about the time into believing it is one time when it is, in fact, another). What happens, however, if we introduce the idea of an "unconscious intention," meaning by that that a person intends to act a certain way, but is unaware of the reasons or causal factors that constitute the intent. The person still acts, but he or she does not acknowledge the reasons for the act or connect the act to the proper intention, which is "unconscious," so that it looks like the person has blundered, or erred, or made a mistake. The person will still ascribe an intention to the act, but because the act is inconsistent with the professed intention, the person is confronted with an inconsistency that is publicly observable as an error.

I shall argue here, in distinguishing 'deception' from 'self-deception, that reference to an unconscious intention adds little of significance to a description of the results obtained from a picture of deception-as-error; but the notion plays an important, even necessary role in making sense out of the concept 'self-deception.' Ordinary linguistic analysis leads us ineluctably to the conclusion that if 'self-deception' is necessarily intentional, the idea of an intrapsychic epistemic deficit will only become coherent if we consider the possibility that the intention giving rise to the self-deceiver's 'error' is operative and being made manifest in action unawares.

There is, to be sure, a real dispute about the role of the "unconscious" in self-deception.[29] We have already seen that 'deception' and 'self-deception' differ with respect to the intention feature--it is contingent in 'deception' and necessary for 'self-deception.' But we must clarify the kind of intention involved in self-deception. Ordinary language requires that we introduce a satellite meaning of intention (i.e. "unconscious intention") in order for 'self-deception' itself to make sense. Intention, even though it is a formally shared feature of both 'deception' and 'self-deception,' cannot simply be transferred from one concept to the other in material particulars. It is assumed here that if 'self-deception' be related to 'deception' as ordinary language suggests, then intention, which is a first-order conceptual feature of 'deception,' ought to be relevant to the concept 'self-deception' in an analogous rather than an idiosyncratic way. An ordinary or typical employment of 'self-deception' suggests that the condition of the person described as 'self-deceived' is this: that the condition is the result of self-directed action, that it is intended, and that the person is in some way responsible for the epistemic situation.

Non-intentional or unintentional 'deception' can be classified as an error, a misjudgment, or a mistake. An unintended 'deception' yields the same result as an error. We must keep in mind, however, that 'error' can describe the result of an "unconsciously intended" self-deception, that is, a self-directed belief-misleading project that has a purpose of which the person in question is unaware. Whether the deception be unintended or unconsciously intended, either description results in an error. On the first description, one can say that a person has arrived at an incorrect conclusion due to an honest mistake or an unintended lapse or blunder: "I forgot to reset my watch after I changed time zones so I was deceived about the time." This means I unintentionally erred and even extended that error to another who inquired about the time, the person I "deceived." I can explain this error by saying, "My memory deceived me," which would appeal to a marginal or satellite use of 'deception,' but not a meaningless or unauthorized use.

On the other hand, according to the second description ("unconsciously intended self-deception"), the error, which is intentional, results from a conflict between competing and contrary intentions, one of which is held unconsciously. The error, then, is not an "honest mistake" or an error simpliciter (i.e., unintended), but is itself the result of purposeful, intended or motivated action. The difficulty is this: What looks to be an error is more than an error. It is, in fact, what we might term a "willful forgetting," an "intended error," a "willful ignorance." Since Freud advanced such descriptions in order to account for certain behavior in the neurotic, I shall briefly present a Freudian perspective on the form of intention that self-deception appeals to, a satellite intention: "unconscious intention."

"Forgetting--that is, a failure to carry out--an intention--points, as we have said, to a counter-will that is hostile to it."[30] In Freudian psychoanalytic theory, the statement "My memory deceived me, hence I erred" can be analyzed such that the resulting error can be traced back to a specific intention at odds with a person's own understanding of the intention. By extirpating that "hidden" intention, one could theoretically explain the dynamic of conflicting intentions, which produces what is publicly observable as an error--a person's "failure to carry out" an avowed intention. According to Freud, intention affects action, but there are cases where the intention that affects action expresses itself contrary to a consciously professed intention. In other words, the person acts contrary to his or her own interpretation of the intention--"I forgot." "I erred." "I blundered." Although a person need not be preoccupied with thinking about what he or she intends to do even in even the most simple descriptions of intention, the Freudian picture is that the agent can dissociate him- or herself from an awareness of an intention that actually governs subsequent action, such an intention being one that disposes the person to act a certain way even though the action is inconsistent with stated aims. Furthermore, Freud says that a person who accomplishes this dissociation does so for certain reasons. Another way to say this is that what will appear as an error is actually intentional or motivated behavior. That is, <u>reasons</u> for committing the error may be inferred even though the person who has blundered or forgotten cannot fathom the reasons. The person will comprehend neither the motives, which are hidden, nor the specific intention satisfied by the behavior, which is manifest as an error.

A person, then, for certain reasons (motive), may, while interpreting his or her own behavior as being consistent with avowed intention B, do something that is inconsistent with intention B though consistent with a contrary but unconscious intention A, such that the result of the action appears to be a mistake or error in terms of intention B. So what may appear to be a simple mistake--a slip of the tongue, forgetting a proper name, mis-writing something, putting a letter in the wrong envelope, all seemingly innocent or "unintentional" mistakes--can be described in terms of a second, "hidden" or "unconscious" intention that conflicts with an avowed or linguistically explicit "reason for action." The result is still an "error"--Freud does not deny this; but it is an error that is intended on some level, a level on which the person is not consciously aware.

Freud traced certain kinds of error to a counter-intention aimed at avoiding displeasure. According to Freud, certain kinds of error could still be acknowledged as errors by the person who forgot or blundered; but the positive and purposeful function performed by the error would be obscure if not thoroughly inaccessible to the individual's primary awareness, by which I mean that level of consciousness where one makes matters linguistically explicit to oneself. Consistent with his stated purpose to make the unconscious conscious, Freud included "error" as a form of <u>parapraxis</u> ("faulty acts": '<u>Fehlleistungen</u>'), which his psychoanalytic method was designed to explain and treat therapeutically. In the end, by referring "error" to the unconscious intention that was aimed at avoiding displeasure, Freud was able to relate 'error' to a theory about the formation of neurotic symptoms:

> . . .in this reason for objecting to remembering a name [this being Freud's example], we come across a principle which will later on reveal its enormous importance for the causation of neurotic symptoms: the memory's disinclination to remembering anything which is connected with feelings of unpleasure and the reproduction of which would renew the unpleasure. This intention to avoid unpleasure arising from a recollection or from other psychical acts, this psychical flight from unpleasure, may be recognized as the ultimate operative motive not only for the forgetting of names but many other parapraxis, such as omissions, errors, and so on.[31]

Thus, a slip of the tongue or pen, or forgetting a proper name, may, as examples of parapraxis, yield a result that is meaningful in terms of "an inescapable hypothesis that there are purposes in people which can become operative without their knowing about them."[32] To take examples from the common life, Freud's own examples, people who forget to pay their debts or return borrowed books may, at the very moment they explicitly deny having ulterior motives for the forgetfulness, actually be acting in congress with a intention of which they are unaware. Freud said about such a person that "he has this intention but knows nothing about it, but. . .it is enough for us that it reveals its presence by producing the forgetting in him. He may report to us that he has in fact forgotten."[33] The actual behavior that is manifest publicly as forgetting is the clue to, and the evidence for, the intention that produced the act.

Taking a psychoanalytic view, a memory-related error may constitute a parapraxis, which, if it were to be be applied to the statement, "My memory deceived me. . .", refers us to an intention of which the person is unaware. The parapraxis in question is to be attributed to an intended action that is made manifest as an error, and the error could be expressed in the language of 'deception.' Such a use would, however, constitute a distinct and qualified description of 'error,' one that would be exceedingly complex when compared to the same statement "My memory deceived me. . ." when one means by that that the error was of the first-order, simple and unintended.[34]

Freud's point was that a certain class of errors, errors associated with forgetting, have a temporary quality, ". . .for in their instance we believe for a time that something is the case which both before and afterwards we know is not so."[35] On this account, error is implicated in a belief-misleading project (i.e., 'deception') that is also self-directed, hence applicable to the concept 'self-deception.' From the point of view of the interpersonal sphere of relations, the kind of "error" Freud describes can be said to specify a belief-misleading project that either 1.) unintentionally, or 2.) by unconscious intention achieves the end of a deception, namely, the creation of an epistemic deficit for which someone is responsible. About this second description another remark or two is in order.

Because I forget to reset my watch after entering a new time zone and subsequently mislead another into believing it is a certain time when, in fact, it is not, one could say that I deceived that other person. My deceptive action would be attributed either to an honest mistake, an innocent or unintended error; or to a forgetting that is itself the result of an unconscious pressure exerted by a counter-will and a counter-intention, a forgetting that has as its purpose (say) the avoidance of unpleasure. A much more detailed description would be required in order to use this particular example as an actual illustration of parapraxis or "willful forgetting." But even the Freudian would agree with the ordinary language analyst that a simple case like this is sufficient to provide an example of an error due to forgetfulness. To describe a deception as "unintentional" and therefore as an error ("I inadvertently told the woman the wrong time because I forgot to reset my watch") on the one hand, and to describe an error as having been produced by an unconscious intention to forget on the other, constitute quite different descriptions. As different as they are, however, they both yield a similar result, namely, an error. Error, I have argued, describes the result of a deception, and in the common life, we do occasionally use 'deception' to indicate error.

Let me review the relevance of this discussion to the interpersonal concept of deception. 'Deception' is a concept ordinarily used to specify the fact of an interpersonal epistemic deficit due to a conscious (linguistically explicit) intention on the part of a deceiver. 'Deception' has been shown to permit uses in which intention is apparently absent (i.e., the honest or innocent mistake). Intention was thus described as a contingent feature of deception. If conscious intention is not necessary for all cases of 'deception,' then about those cases where it is not a necessary feature one may conclude that the deception yields an epistemic deficit unconsciously, whether it was intended unconsciously (to avoid displeasure) or consciously unintended (simple mistake). In either case, the "deceiver" has "deceived" unconsciously and has created an epistemic deficit unawares. The result of the deception is, in either case, to be described as an error, mistake or misjudgment, a temporary state of affairs according to Freud. Without pursuing these issues further, it can be reiterated that error is related to a particular employment of deception. However one might wish to describe what has happened in a case of error-by-forgetting, the result is a belief-misleading project. It is deceitful action directed by one agent against another without the "deceiver's" conscious and intentional cooperation in acts of belief-leading that turn out to be erroneous. However one might wish to describe the intention that leads to the epistemic deficit, the person in question assumes responsibility for misleading another's beliefs. In fact, this responsibility seems to apply even if one's own memory misleads one's own belief. This last point permits us to consider the statement "My memory deceived me, hence I erred" in another light: as a remark about a particular kind of error, one that is intended. Such a remark is relevant to our consideration of the concept 'self-deception.'

h. Deception: Conscious and Unconscious Intention

'Intention,' I have said, is a contingent feature of 'deception.' One can speak of a particular deception being consciously intended, and this is our first-order use, the kind of intention apparent in the Nora-personnel officer example. We are also authorized, however, to speak of unintentional or unconsciously intentional deceptions (i.e., "errors"), employments that constitute second-order uses of 'deception.' Although an unconscious intention is a satellite meaning for intention, the idea of an unconscious intention aids us in our attempt to account for self-deception. Unconscious intention enables us to account for the fact that self-deceivers intend to act in accordance with their belief that p, do so, then seem to be in error about the meaning of their act. Having acted consistently with p, self-deceivers explain their acts in terms of their intention to act in accordance with the belief that not-p, and it is this disparity that leads us to think that self-deceivers are in 'error.'

Consider again the relations involved in 'deception' and 'self-deception.' The conscious intention that makes up a first-order use of 'deception' explains Nora's intentional lie. It does not, however, prove helpful in understanding, much less describing, an instance of self-deception. In fact, if we consider a person who is consciously intending to create an intra-psychic epistemic deficit, it is not clear how--or even that--such a thing is possible. How does a person who believes p to be true go about convincing him- or herself that it is not? How can one sincerely and consciously believe p while also sincerely and consciously believing not-p? This is the philosophical cul-de-sac into which we are led by holding 'self-deception' closely to a first-order model of 'deception.' To escape this dead-end, we must consider a description in which 'self-deception' is rendered coherent as a deception-related concept because the intention feature is necessarily <u>unconscious</u>. To make this move means that first-order use of 'self-deception' will correspond, at least as far as the intention feature is concerned, to a second-order use of 'deception.' The idea that the intention in the 'deception' of 'self-deception' will necessarily refer to an <u>unconscious intention</u> is an idea that will require further scrutiny. An example will illustrate the point and restate the problem.

A man who is riding a ferry in rough waters begins to feel seasick. Can this person, who intends to do something to alleviate his discomfort, simply convince himself that he is not seasick? Can this person, by focusing his attention on some image of serenity unattached to the reality of the boat's swaying motion, wish so much to be stable that the result of the wishing is to alter his actual belief about his condition, which is that he is seasick? Can he effect a substitution of a secondary belief, namely, a belief that he is not seasick (not-p), for his primary belief that he is, in fact, seasick (p), a belief for which his nausea constitutes evidence?

On first glance, it appears that if this passenger were to manipulate his awareness such that a belief that he is not seasick were to result, we would have an example of an intentional deception directed by the self against the self. This example would meet the formal requirements for an analogy to the first-order deception with respect to the intention feature. Were this passenger to believe that he were not seasick, this belief (not-p) would be held in the face of certain evidence to the contrary and would represent an avowal at odds with his own primary awareness, belief or avowal (p), that he is, in fact seasick. The criterion that 'self-deception' have a motive (say: the avoidance of displeasure) and incite action (say: self-convincing through mental repetition) that is intentional (say: aiming to disavow that one is seasick) appears to be satisfied. The question, however, is whether this kind of conscious effort to mislead one's own beliefs comprises an accurate description--or even a good example--of what is meant when one typically says "So-and-so is self-deceived."

The fundamental problem with this example is that it is difficult to ascertain what would count as evidence for a successful outcome to this attempt to mislead one's own beliefs. If the passenger were actually to conquer his nausea and overcome the symptoms of seasickness, by what authority would we claim that his actual condition is in conflict with what he believes to be the case? If the passenger does not believe that he is nauseous and experiences no symptoms of nausea, then he is no longer nauseous. There is no epistemic deficit to be discerned and no seasickness to be observed. We would say that this person has overcome a condition known as seasickness by employing a certain technique (perhaps thinking serene thoughts while gazing at the stable horizon) and that the technique works. We would not normally say that this person is 'self-deceived,' meaning by that that he has knowingly willed his way into believing a false belief, for we have no evidence that the belief is false (now). We could only say that this person is no longer seasick.

On the other hand, if the passenger believes that he is not nauseous as a result of his project to mislead his own belief about his condition, yet evidence exists to contradict that belief--(say: he vomits)--would it be reasonable to assume that the person could continue to believe that he is not sick? I would contend that ordinary use of 'self-deception' does not typically sanction an employment to describe or explain a situation in which a person continues to believe something to be the case in the face of this kind of overwhelming evidence to the contrary. Although the seasick person could hide his peristaltic episode from fellow passengers and deny his malady for face-saving reasons, it would be thoroughly unreasonable for him to deny sincerely to himself that he is sick. Other examples of illness could occasion self-deception, as I shall note in Chapter Three; but this example suggests that a person who vomits and then denies being ill is somehow outside the common life. Such false belief is not only irrational but delusional and inscrutable.

The self-deceived person is not a person who consciously intends to disavow p, as if that could be accomplished by simply willing p to be false. In the common life, people who know that p is worthy of belief but who desire that not-p be true, often experience conflict. When the response to the conflict is something other than self-deception, we should expect that individual to make the conflict linguistically explicit, as in "I believe p is the case though I wish it were not." A self-deceived person, however, is different. A self-deceiver, for reasons that he or she cannot discern, intends to engage in activities that will permit this conflict from becoming linguistically explicit. The self-deceiver acts consistently with an intention to avoid making a conflict between p and not-p linguistically explicit, and it is only possible to enact this intention if the person engaging in self-deception is able to keep the intention itself from becoming linguistically explicit. The intention to keep oneself unaware that one is deceiving oneself, that one does know that p is worthy of belief but is willfully denying p due to a stronger desire that not-p be true, must itself be kept from linguistically explicit recognition. Therefore, the intention that gives rise to self-deceptive activities must itself be unconscious: If I were aware that I intended to deny that p is worthy of belief because I desired that not-p be true, I would have to conclude that "I believe p is the case though I wish it were not." It is self-deception that makes it possible to avoid or postpone such recognition.

A self-deceived person, then, rather than consciously intending to achieve a disavowal of p by willing an avowal of not-p, will "unconsciously intend" that not-p be true. The affirmation that not-p is true can be maintained in the face of evidence to the contrary, but only as long as it is within the realm of rational possibility to argue against the contrary evidence. A point may be reached, however, where evidence disconfirming the truth of a proposition is so overwhelming that further denial expresses profound irrationality.

It has not been established that 'self-deception' constitutes delusional behavior; for I have not, and shall not, argue that 'self-deception' is synonymous with 'delusion,' even though 'delusion' could be said to entail self-deception. Rather, self-deception is a feature of the common life, and as such, it involves less extreme kinds of belief-misleading activities than we would see in the ferry boat passenger who, in the face of overwhelming evidence to the contrary (vomiting) denied to himself that he was ill. If irrationality is involved, it must be so qualified that it is not rendered equivalent to full-blown delusions about the nature of reality. If irrationality is involved in self-deception, it would be expressed in such moderately irrational activities as rationalizing, excuse-making and denial. If that is the case, it is not clear how we are best to characterize self-deception, since these activities are, in addition to appearing irrational, related to information processing and evidential assessment. And if we should discover that the irrational activities of a self-deceiver arise in response to information that is processed as unpleasurable or, more seriously, as threatening to one's sense of well-being (Freud's account of the motive), are we not witnessing a highly sophisticated rational activity that manifests itself in publicly observable behavior that appears irrational?

That a deceptive self-relation includes these kinds of rational activities will be shown. For now, however, let it be said about denials, rationalizations and excuses that they arise as actions intended to fulfill the purpose of some intention, and that the person engaging in these activities is simply <u>unaware</u> that what he or she considers an honest "disagreement" with a particular "interpretation" is really a complicated intentional act aimed at avoiding an linguistically explicit acknowledgment that p is, as the person knows deep down, true. The self-deceiver's interpretive actions appear to us in the common life as mistakes, errors, or blunders. The persistent refusal to acknowledge the best, most precise linguistic interpretation of those acts--the clever though somehow irrational denial--is evidence that the denial is itself an intentional act, an act for which motives may be ascribed. If the self-deceiver is ignorant, it is an ignorance that is willed.

i. Review of Intention Issues

'Deception' and 'self-deception' both appeal to the idea of intention for conceptual coherence, though in different ways and in different degrees. I have made use of the 'deception' analogy in order to clarify how the intention of 'deception' is related to, and might be translated into, 'self-deception,' and several points were noted.

1. A first-order use of 'deception' will include as a conceptual feature a <u>conscious</u> intention (e.g., Nora's lie). A conscious intention to deceive oneself, however, is paradoxical and non-sensical, as I illustrated with the ferry boat passenger who attempts to mislead his own beliefs consciously: the passenger either succeeds in his effort to want to believe he is not seasick, in which case he is no longer seasick, or he holds that belief in a way that seems more extreme than we should want if our case be that self-deception is a feature of the common life. In the first case, there was no epistemic deficit; in the second, the passenger believed falsely that he had overcome an illness in the face of overwhelming evidence to the contrary, thereby exhibiting delusional (extremely irrational) behavior, rather than the more moderately irrational behavior of self-deception. In neither case do we have an instance of self-deception as it is commonly understood.

2. An unintended deception is equivalent to an error or mistake; but an "unintended self-deception," if it makes any sense at all, yields only a euphemism for error. No examples spring to mind where reference to an "unintended self-deception" provides an informative description. 'Self-deception' is never used to signify the lack of intention, motive or purpose in the self-directed project to mislead one's own belief. The conclusion to be drawn,

then, is that although 'intention' constitutes a contingent feature of 'deception,' it is a necessary feature of 'self-deception.' Without intention, 'self-deception' would constitute a conceptual equivalent to error simpliciter, that is, an unintended mistake or error.

3. If an "unconscious intention" be ascribed to a particular feature of 'deception,' it can be shown that this particular qualification yields a result no different from that of an unintended deception. A 'deception' perpetrated either by an "unconscious intention" or "unintentionally" yields only one result--an error. Two satellite meanings of 'deception' yield the result of error: the unintended deception--"I deceived the person who asked about the time because I forgot to reset my watch"--and from "unconscious intention," the kind of intention Freud endorsed.

j. Self-Deception: Unconscious Intentions, Beliefs and Neurosis

To characterize the intention feature of self-deception as necessarily "unconscious" is to move us towards resolving the epistemological paradox often associated with 'self-deception.' "Unconscious intention" implicates "unawareness" in the practical dynamics of intrapsychic relations; and, even more importantly from a philosophical point of view, it refers to a capacity of mind or a condition of consciousness wherein the idea of a deceptive self-relation is rendered logically feasible and formally coherent. Consider the person who has two opposing intentions, one conscious ($\underline{A}$) and one unconscious ($\underline{\text{not-A}}$).

A woman, Jones, intends to do $\underline{A}$, and, as a result of intending to do $\underline{A}$, holds certain beliefs about how best to realize $\underline{A}$ and is disposed to act in accordance with that intention. Jones, however, while making linguistically explicit to herself that she intends to do $\underline{A}$, does $\underline{\text{not-A}}$. In this case, Jones will enact $\underline{\text{not-A}}$ as a result of holding an unconscious intention to do $\underline{\text{not-A}}$. In describing Jones behavior, which includes an explanation of $\underline{\text{not-A}}$ behavior in terms of $\underline{A}$ intention, we are forced to conclude that Jones is a person holding two opposing intentions; for in acting inconsistently with $\underline{A}$ she is acting consistently with an intention to achieve the aim of $\underline{\text{not-A}}$. Moreover, Jones' beliefs about how best to realize $\underline{A}$ could be said to be opposed by an "unconscious" counter-belief to $\underline{A}$, a belief that the best way to realize the intent of $\underline{\text{not-A}}$ is to "forget" the intention to realize $\underline{\text{not-A}}$ and maintain the original beliefs associated with $\underline{A}$. Jones, then, forgets the intent of doing $\underline{\text{not-A}}$, yet acts in accordance with $\underline{\text{not-A}}$. She "enacts" $\underline{\text{not-A}}$, but can only understand her act in terms of an intent to do $\underline{A}$. The result is an epistemic deficit between what she avows ($\underline{A}$) and what she does ($\underline{\text{not-A}}$). The notion of an "unconscious intention" corresponds in this instance to an unconscious belief with respect to how best to realize $\underline{\text{not-A}}$. She wants to realize $\underline{\text{not-A}}$, but because she does not want to acknowledge that desire, she prefers to to interpret her act in terms of $\underline{A}$. This is a complex description, but not an improbable one. People can actually make these moves; and since intention is related to belief,[36] opposing beliefs can find their way into the common life, even our common intrapsychic experience.

The person who consciously intends to do A, but does not-A as a result of an unconscious intention to do not-A, is a person who could be said to be engaged in a self-directed--an unconsciously directed--project to mislead belief. An actual disparity obtains between the beliefs that attend the conscious intention (A) and the beliefs that attend the unconscious intention (not-A). That is, the person has two opposing awarenesses, one conscious with respect to A, one unconscious with respect to not-A. Accordingly, the person satisfies the criteria necessary for ascribing 'self-deception' as those criteria are made available to us from both ordinary language analysis and through the analogy to 'deception.' The analogy to 'deception' is maintained if we can say that contradictory beliefs are held simultaneously by means of an intentional act, the result being that the person is unaware of one of the beliefs. To permit the notion of "unconscious intention" to enter our picture of 'self-deception' is to clarify the meaning of the concept and to validate its use in ordinary language as an intention-related term. Freud's picture of parapraxis, then, looks to be an explanation of what could pass in ordinary language as behavior attributable to 'self-deception.' In fact, this has been claimed about Freud. Theodore Mischel, for example, has written that the Freudian theory of neurosis depends upon 'self-deception' for its explanation:

> I am suggesting that a variety of normal cognitive processes can, as Freud put it, 'provide a pretext for neurotic procedures'; that is, different 'mechanisms of defense' can be construed as intentional but unconscious uses of different forms of thought and perception for the purpose of protecting oneself from the anxiety of an unbearable conflict by fending off consciousness of that conflict. In other words, neurotics attempt to cope with their anxieties by deceiving themselves about their real feelings toward others, and neurotic defenses are different modes of normal cognition that have been distorted by this unconscious defensive aim.[37]

According to psychoanalytic theory, 'neurosis' can be explained by including within its description the dynamics--the purposefulness, the intentional character, the motivational basis--attributable to the concept 'self-deception.' Neurosis necessarily entails self-deception.

This picture of neurosis qua self-deception arises from an interpretation of consciousness. Consciousness is conceived as having a capacity to respond purposefully to directives which are, themselves, unconscious, and even contrary to a conscious intention. To adopt this picture of mind is to conceive of a self that is capable of the dynamic self-relations required for self-deception. That is, the self is capable of so relating itself to itself that it actually holds contradictory intentions (action) and contradictory beliefs (cognition) simultaneously, being motivated to do so with the result that the person is unaware of one of the beliefs, or unaware that he or she is acting consistently with a certain (opposing) intention. By referring to certain "unconscious" mental activities, we affect the description of 'self-deception' significantly, for this "unconscious" feature allows us to say of a person that he or she is both aware and unaware, even with respect to the same epistemic object.

We need not be Freudians to include some notion of "the unconscious" in our operative and normative picture of mind. We need only be observers of human persons. We need only observe persons who seem intent on misunderstanding the meaning of their own action. Including "unconsciousness" in our description of mental life helps us resolve certain philosophical difficulties; for armed with this qualification, we can grasp how an intrapsychic conflict is logically possible and how an intrapsychic epistemic deficit could be ontically occurrent. We can speak coherently about persons who both know and do not know, or believe and do not believe. The "unconscious" provides an actual solution to the epistemic paradox of 'self-deception.'

Although self-deception presents itself as a skein of philosophical difficulties, a single thread enables us to unravel those difficulties--the notion of an "unconscious" intention or belief. Curiously, few philosophers who have studied this topic have adopted this "easy" solution. Few have attempted to explain self-deception by appealing to the "unconscious." Should we do the same, our dilemma would be this: If 'intention' is the crux of the matter with respect to conceptual intelligiblity, then how is that intention to be characterized? I have already shown that certain problems preclude our relying on a picture in which a person <u>consciously</u> intends to deceive him- or herself; I have also claimed that <u>unintended</u> self-deception is simply a euphemism for error. If these uses have been precluded, do we not sabotage our last, best hope for rendering 'self-deception' intelligible by cutting the lifeline that the notion of an <u>unconscious</u> intention or belief provides? This is to state the problem posed by considering the claim that like a first-order 'deception,' 'self-deception' entails purposeful action. In self-deception, the epistemic deficit obtains because it is intended, because one is motivated to "forget" or purposefully to act such that one both knows and does not know, believes and does not believe, is aware yet unaware. Positing "unconsciousness" as a dynamic capacity of mind relieves these contraries of their unresolvable contradictoriness.

Reference to a capacity of human persons to act from motives that are unconsciously held enables us to analyze 'self-deception' such that it reveals itself to be a concept that is (potentially) coherent despite the obvious or apparent paradox that attends a facile description. Freud's notion of unconscious mechanisms and processes has not generally been brought to bear on 'self-deception' to explain what otherwise looks contradictory. Philosophers have been reluctant to make this Freudian move because appeal to "unconsciousness" is considered to be philosophically weak.[38] Because it is considered weak, philosophers have had to assume that 1.) self-deception can be accounted for without appealing to the idea of unconscious intentions and beliefs, and 2.) that such an account would be a stronger account. It would be stronger because it would not resolve the epistemological paradox of self-deception by resorting to such notions as "unconscious believing" or "unconscious knowledge," "multi-selved believing," "unnoticed believing," or "half-believing." Critics charge that these are question-begging notions[39] inasmuch as they rely on "unconsciousness," which is a controversial notion. If one appeals to unconsciousness, the argument goes, one must first render that coherent and intelligible.

I would point out that Sartre's account of "bad faith" in Being and Nothingness constitutes a theory about 'self-deception,' yet Sartre was an outspoken critic of Freud's psychoanalytic (explanatory) theory of the Unconscious. Sartre, however, does not fail to include in his account some notion of unawareness or unconsciousness, though it is not, of course, Freud's particular formulation of "The Unconscious" as a structural repository of mind. Modern philosophers, whether analytic or existential, have approached our topic with a certain suspicion about the unawareness criterion. The challenge of 'self-deception' for the modern philosopher has been to find a way to describe how an epistemic deficit can obtain intrapsychically, how it is possible to be unaware as the result of a process that assumes prior awareness, how a deceptive intrapersonal relation can be understood on the basis of an interpersonal model (i.e., 'deception') without appealing to Freud's hypothetical-explanatory notion of "The Unconscious."

I reiterate the fact that alternative accounts of 'self-deception' abound, and we shall have occasion to examine those accounts in more detail in Chapter Two. Having noted that controversy surrounds the "unconsciousness" criterion, let me turn to another source of problems and postpone further discussion of "unconsciousness" until the next section (2. "Self").

k. Cognition and Action: A Summing Up

In my "ordinary language" consideration of the relation between 'deception' and 'self-deception' I have thus far highlighted two problems. First, whether 'self-deception,' like 'deception,' involves an epistemic deficit necessarily--which it does. Second, whether 'self-deception,' like 'deception,' involves a contingent notion of intention--which it does not. This second problem has introduced us to the idea that 'self-deception' is an action concept that issues in a cognitive result. It has been necessary to question the role of intention as it pertains to the result of 'self-deception,' namely, the creation of an intrapersonal epistemic deficit. This epistemic deficit obtains for certain reasons and can be said to be motivated; yet it is a cognitive result, and it is this cognitive aspect that justifies a description of a self-deceived person as one who both knows and does not know, who is aware yet unaware. These problems--and initial clarifications--have emerged from an ordinary language analysis of 'deception,' the concept that identifies a form of action that will be reflexively transformed in the derivative concept 'self-deception.'

Having considered the intended aim of a self-directed project to mislead one's own beliefs and the cognitive result that obtains when successful (epistemic deficit), let us consider the third feature of the comparison.

1. The "Doing" of Self-Deception and the Wishful Thinker

The description offered previously of a 'deception' (Nora's lie) indicated that the interpersonal deceiver <u>does something</u> to effect the end sought by the deception. Although this may entail acts by omission or commission, out-right lies, "white lies," or even the silence that misleads, the deception obtains because the agent does something to achieve the intended aim. There is action, then, and it is purposeful. If we transfer this feature of an interpersonal deception to an intrapersonal context, this is the problem that emerges: What is it that a self-deceiver does (or can do) to effect the aim of a belief-misleading project? If the intention of the project is to achieve unawareness with respect to some epistemic object, it is clear that something must be done to achieve that aim. If we extract <u>action</u> features from our description, the result would be that no distinction could be drawn between 'self-deception' and a notion like 'wishful thinking.' Such a distinction is necessary, however, for wishful thinking, unlike self-deception, is never described as paradoxical, and we do not think of the wishful thinker in action terms, in terms of doing. Once again, ordinary language provides the necessary wherewithal for ascertaining the specific meaning of the concept 'self-deception.'

A wishful thinker may become self-deceived, but why is the wishful thinking not conceptually equivalent to self-deception? The answer is to be found in deciphering the relation of thought to action in each concept. A self-deceiver and a wishful thinker may both be said to entertain a certain belief p. We can infer that whatever p happens to be in particular, generally speaking p could be said to involve something related to a want or desire, something that is believed will make the person happy. The self-deceiver, however, proceeds to maintain this belief in a way that the wishful thinker does not, in a way that "perverts" the procedures whereby we determine what is and what is not the case.[40] A self-deceiver is motivated by a desire that p be true. Acting intentionally to satisfy that desire, the self-deceiver will discount evidence, rationalize or deny certain interpretations of fact that would usually disconfirm the belief p. These are things the self-deceiver actually does. The self-deceiver engages in certain kinds of belief-misleading activities that shore up the belief even though on some level of awareness (unconsciously) he or she knows that the belief p is weak or unfounded.

The wishful thinker, on the other hand, also desires that p be true, and may even believe it in an occurrent sense; but the wishful thinker does not take action on the desire. When evidence is presented to disconfirm the belief that p is true, the wishful thinker yields to the weight of that evidence and is able to acknowledge that p is not true. Desire does not conquer rational assessment. A self-deceiver, however, does not yield, but actively resists the disconfirmation process. The self-deceiver resorts to rationalizing, explaining away or reinterpreting the evidence consistent with his or her desire that p be true. The self-deceiver, then, will maneuver to avoid confronting the truth about p, thereby avoiding the self-confrontation that would lead the self-deceiver to make his or her desires with respect to p linguistically explicit.

The distinction between self-deception and wishful thinking is not always clear in individual cases, nor in certain discussions, as has been pointed out elsewhere.[41] 'Wishful thinking' is, finally, a way of thinking--perhaps a kind of fantasizing, daydreaming, or hoping--that expresses one's capacity for imaginative conceiving. 'Self-deception,' on the other hand, is a doing something beyond the entertaining of possibilities, or wishing things were different than they are, or wanting something to be the case when, in fact, it is not. Wishful thinking is entertainment--it is a form of imaginative mental gymnastic that is always hypothetical rather than practical. And beyond this, to ascribe 'wishful thinking' to a person is not only to assume that this "entertainment" affords certain satisfactions; it is also to assess the person's beliefs from a perspective of normative rationality. That is to say, 'wishful thinking' is not different from 'self-deception' in that no beliefs are involved. It is different in that a self-deceiver adopts an attitude and does something in conjunction with those beliefs that a wishful thinker is unwilling to do, namely, maintain a belief that p is true in the face of evidence that disconfirms that belief. Does this mean that a wishful thinker is to be adjudged, when the issue is pressed, as rational whereas the self-deceiver is irrational? Ordinary language considerations may help at this point, but only if we remember that the language indicates that the self-deceiver acts, and by acting shows through rational processes the irrational desire that p be true. The irrationality of self-deception, tempered as it is by intrapsychic maneuvers that are of a piece with rationality, is not equivalent to other kinds of irrationality. It would be a mistake, for instance, to equate the irrationality of self-deception with that of delusion.

My position is that 'wishful thinking,' 'self-deception,' and 'delusion' are linguistically and conceptually distinct, though the distinctions may be much easier to stipulate definitionally than with respect to real cases. Although the differences will be clarified only by considering examples, even our formal statements of distinctions may be hard to press into service when considering hard cases. How does one describe the movement from wishful thinking to self-deception? How does one trace the movement from wishing and even believing something to be the case to acting as if it were true and worthy of defense? A further difficulty arises because awareness of ambiguities will not lead us to conclude that the self-deceiver is more irrational than the wishful thinker or irrational simpliciter. After all, the self-deceiver's behavior may provide no obvious clue to self-deception, since a self-deceiver manifests his or her self-deception in quite ordinary sorts of activities--such things as writing letters, conversing with a colleague, or defending a position in a discussion. A self-deceiver is not one who would try to swim the Atlantic or jump from a building believing that flapping arms will provide flight. It is the deluded person who might do such things, for it is the deluded person who reveals by overt behavior that he or she is at odds with the common life. The self-deceiver seems to act rationally with respect to a belief that is valid in the context of the person's hopes and wishes. The self-deceiver's belief may even be consistent with certain facts that could plausibly be construed to support the 'erroneous' belief. One thing is certain: 'self-deception' typically arises at the point where evidence is weighed and interpreted. Self-deceivers pervert the normal processes through which evidence is evaluated, but this does not mean that they are thoroughly irrational--deluded--by so doing.

Ambiguity appears because even though a self-deceiver's belief about p may be valid in a context governed by certain motives, hopes, wishes or fears, there is still sufficient reason to hold that the belief is unsound. Should the self-deceiver persist in that belief beyond the point where the evidence is simply overwhelming, then we would have reason to ascribe 'delusion.' Self-deception is a step short of delusion but also a step beyond wishful thinking. A self-deceiver acts to maintain a belief in the face of disconfirming evidence and resists that disconfirming evidence by failing to acknowledge it as disconfirming. This is unsound from the standpoint of normative rationality. The self-deceiver's epistemic position may not be invalid or even irrational at this point. Part of the problem is simply the nature of the evidence--when is evidence overwhelming, when is there room for reasonable doubt? Evidence is arguable and open to interpretation, and one act may be open to several descriptions. One need only consider how evidence is established as credible in a court of law. It is not the evidence that convicts the defendant, but a judge or jury which renders a decision about the evidence. So, too, a person in self-deception could have evidential grounds and a valid argument in support of his or her belief that p is true. The problem is that the self-deceiver acts as if the belief that p is true actually is true--when there is more room for doubt than belief. A self-deceiver does not want to see room for doubt and decides unawares that his or her valid belief is also sound, thereby ceasing to be skeptical when there is need for skepticism. The self-deceiver opts to believe something when there is ample evidence to disconfirm the soundness of the belief. What evidence convincingly disconfirms a belief? If 'self-deception' is a feature of the common life, and 'delusion' is not, we may simply have to conclude that evidence that can be characterized as 'overwhelming' occasionally arises though it is not typically available or easily accessible, at least with respect to the epistemic objects of self-deception. This last qualification deserves further comment.

III. The Problem of the Epistemic Object

The problem is this: What <u>kind</u> of epistemic object occasions self-deception? Can we deceive ourselves about anything, or is there a particular <u>kind</u> of epistemic object that is necessarily involved in self-deception? I contend that self-deception arises over objects of a certain kind, for only objects of a certain kind can provide the motive for self-deceptive activity.

Keeping in mind the example of the passenger who tried to convince himself that he was not seasick, I would claim that certain epistemic objects are simply inappropriate objects for 'self-deception.' In other words, one cannot deceive oneself about just anything. When I make a computational error in my checkbook I may fly off the handle and deny either my responsibility or that an error actually exists. A simple check of the arithmetic will settle that kind of dispute. We simply appeal to the rules of arithmetical computation and <u>show</u> the error. It is difficult to imagine this kind of example serving to illustrate an instance of self-deception, however, for if I refused to admit the error I must either be ignorant of the rules of addition and subtraction or thoroughly irrational in willfully refusing to recognize the error (to myself at least). Self-deception does not arise over disputes that can be settled by appealing to such a norm. A norm, here, simply refers to the established and culturally accessible rules that govern how we do such things as manipulate variables or ascertain a correct employment of terms. A person ignorant of the rules can be taught the rules. A self-deceiver, however, is one who knows the rules but bends them for some reason. Should he or she defy those rules entirely, the person would be acting from a premise incompatible with the common life, and we would say of such a person that he or she is 'deluded.'

I shall argue below that appeal to a rule-governing authority that regulates operations and assessments--like the rules of arithmetic computation that govern checkbook operations--is irrelevant to self-deception because self-deception requires a different kind of epistemic object. The object in question must be such that it incites one to act defensively, and I shall argue that as a class, these objects impinge on self-image, whence issues the motive for self-deception. If one cannot consciously deceive oneself at will, neither can one simply deceive oneself about just anything; if I am married, how could I convince myself that I am not except I be deluded--thoroughly out of touch with reality. The <u>kinds</u> of epistemic objects involved in self-deception are objects constitutive of one's hopes and wishes and fears. They are beliefs or avowals that, as Herbert Fingarette has argued,[42] implicate one's identity, or, as I shall argue, they are emotions tied to self-understanding, emotions related to love and desire. Very simply, the epistemic objects appropriate to self-deception pertain to self-understanding and a certain perception of oneself, which, as I shall point out, is an image of oneself as a certain kind of person--a moral person. If it be true that only a clever person can undertake the maneuvers required to bring about self-deception, I will show that only a moral person--a person confronted with a challenge to his or her own moral self-image--is a viable candidate for self-deception. We perceive emotionally the epistemic objects that give rise to self-deception; and these objects occasion a response that can so bear on how we interpret our own behavior that distortions in interpretation result, distortions that can be said to be motivated.[43]

n. Action and Cognition: What the Ordinary Language Analysis Reveals

By considering self-deception an action concept rather than simply a cognitive state, we position ourselves to say about self-deception that it is describable in terms of intention (forward looking reasons for action) and motives (backward-looking reasons for action).[44] We position ourselves to consider a wide variety of issues relevant to self-deceptive activity, issues involving cognition and action in dynamic interplay.

We have considered the rationality of self-deception and the objects in relation to which self-deception arises, but we have not attempted to explain how the epistemic deficit actually comes about. Descriptively speaking, we might say that some sort of self-persuading mantra, some kind of verbal repetition that overcomes the person's normal "evidence disconfirming tendencies," is the formal technique that accomplishes the end sought by the self-deceiver. Certain people have been known to recite an abracadabra that transports them from distress to unawareness that an epistemic conflict exists, and these are people we sometimes meet in the common life. I fear it is the case, however, that in the end we cannot adequately explain the causal mechanics that operate the pulleys and levers of consciousness to effect what we term 'self-deception.' Certain neuropsychological research, particularly into the whole area of "split brain" phenomena ("hemisphericity"),[45] may prove helpful in explaining how 'self-deception' is possible from a neurological standpoint. But given the logical problems that even the physiologist needs clarified, we should exercise caution against a too hasty optimism about positive contributions from the "hard" sciences. My interest is not to look into this tangle of issues, since I have taken as the immediate problem the conceptual issue--how to describe 'self-deception' adequately. This may seem a humble task, but it is this humble task that has generated the dispute among philosophers. The philosophers are right. Unless the "convincing theoretical treatment" sought by philosophers is forthcoming, neurophysiological-psychological research can provide only question-begging data, data that can have no application or relevance as long as the conceptual issue remains muddled.

'Self-deception' is a complex concept, and we have attempted to examine that complexity by considering in what respects 'self-deception' is analogous to 'deception.' We have, furthermore, distinguished 'self-deception' from related concepts by considering how we use those other concepts in ordinary discourse. Delusion and wishful thinking are not conceptual equivalents to self-deception. I suggested that wishful thinking connects desire to imagination, while in self-deception desire is connected through imagination to action. Delusion, on the other hand, escapes our requirement for rationality in a more extreme way, not so much perverting our usual procedures for truth determination as defying them. A deluded person escapes reality in a way that the self-deceiver does not.[46]

Substantial problems have emerged from this initial comparison of 'self-deception' to 'deception,' particularly with respect to the action criterion and its relation to the cognitive result. There is no doubt that self-deception is a cognitive concept, for the self-deceiver is one who creates an epistemic gap intrapsychically. But without action components, 'self-deception' would not be a species of 'deception'; for it would mean something other than "the act of deceiving oneself" (OED). It is, however, an action concept as well as a cognitive concept. It entails an act and is motivated, purposeful and intentional like 'deception' proper. But have we resolved our difficulties if ordinary language makes clear that not every action need be intentional or motivated. If I push Jones and in stumbling he closes a door, I cannot attribute the act of closing a door to an intention on Jones' part (or mine). Could it be, then, that 'self-deception' is a similar <u>kind</u> of action? Could it be, as Sartre argued, that one becomes self-deceived much as one falls asleep and is self-deceived much as one dreams?[47] Is falling asleep an action? Does analogy to falling asleep not reiterate our original problem: If my conscious intention were to get some sleep, will not a constant preoccupation with getting to sleep not generate the very condition of anxious attentiveness that effectively prevents me from doing so? I can consciously act to create conditions that make sleep, or self-deception, more likely, for I can do things to alter my focus of attention and take my mind off of a certain obstructive preoccupation; but even so, I can neither will myself to sleep nor simply--consciously--will myself into the epistemic deficit of self-deception.

By raising the issue about action and cognitive awareness, we continue to ask the question about the role of consciousness and how it is possible for me to act such that I deceive myself, i.e., create an intrapsychic epistemic deficit. Let me conclude by saying that an adequate description of 'self-deception' as an <u>action-cognition</u> concept has been suggested, though it will require further elucidation, especially with reference to the "self" that is said to deceive its own self. Yet to be addressed is the problematic issue concerning the relation of action to cognition in a concept that, as ordinary language analysis reveals, entails both.

o. From 'Deception' to 'Self:' Restating the Problem

On the basis of ordinary language considerations, we can say that 'deception' yields a certain result. We can describe that result as a deficit that obtains epistemically between deceiver and deceived. When Nora deceives the personnel officer, a gap appears between what Nora knows to be true about her credentials and what the personnel officer believes to be true. The personnel officer is in error, but not innocently; he has been deliberately misled into believing as true what is, in fact, not true. The descriptive problem we face concerns this question: How can an intrapsychic deficit obtain when the context for it is intrapsychic rather than interpersonal? To say a deceiver knows and the deceived does not know is to describe an epistemic deficit in terms of the relations that govern the concept, in terms of the relations that make the concept 'deception' logically possible as well as ontically coherent. Transferred to self-deception, however, this "two party" relation model seems peculiar and problematic. It seems incoherent to suggest that one person can do intrapsychically what Nora does to the personnel officer. How can one person both know and not know; how can one person play two incompatible, opposing, even contradictory roles simultaneously? It is clear why the philosophers who have sought an analogy to 'deception' generate a picture of self-deception that is, as they term it, "paradoxical."

The philosopher's question is certainly pertinent: How can we describe 'self-deception' such that the result of a particular intrapsychic relation is analogous to our ordinary language notion of 'deception?' If the analogy to deception fails, we shall be confronted with a paradox, and if confronted with a paradox, it can be argued that 'self-deception' is a misuse of language or even an empirical impossibility. The language of 'deception' invokes this paradox. How can a person enact a project to mislead his or her own belief with the result that the person is the victim as well as the agent of that project? In order for there to be a true intrapsychic 'deception,' it looks as if one must believe the very thing one does not believe, or avow as true the very epistemic object that one intends to avoid acknowledging as true. These are clearly descriptions that lend themselves to paradox. Our task, then, is to describe the project whereby we undertake to mislead our own beliefs. How can we achieve the result of self-deception? How can we describe self-deception non-paradoxically when the concept itself seems to point inevitably to a result that is paradoxical--believing p and not-p simultaneously?

This paradox appears inescapable, and were we to hold strictly to the deception analogy we would find ourselves confronted with a notion that could not be described without contradiction. The deception analogy yields a paradox, and analyzing 'self-deception' from the 'deception' pole leads inevitably to this paradox and no further. The paradox can be resolved, but only with the resource to be found in the 'self-' prefix. The paradox will continue to plauge any account that does not attend to the issue of self-relatedness.

Our next chore is to clarify the self-relatedness issue, and we shall do so by examining 'self-deception' from the 'self' side of the linguistic expression. Although the issues here are at least as problematic as--and potentially more complex than--those discussed from the 'deception' pole, they reduce to a problem about the relations governing the concept 'self-deception.' By considering the self-relations governing the concept 'self-deception' we shall come to understand the sense it makes to say that human persons deceive themselves.

2. Self: Holistically Conceived Self-Relatedness

a. Analysis

When we inquire into the meaning of 'self-deception,' we must ask, what is the self that is involved in the deception? What is the meaning of this reflexive word? What function does it perform in elucidating and circumscribing the concept at hand? If we take 'self' to be an independent, autonomous or freestanding noun, do we mean that 'self' is a person? Do we mean a person's consciousness or some controlling feature or characteristic of the personality; or some notion of psychological continuity; or the person's own sense of identity? Is the self a substance? an agent? a locus for converging environmental and genetic conditions that yield a joint effect?[48] All of these questions lead down long and dimly lit philosophical roads which we have not time to travel. My aim here is to identify features of the concept 'self' that are relevant to this inquiry into the meaning of 'self-deception.'

In our everyday discourse "self-" and "-self" serve as reflexive auxiliaries that compound the meaning of certain words, circumscribe the meaning of certain concepts, and, in general, express our everyday perception of reflexive activity. 'Self-deception' is a noun that indicates reflexive activity. It refers to deceptive action that is turned back upon the grammatical subject, so that the ordinary meaning of these words captures the idea that a deception has been circumscribed to a specific set of relations, namely, the reflexive relation of a person to his or her own self. This is quite apparent and, practically speaking, non-problematic.

From a purely linguistic point of view, there is nothing mysterious about 'self-deception' serving to specify a reflexive relation. Neither is the definition of the term unintelligible in its stipulation that 'self-deception' is the "act or fact of deceiving oneself" (OED--my emphasis). Two problems emerge, however, the first of which is whether 'deception' is a concept that lends itself to such reflexive usage. In other words, what sense does it make to say that one can deceive oneself? The second problem, which now requires attention, is this: How do we conceive the self that we assume has the capacity to enact a deceptive self-relation? Is a 'self' capable of being deceived as the result of deceptive action that is initiated and realized intrapsychically? Can a person actually become the victim of his or her own deceptive act?

If we say that 'self-deception' is a reflexively conceived form of deceptive activity, activity that is perpetrated by the self against the self (and for the self), we state the matter in such a way that we actually beg the question about the meaning of 'self'--for now 'self' is functioning as a noun rather than as an auxiliary pronoun, intensifier and prefix. This shift in linguistic function points to an actual shift in meaning. In some respects this is a minor matter, but since our concern here is to ascertain the ordinary language meaning of 'self-deception' and the role of this concept in the common life, it is clear that 'self' has (somehow) been authorized to function in this linguistic community as a free-standing noun and not only as an intensifier or reflexive auxiliary. We commonly hear talk about "the self" as if 'self' were equivalent to <u>person</u>. This is not only a linguistic fact of life, but one which, if accepted as such, can help us avoid certain kinds of philosophical difficulties. Consider William Alston's sage remarks:

> In our ordinary thought we make no distinction between the self, the person, the man/woman, the human being, etc. . . . The term 'self' (usually in compounds) is used for a person when that person is being spoken of as the object of a self-directed cognition, action, or attitude. The 'self' of whom we speak in everyday discourse is in no way to be distinguished from the individual man, and is no more problematical. By maintaining our hold on the everyday conceptual scheme, we will avoid conceptual quagmires and get on to real problems--what functions are involved in e.g., self-control, what determines, or influences their exercise, what are the antecedents and consequences of positive and negative self-esteem, and so on.[49]

The term 'self,' then, has standing as a noun indicating identity, and to the extent that we employ 'self' as a noun related to the the ordinary reflexive meaning, the term has come to serve as a functional equivalent to 'person,' 'individual,' the object of a self-directed action, cognition, or attitude (Alston).

The general context for the meaning of "the self" is clearly <u>psychological</u> and, unlike <u>person</u>, <u>self</u> is confined for the most part to psychological employments.[50] In fact, two uses of 'self' as a free-standing noun can be located in the literature of modern psychology, though we must note that 'self' has emerged as a technical term. Stephen Toulmin has indicated two technical uses for 'self.'[51] The first of these he calls "hypothetical-explanatory." That is, in certain psychological theories, 'self' has been used as a noun to signify and locate the cause, or the source of causes, of action. This represents an employment prominent in the behaviorist picture of psychological reality.[52] A second noun use is that which pertains to a movement in modern clinical psychology to develop a "psychology of the self." In the clinical context, 'self' has been used as a "diagnostic-descriptive" term, and in this clinical use, as Toulmin puts the matter, ". . . the concept <u>self</u> will now be understood as expressing the insights into the complexities and relationships within reflexive conducts of kinds that elude expression in less sophisticated language."[53] If B. F. Skinner is a proponent of the first noun employment, Ernest Wolf and Heinz Kohut are proponents of the second.[54]

The "diagnostic-descriptive" use of 'self' has come to indicate in clinical terminology ". . . a means of characterizing, in significant terms, the different respects in which an agent's active, intentional and affective life may be--or fail to be--organized and integrated."[55] Furthermore,

> To the extent that the resulting clinical descriptions are associated with a more-or-less convincing account of the ontogeny of personality, the psychologist's ideas about the ways in which the actions and feelings of adult agents <u>are</u> integrated or fragmented have implications, also, about the ways in which those <u>came to be</u> integrated and fragmented. Clinical accounts of the <u>self</u>, that is to say, need to be supplemented for theoretical purposes by psychodynamic accounts of the developmental sequences by which individuals can achieve a 'well-integrated' self, and of the vicissitudes which can block such integration.[56]

From this second clinical psychological point of view, 'self' refers to the entire complex of relations that describe the self's ability 1.) to interpret its own experiences, and 2.) to function in the world with coherence, cohesiveness and consistency. This perspective, which begins as a description of the self's relations to its own self, moves beyond description to evaluation; for the degree of cohesiveness, coherence and consistency achieved by a self can be evaluated according to criteria of integration and fragmentation. And inasmuch as this perspective describes the self in the language of responsible action and autonomy, it also invites moral evaluation.

A well-integrated self acquires the ability to exercise self-direction and self-control in a context where co-equal agents are not only competing for certain goods of life, but where other agents are recognized as having co-equal status. In other words, to be a self requires that one recognize other selves as deserving of respect in their claim to equal rights and fair access to the goods of life. A self acquires autonomy to the extent that it recognizes competing and co-equal rights-bearing claimants. Furthermore, the self achieves autonomy only by willingly relinquishing its own self-aggrandizing tendencies. By this act of self-transcendence, the self becomes affectively disposed to acknowledge other agents as co-equal, and the recognition of that status becomes a necessary precondition to its own assumption of autonomy. It is, of course, rational to make this move, either for moral reasons or for interests of self-interest (prudential). Rational though this recognition be, the self, if it is to achieve integration, must endorse the idea of the social community with more than rational assent. The person's heart must be in it as well. If integration depends upon the self renouncing its own imperialistic tendencies, it also depends upon the renunciation being accomplished in a certain spirit--without resentment or emotional resistance.

The picture of self that emerges from this descriptive-diagnostic perspective entails volitional and affective components as well as cognitive--again, it is the entire personality, the complete self, that is being addressed and scrutinized. The integration and fragmentation of the artificially distinct components--emotion, volition, cognition--reveal descriptively and diagnostically to what extent the agent knows his or her own mind ". . . and can put his declared intentions into effect coherently and consistently, over a substantial period of time."[57] Also, this picture of self reveals to what extent a person's self-understanding is realistic and whether the person can ". . . act smoothly and effectively in his dealings in the real world."[58] The well-integrated self does not function in the world cohesively on the basis of cognition alone, for the self that would be well-integrated can be described and diagnosed such that cognition and volition do not appear in essential conflict with affective responses and interpretations.[59]

To describe and diagnose a self as "well-integrated" is to say about the person that he or she has assumed agency. That is, the self is evaluated such that it can be said to be directing particular projects as well as coordinating and directing a more broadly conceived life plan. As an agent, the self perceives how its plans and needs properly relate to those of its fellows. It is therefore more likely to deal with co-agents realistically and objectively, rather than in terms of unrealistic fantasies or unbridled subjectivism; and, as Stephen Toulmin has noted, a self that actually exercises self-control expresses through that control its autonomy and effectiveness as an agent.[60] This is, of course, a psychologically drawn picture of agency, but it is a convenient way to open our discussion to agency through psychology. The self is also the agent that assumes responsibility for organizing the various constituents of selfhood. In portraying the self as a relational complex in which the ability to organize the self into a coherent personality is a task confronting each person, we conceive the self as a moral achievement. The end result of this portrayal is that we derive a picture of a person able to act effectively in the social context as a single, coherent, cohesive, and consistent personality, that is, as a responsible self. And the relational complex indicates the reality of <u>self-relatedness</u>--the relation of a self to its own self.

This picture is, of course, ideal. Clearly the self-mastery required for self-mastery does not come easy. Not everyone can be described and diagnosed as having achieved adequate competence as a coordinator of self-directed projects. The simple fact is that harmonious integration represents a goal that some individuals reach more closely in some respects than in other respects, or at one time better than at other times. In the the common life, most people manage; that is, they are not "self-actualized," but neither are they incapacitated, unable to function, deluded or psychotic. From the point of view of the psychologist seeking to develop a "psychology of the self," it seems that actual failures to achieve that degree of cohesiveness in one's self-relations required for smooth functioning in the "real world" (Toulmin's phrase) will result in the individual either failing to assume, or managing to lose, agency itself. I would add, parenthetically, that a <u>patient</u> (Gk <u>pema</u>: suffering) in this "descriptive-diagnostic" view would be one to whom things "happen," one who suffers, who awaits treatment, whose experiences are incoherent. A therapy based on this particular way of evaluating the self aims at assisting the individual to assume or resume agency--to become a single, coherent, and consistent personality capable of effecting the aims of its intended life plan in a social context, capable of "love and work" to use Freud's familiar phrase.

The use of 'self' as a free-standing noun consistent with this "descriptive-diagnostic" understanding constitutes a use of 'self' that is closely related to, even parasitic on, the ordinary reflexive use. This is to say that we have a familiar experience of reflexive conduct, that it is a distinct species of conduct,[61] and that our everyday use of reflexives in the language of the common life reflects the following: 1.) that 'self' functions as an auxiliary prefix or suffix to indicate that the governing relations are those which turn back to the grammatical subject; and 2.) that by extension of meaning, 'self' functions as a free-standing noun to indicate the complex of intrapsychic relations that actually constitute the person as a person, as an individual, as a self, through relations that can be described and evaluated. Now, of course, we must bring these remarks to bear on our ordinary language analysis of the concept 'self-deception.'

The problem that must be addressed when confronting the issue of 'self-deception' from the 'self' pole is whether the self can be so conceived that we can say that it relates itself to itself deceptively. This is a problematic issue because it can be argued that we have unearthed two distinct senses of 'self,' one of which would negate even the logical possibility of there being such a thing as 'self-deception;' the other of which would enable us to describe 'self-deception' as a species of 'deception'--perhaps to the point of explaining the actual mechanics of its operations.[62] I wish to make this distinction clearer.

I have presented a picture of the self as agent, developing that picture from cognitive, volitional and cognitive components. These components, as I said, play significant roles in the individual's self-relations, which, if they be in discord, yield conflict and fragmentation, and which, if they be well-integrated, yield a consistent, cohesive personality. On the one hand, then, we could understand 'self' as Alston argues, meaning by our noun employment that the person before us is presented as one who is the object of self-directed cognitions, actions and attitudes. Moreover, we added that the person as self can be described in the language of autonomy. A 'self' is therefore the person as he or she is capable of self-direction and self-control, who presents to the world a cohesive and consistent personality. The person before us, then, is a <u>self</u>; and by that we would mean that he or she is integrated such that we encounter an individual, a man/woman, a person--a single, cohesive and consistent personality. This is, I would suggest, a <u>holistic</u> conception, one which renders the ordinary meaning of 'self' <u>qua</u> noun a functional equivalent to 'person,' 'man/woman,' 'individual.' 'Self,' in other words, serves as a convenient shorthand for this holistic notion, and our linguistic community has authorized <u>this</u> term to mean <u>that</u>. This is to stipulate what I shall term the <u>holistic</u> meaning of 'self.'

On the other hand, because 'self' refers us to the ordinary notion of reflexivity, the self can also be conceived as a <u>relation</u>--specifically, the intrapersonal relation of a self to its own self. This picture, though bound to cumbersome and aesthetically displeasing language, is most immediately intelligible when we consider the dynamics of self-relatedness that underscore our ideas of the person in conflict, the person who is experiencing incoherence, who is so present to others that he or she may be described as fragmented or disintegrated. Although technically speaking such description and diagnosis is associated with a "psychology of the self" movement in modern psychology, it is also clear that such description and diagnosis is available to all who observe human behavior and reflect on the experience of intrapsychic conflict. Frank Norris' comment in <u>McTeague</u> that such conflicts are ". . .the old battle, old as the world, wide as the world" aptly describes the self experiencing fragmentation and loss of agency.[63] It hardly needs mentioning that the great religious traditions of the world have addressed themselves to the kinds of conflicts that rob individuals of "inner peace." That persons struggle with themselves is certainly not a new idea; the picture of the self as a relation--as the relation of intrapsychic relatedness--is, for all of its complexity, a picture with which all of us are familiar.

The "relatedness" picture of self constitutes the second notion of self with which I am concerned. It is not inconsistent with the holistic notion; it is in fact complementary and a necessary prerequisite to the development of a holistic notion. What this picture offers is a framework for conceiving intrapsychic relatedness. It refers to the arena where various and often opposing components of the personality dynamically and reflexively interact.

To think of the self in terms of "self-relatedness" is to take into account that several factors affect our capacity to conduct ourselves in the world with self-direction and self-control. Conflicts arise in conjunction with assuming self-direction and self-control, and we settle accounts with ourselves either in the direction of integration, which reflects self-mastery, or in the direction of disintegration, which reflects a loss of agency and self-command. Self-mastery requires what we ordinarily term 'self-knowledge'--

the ability of persons to know their own mind, their own propensities and capacities and inclinations. To know oneself is to be able to act consistently with declared intentions. Furthermore, self-knowledge requires that we recognize our individual standing as one agent in a community of co-equal agents and that we be able to match our conduct to ". . .intentions, capacities and perceived situations."[64] Self-mastery requires self-knowledge, for self-knowledge is required for discerning and then managing the conflicts of selfhood. Self-knowledge is not simply cognitive knowing, but is the totality of understanding that issues from the intrapersonal relations that constitute us as selves. To know oneself is to understand one's own capabilities, feelings, motivations and character; it is <u>ideally</u> a picture in which the self appears without obscurity to its own eye--luminous and transparent--for no content is hidden from the oversight of consciousness. Ideally, and by that I mean that the self-understanding acquired by the self is flawless, the self that knows itself grasps all it perceives and sees clearly all that comes under the purview of consciousness.

I have presented the two ways of stipulating a meaning for the noun employment of <u>self</u>. These are inter-related notions that extend the meaning of the reflexive pronoun 'self.' In a noun employment, the <u>holistic</u> conception represents the current state of self-relatedness, the actual state of integration/fragmentation that presents itself to us, to the world, as this person, John Smith. The <u>relatedness</u> conception refers us to the actual dynamics of a person's self-relations to which we, as observers and outside evaluators, have access inasmuch as we, too, are persons of similar constitution, persons capable of recognizing the manifestations of self-relatedness as they are made available to the outside world. (We know when a person is depressed or anxious or joyous or indifferent, though lacking privileged access to a person's own self-understanding, we may not know immediately the reasons why.)[65] In any event, these two notions are clearly related to each other. To speak of John Smith's <u>self</u> holistically entails some prior ability to describe and evaluate his <u>self</u> as that particular configuration of intrapersonal relations, reflexively conceived relations, that yield the cohesive person who stands before us as John Smith.

To know another person involves some access to that person's self-understanding as it is manifest in the way the person comports him- or herself in the "real world." An encounter with another person is always an encounter with a manifestation of self-relatedness, which is to say that to the extent we evaluate another person as cohesive rather than fragmented, we acknowledge that the person's self-relations have enabled him or her to assume agency, to achieve self-direction and self-control, rather than otherwise. This is what is entailed by speaking about a person's <u>self</u>, taking that to be an extension of an ordinary reflexive notion, though an extension consistent with the relations governed by the concept of reflexivity.

'Self-deception' is a reflexive concept. The linguistic expression refers an occurrent deception back to the grammatical subject, so that the literal meaning of this expression is that some individual, some person, some particular man/woman has deceived him- or herself. From a linguistic point of view, 'self' serves to circumscribe the relations involved in the deception. The actual statement of those relations, however, issues in a description that employs an extended "noun use" of self, which is to say that the self-as-agent acts such that its own self is concurrently made the victim of a belief-misleading project, i.e., a 'deception.' The problem is to ascertain whether this is a coherent notion.

My analysis of deception revealed that a deception is a belief-misleading project involving two person--deceiver and deceived--in an epistemic deficit. If two persons are a necessary condition for a deception, how is it possible for a deception to take place within the context of one person? If we are to hold that 'self-deception' is a meaningful derivative of 'deception'--and not an idiosyncratic linguistic convention that abuses the ordinary meaning of words--'self-deception' must likewise require two parties for the creation of an epistemic gap. But how can one person be two persons? If there are not two persons or parties, how can we properly employ the language of 'deception?' These questions, which must be asked, have proven so difficult that certain philosophers and psychologists have concluded that 'self-deception' is a paradoxical notion that cannot happen.[66]

b. Toward Solution

In order to understand the concept 'self-deception' we must address the problems that emerge from reflecting on the meaning of the linguistic expression. We set out to identify the conceptual difficulties presented by ordinary language considerations, and, at this point, we could content ourselves with having exposed many of those problems. We shall not let matters sit here, however, for we ultimately face an "all-or-nothing" proposition--either it makes sense to say that persons can actually 'deceive' themselves or it doesn't. How is this issue to be decided?

I wish to argue that the holistic and relatedness conceptions of self provide the necessary contextual and conceptual wherewithal that makes it possible to continue our investigation into the meaning of 'self-deception.' This reflexively conceived picture of the self also provides a counterpoint to certain views that are prominent in the self-deception debate. Those philosophers and psychologists who have resolved the self-deception debate by concluding that the concept is contradictory and that one person cannot be the two persons required for a deception have, in my view, misrepresented the holistic notion of self and advanced what is actually a unitary notion of self. These are not equivalent conceptions, even though each of them permits us to speak of a cohesive self, the man, the individual, the person whom we identify as, say, John Smith. The paradox that self-deception invokes is said to be epistemological, but that paradox arises because of an assumption about the self. In order for 'self-deception' to get stymied in contradiction, it must be assumed that the self is not capable of actually opposing itself--of believing p and not-p simultaneously--as ordinary language analysis requires. We must examine now the picture of self that will permit this description and the picture that will not.

Let me say this: In order for self-deception to present an inscrutable paradox, one must assume that the self is an actually unified structure. In other words, the self must be unitary, and by that I mean that in knowing p it is unable not to know p. The unitary conception of self is equivalent to the ideal conception of self mentioned above, the self that is not divided against itself, the self that does not hide from itself or obscure itself to itself. I wish to argue that a unitary conception of self diverges in one significant aspect from the holistic notion I have advanced. That single difference is that the unitary picture does not rely on a prior notion of reflexivity or self-relatedness. In the holistic picture reflexivity and self-relatedness constitute the actual dynamics of selfhood, and it is the manifestation of these dynamic relations in the public world that enables us to speak of self as a functional equivalent to person.

If what we mean by the self-that-is-deceived is actually a unified structure of personality, then our operative conception of self would not function to indicate reflexive self-relatedness. It would not function holistically as the current state of integrated/fragmented self-relatedness, but as a sort of identity monad. That is, the person who stands before us, Jane Smith, is this individual, this person, and this one is to be identified as the self-identical entity or unified structure of personality that we encounter. A unitary view of self would not require us to discern Jane Smith's self-relations, or even consider them. Rather, inasmuch as this person can be identified as Jane Smith, identified with the unified personality entity that we encounter in the real world, this particular person appears to us as a cohesive entity, a single and unified human being, which is named and recognized and interacted with as a single self-identical and actually unified personality. Jane Smith, then, presents herself (her "self") to the world as a unified, single and cohesive entity, and that picture of unity is not distorted or disrupted by a consideration of her mental states, her feelings, her intentions and volitions, which, in this view, are part and parcel of the unity.

On the basis of this unitary conception of self, we can infer that Jane Smith is conscious of herself in such a way that nothing to which her consciousness has access as content can be hidden from the oversight of consciousness. That is, anything that Jane Smith knows or believes is accessible as content to consciousness, so that consciousness is transparent to itself, able to grasp the entirety of its own content. On this unitary and transparent conception of selfhood, persons can be assumed to be conscious of that unity, which is the person's own sense of identity. This is a familiar picture of consciousness and selfhood. Descartes, for one, endorsed this unitary and transparent picture when he asserted that consciousness is common to all operations of the mind (i.e., mind as "thinking substance").[67] Moreover, certain psychologists have supported a unitary view of consciousness,[68] and, as a related development, some psychologists holding this view have adjudged certain psychological 'phenomena' (e.g., "perceptual defense") to be paradoxical, hence impossible features of actual behavior.[69]

A unitary conception of the self and a transparent conception of consciousness yield only one plausible conclusion with respect to the idea of self-deception: it is a contradictory notion that cannot be instantiated. This conclusion obtains because according to this view of selfhood, no structural feature of mind or capacity of consciousness is available to make possible the kind of intrapsychic conflict that opposes and subverts the oversight capacity of consciousness itself. There is no room for "unconsciousness" even in a minimal sense, no room for hiddenness in the structure of the mind. There is no way to conceive of opaqueness in self-relatedness. The point, then, is that if the picture of a unified self and a transparent consciousness were to hold, it would be logically absurd to claim that a single person--a unified and transparent self--can intentionally act to mislead his or her own beliefs and bring about an intrapsychic epistemic deficit. An awareness of, or belief that, p would necessarily negate the possibility of being simultaneously unaware of, or disbelieving that, p. To suggest that the person before us could assume contradictory roles, that as a unified self this person could be both avow the truth of p as agent of a deception and avow the truth of not-p as victim, defies the canons of common sense and the logical requirement that a unitary and transparent self be unitary and transparent. The literal expression, 'self-deception,' would be a logically untenable notion. Furthermore, if there be some phenomenon to which 'self-deception' has been used to refer (e.g., not noticing), then we should scrap this particular linguistic expression and replace it with some other, more adequate expression that does not distort the actual meaning of the words employed, thereby misrepresenting the phenomenon. Whatever that phenomenon might be, it is clear that it cannot be what the expression literally signifies, so the conclusion follows that literal 'self-deception' cannot happen.[70]

The self-relatedness conception of self advanced earlier in this section is incompatible with this unitary and transparent conception of self. The picture I have offered, the picture of intrapsychic relatedness which at any moment can be described and evaluated holistically such that it yields for this person, man/woman, individual this degree of cohesiveness or that degree of fragmentation, is derived from extending the concept of reflexivity from ordinary pronomial use to a free-standing noun use. This move preserves the relations governed by the concept of reflexivity, for it is a move that preserves the dynamics of intrapersonal relations and enables us to speak of intrapsychic conflict.

In response to the <u>unified</u> and <u>transparent</u> picture of self that renders the concept 'self-deception' paradoxical and ultimately unintelligible, I can only say that there is precious little evidence to support such a view. Advocates of non-unitary and non-transparent theories of self have included many observers of human behavior, persons as diverse as Plato,[71] St. Paul,[72] William James,[73] and Freud.[74] The novelists and playwrights who have concerned themselves with characterizing intrapsychic conflicts would include just about anyone's favorite authors. And I would appeal to the experience of my reader. Reflect on your experiences of psychological fragmentation and disunity, and there you will find, in our common life, examples and evidence sufficient to support a relatedness conception of self.

The notion of a unified and transparent consciousness has been radically undermined by Freud's Theory of the Unconscious, which is a theory of structural division in mental life. We need not press Freud's theory into service in order to establish a picture of mental life marked by intrapsychic conflict and division. By observing human behavior, we can say in a a purely descriptive way that a picture of mind is available to us whereby self-conflict, self-relatedness, and self-consciousness[75] reflect a commonplace understanding of human being. This point must be stressed: Even if we were to reject Freud's particular theory as an inadequate "hypothetical-explanatory" model of selfhood, we would still have to deal with Freud's case studies, with Freud's "data," with his observations of persons making manifest intrapersonal conflicts, conflicts that are observable in the common life as experiences of psychic incoherence and personality fragmentation. We would still have to deal with the "descriptive-diagnostic" Freud and the diagnostic fact that persons are capable of acting inconsistently with respect to declared intentions. Freud describes and diagnoses for us case after case of personality fragmentation, of persons whose behavior reveals incoherence and whose acts reflect a lack of self-understanding. Again and again, Freud shows us persons unable to function smoothly in the real world, unable, that is, to assume agency and the command necessary for self-control. Freud's case studies are portraits of people divided in mind and spirit, people who are unable to function in the social context harmoniously, who suffer conflicts so debilitating that they are unable to "love or work."

Freud introduces his readers to individuals who "suffer" from fragmentation and psychic division, persons whose degree of cohesiveness is low, who lack self-knowledge and insight, whose personalities manifest "enigmatic products" both to themselves and to their fellows. It was in light of this kind of description and diagnosis that psychoanalysis announced its therapeutic intention: to intervene in this behaviorally manifest psychic conflict to the end that the afflicted person might begin to work towards re-integration. The goal of therapy was to assist the patient in establishing an integrated self-understanding so that an actual resumption of agency might be forthcoming. "The therapeutic ideal," writes Herbert Fingarette, "is to interconnect all functioning systems and yet not produce an overload of a confusion of systems"; moreover, ". . .the drive toward integration is a drive toward that state where, according to Freud, 'all enigmatic products of life (have been) elucidated.' It is, that is to say, a drive toward meaning."[76] It can be shown from Freud's descriptive and diagnostic data that human lives are replete with severed connections, disintegration, neurosis, and "enigmatic products." Psychoanalysis is a vision of reintegration. A unitary and transparent consciousness represents an abstract ideal behind the theory. It is not the psychological reality with which the practicing psychotherapist works. Neither is it the achievement of the psychoanalytic art.[77]

The perspectives of modern psychology and psychoanalytic theory explicitly support the view of self and self-consciousness argued for in these pages. It is not a view that renders talk about a person, an individual, a man/woman, a particular human being non-sense as that person stands before us as John Smith. Rather, this view maintains that an individual is not present to us as a "self-identical entity" (Fingarette's characterization) but as a self-related psychic complex unique in its particular balance and rational composite. No matter how integrated a person might become in actuality, the language of person never refers to the abstraction of perfect and ideal integration, for person, psychologically speaking, functions to reveal an individual's current state of inter-relatedness: the holistic presentation of self as person. We are not authorized to extrapolate from the holistic notion of person to the self-identical entity conception--the unitary and transparent view--of person, for the evidence of the common life will not support such a move.[78] That we do not experience ourselves as perfectly integrated, that we are not conscious of ourselves or our world in a way that supports a transparent view of consciousness, constitute descriptive and diagnostic facts about our constitution as human persons. That these are facts we know from our own experiences of incoherence and from observing the fragmented behavior of others. What is surprising is that the unitary and transparent position emerges at all--yet it does in philosophical discussions of self-deception.

c. The Paradox Restated and Resolved

Once again I pose the question about the "paradox" of self-deception, this time from the 'self' pole of the expression. How can a person deceive him- or herself when a deception requires (at least) two persons, a deceiver and a deceived? How can one person, one consciousness play both roles? How can a belief-misleading project be directed and enacted by a self against itself such that the actual epistemic deficit required for a first-order deception obtains? How can one person be said to believe p and believe not-p at the same time, when believing p seems to preclude the possibility of believing not-p?

To put the dilemma in these terms is to make it appear that the issue--

hence the puzzle--is strictly epistemological. My contention, however, is that to focus on the logical problem raised by the specter of one person being concurrently aware yet unaware is to misconstrue--and misrepresent--the real issue. The real issue is whether human subjects have an actual capacity for instantiating this "contradiction" as a feature of actual behavior; that is, does it happen that one can so relate oneself to oneself that opposition, even opposition of beliefs, can be said to exist as a feature of that self-relatedness? If we can say this, then the "contradiction" we observe in a person's behavior can be described and evaluated as the behavioral manifestation of an opposition occurrent in the self-relations. Then the paradox refers not to a logical contradiction, but to a way of characterizing an actual intrapsychic opposition. That opposition is manifest in publicly observable ways, and we can observe persons who are unaware of both the disconnectedness in their self-relations and the public manifestation of that disconnectedness. In the common life, we think of ourselves as coherent personalities with discrete identities, not as disrelated, fragmented or disintegrating selves. We conceive of ourselves holistically, even monadicly, for we experience ourselves in the put-togetherness of our personal "identities." Our desire for personality coherence is like a fundamental drive toward meaning; and so strong is that drive that even in the midst of increasing personality fragmentation we continue to refer ourselves to that unified sense of "who I am." This center of self-identity is really the pattern of continuity that we, and others, come to understand as the person I am; but we often trust that sense of self to be more than continuity, which is to say that on occasion we can interpret our own behavior in a way consistent with that pattern while making ourselves unaware that our "sense of self" is not actually unified to the extent we would hope or actually believe. An example will illustrate these points.

An employer, Mr. Jones, wants to be respected by his employees. He therefore acts toward his employees in a way that he believes is consistent with his stated aim--to have their respect. Let us say about Jones that his behavior is interpreted by the employees as being arrogant, haughty and condescending. I wish to say two things: 1.) The employees are in a position to describe and evaluate Jones' behavior towards them as being "arrogant" or "condescending." 2.) Jones himself is unaware that his behavior is, or could be construed as, arrogant. An employee, Ms. Smith, confronts Jones to complain about the way Jones has treated her. Jones is surprised by the confrontation, denies being arrogant, and responds to Smith that in order to hold the respect of his employees, he has acted in a firm but caring manner, a manner he describes as "fatherly." In response to Jones' self-interpretation, Smith says that all the employees have complained about Jones' arrogant attitude and his condescending manner in dealing with his employees.

I wish to say several things about this example. First, it seems quite common that our self-interpretations may conflict with the interpretations of our behavior (and motives) others may make.[79] There may be agreement over the facts: in this case, that Jones acted in several interpersonal encounters in a certain way, said certain things, made certain gestures and so on. Disagreement arises, however, over what the facts mean and how they are to be interpreted. Jones thinks about his relations to his employees as being "fatherly"--caring but firm. His self-perceived firmness, however, is perceived by others as expressing an attitude of overbearingness and exaggerated self-importance. A conflict then, could be said to exist between Jones' own interpretation of his behavior and that offered by those whom Jones encounters. It does not seem far-fetched to suggest that a person could act arrogantly, yet not interpret his actions to himself as expressing an arrogant attitude. Nor does it seem far-fetched to suggest that being confronted with the accusation of arrogance, Jones could express real surprise. Jones' declared intention was to win the respect of his employees, an aim which would be undermined by arrogant behavior. Since Jones obviously would not consciously set out to undermine his declared goal by acting arrogantly, it is clear that he was unaware that he was acting arrogantly. He was unaware that others thought he was acting arrogantly, unaware that his behavior was being interpreted in a way other than, and contrary to, his interpretation.

In addition to noting that an interpersonal conflict over how best to describe Jones' behavior, let me suggest that we have grounds for inferring an intrapersonal conflict. That intrapersonal conflict is manifest in the unawareness, or, to be more specific, in Jones' denial. In denying that arrogance represents an accurate description of his behavior, Jones reveals an intrapsychic opposition. Jones' desire to be respected is pitted against Jones' ability to interpret his own actions. His actions contribute evidence that disconfirm Jones' own self-understanding. Jones, after all, believes he is acting in a "fatherly" way and when confronted with a contradictory interpretation denies that contrary interpretation, perhaps rationalizing that Smith doesn't speak for everyone, or that Smith has stupidly or maliciously misinterpreted his motives and actions. Jones, in effect, denies having any motive consistent with action that expresses arrogant attitudes. His denial reveals to us that Jones himself has not considered his actions or attitudes "arrogant," or "haughty," or "condescending." Smith and her fellow employees, however, think otherwise. Because of an overbearing manner and an attitude where his sense of self-importance is exaggerated, Jones reveals himself to be arrogant. He is experienced as such and "arrogance" is deemed by Smith to be a fit characterization.

Perhaps it could be said about Jones that he is "lying to himself" about his behavior. This might be said because Jones' interpretation of the facts of his behavior constitutes a "belief misleading project" directed by Jones against himself, the result being that Jones believes something to be true, namely, that he is not arrogant, when evidence in the form of a general (here: unanimous) consensus disputes and disconfirms that belief. If Jones can be shown to have acted in a manner consistent with meeting the criteria for ascribing "arrogance," and if an accumulation of evidence shows a consistent pattern of action substantiating this description, then Jones' refusal to acknowledge "arrogance" looks to be the act that creates an epistemic gap. There appears to be a gap between certain facts of behavior about which both Smith and Jones could agree and their respective interpretations. Jones appears to be distorting the most reasonable interpretation of the behavioral data, construing the facts in a certain light, shaping the facts so that they lend themselves to a "fatherly" rather than an "arrogant" evaluation. Accordingly, it could be said that Jones is engaged in an <u>interpretive activity</u> that does not accurately evaluate the evidence of his behavior, that in fact he is "covering up" the best interpretation with one consistent with his declared intentions. That "cover up" appears to be motivated. Jones, after all, knows that "arrogance" is inconsistent with his declared desire to win the respect of his employees, so that Smith's accusation of "arrogance" is denied for a reason. The reason is that Jones desires to preserve a picture of himself as a "fatherly"--caring but firm--employer. This is Jones' self-perception; this is the description of his behavior most consistent with his desire to be respected. He is therefore motivated to preserve this picture and to deny accusations to the contrary. "Fatherliness" is consistent with Jones' desire for respect, and this desire leads to a willful interpretive distortion.

We can say about Jones that he lacks both self-knowledge and insight into how his behavior affects others. His behavior reveals a contradiction between self-understanding and the most reasonable interpretation of this behavior, namely, that the behavior reveals an arrogant rather than a fatherly attitude. The point is not that Jones has misused the language, mistaking "fatherliness" for "arrogance." Rather, Jones knows what 'arrogance' means and does not wish to consider himself arrogant. He has not entertained the possibility of such a characterization, has never made <u>that</u> connection between the behavior and how best to describe it. To say, then, about Jones that he is "lying to himself" about the best, most reasonable interpretation of the behavioral facts is to suggest that Jones knows the facts but refuses to acknowledge them in terms appropriate to the ascription of 'arrogance.' He defends himself from Smith's charge that he has acted arrogantly by interpreting his conduct in light of his <u>declared</u> intentions and motives. What Jones professes about his behavior is inconsistent with the public perception, yet he is able to derive plausible, albeit unsound, reasons for his conduct by continuing to interpret his actions in light of his "fatherly" interpretation. Jones' own understanding of his conduct yields a linguistically explicit intention inconsistent with the public perception; and because actions follow from motives and express intentions, we must conclude that Jones has acted to interpret his behavior in a way that reveals his unawareness of arrogant behavior. Jones own interpretation preserves a certain desired self-image, one consistent with "fatherliness," but his interpretation distorts the behavior. By rationalizing the arrogant behavior and interpreting it as caring but firm ("fatherly")

Jones protects himself from a painful recognition while providing himself with plausible, though ultimately untrue, reasons for his conduct.

This is an example drawn from the common life. It is designed to illustrate how an unconscious motive or a case of "simultaneous awareness/unawareness" might be included in a description of a very ordinary occurrence, namely, the person who shows surprise when informed that his conduct has been arrogant and that this view is widely shared. The point, however, is not that this provides us with a paradigm case of self-deception. The point is that we are able to describe and diagnose quite ordinary instances of persons "acting out" intrapsychic conflict and do so 1.) for reasons and 2.) unawares. Of course not every dispute about conduct in which a person defends him- or herself illustrates a manifestation of intrapsychic conflict. We quite often defend ourselves from an accusation convincingly and justifiably. In the case of Smith and Jones, however, we determined that the arrogance of Jones constituted a generally (nay: unanimously) accepted characterization. Although this may appear unrealistic because we invoked a unanimity that rarely obtains in actual cases, agreement can be reached in our evaluations of conduct. We share the language of the common life, and that language works even when the matter at hand seems open to countless interpretations. Deeper agreements are possible. Whether a public speaker is a good public speaker is an evaluation that must be made by the public. If a public speaker believes him- or herself to be a good public speaker, but the public generally criticizes the person for poor public speaking, then the public speaker is denying the interpretation that matters most. Arrogance is like public speaking. People do not ascribe arrogance capriciously, but according to governing rules and criteria. Just as there are poor public speakers who think that they are good public speakers (with consistently inattentive audiences?), so too there are arrogant people unaware that they comport themselves arrogantly. Our conduct is publicly observable: we ascribe "arrogance" by determining how a person acts "in public." Using the language of the common life, we are able to make judgments about human conduct--whether it is "arrogant" or "fatherly." If my behavior is arrogant, it will be observed as such by members of my linguistic community; and my wanting it to be "fatherly" will not alter the public evaluation.

The Smith and Jones example, then, is a picture of intrapsychic conflict made manifest in publicly observable ways. This is so familiar an experience that examples abound. We could, for instance, be Sartrian about the matter: a man's publicly observable behavior satisfies our commonly shared criteria for ascribing 'homosexuality' yet he denies that he is, in fact, a homosexual.[80] What would appear a logical contradiction on a "unitary self" description, namely, that a person could be a homosexual and at the same time not be a homosexual, can now be rendered intelligible thorough a "relatedness" conception of self: a person displays the sexual preference attributes of a homosexual, but, for discernible reasons, refuses to acknowledge that he is a homosexual; so he denies that he is a homosexual and functions in the world oblivious to the fact that his behavior related to sexual preference presents him to his linguistic community as a homosexual. This individual exhibits behaviorally an intrapsychic disconnectedness: he denies being a homosexual and construes his action such that it does not yield a homosexual interpretation; but the best, most reasonable interpretation of the behavioral facts dictates otherwise. What we describe and diagnose in this instance is not a logical paradox. It is, rather, an intrapsychic opposition made manifest behaviorally. The person acts: the person's interpretation is consistent with a desire not to be thought a homosexual, though the interpretation is inconsistent with the most reasonable interpretation. The intrapsychic opposition is made manifest in the difference between the action, which lends itself to one interpretation (p), and the linguistic activity that offers an alternative interpretation (not-p), which misconstrues the meaning of the facts.

When we say that a person acts such that he satisfies the criteria for ascribing homosexuality, then add that the person's denial exposes a disconnectedness in the person's self-relations, we are not saying that this person cannot be understood or that this situation yields a logical contradiction. We do not have an actual contradiction, only an actual conflict that has the "air of paradox" because we are dealing with one person rather than two. In order to resolve the paradox of self-deception, we must keep in mind the intrapsychic dynamics that are at work. We do have "two parties" to the conflict. 1.) One of those parties is the actual desire associated with an inclination toward "homosexual" preference. This desire is manifest in certain kinds of publicly observable behavior that the person in question interprets one way, but is publicly interpreted another way. 2.) The "other party" to the intra-relational conflict is the contrary and opposing desire not to be associated with the public interpretation ('homosexuality'). This desire generates <u>interpretive activity</u> about the meaning of one's own behavior, though, as I have said about this particular instance, the behavior is more appropriate to a "homosexual interpretation" than to the person's contrary interpretation, which constitutes a denial or rationalizing of the behavior.

The two persons required for a literal deception are not present in this example. We do have, however, "two parties" reflexively conceived, namely, two conflicting and opposing desires; and from this opposition an epistemic deficit obtains between the facts of the behavior and how best to interpret those facts. The person reluctant to acknowledge that his behavior is "homosexual" covers up the best, most reasonable interpretation of the evidence with an alternative interpretation that is itself consistent with a counter-desire, whence the impetus for undertaking a project to mislead one's own beliefs may be said to be located. This counter-desire, in turn, effects a belief about the behavior that is inconsistent with the public assessment as that is dictated by the language of the common life. Supporting the non-homosexual interpretation requires that the evidence itself be distorted such that it is rendered consistent with the belief that the person is not a homosexual (not-p), a cognitive "rationalizing" activity designed to avoid another contrary belief (p) that is too painful to accept. We say, then, that this person is a homosexual but denies it. Furthermore, we can say that his denial represents action consistent with his self-understanding. We can say that this person can (probably) explain the behavioral evidence of his actions as being consistent with linguistically explicit intentions. And we can say of his "subjectivist" interpretation that it reveals an unawareness of the intentions and motives that can be attributed to the actual behavior according to the linguistic conventions of the common life.

The homosexual interpretation arises from public observation, public description and public diagnosis. By observing the person's actual behavior, by hearing his interpretation and the public interpretation that opposes it, we can conclude that an intrapsychic conflict is being made manifest in a public arena by observable action. We can describe that conflict by saying that the person does not want to consider himself a homosexual. He behaves, however, in a way consistent with those criteria that we, as members of a linguistic community, have been authorized to ascribe to behavior that indicates 'homosexuality.' A disparity, then, exists between the person's declared, linguistically explicit interpretation and the public interpretation. We observe that the person is unaware that a "homosexual interpretation" is the best, most reasonable interpretation of the action, so we say that the person is unaware of the dispositions and intentions that give rise to the actual behavior. He "covers up" the best interpretation with another interpretation, one that enables him to avoid the displeasure of admitting homosexual proclivities--which this person does find distressing--while preserving a desired self-image as heterosexual.

In a curious way, then, homosexuality is like public speaking or arrogance: a certain individual could very well express surprise that others consider his or her behavior to mean something contrary to the person's self-understanding. The kind of unawareness to which I refer is not uncommon. It represents, rather, a quite ordinary manifestation of disconnectedness in intrapersonal relations. The descriptive fact of unawareness reflects the fact that a person may be unaware of a certain intention, motive, or emotion, when that intention, motive, or emotion is opposed by a "party" which, in turn, issues in action more amenable to the person's regulative self-understanding. Human persons have the capacity to be unaware as I have described. Human subjects have a capacity for so relating themselves to themselves that the conflict between opposing desires ("parties") yields behavior that is likewise opposed. A denial or rationalization confirms the conflict and the unawareness--were we certain that the actual behavior was contrary to the subject's interpretation.

My position, then, is that the epistemological issues that arise in conjunction with a logico-linguistic analysis of 'self-deception' cannot be addressed independently of the actual relational context within which 'self-deception' obtains--which is the context of self-relatedness, intrapsychic conflict, intrapersonal dynamics. Self-deception does not emerge, then, as a logical problem, but as a configuration of self-relatedness. This configuration is difficult to describe if certain assumptions about selfhood are not challenged (i.e., unitary and transparent view). The <u>self</u>, I have argued, is a logical and legitimate extension or our ordinary pronomial conception of reflexivity and as such represents the capacity of the person for varied, dynamic and complex kinds of intrapersonal relations. Evidence from the common life reveals that there are misconnections in a person's self-relations such that intrapsychic conflict, or what appears to us through disconnected, even "contradictory" behavior, may be inferred. In other words, the current state of the person's self-relations will be accurately described by employing the language of "conflict" and "contradiction."

> For when a man has an attitude which it seems to us he should not have or lacks one which it seems to us he should have, then, not only do we suspect that he is not influenced by connections which we feel should influence him and draw his attention to these, but also we suspect he is influenced by connections which should not influence him and draw his attention to these. It may, for a moment, seem strange that we should draw his attention to connections which we feel should not influence him, and which, since they do influence him, he has in a sense already noticed. But we do--such is our confidence in 'the light of reason.'[81]

The author of these remarks, John Wisdom, goes on to say that these connections are not made linguistically explicit by the person who seems to us to be acting blindly, or out of wrongheadedness or wrongheartedness. That is, the connections are <u>unspoken</u>:

> Whether or not we call the process of showing up these connections 'reasoning to remove bad unconscious reasoning' or not, it is certain that in order to settle in ourselves what weight we shall attach to someone's confidence or attitude we not only ask him for his reasons but also look for unconscious reasons both good and bad; that is, for reasons which he can't put into words, isn't explicitly aware of, isn't aware of at all. . . .[82]

Judgments about unawareness can be made on the basis of observation, and our employment of expressions such as "unaware that" or "unconscious that" represent legitimate characterizations based on our description and diagnosis of "contradictory" behavior.

If consciousness is opaque--rather than transparent--at any given moment, if, that is, consciousness does not have full access to its own contents, then one cannot conceive of consciousness monolithically or monadicly. There can be degrees of consciousness, different ways of being aware, some of which may be beyond the grasp of linguistic recognition at any given moment. It is even reasonable to assume that a self is endowed with a capacity to entertain one awareness at the expense of the another, which is to say that while focusing on A, I "forget" not-A or disregard its importance. Clearly, if the self does have a capacity for entertaining opposing awarenesses, emphasizing one while suppressing its contrary, that capacity is exercised when we observe a person "opposing" him- or herself in some way, unawares.

An "explanatory-hypothetical" Theory of the Unconscious need not be invoked in order for us to observe the disparity between a person' denial of ,say, love and his or her "obvious" affection. We can talk about such things in more modest terms, for we can talk about a person who is disposed to action because of an "unconscious" emotion of love, an emotion that is occurrent though unrecognized. The disconnectedness between the behavior and the self-interpretation is publicly observable even if we lack an undisputed theory to explain the disconnectedness--and I noted earlier that Freud's particular formulation of a theory of Unconscious has not gone unchallenged. For our part, we have not found it necessary to put Jones, the public speaker, or the homosexual "on the couch," so to speak. We have not found it necessary to probe these examples of contradictory behavior as a depth psychologist might, for we do not ferret out the true meaning of the behavior by explaining the contradictions as if they are only intelligible with reference to deep-seated desires repressed into a structural repository of mind, the Unconscious. The point I have stressed is that such contradictoriness is behaviorally manifest and can be observed. And those observations provide the empirical data that allow us to infer that the person's current state of self-relatedness is conflicted, that the person is actually unaware of the best, most reasonable interpretation of his or her own behavior. Although I do not consider the Freudian theory invalid, my concern is only to show that we need not invoke that theory in order to observe the behavior or acknowledge the fact of "unawareness." The common life is sufficient.

While Freud's Theory of the Unconscious is thought by some to be question-begging, as earlier noted, a more common use for "unconscious" is available to us. We can, therefore, speak of emotions, or intentions or motives--even beliefs--as being unconscious--". . .not in the sense of being unsensed, unnoticed, unattended or ignored, but in the sense of being unrecognized, uncommunicable, and unavailable to awareness."[83] The significance of this characterization of unconsciousness is that it supports a self-relatedness picture of self while discounting the unitary and transparent view that would render 'self-deception' literally meaningless. Put positively, this minimal conception of unconsciousness permits us to make sense of the otherwise paradoxical notion that a person can both know and not know, believe and not believe. I have not yet provided an explanatory account of self-deception, but unless the unitary and transparent theory of self and consciousness is adequately challenged--and I believe the common life provides evidence sufficient to dethrone it--we could not inquire further. We could not pursue an investigation beyond the logical impasse created by the idea of one person having to be two persons as the first-order analogue to 'deception' requires.

I would conclude this section by noting that we do have a reason to go on, for the obstacle that stood in our way, the <u>logical</u> impossibility of there being no such thing as literal self-deception has been removed. That logical impossibility has been shown to arise from an unwarranted and inaccurate understanding of the <u>self</u>-that-is-deceived, namely, the unitary and transparent view. My alternative interpretation, based on everyday examples and observations of human action in the common life, supports the idea that the self is not unitary but is, in fact, a complex of intricate relations that are made manifest in behavior as <u>this</u> person, at this moment, being this degree of cohesiveness intrapersonally and that degree of fragmentation. We are able, therefore, to speak of "parties" to an intrapsychic relation, parties which may be in opposition just as conflicting desires are in opposition. Moreover, since we can observe the disparity between a person's behavioral self-interpretation and the best, most reasonable interpretation of that behavior, we can also speak of persons being "unaware" of their reasons for behaving as they do. This supports a theory of opaque consciousness. Together, these two notions, a non-unitary self that is holistically and relationally conceived and a non-transparent consciousness, provide the conceptual wherewithal that can render 'self-deception' intelligible as a concept related to 'deception.'

Recall that a first-order deception requires two persons. My self-relatedness picture of self enables us to speak intelligibly of "two (intrapsychic) parties," conflicting desires, for example. A first-order deception requires that an epistemic deficit be achieved as the result of intentional deceptive activity. That activity prevents the deceived person from acquiring access to the deceiver's knowledge of the facts or his or her (supposedly) true beliefs. My self-relatedness picture of self, in that it pits one term of an intrapsychic relation against another, establishes an opposition sufficient to achieve an analogous result: the person can be said to be aware of certain behavioral facts, but, because he or she denies the best, most reasonable interpretation of those facts (obviously for some reason), that person is engaging in interpretive activity (rationalizing, denying, self-persuasion) that overrides the best, most reasonable interpretation. The person acts to prevent a self-confrontation in which he or she declares the intent of the behavior in a manner consistent with the best, most reasonable interpretation. The current state of self-relatedness, in other words, renders the person before us unaware of the actual motive for the behavior, the reason being that a "subjectivist" interpretation (e.g., <u>this</u> person does not want to think of himself as homosexual, while another person admits the meaning of the facts) has effectively covered up that "unspoken" but actual motive.

To follow up on this last point: A first-order deception requires a motive of which the "deceived" person (victim) is unaware; my analysis of self enables us to attribute a similar unawareness to the self that deceives itself. A self-deceiver acts such that he or she fails to understand the true meaning and the actual motive of the behavior. A self-deceiver does not make the true meaning or the actual motive linguistically explicit to him- or herself because of some reason for wanting to avoid doing so. The true meaning, the actual motive, is therefore hidden. The motive is "unconscious;" the intention is enacted but the significance of the action is misunderstood. Yet it is this very "unconscious" motive that we, as observers, can describe and diagnose as the appropriate motive that renders the behavior intelligible, given our knowledge of human persons and their behavior and given our ability to use the language of the common life.[84] All in all, the criteria for a first-order deception may be modified in a way consistent with the requirements of reflexivity, so that it makes sense to say that a self can act to mislead its own beliefs, that this self has so related itself to itself that the person can be said to be in the grip of 'self-deception.'

The relatedness conception of self affirms a capacity of human persons to engage in complex, dynamic and conflicting intrapsychic relations. This conclusion not only makes a concept like 'self-deception' possible, but, on the basis of ordinary linguistic resources (i.e., referring 'deception' to the reflexive relationship with the grammatical subject), intelligible. Unlike the unitary and transparent picture of self and consciousness, our "relatedness" conception of self connects us to an already existing language. It is ambiguous language in some respects, but it is a language that makes talk of intrapsychic relations and degrees of fragmentation and cohesiveness meaningful. That language, in turn, makes it possible to conceive of 'self-deception' in terms of intrapsychic relations, in terms of the self relating itself to itself such that an intrapsychic 'deception' appears as one possible way in which those relations obtain.

Having taken a look at the problems associated with the notion of a deceptive self-relation, and in light of these remarks concerning a relatedness conception of self, let us consider the issue of the self-deception and paradox as a particular problem.

B. Paradox

As a concept that raises issues of logical and epistemological importance, 'self-deception' has provided modern philosophers with a hard nut to crack. Although several contemporary studies have focused specifically on the logic of a person deceiving him- or herself,[85] the recognition that 'self-deception' invokes a logical quandary goes back further than the philosophy journals of the last twenty-five years or so indicate. Kant, for instance, noted in <u>The Doctrine of Virtue</u> that "It is easy to show that man is, in fact, guilty of many <u>inner</u> lies, but to explain the possibility of an inner lie seems more difficult. For a lie requires a second person whom one intends to deceive, and intentionally to deceive oneself seems to contain a contradiction."[86] The modern preoccupation with the paradox of self-deception, however, seems to have arisen from Sartre's analysis of "bad faith" in <u>Being and Nothingness</u>. In that volume, Sartre wrote the following:

> But consciousness affects itself with bad faith. There must be an original intention and a project of bad faith; this project implies a comprehension of bad faith as such and a pre-reflective apprehension (of) consciousness as affecting itself with bad faith. It follows first that the one to whom the lie is told and one who lies are one and the same person, which means that I must know in my capacity as deceiver the truth which is hidden from me in my capacity as the one deceived. Better yet I must know the truth very exactly <u>in order</u> to conceal it more carefully--and this not at two different moments, which at a pinch would allow us to reestablish a semblance of duality--but in the unitary structure of a single project. How then can the lie subsist if the duality which conditions it is suppressed?

The paradox is clarified when Sartre follows these remarks with this comment:

> To this difficulty is added another which is derived from the total translucency of consciousness. That which affects itself with bad faith must be conscious (of) its bad faith since the being of consciousness is consciousness of being. It appears then that I must be in good faith, at least to the extent that I am conscious of my bad faith. But then this whole psychic system is annihilated. We must agree in fact that if I deliberately and cynically attempt to lie to myself, I fail to completely in this undertaking; the lie falls back and collapses beneath my look; it is ruined <u>from behind</u> by the very consciousness of lying to myself which pitilessly constitutes itself well within my project as its very condition. . . To escape these difficulties people gladly have recourse to the unconscious.[87]

Sartre launches his existential project at precisely this point. In a "hypothetical-explanatory" mood, Sartre proceeds to challenge the non-unitary picture of self and the non-transparent conception of consciousness advanced in Freudian psychoanalytic theory. Sartre rejects Freud's notion of unconsciousness, and this appears to hand "bad faith" or self-deception over to the logicians, who, it seems, are compelled to point out the unresolvable epistemological contradiction involved in the idea of lying to oneself. As a philosopher concerned with coherence, as good philosophers are, Sartre describes in explicit detail the logical impasse into which we are led necessarily by considering the idea of lying to oneself. Were the self as a self-identical and unitary entity to act consciously, act, that is, with all the content of consciousness translucent in and for consciousness, the attempt to lie to oneself would be destined for failure and psychic annihilation. When 'self-deception' is described as the conscious act of lying to one's own self, we confront nothing but paradox and contradiction.

This description of the paradox is derived from modeling 'self-deception' on 'deception of others' such that it appears, as Raphael Demos has written, that in self-deception, a person ". . .believes both p and $\underline{not\text{-}p}$ at the same time."[88] As it stands, this formulation of the paradox implies that from the standpoint of a translucent consciousness, 'self-deception' is equivalent to a person saying "I am lying to myself about $\underline{p}$." This is impossible, however, since knowing that one is deceived about the truth of $\underline{p}$ would preclude being deceived about the truth of $\underline{p}$. If one knew that one intended to mislead oneself about $\underline{p}$, knowledge of that intention would prevent one from doing so. This way of construing the paradox makes it look as if self-deception is that act of a unitary and transparent consciousness whereby one attempts to believe $\underline{not\text{-}p}$ even though one recognizes the truth of $\underline{p}$. This describes the contradiction of not knowing the very thing one already knows. Were this the most accurate description of the paradox of self-deception, we should either have to conclude that self-deception cannot happen--"If the notion of self-deception were really self-contradictory, there would be no such thing as self-deception: for there cannot be any instances of a self-contradictory notion"[89]--or we should have to conclude, along with D.W. Hamlyn, Terence Penelhum, and Canfield and Gustavson, that the idea of a person believing $\underline{p}$ and concurrently not believing $\underline{p}$ ($\underline{p}$ & $\underline{\text{-}p}$) is a formulation that must be avoided.[90]

In any event, modern philosophers of the analytic tradition have taken the contradictoriness entailed by one person believing "$\underline{p}$ and $\underline{not\text{-}p}$" to be the essential obstacle to rendering 'self-deception' intelligible. Various attempts have been made to resolve this paradox. Canfield and Gustavson, for instance, urged a picture in which a human subject, Jones, does not both believe and not believe, but believes in the face of "adverse circumstances." The contradiction is avoided, then, because on this description, it can be argued that when ". . .'Jones deceives himself about P is true, it is true that Jones believes P under belief-adverse circumstances, e.g., circumstances such that the evidence Jones has does not warrant belief in P.'"[91] On this description, Jones is believing p when he ought not to, but that does not entitle us to say that Jones therefore believes p and not-p concurrently. This view was challenged on the grounds that it fails to distinguish which conditions are exclusive to self-deception, since belief under "adverse circumstances" could also be the result of stupidity or naivete. Terence Penelhum, therefore, argued that in order for 'self-deception' proper to obtain, Jones must not only believe in the face of the evidence, but also know the evidence and recognize ". . .the import of the evidence."[92] Penelhum's position was itself challenged by Bela Szabados, who argued that even that qualification will not enable us to distinguish a self-deceiver from one who vacillates, hesitates or lies, since, in Szabados' view, the essential distinction between self-deception and these other concepts lies in the fact that self-deception is motivated.[93] Penelhum had argued that motive was not a necessary conceptual feature of self-deception: "I do not feel prepared to say that a motive must be present, partly because I cannot see any necessary incoherence in the concept of motiveless self-deception in odd cases. . . ."[94] Szabados attacked Penelhum on this point, but Jeffery Foss later scrutinized Szabados:

> Even if we are prepared to believe with Szabados that all self-deceivers and all mere wishful thinkers (vacillators, hesitators, liars, etc.) are exactly alike in that they are in the same state of mind, and even if we are further prepared to believe they can only be distinguished on the basis of the motives and mechanisms that got them into that unfortunate state--even so, Szabados does not specify what these motives and mechanisms must be. So at this date, no amendment or elaboration of the line of attack suggested by Canfield and Gustavson has met with unqualified success.
>   There is, moreover, another problem in the approach used by [Canfield & Gustavson, Penelhum, Szabados]. This problem is that the person who believes in the face of adverse evidence might just be right. If that is so, then he is neither deceived nor self-deceived.[95]

The debate over the paradox rests on a shaky assumption, namely, that the self that deceives itself is unitary and that consciousness is translucent. The paradox, in other words, results from holding 'self-deception' strictly to the first-order deception analogue, where an epistemic deficit can arise because it involves two distinct persons, two distinct consciousnesses in interpersonal relationship. Self-relatedness is not invoked, for the simple description of deception does not require it. To describe 'self-deception' on the basis of ordinary language features, however, is to say that one person can do reflexively what two persons in 'deception' do interpersonally, thereby affirming p and not-p simultaneously, within the context of one consciousness; and this is a move certain philosophers have been reluctant to make.

Another line of attack on the paradox was suggested by Frederick Siegler. Siegler argued that the temporal qualification attached to a 'strong' sense of self-deception, namely, the simultaneity of opposing beliefs, cannot be evidentially established. That is, we cannot generate examples that show us convincingly that a person is holding contrary beliefs at the same time. Neither can we ascertain any criteria that would permit Jones to speak of intentionally seeking to deceive himself: "We could not find evidence for 'Jones believes p and not p,' or for Jones believes not p as a result of his own procedure intended to induce a belief which he believed to be false."[96] Having therefore challenged both a strong (simultaneous) and a weak (non-simultaneous) view of self-deception, Siegler concluded that 'self-deception' serves only a rhetorical function in our language. In other words, when we say that 'Jones deceived himself,' we mean to ask how Jones could possibly believe what is obviously not true, to which Siegler responded "'He really can't.'"[97] Siegler, then, would hold that the notion of 'self-deception' is actually contradictory, and from that an irresistible conclusion follows: that 'self-deception' cannot happen. We have seen this conclusion before, but it is offered here as a logical position that necessarily follows from assuming Sartre's description of the paradox to be correct.

What happens, however, if instead of assuming that the paradox is purely a logical issue, we accept as a premise that self-deception does occur and that the expression itself is meaningful? Can the paradox be eliminated on empirical grounds?

Some analyses of self-deception begin with the quite reasonable assumption that, as one writer put it, "Since it is a datum that we engage in self-deception, the notion of self-deception cannot be more than apparently self-contradictory."[98] The paradox, then, rather than referring to the contradiction whereby one consciously believes the very epistemic object (p) that one does not consciously believe, identifies a less obvious sense of paradox. The contradiction, in other words, is either informal or only apparent. This revisionist description of the paradox holds that persons can believe p while also believing not-p, but the sting of paradox is removed because it is also said that these opposing beliefs can only be held if one of them is not acknowledged or made linguistically explicit (i.e., "unconscious belief"). To formalize the difference somewhat, instead of describing the paradox as (Jones believes p) & -(Jones believes p), a straightforward contradiction, the following revision can be offered: (Jones believes p) & (Jones believes not-p). While this is paradoxical in the sense that one person is holding contradictory beliefs, the idea is that persons are able to hold contradictory beliefs inasmuch as they are capable of not "spelling out" one of the beliefs. As John Wisdom and H.O. Mounce have argued, the human person can hold a belief and act on it without that belief becoming linguistically explicit, communicable, or available to awareness.[99]

My description, based on an analysis of ordinary language features, begins with Jones explicitly professing his belief that p. A simultaneous but opposing belief, a belief that not-p, can be inferred because Jones seems disposed to act contrary to p, and that action is consistent with not-p. An opposition is observed, but Jones appears to be unaware that not-p is the operant belief disposing him to act the way he does. If a motive can be found for Jones not wanting to recognize not-p as the belief governing his actual behavior, we have then identified the necessary and sufficient criteria for ascribing 'self-deception.'

There are everyday examples that fit this description. Consider the case of a woman who believes p when p is "that it is safe to fly." Despite an avowal of p, however, she reveals a nervousness about flying and goes to great lengths and inconvenience to avoid flying. We can say that this woman is disposed to act consistently with an operant (but unconsciously held) belief that not-p, that it is not safe to fly. She believes that it is safe to fly--a justified belief for which there is abundant evidence; but she is disposed to act contrary to her best interpretation of the evidence and does so without ever becoming aware that she also--even "really"--believes that it is not safe to fly. A person, on this view, is deemed capable of being "ignorant" (Mounce), unaware or unconscious that he or she holds a belief contrary to the professed belief. Alan Paskow has written about the the man who mistakenly believes himself to be "compassionate:"

> People are often ignorant of the fact that they hold mutually exclusive beliefs, people do sometimes make contradictory claims because they assume different (but ultimately incompatible) perspectives, and people do "conveniently" forget their motives for adopting a particular course of action. I do not think that any of the proposals thus far considered [a Platonic view: that self-deception is a form of ignorance; David Pears' view: that one can quasi-deliberately lose sight of one's original motive] truly explains the not unusual and in my opinion quintessential kind of self-deception to be seen in my example of the man worried about his lack of compassion. For this man is not, so far as I can tell, wholly ignorant of the fact that he holds a belief contradictory to his professed belief; he does not think to himself something like: "from my sober viewpoint I would admit that I'm probably uncompassionate;" and he does not over time forget his belief that he is uncompassionate. His excessively exasperated, strangely misinterpretive, projective, or compulsive behavior shows that in basic attitude he really does in some sense believe himself, repudiations notwithstanding, to be uncompassionate. If my characterization of this man is right, then the conclusion that a person simultaneously believes p and not-p to be both true, and in the same respect, is unavoidable. Sartre reaches a similar conclusion. . . .[100]

The problem here is that on the one hand, Paskow is trying to account for the fact of contradictory behavior and the observable reality of "unawareness" or "convenient unforgetting;" but on the other hand, he advances a view consistent with Sartre's unitary self and transparent consciousness view. The incompatibility to be noticed is between a "paradox" that is only apparent and one that is actually contradictory. While an "only apparent paradox" would yield a description that looks first to the facts of behavior, then to the logical issues, the "actual paradox" generates one of two irresistible conclusions: either literal self-deception cannot happen because a person cannot both know and not know the same thing in the same respect at the same time, or the observed behavior must be described in more adequate--and less misleading--linguistic expressions. To affirm the human subject's capacity for "convenient forgetting" and for "ignorance" of exclusive, contradictory yet simultaneously held beliefs, is to present a picture of human capability grounded in a non-unitary and non-transparent conception of self and consciousness. To counter that affirmation with the claim that these oppostions derive from perspectives that are "ultimately incompatible" (Paskow) is to advance a unified and transparent picture of self, a picture that yields a necessarily contradictory result.

If pressed, we might say that this description requires for coherence something like Sartre's idea of pre-reflective consciousness. This notion, to be examined in more detail in the next chapter, allows us to account for the "fact" that persons are not explicitly aware of all contents of consciousness at all times. I would add, however, that pre-reflexivity can be so interpreted that it actually counts against Sartre's own picture of consciousness since it can be argued that if, in fact, Sartre does resolve his own paradox (and that is the issue), pre-reflection ought to be considered functionally equivalent to a minimally conceived notion of "unconsciousness." This in turn permits us to see the paradox as "only apparent," so that we in effect resolve the paradox.[101] Sartre then appears not as an enemy of Freud, but as a "descriptive-diagnostic" ally who differed with Freud over the best "hypothetical-explanatory" account.

In the above quoted passage, Paskow attempts to harmonize two logically incompatible notions. Affirming the observable <u>fact</u> of unawareness as manifest in contradictory behavior, Paskow refers behavioral data to a picture of self and consciousness that cannot accommodate them. This data is the product of self-conflict that is only intelligible if it is seen as arising from a contrary, non-unitary and non-transparent picture, which is the picture consistent with a relatedness conception of self. Affirming Sartre's presentation of the structure of selfhood and the capacity of unconsciousness yields, at this point, an actual contradiction. This logical paradox is of such a form that it cannot be resolved in that form. Paskow himself remarks that Sartre "never really solved" the paradox of self-deception as he had himself formulated it;[102] and still others have argued that what Sartre pictured in his description of "bad faith" cannot happen.[103] All I wish to point out is that either of these conclusions is a necessary logical outcome given the premise of a unitary self and a transparent consciousness. Either the paradox is not solved, or the behavior pointed to cannot be described as Sartre describes it.

These conclusions are generated from "the top down." That is to say, the paradox emerges as a formal problem in logic, and that paradox is of such a character that it necessarily precludes a further elaboration of material particulars. The "apparent paradox" view, however, emerges from the material concerns associated with the data of contradictory behavior. On the basis of that behavioral data, we seek a formal description, but in the end derive only an "apparent paradox."

Were we to accept the actual or formal paradox as the true meaning or best description of 'self-deception,' we should be left with a contradictory concept, for we should have a description that is true if and only if it is false--an antimony.[104] Saying "So-and-so is self-deceived," then, would be equivalent to saying that this sentence is meaningful only to the extent that we know it to be literally false, and it would be false because a person cannot both know and not know the same thing in the same respect at the same time. This antimony or formal paradox, however, is mitigated, then disallowed, when we factor into our conceptual system a picture of mind that provides for an actual human capacity for holding epistemic opposition simultaneously. We know from the evidence of the common life that persons are able to entertain contrary beliefs, intentions, and desires. Furthermore, we know that they can profess one belief at the expense of another contrary belief, which can be suppressed or otherwise rendered "unconscious"--not available to linguistically explicit recognition. In order to resolve the paradox of self-deception, we must conceive the self as capable of such maneuvers. We must so conceive the self that we can say that this capacity for being unaware is an actual capacity, and that this capacity is part and parcel of self-relatedness. That a person believes p and not-p is not, then a problem in logic, but a descriptive remark about the dynamics of selfhood, and specifically a reference to one configuration of self-relatedness. If a human subject is capable of holding contradictory beliefs simultaneously, capable of acting on both but acknowledging only the one that is consistent with a governing self-understanding; if a human person can hold opposing beliefs because of a capacity to keep one of those beliefs at bay, unaware and unavailable to linguistically explicit recognition, then the formal paradox does not obtain. Paskow's attempt to collapse these two notions of paradox, the actual and the apparent, into one description must eventually shipwreck, since a kind of "either/or" obtains with respect to how consciousness itself is constituted. It is either unitary or it isn't. One can't have it both ways when each possibility excludes the other on logical grounds.

Any analysis of self-deception that commences with, or issues in, the description of an actual paradox assumes a unitary and transparent perspective on the human person and consciousness. Once the formal paradox is extracted and described, it may be approached in various ways, ingenious and clever ways, and philosophers continue to search for that loose thread that might unravel the tangle of contradiction. As I have argued, however, unless the unitary and transparent picture is abandoned as an inadequate way of conceiving selfhood, no satisfying resolution of the paradox is possible. Unless that transparent picture of consciousness is abandoned, attempts to sort out the logical issues will meet with only qualified success at best, or, more likely, they will further complicate the issues by obscuring that premise, making it appear that the real issue is a logical issue. The real issue, logically, is what follows from assuming that the self is unitary and consciousness transparent. How that assumption is determined is a separate issue to be decided on more than just logical grounds; and that assumption is best examined by invoking a descriptive-diagnostic analysis and by taking into account empirical evidence. Furthermore, were one to claim that Sartre, for instance, does resolve his own paradox, we must understand that such resolution is only conceivable if Sartre himself can be shown to be backing off from a strictly and inflexibly conceived picture of transparent consciousness. As I have suggested, it can be argued that Sartre's notion of pre-reflection does actually enable resolution of the paradox of self-deception since it provides the conceptual room necessary to establish the fact of human "unawareness." One can even argue that Sartre, armed with a non-Freudian, minimally conceived idea of "unconsciousness," is able to resolve the logical dilemma at the same moment he mounts a challenge to the Freudian hypothesis of psychic division and the "Unconscious." The debate between Sartre and Freud can be characterized, as I have already noted, as "hypothetical-explanatory" rather than "descriptive-diagnostic." I shall look into this matter further in the next chapter.

It is worth mentioning that certain writers have attempted to avoid the contradiction of self-deception by denying that the person who believes p and the person who believes not-p are one and the same person. This view advances a perspective that reaches back to Plato's tripartite division of the soul,[105] and, in general, it assumes a perspective with which I am sympathetic if not totally in agreement. Amelie Rorty, for instance, has argued that self-deception presupposes a complex organization of the self,[106] a view I support but one that has been challenged in particulars.[107] Moreover, in response to Canfield and Gustavson, John King-Farlow has argued that a person ". . .is quite often usefully looked at, with major reference to his consciousness, as a large, loose sort of committee. There is a most irregularly rotating chairmanship. The members question, warn, praise, and DECEIVE each other. . . . [Moreover] the deceiver and the deceived are not the same simpliciter.[108]

These positions are headed in the right direction, though the metaphor of a "committee" may be misleading to the extent that it personifies the terms of an intrapsychic relation. Such personification may lead (mistakenly) to the idea that those terms are, in fact, discrete personalities, a true "deceiver" and "deceived," two "persons" rather than two intrapsychically distinct though related "parties." Rorty and King-Farlow have faced another criticism as well:

> I think that all such attempts to explain self-deception by means of an averred multiplicity of the self face the following overwhelming difficulty: either the deceiver and the deceived in any case of self-deception are identical or they are not. If they are one and the same, then this appeal to the multiplicity of the self is false. If they are not identical, then self-deception really is other-deception, and we have no way to tell the two apart.[109]

This criticism, in my view, raises an invalid dilemma, at least with respect to the "relatedness" conception of self. First of all, on the basis of an ordinary language appeal, 'self-deception' can be shown to be a closely related analogue to 'other deception,' since both refer to projects aimed at misleading belief. Inasmuch as it is <u>self</u>-deception and not <u>other</u>-deception, the relations governing the concept 'self-deception' require that the <u>deception</u> be described in terms consistent with a <u>self</u>-that-can-be-deceived. The deception will be modified to the extent required by the governing relations, which is to say that the governing relations will locate and indicate the differences between the two concepts. One need not personify the terms of a self-relation in order to make it look as if what is involved in an intrapsychic opposition are discrete "inner" <u>persons</u>. I have argued that the terms or "parties" of an intrapsychic relation are conflicting desires, intentions, aims, motives, wishes, and beliefs. These conflicting parties dynamically oppose each other intrapsychically. In the context of a self-relatedness conception of self, we can say that the "deceiver" and the "deceived" are the same person, though what we mean is that holistic remark is that the current state of intrapsychic relatedness is such that one term of the relation opposes another. That opposition is made manifest behaviorally in the difference between the self-deceiver's interpretation and the best, most reasonable interpretation of the behavior. That the person is unaware of the true meaning of his or her own actions is the result of interpretive activity that covers up and resists that best, most reasonable interpretation; and the self-deceiver rationalizes or denies or otherwise seeks psychological gain by invoking an alternative interpretation more suitable to certain needs or desires. A gap appears between these two interpretations. One interpretation is enacted in the behavior itself, though this interpretation the self-deceiver denies. The other interpretation is that professed by the self-deceiver, though this explanation is faulty and erroneous. These two interpretations expose a gap that corresponds to the self-deceiver's own epistemic deficit, and we have access to a person's self-deception because that disparity between action and interpretation is manifest in publicly observable ways.

By adopting a self-relatedness conception of self, we find ourselves confronted not with a paradox, but with the fact of inconsistent behavior; and inconsistent behavior provides the evidence to establish that Jones is unaware of the true reasons for his action. We can even conclude that Jones' unawareness obtains for specific reasons and is attributable to an actual intention to avoid awareness. If that reason for action can be isolated, then the awareness begins to appear not as ignorance or a simple mistake, but as action intended to cover up the best, most reasonable interpretation with an alternative "cover story."[110] The cover story stems from some need to interpret one's own behavior in a light that satisfies certain needs that the "real story" cannot. The curious and mysterious thing is that somehow Jones himself recognizes the threat posed by the real story, since it is in response to this threat that the cover up begins. Jones, however, is functionally unaware of the true meaning of his act because the operative interpretation is a "subjectivist" interpretation that prevents a more accurate assessment of the behavioral facts from rising to linguistic explicitness. If this "cover story" or "subjectivist interpretation" can be shown to be motivated--and denials and resistance and rationalization would point this out--one could say about Jones that he appears engaged in a complex process of self-convincing or self-persuasion. What he reveals to us is a self-directed project to mislead his own beliefs, and it results in an epistemic deficit. That deficit obtains between what he knows to be the facts of his behavior (e.g., that he made a public address and noticed certain people falling asleep) and what can be established by means of evidential assessment and proper use of the language of the common life to be the best, most reasonable interpretation of that behavior.

That Jones "covers up" the best, most reasonable interpretation with an alternative so inadequate that it can appear unwarranted, fanciful or expressing a certain "blindness," constitutes a justification for being able to say, in the language of the common life, that Jones is <u>deceived</u> about the true meaning of his behavior, that his beliefs about that behavior are inconsistent with the best, most reasonable interpretation. The denials and rationalizations put forward to support his false belief reveal a lack of self-understanding, and once this false belief is determined to be false and its justification to be the product of wrongheadedness or wrongheartedness, one can say of Jones that he is engaging in interpretive activity that is intended to maintain the "cover up." A description and diagnosis of Jones' behavior that would refer us from observable manifestations of intrapsychic conflicts to the self-relations giving rise to the behavior provide us with a basis for a formal description of the act of self-deception. We conclude that what we are observing is the result of a successfully enacted belief-misleading project directed by Jones against Jones--for Jones.

Were there no intrapsychic conflict giving rise to these two contrary stories (real and cover), we can assume the person would simply accept the real story. But in self-deception this does not happen. The individual has reason to avoid confronting the real story, so that denials and rationalizations are put forward to support a cover story, thereby revealing that the person has acted to avoid self-understanding. This may look like an error or mistake, but the cover story is so maintained that it reveals a "willful ignorance" beyond any simple error. Jones can be said to so relate himself to himself on the basis of an intrapsychic conflict that he acts ("deceiver") to bring about the end of a belief-misleading project, which issues in the unawareness that enables us to say that he is deceived. Unawareness concerning the actual meaning of the facts of the behavior provides adequate evidence to establish an intrapsychic epistemic deficit. If that epistemic deficit can be shown to be the product of intentional activity of which the person is unaware, that it arises from "unconscious motives," then there is justification for concluding that this is no simple error or mistake, but an instance of self-deception.

This is admittedly a complex picture, but so too is the concept 'self-deception' and the phenomenon to which it points. This description, however, does serve to meet the objection of Foss noted above without resorting to the premises so often encountered in the literature of self-deception, namely, that the self is a unitary self-identical entity governed by a transparent consciousness. By avoiding this premise, whence the paradox arises, we are able to avoid describing the dynamics of intrapsychic conflict in terms that urge a metaphorical clarification which may prove misleading. It is necessary to avoid seeking clarification in terms suggesting that the self _is_ a "committee," or worse, that the self is occupied by discrete personality-like entities engaged in battle and vying for supremacy. This is to employ the language of schizophrenia (potentially), a technical and extreme language, and not the language of the self, which is the language of self-relatedness and even an ambiguous language in the common life.

The relatedness conception of self put forward in these pages provides an adequate and defensible alternative to the unitary and transparent picture that would negate the possibility of self-deception on purely logical grounds. This alternative picture discounts the idea that there is an _actual_ paradox, only an intrapsychic opposition that is behaviorally manifest. By invoking this alternate picture we prevent 'self-deception' from becoming like sleeves on a vest.

A self that is capable of intrapsychic relations, of self-conflict and opposing awarenesses, is a self that can deceive itself. Such a self may enact a project to mislead belief such that the person becomes functionally unaware of a dispositional belief that is, despite the unawareness, enacted. Self-deception is, as I have said, a possible configuration for an individual's self-relations.

'Self-deception,' to be sure, is a concept attended by certain logical oddities; but unless certain logical obstacles are removed, obstacles that would preclude this concept from being considered a coherent and meaningful linguistic expression, inquiry could not proceed. It has been necessary, therefore, to avoid shipwreck at the point of paradox. That shipwreck can be avoided only if the source of navigational difficulties can be accurately identified, only if the nature of the paradox is adequately examined. The source I have identified is the 'self' concept--what the self is and how its capabilities are to be conceived.

The picture of self I am advocating would be in agreement with Kant's previously noted remark that ". . .intentionally to deceive oneself seems to contain a contradiction." The force of _seems_ is that the paradox is not actual, but only apparent. That is, the contradiction is not, strictly speaking, a logical contradiction but an existential opposition, and the paradox issue arises because of the ambiguity of our language about self and our sometimes lack of precision in using it. The language of self-relatedness requires care, for the dynamic reflexivity can be lost in monadic uses or metaphors that tend to harden. ('Sich' can easily become 'Selbst.') By refusing to accept a unitary picture of self, we dredge the conceptual sandbar that would run our meaningful, coherent and common life concept of 'self-deception' aground. By disallowing the actual paradox, we remove the only mooring to which the "self-deception cannot happen" position is tied.

We resolve the paradox of self-deception by establishing a clear alternative premise about the self, a premise that is supported by the way we extend reflexives in ordinary language to perform reflexive meaning tasks, a premise that is confirmed by our knowledge of human persons. That premise is that the self is constituted as a complex system of dynamic intrapsychic relations. We want to say, then, that the self is capable of relating itself to itself in a variety of ways, including the form of self-conflict we term 'self-deception.'

If the paradox of self-deception is not actual but only apparent, then the next question is whether the description of the _act_ of self-deception offered in these pages corresponds to a _fact_ of self-deception. It is clear that our typical use of the expression 'self-deception' is meant as a kind of empirical appeal, for we are referring to, describing or identifying some fact of human psychic life and some fact of human behavior. Having examined the "act of deceiving oneself" (_OED_ definition) on the basis of an appeal to ordinary language, let us consider as a separate but related issue the empirical warrants that could be said to attend any actual employment of the concept. Let us consider "the _fact_ of deceiving oneself" (_OED_ definition).

C. Facts

If it could be empirically established that human subjects lack a capacity for engaging in deceptive self-relations, then no argument to the contrary could prevail. Were self-deception to be empirically invalidated, continued use of the expression would be a linguistic oddity. Continued use of the expression could be justified only if a meaning other than the meaning related to the literal terms of the expression were stipulated, which is to say that the rules governing the use of 'self-deception' would be like those governing 'unicorn.' Moreover, there would be no reason to assume that, say, a religious resurrection of the concept (e.g., Kierkegaard's 'double-mindedness') could establish sufficient contextual warrants to authorize a meaningful use in a "religious language game;" for that use, too, makes an empirical claim. It is clear that any employment of 'self-deception' intends to appeal to an empirical particular, to something that actually occurs, to a fact of our experience. If there be no such thing as 'self-deception,' if empirical investigation yields a conclusion about ontic status to the effect that self-deception does not exist, using the expression will not make it so.

Because our ordinary use of 'self-deception' is meant to refer to some fact of human behavior, certain investigators have concentrated on trying to establish the empirical warrants for the concept. Gardner Murphy, for instance, a psychologist with expertise in the field of perceptual phenomena, studied and experimented with 'self-deception' as a form of perceptual avoidance and distortion.[111] Self-deception, he wrote, is associated with a "perceptual distortion of memory and thought."[112]

In Murphy's view, experimental evidence has established that human subjects are capable of perceiving and not perceiving simultaneously ("field-ground" differentiation). That is, human subjects intentionally "screen out" information perceived to be harmful or threatening because they are (somehow) aware that it is threatening. The screening out process occurs unconsciously, and this can be confirmed by follow-up reports. Murphy found, moreover, that perception is affected and distorted by an expectation (belief) about possible satisfactions and possible harm. This in turn affects the motivational ground for the distortion. A perceiving subject, according to Murphy, can report not seeing some item in a stressful picture, but the act of not-seeing constitutes an intentional act that is itself postulated on a broader awareness prior to the distortion. What is perceived and believed to be harmful occasions a stress-reaction that not only distorts the perception, but eventuates in a self-report that the subject believes accurately reports the picture's contents. Focusing attention on a non-stressful figure in the perceptual field is also a not-focusing on stress producing figures. The subject's disposition to believe something about the picture affects the conscious perception; and that conscious perception conflicts with the totality of the picture, despite the fact that the entire picture was scanned. Murphy attributes these intentional perceptual avoidance maneuvers to 'self-deception.'

Although Murphy does not provide a logico-linguistic analysis of the concept 'self-deception,' he does collect data to support the following conclusions: 1.) that subjects may be simultaneously aware and unaware and that they hold contradictory beliefs; 2.) that the screening-out process results in the subject being unaware of one of the beliefs (that something in the picture is harmful) as is evidenced by a self-report; and 3.) that because the screening out occurs in response to objects or stimuli perceived to be (potentially) harmful, a motive may be attributed to the distortion process. Murphy's empirical findings support our ordinary language criteria for ascribing 'self-deception.' He concludes that perceptual defense is parasitic on the concept 'self-deception,' a reasonable conclusion given the experimental findings.

Other research efforts have bearing on the empirical question about 'self-deception.'[113] Studies are available in which self-deception has been mentioned as a factor contributing to the lack of validity in self-reported personality inventories,[114] or as a defining characteristic of all defense mechanisms,[115], or as the explanation for a subject persisting in belief ("maintaining a hypothesis") in spite of evidential disconfirmation.[116] No psychological work on self-deception has been of greater significance, however, than the experimental investigations of Harold A. Sackeim and Ruben C. Gur, both clinical psychologists.[117] Although a phenomenon like selected non-awareness has been related to self-deception in the studies of Murphy and others, prior to the Sackeim and Gur studies there were ". . .no attempts to demonstrate that any given set of behavior conforms to what is meant by self-deception."[118]

Sackeim and Gur devised a procedure for directly investigating self-deception. Their experiments were designed to test the hypothesis that self-deception is a phenomenon for which there are behavioral correlates. Despite the far-reaching implications of self-deception for theories of personality and consciousness, prior to Sackeim and Gur, direct empirical verification of the concept was simply lacking. The point of their studies was to correct the deficiency of empirical data relevant to 'self-deception' and to determine whether there is an actual phenomenon that "fits" the concept.

The Sackeim and Gur studies offer the first direct empirical evidence to support our ordinary and literal understanding of the concept 'self-deception.' The various experiments undertaken during this investigation were designed to test the validity of the empirical appeal that we, the everyday users of the concept, make when we put the linguistic expression to work to describe, explain, refer to, or identify a particular phenomenon of human behavior. The studies were methodologically sophisticated both philosophically and experimentally. They began by isolating the necessary and sufficient criteria of the concept, taking into account the work of such figures as Freud, Sartre, Demos, Fingarette and a wide body of research in the field of modern psychology. Experiments were then devised to see if empirical warrants could be found for the concept identified by their logico-linguistic analysis. Four necessary and sufficient criteria for self-deception were identified:

1. The individual holds two contradictory beliefs (that p and not that p).
2. These two contradictory beliefs are held simultaneously.
3. The individual is not aware of holding one of the beliefs.
4. The act that determines which belief is and which belief is not subject to awareness is a motivated act.[119]

Although the discussion that yields these criteria is rather summarily presented, ordinary language analysis, as I have shown in this chapter, will support this presentation. These criteria take seriously the literal meaning of self-deception, for it shows the concept to be action that yields an epistemic result; it affirms a relatedness concept of self, for it holds that the person can be unaware of a belief for certain reasons, and that the unconsciously held belief opposes a "contradictory" belief. In other words, this statement of criteria withstands philosophical scrutiny and confirms the standard meaning present in our everyday employment of the concept. We need not, at this point, concern ourselves further with the logico-linguistic analysis. I would briefly summarize what Sackeim and Gur did to establish that these criteria have empirical warrants. Let us consider the experiments.

Sackeim and Gur write,

> The question we posed for investigation is whether individuals are engaging in self-deception when they avoid self-confrontation by misidentifying the self as others and when they artificially seek out self-confrontation by misidentifying others as self. Both of these errors involve distortions of reality. Mistaking self for others reflects an avoidance or denial of an aversive event. Individuals who misidentify others as self commit a 'narcissistic' self-projecting response. Our hypothesis, then, is that at least some misidentifications of self or others are instances of self-deception.[120]

The experimental procedures, in other words, gathered empirical evidence to support the claim that we experience an actual phenomenon for which 'self-deception' is an appropriate linguistic indicator.

In the Sackeim and Gur experiment, sixty undergraduate students from the University of Pennsylvania (30 male, 30 female) were told they would be participating in a study of personality and voice discrimination.[121] After filling out a personality inventory, students were taken individually to an experimental room where they read in a normal speaking voice a selected paragraph from Thomas Kuhn's *The Structure of Scientific Revolutions*. The readings were recorded on audio tape. After the voice was recorded, subjects were led to another room where they were fitted with GSR (galvanic skin response) electrodes, then led back to the experimental room where they were connected to a polygraph. Meantime, a subject's voice was edited into a sample, which consisted of voice recordings from other student participants. Each student was then asked to listen to a tape recording of 30 voices and identify those voices either as one's own or another's. In response to hearing the voices, the subject was to push one of six buttons, which were arranged in two sets on either arm of the chair: pushing a button on the left or right would indicate whether the voice was one's own or another's, the particular button pushed would indicate the degree of certainty with which the choice was made. Subjects were to respond as quickly as possible, and after the session, the student was led to another room and given a post-experimental questionnaire.

Although research had been conducted on the phenomenon of non-recognition of the self,[122] the results of previous studies were, as Sackeim and Gur noted, of questionable value, for factors other than 'self-deception' could have brought about the results (e.g., inadequate instruction, poor equipment). Accordingly, Sackeim and Gur sought to ". . .minimize all errors in identification that would be due to factors other than self-deception."[123] Their results of the experiments showed that confrontation with the self is psychophysically arousing, that subjects identified their own voices more slowly than the voices of others, and that hearing one's own voice produced greater changes in skin conductance (GSR) than voices of others. Even when a subject denied hearing his or her own voice, the GSR results indicated that hearing one's own voice produced behavioral changes inconsistent with a simple error. In other words, subjects who heard their own voices were psychophysically aroused, and the behavioral correlates were the same whether the voice was acknowledged as the subject's own or denied. This indicated that a recognition response occurred even if the subject did not believe the voice was his or her own. On some level, some "unconscious" level, the voice was recognized and believed to be the subject's own even if it had been misidentified. Sackeim and Gur concluded that this behavioral data was evidence that the subjects were affirming two contradictory beliefs, for ". . .if the behavioral correlates of a subject who affirms that not-p are identical to those who affirm that p, the conclusion is that the subject who affirms that not-p also believes that p."[124]

Sackeim and Gur concluded that the criterion of contradictory beliefs was established because ". . .those subjects who committed one type of error indicated by their GSR reactivity that when they misidentified voices, at some level of processing correct identification has been made; these subjects, therefore, held contradictory beliefs."[125] A response to hearing one's own voice that elicits the same degree of physical arousal whether the voice heard was correctly (p) or incorrectly (not-p) identified permits us to infer that the subject believes on some level that the voice heard was his or her own (p) despite the misidentification, despite the denial, despite the profession that not-p is true. The "contradictory" responses yield similar behavior correlates. The subject who denied that the voice heard was his or her own still responded behaviorally as if it were his or her own.

Even though the person looks to have made a mistake, the person who disavows the voice as his or her own (not-p) acts as if, responds as if, believes the voice to be his or her own. Were the misidentification a simple error, the kind of arousal measured by GSR would not occur.

The simultaneity criterion--that the contradictory beliefs are held at the same time--was satisfied because self-reports (the subject's professed belief that the voice was or was not one's own) and psychophysical measures were recorded at the same time. If the subject professed a belief that the voice heard was not his or her own (not-p) and the GSR indicated an arousal consistent with a recognition of one's own voice (p), then we have evidence of contradictory beliefs, and these contradictory beliefs were recorded concurrently. "Since the psychophysical measurements were taken concurrent with subject's identification of voices, the second criterion was satisfied by the very nature of the experimental procedure."[126]

The unawareness criterion required that subjects be unaware of the errors they committed during the experiments. Prior to Sackeim and Gur, unawareness had been tested by post-experimental reports from subjects, but these obtrusive measures led to difficulties. One study cited by Sackeim and Gur bemoaned: "The most pressing methodological problem with the present studies is the one that plagues all studies of learning without awareness. There seems to be no entirely defensible method of assessing subject awareness after the experiment."[127] Sackeim and Gur proposed to correct these methodological difficulties by taking one obtrusive measure of awareness and two unobtrusive measures. One of the unobtrusive measures concerned the reaction time required to respond to an "other" stimulus after one had correctly identified one's own voice; the second concerned response time to one's own voice. Unawareness was confirmed by these three measures as follows:

The results of the obtrusive post-experimental report indicated that subjects who had mistaken their own voices for those of others would demonstrate unawareness of that mistake by reporting fewer instances of hearing their voices on the tape than would subjects who did not make this mistake. Only one subject reported that he had mistakenly identified his own voice as another's (false negative response). "Thus, on the basis of this obtrusive measure, virtually all subjects were not aware of having made false negative errors, whereas, about half of the subjects who committed false positive errors lacked awareness of having made these responses.[128] A false positive error is the narcissistic error--mistaking another's voice as one's own.

The first unobtrusive measure took as its hypothesis that subjects who were aware that their own voices had been the previous stimulus would respond faster to the next voice, the voice of another. On the other hand, subjects who mistook their own voices for others' voices should react in the same amount of time to other's voices. This, in fact, happened. The results indicted that the same amount of response time followed errors in identifying empirical claims that attend the concept 'self-deception.' The other 'empirical' studies noted above do not display Sackeim and Gur's sensitivity to philosophical issues. Murphy, for instance, did not conduct a logico-linguistic analysis of the concept 'self-deception' before beginning his study, though the role of the concept 'self-deception' in his study is significant. 'Self-deception' helped Murphy--and Frenkel-Brunswik (noted <u>supra</u>)--to interpret his data by enabling him to correlate certain empirical facts to psychological mechanisms believed to exemplify the self-deception process. In these other studies, 'self-deception' was assumed to be an actual, observable phenomenon of behavior, and that assumption rendered their findings intelligible. The "ordinary language" understanding of self-deception provided sufficient conceptual wherewithal to frame an investigation and interpret its findings. Underlying both the Murphy and Frenkel-Brunswik studies was the assumption that the meaning of 'self-deception' is commonly available in the linguistic community, that it is s was the assumption that the meaning of 'self-deception' is commonly available in the linguistic community, that it is neither a technical signification nor a piece of jargon. In those other empirical studies of self-deception, it was assumed that the term, 'self-deception,' provides linguistic access to an actual feature of human behavior. It was assumed that this language was neither so puzzling as to be contradictory, nor so contradictory as to be an empirical impossibility.

These were safe assumptions. An experimental psychologist like Gardner Murphy is not to be faulted for neglecting to predicate his work on an explicit logico-linguistic analysis of the sort found in Sackeim and Gur. I make this claim because as users of the language, as persons familiar with the complexity of human behavior, we know what the language means and how it means; and we know that the language refers us to an all too familiar feature of our common life. We know about this feature of the common life from observing human behavior and from reflecting on our own experience. We understand the literal meaning of 'self-deception' because the concept has been located within a linguistic system that renders its purpose as a meaningful cipher of communication literally transparent. We have available from ordinary language rules for employing the linguistic expression in a manner consistent with the meaning complex that governs its use.

In short, 'self-deception,' rather than being a piece of non-sense, is, in fact, a way of making sense. The expression is, when correctly employed, of a piece with the system of rationality that holds the linguistic community together. That psychological investigators like Murphy or Frenkel-Brunswik assumed the existence of self-deception before initiating their experiments and used the concept to interpret their findings was thoroughly reasonable; for they trusted the language, and that enabled them to move beyond preliminary questions about ontic status to more intriguing empirical questions.

The "logical" position assumed by both Murphy and Frenkel-Brunswik with respect to the concept 'self-deception,' then, could be stated like this: If we know what self-deception is from analyzing the literal expression, if we understand that the concept makes an empirical appeal, it is only appropriate to look into issues pertaining to as yet unsolved or still mystifying features. Those researchers who think that psychophysical or psychoneurological developments may one day explain self-deception are bringing the latest scientific hypotheses to bear on these very same unsolved and mystifying features. The quest for knowledge continues, and it proceeds on the basis of an assumption about the ontic status of the concept. Only the push by certain philosophical psychologists for whom the paradox of self-deception threw the empirical claims of the concept into question makes the kind of study offered by Sackeim and Gur a necessary back-tracking maneuver.

Without question, if logical issues are permitted to decide empirical issues on the basis of premises that themselves make an empirical claim (i.e., unitary and transparent consciousness), then the need arises to establish the empirical warrants of those premises. The empirical issue will be decided by ascertaining the facticity of relevant conceptual criteria, which in turn will cast light on whether the premise about consciousness is itself empirically warranted. That said, we should not claim that the facticity issue is now definitively settled. The heart of the debate about the facts of self-deception rests with how consciousness is to be conceived, with what capacities we can justifiably attribute to it; and all of this will influence how we interpret data and establish the meaning of the facts. Although Sackeim and Gur present evidence that consciousness is not transparent to itself, it is still possible to claim that whatever this data means, it cannot support a claim for literal self-deception, for it is logically impossible that one can recognize, hence believe that this this voice is one's own while also professing a belief that it is not. In other words, another explanation of the data is called for. While this is possible, those who claim that 'self-deception' cannot happen have not as yet provided a persuasive alternative account of this data.

If self-deception be a fact of the common life, we do not require substantiation or verification from experimental psychologists who publish in obscure literary locations research results about Ivy League undergraduates. If what we need to bolster the claim that self-deception is a feature of the common life is authority, I, for one, am willing to trust Plato, Scripture, Shakespeare, Kierkegaard, or Sartre. But I am even more willing to rely on my own experience, and the experience of others in my linguistic community, in order to establish a claim that 'self-deception' is a meaningful descriptive and diagnostic tool within that community. Sackeim and Gur do provide a body of empirical data for which those who claim that self-deception cannot happen must provide a plausible alternative explanation. But if analysis of the paradox yields an actual contradiction, we must be prepared to grant that Sackeim and Gur will not prove convincing.[136] Until such an "alternative explanation" is forthcoming, it is reasonable to hold that the Sackeim and Gur findings are consistent with our case that self-deception does happen and that the paradox of self-deception is only apparent and can be resolved.

As a result of the "ordinary language" analysis put forward in this chapter, we are able to conclude that 'self-deception' does provide an important landmark on our conceptual map and a meaningful tool for use in our linguistic community. My aim in this section has been to respond to critics who have claimed on logical grounds that self-deception cannot happen, an empirical question that I thought should be addressed with empirical findings. I have therefore extended this discussion of ordinary language features into the empirical realm, a move justified by ordinary language considerations themselves, since 'self-deception' makes an empirical claim. Certain scientific investigators have shown either explicitly (Sackeim and Gur) or implicitly (Murphy or Frenkel-Brunswik), that 'self-deception' is a viable, usable, meaningful and intelligible concept woven into the fabric of our everyday discourse. Of course the datum of use will not, of itself, establish the datum of literal self-deception. But the datum of use does establish that persons using the expression to perform some meaning task do intend to use the expression meaningfully. If, above and beyond this, questions arise concerning empirical warrants, it is necessary to investigate the premise of the objection as well as the empirical issue itself. I have shown that premise of the objection is unsound and itself unsupported by persuasive evidence: where is the data to show that consciousness has access to all its contents, or that the self is actually unified and not capable of profound disunity? I have reported on empirical research results that tend to support the meaning of 'self-deception' as that meaning is available through ordinary language considerations. This has been a kind of technical response to what may be a technical question; but I am convinced that the evidence of the common life is sufficient to support our everyday use in accordance with "ordinary language" criteria ascribability. In the absence of a better, alternative explanation, we may add that there is experimental evidence available, evidence gathered in accordance with strict scientific methodology, that can be used to support the empirical claim made by the concept 'self-deception.' Accordingly, we are justified in saying that 'self-deception' is a phenomenon, a fact about human self-relatedness, and that persons who satisfy the criteria for ascription can be described and diagnosed as 'self-deceived.'

D. Conclusion

My concern in this chapter has been to elucidate problems that attend the ordinary language features of 'self-deception.' My analysis of 'deception' revealed that a first-order deception refers to an intentionally directed project to mislead another's belief. If 'self-deception' be a meaningful analogue to 'deception,' rather than a linguistic oddity--hence an idiosyncratic use of words--that formal picture of an intentionally enacted belief-misleading project must be duplicated. I have presented an analysis that supports this expectation.

'Self-deception' is a species of 'deception' proper, though the relational contexts of each concept differ. The "two parties" in self-deception are not the two persons of 'deception,' but a reflexively conceived intrapsychic relation between opposing desires, intentions, wishes, beliefs and so on. In self-deception, conflicting and opposing--though intrapsychically related-- "parties" interact to create the necessary epistemic deficit. This epistemic deficit is manifest in behavior, in a person acting (unawares) contrary to his or her professed beliefs and declared intentions, thereby demonstrating a degree of personality fragmentation. 'Self-deception' can be described without paradox if we conceive the self as a complex relational system, capable, that is, of self-opposition and intrapsychic disorder, capable of denying what it believes, capable of believing and not believing.

The "paradox" of self-deception, I have shown, arises from assuming that a person is unitary and consciousness transparent, an assumption that precludes self-deception on purely logical grounds. This view, however, is supported by neither the findings of modern psychological science nor the evidence of the common life. (We have even cast doubt on the degree to which Sartre, a major proponent of unitary and transparent consciousness, is able to hold that view consistently and account for the data of unawareness. This is to say that his notion of pre-reflection may provide a minimally conceived notion of "unconsciousness"--else his "paradox" is not resolved.) The paradox, then, is not actual, but only apparent. It is apparent in the fact of intrapsychic opposition, and because we can describe such opposition coherently, there is no reason to abandon the literal meaning of 'self-deception.' 'Self-deception' is a first-order deception--an act with epistemic consequences, an act intended to mislead belief; but because it concerns reflexive self-relations rather than self-other relations, the concept is modified to account for the change in governing relations.

Having analyzed the ordinary language features of 'self-deception' as an <u>act</u>, I then focused on the question of <u>fact</u>. Evidence is available to support the empirical claim we make when we use 'self-deception': When we say that Jones is 'self-deceived' we mean to be describing and diagnosing a fact about Jones' intrapsychic relations as they are manifest in publicly observable behavior. The common life makes relevant evidence available to us--ordinary instances of persons who, for reasons of psychological gain, resist the best, most reasonable interpretation of their behavior, yet who, when admitting their willful error are able to say "I knew that all along." Experimental psychology supports the ordinary language criteria of ascribability. The nature of this data is such that it supports the literal meaning of 'self-deception' and will until such time as an alternative explanation of the data is forthcoming and disconfirms the interpretation offered above.

The ordinary meaning of 'self-deception' as the "act or fact of deceiving oneself" (OED definition) can be shown, then, to be a stipulated shorthand for complex concepts that, when analyzed, permit us to modify a concept like 'deception' in a way consistent with the requirements of reflexivity while not permitting a distortion of the ordinary meaning of 'deception' as a belief-misleading project. The OED definition, which is uninformative as it stands, can be shown to be meaningful if the terms of the definiens are adequately elucidated. I have attempted to show that clarity can be forthcoming and that elucidation may proceed without sacrificing the meaning ordinarily attributed to "self," "deception," "fact" or "act." The kind of analysis undertaken thus far in these pages supports the contention with which I began, that the ordinary language employment of 'self-deception' represents a meaningful cipher of communication within this linguistic community. There is reason to say that the fact of the expression's employment is supported by an intelligible and empirically warranted reference to a phenomenon of self-deception, to which the literal expression provides an adequate, even substantial, bridge of meaning. In fact, it is difficult to imagine an "ideal language" doing more.

This chapter represents the first step in the conceptual investigation proposed in the opening pages of this study. I have looked at problems that attend the meaning of the literal expression and have attempted to resolve those problems with reference to "ordinary language" considerations. Having begun the process of "intimately acquainting" ourselves with 'self-deception,' let us now turn to different interpretations of the concept and address 'self-deception' as a concept that is meaningfully employed in specific contexts of discourse to perform a variety of meaning tasks. Let us consider 'self-deception' as a topic that invites scrutiny from different points of view, that arouses more than one kind of interest.

CHAPTER ONE

[1] See, for example, Plato's Cratylus, 428d: "Excellent Cratylus, I have long been wondering at my own wisdom. I cannot trust myself. And I think I ought to stop and ask myself, What am I saying? For there is nothing worse than self-deception--when the deceiver is always at home and always with you-- it is quite terrible. . . ." See Plato's Collected Dialogues, eds. Edith Hamilton & Huntington Cairnes, trans. Benjamin Jowett (Princeton: Princeton University Press, 1971), p. 462.

[2] Joseph Butler, "Self-Deceit" in Fifteen Sermons Preached at Rolls Chapel, 4th ed. (London, 1749).

[3] See Jonathan Robinson, Duty and Hypocrisy in Hegel's Phenomenology of Mind: An Essay in the Real and the Ideal (Toronto: University of Toronto Press, 1977), esp. pp. 35, 118. See also Hegel's Phenomenology of Spirit, trans. H. V. Miller (New York: Oxford University Press, 1977), p. 401: ". . . hypocrisy, as is commonly said, demonstrates its respect for duty and virtue by making a show of them, and using them to hide itself from its own consciousness, no less from others. . . ."

[4] Sartre has said that Being and Nothingness is "an eidetic analysis of self-deception." Quoted in R. D. Cumming, "To Understand a Man," in The Philosophy of Jean-Paul Sartre, ed. Paul A. Schlipp (La Salle, IL: Open Court, 1981), p. 61.

[5] David Kipp, "On Self-Deception," Philosophical Quarterly 30 (October 1980), p. 305.

[6] Jeffery Foss, "Rethinking Self-Deception," American Philosophical Quarterly 17, 3 (July 1980), p. 237.

[7] David Pears has suggested that M. R. Haight's A Study of Self-Deception, is so concerned with "arid paradoxes" that the study is threatened with paralysis. See David Pears, "When I Disagrees With Me," Times Literary Supplement No. 4073 (24 April 1981), p. 463.

[8] Kipp, "On Self-Deception," p. 305.

[9] For a thorough discussion of other common examples, see Sissela Bok, Lying: Moral Choice in Public and Private Life, passim.

[10] See, for example, Raphael Demos, "Lying to Oneself," Journal of Philosophy 57 (September 1960), pp. 588-594; Frederick A. Siegler, "Self-Deception," Australasian Journal of Philosophy 41, 1 (May 1963); Frederick A. Siegler, "Self-Deception and Other Deception," Journal of Philosophy 60, 22 (24 October 1963), pp. 759-764; Frederick A. Siegler, "Lying," American Philosophical Quarterly 3 (1966); Roderick Chisholm and Thomas D. Feehan, "The Intent to Deceive," The Journal of Philosophy 74, 3 (March 1977), pp. 143-159.

[11] Siegler, "Self-Deception," p. 29.

[12] Deception simpliciter is discussed in Chisholm and Feehan, "The Intent to Deceive," p. 144.

¹³Relevant distinctions are discussed in St. Thomas Aquinas, Summa Theologica, II, II-ii, Question 110 ("Of the Vices Opposed to Truth, and the First of Lying"), (New York: Benziger Brothers, 1947), pp. 1664 ff.

¹⁴This point is made by John King-Farlow, "Deceptions? Assertions? Or Second-String Verbiage?", Philosophy 56, 215 (January 1981), pp. 100-105.

¹⁵Bernard Gert, The Moral Rules: A New Rational Foundation for Morality, (New York: Harper & Row, Harper Torchbook, 1973), p. 103.

¹⁶Henry Sidgwick, The Method of Ethics, 7th ed., (Indianapolis: Hackett Publishing Co., 1907, 1981), "Self-Regarding Virtues," pp. 327-328, argued for an ultimate harmony between 1. Self-interest and 2. Virtue, whence arose his position that a Duty of Prudence was appropriately a moral duty. The Kantian position opposed this: "Neither do we consider the harm that a liar brings on himself; for then a lie, as a mere error of prudence, would be contrary to the pragmatic axiom, not to the moral axiom, and it could not be considered a violation of duty at all.--By a lie a man throws away, and, as it were, annihilates his dignity as a man." From Immanuel Kant, The Doctrine of Virtue, trans. Mary J. Gregor, (New York: Harper Torchbook, 1964), p. 93. For a contemporary discussion of moral versus prudential reasoning see David A. J. Richards, A Theory of Reasons for Action (Oxford: Oxford Clarendon Press, 1971), which is a treatment in the Kantian spirit.

¹⁷There is a religious perspective on deception beyond the moral. Dietrich Bonhoeffer evaluates lying from a religious point of view in "Telling the Truth, Ethics, ed. Eberhard Bethge (New York: Macmillan Co, 1969), p. 369: "The lie is primarily the denial of God as he has evidenced himself to the world. . . the denial, the negation, and the conscious and deliberate destruction of the reality which is created by God and which consists in God, no matter whether this purpose is achieved by speech or silence." See also p. 365 for further elaboration: "Every word I utter is subject to the requirement that it shall be true. . . .An individual utterance is always a part of the total reality which seeks expression to this utterance."

¹⁸Immanuel Kant, The Doctrine of Virtue, p. 93: "A lie (in the ethical sense of the term), an intentional untruth as such, need not be harmful to others in order to be pronounced reprehensible; for then it would be a violation of the rights of others. A lie may arise from mere frivolity or even good nature; indeed, the speaker may intend a really good end by it. But his way of pursuing the end is, by its mere form, a wrong to his own person and a baseness which must make him contemptible in his own eyes." Consider also Kant's statement in Lectures on Ethics, trans. Louis Infield (Indianapolis: Hackett Publishing Co., 1980), p. 229: ". . .a lie is a lie, and is in itself intrinsically base whether it be told with good or bad intent. For formally a lie is always evil; though if it is materially as well, it is a much meaner thing. There are no lies which may not be the source of evil."

¹⁹Kant, Lectures on Ethics, p. 227.

²⁰This point is made in G. J. Warnock, The Object of Morality (London: Methuen & Co., 1971), p. 84: "It is, one might say, not the implanting of false beliefs that is damaging, but rather the generation of suspicion that they may be being implanted. For this undermines trust; and, to the extent that trust is undermined, all co-operative undertakings, in which one person

can do or has reason to do is dependent on what others have done, are doing, or are going to do, must tend to break down."

[21] Kant, Lectures on Ethics, p. 228.

[22] Warnock, The Object of Morality, p. 83.

[23] Rudolf Otto, The Idea of the Holy, trans. John W. Harvey (New York: Oxford University Press, 1923, 1980), p. 52.

[24] Bonhoeffer, Ethics, p. 369.

[25] Reinhold Niebuhr, "The Christian Conception of Sin," in An Interpretation of Christian Ethics (Cleveland: World Publishing Co., 1935, 1963), p. 83.

[26] Kant thought an untruth was a lie ". . .only if I have expressly given the other to understand that I am willing to acquaint him with my thought" in Lectures on Ethics, p. 228.

[27] The evidence issue is discussed in Siegler, "Self-Deception," p. 36.

[28] M. R. Haight, A Study of Self-Deception, p. 108: "If self-deception works as I think, it is often a lie only to other people." See pp. 108 ff.

[29] See the debate between Robert Audi, "The Epistemic Authority of the First-Person," Personalist 56 (Winter 1975), pp. 5-15, who argues that self-deception is only describable if reference is made to the unconscious; and the rejection of this view by John Exdell and James Hamilton, "The Incorrigibility of First-Person Disavowals," Personalist 56 (Autumn 1975), pp. 389-94. See also Audi's rejoinder, "Epistemic Disavowals and Self-Deception," Personalist 57 (Autumn 1976), pp. 378-85.

[30] Sigmund Freud, Introductory Lectures on Psychoanalysis, trans. & ed. James Strachey (New York: W. W. Norton & Co., 1977), p. 72.

[31] Ibid., p. 75.

[32] Ibid., p. 74.

[33] Ibid.

[34] Freud wrote, "It is in general true that only a certain proportion of the errors that occur in ordinary life can be looked at from our point of view. . . . But I cannot believe that this is so in the type depending on forgetting (forgetting names or intention, mislaying)." Ibid., p. 60. My aim here is not to challenge the coherence of the notion of an unconscious intention. Frederick Siegler did challenge it, arguing in "Unconscious Intention," Inquiry 10, 2 (1967) pp. 251-67 that the notion is incoherent. His argument has been rebutted by Robert K. Shope, "Freud on Conscious and Unconscious Intentions," Inquiry 13, 1-2 (Summer 1970), pp. 149-159. Shope argues that Siegler does not prove that the concept of an unconscious intention is incoherent, even though Freud himself failed to prove that such an intention exists.

[35] Freud, Introductory Lectures on Psychoanalysis, p. 26.

[36]Although Donald Davidson has argued that "". . .we do not necessarily believe will do what we intend to do, and that we do not state our intentions more accurately by making them conditional on all the circumstances in whose presence we think we could act ("Intending," in Essays on Actions and Events [Oxford: Clarendon Press, 1980], p. 95), the stronger case is that intention infers belief, since belief is dispositional. According to Bruce Aune ("Intention," The Encyclopedia of Philosophy, IV, p. 199), "Since the disposition characteristic of a minimal intention involves the agent's beliefs concerning the conditions appropriate for its realization and since the dispositions characteristic of more complex intentions involve beliefs concerning the preferred means of realizing them, it is clear that in addition to any purely behavioral disposition an intention will necessarily involve some idea or conception of what is intended." If "unconscious intention" is not incoherent, and if it be considered a legitimate qualification of 'intention,' it is logical to assume that a connection exists between "unconscious intention" and "unconscious belief" similar to that which obtains between conscious intention and conscious belief." This legitimates the subsequent statement in the text.

[37]Theodore Mischel, "Understanding Neurotic Behavior: From 'Mechanism' to 'Intentionality,' in Understanding Other Persons, ed. Theodore Mischel (Totowa, NJ: Rowman and Littlefield, 1974), p. 236.

[38]Consider the assessment of "unconscious" by Lancelot Law Whyte, "Unconscious," Encyclopedia of Philosophy, VIII, p. 185: "For the ultimate purpose of the concept of unconscious mental processes is to link conscious awareness and behavior with its background--a system of processes of which one is not immediately aware--and to establish this connection without losing the benefits of scientific precision. Here lies the weakness of the concept of the unconscious: it cannot be made fully acceptable to the scientific age until some science or union of sciences has provided an adequate conception of the unity and continuity of conscious thought, unconscious cerebral processes, physiological changes, and the processes of growth. In fact, the idea of the unconscious (or some equivalent) can acquire scientific status only after a unified picture of the human organism has repaired the intellectual lesions created by Cartesian and other dualistic or specialized methods." I shall discuss a unitary conception of self in the next section and challenge the adequacy of such a conception. With reference to Freud's particular Theory of the Unconscious, A.C. MacIntyre has criticized it for claiming to be a causal feature that explains certain behavior, when, according to MacIntyre, it does not explain but only describes: "My theory then is that in so far as Freud uses the concept of the unconscious as an explanatory concept, he fails, if not to justify it, at least to make clear its justification. He gives us causal explanations, certainly; but these can and apparently must stand or fall on their own feet without reference to it. He has a legitimate concept of unconscious mental activity, certainly; but this he uses to describe behavior not explain it. . . .Freud, of course, seeks to account not only for neurotic symptoms, but for dreams, slips of the tongue, jokes and the like. Here again it was Wittgenstein who pointed out that what Freud had done was to give not an explanation, but a 'wonderful representation' of the facts" in The Unconscious: A Conceptual Analysis (Atlantic Highlands, NJ: Humanities Press, 1976), pp. 72, 73.

[39]Kipp, "On Self-Deception," p. 305.

[40]This notion of "perverting" the "procedures whereby we establish truth

and falsehood" is made by Bela Szabados, "Wishful Thinking and Self-Deception," Analysis 33, 6; N.S. 156 (June 1973), p. 205.

[41] See Bela Szabados, "Wishful Thinking and Self-Deception," pp. 201-204 for a critique of two theories about the relation of 'self-deception' to 'wishful thinking': Herbert Fingarette, Self-Deception (London: Routledge and Kegan Paul, 1969), p. 19; Patrick Gardiner, "Error, Faith and Self-Deception," Proceedings of the Aristotelian Society, 70 (1969-70), pp. 221-224; reprinted in The Philosophy of Mind, ed. Jonathan Glover (Oxford: Oxford University Press, 1976), pp. 35-52.

[42] See Fingarette, Self-Deception, passim.

[43] The epistemic object for a deception cannot simply be transferred to self-deception. Nora, then, our liar, deceives the personnel officer about her educational credentials; but it would be counter-intuitive to think that she could deceive herself about whether she had graduated from college. This is an inappropriate object for self-deception. Though Nora may be self-deceived, this particular epistemic object will not serve to illustrate the concept. It would be possible to show how Nora's deception leads her to self-deception, but we shall, in the next chapter, offer different examples.

[44] This distinction is made by Anthony Kenny, Action, Emotion and Will, (London: Routledge & Kegan Paul, 1963), pp. 91 ff.

[45] Fingarette has speculated on the relevance of hemisphericity research to self-deception, concluding that the area is promising but awaits further developments. See his appendix, "The Neuropsychological Context of Self-Deception" in Self-Deception, pp. 151-162. Other relevant sources on this question include Harold A. Sackeim and Ruben C. Gur, "Self-Deception, Self-Confrontation, and Consciousness," in Consciousness and Self-Regulation, Advances in Research, eds. G. E. Schwartz & D. Shapiro (New York: Plenum Press, 1978), esp. p. 188. Both R. E. Ornstein, The Psychology of Consciousness (San Francisco: W. H. Freeman & Co, 1972, and D. Galin, "Implications for Psychiatry of Left and Right Cerebral Specialization," Archives of General Psychiatry 31 (1974), pp. 572-583, have argued that, according to Sackeim and Gur, ibid., "the blockage of information from entering the left hemisphere provides the neurological underpinnings of repression" (pp. 188-89).

[46] This distinction was suggested, though not explicitly argued, in Richard Wollheim, "Wish-Fulfillment," in Rational Action: Studies in Philosophy and Social Science, ed. Ross Harrison (Cambridge: Cambridge University Press, 1979), pp. 47-60.

[47] Sartre writes in Being and Nothingness: An Essay on Phenomenological Ontology, trans. Hazel E. Barnes (New York: Philosophical Library, n.d.), p. 68: "One puts oneself in bad faith as one goes to sleep and one is in bad faith as one dreams." The importance of this kind of picture of self-deception as an action concept has ben noted in sympathetic treatments by Fingarette, Self-Deception, pp. 94 ff.; and Stephen Crites, "The Aesthetics of Self-Deception," Soundings 62 (Summer 1979), pp. 107-129. What must be explained is how one could "put oneself" into bad faith unintentionally. Sartre's understanding of the "unconscious" is the issue here, and I shall address that in due course.

⁴⁸The literature on "self" is vast and increasing daily. For collections of philosophical essays, see Bernard Williams, Problems of the Self: Philosophical Papers, 1956-1972, (Cambridge: Cambridge University Press, 1973); John Perry, ed., Personal Identity (Berkeley: University of California Press, 1975); Amelie O. Rorty, ed., The Identities of Persons (Berkeley: University of California Press, 1976). For a discussion of modern conceptions of self-as-substance as found in Locke, Berkeley and Hume, see Risieri Frondizi, The Nature of the Self: A Functional Interpretation (Carbondale: Southern Illinois University Press, 1953, 1971). For the idea that the self is "not an originating agent; he is a locus, a point at which many genetic and environmental conditions come together in a joint effect" see B. F. Skinner, About Behaviorism (New York: Alfred Knopf Co., 1974), p. 168. For a discussion of self-deception as a form of ignorance see B.F. Skinner, Science and Behavior (New York: The Free Press, Macmillan, 1953, 1965), pp. 283-296. For a valuable "philosophical psychology" collection, see Theodore Mischel, ed., The Self: Psychological and Philosophical Issues (Totowa, NJ: Rowman and Littlefield, 1977).

⁴⁹I have argued elsewhere that person is a term or public disclosure and revelation (L. persona: mask) while self is a psychological term expressing a person's own self-relations, a distinction that is necessary because even though self and person are sometimes used interchangeably, they are not identical terms or functional equivalents when we consider actual employments. See my "Self-Deception: A Conceptual Analysis in Three Relational Contexts," pp. 188-89. In this I have learned much from William Alston, "Self-Intervention and the Structure of Motivation," in Theodore Mischel, ed., The Self: Psychological and Philosophical Issues, pp. 67-68. Jung's distinction between person and persona corresponds in some ways to my suggestion about distinguishing self and person. "The concept of 'persona' as introduced by Jung should not be confused with the concept of person; rather, it is to be understood in the opposite direction. Person refers to the innermost center and metaphysical core of man, while persona indicates the manner and way in which an individual appears to his environment and--more or less consciously--represents himself to it" in Josef Rudin, Psychotherapy and Religion, trans. Elisabeth Reinecke and Paul C. Bailey (Notre Dame: University of Notre Dame Press, 1968), p. 76, ft. 9.

⁵⁰See, for example, Clark E. Moustakas, ed., The Self: Explorations in Personal Growth (New York: Harper & Row, 1974). This collection of essays takes as its starting point "Concern for the self with all its contributing attributes and potentials is rapidly becoming a central focus of contemporary psychological inquiry. The selection of recent writings in this book portrays the fundamental unity of personality and presents a framework for understanding healthy behavior. The emphasis is on knowing, exploring, and actualizing the self" (p. xiii).

⁵¹Stephen Toulmin, "Self-Knowledge and Knowledge of the Self," in ed. Mischel, The Self: Psychological and Philosophical Issues, pp. 291 ff.

⁵²See Willard F. Day, "On the Behavioral Analysis of Self-Deception and Self-Development" in ed. Mischel, ibid., pp. 224-49, for an interpretation sympathetic to the behaviorist position.

⁵³Toulmin, "Self-Knowledge and Knowledge of the Self," p. 303.

⁵⁴Ibid., p. 308. See also Ernest S. Wolf, "'Irrationality' in the Psychoanalytic Psychology of the Self," in Mischel, ed., ibid., pp. 203-223, including his bibliography on Kohut, p. 203.

⁵⁵Toulmin, "Self-Knowledge and Knowledge of the Self," p. 313.

⁵⁶Ibid.

⁵⁷Ibid., p. 311.

⁵⁸Ibid.

⁵⁹Modern psychology has taught us that certain of our desires may be in conflict with certain other desires, but this observation is not new. We could find all kinds of examples, though I would mention one picture of this kind of conflict as portrayed in Frank Norris' 1899 novel, McTeague: A Story of San Francisco (New York: New American Library, 1964) where an intrapsychic conflict is behaviorally manifest as follows:

> McTeague [a dentist] straightened up, putting the sponge upon the rack behind him, his eyes fixed upon Trina's face. For some time he stood watching her as she lay there, unconscious and helpless and very pretty. He was alone with her, and she was absolutely without defense.
> Suddenly the animal in the man stirred and woke: the evil instincts that in him were so close to the surface leaped to life, shouting and clamoring.
> It was a crisis--a crisis that had arisen all in an instant; a crisis for which he was totally unprepared. Blindly and without knowing why, McTeague fought against it, moved by an unreasoned instinct of resistance. Within him, a certain second self, another better McTeague rose with the brute; both were strong, with the huge, crude strength of the man himself. The two were at grapples. There in that cheap and shabby dental parlors a dreaded struggle began. It was the old battle, old as the world, wide as the world--the sudden panther leap of the animal, lips drawn, fangs aflash, hideous, monstrous, not to be resisted, and the simultaneous arousing of the other man, the better self that cries, "Down, down," without knowing why; that grips the monster; that fights to strangle it, to thrust it down and back (pp. 27-28).

This is a picture of the self in conflict with itself. Although we could say that this example illustrates the Freudian notions of id, ego and super-ego, we need not invoke these explanatory devices; for this conflict illustrates a fragmented self, a self incoherent and lacking in cohesiveness. We do not need an arcane "scientific theory" in order to understand McTeague; the example is intelligible because of our knowledge about human persons--how passion can affect self-control. A descriptive-diagnostic appreciation of human persons permits us to derive an interpretive structure that enables us to understand the self and its conflicts. I would also note that Søren Kierkegaard, a literary psychologist of more relevance to this study, holds also to a descriptive diagnostic perspective on the self.

⁶⁰Toulmin, "Self-Knowledge and Knowledge of the Self," pp. 311-12.

[61]Ibid., p. 300. See also p. 301 for a discussion of "reflexive conduct," along with the comment that ". . .the concept self. . .[can be] understood as expressing insights into the complexities and relationships within reflexive conduct of kinds that elude expression in less sophisticated language" (see footnote 54).

[62]I would remind the reader that I shall be looking no further into issues of psycho-neurological evidence since any such data is question-begging if conceptual issues are not resolved.

[63]See footnote 60.

[64]See Toulmin, "Self-Knowledge and Knowledge of the Self," pp. 304-05.

[65]We are not dependent upon a verbal report from the anxious individual since we have criteria for ascribing 'anxiety' even if for some reason the person does not admit to anxiety. A "descriptive-diagnostic" analysis of the self enables us to assess whether a person is (say) anxious, if she "knows her own mind," if she knows her intentions, can realistically assess the likelihood of carrying them out, and recognizes and acknowledges her status as one agent among many. Persons reveal publicly the extent of their self-mastery, reveal, that is, to what extent affections, cognition, and volition are harmonized in this particular self. We could expand the list of things that reveal the actuality of a person's self-relatedness: satisfactions with certain relationships, capacities for intimacy and so on.

[66]This is the gist of the argument made by M. R. Haight in A Study of Self-Deception. Haight is not alone in her position, since almost all commentators have referred to the paradoxical nature of the concept. See also Stanley Paluch, "Self-Deception," Inquiry 10 (1967), pp. 268-78, who writes: "There is no doubt about the fact that we talk about people deceiving themselves, but what is not clear is that there are any instances where this way of speaking is best or could not be replaced by other descriptions which do not involve the notion of a deception at all" (p. 277). In concluding that the literal expression is misleading, Paluch suggests abandoning it in favor of fixation, delusion, or idée fixe, which, he argues, are more precisely what 'self-deception' means. For a rebuttal of Paluch's contentions, see David Pugmire, "'Strong' Self-Deception," Inquiry 12 (Fall 1969), pp. 339-46.

[67]See Bernard Williams, Descartes: The Project of Pure Inquiry (Atlantic Highlands, NJ: Humanities Press, 1978), pp. 81-86, for a discussion of Descartes' equation of the mental with the conscious. According to Williams, Descartes concluded that "mental states are fully available to consciousness" (p. 84-85).

[68]The idea of a unitary consciousness provided a working assumption in Wilhelm M. Wundt, An Introduction to Psychology (New York: Macmillan, 1912).

[69]For example, Duncan Howie has argued that research by experimental psychologists on the phenomena of perceptual defense leads to paradoxical conclusions. See his "Perceptual Defense," Psychological Review, 59 (1952), pp. 308-315. Howie not only argued that perceptual defense is an incoherent notion unavailable to direct phenomenological investigation, but he rejected the idea that the mind as a unified structure can oppose itself in systematically distinct acts of unawareness, terming such a claim, following Ryle, a

"category mistake." Howie defended the picture of mind wherein consciousness is unitary. "To speak of perceptual defense is to use a mode of discourse which must make any precise or even any really intelligible meaning of perceptual defense impossible, for it is to speak of perceptual process as somehow being both a process of knowing and a process of avoiding knowing" (p. 301). This is a conclusion consistent with a unitary picture of consciousness, though it is curious that Howie used Ryle to support an essentially Cartesian picture of consciousness.

[70]This is a logical argument based on a certain understanding of 'self' and an ordinary first-order understanding of 'deception.' This logical argument has at times been made as an empirical argument, but it is clear than an empirical conclusion should not be drawn until the premises of the logical argument are empirically substantiated. The problem is that this particular assumption about the nature of selfhood is not only not valid empirically, but empirical evidence actually discounts the idea of a unitary self and a transparent consciousness. The confusion of logic with empiricism constitutes a flaw in certain studies, Paluch's and Haight's being the most notable in psychology and philosophy respectively. The criticism I am lodging has also been made by H. O. Mounce, "Self-Deception," Proceedings of the Aristotelian Society, Supp. Vol. XLV (1971), p. 61, against D. W. Hamlyn, "Self-Deception," ibid., pp. 45-60.

One other point. Were we to argue for a legitimate use of 'self-deception' on the basis of a unitary self and transparent consciousness notion, the most likely candidate for exemplification would be the case of "multiple personality," since one could hold that one person houses separate, distinct, discrete and unified personalities. This picture will not withstand examination, however, since this kind of empirical personality disorder points to the kinds of extreme fragmentation and severe disunity that can obtain in certain rare instances. This kind of "explanation" of 'self-deception' violates our first requirement for an adequate account of the concept as a feature of the common life, which is what the language itself indicates. The "multiple personality" example, in fact, constitutes a kind of evidence that discounts a unified picture of self and supports the alternative "relatedness" conception, for "multiple personality" then represents an uncommon form of mental aberration, but one that is intelligible in terms of the human capacity for relating oneself to oneself in a variety of ways, some of which are pathological and express an extreme--and dangerous--form of incoherence, discontinuity and inconsistency.

[71]See footnote 1, p. 101. Kierkegaard, who in true Socratic fashion affirms a non-unitary and non-transparent picture of consciousness, refers to this passage in The Concept of Anxiety, ed. and trans. Reidar Thomte (Princeton: Princeton University Press, 1980), p. 160.

[72]St. Paul was conscious that he could not square his actions with his intentions. His picture of the self in conflict is nowhere better expressed than in Romans 7.18b-19 (RSV): "I can will what is right, but I cannot do it. For I do not do the good I want, but the evil I do not want is what I do." The picture of the self in conflict is a prominent working assumption in Christian thought. I have discussed this issue in "Toward a Christian Conception of Selfhood," (Unpublished M.A. thesis, Andover Newton Theological School, 1978).

[73]William James writes in Varieties of Religious Experience, p. 228: "I

cannot but think that the most important step forward that has occurred in psychology since I have been a student of that science is the discovery. . . that, in certain subjects at least, there is not only the consciousness of the ordinary field, with its usual centre and margin, but an addition thereto in the shape of memories, thoughts, and feelings which are extra-marginal and outside the primary consciousness altogether, but yet must be classed as conscious facts of some sort, able to reveal their presence by unmistakable signs. I call this the most important step forward because, unlike other advances which psychology has made, this discovery has revealed to us an entirely unsuspected peculiarity in the constitution of human nature."

[74] Freud refers to the Unconscious and the Conscious as "two systems" throughout his essay, "The Unconscious" (1915). See also the essay "Repression" (1915). Both essays are reprinted in <u>Sigmund Freud, General Psychological Theory: Papers on Metapsychology</u>, ed. and intro. Philip Rieff (New York: Collier Books, 1963, 1972). For more information on Freud's picture of a divided or non-unitary self, see David S. Holmes, "Investigations of Repression: Differential Recall of Material Experimentally or Naturally Associated With Ego Threat," <u>Psychological Bulletin</u> 81, 10 (1974), pp. 632-633. See also Sackeim and Gur, "Self-Deception, Self-Confrontation, and Consciousness" for a general discussion and bibliographical materials relevant to the psychoanalytic picture of a non-unitary self. For a discussion of Freud's use of <u>self</u> (p. 305) and for an appreciative interpretation of the psychoanalytic perspective on the notion of a divided self, see Herbert Fingarette, <u>The Self in Transformation: Psychoanalysis, Philosophy and the Life of the Spirit</u> (New York: Harper & Row, Harper Torchbook, 1965). For a quick picture of Freud's position on the self's constitution, see his unfinished but influential essay, "Splitting of the Ego in the Defensive Process," in <u>Sexuality and the Psychology of Love</u>, ed. Philip Rieff (New York: Collier Books, 1974), pp. 220-23.

[75] That these are related notions in the psychoanalytic perspective is a point made by Herbert Fingarette, <u>The Self in Transformation</u>, e.g., p. 312: "'Consciousness of self' is not an awareness of some self-identical identity (i.e., a unitary-transparent picture--LHS); it is, rather, <u>any consciousness colored by intrapsychic conflict and anxiety</u>." This is a view thoroughly consistent with the "descriptive-diagnostic" view presented in these pages.

[76] Ibid., p. 26.

[77] Although I shall discuss Sartre in more detail in both the next section and the next chapter, I should remark on his opposition to Freud. Sartre is a proponent of an existential perspective on the self, which entails in its phenomenological description a <u>transparent</u> view of consciousness. Is Sartre's understanding of self-deception, then, paradoxical? As I shall make clear, it is paradoxical. Does Sartre resolve the paradox? Students of Sartre are divided on this issue, but if Sartre does propose a transparent consciousness view, we should <u>expect</u> it to remain unresolved. For now, let me say: even Sartre, an outspoken opponent of Freud's Theory of the Unconscious provides in his notion of pre-reflection a possible way out ot he paradox of self-deception, since that notion of pre-reflection serves as a <u>functional equivalent</u> to Freud's descriptive-diagnostic view of psychic conflict arising from unconscious and repressed causes. That is, the dispute between Sartre and Freud is a "hypothetical-explanatory" dispute, not a disagreement over "descriptive-diagnostic" facts of human behavior and intrapersonal conflict.

⁷⁸The problem one encounters is that the language of the self is ambiguous. Common sense dictates that when we encounter a person we encounter this essentially unified structure of personality or entity--and this person is pretty much today as he or she was yesterday or will be tomorrow. We therefore operate as if the person were unified, but, as I have argued, we are actually operating with the current state of self-relatedness, which may be different tomorrow. The point, then, is that we assume something by person that is ambiguous inasmuch as a holistic view and a unitary view function around the idea of person as this John Smith whom we encounter, whom we can know, who seems to us continuous as a personality from one day to the next. Our language does not fail us; but it does create an ambiguity where person actually means one thing holistically but may be used as a functional equivalent to a realized-unitary view. The extent of this language problem arises when considering how to describe anxiety. As Fingarette writes (The Self in Transformation, p. 313), "Certain anxiety symptoms (for example, 'nervousness,' faintness) are easy to distinguish. But most often the anxiety motivation of behavior is masked, the behavior frequently being rationalized. Thus the man who has always worked compulsively at his job is likely to be unable to distinguish his behavior from that of industrious and enthusiastic but anxiety-free work. The attempts of others to use language to suggest to him the subtle but profound difference in the 'feel' of the two experiences will most likely be met by him either with incomprehension or defensive scorn or both. When he asks them to describe in 'plain' language how they approach their work, victory is his--for they have to use the very language-forms he does. If someone says that anxiety free work has a kind of absorbed and devoted character, the compulsive replies that those are just the words that describe his work! And he is right." My point, then, is that person, man/woman, individual can likewise be understood from points of view subtly different, yet profoundly different. A unified self is to a holistic self like absorbing and devoted work is to anxiously compulsive work. We use the language to simplify complex notions (person, work), and, in order to draw out the distinctiveness, the kind of qualification we have undertaken here must follow. Actually, our noun use of self may, as I suggested earlier in footnote 49, provide us with the kind of relatedness picture of person that may be overlooked when we use 'person' to identify the person who stands before us as John Smith, who presents this "mask" of person to the external world, who is before us "in person."

⁷⁹See the evidence revealing a wide disparity between student's self evaluations of their abilities and personalities and the interpretations of their supervising faculty in Else Frenkel-Brunswik, "Mechanisms of Self-Deception," Journal of Social Psychology 10 (1939), p. 409-420.

⁸⁰Sartre discusses the person who experiences guilt about his homosexuality, an example illustrating "bad faith." See Being and Nothingness, pp. 63-67. I am using the example of a homosexual to focus on denial, unawareness and reasons (motives) for one's unawareness being manifest in publicly observable ways.

⁸¹John Wisdom, "Gods," in A. G. N. Flew, ed., Logic and Language, First Series (Oxford: Basil Blackwell, 1963), p. 199.

⁸²Ibid., p. 200.

⁸³Michael Fox, "On Unconscious Emotions," Philosophy and Phenomenologi-

cal Research XXXIV, 2 (December 1973), p. 170.

[84]D. M. Hamlyn has written that ". . .reference to motives presupposes the context of a demand for explanation, a demand that action should be made intelligible as an intentional action of a certain sort," thus relating 'intention' to 'motive' in an intimate way. Furthermore, Hamlyn writes that "in some contexts we should almost be inevitably forced to the conclusion that the person concerned was acting intentionally without being conscious of this." And, ". . .if someone definitely appears to do something for some further end and yet seems to be unconscious of what he is doing, we can properly say that he does know what he is doing, though by intentional inattention or something of the sort he has made himself unconscious of what he is doing. That is why it is so plausible to speak of self-deception in these contexts, even in (sic) the invocation of this concept does so little toward showing how unconscious intention is possible." See D. W. Hamlyn, "Unconscious Intentions," Philosophy XLVI, 175 (January 1971), pp. 13, 22. In support of my case, a minimal sense of unconscious that does not invoke (say) Freud's hypothetical-explanatory model, see the following works: Lewis White Beck, "Conscious and Unconscious Motives," Mind LXXV, 298 (April 1966), pp. 155-79; Stuart Hampshire, Thought and Action (New York: Viking Press, 1967), pp. 90-168: "Intention and Action"; Christopher Olsen, "Knowledge of One's Own Intentional Acts, Philosophical Quarterly 19 (October 1969), pp. 324-336. Olsen, for example, writes that "A person is not always aware of everything that he can correctly be said to know" (p. 327). In other words, there is support from the philosophical community for the position I am advancing in the text.

[85]Almost all studies treat the issue of paradox. This is as true of Fingarette's Self-Deception as of Haight's A Study of Self-Deception. The problem of paradox is raised, for instance, in the following studies: John V. Canfield and Donald F. Gustavson, "Self-Deception," Analysis 23 (December 1962), pp. 32-36; John V. Canfield and Patrick McNally, "Paradoxes of Self-Deception," Analysis 21, 6 (June 1961), pp. 140-44; T. S. Champlin, "Double Deception," Mind LXXXV, 337 (January 1976), pp. 100-02; Raphael Demos, "Lying to Oneself," pp. 588-94; Richard Reilly, "Self-Deception: Resolving the Epistemological Paradox," Personalist 57, 4 (Autumn 1976), pp. 391-94; John Turk Saunders, "The Paradox of Self-Deception," Philosophy and Phenomenological Research 35, 4 (June 1975), pp. 559-70. See also David Pears, Questions in the Philosophy of Mind (London: Gerald Duckworth & Co., 1975), pp. 80-96. This article appeared under the same title in an earlier version in Teorema, mono. 1 (1974), and in the same form under a different title, "Freud, Sartre and Self-Deception," in Freud: A Collection of Critical Essays, ed. Richard Wollheim, (Garden City: Anchor Doubleday, 1974).

[86]Kant, The Doctrine of Virtue, pp. 93-94.

[87]Sartre, Being and Nothingness, p. 49.

[88]Demos, "Lying to Oneself," p. 588.

[89]Saunders, "The Paradox of Self-Deception," p. 559.

[90]See D. M. Hamlyn, "Self-Deception," pp. 45 ff.; Terence Penelhum, "Pleasure and Falsity," in Stuart Hampshire, ed., Philosophy of Mind (New York: Harper & Row, 1966), pp. 242-65; Canfield & Gustavson, "Self-Deception," pp. 32-33.

[91] Canfield & Gustavson, "Self-Deception," p. 34.

[92] Penelhum, "Pleasure and Falsity," p. 259.

[93] Bela Szabados, "Self-Deception," *Canadian Journal of Philosophy* IV, 1 (September 1974), pp. 67-68.

[94] Penelhum, "Pleasure and Falsity," p. 259.

[95] Jeffery Foss, "Rethinking Self-Deception," *American Philosophical Quarterly* 17, 3 (July 1980), p. 239.

[96] Siegler, "Self-Deception," p. 42.

[97] Ibid., p. 43.

[98] Saunders, "The Paradox of Self-Deception," p. 559.

[99] The inability to "spell out" is Fingarette's term; Fingarette's model will be discussed in the next chapter. See also H. O. Mounce, "Self-Deception," pp. 66-69.

[100] Alan Paskow, "Towards a Theory of Self-Deception," *Man and World* 12, 2 (1979), p. 180. See also David Pears, "The Paradoxes of Self-Deception," passim.

[101] For a complete discussion of this issue and an argument that Sartre and Freud are both equipped to resolve the paradox in functionally similar ways, see Phyllis Sutton Morris, "Self-Deception: Sartre's Resolution of the Paradox," in Hugh Silverman, ed., *Jean-Paul Sartre* (Pittsburg: Duquense University Press, 1980), pp. 30-49. See the next chapter for a discussion and clarification of Sartre's views.

[102] Paskow, "Towards a Theory of Self-Deception," p. 180.

[103] Consider Lee Brown and Alan Hausman, "Mechanism, Intentionality, and the Unconscious: A Comparison of Sartre and Freud," in Schlipp, ed., *The Philosophy of Jean-Paul Sartre*, who write, p. 578: "Does self-deception with all its Sartrian paradoxical elements actually exist? It seems extremely doubtful. It might of course be otherwise with a range of phenomena associated with Freudian theory. Perhaps Sartre has simply 'deduced' that there must be his sort of self-deception from his general metaphysical claim that man is the being who can take negative attitudes with respect to himself. If he is wrong, and if there be no such thing as he describes, then of course the problem vanishes. But his mistakes are quite independent of the really important things he has to say about Freudian theory and, as we have shown, Freudian theory is independent of what he has to say."

[104] This definition of antimony appears in W.V. Quine, "The Ways of Paradox," in *The Way of Paradox* (New York: Random House, 1966), p. 9.

[105] See G. M. A. Grube, *Plato's Thought* (Boston: Beacon Press, 1935, 1966), pp. 133 ff. for a discussion of this issue. Grube notes, "Plato is brought to the notion of conflict within the individual mind or soul. . . .Far from being a 'primitive view', this is very advanced; one of the most start-

lingly modern things in Platonic philosophy is just this discovery of the importance of conflict in the human mind" (p. 133).

[106]Amelie O. Rorty, "Belief and Self-Deception," *Inquiry* 15, 4 (Winter 1972), p. 387.

[107]Bela Szabados, "Rorty on Belief and Self-Deception," *Inquiry* 17, 4 (Winter 1974), pp. 464-73.

[108]John King-Farlow, "Self-Deceivers and Sartrian Seducers," *Analysis* 23, 6; N.S. 96 (June 1963), p. 135.

[109]Foss, "Rethinking Self-Deception," p. 239.

[110]This term is Fingarette's. See his *Self-Deception*, p. 50; also Crites, "The Aesthetics of Self-Deception," pp. 107 ff.

[111]Gardner Murphy, *Outgrowing Self-Deception* (New York: Basic Books, 1975), esp. pp. 3-60. See also Gardner Murphy, "Experiments in Overcoming Self-Deception," *Psychophysiology* 6 (1970), pp. 790-99.

[112]Murphy, "Experiments in Overcoming Self-Deception," p. 791.

[113]See, for example, the studies by Else Frenkel-Brunswik concerning the "auto-illusion" that creeps into students' self-reports of behavior as compared to a controlled, if not purely objective, evaluation of students by teachers and superiors. A dated, but revealing compilation of data. See Frenkel-Brunswik, "Mechanisms of Self-Deception," pp. 409 ff.

[114]The "K factor" refers to a factor in personality tests that distorts the test results due to unconscious or conscious misrepresentation of the personality by the subject. See Paul E. Meehl and Starke R. Hathaway, "The K Factor as a Suppressor Variable in the Minnesota Multiphasic Personality Inventory," *Journal of Applied Psychology* 30, 5 (October 1946). This study reports, p. 525: "one of the most important failings of almost all structured personality tests is their susceptibility to 'faking' or 'lying' in one way or another, as well as their even greater susceptibility to unconscious self-deception and role playing on the part of the individuals who may be consciously quite honest and quite sincere in their responses."

[115]Ernest R. Hilgard "Human Motives and the Concept of Self," *American Psychologist* 4, 9 (September 1949). In a general discussion of defense mechanisms, Hilgard writes, p. 376: "Another way of looking at the mechanisms is to see them as bolstering self-esteem through self-deception. There is a deceptive element in each of the mechanisms. Rationalization is using false or distorted reasons to oneself as well as to the world outside; using reasons known to be false in order to deceive someone else is not rationalizing but lying. It is entirely appropriate to consider self-deception as one of the defining characteristics of a mechanism." I shall discuss self-esteem and self-identity as providing the *motive* for self-deception in the next chapter.

[116]P. C. Watson & P. N. Johnson-Laird, *Psychology of Reasoning: Structure and Content* (Cambridge: Harvard University Press, 1972). Cited In Ruben C. Gur and Harold A. Sackeim, "Self-Deception: A Concept in Search of a Phenomenon," *Journal of Personality and Social Psychology* 27, 2 (February

1979), pp. 147-48, 169. Hereafter cited as "Gur and Sackeim." The other study by these two psychologists previously noted, "Self-Deception, Self-Confrontation, and Consciousness" will hereafter be cited as "Sackeim and Gur."

[117]In addition to the two articles already cited, Sackeim and Gur have also published "Self-Deception, Other Deception, and Self-Reported Psychopathology," Journal of Consulting and Clinical Psychology 47, 1 (1979), pp. 213-215. Sackeim and Gur provide a superb bibliography on the experimental literature available on self-deception. They refer the reader to accounts of behavioral and attitudinal change in which self-deception has been mentioned, with reference to cognitive dissonance theories, for instance, e.g., L. Festinger, A Theory of Cognitive Dissonance (Evanston, IL: Row, Peterson, 1957); and theories of reactance, e.g., J. W. Brehm, A Theory of Psychological Reactance (New York: Academic Press, 1966).

[118]Gur and Sackeim, p. 149.

[119]Ibid., p. 149.

[120]Ibid., pp. 149-50.

[121]Ibid., p. 152. See pp. 152-53 for an extended discussion of methodological considerations.

[122]Sackeim and Gur, pp. 172-73. Specific studies and results are discussed on these pages.

[123]Ibid., p. 173.

[124]Ibid., p. 174.

[125]Gur and Sackeim, p. 156.

[126]Ibid.

[127]D. G. Martin, G. A. Hawryluk and L. L. Guse, "Experimental Study of Unconscious Influences: Ultrasound as Stimulus," Journal of Abnormal Psychology 83 (1974), p. 604; quoted in Sackeim and Gur, p. 178.

[128]Gur and Sackeim, p. 156.

[129]Sackeim and Gur, p. 179.

[130]Gur and Sackeim, p. 157.

[131]Ibid., p. 161.

[132]Ibid., p. 162. See pp. 162-63 for a summary of method.

[133]Ibid., p. 166.

[134]This defines "fact" in Angeles, Dictionary of Philosophy, p. 93.

[135]Ibid., pp. 74-75. This definition of 'empirical' reads as follows:

"Referring to knowledge founded on experience, observation, facts, sensation, practice, concrete situations, and real events."

[136]One could reasonably dispute the Sackeim and Gur findings, and I have discussed this issue at length in "Self-Deception: A Conceptual Analysis in Three Relational Contexts," pp. 202-204. I would note, however, that GSR polygraph results do provide a psychophysical measurement, and our experience in the common life with anxiety or stress does permit us to say that physical responses accompany these mental states; not always, but sometimes, even often. The Sackeim and Gur findings can be provisionally accepted because their interpretation that the errors in voice identification are stress related appeals to a certain kind of argument, a "how-else-do-you-explain-it?" explanation that is uncommon in neither philosophical nor scientific circles. For more on alternative explanations see, Peter Donovan, Interpreting Religious Experience (New York: Seabury Press, Crossroad Book, 1979), pp. 89 ff.; also Basil Mitchell, The Justification of Religious Belief (New York: Oxford University Press, 1973, 1981), pp. 123-24.

CHAPTER TWO

SELF-DECEPTION: THE PERSPECTIVE OF PHILOSOPHICAL PSYCHOLOGY

'Self-deception' is a psychological concept. As a proper object of psychological inquiry, 'self-deception' refers us to the mental and behavioral characteristics of individuals[1] as those characteristics reveal a particular form of self-relatedness. As a concept, moreover, 'self-deception' is also subject to philosophical scrutiny. When I say that 'self-deception' is subject to analysis from the perspective of philosophical psychology I mean that 'self-deception' is a psychological concept the meaning of which is subject to our thoughtful scrutiny. Through philosophical investigation, we undertake the critical task of analyzing the concept such that we arrive at a description that, in this case, corresponds to our best determination of that to which the linguistic expression points. In order to become "intimately acquainted" with 'self-deception'--my purpose in this study--it is necessary to examine this psychological concept philosophically. I begin with a question.

"What particular interest does philosophical psychology take in self-deception?" The answer to this question is quite simple: "The problem of self-deception is the problem of how to describe self-deception without contradiction."[2] The paradox of self-deception, I have said, is a problem generated from ordinary language considerations. I have offered the view that the paradox refers to an actual intrapsychic opposition, which renders the paradox only apparent and not a logical contradiction. This clarification eliminates the primary obstacle to conceptual elucidation, though we have yet to examine the concept--beyond paradox--from the point of view of the philosophical psychologist. The essential problem confronting a philosophical psychologist is whether it can be shown that 'self-deception' is the meaningful cipher of communication that typical linguistic users assume it to be. The following remarks by Alan R. Drengson restate the problem:

> We do not normally find anything puzzling about saying that someone is deceiving himself. Some philosophers have, nevertheless, found that their attempts to describe what is involved in self-deception run into difficulties. Indeed, some philosophers have claimed that attempts to describe self-deception in detail lead to paradox. Recent analyses of self-deception have been directed, at least in part, at removing the alleged paradox.[3]

My interest in this chapter is to examine self-deception from the specific view of philosophical psychology. I concede that, philosophically speaking, our aim should be to find one paradigm case that would permit us to establish a standard against which all other instances might be measured, that would allow us to say all that is necessary in order to describe the concept adequately. The psychological task, however, in that it tends to focus our attention on particular instances, seems resistant to such formalized treatment. As André Gide remarked, "You may be sure that in psychology there are nothing but individual cases and that, in a case like yours, too hasty generalizations may lead to the most serious errors."[4] There is sound counsel in this remark, counsel, I for one, shall try to heed.

My proposal, then, is to consider, first of all, examples of self-deception. I shall use a fictional, a quasi-historical, and a philosophical example, each of which I shall be prepared to defend as illustrations of the concept 'self-deception.' I shall then discuss various philosophical treatments of self-deception, each of which represents a different analysis within the parameters of the "philosophical psychology" perspective. These various approaches will be tested for adequacy with the litmus of "common life" considerations. I shall conclude with my own "emotional perception" proposal, which attempts to account for the complexity of individual cases. It draws on the strengths of the various other accounts while avoiding obvious weaknesses. I shall argue that "emotional perception" is the most adequate way of conceiving 'self-deception,' for not only is it coherent, but it is consistent with the "ordinary language" analysis offered in the previous chapter.

A. Three Examples of Self-Deception

In order to make the case that self-deception is a feature of the common life, we must be able to analyze instances of self-deception as they arise in our common life together. Our ultimate appeal, in other words, is to a familiar experience, which it is then our task as philosophers to describe coherently. One philosophical approach

> consists in examining instances in which men are said to be self-deceived and, without prejudging the issues in deference to existing vocabulary, try to see what actually happens. If this is done, we shall (I suspect) find analogies and similarities with cases of deception proper that are sufficient to make the reflexive extension of the concept appear, within limits, reasonably appropriate. But the instances themselves will form a variegated spectrum, and the analogies can in any event never be more than partial ones. Which we select, which we find it most natural to press, will no doubt be partially determined by our particular moral viewpoint or conception of human nature.[5]

How we select examples, then, poses difficulties because our selections will expose assumptions and reflect operative presuppositions. The examples I am proposing as instances of 'self-deception,' in addition to providing illustrations of relevant conceptual features, have the virtue of not being idiosyncratic or extreme instances of behavior. That is to say, they are examples that appeal to our experience--even if fictionally and imaginatively; and because of that appeal, they command our attention and will require analysis. These examples, I admit, are not instances of "normal" behavior; but self-deception is not a normal psychological condition. It is, rather, a psychological phenomenon with which we are all familiar, which is to say nothing more than this: it is familiar rather than normal. The examples to be put forward reflect my own operative assumption that self-deception is a feature of the common life. Accordingly, my reader should not expect me to present examples of extreme personality breakdown (i.e., schizophrenia). Rather, these examples will reflect a more mildly conceived and enacted fragmentation process that we experience in the common life and refer to in ordinary parlance as instances of 'self-deception.'

Because my first example is purely fictional, I would note that a certain kind of criticism attends this *type* of example. It is reasonable to argue, after all, that ". . .it is quite easy for novelists or philosophical theorists to describe hypothetical states of mind in terms that attest to the reality of self-deception without this at all sufficing to guarantee that such states of mind ever, in reality, occur."[6] Although this position has obvious merit, it does not do justice to the truly skillful author, the author who can create characters whose mental states appeal to the reader's experience.

An author's ability to illuminate character by describing psychological dynamics and charting action based on psychological development is fundamental to the artistic challenge. Writers of fiction illustrate psychological concepts through the creation of character; we know what jealousy is, for example, from the common life, but we know more about it if we attend a performance of *Othello*. We do not normally judge an artistic achievement on the basis of the artist's ability to suggest a *hypothetical* state of mind, for a hypothetical state of mind would be so foreign to our own experience that the appeal would be abstract, if not unintelligible. We are more apt to applaud a fictional creation if we are able to adjudge the conceptual illumination, or the character, as successfully drawn and consonant with a broader appeal to our shared knowledge of human persons. Certain masterpieces of fiction, then, build upon what we already know, reaching into the psychological hinterland of motives, intentions and purposes that are part of the action and the character. In "real life" these are often obscure. In my reading of fiction, many of the passages I underline catch me up because of something that rings true to my experience, even if it is to imagined experience or my experience of imagination. The successful author bridges through aesthetic form an imagined character's experience and my own, and in so doing makes that character's problem or situation quite "real." To the extent that an author can accomplish this--there are authors who have used 'self-deception' in a fictional context to illuminate character and conflict and who have appealed to my experience by so doing--it seems that the appeal is not to a purely "hypothetical state of mind."[7]

Of course, as my reader should by now expect, the view I have just advanced has its detractors. Anthony Palmer, for instance, has argued that the artist has an actual advantage over the philosopher when it comes to elucidating 'self-deception.' Palmer's view is that "characterizing" self-deception in a fictional account, in the sense of <u>creating character</u> as opposed to <u>describing character</u>, constitutes a way of <u>showing</u> that which cannot be satisfactorily <u>described</u>. Palmer's case is that philosophers are interested in description, and "If we operate in a descriptive mode our aim has to be the elimination of contradiction. We could not say of an illogical world what it would be like. Contradictions will not bear standing; they lack sense."[8] His point relevant to self-deception is that inasmuch as a description of self-deception shows us a character's contradictory state of mind, and that contradiction is behaviorally instantiated, philosophy will get stuck at the point where the contradiction must be put into words and described. Palmer, then, argues that

> It would be wrong, however, to draw from this conclusion that we can only be led to understand that which is not contradictory, or that which bears stating, for this would be to suppose that the descriptive mode of characterization is the only one open to us, which it is not. In their efforts after understanding, human beings are not only describers and staters, they are also creators, and in that way can come to understand, and lead others to understand, things which would be closed to them. [Philosophers] have been inclined to think that little weight should be placed upon truths which cannot be stated, and rightly so when such claims are decked out in talk almost mystical in nature about things which only those possessors of sensitive souls known as artists have the wherewithal to penetrate. But stripped of its mystical aura the artist's claim not only makes sense, it is valid.[9]

Palmer's view, then, is that the contradiction implicit in any description of self-deception will arise as a logical impasse to prevent further description of behavioral realities: "This may baffle description but . . .there is a sense in which it does not baffle characterization."[10] The reason that it does not baffle characterization is, in short, that novelists can show in their creation of character what neither they nor philosophers can describe.

Although I want to affirm both the fact of human creativity and the value of it (even in philosophical discussions); and while I want to agree that a novelist can show us through the "creation of character" what a philosopher might have trouble describing; it nevertheless strikes me that the distinction being pressed by Palmer is somewhat artificial. "Characterization," after all, is a kind of description. Furthermore, the kind of artist inclined to introduce an audience to truths which cannot be stated--whatever those would be--would probably not opt for a linguistically-related medium in the first place. I would want to say that the distinction to press is this: that a philosopher interested in describing 'self-deception' does so by a direct communication about the concept, by an appeal to knowledge by description, a knowledge that such-and-such is the case (Ryle), that it satisfies certain criteria, and that it conceptually instantiates when the criteria are satisfied. The literary artist, however, is ostensibly involved in an effort the end of which is to satisfy certain aesthetically conceived aims. In pursuit of those aims--whatever they be--the writer may indirectly communicate something about the nature of certain concepts, showing how a person's greed or jealousy or self-deception influences the course of action and reflects the values, beliefs and development of the character. Shakespeare's Othello, then, provides us with a more richly textured conception of 'jealousy' than we might have otherwise held or imagined or experienced. Now we see how jealousy can be implicated in human tragedy and so on. That insight is gained as a result of a description of character and action, i.e., "characterization." That "showing" by characterization is not incommensurate with another kind of description, that which is commonly associated with philosophical description.

I am led to the conclusion that if a novelist were to create a character about whom we could say "This character is self-deceived" and then added that the picture of self-deception is, conceptually speaking, an actual paradox, then that actual paradox would only obtain if the conception of consciousness attributed to the character is shown to be unitary and transparent. This, in fact, cannot be shown; in fact, the only literary example I have at my fingertips where an author deliberately forces a character to play with the actual paradox of self-deception as an existential possibility is Kierkegaard's Aesthete, who attempts as a project to deceive himself consciously and deliberately. This, of course, fails, which is why first volume of Either/Or leaves the Aesthete on the verge of madness.[11] In other literary instances where the concept 'self-deception' is pressed into service, the author is illustrating action attributable to self-conflict and psychic fragmentation. I would have to ask how such characterization is essentially different from a philosopher who examines the concept, considers examples, then tries to present a coherent account. If the concept 'self-deception' is "characterized"--as opposed to "described"--as an actual paradox, the picture of self-deception in both cases would force the same logical conclusion: either the phenomenon being characterized is not literal self-deception, or 'self-deception' is being used idiosyncratically, used, that is, in an inappropriate manner to describe what other linguistic expressions could more adequately and accurately describe.

All of this is to suggest that Palmer, too, operates from a unitary and transparent view of consciousness, since he argues that self-deception is an actual paradox: that one person is both deceiver and deceived, which is the juxtaposition of opposing roles in one consciousness that cannot be coherently described. I would argue, however, that because the paradox can be shown to be only apparent, the opposition that Palmer detects can be coherently described. The opposition between a character's behavior in a fictional setting and that same character's interpretation of that behavior simply points to the complexity--and the conflict--of the character's intrapsychic relations. The literary artist, in other words, is not showing us a "truth that cannot be stated." The literary artist is showing us, rather, a "person" whose self-relations configure such that self-deception obtains. We discern the self-deception in the difference between the character's behavior as described by the author and the character's own understanding of the behavior, to which we, as readers, are privy.

The value of a literary example? My view is that the probing and patient investigator who presents us with a self-deceived character is able, as a literary creator, to portray the particularities of intrapsychic conflict in their manifest concreteness. We can therefore evaluate a character's self-deception with a certainty that is often not possible with actual persons. After all, an actual person, whose secret musings are protected by privileged access, could be trying to deceive us with his or her contradictory behavior, for self-deception can be feigned. Furthermore, because literary artists are able to present the particularities of intrapsychic conflict in a manner consistent with their aesthetic intentions, we as readers can discern that the character in question is rationalizing, or offering by strong denials a plausible but untrue interpretation of his or her own actions, thereby exhibiting behavior consistent with an instance of self-deception. The mental state is not hypothetical, the character is. The character becomes "real" to the extent that he or she behaves in a recognizable way and reveals a recognizable recognizable self-conflict. In situations, conflicts and action, characters reveal their reasons for wanting to mislead their own beliefs, so that in the end, if it is self-deception a character has fallen into, the reader comes to conclude that the character does not know about him- or herself what the reader knows. Moreover, a fictional context is so constructed that it can provide the detail necessary to understand the complexity of the intrapersonal conflict and to appreciate the psychological gain that the character derives from a "cover up." If it is the author's purpose to exhibit a case of self-deception, that author will control the materials of composition and characterization so that 'self-deception' fits as an adequate and intelligible description of the character's action--and mental state.

In sum, then, the value of a literary example is to be derived from the access that is provided to the character's self-understanding. The author is able to reveal the nature of a character's self-relations in an explicit way, thereby familiarizing the reader with the--so to speak--"conflicting parties." Philosophers do not usually undertake the painstaking work of constructing, then probing, the self-deceiver's intrapsychic relations, preferring instead to focus on issues of conceptual coherence. A literary artist out to portray a character in the grip of self-deception, on the other hand, can be expected to so portray a character that a typical reader would conclude "This character is self-deceived." Such an artist could only accomplish this, however, if he or she invokes a non-unitary and non-transparent view of consciousness. Literary artists like Henry James, George Eliot, Nathaniel Hawthorne, and Herman Melville deal with the contradictoriness of human behavior to be sure, but that contradictoriness is a coherent manifestation of intrapersonal conflict, not an actual paradox that somehow shows what "cannot be said." We do have access through character and action to the "parties" that give rise to opposition in the character, for we have a language of selfhood, ambiguous though it be at times. I would add that the aesthetic challenge that confronts an author is, in my view, to create a *self* through characterization, to portray a self as it expresses its manifold capacity for intrapsychic relatedness. By creating character that is complex, that is fragmented and divided and even obscure to itself, the literary artist provides access to fictionally drawn-- but in a sense "actual"--instances of self-deception. To deny the possible validity of a psychological description because it is presented fictionally would be equivalent to denying the relevance of any hypothetical person to psychological actualities. If pushed, this fallacious move would prevent any fictional presentation from bearing relevance to the common life,[12] and the fictional example is too important a resource to be denied in this or any other study of psychological concepts.

My fictional example is taken from the André Gide novella, The Pastoral Symphony.[13]

The story concerns a pastor who is married and has several children. Upon being summoned to an obscurely located rural home where an old woman has died, he discovers a blind girl whom he decides to take home because, as he says, ". . .it came upon me suddenly that God had set a kind of obligation in my path and that I could not shirk it without cowardice."[14] All of the attention that he subsequently lavishes on this girl is referred back to a motive of Christian duty and charity.

The blind girl, Gertrude, is a young woman socially debilitated by her blindness and by her impoverished, silent life with the old woman. The pastor undertakes to teach the girl how to converse, and in time she learns to read Braille. A "Helen Keller-esque" breakthrough occurs from painstakingly patient attention, after which Gertrude rapidly progresses in her conquest of speech. Gertrude begins to emerge as a quite lovely and mature young woman. She is graced with many endearing qualities.

The story of the pastor's relationship to Gertrude is presented as the account kept by the pastor in a journal. The journal reveals that the pastor's relationship to Amelie, his wife, is marred by bickering and petulance, the pastor occasionally confiding to his diary that Amelie is unappreciative of his attempts to enact Christian charity. Gertrude is a particular bone of contention. Amelie accuses her husband of spending more time with her than with any of their own children, and, as the journal reports, Amelie is forever dropping cryptic remarks about Gertrude, which the pastor reports but does not understand. "The only pleasure I can give Amelie is to refrain from doing the things she dislikes," the pastor writes, and he observes that his wife's capacity for "negative love" is the most he can expect of her.[15]

The journal reveals to its readers that the pastor has fallen in love with Gertrude. The pastor will not admit this to himself, for he understands his love for Gertrude to be the fulfillment of a duty of Christian charity. Any other kind of interpretation--say, an erotic interpretation--would constitute sin in the pastor's own eyes. It becomes clear, however, not only in the teaching situations, but in his taking Gertrude to concerts and accompanying her on long intimate walks, that the pastor's love is other than he believes it to be. For his part, the pastor often quotes Scripture to himself to justify (rationalize) his belief that his motive is Christian charity. On that score, too, it is clear that the pastor is misconstruing the most reasonable sense of the passages he cites. Moreover, that the pastor has fallen in love with Gertrude is clear to all around him, particularly Amelie, who remarks in one of her "ill humors" as the pastor calls them, "If I had to warn you of everything you can't see for yourself, I should have my work cut out for me."[16] The pastor's response is quite revealing: "What did she mean by this insinuation? I did not know or care to know, and went on, without attending to it."[17]

A month passes. The pastor returns to his journal, but before adding new entries, he pauses to read his previous entries. He reflects on what has transpired. Suddenly, while reading his own account of his relationship to Gertrude, he is able to see what he had not been able to see heretofore, namely, that he has been deeply and erotically "in love" with Gertrude. His wife's formerly mysterious remarks are now illuminated as insights into his behavior rather than as sniping. The pastor acknowledges his mistaken interpretation of his love for Gertrude. He sees that he has been persuading himself that his love was innocent and disinterested, when now he understands that it was erotic. The pastor reflects,

> Now that I dare call by its name the feeling that so long lay unacknowledged in my heart, it seems almost incomprehensible that I should have mistaken it until this very day--incomprehensible that those words of Amelie's that I recorded should have appeared mysterious--that even after Gertrude's naive declarations, I could still have doubted that I loved her. The fact is that I would not then allow that any love outside marriage could be permissible, nor at the same time would I allow that there could be anything whatever forbidden in the feeling that drew me so passionately to Gertrude.
> The innocence of her avowals, their very frankness, reassured me. I told myself she was only a child. Real love would not go without confusion and blushes. As far as I was concerned, I persuaded myself I loved her as one loves an afflicted child. I tended her as one tends a sick person--and so I made a moral obligation, a duty, of what was really a passionate inclination. . . .I misunderstood my real feelings,

and even as I transcribed our talk, I misunderstood them still. For I should have considered love reprehensible, and my conviction was that everything reprehensible must lie heavy on the soul; therefore I felt no weight on my soul, I had no thought of love.

These conversations not only were set down just as they occurred, but were also written while I was in the same frame of mind as when they took place; to tell the truth, it was only when I reread them last night that I understood. . . .[18]

After this self-confrontation, after admitting that his love was romantic and erotic rather than of a piece with Christian agape, the pastor refuses to undergo self-censure. Having acknowledged the true nature of his love for Gertrude, he decides there is nothing wrong with such love. Yet he is concerned about theological ethics and personal integrity, so he resorts once more to quoting Scripture, this time seeking to justify his belief that this love for Gertrude is the real meaning of the Gospel message. His exegesis is once again creative but idiosyncratic. The story is finally resolved after surgery restores Gertrude's sight. The pastor has feared an operation because, as he tells himself, Gertrude might be disappointed or endangered by the results; though it is clear to the reader, because of a sub-plot involving the pastor's son, Jacques, who is also attentive to Gertrude and with whom Gertrude has shown romantic interest, that the actual reason for the pastor's vacillation is that he fears he will lose Gertrude to his own son. Jacques and Gertrude do love each other, and the pastor, who does not acknowledge the threat posed by Jacques, decides to send his son away. Only then does the pastor withdraw his objections to the operation. Gertrude's sight is restored, though she is plunged into despair at having lost Jacques and seeing the pastor. The tragic denouement is that Gertrude attempts suicide by throwing herself into a river, and although she does not kill herself, she contracts pneumonia and from this she dies. Before she dies, she tells the pastor that it is Jacques she loves, not him; and that revelation, accompanied by Gertrude's death, awakens the pastor to a realization that he has built a false and illusory world. He has deceived himself, and the story ends with the pastor on his knees, seeking forgiveness from Amelie and God.

Gide's story shows the reader how a self-directed project to mislead belief can be enacted and how an intrapsychic epistemic deficit is manifest behaviorally. That the pastor acknowledges his self-deception, on two separate occasions, confirms this conclusion. Briefly, the pastor has deceived himself about the nature of his true feelings for Gertrude. He knows he loves her, but at the same time he can only acknowledge that love in terms appropriate to a Christian interpretation. The best, most reasonable interpretation of his love is that it is erotic and romantic. But because the pastor considers such love inconsistent with his own professed values and standards, he interprets his love such that he can continue to profess those values and standards. We can say, then, that the pastor knows he loves Gertrude at the same time he knows he does not love her. He will not interpret this clearly erotic love as erotic because it is not his desire to love her that way. In his own eyes, such love would be "reprehensible."

In this story, a contradiction is apparent in that the pastor loves Gertrude at the same time he does not love her. That contradiction, however, is resolvable because each term of the opposition can be traced to a conflict of self-relatedness; that is, each term of the opposition is attended by intention and belief consistent with the term, and each term is made manifest behaviorally. The behavior itself is attended by two opposing interpretations. There is first of all a "true" interpretation, and the reader and Amelie have access to this: that the pastor loves Gertrude in an erotic way. The false interpretation, on the other hand, is that which the pastor professes, the interpretation he makes linguistically explicit to himself. This false interpretation is the interpretation most consistent with the pastor's commitments to certain overriding values (i.e., marital fidelity, Christian duty to help the weak and care for the needy). It is also the interpretation most likely to provide psychological gain, since he is able to avoid the pain of admitting that his love is of a reprehensible sort. The pastor's commitment to a Christian self-image makes it possible to discern a motive for his "erroneous" interpretation of his love, and this error is no simple mistake that anyone could carelessly make. The gain is that the pastor can behave in a manner that expresses eros while at the same moment avoiding the interpretation that would cause him emotional trauma. Because the truth that he is acting--in his own terms--"reprehensibly" would be painful to admit, the pastor misleads his own beliefs about the nature of his love so that he can acknowledge affection for Gertrude while interpreting that affection in terms consistent with Christian charity. Reprehensible love is made laudable.

The pastor's interpretation of his relationship to Gertrude is plausible, but not the best, most reasonable interpretation. His love for Gertrude reflects two opposing desires: the desire to love Gertrude passionately and erotically; and the desire not to love Gertrude this way, but another way (Christianly). The pastor's behavior reveals in a publicly observable way an opposition taking place intrapsychically between these two opposing desires. We see this in the behavior itself, which is erotic, and in his interpretation of that behavior, which is not erotic. The pastor attempts to resolve the conflict by engaging in interpretive activity that distorts and evades the best, most reasonable interpretation of the facts. Clearly he does so for reason of psychological gain. As a married man, as a minister committed to normative values concerning monogamy and the impermissibility of adulterous desires, the pastor has an easily discernible motive for an interpretive "cover up." He does not want to perceive himself as a person whose desires are illicit and unworthy of one with his vocational calling. Others around the pastor see the true nature of his activities and feelings--we as readers see it--but because of his self-persuasion efforts, the pastor is able to evade facing the "true" interpretation of his love for Gertrude, the interpretation the pastor considers "reprehensible." The pastor succeeds in deceiving himself.

When the pastor finally does face up to the true nature of his love, we as readers find that this self-confrontation provides the occasion for a second instance of self-deception. In this second act of self-deception, the pastor rationalizes his now accepted erotic love by finding religious sanction for it. He now understands his love for Gertrude as the true meaning of the Gospel message, though this new interpretation is inconsistent with his former view that erotic love outside marriage is "reprehensible." The pastor, however, deceives himself on this matter, for he is finally unable to overcome the former view to which he was deeply committed. Though he could have experienced a true change of mind, the pastor eventually recognizes that he is misreading the texts, for he admits finally that they do not sanction his erotic love for Gertrude. Throughout, the pastor's actual behavior, as he recounts it, reveals that his own interpretation of that behavior is based on a willful misconstrual of fact.

The ordinary language criteria for ascribing self-deception can be shown to apply in this example. The pastor knows he loves Gertrude (p), but at the same time (simultaneity) he has reason (motive) to keep himself from being explicitly aware of that fact. So he denies that his love is erotic (not-p), and covers up the best, most reasonable interpretation with an alternative "Christian" interpretation that enables him to evade the true meaning of his behavior. An epistemic deficit obtains between the two interpretations, between the two beliefs. Love of Gertrude constitutes the object in relation to which self-deception obtains.

The pastor, then, acts in a way that is consistent with an erotic desire. That desire manifests itself in publicly observable behavior, and it is the behavior that permits characters in the story and readers of the journal to conclude that his love for Gertrude is erotic, passionate, romantic. At the same time, however, the pastor is disposed to act according to an opposing desire, a desire not to love Gertrude erotically, and it is this counter-desire that issues in his conscious interpretive activity. That counter-desire is behaviorally manifest in the pastor's own linguistically explicit interpretation; and this interpretive activity permits him to keep himself unaware that his behavior amounts to erotic desire. The unawareness--the interpretive activity giving rise to the alternative "Christian" interpretation--is not recognized as motivated behavior, and the pastor is able to escape self-censure. He is able to interpret his acknowledged affection for Gertrude in a manner that is not reprehensible. Christian charity is the foundation for the pastor's explicit self-understanding, but the true nature of his love continues to show through. And although the pastor is not explicitly aware of his love as erotic, on another level he is. He perceives a threat from the very erotic interpretation that he does not acknowledge, and it is in response to this perceived threat that he undertakes to mislead his own beliefs, seeking to avoid self-censure by an interpretive "cover up." His behavior betrays him--to us and finally even to himself. We as readers have known all along, for the pastor's journal has described Gertrude in language that spells our a desire incommensurate with simple Christian charity:

> I noted this date as if it had been a birthday. It was not so much a smile as a transfiguration. Her features flashed into life--a sudden illumination, like the crimson glow that precedes dawn in the high Alps, thrilling the snowy peak on which it lights and calling it up out of darkness--such a flood it seemed, of mystic color; and I thought too of the pool of Bethesda at the moment the angel descends to stir the slumbering water. A kind of ecstasy rapt at the sight of the angelic expression that came over Gertrude's face so suddenly, for it was clear to me that this heavenly visitor was not so much intelligence as love. And in a very transport of gratitude I kissed her forehead and felt that I was offering thanks to God.[19]

I contend that this is the voice of passion speaking. These are the words of a lover inspired to poetry and metaphor as he experiences rapture at the sight of his beloved. I also contend that Christian duty and charity, being directed elsewhere that at panegyric, are not provisioned to find on the occasion of a young woman's smile an object suitable for such an outburst of fervent feeling. The pastor loves Gertrude. He believes that Gertrude is a fit subject for passionate, erotic longing; and inasmuch as his love contains a cognitive core in which Gertrude is judged to be an "emotional object" above all others, he even "believes" her to be more worthy of this erotic longing than his own wife. This "belief" is "unconscious"--it is to be contrasted with the conscious profession of belief that Gertrude is worthy of Christian charity due to her helpless condition.

Analysis of the pastor's behavior reveals two opposing beliefs. On the one hand, he believes that Gertrude is an appropriate object of erotic love. Consciously, the pastor acts to interpret his behavior as consistent with his desired self-image--the duty-bound pastor and family man incapable of emotional indiscretion. Consciously content with loving Gertrude in a Christianly way, the pastor is possessed of a contrary belief (not-p), which could be described as a belief not to love Gertrude passionately and erotically. The pastor's publicly observable behavior, however, manifests the "unconscious intention" to act consistently with an occurrent, though not explicitly professed desire to love Gertrude passionately and erotically. Keeping in mind William James' practical dictim, "Belief is measured by action," let us say that the unconscious belief that Gertrude is an appropriate target for the pastor's erotic desire is, as a matter of fact, enacted. In light of the pastor's distorted Christian interpretation, therefore, the action consistent with p is itself present, though the pastor is unaware that his action springs from his disposition to act consistently with p. For discernible reasons, the pastor suppresses his belief that p by covering up what he unconsciously perceives and believes--that his love for Gertrude is erotic. These opposing beliefs represent opposing desires and opposing intentions, and these are the "parties" of intrapsychic opposition. The terms co-exist in one consciousness, in terms of one person's self-relatedness, expressing one person's capacity for experiencing conflict and fragmentation.

Because the pastor professes a belief that his love for Gertrude is non-erotic while he enacts a belief--a belief of which he not explicitly aware--to the contrary; and because we can discern a motive for his "cover up" of that primary, though now unconscious belief due to his religious views and the normative action guides that attend them, it is clear that Gide's pastor exhibits an instance of self-deception. The pastor acknowledges that he loves Gertrude; but for reasons of psychological gain, he acts to avoid confronting the true nature of that love, opting for a false interpretation more compatible with his self-image and self-understanding. To say, therefore, that the pastor is aware, yet not aware, or knows but doesn't know, is not to speak the language of logical contradiction; it is to speak the language of the self as that language expresses the complexity of self-relatedness--where opposition is possible between competing beliefs, desires, intentions, and emotions. The next two examples will contain less detail, but a similar kind of analysis can issue from them. These examples will further illustrate the idea of a belief-misleading project directed by the self against the self.

My next example is taken from an article by John Exdell and James R. Hamilton, as modified and extended by Robert Audi.[20] The example is quasi-historical in that it deals with an actual historical personage and an actual occasion for conflict. Certain details, however, are not asserted as being verifiable historical events. I would add that there are historical examples available for our use (e.g., Chamberlain, Munich and the Nazi threat), particularly autobiographies, but the kind of historical investigation required to ascertain an instance of self-deception would require historical research and a perspective on "psycho-historical" issues beyond the scope of the present inquiry.[21]

The Cambodian army, under attack by insurgent forces, is nearing defeat. Lon Nol and his associates have but one option left, which is to flee the country. "But Lon Nol--normally a shrewd and perceptive man--has lost his ability to see things as they are."[22] When consulting with his aides, President Lon argues that solidarity is required. If his supporters will but stick together, he is certain that his government can withstand the threat:

> Knowledgeable friends urge him to abandon the struggle. He

disputes their predictions and rejects their advice. A respected general informs him that the army is beaten only to find himself under suspicion of disloyalty. President Lon is sustained throughout by the conviction that American air support will pull him through. But here too he is out of touch. The American government is clearly resigned to his defeat and is already seeking an accommodation with the enemy.[23]

When Lon Nol's advisors confront him with evidence of imminent disaster, Lon argues against the significance of the evidence. Yet, curiously, ". . .we find him enquiring--as if concerned only with a weekend vacation, to be sure--about the condition of his private plane, which would be his means of escape."[24] President Lon decides to order an attack. Although he reassures his advisors that such a move will lead to victory, his advisors note that the President is not displaying the kind of confidence they have come to expect of him. Lon knows as a fact that insurgent forces are on the move. He interprets this fact, however, as if his position of power were assured and the threat not potentially fatal. He expresses this belief by giving an order to attack, which his advisors argue against. Lon responds by shutting off debate. He appeals to his authority as military commander, and when he does try to counter his advisors' arguments, he seems to lack conviction and his arguments are weak.

At this moment, Lon Nol is self-deceived. He declares his belief that his government will survive and repel the insurgent forces (p) and orders action consistent with this belief (attack). Yet he acts contrary to this belief. He refuses to hear a litany of bad news, argues with trusted advisors and shuts off debate, and checks to see if his plane is ready to go. He is seemingly unaware that he also believes that disaster is about to befall him (not-p). Lon Nol is aware of the threat, for he acknowledges the strength of the enemy. But he persuades himself that the evidence counting for an inevitable insurgent victory is itself not persuasive. By willfully interpreting two conditionals as already established facts--that solidarity at home and help from America will assure the survival of his government--he discounts his advisors' interpretations and professes his belief that he will prevail. This belief is plausible given the conditionals, but, as subsequent events confirmed, it is clearly not the best, most reasonable interpretation of the facts.

Two contradictory beliefs are evident--a belief in victory (p) and another belief that defeat, not victory, is imminent (not-p). He acts on both beliefs--by professing the one through interpretive activity (p); by checking his plane, shutting off debate, arguing without conviction, which are all actions consistent with a belief--even if "unconsciously" held--that not-p. Furthermore, since our common life experience with political leaders permits us to say in general that their power is so dear to them that the prospect of relinquishing power poses a distressful prospect, we can safely infer a motive for Lon Nol's refusal to process information through normal channels: he holds supreme power; he loves his power; and he cannot face the prospect of losing that power, especially in an ignominious manner. His "unawareness" of impending disaster is the result not of innocent error or ignorance, but of interpretive activity for which a motive may be reasonably inferred.

Lon Nol refuses to admit that he is about to lose his government. Yet he acts consistently with an awareness to the contrary--an awareness that he does not make linguistically explicit, that is "deep down" or suppressed. Lon Nol, then, can be said to be self-deceived. His publicly observable behavior contradicts his professed belief: he knows "deep down" that all is lost. His refusal to admit defeat is not simple pig-headedness, for ". . .Lon Nol can be seen as acting to overcome his own natural tendency, as a 'shrewd and perceptive man,' to follow the evidence where it leads, rather than just stubbornly refusing to acknowledge its force."[25]

My third example of self-deception comes from a British philosophical text of some importance in the history of American philosophy, since William James' influential essay, "The Will to Believe" was written in response to it. Though concerned with other matters, William Clifford's essay, "The Ethics of Belief," begins with an example of self-deception:

> A shipowner was about to send to sea an emigrant-ship. He knew that she was old, and not over-well built at the first; that she had seen many seas and climes, and often had needed repairs. Doubts had been suggested to him that possibly she was not seaworthy. These doubts preyed upon his mind, and made him unhappy. He thought that perhaps he ought to have her thoroughly overhauled and refitted, even though this should put him to great expense. Before the ship sailed, however, he succeeded in overcoming these melancholy reflections. He said to himself that she had gone safely through so many voyages and weathered so many storms that it was idle to suppose she would not come safely home from this trip also. He would put his trust in Providence, which could hardly fail to protect all these unhappy families that were leaving their fatherland to seek for better times elsewhere. He would dismiss from his mind all ungenerous suspicions about the honesty of builders and contractors. In such ways he acquired a sincere and comfortable conviction that his vessel was thoroughly safe and seaworthy; he watched her departure with a light heart, and benevolent wishes for the success of the exiles in their strange new home that was to be: and he got his insurance-money when she went down in mid-ocean and told no tales.[26]

The obvious drawback of this example is its lack of detail. The shipowner is portrayed without bringing us into any profound degree of psychological familiarity. Certain of his actions--and his reflection on possible action--is not spelled out. We could enhance the example by including certain kinds of detail: that the shipowner refused to acknowledge his captain's complaints about structural deterioration and unseaworthiness; that the shipowner decided to wait for a later ship to send some valuables consigned to him for shipment, even though this ship could get them delivered to their destination by their due date; that the shipowner refused to allot this ship its usual amount of stores, cutting it back to a bare minimum; that the shipowner, having received word to come as quickly as possible to the same destination as the ship, decides to postpone immediate departure in order to get necessary papers in order. Despite the lack of such detail, the example as it stands can satisfy our "ordinary language" criteria of self-deception.

The shipowner believes that the ship is unseaworthy (p). Certain doubts prey on his mind, but after considering the expense of reoutfitting the ship (motive), he comes to consider the seaworthiness issue in light of certain facts (number of safe voyages, weathering of many storms) and entertains a plausible belief that the ship could make one more voyage, hence it is seaworthy (not-p). He engages in interpretive activity aimed at acknowledging the belief that the ship is seaworthy and convinces himself that it is, as his light heart (clear conscience ?) confirms. He stifles his initial doubts and misgivings by engaging himself in this interpretive activity, even going so far as to quash any lingering doubts by invoking Providence.

The shipowner buttresses his professed belief that the ship is seaworthy by invoking Providence. Providence, he thinks, (and not clear evidence of seaworthiness) will guarantee one more journey. Clearly the shipowner does not want to invest in the up-keep of this vessel (motive), and because of this desire not to expend funds, he "reevaluates" the situation, overcomes his doubts, and distorts the evidence of unseaworthiness. In the end, he acts in a manner consistent with his desire not to allocate funds for repairs. It is significant that in Clifford's discussion of the example, it is the final Providential "rationalization" that is the true culprit: reliance upon Providence in the face of empirical evidence to the contrary enables the belief-misleading project to succeed--the belief that Providence will oversee the safe journey of the ship and its precious human cargo.

Does the shipowner hold contradictory beliefs simultaneously? He certainly acts--and feels--as if the ship is seaworthy as it sets sail; but do we know that he is no longer entertaining doubts? I would contend that the shipowner's reliance upon Providence is evidence that the doubts are still there, even if they are no longer linguistically explicit, even if a professed belief that the ship is seaworthy has suppressed those doubts. The significance of the evidence counting for unseaworthiness has been distorted by an overriding--and motivated--interpretive scheme. The shipowner, in other words has banished evidence for unseaworthiness from continued attention and conscious preoccupation (doubt). And the fact of his sudden reliance upon Providence, rather than on the actual, empirically determined assessment of the vessel's seaworthiness--seaworthiness being the best, most reasonable justification for believing that a ship will arrive safely at its destination--counts as evidence that his doubts persist; for the doubt (or belief that $\underline{p}$) is manifest in his rationalizing activity and explains why such activity occurs in the first place.

Clifford is not explicit about the simultaneity of opposing beliefs. In fact, he makes it look as if the shipowner does not hold the contrary beliefs simultaneously, but holds one at one moment, another at another moment, thereby indicating a temporal gap, which, incidentally, is one strategy for eliminating the paradox of self-deception. The simultaneity and opposing beliefs criteria are met, however, because the shipowner is forced, even as the ship sets sail, to invoke Providence in order to see the ship safely to port. By doing that, he believes safe arrival depends upon God and not on the seaworthiness of the vessel itself. He is not explicitly confident in the vessel; rather, he is confident that God will provide. This is curious to us as outsiders because the shipowner at one point entertained explicit doubts, which he then overcame by appealing to God's mercy. I believe these interpretive maneuvers provide behavioral evidence that the doubts that had been stifled were just that: stifled, not extinguished. The doubts are still affecting behavior and influencing interpretive activity. The shipowner does not allay his doubts by being assured that the seaworthiness problem is resolved. On the contrary, his move is actually equivalent to saying "Only God can see this ship safely to port--and, by the way, I trust that God see it safely to port, for God would not let the innocent die."

The invocation of Providence for the purpose of seeing the ship safely to harbor does constitute a "rationalizing" activity vis-a-vis the stifled belief that the ship was, in fact, unseaworthy. Clifford intends to make this point about rationalizing (i.e., holding a plausible but untrue belief) for the purpose of his moral argument against believing upon insufficient evidence. My case for self-deception, however, is based on the fact that one can reasonably expect a seaworthy ship to reach its port of destination safely, for it is in the nature of things--it is a feature of the common life--that seaworthy vessels will journey to their destinations successfully while unseaworthy vessels will either meet with disaster or arrive only by luck--or, yes, perhaps Providence. The point, though, is that if the ship were seaworthy, and the shipowner believed that and that alone, he would not have to opt for another belief justification process, one outside the normal process by which judgments about the prospect of a ship arriving safely to port are made. He would not have to depend so mightily upon Providence for his comfortable conviction that all is well.

A shipowner who believed his ship to be seaworthy might, were he a religious fellow, still call on Providence--to bless the voyage with calm waters, good winds, and so on. He would not, however, ordinarily depend upon Providence the way Clifford's shipowner does--to provide safe passage for the innocent emigrants by the miracle of divine intervention. In the common life, the safe arrival of unseaworthy vessels to their port of destination constitutes something unexpected, something "lucky," something out of the ordinary--even miraculous. The shipowner, however, is revealing in his reliance upon Providence a lack of reliance upon his equipment, making the prospect of a successful voyage not a normal expectation or a normal course of events in the natural world, but a sort of miraculous achievement unattainable without divine intervention. The shipowner invokes Providence, then, in order to guarantee safe passage when safe passage cannot be otherwise assumed. In the common life, determining seaworthiness is equivalent to determining the prospects for a safe voyage. The shipowner sends to sea a ship believing it to be seaworthy, yet he also sends it out relying not on its seaworthiness to see it safely to its destination, but on miraculous prospects (divine intervention). That he is able to justify his belief in seaworthiness in the face of evidence disconfirming that belief is the result of the shipowner's having been engaged in a project to mislead his own beliefs. Inasmuch as there are two opposing beliefs present, and we can say on the basis of behavioral evidence that they are present simultaneously; and because the shipowner is unaware of one of those beliefs yet acts in accordance with it; and because he has a motive for acting as he does since he neither wants to spend the money needed for refitting nor does he want to think of himself as one who would endanger human lives for financial gain--a distressing conflict to be sure--the shipowner in Clifford's example can be said to illustrate an instance of self-deception.

In Clifford's view, the fact that theistic belief (a belief that Providence will protect the passengers) can be used to justify actions that would otherwise be deemed impermissible due to the insufficient weight of the evidence itself, and the fact that theism can be used to "stifle doubts" to the end that personal injury or preventable death can result, count as a moral argument against theistic belief itself.[27] Clifford accuses the shipowner of being directly responsible for the passengers' deaths and condemns the kind of belief that enabled the shipowner, "with sincere and comfortable" conviction, to put the ship to sea. Self-deception does, in many instances, raise issues of substantial moral importance; and it is clear that Clifford's example of the shipowner is one such instance. The moral argument is not my direct concern at the moment, though this example, as given, would clearly support Clifford's judgment by implicating theistic belief in morally impermissible action. A philosophical-psychological approach can certainly lead us to ask moral questions, for clearly certain psychological phenomena point beyond issues of description to issues of meaning and value. For now let me say that I shall discuss moral problems in due course (Chapter 3), for they deserve specific treatment. Let Clifford's shipowner be kept in mind, however, for it introduces issues that will enable us to shift our investigation from the arena of philosophical psychology to ethics.

B. In Search of a Model

In this section, I wish to consider the kinds of interpretive proposals that have emerged from the perspective of philosophical psychology. I shall consider five models: the cognition model, the translation model, the action model, Freud's multiple agent model, Sartre's voluntary dialectical model, and my own synthetic model, based on an "emotional perception" account of self-deception. I shall test the adequacy of these proposed models by considering the extent to which they conform to the ordinary language analysis offered in the previous chapter.

1. The Cognitive Model.

The cognition model characterizes self-deception in terms of knowledge, belief and thought. To use a by now familiar expression, this model conceives of self-deception as the state of epistemic deficit. Another way to say this is that as an epistemic state, self-deception is not to be described as an act, so that a proponent of this model would claim, as, for instance, Robert Audi has claimed, ". . .that one can get oneself into a state of self-deception without any act deserving that name. I do not believe it is an act."[28]

Because the cognition model defends the view that self-deception is first of all a state, and secondly that it is a state to be characterized in terms of knowing, believing or thinking, the cognitivist runs into a familiar problem, namely, that associated with the epistemological paradox. How is one to describe the state of mind in which one person holds contradictory beliefs, or believes p while also knowing "deep down" that not-p? Resolution of this cognitive impasse will depend upon being able to show how it is possible for a person to believe and not believe simultaneously; and if that cannot be shown, then the attempt to render 'self-deception' intelligible in terms of a cognitive model must be abandoned. We must, that is, either adjudge 'self-deception' to be a literally meaningless linguistic expression or seek another kind of solution through the resources of another kind of model. One thing is certain. On a cognitive model, self-deception is a problematic concept, even if it be shown that the concept is not actually contradictory. A paradoxical opposition is unquestionably evoked in our ordinary linguistic use of 'self-deception, for we do mean to say that a person does not know what he or she knows; and although this paradox can be resolved, the idea that person believes "deep down" what he or she will not acknowledge is constitutive of the cognitive state to which we refer when we say that a person is self-deceived.

Herbert Fingarette has pointed out that "Paradoxes arise in connection with self-deception when we characterize it in terms of belief and knowledge, or in terms of 'perception' language such as 'appear' or 'see.'"[29] For those who adopt what Fingarette has called the "cognition-perception" family of terms, the overriding concern will be to formulate a coherent account of the self-deceiver who "sees" what he "cannot see." A self-deceiver, in other words, is one who is unable to see through a smokescreen of one's own making. The person cannot perceive his or her own fakery and ". . .makes it appear to himself that something is so."[30] That a person is <u>unaware</u> of his or her own deception, and the psychoanalytic reference to <u>unconscious</u> wishes, fantasies or desires,[31] constitute additional ways of saying that which the cognitivist insists be said: that the person who is self-deceived exhibits a cognitive division between one belief, which is professed or avowed, and another opposite belief, which is present but not avowed. The less subtle and more problematic way of stating this is that the self-deceiver believes to be true what he or she knows is not true.

Prominent cognitivists include such figures as Canfield & Gustavson, Demos, Siegler and Penelhum, all of whom I have had occasion to mention. Their work has been extensively critiqued by Fingarette[32] and Szabados.[33] I would only add that the criticism of these cognitivists amounts to one of two charges: either the cognitivist has failed to eliminate the paradox in its entirety, or the account leaves out some feature essential to self-deception <u>per se.</u> Because of the inadequacy of these cognitive accounts, all of which fall before one of the two criticisms, should we then simply abandon the cognition model? My response is that an ordinary language analysis will not permit us to dispense with the cognitivist perspective. Self-deception, after all, <u>results</u> in an epistemic deficit, and without this reference to an epistemic result, there can be no literal self-deception. If we cannot eliminate the cognitive feature of the concept, then we must ask: Is there a cognitivist account of self-deception that is consistent with ordinary language analysis, yet avoids falling into the errors so carefully identified by Fingarette and Szabados?

In light of the attention given self-deception in the philosophical literature, and in light of specific attempts to subject self-deception to more sophisticated epistemological scrutiny,[34] it should come as no surprise that more adequate cognitive accountings of self-deception have appeared. One should expect a revised cognition account to be appreciative of the critical developments that have made other analyses possible, yet make the case that self-deception is--despite the alternative views--essentially a cognitive concept and intelligible as such. Although more sophisticated treatments have appeared since the days of Canfield & Gustavson, one feature has remained constant: central to any cognitive account of self-deception is the concern for eliminating the epistemological paradox. For the cognitivist, it is the epistemic deficit--the gap between p and <u>not-p</u>, that obstructs a coherent accounting of the concept, for this deficit points to a cognitive configuration that cannot be described without invoking a paradox.

A recent attempt to account for self-deception using the cognition model has been offered by Kent Bach.[35] Bach's account is sophisticated, though it has a wrinkle or two for both the "ordinary language" analyst and the cognition analyst. For instance, he argues that self-deception requires motive, an action feature, in its description. Although we should recall that the ordinary language analyst would insist on saying that this action feature is necessary for an adequate accounting of 'self-deception,' in itself, "motive" might appear out of place in a cognitivist account. Not only is motive an action feature more of a piece with an action model, but, as I mentioned earlier, Penelhum, one of the original cognitive theorists, argued that self-deception could be described adequately without reference to motive. If this appears to be an inconsistency, Bach makes another claim that, in itself, is as damaging to the ordinary language analyst as to the cognitivist, namely, ". . .self-deception is not necessarily a matter of belief at all."[36] Having said this, Bach is able to provide an account that does describe, in cognitive terms, the necessary epistemic deficit, though he chooses terms that are not usually employed to describe the gap between what a self-deceiver believes with respect to p and its concurrent counter-part, not-p. After claiming that self-deception is not essentially a matter of belief at all, Bach offers the following explanation, which introduces a new way of using certain cognition terms for the purpose of clarifying the self-deception debate:

> A person who believes that p (or that the evidence heavily favors p) can deceive himself that not-p without having to get himself to believe not-p. Consider that the occasion for deceiving oneself arises only insofar as the touchy subject is thought of, and so if the person believed that p (while desiring not-p) but it never occurred to him that p, he would have no occasion to deceive himself. Accordingly, what matters in self-deception is not the belief that p per se but the occurrence of the thought that p, especially on a sustained or repeated basis.[37]

Bach's case is that a self-deceiver believes p at the same time he or she desires not-p, ". . .and what he does is to avoid the sustained or recurrent thought that p."[38] I include Bach as a cognitivist, then, for several reasons. First, because he argues for an epistemic deficit between a belief that p and the thought that not-p, which I take to be a distinction relevant to a cognition model. Second, because he argues that a self-deceiver is able to avoid the sustained or recurrent thought that p by three activities-- rationalization, evasion, and jamming--which are all cognitive in nature. Third, because the three ways he identifies for deceiving oneself are to be viewed as having in common ". . .the state that they yield or preserve, that of being self-deceived."[39] Fourth, because even though he includes motivation in his description of the self-deceiver's activity, the motivation is considered to be a special kind of psychological causation that does not entail a reference to intention, intention being, in Bach's view, necessarily available to consciousness. Finally, because in distinguishing his picture of self-deception from "bad faith," Bach baldly states that ". . .self-deception proper concerns cognition (i.e., thinking and believing)."⁴⁰

Bach's argument rests upon a distinction between **thinking of** and **believing that**. His position is that thinking is a cognitive activity that does not necessarily imply believing. Bach does not hold to the traditional distinction between dispositional and occurrent belief. Rather, Bach means by believing only the dispositional sense. He therefore does not support the notion of an occurrent belief, preferring **thinking** to **occurrence**. His justification for this distinction is that persons entertain thoughts in an occurrent sense, thoughts that are not actual beliefs (e.g., the thought that the moon is made of green cheese); and we all have beliefs ("countless") that are not occurrent at any moment. "Whereas both thinking of and thinking that are mental occurrences, thinking involves at least momentarily assenting to or judging that p. This, I claim, does not entail believing that p, even for a moment."⁴¹ He adds, "Unlike thoughts beliefs are states, not occurrences."⁴²

This distinction between thinking and believing that p allows Bach to account for the fact that a person need not have thought everything he believes and ". . .also for the fact that his thoughts do not inevitably correspond to his beliefs and that they are not invariably what he thinks they are."⁴³ Bach's case, then, is that self-deception constitutes that mental state wherein a person is motivated to avoid the thought of p, not simply because he cannot bear the thought of p (which he can't), but because he has reasons for avoiding the thought that p. Those reasons issue in cognitive processes or techniques (rationalization, evasion, jamming) that enable the person to avoid the thought p while maintaining his or her own rational standards. The picture that develops, then, looks something like this: The self-deceiver holds a desire that **not-p**. That desire is opposed by a disposition to act (belief) consistent with p. The desire that **not-p** and the belief that p, when conjoined, cause the person to accept reasons for avoiding the thought that p. The person's rationalization, evasion or jamming represent specific cognitive activities whereby the person comes to accept reasons he or she would normally reject. The self-deceiver "does not realize that his desire that not-p and his belief that p combine to motivate him to fabricate and accept that reason as warrant for avoiding the thought that p."⁴⁴ Bach adds, "If this aspect of his doings were intentional, then there would be something paradoxical about the fact that he could coherently and successfully contrive not to think what he believes but something to the contrary instead. Though motivated this is not intentional."⁴⁵

Bach's picture, then, avoids an epistemological paradox by discounting any notion that the person acts intentionally (i.e., consciously) to engage him- or herself in a belief-misleading project. Yet the person can be said to engage in cognitive interpretive activity that effectively shields some actually held belief from explicit awareness (thought). About such a person's self-understanding it can be said there is a blind spot. Furthermore, Bach makes reference to a minimally conceived notion of unconsciousness, when he says, rightly, I think, that

> We need not posit repression to account for what happens. What happens is that the self-deceiver, even when confronted, lacks some awareness at some point. If he admits the weakness of his earlier reasoning, he may bolster it with further considerations but not recognize their weakness in turn. No matter how far his accuser (friend, psychiatrist) goes and no matter how much is conceded, there is always room for further considerations or reconsiderations of previous ones. His accuser may call this 'resistance,' but as long as there is something about what he is doing whose violation of his own rational standards he does not notice, he can continue to deceive himself. He is motivated to avoid the thought that p, but this does not mean that he is motivated to go to endless lengths.[46]

This, then, is Bach's case in a nutshell. It is a cognitive case to be sure; but it is a cognitive analysis that unlike many of its predecessors essentially meets the ordinary language criteria for ascribing self-deception. Bach's analysis conveniently--to my mind--describes in a non-paradoxical fashion a self-directed belief-misleading project that yields an epistemic deficit. It permits us to speak of opposing cognitive particulars (belief that not-p and thought that p) simultaneously, of there being a discernible motive, of unawareness attending one of the cognitive particulars. We can ask, however, whether Bach elucidates our examples of self-deception. Does Bach's account square with the results of our ordinary language analysis?

In each of the three examples--the pastor, Lon Nol and the shipowner--the self-deceiver is disposed to act in accordance with a desire (or belief) that not-p: not to love Gertrude erotically, not to plan for victory over insurgent forces, not to overhaul the vessel. Include, then, the fact that for certain reasons (motive), the individual wishes to avoid the thought that p. which, in each example, would be an actually occurrent cognition. The "thought that p" is the thought that such love as the pastor has for Gertrude is of a sort that the pastor himself considers reprehensible, or the thought of defeat advanced by military advisors, or the doubts that prey on the shipowner's mind. In each example, the thought that p combines with the desire (dispositional belief) that not-p with this result: the exemplar in question is motivated to avoid the thought that p and will engage in interpretive activity so that the occurrent epistemic deficit between the thought and the belief will be weighted on the side of the belief--to the exclusion of the thought. In each instance, the self-deceiver can be seen to be persuading himself that p is either not true or that it is undeserving of the evidential force others accord to it (e.g., the pastor's wife, Lon Nol's advisors). The self-deceiver evaluates the thought that p such that the thought that p is, as presented, essentially incompatible with a counter-desire or belief. The self-deceiver, in other words, uses his cognitive powers to avoid the thought that p. It is excluded from conscious recognition or crowded out by the force of a cognitive act consistent with what the self-deceiver prefers--for certain reasons--to hold as his true reason for action.

The pastor, then, avoids the thought that p, but only so far; he will not go to endless lengths. Lon Nol is left awaiting disaster, avoiding the thought that disaster is imminent (p), but will, in the end, flee the country. We lack sufficient information to know whether the shipowner accepted his insurance money without any sense of personal responsibility, but one could reasonably assume so. In each instance, the self-deceiver effectively utilizes certain cognitive techniques (rationalizing, evading or jamming) to persuade himself that a certain thought is not worthy of being entertained seriously as a candidate for belief. Each self-deceiver is able to avoid admitting the thought that p--that the pastor's love is erotic, that defeat is imminent, that the ship will sink despite Providence. We can find in all these examples the features that will allow for self-deception on Bach's account. We can discern an epistemic deficit between a (dispositional) belief that not-p and the thought that p. We can attribute a motive for the resulting unawareness wherein the self-deceiver accepts reason he would not normally accept, for according to Bach, avoiding the thought that p is a motivated behavior. Bach's case, then, appears to be consistent with the findings of our ordinary language analysis; yet, because his descriptive terms are neither those of the ordinary language analyst nor the traditional cognitivist, a couple of points need to be clarified.

My ordinary language analysis has determined that an epistemic deficit is a necessary feature of self-deception. That analysis did not, however, establish that self-deception is a state of mind or only a state of mind. An ordinary language analysis is chary of separating the process whereby self-deception obtains or is maintained (rationalization, evasion, jamming) from the result of that process, i.e. the "state" of epistemic deficit. Bach's care in including these "action" considerations makes it appear that Bach himself has avoided this separation of process and result. A critique of Bach from the "ordinary language" side of things, then, amounts not so much to a charge of inadequacy per se as to a quibble with the way these action considerations have been formulated within a cognition perspective. At the moment, my point is that the relation of action or process to result is an important consideration not only because as an analogue to deception, self-deception refers us to a particular form of relationally governed deceptive activity; but because an analysis put forward strictly or only in cognitive terms opens one to an "action" critique of the sort advanced by Fingarette or Szabados. As Szabados has put the matter:

> [To] say of someone that he is self-deceived is not merely to say that he is in a certain state of mind; ascription of self-

deceit also involves an appraisal as to how the person in question got into that state of mind and how he sustains himself in it. To leave out such 'dynamic' features of self-deception is bound to result in an inadequate account."[47]

Bach's account does include these 'dynamic' features, albeit under cognitive rubrics. And in fairness, how those dynamic features are there (via cognition) is not as important as the fact that they are there. As a cognitivist, however, Bach is an anomaly. Other cognitivists have not included such "action" considerations in their accounts, and their accounts have subsequently proven inadequate. Bach does not fall under the "action" criticism as other cognitivists do (Demos, Siegler, Canfield & Gustavson, Penelhum). Again, Bach is an exemplar, a "best cognitivist account" representative, who, in my view, avoids the pitfalls of his predecessors while managing to present a coherent account in terms appropriate to a cognition model. Bach's cognitivist account, then, not only eliminates the paradox,[48] but it withstands the criticism to which the cognition model in general falls prey. In more than a quibbling mood, I would say that inasmuch as Bach makes a case that "self-deception proper concerns cognition," that claim must be amended to say: self-deception proper is a dynamic process whereby the self so relates itself to itself that it is able to mislead its own beliefs, the result being that an epistemic deficit (cognitive state) results. Both process and result are necessary for an adequate description of self-deception. This amended version is consistent with the "ordinary language" view, which is to say with Szabados and against the strict cognitivist, that self-deception is not merely a state or only a state, for self-deception does refer us to the "act of deceiving oneself" (OED).

Despite obvious strengths, Bach's account does raise certain difficulties. Those difficulties may be traced to Bach's failure to provide an example that illustrates his account of self-deception. This is more significant than one might at first realize, as I shall explain. And even though I have shown that certain examples of self-deception can be used to support his account, appeal to example also exposes imprecisions in formulation or actual deficiencies.

In comparing Bach to the ordinary language analysis, it seems that the distinction between "thinking that p" and "believing that $not\text{-}p$" is functionally equivalent to the ordinary language distinction between "believing that p" and "believing that $not\text{-}p$." Bach's case permits us to speak of an epistemic deficit, of a person achieving unawareness of "the thought that p," and it enables us to say that the act that determines what is, and what is not, subject to awareness is a motivated act. There seems to be, then, a formal agreement between the perspectives.

Having noted that formal agreement, however, we must attend to material differences. And once these differences are considered, it is not entirely clear how that formal agreement actually obtains. For instance, on Bach's account, "thinking that p" is not to be associated with dispositional belief. If it be put in terms of 'belief' at all, "thinking that p" would be equivalent to occurrent belief. Bach, however, claims that the thought that p as is not necessary for believing that p (dispositionally). In fact, Bach declares ". . .I deny that occurrent belief is believing at all"--hence his preference for "thinking that."[49]

The ordinary language analysis, however, requires two contradictory beliefs, both fully dispositional since both are behaviorally enacted. As I have argued, we have access to the opposition between p and not-p through the person's publicly observable behavior: we observe that a person does not understand his or her own action; we observe that a person is denying or evading a painful truth. Such behavior is governed by dispositional belief, for the opposing beliefs dispose the person to act in a contradictory way.

It is possible to ascribe self-deception because there are people--we call them self-deceivers--who actually enact opposing beliefs. Each of those beliefs is manifest in action: one is the behavior itself (the best, most reasonable interpretation of which the person is unaware) and the other is the occurrent interpretation which is held to be true by means of an intentional act of linguistic interpretation that does not square with the facts of the behavior. To take an example: the pastor's belief that Gertrude is worthy of his erotic longing is behaviorally manifest (p). This corresponds to Bach's notion of a dispositional belief, which, in this instance, is suppressed. It "occurs" to the pastor that he loves Gertrude, but the pastor's occurrent belief is that he loves Gertrude in a Christian--not an erotic--way (not-p). What Bach fails to account for is that this occurrent belief that not-p is the result of a dispositional belief--that Gertrude is not a fit subject for his erotic longings--that is behaviorally manifest in the interpretive activity, in the rationalizing, evading or jamming. In other words, the pastor is disposed to enact not only p, which is suppressed, but not-p which is manifest in interpretive activity that sustains the "thought that not-p" in the face of evidence disconfirming it. The pastor is not only disposed to act on p, but his reasons for acting to "cover up" this belief are sufficiently strong that he acts on his belief that not-p as well. His occurrent cognitive state entertains not just a thought that not-p, but a fully dispositional belief that not-p, which is manifest in the linguistic activity of, say, denial.

On Bach's account, that the pastor loves Gertrude erotically is entertained as an occurrent thought, for the pastor, when entertaining this thought, condemns the kind of love this represents. He considers this "thought that p" an illicit love, and evades the fact that his own condemnation of such love pertains to his own feelings toward Gertrude. So the pastor contrives to avoid the thought that his love is adulterous. The point, however, is that according to the pastor's own rational standards, he is an adulterer. He has been acting "adulterously," and he has been acting consistently with a dispositional--though "unconscious--belief or desire that p.[50]

The "thought that p" is present as an occurrent thought (or belief) that the pastor has reasons (motives) for wanting to avoid, and he is able to act purposely (rationalizing, evading, jamming) in order to actually avoid the thought that p. What is unclear in Bach's account is that this "thought that p" is not associated with a dispositional belief; and this can only mean that the "thought that p" is not manifest in behavior. For Bach, this thought that p is only an occurrent thought in relation to which certain kinds of cognitive activity commence to the end that the thought is banished from conscious consideration.

The difficulty is that if the "thought that p" is not tied to a fully dispositional belief that p, how could one ever acquire access to the actuality of self-deception? In other words: If the pastor wishes to avoid the "thought that p" (that his love is erotic), how can his dispositional belief that not-p (that he's acting Christianly) be evidence for self-deception? Is it not necessary that his behavior also show itself to be consistent with the "thought that p"? How else could we observe a behavioral contradiction, infer an intrapsychic opposition, and ascribe self-deception?

My question to Bach, then, is that if the important part of self-deception is what is occurrent as a thought--". . .what matters is what occurs to the self-deceiver, not what he believes in the full dispositional sense"[51]-- how could we--or the pastor's wife--ever observe it? Since an occurrent thought or belief is not "action related," neither intentional nor necessary for any dispositional belief, that occurrent thought would not be behaviorally enacted. We would not see it--we could observe no contradiction between the action and the self-deceiver's interpretation. How, then, could we ever ascribe self-deception?

The ordinary language analysis permits us access to contradictory beliefs because those beliefs, both fully dispositional, govern publicly observable behavior. How could we discern the occurrent "thought that p," which constitutes the epistemic object of self-deception for Bach, if that thought is not associated with behavior and with the belief that governs the behavior? I am inclined to think that the reason Bach fails to provide us with a full-blown example of self-deception is that on his account there is no way to discern the involvement of the "thought that p" in the self-deception except by hypothesizing it. There would be no observable behavioral correlates that could be used as evidence to support a claim that this "thought that p" is present and that it is a dynamic factor in the state of self-deception.

There are, then, difficulties with Bach's account. His formulation of an epistemic deficit in terms of a dispositional belief and a "thought that p" is a problematic formulation if we try to show how this deficit plays itself out. Bach provides no such example, and this may be a significant flaw in his account. One other problematic area seems worthy of mention. Bach argues that self-deceivers act (rationalizing, evading jamming) but that what they realize in their state of self-deception is motivated but not intentional. A self-deceiver does not, of course, tell himself that he must do something in order to accept reasons that he would normally reject, as if he could consciously contrive not to think what he is already thinking. To the extent that Bach is saying that the state of being self-deceived is not the result of purposeful action, but only a state for which a psychological cause (motive) may be found, it seems that this cognitive account may fall prey to a specific criticism leveled against cognition models in general:

> [Self-deception] necessarily contains within itself a certain purposefulness. The element of internal purposefulness is reflected in such phrases as 'persuades himself to believe', 'makes it appear to himself', 'lies to himself'. [In] their anxiety to resolve the supposed paradox in maintaining that a person holds two incompatible beliefs, Demos, Siegler, Canfield and Gustavson, and Penelhum all fail to appreciate that the deep paradox of self-deception lies not in that at most mildly cognition, but in the element of knowing, intentional ignorance.[52]

Analysis of Bach's use of 'motivation' and 'intention' would take us far afield, but a problem is to be noted here. Bach himself acknowledges this when he admits to using 'motivation' in a peculiar sense: "Although I know of no explicit precedent for my formulation, I believe (but will not show) it to be implicit in much psychological discourse."[53] Bach's account, then, despite the fact that such activities as rationalizing or evasion are considered to be motivated, runs the risk of yielding a conception of self-deception that is neither purposeful nor the expression of human agency. My case is that "unconscious intention" or "unconscious motive," which are also prevalent terms in psychological discourse, provide a more adequate descriptive foundation for an account of self-deception than Bach's terms allow; and the descriptive power of these terms is such that their use will not run the risk of denying that self-deception is a dynamic process, or that 'self-deception,' despite the fact that it results in a cognitive state, is also an **action** concept.

Despite certain specific difficulties, Bach's account of self-deception is remarkable in its extension of the cognitive model. The problems that do arise, can, I believe, be associated with the fact that Bach is pushing certain action concepts into a model, into a mode of discourse, that is many respects ill-equipped to handle them. Even as it stands, certain proponents of a cognition model might not recognize Bach as a comrade or true heir. In Bach's analysis of self-deception, the cognition model is pushed to the furthest reaches of the cognition resource. Bach has learned from certain "action analyses" but has not accounted for the epistemic deficit in non-cognitive terms. The result is that he has avoided many of the obvious problems of a cognition account, while retaining certain necessary cognitive components that "actionists" might tend to discount or overlook. There is, however, a fundamental compatibility between Bach's account and the ordinary language account proffered in the first chapter of this study.

2. The Translation Model[54]

The translation model of self-deception asserts that 'self-deception' functions linguistically either as a euphemism or a metaphor. The concept 'self-deception' does not mean what the language itself indicates, but refers to some concept other than that which obtains from formal analysis of the literal expression. Translationists accept the epistemological paradox of self-deception as a legitimate difficulty, but they resolve that difficulty by arguing that the literal notion of a self actually 'deceiving' itself is a logical, hence an empirical, impossibility. From this two things follow: First, no one really 'deceives' him- or herself; that is, no one is able to create an intrapsychic deficit that corresponds to the epistemic deficit obtained from an interpersonal deception. Secondly, the literal expression 'self-deception' can be <u>translated</u> into better, more accurate literal expressions on any occasion when it is used.

The most detailed and explicit translational account of self-deception is to be found in M. R. Haight's <u>A Study of Self-Deception</u>. Haight's analysis of the literal expression leads her to conclude that the split between "deceiver" and "deceived" required for an intrapersonal deception cannot obtain intrapsychically. As Haight puts it, because one person cannot hold contradictory beliefs simultaneously, "I have argued that self-deception is literally a paradox. Therefore it cannot happen."[55] Haight holds that the notion that one person can be both deceiver and deceived, that one consciousness can both believe and not believe the same epistemic object, amounts to a logical contradiction, and this has observable empirical consequences. On Haight's view, because a paradox attends any use of the expression 'self-deception,' we are likely to speak non-sense when using it. To avoid meaningless speech, we must qualify 'self-deception' so that its true meaning is recognized, and that true meaning is something other than what the literal expression indicates.

This analysis revolves in a cognitive orbit, and it takes seriously the relation of 'self-deception' to self-other 'deception.' The virtue of holding 'self-deception' accountable to the linguistic facts demanded by a strict first-order use of 'deception,' however, is subverted in my view because Haight invokes the picture of consciousness in which one consciousness cannot oppose itself and direct itself into purposeful unawareness. She invokes, in other words, the fallacy of transparency. Haight collapses her logical argument such that it yields a necessary <u>empirical</u> conclusion--self-deception cannot happen. It is methodologically fallacious, however, to determine the status of an empirical claim by relying solely on logical considerations, especially when the question at hand is an empirical question for which relevant empirical data supporting the "actuality" of the contradiction is available (Sackeim and Gur). Haight's assumption that a person is incapable of holding opposing roles and opposing beliefs can be refuted by clarifying the nature of self-relatedness, by determining the capacity of the self to so relate itself to itself that it can, in fact, oppose itself. Furthermore, in that intrapsychic opposition, the self can be shown to act in accordance with beliefs and intentions that are present, but unavailable to linguistically explicit and self-conscious reflection. Rather than critique Haight's assumption further, let us ask, "How does she 'translate' self-deception?"

Haight's view is that self-deception is really of a piece with "lying" or, if the deception be non-verbal, "pretending."[56] According to Haight, self-deception is really a form of other-deception. Human persons are capable of "pretending to pretend." This means that if a person has some reason for wanting to be thought self-deceived, that person can feign self-deception in order to mitigate responsibility for the lie or pretense, thereby avoiding the full brunt of moral censure. Such individuals are not literally self-deceived; rather they have lied, the lie has been discovered, and rather than admit to having lied, they choose the appearance of self-deception since this permits them to act "as if" they were innocent--unaware--of intentional, deceptive wrongdoing. Behind this scenario lies the assumption that self-deceivers are always capable of spelling out the lie being perpetrated:

> To sum up: any particular self-deception could, some or all of the time, be mere pretense, so far as some or all of the lookers-on can tell. I suspect that the kinds of pretense are endless. [But] it will seem an inept and eccentric pretense by ordinary standards; and even if we suspect that it is one, we cannot be quite sure. This is because the lie (if it is one) is not--or not essentially--about anything we can check. It is about the liar's state of mind, including his (cognitive) belief; and believers and pretenders may look exactly alike. So can those who pretend from compulsion and would perhaps not like to, and those who pretend from choice: if he does not mind being branded a self-deceiver, a deliberate liar may get away with a lot.[57]

This is not literal self-deception, but 'self-deception' being used as a mask for interpersonal deception. I agree that this is a possible case, and that a person might wish to appear self-deceived in order to avoid moral censure. Such an instance would illustrate what Ryle meant by "double bluffers."[58] But Haight's case raises its own curious problems. After all, if I were to pretend to be self-deceived in order to avoid moral censure and "get away with a lot," that could only be accomplished if my linguistic community, my potential censors and accusers--"others"--understood by self-deception that the behavior I am exhibiting is consistent with my being, so to speak, a "victim of my own action." I could only feign self-deception if my linguistic community understood literal self-deception and were willing to ascribe it to my behavior. It is reasonable to assume that 'self-deception' would only be ascribed if I met (or even seemed to meet) certain accepted criteria. I could only feign self-deception if the ordinary language meaning of the concept were being pressed into service by my linguistic community, and I, knowing that meaning and knowing that people trust the language to be meaningful, did all I could to make certain my behavior certified their observation that I was, in fact, 'self-deceived.' Haight's case is, from an ordinary language perspective, highly problematic and perplexing. For Haight's case to be successful, everyone who thought I was deceiving myself would be literally mistaken; but the problem is that I am behaving in a way that my community recognizes as literal 'self-deception.' Haight's claim amounts to saying that if my linguistic community understood the <u>real</u> meaning of my behavior, it would see that behavior not as an instance of literal self-deception but as a pretense, and it would call me either a liar or a pretender.

Haight's case is parasitic upon the ordinary language meaning of self-deception, a meaning that is, according to Haight, false. The pretense position depends upon the fact that the linguistic community actually agrees and operates with the literal meaning of the concept--else the pretense could not work. Curiously, that observation--that the community does in fact use the expression in a literal way--seems correct, but I would contend that the linguistic community's literal understanding of 'self-deception' counts against Haight's own analysis. That analysis turns a picture of self-deception and the common life upside down, for the argument is that the ordinary language understanding, the literal meaning of the concept, is not to be trusted --though she trusts it to be accepted literally by the linguistic community, which then falls prey to the pretender. Pretending to be self-deceived when one is not requires that the literal meaning be mistakenly ascribed, that the deceived person be willing to mitigate responsibility by acknowledging that the pretender is manifesting behavior appropriate to 'self-deception.'

Not only is Haight wrong that this is the true meaning of self-deception, but her argument begs the question, "How did the linguistic community make this horrendous mistake?" The account accuses the linguistic community of ignorance and linguistic negligence, as if 'self-deception' is only properly used when referring to scoundrels. In claiming that the language does not mean what it says, Haight's account comes down to this: "Can we trust the language?" The linguistic community has placed its trust in this misleading language because, I should think, this language corresponds to a particular feature of human experience. The phenomenon identified by the literal expression, while it may indeed be a pretense on the part of the 'self-deceiver,' is yet manifest as behavior that corresponds to what I understand by 'self-deception'; and it is this understanding that I share with the pretender that makes the pretense to being self-deceived possible. I can be deceived into thinking another person is self-deceived, but only if the language works, only if the deceiver appeals to the literal concept successfully, which is to say that both the deceiver and I must agree on the literal meaning of 'self-deception.' Let me reassert that ordinary language analysis is rooted in the idea that the linguistic community not only knows what it means when it employs the literal expression 'self-deception'--and knows <u>how</u> to apply it; but that its understanding of the literal expression can be substantiated by conceptual analysis and by empirical appeal. In other words, the language can be trusted.

Haight translates 'self-deception' into other-deception, into lying and pretense. What other concepts might the metaphor of 'self-deception' refer to or, to more accurately capture the critical thrust of this model, with what other concepts has 'self-deception' been confused?

Some translations appear unexpectedly. When attempts to elucidate the concept 'self-deception' fail in some respect, other concepts present themselves as functional equivalents, whence the question, "How is self-deception different from such-and-such?" Canfield and Gustavson, for instance, argued that a person who believes <u>p</u> such that the evidence does not warrant belief that <u>p</u> is, under "belief adversive circumstances, self-deceived.[59] Were this the criterion necessary and sufficient for ascribing 'self-deception,' how could one distinguish self-deception from <u>ignorance</u>? An ignorant person would satisfy the Canfield and Gustavson requirement for self-deception, for an ignorant person could believe <u>p</u> in circumstances where the evidence does not support the belief.

What if the person were aware of the evidence counting against belief in <u>p</u> (Lon Nol), but believed <u>p</u> nonetheless, realizing where that belief might lead? Is this a sufficient improvement that would more accurately circumscribe the meaning of 'self-deception'? Without further qualification, such an instance would better fit our ordinary notions of <u>stubbornness</u> or <u>pigheadedness</u> (which lack the "unawareness" criterion of self-deception), or, as Szabados sees it, <u>stupidity</u> or <u>dullwittedness</u>.[60] An ordinary language analysis would argue that these terms cannot be translated into what is, properly speaking, self-deception.

To reiterate a point made earlier: 'Self-deception' is distinct from <u>wishful thinking</u>. The case has been made in cognitive terms that "Wishful thinking need not involve any reasoning or semblance of reasoning."[61] In action terms, wishful thinkers wish, that is, they entertain possibilities for action, but in the end they do not act on those wishes in the face of contrary and disconfirming evidence. Wishful thinking may very well precede self-deception; but so too might vacillation and emotional ambivalence, neither of which is conceptually equivalent to self-deception. A person is always free to change his or her mind, to be undecided or to waiver. That persons experience distress and confusion when confronted with a course of action, not knowing for certain what to do or which course to choose, is another familiar feature of our common life, but it is not self-deception. Neither ambivalence nor vacillation involves the suppression of belief that identifies the self-deception "cover up." And the fact that a person may vacillate or experience ambivalence does not mean that self-deception will necessarily result.

Another candidate for translation involves the "blindness" metaphor. An ordinary language analysis reveals that even though they may seem blind, self-deceivers actually perceive what they seem unable to recognize. That is, they react to objects that they perceive as distressful, thereby exhibiting a blindness that is publicly observable as the self-deceiver's mistake or "error." This apparent blindness, however, results from a prior seeing, a prior scanning and recognition. Self-deceivers are not "intellectually blind," if by that we mean that some impediment to sight beyond the person's control is responsible for the blindness; for their blindness is chosen. It is a response to seeing. "Being blind" and "putting blinders on" are distinct ways of talking. The self-deceiver is one whose blindness is acquired by "putting blinders on."

Is self-deception perhaps commensurate with biased thinking? One could argue that because a self-deceivers evade the normal processes of evidential assessment, they are simply caught in the grip of biased thinking, and that explains their apparent irrationality. This possible translation for self-deception fails because self-deceivers make an effort of some sort to bring about this irrationality--in fact wills it--and the irrationality is itself uncharacteristic of the person. A biased person is one whose irrationality seems quite characteristic and effortless. There is a kind of "uncharacteristic irrationality" that has its genesis in fatigue, drugs, shock, alcohol, or befuddlement, but none of these are candidates for translation since self-deception as a motivated and self-serving behavior is not conceptually equivalent to an ordinary instance of "uncharacteristic irrationality."[62]

We have so analyzed 'self-deception' that it is possible to distinguish it from related concepts. I have maintained that self-deception is not, strictly speaking, a technical term. On the other hand, I must also claim that the criteria for ascribing the concept are specific enough to qualify it as rule-governed concept, one which is not translatable into other more broadly drawn notions like ignorance, stupidity, wishful thinking or intellectual blindness. A survey of the philosophical literature on self-deception reveals that analyses of the concept often fail to distinguish self-deception from these other concepts. Clearly, an account of self-deception fails to the extent that it renders the concept amenable to translation into one of these other concepts.

The relation of self-deception to hypocrisy is a more subtle issue. Generally speaking, a hypocrite is one who, for reasons of personal advantage, breaks in private a moral rule or standard advocated in public. A sticky problem arises over the issue of sincerity. We normally ascribe sincerity to persons who act and speak with conviction, who believe not only what they are saying, but who believe themselves to be sincere. In other words, we certify sincerity by appealing to the person's own sense of his or her sincerity. The problem, then, is whether the hypocrite is sincere or insincere, for if sincere, it looks as if the hypocrite may really be self-deceived. Can 'self-deception' be translated into 'hypocrisy'?

The question about sincerity is difficult since a self-deceiver will rationalize or deny sincerely, hence no hypocrisy. Yet a total description of the intrapsychic opposition reveals that the self-deceiver is not of one mind but is acting in congress with opposing beliefs. This could permit us to ascribe insincerity, since in one sense--and on some level--the self-deceiver believes that a professed denial or rationalization is not true. I wish to distinguish self-deception from hypocrisy while also making clear that they are related--and often actually related--concepts.

Was it hypocrisy Hume had in mind when he wrote, "Our predominant motive or intention is, indeed frequently concealed from ourselves when it is mingled and confounded with other motives which the mind, from vanity or self-conceit, is desirous of supposing more prevalent"?[63] If this be hypocrisy, how is it to be distinguished from Ryle's observation that people commonly "deceive themselves about their own motives."?[64] Ryle argued that a hypocrite is one who "pretends to motives and moods" he or she does not really have,[65] and R. M. Hare has characterized the real hypocrite as one who backslides purposefully, that is, one who uses subterfuge to reconcile him- or herself to a moral language that is not fully universal or prescriptive, but who nevertheless knows what he or she is doing.[66] And Szabados has argued that certain instances of self-deception entail hypocrisy.[67] A self-deceiver rationalizes, which is to say that he or she employs accepted rules or reasoning but abuses those rules by employing them to suit some self-interested purpose. When a self-deceiver pays "lip service" to possible doubts, doubts about his or her own rationale, or questions his or her own motives, yet "pretends otherwise" to himself and others, the self-deception can be characterized as also of a piece with hypocrisy.[68] Szabados sees the entertaining of the thought that p, the thought that is to be avoided (to use Bach's formulation), as not only being of a piece with self-deception, but also "hypocritical to an extent."[69]

No doubt, as in the case of the shipowner, a self-deceiver may be hypocritical in paying lip service to a doubt but rationalizing it away. For the moment, however, I would hold to our more standard idea of a hypocrite as one who breaks a rule in private that is advocated in public, who does so for reasons of personal gain. This characterization is sufficient to qualify and distinguish the hypocrite from the self-deceiver who, in a very real sense, does not know what the hypocrite knows. Self-deceivers are not "of one mind" in their experience of self-deception, yet, because they are deceived, they believe that they are. In other words, they deny or rationalize with the single-mindedness of the sincere person, for they profess a certain belief as true (p). But not-p is also believed unawares, which is to say that self-deceivers are, like hypocrites, double-minded; but, being self-deceived, they are not aware that their behavior conforms to 'hypocrisy.' In one sense all self-deceivers are hypocrites, for self-deceivers are double-minded and act contrary to their professed beliefs. Yet hypocrisy is nonetheless a distinct concept in that it lacks the unawareness criterion required for self-deception. Because of this crucial point of conceptual differentiation, one must conclude that 'hypocrisy' is related to, but not to be translated as, 'self-deception.'

3. The Action Model

The action account of self-deception challenges the cognition model premise that self-deception is a mental or epistemic state that overcomes one. Sartre asserted the challenge this way: "One does not undergo his bad faith, one is not infected with it; it is not a state. But consciousness affects itself with bad faith. There must be an original intention and a project of bad faith."[70] The premise of the action model is that self-deception is intentional and that the act of deceiving oneself is to be characterized as a project--a voluntary undertaking that issues from certain causes to certain desired ends by means of specific activities.

According to the action model, self-deception is not conceived in cognitive terms, as if self-deception were a mental state where opposing beliefs give rise to erroneous conclusions, but in terms of volition, as if the concept referred to a problem in self-understanding. It points to a failure to know oneself that itself arises from a desire not to know oneself, a desire, that is, to act such that a mistake or error in self-understanding inevitably results. That result is pictured as having been willed; for the self-deceiver will not err about just anything, but only about those articles of awareness that can affect action--the person's aims, reasons, wants, beliefs, attitudes, emotions, and so on. Self-deception is motivated activity. It is manifest behaviorally and expresses through its mechanisms purposefulness.

Herbert Fingarette's analysis of cognitive accounts in his outstanding and influential monograph, <u>Self-Deception</u>, concluded that the cognitivists were either unable to eliminate the paradox of self-deception or did so by abusing the distinctiveness of the concept--making it, in other words, "translatable." Fingarette's proposed solution to the paradox impasse was to set aside the cognitive model in favor of an action model. Rather than conceiving of self-deception in the language of belief or the through the metaphor of perception, he chose to employ the language and metaphors available within the "action-volition" family of terms. Fingarette, whose analysis of self-deception is still the outstanding action account, argued that belief is not central to an adequate understanding of the concept. The truth of this claim was to be borne out by the superior strength of his alternative action account, a brief review of which is in order.

According to Fingarette, self-deception results from our unwillingness to "spell-out" certain engagements in the world. A self-deceiver is one whose disavowal obtains those engagements generate a painful conflict between one's actual behavior and one's self-understanding or "identity." Self-deception is what one does in order to avoid becoming "explicitly conscious"[71] about some part of one's engagement in the world, and what is at stake is not belief but action. The engagement requires the agent to do something that ". . .only the agent can do for himself."[72] The self-deceiver ". . .is unable (by virtue of his tacit commitment) to spell this fact out to himself or to anyone else. [He] does not, cannot, express the matter explicitly at all. He tells us nothing but what he tells himself."[73] Drawing on the resources of existential thought and psychoanalytic theory, Fingarette elucidates the phenomenon of self-deception by describing the self-deceiver's purposeful strategy of disavowal. An "action-volition" model of self-deception enables him to do this.

Fingarette's proposal is that we must think about becoming conscious as something we do rather than as something that happens. Consciousness requires a model in which ". . .we are doers, active rather than passive. To be specific, the model I suggest is that of a skill."[74]

> The specific skill I particularly have in mind as a model for becoming explicitly conscious of something is the skill of saying what we are doing or experiencing. I propose, then, that we do not characterize consciousness as a kind of mental mirror, but as the exercise of the (learned) skill of 'spelling-out' some feature of the world as we are engaged in it.[75]

Fingarette means by "spelling-out" "to be explicitly aware of" or "to pay conscious attention to."[76] It is a way of being engaged in the world: it is "something we can do."[77] Spelling-out can itself be spelt-out, though a "special reason" is required. "Rather than taking explicit consciousness for granted, we must come to take its absence for granted; we must see explicit consciousness as the further exercise of a specific skill for a special reason."[78] In order to exercise the skill, one must determine whether there is adequate reason for spelling-out the engagement, and this itself constitutes an exercise of the skill, a way of being engaged in the world. It is on this pattern of conceiving a person's exercise of awareness that Fingarette constructs his action theory of consciousness.

Fingarette shows that this "spelling-out" theory of consciousness is relevant to self-deception. Self-deception is the action whereby an individual refrains from exercising his or her skill in spelling-out. In other words, "We avoid becoming explicitly conscious of our engagement, and we avoid becoming explicitly conscious that we are avoiding it."[79]

> In general, the person in self-deception is a person of whom it is a patent characteristic that even when normally appropriate he persistently avoids spelling out some feature of his engagement in the world. Sometimes we see this as an 'inability' to spell-out: The self-deceiver is 'unable' to admit the truth to himself (even though he knows in his heart it's so).

> There is a kind of genuineness to his 'ignoring'; it is not simply hypocrisy, or lying or duping of others. Yet we also feel that in some sense, he <u>could</u> admit the truth if only he <u>would</u>.[80]

The "inability" noted by Fingarette is not the result of a lack of skill or strength: "[It] is the adherence to a policy (tacitly) adopted."[81] The self-deceiver adopts a policy of not spelling-out, which, in other words, constitutes a "self-covering" policy that is made manifest in what Fingarette insightfully calls a "cover story."[82]

> For a natural consequence is the protective attempt on the part of the person to use elements of the skill he has developed in spelling-out as inventively as possible in order to fill in plausibly the gaps created by his self-covering policy. He will try to do this in a way which renders the 'story' as internally consistent and natural as possible, and as closely conforming as possible to the evident facts. Out of this protective tactic emerges the masks, disguises, rationalizations, and superficialities of self-deception in all its forms.[83]

Once the "cover story" is operational, the self-deceiver exercises his or her rational capacity in order to enhance and further support the self-covering policy. When a person is self-deceived, the self-covering policy cannot be explicitly acknowledged or spelt-out. This itself looks paradoxical, for a self-deceiver successfully avoids spelling-out, but only because he or she adopts a policy aimed at avoiding spelling-out. Ronald de Sousa has referred to this paradox in Fingarette's account, observing that the policy of self-covering ". . .cannot be spelt-out, for that would involve spelling out what its policy covers--which is what the policy forbids."[84] The paradox indicated here, however, does not yield a logical contradiction. Fingarette's account does not assume that policies and engagements are automatically conscious despite their intentional or purposeful nature. Neither does Fingarette assume spelling-out is a necessary condition for the failure to spell-out. What can be said is that an actual failure to spell-out will be manifest in the self-deceiver's behavior as a kind of blindness or ignorance.[85]

Fingarette's conceptual levers all rest on motive, which is the model's fulcrum. In order to grasp Fingarette's formulation of self-deception as motivated action, certain relevant considerations must be kept in mind. First of all, the policy of refusing to spell-out is related as ". . .a concomitant to a far more fundamental maneuver,"[86] namely, the disavowal of an engagement as one's own. Secondly, it is around one's avowals, around the facts that one spells-out as constitutive of one's own world, that one is able ". . .to define one's personal identity for oneself."[87] Self-deception, then, concerns one's disavowals. It is <u>disavowal</u>, rather than some notion of a privileged access to the contents of one's own consciousness, that provides the special authority that attends a person's spelling-out his or her own identity. Personal identity, for Fingarette, is the synthesis or integration that develops in the course of a person's growing up and maturing, since ". . .with the emergence of one person in the individual, there is a tendency for increasing correlation between what is avowed by the person and the actual engagements of the individual."[88] (Fingarette means by person here what I earlier discussed in terms of self, for the person who can identify oneself to oneself as a particular person has acquired a capacity exclusive to the self.)[89]

Fingarette invokes a picture of the self-as-community. That community is comprised of quasi-autonomous and distinctive members, which include "reason-motive-feeling-aim-means-and moralistic reactions."[90] These members come together to function inter-dependently and, one would hope, harmoniously. When one avows one's identity and identifies oneself to oneself as this particular person, he or she achieves, ideally, the synthesis or integration of selfhood.

Because it involves a pattern of behavior in conflict with one's self-image, self-deception entails a necessary disavowal of one's identity. The identity feature provides the motive for the self-covering policy. According to Fingarette, a conflict in the community of the self may reach a point where one's pattern of conduct painfully conflicts with one's avowed identity. Self-deception obtains when, for reasons of preserving an avowed identity, a person disavows certain engagements as one's own. When an individual is engaged in action that does not square with his or her avowed personal identity and resorts to a self-covering policy in order to maintain that identity, the result is self-deception:

> [An] individual will be provoked into a kind of engagement which, in part or in whole, the person cannot avow as his engagement, for to avow it would apparently lead to such intensely disruptive, distressing consequences as to be unmanagably destructive to the person. The crux of the matter here is the unacceptability of the engagement to the person. The individual may be powerfully inclined towards a particular engagement, yet this particular engagement may be utterly incompatible with the currently achieved synthesis of engagements which is the person.[91]

Fingarette's account eliminates the familiar epistemological paradox; but more importantly it refocuses our attention on the moral issue raised by this action concept. A person's motive for self-deception is tied to a desire to preserve an avowed identity, and this identifies a project of essentially moral significance. Such a project requires some degree of personality integration, so it appears that the person who adopts the self-deception project is an agent already moving in the direction of accepting responsibility for the self one is.

Self-deception, then, if it invokes a paradox at all, invokes a moral rather than a logical paradox. On the one hand, the attempt to preserve one's identity is constitutive of a moral effort. On the other hand, self-deception is simultaneously a disavowal of responsibility for those actions or engagements that prove incompatible with that sense of identity. The self-deceiver, then, is simultaneously avowing and disavowing responsibility. For Fingarette, the self-deceiver is neither to be condemned for his or her self-deception (as in existential-Sartrian analysis) nor non-judgmentally excused (as in the "de-moralized" Freudian analysis). Self-deceivers, rather, are to be urged to self-acceptance so that they can avow their engagements, being ". . .helped to go to the limits of [their] courage, but not beyond the breaking point. This is precisely what the ideal therapist would offer."[92] Morally speaking, self-deception is an ambiguous condition, and Fingarette embraces that ambiguity as a check on the tendency of moralizers and de-moralizers alike to overlook the complexity of the self-deceptive act.

Fingarette's analysis involves philosophy and psychology in a dialogue. Because Fingarette argued that self-deception is implicated in common forms of neurotic defense, he located the topic in a broader conversation than had been previously envisioned. Due in large part to Fingarette's efforts, self-deception has been set in a larger, inter-disciplinary context where contributions have been welcomed from psychoanalysis, action theory, and moral analysis, a framework of inquiry that can be endorsed by the "philosophical psychology" perspective. All who study 'self-deception' owe Herbert Fingarette a debt of gratitude, for he managed to shift the focus of inquiry away from the paradox (logic) to questions about action (existence). He asked a new question and set a new agenda of issues, and I, too, sing his praise.

A few interpretive and critical remarks about this action model are in order.

It is important to note that our examples of self-deception can serve to illustrate Fingarette's account, which is itself richly illustrated. The pastor, for instance, refuses to spell-out the true nature of his engagement with Gertrude. He devises an elaborate "cover story" that is in some respects plausible and pertains to certain facts. That cover story is that he acts from Christian duty and that the love he feels for Gertrude is pure (non-erotic) Christian love. This "Christian interpretation" is consistent with the pastor's religious and moral vocation and his identity as a minister and preacher of the Gospel. To behave or even feel otherwise would, according to the pastor's own interpretation, constitute reprehensible behavior. The pastor's behavior, however, reveals that his love is erotic. His avowal of a Christian identity, therefore, is simultaneously a disavowal of his engagement with Gertrude. He refuses to accept his engagement with Gertrude "as his own," so he disavows his engagement as erotic even as he continues to enact his erotic desires. Being motivated by a desire to maintain his avowal of Christian identity, the pastor refuses to spell-out his engagement with Gertrude. When coupled with the fact that he simultaneously disavows his erotic passion, which is manifest behaviorally despite the disavowal, this description provides us with an action-volition account of an instance of self-deception. On the action-volition model, the self-deception results from disavowing an engagement that is the pastor's own. It obtains because of the pastor's skill at spelling-out his avowed identity (Christian) while not spelling-out the true nature of his engagement with Gertrude (erotic).

Our two other examples fit this action account as well. Lon Nol's avowal of his identity as a powerful leader is in conflict with the prospect of defeat and humiliation. He refuses to spell-out his engagement relative to the prospect of being forced to flee the country and admit defeat. The shipowner's disavowal of his engagement with respect to evaluating the seaworthiness of the vessel expresses the fact that he disavows any image of himself as a person willing to endanger innocent lives entrusted to his care. He does not identity himself--or so we can surmise--as an immoral man, and he skillfully creates a cover story (Providence) that enables him to put an unseaworthy vessel to sea while confident of its chances for safe arrival. At the very moment he acts immorally by authorizing an unseaworthy vessel to put to sea, the shipowner enacts a self-covering policy that permits him to disavow the act of sending innocent persons to probable death as "his own." Though his act is immoral, the cover story permits him to do what he does, and that cover story indicates that on some level of awareness, the shipowner avows responsibility for what he is doing, else his disavowal of responsibility would be no indication of self-deception, but simply an honest error or mistake in judgment. Clifford clearly meant to indicate by his example that this particular tragedy at sea was no simple error.

Fingarette's model can be used to elucidate many examples of self-deception. Moreover, there is a general compatibility between the action account and the ordinary language analysis, the issue of 'belief,' of course, being the exception. If, for the moment, we substitute "avowal" for "belief," it can be said that Fingarette's action model provides us with an "avowal-misleading" project whereby a deficit arises between what is avowed (identity) and what is disavowed (the particular engagement). This deficit is not epistemic according to Fingarette, only the difference between what is avowed and what is disavowed. The self-deceiver is not explicitly aware of the disavowal, and this unawareness occurs because of the person's skill in not spelling-out. The self-deceiver can be said to hold contradictory avowals simultaneously. One of those avowals is consistent with the self-deceiver's self-image (identity), and of that he or she is explicitly aware and able to spell-out. At the same time the self-deceiver is not aware of the engagement because he or she has skillfully maneuvered such that the engagement in question can be kept from explicit awareness (disavowal). The unawareness results from action (i.e., not spelling-out) that is motivated. The motive for disavowing an engagement as one's own is attributable to a desire to maintain one's identity, which, as is clear, conflicts with the behaviorally manifest, publicly observable engagement.

Despite the fact that Fingarette's action account is compatible with our ordinary language analysis of self-deception, this compatibility depends solely on identifying "belief" with "avowal." Fingarette, of course, refused to integrate the two terms. Believing that "avowal" provided the necessary action corrective to belief, Fingarette used this non-cognitive term as the cornerstone in a project to reconstruct the concept 'self-deception.' Since "avowal" performed these non-cognitive functions, Fingarette's position was certainly understandable. The difficulty, however, is that unless some kind of reconciliation is effected between "belief" and "avowal," the ordinary language and the action accounts cannot be rendered compatible. The question is whether there are grounds for such reconciliation. I believe such grounds exist, and I shall spell that position out directly. I shall advance the criticism that Fingarette's account is, as it stands, inadequate, for in distinguishing "avowal" from "belief" as he does, Fingarette misconstrues the nature of cognition. Due to this misconstrual, Fingarette's shift in emphasis from metaphors of "cognition" to metaphors of "action" will not enable us to account for self-deception--not if "avowal" is construed to mean cognition-free. Is there any justification for pushing "belief"--the ordinary language term for describing the deficit that obtains in self-deception--as a more adequate term than "avowal," the action model term? I think there is.

Fingarette's action model rests on the supposition that cognitive accounts are essentially focused on an epistemic object, on an object of belief or knowledge. Self-deception, however, obtains with reference to a variety of <u>other kinds</u> of objects. According to Fingarette, self-deception arises in relation to ". . .such matters as one's own attitudes and wishes, ones's hopes and fears, as well as one's beliefs."[93] The traditional cognition accounts cannot account for this kind of self-deception, while the action account can. No doubt, Fingarette's account represents a valid corrective to those cognitive accounts he examined and found wanting (Demos, Penelhum, Canfield and Gustavson). But Fingarette's own conception of "avowal" as a notion that necessarily excludes belief proves a puzzling and inadequate corrective. I hold <u>contra</u> Fingarette that "avowal" cannot be rendered truly intelligible without cognitive referents. In fact, I would argue that "avowal," even as proposed by Fingarette, necessarily entails belief, a claim that requires further explanation.

The "non-cognitive" objects that Fingarette poses as appropriate objects for self-deception can be shown to have a "cognitive core." An emotion, for instance, can be said to have an object, which is to say that some cognitive activity (belief, judgment, evaluation) must obtain in order for the object in question to be constitutive of <u>this</u> rather than <u>that</u> emotion. There is a logic to emotion, a rational structure or grammar whereby an emotion is logically connected to a particular epistemic object. We appeal to this logic of emotion when we determine that someone's emotional response is either appropriate and understandable or defiant of that logic and seemingly "irrational." Not only are emotions constitutive of an evaluation process, which is necessarily cognitive, but emotions themselves can be cognitively evaluated. We can say that a particular emotion is inappropriate or unintelligible. An emotional response that is inappropriate to the object defies the normal logic or grammar of emotion, thereby rendering the emotional response itself subject to the evaluation that the response is inappropriate. According to criteria governed by any particular emotion, one may judge that a given affective response is unwarranted by the particular object. The person who perceives an epistemic object and reacts with emotion can be said to have responded in a way governed by the normal logic of the emotion--or not. As we evaluate emotion we can discern instances of "irrational" response, and 'irrationality' here means that one's affective response to an epistemic object fails to accord with our understanding of how emotions work in the common life.

These are judgments that can be--and are--made about emotions and their objects. My point is that emotions, in that they refer us to epistemic objects that we perceive and evaluate, can be said to have a cognitive core. They are not simply "feelings," which are episodic and which may or may not attend a particular emotion. I do not simply love, I love someone. By saying I love a particular person, I mean by that that I have evaluated this person in a way that is special, perhaps even peculiar--I <u>believe</u> that this person is to be cherished in a way that sets this person apart from the many other people I know. My love is constitutive of an act of the utmost discrimination, and the emotion is unintelligible if this discrimination is not apparent in my enacting that emotion, in my actual loving my beloved. It seems inescapable that the emotion of love (or hate, or fear, or jealousy) entails as a necessary feature a cognitive core of belief, evaluation, judgment, discrimination, all of which are appropriately <u>cognitive</u> terms. This is, as far as I am concerned, a standard interpretation of emotion not only in the philosophical literature but in the common life itself.[94]

The view I have just presented challenges Fingarette's position that certain objects of self-deception are essentially non-cognitive (emotions, attitudes). Were I to claim that self-deception obtains with respect to love, that I disavow a love that is my own, I am still implicitly committed to the view that love itself has a cognitive aspect. Love, too, has a cognitive core, and to analyze love is to say that love entails certain kinds of cognitive activities and that with respect to the object of my love--with respect to this person and my beliefs, decisions, evaluations and so on--a logic or grammar clearly obtains. Without this cognitive core, I should be unable to determine whether my occurrent feeling or experience is "love" or some other emotion or feeling. "Love" makes the connection between me and my beloved, between the pastor and Gertrude. The pastor deceives himself about the nature of his love, mistakenly believing that his affection for Gertrude is agape-like and selfless rather than erotic. Were the logical connection between the pastor's avowal of affection and the object of that affection to be concealed, one could not identify the emotion involved or understand the significance of the pastor's actions. The point, however, is that we can make those connections and understand, just as the pastor's wife understands. Emotions are activities with a cognitive core, not passive states which simply happen to one, over which one has no control, no power to discriminate or make decisions and judgments. Emotions can give rise to self-deception, but not emotions divorced from these cognitive components where the object of the self-deception is constituted. Emotion stripped of its cognitive core would not be, strictly speaking, an emotion at all, but an unintelligible and untargeted feeling state as likely to be caused by too much salt in the diet as by human passion.

Fingarette's case that an emotion can be the object of self-deception is descriptively correct. His picture of emotion, however, is so inadequately drawn that the case he makes to support the truth of that description contradicts the force of his action/non-cognition theory of self-deception. On this one point of "belief" Fingarette's whole position proves to be otiose as an alternative to the cognition model. I do wish to affirm that Fingarette is right to point out the inadequacy of certain cognition accounts, hastening to add that the ". . .deep reason for the inadequacy of the 'cognition model of consciousness' is that the 'cognition model' of cognition is wrong."[95] The objects that Fingarette points to as alternative objects of self-deception unaccounted for by certain cognition accounts are not themselves without cognitive referents. They therefore should not be conceived as unrelated either to cognition or, more precisely, to belief itself.

Fingarette's use of the term "avowal" raises another difficulty. Fingarette's notion of "avowal" is, in my view, inadequately drawn; and contrary to Fingarette's position, I believe that avowal can be shown to be a cognition term, one that actually entails belief. Let it be remembered that Fingarette convincingly establishes that previous accounts of self-deception formulated around "belief" were flawed. Although Fingarette's criticism is incisive--and true--the inadequacy of previous cognition accounts is no cause for gutting cognition from self-deception at a stroke. My case against Fingarette rests on the position that our everyday use of the concept 'self-deception' is meant to refer us to behavior governed by contradictory beliefs. That view may appear paradoxical, but if a cognitive paradox arises because of the contradictory beliefs criterion, that does not mean that the concept is necessarily incoherent. An account that fails to resolve the paradox in cognitive terms is simply an inadequate account. There is no self-evident, or even convincing argument that justifies abandoning cognitive terms altogether. One can, however, find many substantial reasons for retaining those terms. It is incomprehensible to me to think that my avowal of self-identity can somehow be divorced from my beliefs. My beliefs are a part of who I am. Who I am is inextricably tied up with the person I believe myself to be. Alan R. Drengson has made a similar point: ". . .beliefs are involved in a person's self-identity. Part of my self-image involves seeing myself as a person with certain beliefs."[96] Drengson concludes that "It would seem that the shift in analysis that Fingarette proposes is at best unnecessary."[97]

Of all the criticisms that can be leveled at Fingarette's action account --and there are several others[98]--the fact that "belief" is entailed by exactly those terms that Fingarette presents as divorced from cognition seems to me to be the most damaging. Avowal of identity must certainly involve some reference to what I <u>believe</u> myself to be. In conjunction with this cognitive picture of avowal is the fact that an <u>emotional</u> object of self-deception likewise can be analyzed such that a cognitive core of belief can be precipitated. When taken together, these two reinstatements of cognition show that Fingarette's conception of cognition is inadequately drawn. Furthermore, the fact that belief is incompatible with these terms he considers non-cognitive means either that he has escaped acceptable limits of standard linguistic usage (idiosyncratic definition) or he was operating with a mind to establish a cognition/action "either/or" that is, upon reflection and analysis, more party to a "both/and" configuration. Certainly the dichotomy between action and belief is not as strained as his account would indicate, and the position taken in the present study, namely, that action is governed by belief, will brook no such compartmentalizing of terms. Clear distinctions, in this particular case, adversely affect conceptual clarity.

If we move to substitute "belief" for <u>avowal</u>; and if we mean by avowal an <u>acknowledgment</u> (Fingarette's word) that includes cognitive as well as action features, then Fingarette's account fares quite well as an account compatible with ordinary language analysis. To do this, however, has the unfortunate effect of rendering Fingarette's major conceptual move superfluous. I maintain that substituting belief for avowal can be effected by invoking the law of parsimony. If avowal, as well as emotion, entail cognitive cores, then "belief" constitutes the leaner and clearer description of the terms necessary for describing self-deception. Fingarette's account can be harmonized with the ordinary language analysis, but not as it stands. Such harmonization can occur only if we bring cognition (belief) back into the picture as a more adequate way of formulating the meaning of "avowal" and "self-deception objects." Fingarette's terms themselves permit this move, as I have shown, thought Fingarette himself will not. I am forced to conclude that as it stands, Fingarette's action account has not merely compensated for the mistakes of previous cognition accounts, but has over-compensated. Fingarette errs on the side of action to the same degree that the cognitivists whom he criticizes err on the side of cognition. As my analysis shows, it is already clear that both action and cognition are required, for our everyday use of 'self-deception' provides us with idioms that permit us to understand by that expression that a person is acting such that he or she is unaware of the significance of the action, that he or she is acting consistently with an "avowal" of which the person is not explicitly conscious. That meaning of 'self-deception' is literal to the extent allowed by governing relations, and the concept is used to bear out a fact of our natural history, of our lives as members of a linguistic community. The cognition model, built as it is on the foundation of belief, must not be considered the model that stands in radical opposition to, and is to be preferred to, an action model. As de Sousa has written, ". . .the dichotomy of self-deception lies <u>within</u> the concept of belief itself. Belief and knowledge are indeed involved--quite literally and not as 'models'--in self-deception."[99]

4. Freud and Sartre: Two Other Models

The possibilities for adequately conceiving and describing self-deception have not been exhausted by the three models considered thus far. I propose to consider the models that have been associated with Freud and Sartre, though I must make clear that I am opting for a description of general contours. This is not to be an an in-depth exegetical study, for that would unduly delay our departure for contexts of meaning governed by other relations and forms of discourse.

a. The "Different Selves" or "Multiple-Agent" Model (Freud)

The advocates of any conceivable model of self-deception must jump an imposing hurdle in order to establish for their particular account a claim of adequacy. To put this hurdle in the form of a question, "How can a model be devised so that paradoxes, either moral or epistemological, can be avoided while the intentional and purposeful nature of what we ordinarily mean by 'self-deception' is retained?"

In some respects, it looks as if a model that is engineered on the idea that the human person entails "multiple selves" is a fitting, even obvious solution, since the postulation of several selves would permit us to speak of self-deception as an actual, intentional, first-order deception between discrete persons, deceiver and deceived. The "multiple-agent" model, as it has been called, has several contemporary proponents, but Freud has been considered its classic representative.[100] One would require a detailed presentation of the Freudian meta-psychology to understand how Freud actually acquired status as exemplar of this perspective, a task to large for present purposes. I can, however, lay out the general outline of the "multiple-agent perspective," offering an interpretation of Freud that is, I hope, sound if not exhaustive. I shall also offer critical remarks concerning the ability of this perspective to resolve paradoxes, arguing that "multiple-agency" is an inexact and inadequate way of picturing the self, a way that violates the spirit and intent--as well as the formal content--of the reflexively conceived picture of self-deception yielded by ordinary language analysis. Freud's actual relation to this "multiple-agent" theory will be clarified.

The multiple-agent theory argues that a literal first-order deception will account for the fact that within the context of one consciousness, an individual can simultaneously deceive and be deceived, both believing that p while duping itself so that it also believes not-p. The literal first-order deception obtains by transferring 'deception' from an interpersonal context of two persons to an intrapersonal context of two persons (multiple agents), thus rendering the concept intelligible. Although this is a highly questionable view, as I have previously indicated, we ought to consider this perspective because it provokes a serious question, namely, at what point do certain metaphors for intrapsychic division become mere linguistic markers for actual, discrete intrapsychic personalities? At what point do we render our metaphors non-metaphoric and their value in suggesting or disclosing a reality in tensive language otiose? I have argued that the the language of the self is ambiguous. If that be true, it follows that metaphoric ("tensive") language would be ideally suited to the task of expressing the reality of self-relatedness, for that reality is itself a reality of living tension.[101] The fact, however, is that certain metaphors for "self-relatedness" are translated from tensive to explanatory language, sometimes by the very persons who opted for the tensive language in the first place. We face a linguistic problem.

In Chapter One, I noted John King-Farlow's proposal to conceive of the self as a large loose committee with an irregularly rotating chairmanship:

> The members question, warn, praise and DECEIVE each other. [The] one who at present holds the chair (and the chair is not to be identified with consciousness or fullness of assent) is in the best position to cow or gull the others. They debate, share jokes, crosscheck the facts about yesterday's sensations, and carry on group activities very much as would a group of flesh and blood individuals. Some fall half asleep from time to time and many more are caught off guard by various factions within the committee and driven out into the corridor to stamp their feet or moan distractingly through the keyholes.[102]

The value of this particular metaphor is that the language of 'committee' discloses something about selfhood. This metaphor provides, as King-Farlow himself believes, a context within which one is able to conceive of the individual person in a state of intrapsychic conflict while saying neither that "deceiver" and "deceived" are one and the same person simpliciter nor that they are discrete persons. Note, however, that the parties in the relation are compared to discrete personalities. As such, misunderstanding is possible, for one could move to harden the language of metaphor to the point that the metaphor gives way to the language of explanation, as in "The self is composed of discrete personalities."

Amelie Rorty, with a similar kind of move in mind, has offered a view of the self-as-city, a model she conceives as "archeological." The self, that is, conjures the image of a modern, rationally laid out city, that is, like modern Paris, superimposed on the older, medieval Paris. The rational plan of radial avenues covers the old city, which was marked by small lanes and alleyways, autonomous neighborhoods ("loose confederations of neighborhoods"), guilds and conflicting interests.[103] "The two cities both serve and block each other's operations."[104] If the self be conceived via this metaphor, the pathways and strata constitutive of a self-in-conflict are "tensively" disclosed and the complex "archeology" of the self is revealed. This is a promising metaphor to be sure, but a problem arises because the metaphor lends itself to translation, as when Rorty herself explains "It is not the same agent who accepts one judgment but acts on another, or the same person who both knows and does not know what he is doing."[105] Here the metaphor gives way to explanation. Does the city metaphor authorize this particular conclusion about which discrete person is doing (or believing) what in self-deception? Does intrapsychic conflict require that one act as one discrete agent in opposition to oneself as another discrete agent as if one substantive self can deceive another substantive self? The case has been made that this picture of selfhood arises in Freud, so that the question appropriately addressed to Freud is this: "Is there a real 'I' amid these persons-in-conflict?" Is there, in other words, a multiplicity of minds within the mind of an individual person.

In order to respond to these questions, the general form of the "multiple-agent" theory must be considered, and Freud, for some, is the natural place to turn. The case has been made that nowhere has this theory been more spectacularly developed than in Freud's psycho-dynamic theory of conscious and unconscious mental activity.[106] On this view, Freud's system can be said to have divided the human person into discrete agencies (what one might think of as "homunculi"), or, as Raziel Abelson has said of Freud's theory of id, ego, and super-ego, the system constitutes a "division of the agent into sub-agents" such that in self-deception, ". . .one or two of these agencies deceives a third. The id, or the super-ego and id, hoodwink the ego" with the result that self-deception ceases to be of a piece with reflexive activity but is now ". . .reduced to ordinary deception of others."[107] The simplest statement of Freud's multiple-agent theory is that self-deception is the result of primordial forces (instincts) and painful affects that can be interpreted on some level of consciousness to be unacceptable. The "unacceptability" is acknowledged only tacitly and indirectly, but one responds to it nonetheless. The activity of response is to be characterized as resistance and repression; the view of self-deception being invoked pertains to the mechanisms of defense that identify neurotic response.

I wish to ask three questions of this view. First: If it be assumed that this view of "multiple-agents" accurately portrays Freud's position, what problems will this pose for analyzing 'self-deception'? Second: Does multiple-agency accurately portray Freud's position? Third: If it is not an accurate portrayal, what can be said about self-deception from a psychoanalytic perspective? We are really asking whether self-deception can be inferred from Freud's theory of unconscious mental activity. We must resolve whether Freud himself offers a view of 'self-deception' amenable to an ordinary language analysis, or whether his picture of resistance-anticathexis-repression so construed that it does not lend itself to assimilation by the concept 'self-deception.'[108]

If the move be made to understand by 'self-deception' that the id, or id and super-ego, conspire to dupe the ego, several unacceptable consequences necessarily follow; and these consequences follow even though preliminary analysis might indeed indicate that this "homunculi" ("little men") perspective avoids logical paradox while preserving action features. Sartre's criticism of Freudian psychoanalysis in Being and Nothingness is relevant at this point. Sartre accepted the blind instinctual force and therefore thinglike nature of the id, but he characterized it as a homunculus or a discrete entity that functioned to express the undifferentiated energy of unconscious libido. As a result of that understanding of Freud, Sartre criticized the "multiple-agent" view, since he held that this thinglike mechanism is capable of discerning what is acceptable to consciousness and what is not. This mechanism, the "censor," Sartre conceived as a single entity that must both know and not know what it knows, and from this Sartre concluded that Freud's psychoanalytic perspective is forced to paradox, since

> [We] perceive that the censor in order to apply its activity with discernment must know what it is repressing.
> But it is not sufficient that it discern the condemned drives; it must also apprehend them as to be repressed, which implies in it at the very least an awareness of its activity. In a word, how could the censor discern the impulses needing to be repressed without being conscious of discerning them? How can we conceive of a knowledge which is ignorant of itself?[109]

Sartre's case, in short, is that Freud's move to split the "psychic unity" (Sartre's assumption) in two only results in a repositioning of the paradox. The paradox has been removed from the arena of consciousness, from the idea of one consciousness self-consciously undertaking to deceive itself, to the arena of unconsciousness, where the preconscious censor "consciously" undertakes to do the work of the agent of self-deception. The censor knows what it is censoring: "Thus on the one hand the explanation by means of the unconscious, due to the fact that it breaks the psychic unity, cannot account for the facts which at first sight it appeared to explain. . . .We find that the problem which we had attempted to resolve is still untouched."[110]

For Sartre, then, Freud's theory emerges as an absurdity, for the result of Sartre's critique is a complete reduction of psychoanalytic method in general. Sartre's own view, as previously mentioned, is premised on a Cartesian picture of mental life that is itself faulty and open to challenge. I would note, however, that Sartre's critique of Freud is really a critique of the "multiple-agent" theory, and that his critique is valid as it stands. Any multiple-agent view is subject to Sartre's criticism that the paradox is repositioned, not resolved.

Other problems attend the "multiple-agent" theory. For instance, on a multiple-agent theory, no person is free, and because of that, no person can assume responsibility for his or her self-deception. If a person's actions are the result of separate sub-agents over which he or she has no control, then the actions are not "one's own," but are determined by causal forces over which no control can be exerted. A self-deceiver is a victim, not an agent. A more serious difficulty with multiple-agency is that on this view, reflexivity is lost. The human person is not conceived as a self-related agent capable of reflexive integration and disintegration, but as the split that obtains in unified psychic life, which is to say that genuine psychic integration is impossible. A third difficulty is that a regress is involved in that each of the different selves could itself be capable of 'self-deception.' Not only is this counter-intuitive, but this is conceptually impossible in the case of the undifferentiated id, one of the sub-agents.

These are criticisms of the multiple-agent view, some of which Sartre himself advances. Do they in fact pertain to Freud in particular? My equivocal response is that Freud does accept contradictoriness as a fact of mental life. To move from that understanding to multiple-agency, however, is somewhat misleading, and, finally, it is not an adequate way to characterize that contradictoriness. Sartre's criticism deserves a response. Sartre is critical of a certain account of repression, that account which presents a libidinous homunculus as the undifferentiated and blocked energy of the unconscious libido in thinglike terms, like a discrete entity, perhaps even an agent or separate self. Sartre, however, does not address that later and clearer account of repression offered by Freud in both <u>Beyond the Pleasure Principle</u> and <u>The Ego and the Id</u>. Freud's later account of repression is one in which the <u>ego</u> includes <u>both</u> conscious and <u>unconscious</u> activities. It is the ego that engages in purposeful construction of defenses against instinctual processes. As one writer has put the matter, "In his later work, then, Freud claims intentional status for the ego's efforts to keep itself unconscious of what it is doing to maintain that unawareness."[111]

Freud's later formulation of repression is incompatible with a multiple-agent theory. It is, in other words, incompatible with the actual theory that Sartre holds up for criticism. Freud held that mental conflict arises from a conflict of ideas, and that an agency, the ego, which includes within its domain actual unconsciousness--"We have thus come upon something in the ego itself which is also unconscious. . ."[112]--is the agent of resistance and repression: ". . .there can be no question but that this resistance emanates from (a person's) ego. . . ."[113] The ego, then, is not merely a victim of forces; neither is it opposed by a distinct and discrete homunculus (id) that imposes unconsciousness upon it. The point, rather, is that unconsciousness is due to ego function and expresses ego-directed repressive-resistant activity. This picture clearly portrays an agent at work. That agent is not, however, the id or a blind instinctual force of unconscious energy--it is the ego. It is the ego that Freud conceives as a complex agent, one which can itself "split" in the process of defense. This splitting identifies ego-activity, the result of which is that the total picture of what we might term "self-deceptive activity" is of a piece with the picture of "self-relatedness" argued for throughout these pages.[114]

Freud, of course, means several things by repression, and his understanding of "unconsciousness" must likewise be subjected to textual clarification. One does find in Freud, however, a certain reluctance to "personify" these alleged homunculi--". . .the hypothesis of the super-ego really describes a structural relation and it not merely a personification of some such abstraction as that of conscience"[115]--and the dynamic, topographical or systemic senses of "unconscious" eventually give way in Freud's pages, for purposes of clarification, to a descriptive sense. "The oldest and best meaning of the word 'unconscious' is the descriptive one," Freud writes, then adds, ". . .we call a process unconscious if we are obliged to assume that it is being activated at the moment we know nothing about it."[116]

In D. M. Thomas' novel, The White Hotel, a fictionalized Sigmund Freud writes of the main character, a neurotic woman, Frau Anna G., that "What she had in her consciousness was only a secret and not a foreign body. She both knew and did not know. In a sense, too, her mind was attempting to tell us what was wrong; for the repressed idea creates its own apt symbol."[117] Though Freud did not actually write these words, he could have. Freud nowhere employs the language of "unconscious belief;" but even if we were to argue that the idea of unconscious belief is inconsistent with the system "Unconsciousness," we could not conclude that the idea of such belief is also inconsistent with the descriptive sense of unconsciousness that can be attributed to both ego and super-ego activity.[118] The patient who resists the analyst performs work related to ego-activity--the work of creating an epistemic deficit--and the resulting unawareness reflects the purposeful nature of that activity. Unconsciousness, descriptively presented, is not, therefore, the result of a surging force that victimizes the person, robbing the person of freedom and all responsibility as well. Freudian psychoanalysis, rather, presents a theory about unconsciousness and the self's struggle for self-mastery that assumes a context of freedom. It is in the context of freedom that the neurotic comes to accept responsibility and resume functioning in the world as one who can love and work. As Phillip Rieff has so ably pointed out, while freedom in the social sphere may be no more than a metaphor, Freud avowed an "inner freedom" that can be said ". . .to exist only within the person, when there is a right balance among the psychic parts."[119]

All of these points lead to the following conclusion: Sartre was critical of an multiple-agent theory that posits an entity-agent (censor) that effectively robs a person of freedom. But neither that criticism, as formulated by Sartre and reported by Abelson, squares with the ego-activity view of repression and resistance so prominent in Freud's later writings. Freud, then, is not really a proponent of the multiple-agent theory; which means that the view under attack in Sartre's Being and Nothingness is not Freud's. Certain students of Freud and Sartre have noted this fact.[120]

We can conclude about Freud and multiple-agency is that Freud disavows this model as an adequate way of conceiving mental activity and psychic structure. Multiple-agency ought not to be interpreted in a literal way as a Freudian concept. If we invoke a "split-ego" view, however, a view consistent with Freud and Fingarette but inconsistent with a multiple-agency, the picture of intrapsychic conflict that arises is commensurate with a reflexively conceived picture of self-relatedness. The unconscious and the super-ego indeed represent agencies, as Freud sometimes says, but his metaphors do not personify these rational structures, and, more importantly, he refers these agencies back to the ego, which is properly the agent that enacts through available mechanisms repression, resistance, and, by extension, self-deception. Freud offers a picture of mind in which self-relatedness emerges from a certain way of describing ego-activity. What obtains as a result of this conception of self-relatedness is literally a notion of ego-reflexivity.

If we accept the view that the ego is capable of reflexive self-relations, we can also interpret repression and resistance as purposeful ego-activities. No logical paradox raises its head, only a psychological opposition manifest in behavior as a contradiction due to the "ego-split." The ego acts against itself, but reflexively and as two parties, not as two discrete homunculi. On this ego-reflexive view, an epistemic deficit results. The person experiencing "ego-split" exhibits, say, resistance to analysis, and due to that observed resistance it is possible to say that he or she is simultaneously aware, yet unaware. The unawareness results from the ego assessing the nature of a threatening epistemic object and responding to the subsequent intrapsychic conflict by employing the mechanisms of resistance. Of course, the ego need not do so, but it may do so if it has sufficient cause for so acting. Such defensive maneuvers can always be avoided if the self can become master of its own house. As Freud says, if you "Look into the depths of your soul and learn first to know yourself, then you will understand why this illness was bound to come upon you and perhaps you will thenceforth avoid falling ill."[121] "The blame, I must tell you lies with yourself."[122]

The defensive behavior apparent in resistance is motivated by the ego's unwillingness to accede to the instinctual demands of the libido. The ego desires to defend itself from awareness, to keep what it perceives to be distressing at a distance; for the displeasure of admitting the libidinal desire to consciousness is more than the pleasure to be derived from satisfying the instinct itself. (Consider the case of Gide's pastor.) Freud says that ". . .the soul is not a simple thing; on the contrary, it is a hierarchy or superordinated and subordinated agents, a labyrinth of impulses striving independently of one another towards action, corresponding to the multiplicity of instincts and of relations with the outer world, many of which are antagonistic and incompatible,"[123] these "agents" are unable to <u>act</u> without reference to "the highest agent," the ego. The ego is deceived into complaisance with respect to the information it is processing, information it assumes to be correct and trustworthy. These "agents" Freud refers to are not like distinct homunculi fighting for control against the ego-homunculus, but more like metaphorical agents in conflict with each other within the context of ego-agency itself. Even in the passage just quoted, it is clear that an epistemic deficit obtains as the result the ego's antagonistic relation to itself, a description that supports a self-relatedness concept of self. The self-relatedness concept of self is at odds with both the "unitary and transparent" view of consciousness on the one hand, and with the multiple-agency theory of personality, and intrapersonal conflict, on the other.

The multiple-agent theory, problematic, even paradoxical as it is, can be maintained only by denying human freedom (Sartre) or agency (Abelson) and by positing a <u>moral</u> paradox--that one is not responsible for one's own act of unawareness. None of these things does Freud endorse as acceptable losses, neither freedom, nor agency, nor responsibility. Sartre's error in attributing such a view to Freud aside, the validity of his criticism helps to establish that the multiple-agent view of self invokes an untenable, and unreflexively conceived, notion of self-deception.

A final issue concerns the role of self-deception in a psychoanalytic schema. We begin by recognizing that "Traditionally, Freudian psychoanalysts have not addressed the problem of self-deception under that name."[124] Traditional psychoanalysis has addressed the issue of self-deception in the language of unconscious defense, mechanisms of defense, censorship and resistance, all of which are related to neurosis, all of which could be said to imply a theory of self-deception, even a theory, as Mischel put it, of neurosis <u>qua</u> self-deception.[125] We can, of course, impute a theory of self-deception by means of the language and conceptual parameters of defense and resistance, though there is no appeal to the authority of Freud himself because he did not analyze 'self-deception' <u>per se</u>. It is significant that in light of this lack of appeal to authority, psychoanalytic interpretations of 'self-deception' have arisen, and the same kinds of disputes about the meaning of the concept found in the philosophical community reappear in the psychoanalytic community. While Mischel believes 'self-deception' can be translated into 'neurosis,' Roy Schafer has concluded that the literal expression 'self-deception' is a "misnomer," a linguistically misleading expression for a phenomenon having to do with persons attending faultily to their own actions.[126] In a sense, this amounts to saying that literal self-deception cannot happen.

Despite this in-house debate, I believe Freud does permit us to infer 'self-deception' from his theory. We can do so by considering again the purposeful activity of the ego defending itself from perceived harm, displeasure or distress. Freud gives us the fact of contradictory behavior and describes the unawareness attending it. Both of these publicly observable phenomena are presented as purposeful and motivated and consistent with ego-activity. Although Freud does not give us, strictly speaking, "contradictory beliefs," this feature, too, can be inferred if one can 1.) permit the contradictory behavior to be a consistent manifestation of mental conflict; 2.) if that mental conflict can be perceived as purposeful ego-activity reflecting an "ego-split;" and 3.) if the ego-split can itself be interpreted as the reflexive activity of a divided agent whose contradictory actions are both governed by belief, one conscious (the patient's professed understanding of his or her behavior), one unconscious (that belief which the patient resists acknowledging but which can be ascribed to the behavior itself since the behavior is governed by belief). To accept the position governed by these conditions is to understand how some of Freud's most profound interpreters meaningfully--and correctly--use the language of 'self-deception' to interpret central features of psychoanalytic theory. Philip Rieff, for instance, will say that for Freud, our inner nature lies hidden, that Freud not only "supports the Nietzschean idea that 'One's self is well-hidden from one's own self," but calls into question "all self-insight, intuitive as well as intellectual":

> Not only does Freud anticipate that, when a patient offers a seemly account of his conduct, the analyst will be able to detect aggressive or erotic motives which the patient's account has concealed. More damaging to the pride of self-insight is the fact that, even as he charges that real motives are generally hidden behind some rationalization, Freud denies the importance of the conscious lie, the deliberate deception of others. It is for its continual self-deceptions that he reproves the ego.[127]

The ego is capable of deceiving itself because the ego is capable of enacting a reflexively conceived split. I would note that Freud uses "ego" two ways, one of which is a reflexive or intra-relational meaning, the other being comparable to what I have termed the 'holistic meaning of self,' where it is not one aspect of self being referred to but the self-as-a-whole.[128] Having made that distinction, let me say that once it is recognized that the ego (or person, or patient, or self) reflexively conceived is deemed structurally capable of "deceiving" itself, it is also possible to grasp more clearly the aim of psychotherapy, which is the education of the ego[129] and its "strengthening."[130] The psychotherapist is one who helps the ego to <u>know</u> itself, so that the operative psychoanalytic principle is that "'To know thyself' is to be known by another";[131] and from this therapeutic relationship wherein self-understanding is achieved, a "cure" is effected, which is to say that the ego is reintegrated and made strong enough to carry on the organizational work of self-relatedness, balancing the demands placed upon by the id, the external world, and the super-ego. In conjunction with this therapeutic consideration, the requirement that a potential analyst submit to analysis as part of the therapeutic training has as its aim the increase of the candidate's ". . .ability to converse with his or her unconscious well enough to recognize the unconscious motivations of others" and "to recognize the maneuvers of self-deception."[132] Students of psychoanalytic theory and practitioners of the art can, then, employ the language of 'self-deception' to clarify the nature of the problem addressed by psychoanalytic theory and encountered in psychotherapy--resistance to "working through" the meaning of one's own behavior. Psychoanalytic training is designed to help the candidate encounter, identify and treat the tendency to resist one's own unawareness of the "best, most reasonable interpretation."

Self-deception, then, is implied by psychoanalytic theory, for that theory assumes a certain capability of the self--the capability to forget actively and purposefully; to achieve unawareness of what one knows, believes or wishes; to resist and repress in order to keep oneself from explicitly "spelling-out" the nature of one's conflicts and the meaning of one's behavior. All of these remarks are intelligible within a relatedness conception of self, which is a picture framed in terms of psychic integration/disintegration or ego-alienation. This picture of self obtains from the experience of encountering a self (holistically conceived) as it presents itself to the world in the current (fragmented/integrated) state of its self-relatedness. That state of self-relatedness is manifest in certain behavior to which one may ascribe, in a meaningful way, the reflexively conceived and psychoanalytically supported concept, 'self-deception.'

It may seem that the distinction being pressed here between a relatedness conception of self and a multiple-agent theory is fuzzy or nit-picking. Many consequences follow, however, from the way in which we describe the constitution of the human person as self. If we permit our language to harden, if we permit "id/ego/super-ego" to achieve conceptual status as homunculi,[133] as discrete agents capable of deceiving the self just as one person deceives another person, it follows, as Sartre pointed out, that the self-deceiver is neither free nor responsible. The whole action character of self-deception is called into question, and the ordinary language meaning of the concept is threatened. Since we know that Freud intended neither to absolve persons of responsibility for breakdowns in their psychic integration--even their dreams![134]--nor to deny human freedom, we are forced to conclude from the way Freud himself talks about the constitution of the human person that ambiguity attends the very language of self or ego disclosure. I believe Freud does provide an accurate "ordinary language" description of self-deception, one in which an epistemic deficit results. Consider his observation that obsessional neurotics avoid conflict by an <u>act</u> that can only refer to 'self-deception':

> But there is no doubt that before becoming conscious they have been through the process of repression. In most of them the actual working of the aggressive instinctual impulse is altogether unknown to the ego, and it requires a good deal of analytic work to make it conscious. . . . What happens is that the affect left out when the obsessional ideal is perceived appears in a different place. The super-ego behaves as though repression had not occurred and as though it knew the real wording and full affective character of the aggressive impulse, and it treats the ego accordingly. The ego which, on the one hand, knows that it is innocent is obliged, on the other hand, to be aware of a sense of guilt and carry a responsibility which it cannot account for. . .and the contradiction in the ego merely shows that it has shut out the id by means of repression while remaining fully accessible to the influence of the super-ego.[135]

In light of this passage, Mischel has written of Freud that

> his point may be, not that we are to conceptualize the person in terms of homunculi, but that the neurotic has avoided the conflict by deceiving himself: his lack of awareness is motivated, he has made himself unconscious of an incompatible impulse which he knows, in one sense of that term, to be his. And he can do that only insofar as he can also keep himself unconscious of the technique he is intentionally using to deceive himself.[136]

The problem one encounters is that Freud does not seem to mean that personality is constituted by discrete intrapsychic agents, but from a self's relations to its own self as differentiated by certain linguistic conventions. These conventions refer to the intrapsychically related parties constitutive of selfhood. Difficulties arise over interpretation, however, because Freud himself, being a gifted writer and one apt to use metaphor, uses language suggestive of "persons" or "things." All of this is to say that Freud's language is itself ambiguous in many respects. Clearly, "id, ego, super-ego" are used as nouns, as persons or things, and one can even find Freud hardening the metaphors when he "personifies" the ego, refers to the super-ego as an agent or casually mentions that the id has intentions. Do not all of these "thing" or "person" images or mental life reflect a multiple-agent reality?

The language of the self--ambiguous though it be--permits us to employ many kinds of analogies and metaphors in order to clarify the nature of the relational reality to which this metaphorical language of "person" or "thing" points. It must be recognized that the language of the self is intelligible not because it is concrete, but because it enables us to understand in a tensive language ("reflexivity") a tensive reality. The language of self moves us to employ metaphor and impose analogies so that we might understand more precisely the reality of dynamic self-relations. Freud himself often makes such linguistic moves, using metaphorical language or analogies to describe the nature of self-relatedness. He uses, for instance, an analogy to "the state" or--shades of Plato!--a "rider" (ego) bridling his unruly horse (id, passion).[137] Freud even wrote at one point, "Analogies, it is true, decide nothing, but they can make one feel more at home."[138] This feeling of being at home means that one can have linguistic access to the complexity of self-relatedness. Freud uses nouns to describe the "parties" to the intrapsychic relation, and, as I have said, the reason one would resort to metaphors of "state" or "city" or "committee" or "id/ego/super-ego"--all of which are nouns--is that these nouns help us to picture and make concrete what are actually adverbs. All of these metaphorical nouns can be viewed as linguistic conveniences for realities which, had we a non-ambiguous language for them, would express the modifying of action: the action associated with intrapsychic relatedness and the action of reflexivity.[139]

Has "ordinary language" proved itself inadequate? My answer is no. The point is that the ambiguous language of the self must resort to metaphor in order to preserve the tensive character of the referents themselves. We do not lose meaning by employing "poetic" language--we acquire it. We enable ourselves to grasp meaning with a clarity that descriptive and scientific language does not provide. In a sense, the language of poetry and metaphor is put to work to convey something that an explanatory language could not do nearly so well. This is not a problem new to Freud: "Plato was attuned to this problem, though he did not wish to be taken too literally; 'master of oneself' does not really mean there are two people within one person. Yet he provided no alternative way of speaking."[140] While I shall shortly point out what the literal language might look like, I want to defend the metaphor as meaningful, as actually a closer referent than could otherwise be devised. On the basis of this picture of a language of the self, we can begin to sum up our findings.

The essential flaw in the multiple-agent theory is that the view assumes the referents of the "thing/person" language to be, ontologically, things or persons--nouns. It is not at all clear that this is the case, and, given a self-relatedness conception of psychic life, it is even counter-intuitive. We require a language of self, and noun language serves to make self-relatedness intelligible. Yet the nouns perform essentially adverbial tasks, which is to say they serve as metaphors for the activity of self-relatedness. If we take the "id/ego/super-ego" as literal nouns and not as noun metaphors for adverbial functions, we gain concreteness at the expense of meaning. If, on the other hand, we use the nouns to perform adverbial functions, we work the language in an almost poetic mood to perform a difficult meaning task: expressing a tensive reality in a tensive language. The view I am advancing here may be controversial, but it is not lacking in support from the psychiatric community. And clearly, the language of metaphor has been recognized and employed by professionals and non-professional psychological observers to preserve the ambiguity of self-relatedness and the meaning of reflexivity. By holding that view, we can speak about the self in terms of "multiple selves," or say that the personality is constituted by "id/ego/super-ego," doing so without thereby committing ourselves to idea of "multiple personality," by which we mean an extreme psychotic fragmentation of unusual complexity and ego loss of rare occurrence. Multiple-agency in this latter sense has nothing to do with "self-deception and the common life."

One last point. The language of self is, as I have said repeatedly, ambiguous. Should one attempt to explain self-relatedness in its own terms one may wind up speaking of the self as Kierkegaard's pseudonymous author, "Anti-Climacus," spoke of it in The Sickness Unto Death: "The self is a relation that relates itself to itself or is the relation's relating itself to itself in the relation; the self is not the relation but the relation's relating itself to itself."[141] To the extent that this is intelligible, it is so because even here "self" is serving as a noun, serving an anthropomorphic interest. This statement, however, does have the virtue of focusing our attention away from the self being a relation to the self in relation, and this points us to the activity of self-relatedness that is the self.

Kierkegaard's statement is not unintelligible, but neither is its meaning simply self-evident. As a matter of fact, what is self-evident about this statement is sometimes overlooked. What we have here is language made all the more complex in that it attempts not to personify or anthropomorphize; yet, even this language of self-relatedness, for all of its descriptive accuracy, requires deciphering. And to decipher it requires metaphor. Freud's picture of "ego-split" and his metaphor of "id/ego/super-ego" represented an attempt to decipher the action of self-relatedness in a language of mental topography and intrapsychic dynamics. Kierkegaard reaches for the metaphors of self-relatedness by describing and diagnosing behavioral manifestations of self-relatedness. In other words, his technique as a poet-dialectician is to reveal concrete individuals in differing spheres of existence and interest. Kierkegaard's twist is to move from metaphors of self to self as metaphor.

Still, Kierkegaard's words seem to mystify. It is as if we approach the language of self-relatedness by looking behind it, beneath it, under it, over it--but what is self-evident, what is evident in the words themselves? One of Kierkegaard's most astute interpreters has referred to the above quoted passage as "gobbledygook,"[142] and, as some readers may be aware, comedian Woody Allen has often referred to this passage in routines that lampoon philosophy. This tells us that the language of self-relatedness is not only ambiguous--it is comic. It is comic because it is the language of freedom, a language that cannot be determined or constrained, a language of spirit--free of "definition, derivation, and demonstration"[143]--a language of self-consciousness that is as inscrutable as Duck Soup was to the movie that bore that title. Metaphors like "id/ego/super-ego" point with linguistic precision to relations that would elude conceptual grasp without them. Yet, to harden that language, to turn from the language of metaphor to the language of explanation, is to overlook the tensive character of the metaphor itself. It is to miss the activity, the freedom, even the humor. For the language of self-relatedness is ambiguous, just as the reality to which it points is ultimately mysterious. That mystery and ambiguity may be more appropriately grasped when, prior to philosophical investigation, we pause to see the "gobbledygook," the non-sense, which is the comic language of freedom.

The problem of self, which is ever of concern in a treatment of 'self-deception' is very much a language problem. If the language of self is ambiguous, if it "laughs" at our grave attempts to harden, anthropomorphize, personify or thingify it, then we have the option of either creating a new language of freedom filled with recondite neologisms--the path followed by Heidegger and Sartre, and more recently by Mary Daly; or we can pursue ordinary language into metaphor and analogy and see the ambiguity made less obscure and the mystery more intelligible--the path followed indifferent ways by both Kierkegaard and Freud.

I conclude this discussion on an equivocal note. Having disavowed "multiple-agent" as an appropriate metaphor of self, I do wish to reiterate that it is not so much the language of agents to which I object as it is a particular, non-metaphorical way of interpreting that language. Of course the language of self can be used metaphorically; what must be recognized is that it is sometimes most metaphorical when it seems least so. As members of the linguistic community, we are authorized to make certain moves consistent with the language and meanings we all more or less share. It is possible, therefore, to refer to the activity of the self in terms of "different selves," "committees," or "cities," or a "second self" (Frank Norris), even in terms of agents or agencies, personifications and anthropomorphisms. My qualification is that this concrete language must not itself be set in concrete. It must not be allowed to harden such that it detracts from the tensive nature of the referents which the metaphors do so much to express in the language of everyday. If the language of self is ambiguous, it is because it is also the language of freedom. We would do well to remember that the language of freedom will celebrate our attempts to "pin it down" and "get it right" by exposing itself in linguistic forms that may be, literally, comic nonsense or gobbledygook. To fail to see the comedy may be to fail to see the meaning as well. It is not that the meaning is not there, but that this language of the self expresses a freedom that preconditions all of our rational and linguistic determinations--yet the language itself cannot be determined. In an ironic, even paradoxical way, it is "gobbledygook" that makes this clear, even intelligible. Freedom of self-consciousness--spirit--is prone to be overlooked in our rush to solve linguistic puzzles, in our grave attempt to analyze, decipher, and clarify that which eludes exact definition and unambiguous, explicit statement. Were we better poets and philosophers, we would perhaps concede this more readily.

Sartre worked to preserve the freedom of the self-conscious agent against the hard language of a "multiple-agent" view. Freud's language of "ego" can likewise be interpreted as a language of reflexivity (ego/ego-activity/ego-split) consistent in general form to what I have referred to as the language of self-relatedness, since for Freud, the ego is in a "dependent relationship to the id and the super-ego."[144]

b. Sartre's Dialectical Model[145]

Freud did not broach the topic of self-deception in an explicit way; neither did he pause to consider many of the issues that would trouble later philosophers. The same cannot be said of Sartre. Sartre did consider the philosophical issues raised by the topic of self-deception; and, in fact, he used 'self-deception'--albeit in terms of 'bad faith'--to commence an ontological inquiry into the nature of consciousness. Sartre launches his magnum opus, Being and Nothingness, by considering the ways in which the idea of "lying to oneself" entails "bad faith." A person practicing bad faith is, according to Sartre, ". . .hiding a displeasing truth or presenting as truth a pleasing untruth. Bad faith then has in appearance the structure of falsehood. Only what changes is the fact that in bad faith it is from myself that I am hiding the truth."[146]

Sartre plunges his reader into the difficulty of conceiving of a person undertaking a project, which, on the one hand, has in appearance the structure of falsehood, but which, on the other hand, is a "single project" in a "unitary structure." This formulation is logically incompatible with the structure of falsehood, for falsehood requires a duality: liar and lied to, deceiver and deceived. This description of bad faith pictures an other-deception conducted by the self against the self. It is, in other words, a picture whereby self-deception strictly retains the formal features of other-deception. Difficulties arise, however, because in self-deception this kind of easily intelligible duality is lacking. Unlike other-deception, ". . .the duality of the deceiver and the deceived does not exist here. Bad faith on the contrary implies in essence the unity of a single consciousness."[147]

As Sartre presents the issue in terms of a unified consciousness, bad faith or self-deception clearly invokes paradox. Again the question, how can one consciousness both know and not know concurrently, believe and not believe the same thing at the same time? That a paradox arises from the idea of a person intentionally deceiving him- or herself is inescapable; that the paradox must be resolved is the philosophical challenge of 'self-deception.' Does Sartre resolve the paradox? Although scholarly opinion on this issue is divided, I see two possibilities: either Sartre fails to resolve the paradox, or he resolves it by invoking a notion of "unconsciousness" that is, strictly speaking, incompatible with Sartre's own theory of a unitary and transparent consciousness. Which is it?

The way to answer this question responsibly is to undertake an exhaustive investigation of Sartre's writings on bad faith and consciousness. Let me say, however, that textual analysis will yield no self-evident results. In fact, commentators on the Sartrian text have reached no interpretive consensus, and the textual evidence appears inconclusive. The argument has been made, for example, that Sartre's notion of a "pre-reflective" consciousness is a "rough equivalent" to a psychoanalytic notion of unconsciousness. Yet that very contention has been explicitly denied elsewhere on the grounds that pre-reflective consciousness is ". . .simply the everyday consciousness in which for the most part we conduct our lives without explicitly thinking about ourselves."[148] Moreover, the case has been made that "in the strict sense of successfully and completely hiding a truth from oneself, within the unity of a single consciousness, 'lying to oneself' is not possible for Sartre,"[149] while another commentator argues that "Sartre suggests a way out of bad faith as well as presenting a solid and coherent account of self-deception."[150]

Up to this point, all of my references to Sartre have taken his picture of a unitary and transparent consciousness quite literally--and there is no reason not to do so. It is by taking this picture of consciousness literally that one arrives at a formulation of the epistemological paradox of self-deception. Fingarette, for instance, asks, ". . .assuming with Sartre that consciousness is 'transparent' and 'unified', that in the nature of the case there can be nothing unconscious in consciousness, how can we get into a condition where we do not know what we know?"[151] Or: "Can one and the same 'unified' consciousness both believe and not believe?"[152] Fingarette classifies Sartre as a proponent of a "cognition-perception" model of self-deception, "consciousness" and "awareness" being for Fingarette terms compatible with the family of terms associated with the cognition model. His criticism of Sartre, then, is that as a cognitivist, Sartre, like all other cognitivists, ends in paradox; that his account is not truly "intentional" since bad faith is something that "happens" to one, like falling asleep, even though one "puts" oneself into it;[153] and, while acknowledging that his own idea of "spelling-out" derives from Sartre, Fingarette also makes the case against Sartre that ". . .there can be no question that the refusal to reflect is a possibility inherent in Sartre's ontology of consciousness, though he himself never makes this policy explicit or capitalizes on it."[154]

Although the case has been made that Sartre is a total voluntarist who evokes the "moral paradox" of self-deception,[155] Fingarette seems to accuse Sartre of failing, in the end, to develop a satisfactory voluntarist conception of self-deception. Because of the lack of an adequate "action model," Sartre, according to Fingarette, is left holding an ontology that begs, rather than resolves, the most pressing and problematic issue surrounding self-deception, namely, how is one to account for self-deception such that one adequately resolves the epistemological paradox?

I wish to offer here an interpretation of Sartre that claims that Sartre's picture of consciousness does allow us to say that a person can be "wholly" conscious without also "knowing" the total contents of consciousness. I hold that Sartre's presentation of consciousness and bad faith can be shown to be consistent with an "action model" that stresses the purposeful nature of self-deception, which is to say that Fingarette's model is deeply indebted to Sartre as Fingarette himself acknowledges.[156] There are even grounds for asserting that Sartre holds to a view that the self is a synthesis, which invokes a picture of self-relatedness, and that his view contradicts his avowed "unitary and transparent" consciousness perspective. If these claims can be supported, Sartre's picture of self-deception will essentially satisfy the ordinary language analysis of self-deception, an incidental though important result. If a connection can be made between that ordinary language view and Sartre's own, then Sartre can be used to support the view advanced in these pages. The following analysis of Sartre, then, will attempt to make this connection without resorting to tendentious argument and rely on Sartre's texts without, I hope, "proof-texting."

When Amelie Rorty writes about self-deception that her aim is to show "contra Sartre, that it is logically possible"[157] to rid oneself of self-deception, she implies that Sartre is trapped by his epistemological formulation of self-deception and that from this paradox there is no exit. Rorty, like Fingarette, accuses Sartre of holding to a cognitivist model of self-deception, which is to say that Sartre's view of self-deception is strictly dependent upon a first-order model of other-deception, whence the paradox obtains. As I stated in the "multiple-agent" section, Sartre himself rejects the model of other-deception as being sufficient to render bad faith coherent. Sartre, in fact, uses the other-deception model in order to set up the initial difficulty--the epistemological paradox entailed by the prospect of a single unified consciousness knowing and not knowing simultaneously. My view is this: Sartre does attempt to resolve the paradox, but he does so only after making clear what the paradox is. His description is not his solution.

If the obvious "multiple-agent" solution to the paradox of self-deception is inadequate, as Sartre's critique of that model demonstrates, then one must look to the nature of consciousness itself in order to account for the phenomenon of bad faith. Sartre believes that bad faith is endemic to the human condition and that it is so as a consequence of freedom. Given this understanding of the phenomenon, Sartre's move is to provide a metaphysical/ontological interpretation of the paradox by positioning the phenomenon of bad faith (i.e., self-deception) within the context of a dialectic of consciousness itself. Sartre's position is that consciousness is "non-thetic" (pre-reflective) and aware of itself. In reflection, therefore, which is the attempt by consciousness to become its own object. ". . .consciousness exists as a translucent consciousness of being other than the objects of which it is conscious."[158] Sartre holds that consciousness is always conscious of something, and in unreflective, non-thetic or pre-reflective consciousness (the pre-reflective cogito), "there is no knowledge but an implicit consciousness of being conscious of an object."[159] These distinctions enable Sartre to make the case that all consciousness is consciousness of consciousness, which is to say that consciousness is fundamentally and structurally dialectical in nature. By that Sartre means that one can actually point to ". . .the fact that the nature of consciousness is to be what it is not and not to be what it is."[160] When one asks whether it is possible, on Sartre's account, to conceive of a person knowing and not knowing, or believing and not believing, being aware and not aware--at the same time--one must refer that question to a dialectical model of consciousness.

For Sartre, this dialectical conception permits us to say that "We have to deal with human reality as a being which is what it is not and which is not what it is."[161] Several consequences follow from this dialectic, which, as the somewhat inclusive title of his volume indicates, is a dialectic of being and nothingness, or, to put it in more suitable terms for his discussion of bad faith, the dialectic of facticity and transcendence. By facticity Sartre means those things that pertain to human reality in a factual way, such things as one's "body, its height, color, weight, and our entire past--when and where we are born, as well as what we have actually done. . .[and] what is actually happening to us."[162] In that human persons are able to transcend their facticity, which points to the inability of persons ever to identify themselves completely and actually with their facticity, persons can know their own facticity, examine it, and, by adopting a perspective from which they can interpret their relation to their own facticity, transcend it. Consciousness is never perfectly identified with one's facticity, nor transcendence with purely unrealizable possibilities. Transcendence is associated with "believable ways of behavior."[163]

The dialectic of facticity and transcendence makes it possible to say that human subjects are never what they are in their facticity alone, never the human reality of body as being-for-itself, but always exist as a being-for-others, as an object of knowledge for ourselves and others. This is to say that our consciousness of facticity is also a relation of transcendence. The "attitude" of bad faith arises because in the structure of consciousness itself, one is "not what one is" (facticity) but is the consciousness of being what one is as that is known to us in our relations with others. Consciousness of being what one is (facticity) therefore expresses a negation of what one is inasmuch as such consciousness is also a manifestation of an accompanying consciousness of transcendence. This is one way to express the dialectic of consciousness implicated in bad faith. To illustrate this: Gide's pastor is in bad faith with respect to Gertrude because he has a desire for Gertrude that is "being-in-itself." That desire, however, is negated by his transcendence, his "being-for-itself," which is his repudiation of that desire by his intellectual and Christianly interpretation. This transcending being-for-itself is, in other words, a simultaneous negation of an actual erotic desire for Gertrude (facticity). Gide's pastor expresses some of the same tendencies as the disingenuous flirt, Sartre's own example, and is subject to the same critique.[164] Like the "flirt," the pastor "refuses to apprehend the desire for what it is" and "engages" himself such that he "does not notice" that his actions are those of a lover rather than a spiritual counselor.[165] The pastor could say, along with Sartre, that "thanks to my transcendence, I am not subject to all that I am,"[166] and because the pastor represents himself to himself much as Sartre's waiter, the pastor could also say, "I am a pastor (or waiter) in the mode of being what I am not."[167] Sartre's examples, like the example of Gide's pastor, serve to illustrate various aspects of bad faith or self-deception,[168] for what we encounter are persons who are "perpetually absent" to their facticity, to their bodies (as being-in-itself), even to their own acts:[169]

> What unity we do find in these various aspects of bad faith? It is a certain art of forming contradictory concepts which unite in themselves both an idea and the negation of that idea. The basic concept which is thus engendered, utilizes the double property of the human being, who is at once a facticity and a transcendence. These two aspects of human reality are and ought to be capable of valid cooperation.

Coordination, however is just what bad faith prevents. Sartre continues:

> But bad faith does not wish either to coordinate them nor to surmount them in a synthesis. Bad faith seeks to affirm their identity while preserving their differences. It must affirm facticity as being transcendence and transcendence being facticity, in such a way that at the instant when a person apprehends the one, he can find himself abruptly faced with the other.[170]

What Sartre is saying, then, is that a self-deceiver is one who is engaged in a project to retain an "internally" contradictory state of affairs. Furthermore, that project has as its aim the attempt to flee from oneself, to maintain "perpetual absence" from one's own acts:

> We can see the use which bad faith can make of these judgments which all aim at establishing that I am not what I am. If I were only what I am, I could, for example, seriously consider an adverse criticism which someone makes of me, question myself scrupulously, and perhaps be compelled to recognize the truth in it. But thanks to transcendence, I am not subject to all that I am. I do not even have to discuss the justice of the reproach. . . .I am on a plane where no reproach can touch me since what I really am is my transcendence. I flee from myself, I escape myself, I leave my tattered garment in the hands of the fault-finder. But the ambiguity necessary for

bad faith comes from the fact that I affirm here that I <u>am</u> my transcendence in the mode of being a thing.[171]

The human capacity for transcendence is what makes bad faith a possible way of being in the world. Sartre presents a picture of consciousness in conflict with itself, consciousness alienated from being-in-itself. Sartre has not dropped the language of a "unitary and transparent" consciousness, but, as these quoted marks reveal, a person in bad faith is a person who is acting to prevent the conflict between transcendence and facticity from resolving itself in a coordinated synthesis. Bad faith is what Freud termed the "ingenious solution"--the attempt to have two contradictory things at once. Although Sartre wants to affirm the possibility of coordination, it is clear that the self is not synthesized at the moment bad faith is operative. The dialectic model explains self-deception as a condition or state of psychic disintegration. The self is intentionally seeking to avoid synthesis and to flee from the unitary and transparent consciousness that "I am."[172] "On all sides I escape being and yet--I am." "The goal of bad faith [is] to put oneself out of reach; it is an escape."[173] And, in the dialectic model of consciousness, bad faith shares structural similarity with its antithesis, sincerity:

> Thus the essential structure of sincerity does not differ from that of bad faith since the sincere man constitutes himself as what he is <u>in order not to be it</u>. This explains the truth recognized by all that one can fall into bad faith through being sincere. Total, constant sincerity is a constant effort to dissociate oneself from oneself. A person frees himself from himself by the very act by which he makes himself an object for himself. And what is the goal of bad faith? To cause me to be what I am, in the mode of 'not being what one is,' or not to be what I am in the mode of 'being what one is.'[174]

Sincerity is itself, on Sartre's conception, bad faith, for sincerity shares with bad faith the condition ". . .that human reality, in its most immediate being, in the intrastructure of the pre-reflective <u>cogito</u>, must be what it is not and not be what it is.'[175]

Can one picture a person not in bad faith? For Sartre this is, of course, possible, for all that would be required is for persons to be what they are (authentic) and not seek escape, whether in bad faith on the one hand, or in ideals of honesty on the other. Both options describe the person in flight. (The language of "flight" is similar to Freud's "anxiety"--see footnote 144, this chapter.) Both of these possibilities represent attempts to dissociate oneself from oneself, to transcend oneself by making oneself an object (in the mode of a thing) <u>for</u> oneself. This is not only to deny being, but to gain nothingness. Nothingness supports being and makes consciousness itself possible. "If man is what he is, bad faith is forever impossible and candor ceases to be his ideal and becomes instead his being. But," asks Sartre as rhetorically as an Christian theologian considering the fallenness of human nature, "is man what he is?"[176] Sartre's answer is that our condition is one of alienation from the being that we are.

This picture of consciousness provides Sartre with the structure of being that renders bad faith conceivable. Yet all is not resolved. Even if the structure of bad faith is clarified, there is a content matter in need of attention. As Sartre puts it, "The true problem with bad faith stems evidently from the fact that bad faith is <u>faith</u>."[177] Bad faith is neither a cynical lie nor certainty; it is, rather, a belief-related concept: "If we take this belief as meaning the adherence of being to its object is not given or is given indistinctly, then bad faith is belief; and the essential problem of bad faith is a problem of belief."[178]

The description of bad faith offered by Sartre at this point establishes that by an <u>act</u> of faith, by volition, and by an assessment of evidence, self-deception aims to achieve a belief about the truth of things. What one believes will be incompatible with good faith, for what one apprehends as true is negated in order to serve what one <u>wants</u> to be true. What one wants to believe as true becomes an operant and consciously held belief that one has also willed: "Bad faith apprehends evidence but is resigned in advance to not being fulfilled by this evidence, to not being persuaded and transformed into good faith. It makes itself humble and modest; it is not ignorant, it says that faith is decision and that after each intuition, it must decide and <u>will what it is</u>."[179]

The evidence in question here is of a specified kind, namely, nonpersuasive. A self-deceiver, then, "decides" to persuade him- or herself that something is true (<u>p</u>), but only because a prior awareness (<u>not-p</u>) counts against that belief that <u>p</u>. That prior awareness permits the person to assess the evidence such that its persuasive character is disvalued. It is nonpersuasive evidence that is given credence by a consciousness that, in a very real sense, also knows (pre-reflectively) that the evidence is not persuasive. Consciousness "decides," however, to opt for bad faith, which is ". . .a faith which wishes itself not to be quite convinced."[180] Sartre's account of bad faith is one wherein persons try to persuade themselves about the truth of things by engaging in interpretive activity at odds with things as they are in their facticity. On Sartre's analysis, if one actually persuades oneself that something is true, doing so on the basis of non-persuasive evidence, then one has acted consistently with an intention to escape from one's own being. In Sartre's terms, one aims at "being what I am" in a mode of "not being what I am." The entire bad faith enterprise consists in a project, a dialectical project, aimed at flight from self. It is a project so conceived that to understand it is to understand that bad faith presupposes itself:

> We must note in fact that the project of bad faith must be itself in bad faith. I am not only in bad faith at the end of my effort when I have constructed my two-faced concepts and when I have persuaded myself. In truth, I have not persuaded myself; to the extent that I could be so persuaded, I have always been so. And at the very moment when I was disposed to put myself in bad faith, I of necessity was in bad faith with respect to this same disposition. For me to have represented it to myself as bad faith would have been cynicism; to believe it sincerely would not have been in good faith. The decision to be in bad faith does not dare to speak its name; it believes itself and does not believe itself in bad faith; it believes itself and does not believe itself in good faith.[181]

In other words, one effects bad faith only when one is already operating in the context of bad faith. The bad faith is hidden from linguistically explicit recognition, so one is "unaware"; yet if one be in bad faith, one has pre-reflectively "decided" to act consistently with one's disposition to accept non-persuasive evidence as persuasive. As Sartre presents matters, one does not enter this circle of bad faith reflectively (thetically) or through conscious deliberations. This is an important point since Sartre is therefore refusing to accept his own description of the epistemological paradox as the central issue. The idea that one can deliberately and consciously lie to oneself is a paradoxical formulation that does not obtain on Sartre's premise of a "unitary and transparent consciousness": I cannot consciously set out to lie to myself, but I can enter the circle of bad faith pre-reflectively. And at this pre-reflective level, which is a level of not "knowing," consciousness can be said, in the language of action, to "decide" for bad faith. It is the pre-reflective "decision" that enables a self-deceiver to "put" him- or herself in bad faith "as one goes to sleep."[182]

Because Sartre's account of bad faith seems to describe a picture of "not spelling-out," we might be tempted to construe it as an alternative description of the action model. But to think of this as an action account--and nothing more--is to misrepresent it. Certainly, an agent performs the work of of avoidance and disavowal--the agent of consciousness as it is alienated from being, the agent of "for-itself" seeking flight from "being-in-itself." In bad faith, the self-deceiver is caught between a desire for being-in-itself and a contrary desire to negate being. Consciousness operates from a wish or desire to flee from being, and it is this desire for escape that constitutes the motive for bad faith, the motive for forming contradictory concepts and seeking the "ingenious solution" of affirming their identity while also recognizing their differences. This "ingenious solution" works because consciousness can refuse to acknowledge its own responsibility for its own decision by <u>denying</u> that it is in bad faith.[183] As Sartre says, this decision "dare not speak its name." This is a picture of "not-spelling out" an engagement in the world; it is a picture of a person unaware of the meaning of his or her own acts and--at least up to this point--seems thoroughly consistent with Fingarette's action model.

Sartre, however, moves his analysis in the direction of <u>belief</u>, and it is this move that Fingarette does not endorse. The faith of bad faith, according to Sartre, is also implicated in the flight from freedom and being and therefore reflects the nature of consciousness itself. If bad faith, as faith, entails belief, then the belief must itself express the dialectic; and according to Sartre it does. Sartre spells this dialectic out by saying that every belief possesses its own antithesis; for whenever one confronts one's own beliefs as objects of consciousness, one <u>knows</u> (reflectively) what one believes, which is to make certain as <u>knowledge</u> what was uncertain as <u>belief</u>. In other words, every belief holds its own negation because "To believe is to know that one believes, and to know that one believes is no longer to believe."[184] Furthermore, the dialectic is made manifest in the constant questioning that consciousness directs to itself, so that "belief is a being which questions its own being, which can realize itself only in its destruction, which can manifest itself to itself only by denying itself." Sartre then adds, characteristically, "To believe is not-to-believe."[185]

Sartre's picture of consciousness and the role of belief in bad faith issues in a description compatible with the ordinary language position that self-deception is a project to mislead belief that results in an "epistemic deficit." In Sartre's terms, bad faith is a project that attempts to flee being by taking refuge in "not-believing-what-one-believes."[186] Bad faith <u>is</u> the contradictory beliefs held by consciousness, and we say about bad faith that it does "not succeed in believing what it wishes to believe. But it is precisely as the acceptance of not-believing what it believes that it is bad faith."[187] Here, then, we arrive at a description of consciousness revealing through bad faith "an inner disintegration in the heart of being, and it is this disintegration which bad faith wishes to be."[188]

> Bad faith seeks to flee the in-itself by means of the inner disintegration of my being. But it denies this very disintegration as it denies that it is itself bad faith. Bad faith seeks by means of 'not-being-what-one-is' to escape from the in-itself which I am not in the mode of being what one is not. It denies itself as bad faith and aims at the in-itself which I am not in the mode of 'not-being-what-one-is-not.' If bad faith is possible, it is because it is an immediate, permanent threat to every conceivable project of the human being; it is because consciousness conceals in its being a permanent risk of bad faith. The origin of this risk is the fact that the nature of consciousness simultaneously is to be what it is not and not to be what it is.[189]

This overview of issues relevant to Sartre's picture of self-deception, a picture drawn from a dialectical model of consciousness, provides the conceptual wherewithal for grasping the nature of self-deception as epistemic and action-related. Bad faith is a manifestation of the being of consciousness. It is a phenomenon endemic to the human condition, and it illustrates the dialectic nature of consciousness itself. As a "belief-misleading project," bad faith aims at so affecting consciousness that one will believe and not believe, a contradictory state of affairs brought about by the activity of consciousness itself. Consciousness is the agent that, according to Sartre, "stands forth in the firm resolution <u>not to demand too much</u>, to count itself satisfied when it is barely persuaded, to force itself in decisions to adhere to uncertain truths."[190] Just as the ontology of consciousness reveals that the project of bad faith is a "decision in bad faith on the nature of bad faith,"[191] so, too, the structure of belief reveals that every belief includes its own negation. Every belief reflects the structure and nature of consciousness, so that Sartre is able to say, "Every belief is a belief that falls short; one never wholly believes what one believes."[192] The question at this point is not whether Sartre can assert without incoherence the proposition that one can hold contradictory beliefs simultaneously; the question is how Sartre can do so given his premise of a unitary and transparent consciousness? To this question we now turn.

It should be clear that to ask "How can Sartre allow for self-deception?" is to ask about Sartre's conception of consciousness. What is its structure? What are its capacities? Given the above overview of Sartre's position on this issue, the answer to the question about a unitary and transparent consciousness holding contradictory beliefs will require us to say this: Sartre can allow for contradictory beliefs because on his conception of consciousness, contradictory beliefs express the way human beings exist in the world. Human beings, that is, are conscious subjects who are not what they are and are what they are not. Contradictory beliefs are part and parcel of existence as consciousness <u>exists</u> in the mode of "being-for-itself." Contradictory beliefs express a contradictory effort on the part of consciousness to reach for being and nothingness-at-the-heart-of-being. Contradictory beliefs express the dialectical nature of human being as that nature is defined as the attempt to combine the "for-itself" with the "in-itself." Such an effort is, by definition, contradictory and, incidentally, doomed to fail: "Man is a useless passion."[193] Self-deception is, in other words, a contradictory effort in which one attempts to be what one is when one also wishes to flee from the being that one is. This is how human beings exist and what they actually do.

Human reality is, according to Sartre, act,[194] and the project of bad faith represents the act of deciding not be be what one is. The person acts to believe what he or she does not believe--not wholeheartedly. The contradictoriness, then, constitutes a fact of life. Contradictoriness is what obtains when one exists in the "for-itself," in the dialectic manner of the "for-itself." Inquiry into the ontology of consciousness reveals this contradictoriness, so that when one enquires into the nature of consciousness, one discovers contradiction; and contradiction presents itself as an essential way of characterizing human reality as it enacts flight from being. To be caught up in this contradiction is what it means to exist as a conscious subject.

To be in bad faith means that one puts oneself in bad faith (action), but it also means that a consciousness divided against itself has acted to opposes one set of beliefs with another. What is apparent, then, is that contradictory beliefs constitute a phenomenon of human existence and make manifest the dialectical nature of consciousness. Consciousness itself is equipped to accommodate contradictory beliefs because consciousness is itself that structure which enables the flight from being to be enacted as a project to mislead belief.

For Sartre, bad faith is a clue to human reality and to the reality of consciousness. Self-deception is not only a possibility of consciousness; it is the inescapable risk at the heart of consciousness. To elucidate the phenomenon of bad faith is to elucidate the nature of consciousness itself. Given this assessment, Sartre intended to develop a picture of consciousness that would adequately account for the fact of bad faith, that would proffer a theory of structure that could accommodate and sanction the contradictoriness of human reality.

Sartre argued that consciousness is that structure of being that allows being to deny itself. Consciousness is that structure that enables being to mislead itself, to enact projects that are contradictory, to deceive itself. The contradiction Sartre described did not set up a logical problem to be solved--rather, it was itself a resolution to the problem of being and to the problem of being conscious. Sartre resolved the paradox of bad faith by identifying the "for-itself" as that aspect of being that opposes being. The "for-itself" is what it is, but it is by definition not "being-in-itself." Therefore, not to be what one is is to be this: a contradiction. And this is what we are. And what we are we are because we are what we are not. The contradiction is, in another sense, resolved because consciousness is identified as the structure that permits contradictory beliefs to obtain. The "for-itself" identifies this structure, and it is analytic that what it is is a contradiction. For Sartre, then, logic doesn't decide the facts--the facts yield a description for which a logic must be devised.

Sartre's formulation will not permit one to draw the conclusion that self-deception "cannot happen." Quite the contrary. The phenomenon of bad faith is itself neither a logical nor an existential impossibility since there is a structure available (consciousness) that permits contradiction to obtain in the form of opposing and contrary beliefs. This structure accommodates the contradictoriness in human reality that Sartre describes, and his dialectically conceived picture of consciousness allows for the human subject to be simultaneously aware and unaware, to be unaware of one of the beliefs even though the subject is engaged in action properly associated with--and governed by--the unavowed, disavowed, or unconsciously held belief.

Sartre resolves his original epistemological paradox by, first of all, refusing to describe self-deception as a person's conscious plot to lie to him- or herself; and, secondly, by appealing to a dialectical model of consciousness that accommodates cognitive opposition. These moves permit a description of intrapsychic opposition without also committing Sartre to the view that one must be fully aware of both of the beliefs. Sartre posits a pre-reflective awareness, which is a specific level of consciousness wherein one can be said not to know--know in the sense of forming judgments. Pre-reflective awareness, when combined with Sartre's picture of self as having temporally distinct aspects (past, present and future), and when added to the distinction he draws between the self as aware "for-itself" and "for-others," enables Sartre to picture a self deceiving itself. I shall say more about the last two features shortly, using an example, but the more immediate point to note is that Sartre pictures the self as of composite of relatedness. The various aspects of that composite are reflexively and dialectically related and in need of integration; and at no point is the self ever perfectly coordinated. By referring to structures of consciousness which are also aspects of the self, it is possible to say that one form of that disrelatedness may permit us to picture a self deceiving itself. To say that one person may be both deceiver and deceived does not mean, however, that one must be at any given moment wholly one or the other. No one aspect is all of myself, myself grasped "wholly."

Although we find Sartre able to resolve the paradox of self-deception, a confusion may persist due to the picture of consciousness he advances, a picture in which oppositions or contradictions (say: between beliefs) are permitted to stand. An analytic philosopher might ask, "Is this not a confusing picture of consciousness, unintelligible and riddled with paradox?" Although my answer to this is finally "No," I would note here that problems attach to Sartre's idiom. Due to a penchant for neologisms, Sartre opts for language that is cumbersome, and his explanations sometimes seem needlessly abstract. Sartre is, however, a deft illustrator of his philosophy, and, no doubt, each of the three examples of self-deception presented in this chapter --the pastor, Lon Nol and the shipowner--could be said to represent decisions in bad faith, decisions that effect a project of bad faith.

For those uncomfortable with Sartre's idiom, let me suggest that the essential Sartrian picture of bad faith can be illustrated in a mythical-poetic language that relies upon a more familiar symbol system. Consider the Genesis account of Adam in the Garden. Adam is created as "being-in-itself." He is what he is, which is to say he is neither alienated from being nor is he a subject transcending himself. But neither is Adam truly conscious. Because he is what he is, a perfect identity, his awareness is opaque and uninvolved in projects (decisions) to flee from being or to transcend his facticity. Then Adam experiences temptation by encountering an "other." He emerges from his dream-like state to consciousness. He begins to question himself, to objectify himself to himself, to idealize himself and imagine himself in other possibilities of being (God). His awakening to consciousness is an awakening to anxiety, alienation, and shame. He is faced with a decision. His grasp at the fruit of the knowledge of good and evil is a decision in which being moves toward consciousness and therefore away from being. Once conscious, Adam cannot return to his primal innocence. He cannot return to the opaqueness of "being-in-itself." Adam finds himself in a situation where he is no longer synthesized as "being-in-itself." His situation is now such that any synthesis of his conscious yet divided self will be of his own making.

Adam's task, like ours, is to attempt a synthesis between aspects of the self, between that which is what it is not (future self) and that which is not what it is (series of past acts). Alienated from being, from his original being-in-itself, Adam must now direct his actions to accord with the future ideal self whereby his life is given meaning, continuity and unity--the standard against which any project of bad faith will be measured. On Sartre's view, Adam could very well be unaware of this future ideal self yet still be pre-reflectively engaged in it as an unacknowledged avowal. Or, to be more precise, Adam could be aware but not know, so that any attempt to undertake a project that represents flight from being would constitute a knowing in conflict with a deeper awareness. Adam is in bad faith to the extent he successfully persuades himself to believe as true that which is not supported by the evidence. And what he comes to believe conflicts with his engagements as they present themselves in the world to others; and they conflict with his own deeper, pre-reflective awareness, which is itself in accord with the self-knowledge that becomes one's own through the mediation of others.[195]

A theologian would say that Adam has fallen, that he has rebelled against God, that he has sinned. Sartre would say Adam is conscious, a being-for-itself engaged in a project aimed at escape from being. Both would agree that Adam is now, after the fall, in a situation of conflict--he is no longer true to his nature. Both would agree that this condition is endemic, whether in terms of "original sin" (theologian), or in terms of being conscious and separated from one's true identity as being-in-itself (Sartre). I shall push the comparison no further, but I do believe that Sartre identifies in ontological terms a problem relevant to the theologian. The theologian faces the fact of human alienation from being (or the Source or Ground of Being), which, in turn, affirms the notion that we are not what we are, a condition of contradiction that is the human condition. This condition, for both Sartre and the theologian, is inescapable. Bad faith becomes a way of characterizing in the language of ontology what is conceived in religious terms as fallenness and sin--decisions made in bad faith which spontaneously determine our being as we exist as conscious subjects "for-itself."

Having attempted to discern more clearly the Sartrian picture of consciousness, which has been revealed by analyzing the phenomenon of "bad faith," let me conclude by addressing the problem of a unitary and transparent consciousness. We must acknowledge that Sartre himself does not mean to imply by his picture of consciousness that human subjects cannot be "fragmented," "unconscious," or even exempt from the need for psychotherapy. Perfect coordination of the various aspects of selfhood is an ideal. Again, the idea of the self-as-a-synthesis, or a self that has achieved this or that level of integration, does not require that any particular self is perfectly integrated or actually synthesized. Sartre's picture of the self as including past, present, and future aspects reveals that the self is always struggling for synthesis in its existential situation; but he nowhere states that it is actually synthesized or perfectly coordinated. Such synthesis would occur, or so I take it, only with respect to "being-in-itself" (Adam before the temptation). For Sartre, however, "being-in-itself" is opaque: being-for-itself, which by definition is not being-in-itself, is therefore unitary and transparent. That is, it is being-for-itself that is consciousness, and consciousness can conceive of itself as a unitary structure ("I am who I am"). It can see the content of its own consciousness even if it does so in "bad faith" and while fleeing from being. The question, however, is whether Sartre means by this that consciousness, which takes itself for its object, has access to all the contents of consciousness?

The notion of a "unitary and transparent" consciousness commits one to the view that consciousness has access to all its own contents. This is the meaning of "unitary and transparent" given ordinary linguistic features. This ordinary linguistic meaning is operative in those accounts of self-deception that deny the human capacity for simultaneous knowing and not knowing, believing and not believing, avowing and disavowing. I have held Sartre up as a proponent of this perspective. At this point, however, I must argue that Sartre's ability to resolve the paradox of self-deception rests on his ability to mean by "unitary and transparent" consciousness something other than this ordinary language meaning. In other words, Sartre has developed a technical and specialized use for "unitary and transparent" terminology. He so qualifies the notion of a "unitary and transparent" consciousness that he is able to conceptualize consciousness in a way that one might assume is incompatible with those terms. He conceives the human subject as being capable of being unaware of something that the subject is also pre-reflectively aware. He conceives the human subject as being aware but does not know, who is "unconscious" of his or her decisions and how he or she is actually engaged in the world "for others." Under the rubric of a unitary and transparent consciousness, Sartre presents a picture of consciousness persuading itself to believe something on the basis of unpersuasive evidence, doing so for reasons of preserving one's identity in way that is continuous with one's past acts and one's ideal future self. In short, he portrays a fragmented self divided against itself.

Is Sartre able to present a coherent picture of a human subject deceiving him- or herself under the conceptual umbrella of unitary and transparent consciousness? My answer to this question is, unfortunately, yes and no. No, if by that we mean that one can decide voluntarily and consciously (reflectively) to lie to oneself. This is as paradoxical to Sartre as to any analytic philosopher. Yes, if by that we understand that consciousness is capable of being aware (non-thetically) while simultaneously disavowing that of which it is aware. Yes, if by that we understand that the self is not unitary as an <u>actuality</u>, but as an ideal only; and that in the midst of fragmentation, one may "purposefully," yet "unconsciously," undertake actions to preserve one's identity. That is, Sartre makes it possible to say that in order for me to maintain a sense of meaning and continuity in my self-understanding, I may undertake a project to keep my identity consistent with my past and future self. And this project enables me to do so while keeping the true meaning of my acts is unavailable to my own reflection. "Consciousness is unitary and transparent"--but Sartre does not mean by that that I am unified, as if perfectly coordinated, or that I have access to all the contents of consciousness, as if that were what "transparency" or "translucence" meant.

Sartre does not conceive consciousness as having contents to which the self, or one's ego, is related. There is no transcendental ego that is capable of fashioning the contents of consciousness into intended objects of consciousness. Consciousness, rather, as Sartre argues in <u>The Transcendence of the Ego</u>,[196] is a spontaneity, and objects exist <u>for</u>, not <u>in</u>, consciousness. Consciousness is always a transcending toward objects, objects thereby being rendered fit for phenomenological analysis with consciousness present to objects in relation to the world and to others. Without going further into the "contentless" consciousness issue, which was, incidentally, the origin of Sartre's dispute with Husserl, let me reiterate the point important for this discussion, namely, that Sartre does provide room in his picture of consciousness, particularly in his pre-reflective (non-thetic) picture of essential self-consciousness, for actual "unawareness" to obtain relative to a more basic "awareness." There is also room in that picture for what we might term "intrapsychic" conflict. Sartre's picture of a unitary and transparent consciousness does not commit him to a view of privileged access,[197] a view that he denies even though he considers self-understanding or first-person evaluation crucial data. In this he and Freud are in agreement. And Sartre adds in his discussion of an existential psychoanalysis the following:

> Existential psychoanalysis rejects the hypothesis of the unconscious; it makes the psychic act coextensive with consciousness. But if the fundamental project is fully experienced by the subject and hence wholly conscious, that certainly does not mean that it <u>must</u> by the same token be <u>known</u> by him. Quite the contrary.[198]

A lot rides on this last qualification. It seems clear that Sartre is not equating a unitary and transparent consciousness with a perspective that necessarily--by definition--excludes any and every notion of "unconsciousness." In this passage, Sartre is disputing Freud's Theory of the Unconscious, which, as I have already explained, Sartre misrepresented in important respects. What Sartre is saying is that consciousness grasps the whole, but is able, because of bad faith, to <u>see</u> (or <u>know</u>) only a part. If Sartre meant by "unitary and transparent" that self-deception must mean a reflectively conceived and linguistically explicit lie to one's own self, Sartre would have presented himself with a paradox he could not resolve. He goes to great lengths to formulate the paradox this way, but he explicitly rejects the idea that a strict model of other-deception will adequately inform us about the nature of consciousness or the dynamics of intrapsychic deceptive relations. Sartre sought to resolve the paradox of simultaneous believing and not-believing, and <u>Being and Nothingness</u> is his attempt to do so. He resolves the paradox of self-deception via his theory of consciousness, which is dialectical and compatible with a self-relatedness and holistic conception of self.

Sartre's theory of consciousness proffers the view that consciousness is capable of grasping the whole while seeing only a part of what it grasps. It is this dual capacity, which is actually a structural feature of mind, that provides the psychic division necessary for "inner conflict," and it is this dual capacity that is required for Sartre to present coherently a non-paradoxical picture of self-deception.

The interpreters of Sartre who hold that Sartre fails to resolve his own paradox have been mislead at precisely this point: the meaning of "unitary" and "transparent." It is clear that self-deception could not happen given the premise of an actually unified and transparent consciousness; for then consciousness, knowing all it perceives, could not mislead itself about what it knows. Were consciousness transparent, one would achieve privileged access to the entire contents of consciousness and affirm an identity such as this: "As a unitary consciousness, I am what I am, I know what I am--and that's all that I am." Sartre, however, rejects this understanding. Sartre claims that a unitary and transparent consciousness commits one to a view where the human subject can be aware yet unaware. On the picture of consciousness he advances, Sartre claims consciousness is capable of deciding for projects in essential conflict with self-consciousness and identity, so that contrary to ordinary language meaning, "unitary and transparent" consciousness means that "I am what I am not and am not what I am." This is asserted ambiguously, though not paradoxically. "Not knowing" on Sartre's view means that consciousness can apprehend and achieve awareness without that awareness becoming <u>fully</u>, actually knowable. It is even possible to say that an epistemic deficit obtains because a subject can actually grasp pre-reflectively or non-thetically what he or she does not reflectively <u>know</u>:

We are not dealing with an unsolved riddle as the Freudians

believe; all is there, luminous; reflection is in full possession of it, apprehends all. But this 'mystery in broad daylight' is due to the fact that this possession is deprived of the means which would ordinarily permit <u>analysis</u> and <u>conceptualization</u>.[199]

Here, then, is the form of the epistemic deficit: due to purposeful activity on the part of a human subject, who is conscious and therefore capable of transcendence, that which is apprehended may be prevented from becoming linguistically explicit, fully recognized or avowed. On Sartre's dialectical model of consciousness, self-deception is like a mystery in broad daylight.

What we must recognize is that Sartre did not aim to eliminate "unconsciousness" or "unawareness" as descriptive features of human behavior and action. On the contrary, he assumes such features. His theory of consciousness was designed to account for the phenomenon of unawareness and contradictory behavior in a way that did not beg questions about human freedom--the source, Sartre believed, of Freud's failure. The fact that Sartre did not deny the phenomenon of human unawareness provides the necessary qualification that permits one to say that on Sartre's account, even as expressed in the language of "unitary and transparent" consciousness, a human subject is so constituted as to be capable of being <u>unaware</u>, yet <u>aware</u>, or capable of simultaneously believing <u>p</u> and <u>not-p</u>. Furthermore, human subjects are capable of being unaware of one of the opposing beliefs since we can refuse--though not voluntarily in a reflective sense--to avow an engagement in the world as our own. We can refuse to analyze and conceptualize a belief we holds nonthetically though others can attribute that belief to us by observing the behavioral acts. That is, self-deceivers act such that they interpret their own actions as being consistent with a belief about those actions, which is the interpretation they wish; yet this very move also constitutes a refusal to avow or consciously appropriate the belief which <u>others</u> more readily adjudge to be the true belief (the best, most reasonable interpretation) governing the action. Self-deceivers, then, do not know the true meaning of their acts, and that reveals the unawareness. Such unawareness is seen as the result of motivated action, of decision, of an actual "project" aimed at the misleading of belief.

Reflective human subjects on Sartre's view are capable of engaging in a project the meaning of which escapes them. The subject intends--though not <u>fully</u> aware of the intention--to flee being by engaging in the bad faith project, which allows the person to believe and not-believe. In bad faith, a self-deceiver engages in interpretive activity that is based on unpersuasive evidence. That evidence the subject wishes to take as persuasive since by so doing he or she will believe something that is consistent with past action and future self. This is an "identity" motive--Fingarette owes this feature of his account to Sartre--that initiates the project aimed at the misleading of belief so that the belief arrived at is a belief that is also an escape from being--bad faith. In short, this is an account that includes both action and cognition features. It is complicated, perhaps, but not paradoxical.

Sartre does not deny that the self can experience conflict, that it can be disintegrated, fragmented or uncoordinated. Sartre argues just the opposite. In fact, his picture of consciousness as "for-itself" is, by definition, consciousness in conflict. Were Sartre committed to the notion of a unitary and transparent consciousness in what I would term its literal, ordinary language appeal, his reductio of Freudian psychoanalysis would constitute a reduction of psychoanalysis in general, since psychoanalysis is premised on the idea of "inner conflict" and "unawareness," notions inimical to what we would ordinarily mean by "unitary and transparent consciousness." Sartre, however, proposes his own version of psychoanalysis in the latter sections of Being and Nothingness. How can we account for this? My view is that although Sartre's "existential psychoanalysis" is markedly distinct from Freud's version, it is a consistent development within the ontological enterprise itself. That is, "existential psychoanalysis" is a logical step in Sartre's unfolding philosophical project. If one accepts the kind of meaning I have attempted to present for "unitary and transparent" consciousness, Sartre's account of self-deception falls into place as coherent and non-paradoxical; and Sartre need not defend his belief that under the rubric of "unitary and transparent consciousness" "psychoanalysis" is still a necessity, since his presentation of consciousness has, like Freud's, showed us a self broken and in conflict, needing aid and able to find, through the "other," healing.

c. **Conclusion**

Sartre and Freud are not on intimate terms in the sense that each could comfortably converse in the other's lingo. That is a fact, and Sartre's criticism of Freud is sufficient to establish that as a fact. On the level of explanation, Sartre and Freud are doomed to endless and fruitless argument. If they could establish a bond of unity at all, certainly it would not be between the language of metapsychology and the language of ontology, both explanatory languages. Yet this too needs to be said: neither are they thoroughly estranged interpreters of the human experience. Operating from the assumption that some translation is both possible and profitable, I have presented Sartre and Freud to highlight an actual similarity: To the extent that one can say of both Freud and Sartre that each has attended to the phenomenon, and to the concept, of self-deception, they are--must be--in essential agreement as to the particularities of conceptual content. Both accept the reality of intrapsychic conflict; both conceive consciousness or the mind as being so structured that it is capable of keeping from explicit linguistic avowal some belief that is attributable to the subject's behavior by an outsider--Freud's analyst or Sartre's "other." Both agree on the cognitive nature of the result, the epistemic deficit that obtains, and it can be inferred on either account that opposing beliefs simultaneously held are manifest as the observable difference between the subject's professed interpretation and the best, most reasonable interpretation of his or her acts. Both agree that the subject's "unawareness" of the true meaning of the behavior obtains as the result of intentional and purposeful activity--a self-directed "belief-misleading" project if you will.

If it can be demonstrated that the phenomenon of "resistance" on the one hand, and the denials of "bad faith" on the other, are part and parcel of what we ordinarily mean when we ascribe 'self-deception.' We then find ourselves in a position to appreciate two views previously mentioned; first, the view that all neurosis entails self-deception (T. Mischel), at least with respect to the phenomenon of resistance and the notion of "mechanisms of defense."[200] Secondly, we are in a position to appreciate Sartre's own remark to the effect that Being and Nothingness was conceived and executed as an eidetic analysis of self-deception.[201]

In this section, I have attempted to demonstrate how one would go about supporting these assertions, not as an exercise in eisegesis, but as interpretations warranted by a study of Freud's meta-psychology and Sartre's ontological project. My case is simply this: If Sartre and Freud are addressing themselves to the topic of self-deception and not to some other concept or phenomenon, then we should reasonably expect them to be addressing the same thing, namely, some phenomenon of human experience for which 'self-deception' serves as an adequate and accurate linguistic marker. I believe this to be so, and inasmuch as that belief is itself warranted, both Freud and Sartre can be said to be addressing a phenomenon for which the necessary and sufficient criteria for ascribing 'self-deception' appropriately apply.

C. Synthesis: The Emotional Perception Account

From the perspective of philosophical psychology, 'self-deception' is a problematic concept. The difficulties involved in analyzing the concept are apparent in the wide variety of accounts, in the striking difference of opinion over what self-deception is--if it "is" at all--and how one is to understand it. A consensus about normative conceptual status has not obtained, and the controversy has led to diametrically opposed interpretations, like that between the strict cognitivist and the strict action proponent. A strict cognitivist will affirm the epistemic nature of the concept, diminishing if not altogether denying action features. On the other hand, a strict action account will discount "thought, belief, and knowledge" altogether, doing so in order to emphasize the action character of the concept. Both of these "extremes" emphasize a necessary feature of conceptual content, a feature accessible through ordinary language analysis; but each is inadequate to the extent that it excludes the other.

In this chapter we have examined various models of self-deception, and the strict accounts we have found wanting. The strict cognitivist who denies action features eliminates the purposeful character of self-deception, and this reduces self-deception to error or mistake. Different difficulties arise for the strict action proponent, who will beg questions about cognition--thought, knowledge and belief. Fingarette was shown to be operating from an inadequate notion of cognition, and I criticized his action account because it is inconceivable that one could picture "avowal" or a "motive of identify preservation" without reference to belief. Without cognition, it is not clear that one can speak of human action, for human action expresses intent and purpose and is governed by belief. That we might not always be aware of our purpose or belief is not only a familiar experience, but it is this everyday form of unawareness that provides grounds for saying that the belief governing our action is itself "unconscious." And it is by knowing persons in the common life that we come to understand that this "unconsciousness" is motivated--there are reasons why we do not want to recognize the meaning of our behavior. It is on the basis of this picture of unawareness that we can say that in self-deception one cannot "spell-out" an engagement in the world--an engagement that is one's own but which one disavows as one's own.

The problem with the translation models is that they rid us of the concept 'self-deception' as that concept is meaningful in the common life. It is a question-begging model that asks us to retire 'self-deception' from everyday discourse. It is not, however, at all clear that self-deception "cannot happen." Neither is it self-evident that 'self-deception' is meaningful only as a linguistically misleading expression. The evidence of the common life counts against both of these claims. The translation models can be shown to be inadequate because of unjustifiable assumptions about the nature of human consciousness and its capacity for opposing itself. Such accounts deny that human beings are capable of accommodating contradictory beliefs simultaneously and can engage in activities designed--even if unawares--to cover up the best, most reasonable interpretation of their actions. It is clear that in many familiar situations a person's unawareness may seem to provide psychological advantage--that it does not result from an innocent error or stupid blunder, but is a clever, even intricate scheme to keep awareness away. This claim can be appealed to the common life, for this phenomenon of intentional cover-up is a fact of our psychological experience. We can reflect on situations where this has been the case in our own experience; and we can observe it frequently in others. A non-problematic translation of 'self-deception' has not been put forward and is not likely to be.

Sartre and Freud eliminate the paradox of self-deception by postulating their respective theories of mental life on a model of integration/disintegration. Both models establish that there is a human capacity for enacting opposing beliefs, that the result of such opposition may be that one of those beliefs is acted upon while the meaning of the act is prevented by a "belief-misleading project" from becoming linguistically explicit and available to the subject him- or herself. Freud's picture of ego-activity and Sartre's theory of dialectical consciousness provide pictures of mental life in essential agreement with the requirement that self-deception be conceived reflexively, in terms of self-relatedness. Both Freud and Sartre include <u>action</u> and <u>cognition</u> in their accounts, thus providing grounds for a coherent account of self-deception, one compatible with ordinary language features. This harmony of ideas on the self-deception issue does not mean, of course, that Freud and Sartre agree on other theoretical or explanatory issues of importance.

As one surveys the various analyses of self-deception, it becomes clear that the best account available from the perspective of philosophical psychology is one that is able to eliminate paradox while accommodating both cognitive and action features. Those accounts that deny one aspect or affirm one at the expense of the other can be shown to be inadequate to the extent they fail to synthesize action and cognition into one coherent account. The distinction Fingarette draws between "action-volition" and "cognition-perception" families of terms is only helpful if the distinction clarifies how the concept 'self-deception' reaches into both. Those families are inter-related, and to miss or deny that inter-relatedness is invite paradox or beg questions. As John Turk Saunders has written--and this view supports my own--

> [The] 'volition-action' family of terms is so laden with notions having to do with belief, perception, consciousness and knowledge that a non-paradoxical account of self-deception cannot be advanced in terms of the latter family without also being advanced in terms of the former family ['cognition-perception']. The two families crucially overlap.[202]

My position is that an account of self-deception will only prove adequate if it conforms to ordinary language analysis. The ordinary language analysis presented a "synthetic" account of self-deception, for it described a project directed by the self (action) aimed at (intention) the misleading of belief (cognitive result). The three examples of self-deception presented in this chapter can be so analyzed that they exhibit the action-cognition character of the phenomenon. If we were to interpret the pastor, Lon Nol, or the shipowner in light of action alone, or only cognition, the inevitable problems would arise. Analysis of behavior, however, allows us to infer that the ignorance or failure in self-understanding exhibited by these self-deceivers is, in fact, motivated, which is to say that a coherent account must include the fact that a cognitive result obtains (epistemic deficit) for certain action-related reasons. 'Self-deception' is what it says it is--and because it is, it is to be regarded as a meaningful cipher of communication in the common life.

Ordinary language analysis yields a normative view of the concept 'self-deception.' The result of that analysis meets our requirements for conceptual adequacy. I have accepted the givens of the philosophers who have looked into the topic, and I have taken seriously the problem of paradox as they have formulated it. Self-deception is, after all, a problem because it seems paradoxical. The ordinary language analysis, however, is not cowed by the paradox or thwarted in its efforts to resolve it. The ordinary language analysis yields the conclusion that because of the capacity of human consciousness to maintain unawareness of a belief for reasons of psychological gain, yet to act on that belief because "action is governed by belief," what appears logically contradictory is not actually contradictory but descriptive of certain facts. The contradiction that one person can hold two contradictory beliefs simultaneously can be explained, thus resolved, by showing that both beliefs are simultaneously enacted. The description will point to the ability of persons to profess one belief at odds with their own behavior yet consistent with a self-image (p), while suppressing a belief inconsistent with self-image yet so held ("unconsciously") that one is disposed one to act on it (not-p). And self-deceivers do act on it. The paradox can be eliminated as a problem in logic; but that does not mean that opposition is done away with: the intrapsychic conflict is manifest in a publicly observable behavioral opposition.

Is the synthesis of action and cognition that arises from ordinary language analysis beyond controversy? Clearly not. The entire picture of "unconscious belief" or "unconscious intention" needs more specific attention from philosophers, particularly action theorists. I would offer as an opinion that there is a certain strain in the modern analytic tradition that has resisted investigation of such notions for reasons that spring as much from bias as from adherence to principles of logic. Clearly, in the view of this analytic perspective such notions are considered question-begging. And I say "bias" because logical assertions are sometimes put forward as empirical assertions without attending to empirical evidence. Empirical findings, however, are available to challenge the premise of the logic, be those findings in the form of Sackeim and Gur experiments or reflections on the common life.

The assertion that self-deception cannot happen because the concept is literally a paradox is based on an assumption that logic is larger than life. There is evidence available to support the contention that there is conflict and unawareness present in the common life of human persons--not only from psychologists, but from the observations of poets, playwrights, novelists, philosophers, and all those who reflect on their own experiences of "unawareness" and conclude, "I knew that all along." I am not saying logic has no place here, only that the premises of the logic that claims "self-deception cannot happen" are themselves question-begging and controversial. My use of "unconscious belief" has been a logical inference based on the evidence of publicly observable behavior and first-person interpretations of that behavior. There are no doubt certain philosophers who would hold that "belief" is necessarily confined to linguistically explicit propositions, thereby discounting my view. I contend, however, that action theorists and philosophers concerned with psychological concepts may, in the future, provide further clarification and support for the notion I have adopted as operative and normative, namely, the view that action, inasmuch as it is human action, is governed by belief; and that action that is misunderstood or misinterpreted, or that is linguistically unavailable to the agent for discernible reasons of psychological gain is still, to extrapolate the empirical dictum enunciated by William James, "action measured by belief."[203]

For a human subject to act, yet to be unaware of the meaning of his or her act, and for there to be psychological gain in the fact of the unawareness --judgments that can be made and commonly are made--constitute the interpersonal experience to which my own analysis appeals. I find incoherence neither in the the idea of an "unconscious belief," nor in the idea that such a belief may dispose one to action. I do recognize that this view may be challenged, but those who would challenge it and conclude that it is incoherent would also deny that self-deception is a feature of the common life. I have conceded that 'self-deception' is a problematic concept, and I have presented the positions of those who would deny on logical grounds that there is an empirical phenomenon that fits the ordinary linguistic meaning of 'self-deception.' My analysis in these pages addresses those objections to the extent that they can be addressed in the spirit of dialogue and debate. No discussion seems profitable, however, with one who would deny self-deception a priori on the grounds that it is actually a logical contradiction and that to impute 'self-deception' is to impute something that cannot possibly be.

Another difficulty has to do with how to conceive consciousness, mind, or the reality of mental functioning. Sartre's language of "unitary and transparency" is difficult language in that it can be taken to mean that a unitary and transparent consciousness not only excludes any possibility of intrapsychic conflict, but disallows any functional view of unconsciousness--except as ignorance or error. What must be said in support of Sartre's notion--and the idea of a unitary consciousness or mind (self-consciousness) arises in the thought of figures as diverse as Augustine, Kant, and Chisholm--is, for present purposes, this: The idea of an unawareness that is parasitic on a prior, linguistically unavailable or unrecognized awareness must be included in any positive and coherent account of self-deception. Even Sackeim and Gur, outspoken opponents of a "unitary and transparent" consciousness, include in their analysis a reference to a prior recognition on which a measure of anxiety can be based, which is to say that here, too, one finds an assumption that the subject is aware on some level "deep down." That this happens is not so much in dispute as how or why this is possible--and the how or why is certainly not adequately explained by asserting that human consciousness is so constituted as to make this unawareness a possible way of being conscious. That becomes a descriptive remark which occasions the kind of explanatory treatments one finds in Sartre or Freud. The point is that one who deceives oneself about p must in some "unconscious" sense recognize the significance of p and form some kind of judgment about p prior to--and in opposition to--one's declared statement about p. I want to say that this picture of consciousness, which is ingredient in any adequate account of self-deception, can be described, experienced, reported, and logically inferred from publicly observable behavior.

Even though I have examined certain descriptions of 'self-deception' within the contexts of certain explanatory systems, I have not attempted to critique those systems, even synthetic ones like Sartre's or Freud's, except to point out the extent to which the picture of self-deception presented in the context of those systems preserves the integrity of the concept 'self-deception' and accounts for the concept coherently. All of the explanations as to why self-deception obtains, why human subjects are in conflict and psychically uncoordinated, are presented against a backdrop of theory that is--if nothing else--controversial. Detractors are legion.[204] And, when coupled with our inability to explain without controversy how certain psychophysical structures, processes or events are related to the actual instantiation of self-deception, one is led to conclude the following: Beneath descriptions, which themselves have become for philosophical psychologists the problematic features as well as the object of study and inquiry, there lies a deeper unknown about human persons and how they are constituted. Dispelling the problems associated with adequate description leads one to consider possible explanations, which, in the end, must remain speculative. In the end, one is left wondering about the mystery of consciousness and the mystery of being human. Currently there is no explanation available--be it psychological, philosophical, ethical or religious--that escapes the dilemma of being an "alternative explanation," and which, from the point of view of philosophical psychology itself, is free of question-begging features or is not steeped in arguable assumptions and controversy.[205]

A final issue concerns the nature of the object of self-deception and what I take to be a related issue: the motive for self-deception. Fingarette has made the case, persuasively I think, that self-deception is a result of one's attempt to preserve one's sense of identity in the face of certain actions that challenge it. In other words, the object of self-deceptive activity, whatever it be in particular, is perceived--on some level of awareness "deep down"--to be threatening to one's sense of personal continuity. As such one's response to that threat becomes denial or disavowal, which is then enacted in a project to mislead one's beliefs. In the idea "identity" we find the spur for self-deceptive activity: We deceive ourselves in response to a perceived threat. What is threatened is our sense of personal identity.

Specifying "identity" as the motive for self-deception helps to clarify the nature of that object in relation to which self-deception obtains. Identity, however, does not of itself indicate the kind of moral complexity involved in self-deception, not does it provide the most concise characterization of the "object." I shall remark on each of these issues, then outline a constructive "synthetic" account of self-deception. My emotional perception account of self-deception is offered in the spirit of the "philosophical psychology" perspective that has been my concern in this chapter.

The case can be made that self-deception is morally ambiguous inasmuch as a self-deceiver's cover-up attempts to preserve a self-image that is itself constructed for moral reasons, though the defensive deception activity appears to be undertaken not for moral reasons, but for reasons of prudence (self-interest). By this I mean that persons understand themselves to persons of a certain sort: they affirm the action-guides of a moral community and believe themselves to be morally constituted individuals. Identity hangs on a long term pattern of behavior that can be projected into the future; and it hangs on self-knowledge, which is acquired from persons learning to confront themselves reflectively: chiding, accusing, admonishing and praising themselves as they seek to live consistently with moral ideas, even the ideal of moral perfection. Self-deception can arise whenever our actions have been such that they violate that sense of identity or contradict our moral self-image. Of course, one need not deceive oneself when such a violation occurs. One can "own up to" the violation and admit that one deserves censure. But one can also "dis-own" it, refusing to admit that the meaning of the action is such that it constitutes a violation or merits censure. If one opts for the self-deception route, one will have perceived one's own failure to adhere to avowed norms of right conduct. The prospect of admitting this failure would occasion psychological trauma. So painful and distressing is the prospect of admitting what "deep down" one "knows, believes or perceives" to be action meriting self-censure, that one opts to situate oneself such that direct, linguistically explicit self-confrontation is postponed, delayed, avoided. This is describable as flight from moral responsibility. On the other hand, this is flight in the midst of the moral context. The individual perceives that the moral self-image has been violated by action that is one's own, action for which the individual alone is responsible. In seeking to preserve one's identity, one is seeking to preserve the conditions of moral being; yet, by enacting a "belief-misleading project," one is acting from a self-interested (prudential) reason. One's aim is to avoid the censure of conscience and to evade what is "perceived" to be the inevitable pain of self-recognition.

A self-deceiver attempts to evade the truth by refusing to inquire into the meaning of his or her own actions, preferring to interpret those actions in a way consistent with a general pattern of past acts and future ideals. Actions that do not obviously conform are "rationalized." That is, they are "excused" by reasons that fit the self-image but not the act itself. An actual disruption in the pattern does occur, however, and the self-deceiver's refusal to inquire into the meaning of that disruption leads to a situation where, morally speaking, the person can be said to be violating a self-regarding duty to "know thyself."[206] There is ambiguity here, as well as a moral context. The ambiguity is that only a morally constituted person can be a candidate for self-deception; yet the specific reasons for the self-deceptive action are not solely directed to the end of preserving a moral self-identity. More to the point, the self-deceiver who perceives the threat to the self-image is motivated by a desire to avoid pain. The reasons for action are self-interested, prudential, rather than purely moral. Moral identity is preserved only by acting consistently with one's moral self-image. The self-deceiver has violated that self-image in some way; deep down he or she knows it; and because it would occasion pain and distress to acknowledge this failure, the self-deceiver is possessed of reason (motive) to cover up the best, most reasonable interpretation of the inconsistent action.

We are describing a volitional conflict. In self-deception, one decides to act with respect to p, but one also decides not to acknowledge as one's reason for action those reasons consistent with a belief that p. To the outsider, the observer, the friend of the self-deceiver, it is apparent that the self-deceiver has deceived him- or herself about the nature of the motive for disruptive action. This is to say that a person's declared intention with respect to the action in question is at odds with an ascribable motive: a self-deceiver, as an aspect of the self-deception, is deceived about the meaning of action and the reasons for the action. Self-deceivers interpret their reasons for action as being consistent with an avowed moral self-image, though they wrongfully interpret the action, being motivated to do so by prudential reasons (i.e., pain avoidance). In seeking to preserve identity and avoid the pain of self-confrontation, self-deceivers undertake to mislead their own beliefs, which results in the creation of an epistemic deficit. The deficit appears between a prudential motive, which is acted on and governed by certain beliefs despite the fact that those beliefs are not explicitly acknowledged by the self-deceiver; and the professed motive, which is acknowledged and consistent with the person's moral self-image but which is not true.

Self-deceivers deceive themselves about their reasons for action, but to identify motive is not to identify the original object in relation to which the self-deception obtains. The original object must be an object of a certain quality. The original object must be "perceived" to be "threatening," for it is in response to an object perceived to be threatening that one undertakes a project to mislead belief. We must ask why that epistemic object appears threatening. This is an issue philosophical psychologists have generally failed to address. It is, however, a crucial question relevant to any attempt to anatomize the concept 'self-deception,' and it provides an opportunity to present another sort of account, which I here propose.

It is clear that one cannot deceive oneself about just anything. As I noted in the first chapter, to be deceived about such things as whether one is a college graduate or married is to be <u>deluded</u> about the nature of reality. To be deluded is to have lost a grip on those minimal facts of one's identity required for participation in the common life. This is not the case with self-deception. We must ask other questions: "What is it about the object that is perceived to be threatening that occasions the response of self-deception?" "What feature or quality do the objects that occasion self-deception share?"

My response to this question is that for an epistemic object to serve as an occasion for self-deception, that object must constitute an passional interest at odds with another passional interest. A passional interest, to define it, is any interest that effects a movement of the self toward synthesis. A concern for one's moral identity constitutes such an interest. In self-deception, however, one is attempting to preserve this identity in the fact of a challenge to that identity posed by another particular epistemic object--an object perceived to be threatening to that identity. The care, the concern, the love that is invested in one's commitment ("passional interest") to an identity, the reflexive care that is involved in the human project to achieve self-synthesis, is opposed by an object believed "deep down" to be threatening. The object perceived to be threatening, then, provides the occasion for self-deception. It can only threaten, however, if it is also an object related to reflexive care--it must be a desired object and desired because one perceives the object to be worthy of possession and capable of satisfying some identity-related need. The catch is that this desired object is also (simultaneously) perceived in light of one's moral self-understanding to be inimical to one's self-image. As I shall explain, one wants it but doesn't want it. The object occasions care at the same time it is perceived to be contrary to what one loves, values and cares about--or ought to. What occurs is that one's care is divided, and, as a result, one experiences a holistic sense of self that is, in fact, a false synthesis, a synthesis that one refuses to acknowledge as false.

The person who is self-deceived is unaware that the epistemic object in relation to which one deceives oneself is of a threatening nature--though the self-deceiver "believes" it to be so "unconsciously." The true nature of the object-as-threatening is suppressed, resisted, and disavowed by the self-deceiver, as is the knowledge that this object is also desired (which is why it is threatening). The question, then, is "How does the self-deceiver perceive, know or believe in the first instance that the object is of such a character that it constitutes a threat to the subjects self-image or identity?" I suggest here that a positive account of the self-deception phenomenon should proceed on the basis of a "cognition/action" theory of <u>emotion</u> in order to <u>explain</u> what has been described in these pages as 'self-deception.'

On the account I am here proposing, the object perceived to be threatening is cognitively available as an object to a knower. The knower, however, does not make his "belief" that the object is threatening linguistically explicit. That does not mean that the object cannot be grasped cognitively; neither does it mean that its "threatening quality" is beyond the ken of epistemic apprehension. My view is that the object in question is grasped as an epistemic object through the emotions. In other words, there is an "emotional perception" of the object. This means, first of all, that the subject perceives an object, such perception being a function of <u>cognition</u>. Beyond this act of perception, however, the subject also apprehends that the object is of a certain quality, which is to say that it is capable of "affecting" one's behavioral response and one's action in relation to it. One perceives, albeit unawares or pre-reflectively, that this object disposes one to act in a certain way. By making this connection between perception and behavioral response, we lend credence to the idea that emotions--or "affections"--are, as certain philosophers have concluded, <u>action</u> concepts.

Self-deception obtains when a person so perceives an epistemic object that he or she reacts by refusing to make linguistically explicit the true meaning of that object. The self-deceiver interprets the object in a rational way, explaining the object in terms compatible with one's self-image. The professed interpretation, however, is at odds with the best, most reasonable interpretation of the object. The self-deceiver is aware of that best, most reasonable interpretation, not in a linguistically explicit way but as it is perceived through the emotions. In other words, one understands the meaning of that object through an emotional perception of its "threatening" quality. Self-deception, then, obtains in relation to an object (cognition), and the object is of such a quality that it disposes one to act by "affecting" one's behavioral response (action). This "emotional perception" occurs on a level of apprehension that is cognitive yet not linguistically explicit.

This account is based on the common life understanding that to be versed in the language and grammar of emotion is to have acquired competence in comprehending the emotions themselves. We acquire competence by learning to make linguistically explicit non-linguistically explicit affections. This is a complex, though quite ordinary process, and it includes such things as our acquiring the ability to identify an emotion's appropriate object, to differentiate one emotion from another, and to develop a discriminating linguistic repertoire. All of these meaning tasks related to the language of emotion are of piece with acquiring self-mastery. Linguistic discrimination accompanies emotional development, and to acquire this repertoire of emotion is to account for the diversity and depth experienced in one's affective life. In self-deception, we perceive an object <u>emotionally</u>. We can be said to hold a certain belief about the object in relation to which we deceive ourselves, namely, that it is threatening. But our linguistically explicit evaluation of the object about its threatening quality is so construed--and distorted--that our professed belief about the meaning of that object conflicts with the original emotional perception. In self-deception, our non-linguistically explicit awareness, which is of a piece with "unconscious belief (<u>p</u>)," is opposed by interpretive activity that yields a linguistically explicit evaluation of the object and its meaning. What is made linguistically explicit is an opposing belief, that <u>not-p</u>. This conflict would not lead to the enacting of a belief-misleading project save for a concern (motive) to preserve one's self-image or identity. Some object, whatever it be in particular, is emotionally perceived--believed--to be threatening to that identity, and it is in reaction to that emotional perception and as a response to the desire to preserve one's identity from threat that one begins to construe the object in a linguistically explicit way so that a "non-threatening" interpretation results. Thus, one can be said to believe some object to be threatening (p) and yet not believe it to be threatening (not-p).

An adequate account of the emotions will support this view of things, for an adequate account of the emotions will entail a cognitive aspect for the emotions themselves. Emotions have objects, and those objects are discerned--perceived--cognitively. That emotions have objects is a necessary feature of emotions, and analysis of the language of emotion will bear this observation out. That we can recognize and identify an emotion with respect to its appropriate object is a familiar experience, and we can even discern when mistakes are made in relation to the object. That we are able to be linguistically accurate in our use of the language of emotion is neither necessary to having an emotion nor being aware of its appropriate object. It is a commonplace, after all, that we can respond emotionally to objects without being able to identify the object correctly: we can make errors about emotions as we can make errors about anything else. Lack of self-knowledge is sufficient to explain why one might be in error as to which object is appropriate to the emotion in question. Having said that, let me offer the view that an emotion is a way of construing or "seeing-as" (cognition-perception family of terms) that disposes one to action.

My claim is that self-deception arises in response to a perceived and believed threat to some value or interest deemed integral to one's sense of identity (passional interest). That we can engage in projects to mislead our beliefs indicates that when we perceive a certain epistemic object as threatening, we are disposed to act on that perception in a way that "affects" beliefs themselves. To construe an epistemic object as threatening is to be disposed to act in a certain way consistent with that perception. This construal is dispositional and intentional, not merely mistaken; again, it is in light of a particular interest (reflexive care, identity) that one responds to the object this way rather than that. It can be said, then, that the phenomenon of self-deception arises when an emotion obtains such that one undertakes a project to enact a disposition to "construe-as-threatening" a perceived object. We can construe an object as threatening without acknowledging in a linguistically explicit way that we are aware either of the threatening nature of the object or that the object is the appropriate object for our affection (or passional interest). We can enact such a project without being explicitly aware that we believe the object to be threatening, without being explicitly aware of the disposition to act, which is itself governed by the emotional perception. Emotions have objects, but only self-knowledge and acquired competence in the language of emotion will enable us to construe an emotion accurately, that is, in terms of its appropriate object.

My case is that we can apprehend via the emotions that a perceived object is of a certain affective quality (i.e., "threatening"). Furthermore, this "emotional perception" of the "threatening" quality of the object is a perception that precedes any attempt by individuals to interpret--to make linguistically explicit--to themselves the nature of the object. There is, then, an emotional perception prior to the uniquely human attempt to reflect on the nature of the perceived object. We perceives the quality of an object prior to putting into propositional form a claim that the perceived object is threatening, or worthy of love, or cause for jealousy and so on. I am distinguishing simple cognitive perception that perceives only an object from perception that perceives the emotional or affective tone of an epistemic object.

I propose the view that it is through "emotional perception" that one sees (cognition-perception family of terms) the object, but also experiences more than the object, namely, the "feeling" that it is an object of, say, a threatening quality. To see the object, then, is to be affected, and to be affected is to be disposed to act in accordance with what on sees (action-volition family of terms). Ordinarily, to perceive a threat affects one such that one either seeks flight from the threatening object (and experiences anxiety), or one seeks some kind of accommodation that has the effect of diminishing the threatening quality. My case is that this notion of "emotional perception" accounts for the gap between perception of an object and belief that it is of a certain quality, and one's professed belief about that object, a linguistic interpretation at odds with the original perception. A behavioral gap obtains. It is a gap between a person's action and a person's interpretation of that action, which does not square with the best, most reasonable interpretation. To make this case is to say that a gap exists between perception (non-linguistic, but still cognitive) and linguistically explicit reflection wherein one explains or interprets the action.

Within this gap, there is room for error or mistake, since one can be ignorant or otherwise incapacitated with respect to making linguistically explicit connections that are consistent with the linguistic community's general rules for putting this object in relation to that emotion. Education and training in the language and grammar of emotion is the obvious remedy for such "error." For a self-deceiver, however, the error or misinterpretation is not attributable to an unintentional mistake. Rather, the error appears to have "reasons for action" behind it. The interpretation that the self-deceiver explicitly professes constitutes a behaviorally manifest unawareness as to the meaning of his or her own actions. The unawareness obtains for certain reasons. It is unawareness motivated by a desire to avoid what has already been perceived as threatening. Self-deceivers act contrary to the best, most reasonable interpretation of their action; and they do so because they also desire to interpret their own behavior in terms that express the unity and integrity of their self-identity: what has been perceived is construed emotionally as threatening to that identity. The "identity motive" supplies reasons for action that enable individuals to maintain a posture of linguistic explicitness with respect to a "cover story." The self-deceiver accomplishes this, however, by keeping from linguistic explicitness the "real story," now disavowed.

There is, then, a gap between perception of an object, which is also an "emotional perception" in that the perception "affects" one and disposes one to act, and one's linguistically explicit and propositional interpretation of the perceived object. The gap here appears to be an error, but what this pictures is a motivated or intentional error, a "willful error" that the person wants and desires. The person has reasons for acting such that he or she avoids making this emotional perception linguistically explicit.

To have "reasons for acting" (motive) consistent with an emotionally perceived object, and also to perceive the object in question as opposed to one's own self-image or identity, whence the threatening quality of the object arises, is to picture a conflict. The intrapsychic opposition obtains between the object of reflexive care, which is one's own self (self-image or identity), and the epistemic object, which is perceived as threatening to that identity and which therefore disposes one to act defensively. These terms of opposition, the object of reflexive care and the object perceived-as-threatening, constitute the dynamically related "parties" involved in self-deception.

To perceive an object as threatening and to respond to it surely does not require that an individual acknowledge the object as threatening in a linguistically explicit profession of belief. All I mean by this is that we are not required to be accurate in our identification and understanding of the object in question in order for the perception itself to occur. There is room for error, mistake, misjudgment and illusion. And if there is such room, it is possible to take the short but significant step toward saying that under certain circumstances and for certain reasons, a behaviorally manifest error may be the result of intentional action aimed at keeping oneself unaware of the true nature of the object, one's intention being the desire to avoid distress and psychic pain. It is possible to say this if one accepts as coherent the notion of an "unconscious belief" and "unconscious intention," if one accepts such notions as ingredient in certain kinds of action. These would be actions the meaning of which the subject in question refuses--for certain reasons--to understand in accordance with the best, most reasonable interpretation. These would be actions that are incongruous with one's self-image, actions that can therefore be attributed to a project aimed at preserving self-image against a threat to it, actions motivated by a desire for psychological gain.

On the account I am putting forward, a person can be said to perceive a given object emotionally, that is, perceive it to be of a certain affective quality. I have also said that the particular quality in question is a "threatening" quality; and the perception of this threatening quality occurs prior to reflection, prior to the act of interpretation whereby the person makes this quality linguistically explicit to him- or herself as a professed belief. It is, of course, believed to be threatening as a result of the original perception, but this belief is held at bay: it is linguistically inexplicit, an "unconscious" belief. But the question can still be asked, "What exactly is the affect of this emotional perception?" In other words, why is this object perceived to be threatening?

Prior to the act of self-deception, prior to the denial or "cover up," the person who perceives a threatening object perceives that this epistemic object, whatever it be in particular, is inimical to the continued coherence and integrity of the object of reflexive care (self-image or identity). Prior to the act of interpreting the object perceived as threatening, then, the person attaches a quality to the object non-linguistically (i.e., "threatening) and by this act of perception discerns that the object will cause pain and distress. In short, one perceives that pain and distress will be experienced if one acknowledges the object in a linguistically explicit way, if one makes the "unconscious" belief conscious. And it is this pain and distress that occasions the self-deceiver's attempt to evade the true meaning of the object by engaging in other interpretive maneuvers, including rationalization, denial and "cover up."

An emotional perception that the object in view is of a threatening quality provides the occasion for interpretive activity whereby the perceiver makes the object linguistically explicit to him- or herself. The perceived threat may be made linguistically explicit either accurately or inaccurately, either by acknowledging it or by denying it. The question that begs our attention is this: "Why would a person engage in a project to evade the best, most reasonable interpretation of that object?" Why would a person make interpretive moves that have as their aim (intention) a cover up of the best, most reasonable interpretation of the object? We must understand that this threatening object is threatening for a specific reason.

I am advancing the view that the object perceived as threatening is so perceived only in relation to the object of reflexive care (self-image). It must be kept in mind that reflexive care constitutes a desire for psychic integration and personal unity. That is to say that this desire expresses love of self; for in seeking personal unity and psychic integration one is expressing the desire for greater unity that identifies love itself. This desire for greater unity, this love, is qualified by the relational context of the self--the self in relation to its own self. With that as a necessary backdrop, let me add that the object perceived to be threatening to project of personal integration and unity (expressive of reflexive care) is an object the self will resist appropriating and acknowledging as "one's own." To reiterate the point: the object is perceived to be discontinuous with one's own self-perception and "adjudged" to be inimical to one's own sense of regulative identity. Here, then, is the nub--and the rub--of the issue. The object perceived to be threatening to one's own identity is also an object that the person desires. The object of self-deception must be of such a character that its perception is not simply ignored or evaluated as of no "passional" interest. The object is perceived to be an object that "threatens" one's self-image. The question is "Why?"; what is it about this object that provokes one to characterize this object pre-reflectively, to construe it as or "see-it-as" threatening?

The threat that one perceives with respect to the object of self-deception is not to be likened to the threat posed by a savage beast. A savage beast that lunges at me I perceive to be a threat to life and limb, so that I immediately take flight in order to save my skin. The object of self-deception does not pose this kind of threat for the object is not that kind of object. The object of self-deception poses a threat because I seek to possess it, grasp it, make it mine. I do not "care" for the wild beast, only myself. But I could care for someone like Gertrude, or political power, or my wealth while also caring for the object of reflexive care--me. The problem is that in self-deception, my care is divided. At the very moment I perceive this particular object and in seeking to possess it have actually grasped at it through my desire, I also perceive the object to be of such a quality that I would be forced to revise my self-understanding were I to acknowledge this care. The threat, in other words, is provoked by my perception that I actually desire to possess the very object that I wish to disavow. I perceive that by acquiring this object "as my own" I am at the same time losing (or threatening to lose) the integrity and continuity of self as expressed by my reflexive care. That is, I perceive the object to be of such a character that I will not willingly appropriate it into my current regulative system of reflexive care. It conflicts with my own system of self-understanding. But I still want it. To acknowledge that I still want it, to acknowledge that I am not only disposed to "grasp" it as my own but have actually grasped at it, would be to experience a sort of disillusionment or even shame in the face of my regulative self-understanding. It is as a matter of "shame avoidance" that I embark on a project interpretive activity aimed at "disavowing" that this object, with which I am passionately engaged, is "mine." I deceive myself only about those objects I desire.

I can, of course, acknowledge this object of care, desire, love, as mine, for I have the option of making the character of that object linguistically explicit. But to make the correct and accurate connection would be to acknowledge to myself that I have cares, desires, and passional interests inconsistent with, and potentially destructive of, my self-understanding. This is a disagreeable option, even for the person who chooses to make the unconscious conscious, for it does entail pain and psychic distress. Furthermore, one has a sort of self-regarding duty to preserve one's self-understanding, for to lose what one perceives as the continuity and integrity of one's own personality is to lose one's autonomy as a competent agent capable of presenting oneself holistically, as a person, to the moral community. This is to push a conflict over opposing desires into the realm of moral conflict, with the result that denial seems to be justified on grounds of self-defense. One's aim now becomes to defend one's "integrity" from disintegrating influences. A moral description, however, is fraught with difficulties, for what one is defending one's self-image against is some aspect of one's own self that one does not want to acknowledge as one's own. In other words, the disintegrating influence is not an outside aggressor, but one's own desire. And the irony is that inasmuch as it is an object of desire, the object perceived to be threatening expresses an aspect of reflexive care. To want or desire this object, whatever it be, expresses some aspect of one's own self. The desire is itself very much "one's own." The issue is whether one can "own up to it" or whether doing so is perceived to be a greater threat, a more distressing prospect, than acknowledging that one has desires incompatible with one's own self-image.

I could acknowledge the object as my own, thereby affirming that this desire for the object means that I am disposed to act against my own self-image. But this would also mean that I am disposed to work for my own disintegration by seeking to possess those very things which I believe conflict with my own sense of integrity. To "confess one's sins" is to do just this: to acknowledge that one acts as one's own agent of disintegration. On the other hand, I could act consistently with my regulative and integrating self-image and resolve to protect myself from threats of disintegration, even those threats that arise from my own desires, desires that are constitutive of my actual identity, desires that are part and parcel of "who I am." I can deny the desire; I can deny the object of desire as an object of desire; I can deny that this desire expresses a constitutive aspect of my own identity. I can even justify that denial by so construing the facts that I make a plausible case that such desires are not part and parcel of my identity. Such denial is how I maintain my sense of self, my sense of personal integrity, cohesiveness and agency, my sense of self-worth. Yet to do this is to deny who I am and how I am constituted. To do this is to "thingify" one's own identity with a self-image that conflicts with the actual constituents of selfhood. I achieve disintegration under the illusion that I am preventing it. So it is this conflict between desiring to possess an object that one perceives-as-threatening and desiring to prevent oneself from experiencing disintegration as a result of having that desire that leads one to opt for self-deception. Before making the best, most reasonable interpretation linguistically explicit to oneself, the self-deceiver enacts a project to mislead belief in order to prevent oneself from acknowledging that what is perceived-as-threatening is actually an object of desire and constitutive of "who one really is."

Is this "emotion theory" of self-deception consistent with "ordinary language" analysis, whence our normative picture of self-deception derives? Is it a "synthetic" account as philosophical psychology will require? Do the three examples of self-deception presented in this chapter illustrate this particular account of self-deception?

To take the last question first. It is clear that each of the examples of self-deception illustrates a conflict between opposing desires. The pastor has a desire to maintain his self-image as a morally up-right Christian. That desire is countered by a desire to love Gertrude erotically, a desire he acts on, a desire that in his own eyes is illicit. What does the pastor do? He "perceives emotionally" his erotic desire for Gertrude. This desire conflicts with his self-image, however, so whatever he does to enact his erotic desire is interpreted according to regulative system of self-understanding: the Christian interpretation. He interprets his loving acts not only as consistent with his desire to fulfill a charitable impulse but as sanctioned by his Christian self-understanding. Great psychic distress would attend his doing otherwise, and because he perceives this, he acts to preserve his identity. Preserving that identity, then, provides him with a motive for interpreting his caring in a Christian rather than an erotic manner.

As an object of erotic desire, Gertrude conflicts with the pastor's constitutive and regulative self-image. That image, in that it obtains from a desire for integration and unity, expresses reflexive care. The other "illicit" desire, the erotic desire to possess Gertrude, is also constitutive of the pastor's self, for he unconsciously believes Gertrude to be worthy of his love and erotic longings. The difficulty--the conflict--is that this desire is perceived to threaten the regulative self-image. Faced with a fissure in the heart of love itself, faced with a conflict of desires, the pastor opts not to admit that he loves Gertrude passionately, for he does not wish to incur the guilt that he believes would attend such an admission. Rather, he attempts the "ingenious solution" of possessing both objects of desire at once, both the self-image, which he retains and professes, and Gertrude, whom he continues to desire and act passionately toward. He can only do this by refusing to acknowledge in a linguistically explicit way that his engagement with Gertrude is, if the "real story" be told, an erotic and illicit engagement. What the pastor substitutes for the real story is a cover story, and it is this professed cover story consistent with the regulative self-image, which the pastor believes to be true, that permits him to act erotically under the guise of a Christian interpretation. A similar kind of desire conflict can be seen in Lon Nol and the shipowner. Lon Nol desires to preserve his self-identity as an invulnerable and powerful political leader who can summon his loyal people to defend the nation and his authority; yet he is also a person capable of perceiving that his desire for survival may be such that he would rather face the ignominy of defeat than perish in a <u>coup</u>. His ingenious solution is to deny the threat of defeat while calling to see if his escape plane is ready. He loves his power just as the shipowner loves his money. The shipowner so desires to maintain his financial resources that he is able to persuade himself that he is not responsible--but God is--for the seaworthiness of his ship, that he is not acting immorally in sending an unseaworthy ship to sea when he "knows deep down" that only an expenditure of his wealth will reasonably insure safe passage. His desire to maintain a moral self-image conflicts with his desire to act in a way that he perceives is immoral.

Each example pits a desire to preserve an identity against a desire to possess some object that is perceived and adjudged (i.e., "believed") to be incompatible with the identity, hence "threatening." In self-deception, the conflict between contrary desires generates the activity whereby the individual seeks an ingenious solution, namely, to have both at once. While this may look paradoxical, in fact the contradiction is an accurate description, for the desire to preserve one's identity and the desire to posses an object "unconsciously believed" to be threatening are both expressions of reflexive care. Both are constitutive of the person one is. The problem is that one does not believe the object of desire can be appropriated into one's identity without fragmenting and rendering incoherent the holistically conceived person one believes oneself to be. The self-deceiver's solution, then, is not to acknowledge that the object of desire perceived to be threatening is constitutive of one's self and expressive of one's reflexive care; rather, the self-deceiver's solution is to grasp at the object of desire and appropriate it--and act in relation to it--while denying that the object is desired, that the object has aroused one's passional interest, that the desire is constitutive of the self one is. One defers to the passional interest involved in preserving one's self-identity, thereby denying that a separate--though related--desire is also one's own. In short, the self-deception solution is to believe on the one hand that one is a person of a certain sort, a person whose past acts and future prospects are continuous with a regulative self-image governing one's behavior; while, on the other hand, one also believes, albeit without acknowledging it, that a certain object of desire, a certain object constitutive of one's passional interests, is "threatening" to that self-image and therefore to be denied "as one's own."

Just to recapitulate this "emotional perception" account as a theory consistent with a synthetic action-cognition account and the ordinary language analysis: A belief that p is opposed by a belief that $\underline{not\text{-}p}$, since, say, the belief that $\underline{not\text{-}p}$ constitutive of one's self-image will regulate what one is willing to accept in linguistically explicit ways as "one's own." The belief that p, however, is suppressed. The suppressed belief is associated with a certain cognitive evaluation of an epistemic object (i.e., perceived emotionally) that is one's own but in relation to which one acts without "spelling-out" one's engagement as one's own. In other words, one acts consistently with respect to p, but disavows that belief as one's own. This disavowal is accomplished by interpreting the behavior that issues from p in a way that is consistent with $\underline{not\text{-}p}$. What one professes to believe about the meaning of one's behavior ($\underline{not\text{-}p}$) is contrary to the act but consistent with one's self-image.

An epistemic deficit between the best, most reasonable interpretation of the act and the person's self-evaluation appears. That deficit reveals the fact of contrary beliefs, one of which the subject resists acknowledging "as one's own." The belief that governs action (p) is manifest in behavior, though the person is not aware that it is p governing the action and disposing one to act the way he or she does, just as we say that the pastor is unaware that he love Gertrude erotically. One can impute a motive to this unconscious belief. In refusing to spell-out his engagement with Gertrude as his own, the pastor's denial becomes something other than an innocent error. It is manifest as the result of intentional interpretive behavior. Given his social and professional status and his personal commitments to certain values embodied in his Christian faith, it requires little imagination to discern that the pastor has reasons for denying his erotic love. He desires to preserve his identity as a moral Christian while avoiding the distress occasioned by his belief that Gertrude is an appropriate subject for his erotic longing (belief that p). That is the pastor's conflict, and he resolves it by (temporarily) deceiving himself. The pastor's belief that p is a belief that can be imputed despite his denials. But it is also clear that the pastor has good prudential reasons for keeping his belief that p unavailable to his own reflective, linguistically explicit consciousness. For the prudential reason of maintaining a self-image that will not condone his illicit desire, the pastor interprets his relationship to Gertrude in a way that refuses to spell-out his belief that p. He therefore acts to endorse through various devices (rationalizing, excusing, jamming, and so on) the belief that not-p is true, a belief he professes in a linguistically explicit way, but a belief that appears in the guise of a "cover story," His cover story distracts him from the contrary belief that is also his own (p), a belief that is suppressed. The pastor's Christian interpretation is not the best, most reasonable interpretation of his own action, of his own relation to the acts and behavior associated with and measured by his belief that p.

This "emotional perception" theory of self-deception conforms to the notion of a project directed by the self to the end of misleading belief. It results in an epistemic deficit: the gap between a linguistically explicit belief that not-p is true and a simultaneously held belief that p, which is also one's own, also based on cognitive activity, but in relation to which one acts to avoid "spelling-out."

This action/cognition picture of emotion provides the framework for a coherent accounting of self-deception. The criteria obtained from ordinary language analysis apply, and we satisfy the dual requirement that self-deception be dynamic action as well as cognitive state by appealing to emotional perception, emotion being a "seeing-as that disposes one to act." Self-deception is to be explained as that phenomenon of mental/emotional life that is made possible by our uniquely human capacity for perceiving the very object we deny seeing because we do not want to see. The objects of self-deception must be of such a character that they incite one's passional interest. They must also be objects that are "perceived" to be one's own on a pre-reflective level. This explains why I can deceive myself about love or power, money or morality but not about whether I am married or have received a college degree (delusion). The former objects are related to my passional interest and occasion a conflict within my reflexive care while the later are related to the most basic external facts of identity. To deny that I am married when I am points to behavior so aberrant that it cannot be said to constitute the experience of self-deception in the common life.

We deceive ourselves in relation to epistemic objects that we both desire and do not desire. The object must be constitutive of our emotional awareness --the pastor does, after all, desire Gertrude, and we must accept this as a fact of his emotional awareness. To grasp that object through desire is to express the fact that one's desires, even those not acknowledged as one's own, are of a piece with one's regulative reflexive care. Self-deception requires this emotional context, this context of conflicting desires. The self-deception, then, is manifest in behavior as a refusal to acknowledge that a given object that incites one's actual desire and expresses one's own reflexive care conforms to our image of ourselves. Self-deception refers us to a conflict of desires whereby one acts to avoid acknowledging certain objects of desire as objects of one's own passional interests, as desires constitutive of the person one truly is. We do not deceive ourselves about matters of no interest, matters about which one can be said to be indifferent. We deceive ourselves about things we desire, yet do not want; or, if we use a classical notion of indifference (<u>ignorantia affectata</u>), we exhibit in our self-deception the indifference related to not wanting to know, not wanting to acknowledge (avow) claims that would require commitment and continued participation (engagement). On this emotions theory, self-deception can be said to express a failure in self-understanding, a failure in self-knowledge that is no simple error. That failure to understand is motivated by a prudential reason in relation to which one acts to preserve identity and self-image. The fundamental object of reflexive care and and passional interest is one's self-image, one's self-understanding. The epistemic deficit that obtains reflects the fact that one has acted to render oneself oblivious to those desires that threaten the object of reflexive care (self-image) even though the desire is itself one's own. The ignorance is, quite literally, willful. Self-deception is, on this emotional perception account, rendered coherent because an epistemic object has been construed as threatening through a system of awareness that is fundamentally affective or emotional. By means of this regulative emotional system, we are capable of perceiving an object as threatening without that threatening quality itself being "spelled-out."

The perspective of philosophical psychology requires that the concept 'self-deception' be described coherently and non-paradoxically. I have argued that a "synthetic" action/cognition description of the concept will permit one to do that, and that certain explanations that are synthetic in nature-- Sartre's, Freud's, or an emotional perception account--advance our understanding of the concept 'self-deception.'

CHAPTER TWO

[1] Although it is a psychological concept, 'self-deception' is relevant to the sociological phenomenon of false consciousness. For a discussion of false consciousness as a social parallel to individual personality disintegration, see Joseph Gabel, False Consciousness: An Essay on Reification, trans. Margaret A. Thompson (New York: Harper & Row, Harper Torchbook, 1962, 1978), p ix ff., p. 140 ff. See also Peter A. Berger, The Sacred Canopy: Elements of a Sociological Theory of Religion (Garden City, NY: Doubleday & Co., Anchor Books, 1969), pp. 92-101. This study will not explore this sociological dimension since we are restricted to individual behavior (psychology).

[2] Szabados, "Rorty on Belief and Self-Deception," p. 464.

[3] Alan R. Drengson, "Critical Notice: Herbert Fingarette, Self-Deception," Canadian Journal of Philosophy III, 3 (March 1974), p. 475.

[4] André Gide, "Letter to an Unidentified Correspondent 17 April 1928," reprinted in Madeline, trans. Justin O'Brien, (New York: Bantam Books, 1968), p. 86.

[5] Gardiner, "Error, Faith and Self-Deception," p. 51-52.

[6] Kipp, "On Self-Deception," pp. 305-06.

[7] One needs "for instances." I would note that the discussion of self-deception in Hawthorne's The Scarlet Letter (Chillingworth's tirade against Arthur Dimsdale, whom Hawthorne describes as unable to deceive himself); Arthur Donnithorne who, as a deceiver, becomes a self-deceiver in George Eliot's Adam Bede; or the Hyacinth who fails to accede to his own attempts at "self-flattery" due to his well-developed humility in Henry James' The Princess Casamassima. All of these are intelligible in their fictional context, all seem to describe states of mind that render the character's behavior intelligible. There is an appeal beyond "hypothetical states of mind" in the well-drawn psychological novel, these examples coming from recognized masters.

[8] Anthony Palmer, "Characterizing Self-Deception," Mind LXXXVIII, 349 (January 1979), p. 57.

[9] Ibid., pp. 57-58.

[10] Ibid., p. 54.

[11] I shall discuss this example in more detail in the next chapter and there present textual evidence for this assertion.

[12] The view has been put forward that fiction provides an actual occasion for the reader becoming self-deceived via his or her emotional involvement in the "make believe" of fiction. See Jerry L. Guthrie, "Self-Deception and Emotional Responses to Fiction," The British Journal of Aesthetics 21, 1 (Winter 1981), pp. 65-75. I would argue that fiction can occasion actual emotions and intensify the experience of emotion due to aesthetic enhancements (e.g., the music in film, the beauty of the writing in fiction). That the world I enter aesthetically is a "false world" (Guthrie) need not lead to Guthrie's claim that my emotional response to fiction is akin to self-deception.

[13] André Gide, The Pastoral Symphony in Two Symphonies, trans. Dorothy Bussy (New York: Alfred A. Knopf, 1954). Anthony Palmer, "Characterizing Self-Deception," has written, "Self-deception is a persistent theme in the work of André Gide" (p. 51). The Pastoral Symphony has often been used to illustrate self-deception. See references to this work in Drengson, "Critical Notice," pp. 482-83; Anthony Palmer, "Self-Deception: A Problem About Autobiography" (p. 71) and T. S. Champlin, "Self-Deception: A Problem About Autobiography" (p. 88) in Proceedings of the Aristotelian Society, Supp. Vol. LIII (1979).

[14] Gide, The Pastoral Symphony, p. 145.

[15] Ibid., p. 177.

[16] Ibid., p. 191.

[17] Ibid.

[18] Ibid., pp. 201-202.

[19] Ibid., pp. 163-64.

[20] Audi wrote in "The Epistemic Authority of the First Person," that sincere disavowals of knowledge can be false because ". . .S can know that p without being conscious that he knows it; and secondly, sincere disavowals of belief may be false even if S does not have an unconscious belief that p" (p. 5). Self-deception for Audi is a state in which a person sincerely avows the opposite of what he unconsciously knows to be true; and this claim for unconscious knowledge was disputed by Exdell and Hamilton, "The Incorrigibility of First Person Disavowals." In his subsequent rejoinder, "Epistemic Disavowals and Self-Deception," Audi challenged the Lon Nol example as given by Exdell and Hamilton. Exdell and Hamilton had denied that the model of "other deception" was applicable to 'self-deception' and by denying a role for unconscious knowledge in their argument that first-person disavowals are, if sincere, incorrigible, they invoked a Cartesian view of mind and a "transparent" view of consciousness. They held self-deception to be not a conflict state, but a state of ignorance caused by psychological incapacity. Audi's rejoinder adds certain details to the Lon Nol example in order to show what would have to happen behaviorally in order to self-deception to be illustrated. I present a version of the Lon Nol illustration and include those modifications as necessary features of the description.

[21] Problems with actual historical examples I have addressed in "Self-Deception: A Conceptual Analysis in Three Relational Contexts," pp. 380-83. Actual historical examples of self-deception are dealt with by R. Lance Factor, "Self-Deception and the Functionalist Theory of Mental Processes," The Personalist 58 (April 1977), pp. 119, 122 (e.g., Nixon); Hannah Arendt, Eichmann in Jerusalem: A Report on the Banality of Evil (New York: Penguin Books, 1963, 1980), pp. 51-52 (e.g., Eichmann); Stanley Hauerwas and David B. Burrell, "Self-Deception and Autobiography: Reflections on Speer's Inside the Third Reich," in Stanley Hauerwas with Richard Bondi, Truthfulness and Tragedy: Further Investigations into Christian Ethics (Notre Dame: University of Notre Dame Press, 1977), pp. 82-98.

[22] Exdell and Hamilton, "The Incorrigibility of First Person Disavowals,"

p. 392.

²³Ibid., pp. 392-93.

²⁴Audi, "Epistemic Disavowals and Self-Deception," p. 382.

²⁵Ibid., p. 382.

²⁶William K. Clifford, "The Ethics of Belief" from Lectures and Essays, reprinted in Problems and Perspectives in the Philosophy of Religion, eds. George I. Mavrodes and Stuart D. Hackett (Boston: Allyn and Bacon, 1967, 1969), p. 20.

²⁷The shipowner's distortion of the evidence includes a distortion of a normal justification process as well; and in my view, it is clear that the shipowner is deceiving himself about Providence, since I know of no theists who, if confronted with the evidence that gave rise to the shipowner's original doubts, would have willingly boarded that ship. In fact, I suspect that the shipowner would have refused to board his own ship if pressed to do so by some higher authority--despite his light heart. On my analysis, no general condemnation of theistic belief follows from this example. I know of no argument that supports a contention that the theist is prone to disregard the evidence of, say, unseaworthiness, in order to test the power of Providence. By the same token, I cannot imagine a reasonable theist who would insist on boarding a plane if it were known that the plane had worn control cables, a faulty fuel pump, and was popping rivets. Theologically, to board such a flight to invoke Providence for the purpose of insuring safety--which is equivalent to relying on luck or superstition --would be an act that tempts God. This would constitute a case of theological self-deception. Contrary to the shipowner, a theist who believes that God acts providentially could still be expected to join Clifford in his condemnation of the shipowner, despite the shipowner's invocation of Providence. The shipowner is guilty of the worse kind of casuistry--the kind that gets people killed. Clifford's shipowner is mentioned in Szabados, "Self-Deception," pp. 63-64.

²⁸Audi, "Epistemic Disavowals and Self-Deception," p. 384.

²⁹Fingarette, Self-Deception, p. 34.

³⁰Ibid.

³¹Ibid.

³²Ibid., pp. 12-33.

³³Szabados, "Self-Deception," pp. 52-55.

³⁴Self-deception can be accounted for by the kind of functionalist theory of knowledge put forward by Gilbert Harmon, Thought (Princeton: Princeton University Press, 1973). R. Lance Factor, "Self-Deception and the Functionalist Theory of Mental Processes," Personalist 58 (April 1977), pp. 115-123, attempts to make this case explicit. I consider my ordinary language account compatible with Harmon, specially at the point where Harmon refers to "unconscious inference" (pp. 178-79). Factor is more problematic since his idea of self-deception is sketchy. He is more willing than I to abandon other-decep-

tion as an analogue to self-deception, and he seems to eliminate unawareness as a necessary conceptual feature of self-deception. In a peculiar way, Factor falls victim to the "transparency" fallacy that I have attempted to identify and refute.

[35] Kent Bach, "An Analysis of Self-Deception," Philosophy and Phenomenological Research XLI, 3 (March 1981), pp. 351-70.

[36] Ibid., pp. 353-54.

[37] Ibid., p. 354.

[38] Ibid.

[39] Ibid., p. 362.

[40] Ibid., p. 369.

[41] Ibid., p. 354.

[42] Ibid., p. 355.

[43] Ibid. I would note certain qualifications offered by Bach: "This is not to deny, of course, that usually what a person thinks and thinks he believes, is in fact what he believes" (p. 355); and "I should add that we cannot assume a person always to believe what he thinks he believes, for then we would be arbitrarily ruling out the possibility of error of one's beliefs" (p. 356).

[44] Ibid., p. 369.

[45] Ibid.

[46] Ibid., pp. 367-68.

[47] Szabados, "Self-Deception," p. 54.

[48] The paradox is overcome, according to Bach, as follows: "The key is to distinguish what the self-deceiver thinks, when the touchy subject comes to mind, from what he believes." Normally, the state of believing that p causes one to think that p whenever the thought that p occurs, but the state of being self-deceived overcomes this tendency" (p. 368). This picture allows one to say non-paradoxically that a person who believes not-p can think of p, but, being motivated to avoid the thought of p, this person can enact an interpretive program, which enables him or her to avoid the thought that p--a process only possible if the significance of p is recognized prior to initiating the avoidance maneuvers.

[49] Ibid., p. 354.

[50] I believe self-deception requires the postulating of unconscious belief or desire or intention and that there is nothing incoherent about doing so. For a modern action theory defense of this position, see Alvin I. Goldman, A Theory of Human Action (Princeton: Princeton University Press, 1970), pp. 122-25.

[51] Bach, "An Analysis of Self-Deception," p. 357.

[52] Fingarette, Self-Deception, p. 29.

[53] Bach, "An Analysis of Self-Deception," p. 365.

[54] I borrow this characterization from Abelson, Persons, p. 97.

[55] Haight, A Study of Self-Deception, p. 73.

[56] Ibid., p. 108.

[57] Ibid., pp. 118-19.

[58] Ryle, The Concept of Mind, p. 174. See his remarks on pretending, pp. 256-64.

[59] Canfield and Gustavson, "Self-Deception," p. 34.

[60] Szabados, "Self-Deception," pp. 54-55. (Stupidity lacks the intentional or motivations feature of self-deception.)

[61] Bach, "An Analysis of Self-Deception," p. 351.

[62] Biased thinking and uncharacteristic irrationality are discussed by Bach, ibid., pp. 351-52.

[63] David Hume, "Of Self-Love," in An Inquiry Concerning the Principles of Morals, ed. Charles W. Hendel (Indianapolis: Bobbs-Merrill, 1957), p. 117.

[64] Ryle, The Concept of Mind, p. 162. Ryle argues against invoking a "phosphorescence-story" to explain mental occurrences or events. He writes, "[there] is no contradiction in asserting that someone might fail to recognize his frame of mind for what it is; indeed it is notorious that people constantly do so. They mistakenly suppose themselves to know things which are actually false; they deceive themselves about their own motives. . . .If consciousness was what it is described as being ["self-luminous"], it would be logically impossible for such failures and mistakes in recognition to take place" (p. 62). Ryle, then, does not take the idea of deceiving oneself to be paradoxical because he does not hold to the notion of consciousness (i.e., transparent or self-luminous) that would require it to be so, a conclusion consistent with my own.

[65] Ibid., p. 177.

[66] R. M. Hare, Freedom and Reason (New York: Oxford University Press, 1963, 1972), pp. 77, 82. Hare mentions self-deception in the context of moral backsliding (akrasia), p. 83, which is a general issue to be addressed in the next chapter.

[67] Bela Szabados, "Hypocrisy," Canadian Journal of Philosophy IX, 2 (June 1979), pp. 195-210.

[68] Ibid., pp. 209-210.

⁶⁹Ibid., p. 210.

⁷⁰Sartre, *Being and Nothingness*, p. 49.

⁷¹Fingarette, *Self-Deception*, p. 45.

⁷²Ibid., p. 47.

⁷³Ibid., p. 62.

⁷⁴Ibid., p. 38.

⁷⁵Ibid., pp. 38-39.

⁷⁶Ibid., p. 45.

⁷⁷Ibid., p. 43.

⁷⁸Ibid., p. 42.

⁷⁹Ibid., p. 43.

⁸⁰Ibid., p. 47.

⁸¹Ibid., p. 48.

⁸²Ibid., p. 50. For an illuminating discussion of the "cover story" phenomenon, see Crites, "The Aesthetics of Self-Deception."

⁸³Ibid.

⁸⁴Ronald B. de Sousa, "Review Discussions: Herbert Fingarette's *Self-Deception*," *Inquiry* 13, 3 (Autumn 1970), p. 311.

⁸⁵Fingarette, *Self-Deception*, p. 134.

⁸⁶Ibid., p. 66.

⁸⁷Ibid., p. 70.

⁸⁸Ibid., p. 87.

⁸⁹Ibid., p. 91.

⁹⁰Ibid., p. 85.

⁹¹Ibid., p. 87.

⁹²Ibid., p. 143.

⁹³Ibid., p. 33.

⁹⁴See, for example, Anthony Kenny, *Action, Emotion and Will* or William Alston, "Emotion and Feeling," *The Encyclopedia of Philosophy*, Vol. II, pp. 479-86. See also the general collection of essays in Amelie O. Rorty, ed.,

Explaining Emotions (Berkeley: University of California Press, 1980), especially essays by Rorty and de Sousa. See also Edward Walter, "The Logic of Emotion," Southern Journal of Philosophy 10, 1 (Spring 1972), pp. 71-78.

[95] de Sousa, "Review Discussions," p. 319.

[96] Drengson, "Critical Notice," p. 478.

[97] Ibid.

[98] For a discussion of literature responding to Fingarette's analysis, see my "Self-Deception: A Conceptual Analysis in Three Relational Contexts," pp. 389-90.

[99] de Sousa, "Review Discussions," p. 319. See also Szabados, "Self-Deception," for another position that holds that self-deception must be analyzed such that both cognition and action are involved.

[100] Abelson, Persons, pp. 96-97.

[101] For a discussion of "tensive language" and its relation to what I have called the "language of the self," see Philip Wheelwright, Metaphor and Reality, (Bloomington: Indiana University Press, 1968, 1973), pp. 46 ff.

[102] King-Farlow, "Self-Deceivers and Sartrian Seducers," p. 135.

[103] Amelie O. Rorty, "Self-Deception, Akrasia and Irrationality," Social Sciences Information 19, 6 (1980), p. 906.

[104] Ibid.

[105] Ibid., p. 920.

[106] Abelson, Persons, p. 96.

[107] Ibid.

[108] In "Repression" (1915), Freud writes that repression obtains when "a sharp distinction has been established between what is conscious and what is unconscious: that the essence of repression lies simply in the function of rejecting and keeping something out of consciousness." Reprinted in General Psychological Theory, p. 105. In Ego and the Id, trans. Joan Riviere, ed. James Strachey (New York: W.W. Norton & Co., 1960, 1962), Freud writes "The state in which the ideas existed before being made conscious is called by us repression, and we assert that the force which instituted the repression and maintains it is perceived as resistance during the work of analysis" (p. 5). For a more complete discussion of the relationship of resistance to repression see Paul Ricoeur, Freud and Philosophy: An Essay on Interpretation, trans. Denis Savage (New Haven: Yale University Press, 1970), pp. 138-141, ft. 58.

[109] Sartre, Being and Nothingness, pp. 52-53.

[110] Ibid., p. 54.

[111] Phyllis S. Morris, "Self-Deception: Sartre's Resolution of the

Paradox," p. 45.

[112] Freud, The Ego and the Id, p. 7.

[113] Ibid. For more on Freud's idea of resistance and intrapsychic conflict see his New Introductory Lectures on Psychoanalysis, trans. and ed. James Strachey (New York: W. W. Norton & Co., 1933, 1965), Chapter XXXI, "Dissection of the Personality," esp. p. 61. Freud claims that the "agency" of the super-ego performs this work of repression, but my point is that this "agency" has already been characterized as a structural relation that is not to be personified as an actual agent or homunculus independent of the ego. Psychic conflict need not arise in actual splitting of the ego, but it can, as in neurosis, and it can even lead to actual insanity (psychosis). For a distinction, see Sigmund Freud, The Question of Lay Analysis, trans. and ed. James Strachey (New York: W. W. Norton & Co., 1950, 1969), pp. 30-32.

[114] See Freud's unfinished essay, "Splitting of the Ego in the Defensive Process" (1938) in Sigmund Freud, Sexuality and the Psychology of Love, ed. Philip Rieff (New York: Collier Books, 1963, 1974), pp. 220-23. It is this essay that Fingarette employs to resolve the contradiction of self-deception, for he picks up on Freud's use of "disavowal" to make a case that the ego can "split" such that it faces a counter-ego, the behavioral result being that patient, according to Freud, "replies to the conflict with two contrary reactions, both of which are valid and affective" (p. 221). "Both parties to the dispute obtain their share. . . .The two contrary reactions to the conflict persist as the centre-point of a split in the ego" (ibid.)--my emphasis. This view is consistent with my ordinary language analysis for it preserves the intentional character of self-deception in the midst of contradictory behavior, and it permits us to attribute the behavior to "parties" in conflict, not homunculi at war.

[115] Freud, New Introductory Lectures on Psychoanalysis, pp. 57-58.

[116] Ibid., pp. 62, 62-63.

[117] D. M. Thomas, The White Hotel (New York: Pocket Books, 1981, 1982), p. 115.

[118] Thomas Donaldson, "Psychoanalysis and the Practical Inference Model," Philosophy Research Archives IV (1978) argues that even though idea of "unconscious belief" is not itself problematic or paradoxical, the fact that Freud does not resort to this language prevents him from being able to make "unconscious inferences." "Unconscious belief," therefore is a corrective; for more detail on this issue see my "Self-Deception: A Conceptual Analysis in Three Relational Contexts," pp. 393-94.

[119] Philip Rieff, Freud: The Mind of the Moralist, 3rd ed., (Chicago: University of Chicago Press, 1959, 1979), p. 255.

[120] See, for instance, Morris, "Self-Deception: Sartre's Resolution of the Paradox," p. 45 and the following works: Lee Brown and Alan Hausman, "Mechanism, Intentionality, and the Unconscious: A Comparison of Sartre and Freud," which concludes about Sartre's treatment of Freud, ". . .his mistakes are quite independent of the really important things he has to say about Freudian theory and, as we have shown, Freudian theory is independent of what he has to

say" (p. 578); and Richard Wollheim, Sigmund Freud (Cambridge: Cambridge University Press, 1971, 1981), who supports this position, p. 181.

[121]Sigmund Freud, "One of the Difficulties of Psychoanalysis" (1917) in Sigmund Freud, Character and Culture, ed. Philip Rieff (New York: Collier Books, 1963, 1972), p. 189.

[122]Ibid. p. 188.

[123]Ibid. p. 187.

[124]Roy Schafer, A New Language for Psychoanalysis (New Haven: Yale University Press, 1976, 1978), p. 234.

[125]See Chapter One, ft. 37, p. 106.

[126]Schafer, A New Language for Psychoanalysis, p. 234.

[127]Rieff, Freud: The Mind of the Moralist, p. 69.

[128]The "holistic" conception of self appears in various places, including "Some Additional Notes on Dream-Interpretation as a Whole--B. Moral Responsibility for the Content of Dreams" (1925) in Sigmund Freud, Therapy and Technique, ed. Philip Rieff (New York: Collier Books, 1963, 1977), p. 255; and the equation of "ego" and "patient" is also made in Freud, The Question of Lay Analysis, p. 59. The self-relatedness picture of self appears in The Ego and the Id; the chapter "The Dissection of the Psychical Personality" in The New Introductory Lectures, p. 51-71; The Question of Lay Analysis, pp. 25-68; "Mourning and Melancholia" (1917) in Sigmund Freud, General Psychological Theory, ed. Philip Rieff (New York: Collier Books, 1963, 1972), pp. 168-69; and in "My Contact with Josef Popper-Lybnkeus," in Freud, Character and Culture, pp. 303-304. In reference to my claim that the language of self is ambiguous, James Strachey has written in his introduction to The Ego and the Id that Freud had two uses of "ego"--one holistic, the other as an intra-related yet particular function and aspect of mind, that "It is not always easy. . .to draw a line between these two sense of the word" (p. xiv).

[129]Freud, The Question of Lay Analysis, p. 33.

[130]Freud, New Introductory Lectures on Psychoanalysis, p. 69.

[131]Rieff, Freud: The Mind of the Moralist, p. 69.

[132]Erik H. Erikson, Young Man Luther: A Study In Psychoanalysis and History (New York: W. W. Norton & Co., 1958, 1962), p. 152.

[133]"Ego/id/super-ego" has been termed a set of "homunculi" by Ronald de Sousa, "Rational Homunculi" in ed. Amelie O. Rorty, The Identities of Persons, p. 217.

[134]Freud, "Some Additional Notes on Dream Interpretation," p. 223-226.

[135]Sigmund Freud, Inhibitions, Symptoms and Anxiety, trans. Alix Strachey, ed. James Strachey (New York: W. W. Norton & Co., 1959), p. 43.

[136] Mischel, "Understanding Neurotic Behavior: From 'Mechanism' to 'Intentionality,'" p. 235.

[137] Freud, New Introductory Lectures on Psychoanalysis, pp. 68-69.

[138] Ibid., pp. 64-65.

[139] That "ego/id/super-ego" are really adverbs has been argued, I think persuasively, by Roy Schafer, "The Idea of Resistance," International Journal of Psycho-analysis 54 (1973). See also his A New Language for Psychoanalysis.

[140] Bennet Simon, "Plato and Freud: The Mind in Conflict and the Mind in Dialogue," Psychoanalytic Quarterly XLII, 1 (1973), p. 103.

[141] Søren Kierkegaard, The Sickness Unto Death, ed. and trans. Howard V. Hong and Edna H. Hong (Princeton: Princeton University Press, 1980), p. 13.

[142] Louis Mackey, Kierkegaard: A Kind of Poet (Philadelphia: University of Pennsylvania Press, 1971, 1972), p. 135: "This is not the gobbledygook it seems to be, though there is good reason why it seems so."

[143] Ibid., p. 136.

[144] Freud, Inhibitions, Symptoms and Anxiety, p. 21. Anxiety can be concealed, according to Freud, even from the person him- or herself (p. 54), and behavioral correlates may attend it. Anxiety is not itself a biochemical entity, but a relationship between a person and a threatening environment, "and the neurophysiological processes follow from this relationship" (Rollo May, The Meaning of Anxiety [New York: Pocket Books, 1950, 1977], p. 65).

[145] Sartre's picture of mind provides a functional equivalent to "unconsciousness" in the idea of "pre-reflection," and I shall discuss this point in this section.

[146] Sartre, Being and Nothingness, p. 49.

[147] Ibid.

[148] Michael W. Martin, "Sartre on Lying to Oneself," Philosophy Research Archive IV (1978), p. 30, C-10. Martin cites as a proponent of the "rough equivalency view," H. Spiegelberg, The Phenomenological Movement (The Hague: Martinus Nijhoff, 1971), II, p. 487 (ibid.).

[149] Ronald E. Santoni, "Bad Faith and 'Lying to Oneself,'" Philosophy and Phenomenological Research XXXVIII, 3 (March 1978), pp. 394-395.

[150] Morris, "Self-Deception: Sartre's Resolution of the Paradox," p. 49.

[151] Fingarette, Self-Deception, p. 95.

[152] Ibid.

[153] Ibid., p. 94.

[154] Ibid., pp. 98-99.

[155] Abelson, Persons, p. 97.

[156] Fingarette, Self-Deception, p. 7: "My aim is to show that there is a remarkable parallelism between Sartre's doctrine and my own account--with the further demonstration that, by the use of my own account, translated into Sartrian terminology, Sartre's own version can be freed of much of its terminological incoherence and surface paradox." I am using an ordinary language analysis to do the same thing, with quite different results. My case is that an ordinary language analysis will reveal that Sartre's account is actually less of a problem and more adequate as an account than Fingarette's.

[157] Amelie O. Rorty, "Belief and Self-Deception," Inquiry 15, 4 (Winter 1972), p. 399.

[158] Sartre, Being and Nothingness, p. 633. Glossary item.

[159] Ibid., p. 629. Glossary item.

[160] Ibid., p. 60.

[161] Ibid., p. 58.

[162] Joseph S. Catalano, A Commentary on Jean-Paul Sartre's "Being and Nothingness," (New York: Harper & Row, Harper Torchbook, 1974), p. 82.

[163] Ibid., p. 83.

[164] Sartre, Being and Nothingness, pp. 55-56.

[165] Ibid.

[166] Ibid., p. 57.

[167] Ibid., p. 60.

[168] I would point out that Walter Kaufmann has translated "bad faith" as "self-deception" in Existentialism from Dostoyevsky to Sartre (Cleveland: World Publishing Co., 1956), p. 222.

[169] Sartre, Being and Nothingness, p. 60.

[170] Ibid., p. 56.

[171] Ibid., p. 57.

[172] Ibid., p. 60.

[173] Ibid., p. 65.

[174] Ibid., pp. 65, 66.

[175] Ibid., p. 67.

[176] Ibid., p. 58.

[177] Ibid., p. 67.

[178] Ibid., p. 68.

[179] Ibid.

[180] Ibid.

[181] Ibid., pp. 67-68.

[182] Ibid., p. 68.

[183] On "denying" see ibid., p. 70.

[184] Ibid., p. 69.

[185] Ibid.

[186] Ibid.

[187] Ibid.

[188] Ibid., p. 70.

[189] Ibid.

[190] Ibid., p. 68.

[191] Ibid.

[192] Ibid., p. 69.

[193] Ibid., p. 615.

[194] Ibid., p. 478.

[195] Ibid., p. 195.

[196] Jean-Paul Sartre, The Transcendence of the Ego: An Existentialist Theory of Consciousness, trans. and intro. Forrest Williams and Robert Kirkpatrick (New York: Noonday Press, 1957).

[197] Sartre, Being and Nothingness, p. 570. Comparing his psychoanalytic theory to Freud's Sartre writes here, "Both our psychoanalyses refuse to admit that the subject is in a privileged position to proceed in these inquiries concerning himself." I have consistently referred to the idea expressed here as the "opaqueness" of consciousness, since consciousness can act to avoid seeing itself in the wholeness of its initial grasp. This is not Sartre's use of "opaqueness," but I find Sartre's technical use to be a reversal of the ordinary linguistic meaning. That reversal is one of the problematic features of his account, one which has led Sartre's critics to charge that given his "unitary and transparent" view of consciousness, he is unable to resolve the paradox of self-deception.

[198]Ibid.

[199]Ibid., p 571.

[200]See Chapter One, footnote 37.

[201]See Chapter One, footnote 4.

[202]Saunders, "The Paradox of Self-Deception," p. 570.

[203]William James, "The Will To Believe," in The Will to Believe and other Essays in Popular Philosophy (New York: Dover Publications, 1956), p. 29, ft. 1.

[204]I, too, am a critic and detractor. I do not wholeheartedly endorse Sartre's position on consciousness. I support his synthetic view of self-deception and seek to understand how that view is connected to his broader conception of consciousness. But this is a concern separate from a wholesale critique of his theory of consciousness. For example I agree that in Sartre's terms there is no ego in unreflected consciousness--and no object of knowing--but I disagree with Sartre's claim that consciousness contains no content, or that the content is the object, or that all the descriptive features of an intentional situation are comprised by the object of awareness itself. Since behavior can be affected by what one thinks about, I hold contra Sartre that there are descriptive properties of mind. For present purposes these are extraneous issues.

[205]I would point out that St. Augustine's mnemonic epistemology has more room for satisfying the criteria of self-deception and even explaining the concept than contemporary analytic approaches that operate exclusively from sense experience and analyticity as the basis of knowing. Augustine's epistemology that knowing is actually recognition of that which is already known but only intimated to the knower is premised on the idea that the self experiences conflict between opposing wills. One's disquietude is stilled in the recognition of truth (Christ). Recognition provides the occasion to recollect oneself and cease the restless quest. Inner conflict, then, is a premise of knowing, and the fact of inner conflict points to the heart of the human mystery. Although Augustine's Christian explanation is certainly controversial--even for Christian believers--his explanation does account for human disquietude (anxiety) and the inner conflict necessary for self-deception. This is to suggest that it might prove profitable to look again at a mnemonic epistemology as relevant to our contemporary discussions of self-deception.

[206]The self-regarding duty to "know oneself" is discussed by Kant, Doctrine of Virtue, p. 107. Whether self-regarding duties are appropriately moral --as distinct from prudential--is controversial. Thomas E. Hill, "Servility and Self-Respect," Rights, ed. David Lyons (Belmont, CA: Wadsworth Publishing Co., 1979) has noted, p. 122, that "Recent philosophers tend to discard the idea of a duty to oneself as a conceptual confusion." My view is that practically speaking certain self-regarding duties constitute a condition for morality, and, normally, situations do not arise where violations of self-regarding duties (say, not to commit suicide) are not implicated in a community of concern. On that basis, one could uphold the principle that suicide is to be censured on moral grounds--on the grounds that the community interest is

involved. By the same logic, however, violating a self-regarding duty would not amount to a moral infraction, strictly speaking, so long as the prudential action did not prove inimical or offensive to the community interest. I shall address this issue again in the next chapter.

CHAPTER THREE

SELF-DECEPTION: THE ETHICAL AND RELIGIOUS PERSPECTIVES

In order to acquire an "intimate acquaintance" with self-deception, it is necessary to understand what the concept means and how it is used meaningfully. Holding to the theory that meaning is a function of use, this study began by offering a logico-linguistic analysis of the concept. 'Self-deception' was shown to be a self-directed project (action) aimed at the misleading of belief (cognition). Self-deception occurs when one has so acted that an epistemic deficit obtains between opposing beliefs, both of which are enacted, though for certain reasons (motive) one of the beliefs is held unawares. The next move in the analysis was to show that philosophical psychology was an interested party in this discussion,[1] for 'self-deception' is a psychological concept that cries our for philosophical clarification.

Philosophical psychology represents a particular expression of interest and a particular context for analysis. The philosophical psychologist seeks to obtain a picture of self-deception that is both free of incoherence and descriptively and diagnostically accurate. After reviewing major positions on the topic from this point of view, I offered a "cognition/action" theory of self-deception that could meet the objectives of the philosophical psychologist without resorting to certain of the highly controversial theoretical commitments of a Freud or Sartre.[2] My synthetic "emotional perception" proposal, and the critique of other models from which it emerged, was meant to contribute to the discussion about self-deception in a particular way, in a way that accepted the questions and commitments of the philosophical psychologist. A more far-reaching methodological point can now be made explicit. Although the approach to the question of self-deception from the perspective of the philosophical psychologist is certainly necessary, that perspective does not exhaust either the questions that can be asked or the resources that might be drawn upon in order to acquire "intimate acquaintance." The perspective of philosophical psychology is a particular method of inquiry, one that limits the scope of inquiry by means of a commitment to certain governing relations (the self-relations of psychology). Philosophical psychology sets an agenda of issues and holds to certain procedures for investigating those issues; and the governing relations guide the inquiry and authorize particular ways of using relevant concepts. The present study is concerned with this methodological point, for a methodology that authorizes a shift in governing relations will affect the question we ask and expose the kind of concern being brought to bear by the inquirer. This is a statement worthy of note as we attend to the concept 'self-deception' from other angles.

I am proposing at this point that we consider other perspectives and methodological commitments. There are other interests to be considered and other questions to be asked, and the quest for "intimate acquaintance" demands that they be examined and their contribution assessed. The point I would stress is that a shift in perspective will be accompanied by a shift in governing relations. What this means in particular shall be made clear as we proceed.

In this chapter, I shall consider two other perspectives that enter into the discussion about self-deception as "interested parties." One of those parties is the moral perspective, the other religious. Both perspectives represent particular ways of approaching the issue of self-deception. Each perspective asks its own questions, and in neither case is the question it asks that of the philosophical psychologist. Each perspective accepts the findings of the ordinary language analysis, however, for if 'self-deception' is not a coherent and intelligible concept in our common linguistic life, a moral or religious use of the concept will only compound the confusion. The influence of context can only make itself felt if the inquiry proceeds having already accepted the linguistic community's understanding of the concept 'self-deception,' which is to say that an ethical or religious employment of 'self-deception' will be parasitic on that common life, ordinary language understanding. Both the moral and religious perspectives express interests and call forth a context of meaning that one who would become "intimately acquainted" with self-deception must consider. I wish to say a few more things about this shift in perspective before proceeding.

In the moral or ethical sphere, meaning is governed by practical reason. To conceive of this sphere broadly requires that we attend to the subject matter of ethics: freedom and its use, action and choice. Practical reason is concerned with issues of value; and to think practically in the moral sense is to ask why one way of acting is preferable to another. To ask a moral question is to ask what kinds of reasons enable one to choose a course of action; and to make a moral decision is to evaluate action in a context of freedom. In this broad sense, an action is adjudged "moral" or "immoral" depending on how one chooses to act relative to certain fundamental purposes or goods of life: life itself, aesthetic experiences, psychological integrity, friendship, practical reasonableness, play and so on. Moral action is free action, action in which we assume the responsibility of freedom by our choices--in what is chosen and how it is chosen. When we abuse this freedom and renege on our responsibilities, we act in violation of the fundamental goods of life. When we act immorally, we infringe upon the freedom of others and cut ourselves off from those goods of life, failing thereby to assume responsibility for self-determination. From a moral point of view, self-determination expresses the "good" of moral interest, for it is through self-determination that we fulfill ourselves as moral persons in community with other co-equal centers of meaning and value (other persons).

From another point of view, however, the meaning of "moral" and "immoral" can be shown to a value distinction governed by certain relations. This is not to deny the broader conception, but it interprets that broader meaning in terms of a <u>relational</u> distinction. Psychology, we have seen, takes as its governing relations the idea of self-relatedness and its manifestations in human behavior. The moral sphere, however, to conceive it as a sphere of interest and commitment governed by certain relations, takes as its governing relation the idea of other-regardingness. In other words, the moral sphere is concerned with the actions and choices of human persons who are, in a context of freedom, also in community. This does not mean that the moral sphere is not concerned with self-relatedness. The point, rather, is that because ethics is concerned with human action in the social community and how reasons for action are established, the "other" is always a consideration, always the context. Even when one acts for reasons of self-interest, without apparent regard for others, that action is to be evaluated relative to the moral community. When considering self-deception, the question arises whether self-deception is, as a form of deception, an immoral action. In this chapter, I shall address this question by referring to the relational context governing the moral sphere of interest and commitment. As a related issue, we must consider whether a moral "translation" for self-deception is available. To be specific, in the moral sphere, does self-deception really refer to some kind of "weakness of will" or <u>akrasia</u>?

I shall look into these questions. When investigating the relation of self-deception to <u>akrasia</u>, I shall show how the concepts have sometimes been confused. The idea of "voluntary ignorance" (self-deception) has been mistaken for "voluntary wrongdoing" (<u>akrasia</u>); and I shall discuss these two notions, showing that self-deception is not entailed by <u>akrasia</u>; neither is it a conceptual equivalent. We shall take note of the fact that from a moral point of view, self-deceivers seem to violate a <u>prima facie</u>, or even an absolute duty-- the duty of persons to be honest with themselves. In relation to that obligation, the self-deceiver seems to exhibit an instance of <u>akratic</u> action by opting for the dishonesty of self-deception rather than the honest self-confrontation required for self-knowledge and truthful self-understanding.

I shall also consider the curiosity that even though self-deceivers violate the duty of self-honesty, we are reluctant to also say of self-deceivers that their action merits moral censure. I think we can address this issue if, on the basis of governing relations, we distinguish moral and prudential reasons for action. After all, it makes a difference in the moral sphere (broadly conceived) to say that a person violates a duty with respect to others ("immoral action") and to say that a person acts in a way that is not in the interest of his or her own well-being as a moral agent ("prudential <u>akrasia</u>"). I will show that self-deception cannot be assessed as "always immoral;" but I shall hold that a self-deceiver acts as an <u>akrates</u> with respect to certain <u>prima facie</u> obligations. By drawing this distinction, we can hold the self-deceiver responsible for the self-deception while holding that an obligation not to deceive oneself may be permissible under certain conditions. As an example will show, exceptions to the rule that one ought not to deceive oneself do arise, which means that in certain instances self-deception can be said to contribute to a person's well-being and to the well-being of the moral community.

The moral point of view, then, leads us to conclude that self-deception does not impose an absolute moral qualification whenever the phenomenon occurs. It is, even as an _akratic_ act in the _prima facie_ sense, a concept that can attend either moral or immoral acts; but as I shall argue, the acts in question can always be analyzed such that the self-deception can be extracted so that the evaluation "moral" or "immoral" can be said to depend on something other than self-deception. This is not an empty conclusion. It is, rather, a clarification of the concept 'self-deception' in light of the interests and commitments of the moral point of view.

The kind of morally neutral assessment that obtains from ethical analysis does not obtain in the religious context. The religious sphere is a context of meaning and value governed by _ultimate_ commitments and a relation I shall term the "God-relationship." To speak about self-deception in terms of the God-relationship is to say that the act of deceiving oneself is directed in a fundamental way to God or "before God." The practical consequence of "theological self-deception" is that one misleads one's own beliefs about the possibility made available by God for relationship with God. In this sphere of meaning and value, God's existence is not in question--it is assumed. Self-deception, then, obtains in relation to one's being related to the _appropriate_ object of religious interest, God. In other words, to mislead one's own beliefs in terms of the God-relationship is to mislead one's own beliefs about one's own ultimate concern or infinite interest. As a theological self-deceiver, one will wind up disrelating oneself to God. Typically, this takes the form of non-belief or disbelief, which are misrelations to God that indicate _sin_. There are two forms that theological self-deception can take, the classic formulation of sin as pride, the other the more modern notion of sin as despair. I shall look into each of these notions, showing that the theme of sin-as-pride-as-self-deception is prominent in Christian thought from a variety of perspectives and traditions, and that to accuse a person of sin as also to accuse a person of theological self-deception. The meaning for 'self-deception' authorized in the religious sphere is this: that one misleads one's own beliefs about the truth of the God-relation, a truth that the religious perspective claims is available to all. I shall also consider Kierkegaard's notion of sin as despair. This, too, informs us about the meaning self-deception, for Kierkegaard relates self-deception to sin and to disrelation to God. To be self-deceived in the religious context means that one is a sinner and disrelated to God; and I shall report on this religious employment of the term 'self-deception.' I begin, however, by subjecting self-deception to moral scrutiny, looking at this concept from the moral point of view.

A. The Moral Perspective

Self-deception raises several issues of moral importance. Generally speaking, these issues fall under one of two headings: moral translation and moral assessment. The first issue is whether self-deception can be translated into any particular moral concept. It has been suggested that akrasia ("weakness of will" or "voluntary wrongdoing") provides a moral version of self-deception This is a suggestion with merit, though not without problems. I shall consider the relation of akrasia to self-deception.

The second issue concerns the use to which 'self-deception' may be put as a term of moral evaluation. The issue here is whether the self-deceiver is acting immorally when he or she undertakes to mislead belief. I shall examine the moral status of 'self-deception,' arguing that even if a self-deceiver does violate a self-regarding duty not to deceive oneself, that violation does not necessarily entail that the self-deception is itself immoral. I shall examine circumstances in which the self-regarding duty not to deceive oneself can be abrogated with impunity for three reasons: because no clear issue of justice is involved; because the violation does not conflict in any essential way with other-regarding duties, which affects our use of moral concepts; and because examples can show that self-deception, rather than being immoral, contributes to a person's well-being and even promotes the well-being of others in certain cases.

I shall begin my moral analysis by clarifying the relation of self-deception to akrasia. Although I shall refer to different accounts of akrasia, my purpose is not to provide a history of philosophy study but to show that the concept of "voluntary wrongdoing," which, incidentally, has a history in Western philosophy, can be conceived in certain ways that are relevant to the moral assessment of self-deception.

1. Self-Deception and Akrasia

'Self-deception' and akrasia (literally: "incontinence") are related concepts. In fact, Catherine Wilson has argued that self-deception is ". . .a particular variety of weakness of the will,"[3] a position that seems to translate the psychological concept 'self-deception' into terms of moral evaluation. 'Self-deception' and akrasia, however, are also distinct concepts, and commentators have generally affirmed the distinction, even when a formal similarity between the two has been noted.[4] The nature of that formal similarity can be traced to the fact that akrasia, like self-deception, can be described coherently, in terms of self-relatedness, or incoherently, as a paradox that "cannot happen." Sometimes referred to as the "Socratic paradox," akrasia has been thought a paradoxical notion since Socrates asked in the Protagoras (351b-358d) whether a rational person could knowingly pursue evil.[5] I shall briefly sketch a picture of akrasia with an eye to showing why self-deception is a distinct concept not lending itself to translation under the rubrics of akrasia, "backsliding," "weakness of will." I do not intend to deny formal similarities or to show that the concepts are unrelated. My aim, rather, is to so distinguish the two concepts that an unwarranted conclusion that might be drawn is not drawn, namely, that every instance of akrasia is also an instance of self-deception.

a. Akrasia: Voluntary Wrongdoing

What is meant by akrasia? Strictly speaking, akrasia, a term employed and analyzed by Aristotle in the Nicomachean Ethics (Book vii), refers to a condition of character where one knows what one should do but does not do it. The concept refers to an agent's lack of self-determination, self-discipline, self-direction, or generally speaking, will power. Because of the privative nature of the concept, it is often employed or translated as a form of weakness--weakness of will or moral weakness.

Akrasia appears in the literature of moral philosophy under a variety of "translations:" "weakness of will," "incontinence," "unrestraint," "backsliding," "moral weakness," "psychological weakness," and "powerlessness." To complicate the picture, these several meanings can be subjected to analysis, which is to say that they can be shown to be different from one another to various degrees. Gwynneth Matthews, for instance, has identified several distinct meanings for "weakness of will:" "putting off the evil moment," "backsliding," "irresolution," "being persuaded against one's better judgment," "being too easily discouraged," "being unable to bring oneself to do something," "being overcome with desire, or "being unable to resist temptation."[6] Donald Davidson, on the other hand, has offered a broad notion of "weakness of will"-as-incontinence in these terms: "An agent's will is weak if he acts, and acts intentionally, counter to his own best judgment; in such cases we sometimes say he lacks the will power to do what he knows, or at any rate believes, would, everything considered, be better."[7] Raziel Abelson's formulation of "weakness of will," a notion he relates to self-deception and which he sees as being caused by mistaken judgments about one's own intentions, is this: "To be able to bring ourselves to do what we sincerely want to do, or to be unable to refrain from doing what we do not want to do."[8] And R.M. Hare's analysis of "backsliding" yields a picture of a psychological inability, for a backslider is the individual who cannot do what he thinks he ought.[9]

Whatever linguistic expressed is used to delimit conceptual parameters vis-a-vis these various characterizations or "definitions," it is clear that the terms themselves--"incontinence," "weakness of will," "backsliding,"--all participate in a general meaning complex related to a notion of voluntary wrongdoing. I have pointed these several expressions out because to do so is to indicate a complexity of meaning, which is to say that each expression provides an opportunity for meaning discrimination. Yet it is also clear that however one might distinguish, say, "backsliding" from "weakness of will," or "unrestraint" from "psychological inability to do what one ought," there is an undeniable family resemblance running through the diverse linguistic formulations. Analysis reveals that the linguistic discriminations are made with respect to the more generally conceived notion of <u>voluntary wrongdoing</u>, which it is now my purpose to consider.

For the sake of simplicity, and without exploring the moral and rational contingencies of <u>akrasia</u>,[10] I shall for purposes of this discussion retain a concept that means "voluntary wrongdoing" and identify that meaning complex with the stipulated term, <u>akrasia</u>. The "voluntary wrongdoing" designated by this concept is admittedly a broad notion, and one could say it is so broad that it would include any vice or notion of sin. My purpose in construing the meaning of the concept this way, however, is to point to human action that expresses a particular form of intrapsychic conflict. By "voluntary wrongdoing" I mean that given certain preferences and desires that are one's own and in the face of deliberation about how to act, a person may voluntarily act contrary to his or her understanding about the best course of action to take, even when free to do otherwise (i.e., not psychologically constrained: compulsion). A voluntary wrongdoer (<u>akrates</u>), then, acts such that the action violates his or her best judgment. What is being pointed out here is a conflict between a belief to which one attaches great value ("best") and a certain opposing desire. A voluntary wrongdoer is one who acts in accordance with the desire and against the "best" judgment. The idea of voluntary wrongdoing (<u>akrasia</u>) may be clarified with an example or two.

A well-known example of "voluntary wrongdoing" that shares features with my interpretation of <u>akrasia</u> is St. Paul's confession in Romans 7.15-20 (RSV). St. Paul describes what the RSV commentators describe as an "inner conflict."[11] I must note that certain of the remarks in the passage from which the following statements are extracted could lead one to conclude that St. Paul is disavowing responsibility for his action by blaming the power of sin over one's "inmost self" (v. 22). This interpretation, however, is not supportable in the main, and other authentic Pauline passages explicitly argue against it (e.g., Romans 1.31-2.5). St. Paul, then, is not expressing his belief that persons are not responsible for their sinful acts. My interest is not in theological disputation or exegesis. I seek, rather, a description of voluntary wrongdoing, and I find such a description in Paul's <u>Letter to the Romans</u>. I have excised those "controversial" parts of the text that do not bear on the illustration of <u>akrasia</u>. This excised picture of the phenomenon whereby persons act against their one's own best judgment reads as follows:

> "I do not understand my own actions. For I do not do what I want, but I do the very things I hate. I can will what is right, but I cannot do it. For I do not do the good I want, but the evil I do not want is what I do."

The point of this passage is not that Paul does not understand the best course of action. If he be believed, Paul does, in fact, know what is best. He knows the "right" thing to do. He can even will to do the best, right thing. The problem is that despite the human person's understanding about what is known and willed, persons often cannot actually do what they know they ought. This failure, too, persons can know and understand. It is this failure "to do" that occasions the perplexity. Paul is right then to say that it is his own actions that he does not understand, since he violates his own conception of the good. Although he does not understand why this happens, he understands that it occurs and that he is responsible for this "voluntary wrongdoing." Akrasia is the remainder left when we subtract what we actually do from what we know to be the right or best thing to do, which we are capable of acknowledging as an "ought."

As a second illustration, let me modify the pastor and Gertrude story in order to illustrate akrasia without self-deception.

The pastor finds Gertrude helpless and blind. Acting from motives of Christian charity, he takes her into his home to comfort, befriend and care for her. As his teaching and general attention begin to have positive results, the pastor becomes aware of a change in his feelings toward Gertrude. He begins to take increasing pleasure in her company. The pastor, whose marriage has been less than satisfying, begins to feel a gap in his life fill again with the joie de vivre. As Gertrude achieves one breakthrough after another, as she begins to emerge from her sufferings as a person of charm and beauty, a person to be admired rather than pitied, the pastor experiences an attraction to her of such a character that he recognizes it to be erotic longing. He also recognizes this love to be unsuitable to his social station and his moral self-understanding, for such love is inconsistent with both his role as a minister and his conjugal responsibilities. In other words, the feelings he has for Gertrude are not appropriate to a member of the clergy who is caring for a needy person, not to mention their inappropriateness for a good Christian father and husband who has a visitor under his roof. He admits to himself that he has fallen in love with Gertrude, yet he feels bound by Christian duty not to forsake his family charge. He therefore conceals the fact of his love for Gertrude, choosing to do so by various ruses and deceptions in order to divert suspicion. For instance, he adopts a "distant" attitude toward Gertrude when they are in the company of others. But the conflict of desires continues to brew. Torn between his desire for Gertrude--a desire he considers illicit--and a desire to do his Christian duty, the pastor finally can bear the strain no longer and decides to leave his family and forsake his pastorate. He and Gertrude spirit themselves off to an undisclosed location.

The story does not end here. The pastor is a reflective man. It is clear to him that in fleeing with Gertrude, his behavior has merited moral censure. In fleeing with Gertrude, he repudiated his identity and sense of self. He realizes that he has acted in a way that violates his own sense of what he ought to have done. In other words, the pastor understood what the best course of action was; yet, despite that awareness, he acted in accordance with the least preferable (worst) course. How many times has he condemned adultery and family faithlessness? How many times has he read Scripture and believed the explicit injunctions of Scripture to be right in condemning action such as his? The pastor, then, admits to himself that in fleeing with Gertrude he has violated his own best judgment, which even now is not obscured from view. Accordingly, he tells himself that he has acted hypocritically. Furthermore, he experiences remorse for having allowed his desire for a certain pleasure to distort his priorities and subvert his character, for in violating his own preferences, he has acted uncharacteristically. Due to a weakness of will, the pastor has allowed himself to act in accordance with a "worst" preference, and it is this that has proven the stronger motive. He blames himself for his wrongdoing, which he understands to have been done freely and without compulsion. He now begins to view himself as unworthy of happiness with Gertrude. Overcome with regret, the pastor finds his pleasure with Gertrude poisoned. The experience of remorse that sets in eventually brings the pastor to another decision. He decides to leave Gertrude, return home, seek forgiveness, and resume his family responsibilities. All of these things he does.

b. Self-Deception and Akrasia: Distinct Concepts

Neither of these descriptions illustrates self-deception. Neither St. Paul nor the pastor is engaged in a project to mislead belief. Neither demonstrates in publicly observable ways that he is unaware of the best, most reasonable interpretation of his action, nor that his actions conflict with his self-image or with a desire to be a person of a certain sort, whether as a person who knows and wills what is good (St. Paul) or who knows and wills what is required by Christian duty and familial obligation (pastor). No epistemic deficit obtains between contrary beliefs simultaneously held, nor does the interpretive activity indicate that one is intended. There is no evident "cover story" in place (except as a conscious deception: the pastor), no attempt to banish from conscious reflection and deliberation a "real story." The "real story," which is a story of voluntary wrongdoing, is owned up to in frank, direct and explicit acts of self-recognition and self-confrontation--and without the aid of the self-deception poultice. There is psychic distress, of course. It has been occasioned by the self-confrontation. But there is no effort in either case to rationalize away or deny that distress. In neither instance does the individual act to construe what is not there or misconstrue what is. The interpretive activity does not express action motivated by a desire to "save face" and avoid self-confrontation. On the contrary, the akrates seems to avoid avoiding self-confrontation so concerned is he that this distress be made linguistically explicit and accurately interpreted.

In short, these examples do not portray persons engaged in self-directed belief-misleading projects that result in actual epistemic deficits and observable "unawareness." We can discern contradictory beliefs simultaneously held, for the belief that one ought to act in accordance with self-image or an ideal future self (p) is opposed by a contrary belief that one has in fact not done so (not-p). But there is no "ingenious solution," no cover up of the best, most reasonable interpretation with clever interpretive activity that distorts the meaning of the person's own acts and behavior. One does not find any trace of the crucial "unawareness" criterion necessary for the ascription of 'self-deception.'

That the akrates experiences distress as a result of realizing that he or she has failed to act consistently with the preferences that are constitutive of character or self-image is not to be denied. Unlike the self-deceiver, the akrates makes the "threat" posed by this failure linguistically explicit.

The akrates acknowledges this failure to him- or herself. The desire to resolve the conflict is so strong that the "weak" choice may have even seemed a temporary "best" choice in a more largely conceived strategy to resolve the situation of conflict; but even so, at no time does the akrates suppress the fact that the behavior violates a best choice. Furthermore, while a self-deceiver will present behavioral evidence that suggests "overwhelmingly" that a recognition lies behind the denial,[12] the akrates will not do so. The akrates may opt to hide or deceive others about his or her awareness. I suggested such a 'deception' in the pastor case, for it seems possible that "[a person] can voluntarily perceive, categorize, intend and decide in ways that violate his primary preference, and do so without being self-deceived about what he is doing."[13] This is a point of contrast worthy of note. A self-deceiver and the akrates resolve the conflict between opposing desires in different ways. The akrates does not allow the identity-preservation desire to override a conflicting desire to grasp at what is perceived to be "threatening" to that self-image, even though the act itself violates avowed preferences and the recognition of that occasions distress. Another way to put this is that self-deceivers situate themselves to avoid experiencing remorse; akrates do not. Remorse is a necessary feature of akrasia, and the akrates necessarily experiences it. And because of that remorse, the akrates is likely to reform, as Aristotle indicated.[14] Self-deception and akrasia can be distinguished descriptively; but an evaluation can also be made. From a moral point of view, the fact that we can avoid remorse and prevent self-reform by deceiving ourselves means that self-deception is more "dangerous" than akrasia. This is because

> [Self-deception] blocks the movement to correction, blocks the logical rational process oriented towards truth. Akrasia

blocks zweckrationalität without necessarily blocking its own correction. Indeed Aristotle distinguished vice from akrasia by noting that the regret characteristic of akrasia can be efficacious in self-reform.[15]

The kind of reform at issue here is more easily seen with respect to the pastor than St. Paul. One would expect the pastor to repent and to seek reintegration into his moral community by means of a resolve never to act this way again, never again to behave as he did with Gertrude. Whether his community accepts him back without severe recrimination is moot, and the conditions it attaches to his reentry (e.g., penance) are matters of speculation. The central concern is the pastor's own inward movement to rehabilitate himself in that community and realign himself with his own first-order preferences to do the good. Regret or remorse spur such inward movement.

St. Paul's reflection goes deeper, for it expresses the despair of one who seeks moral perfection (say: the conjunction of virtue and happiness) in the face of a sobering realization. That realization is that such perfection, even for one who, like St. Paul, is "blameless" according to certain culturally enshrined action guides (Philippians 3.6), is unattainable. St. Paul's realization that there is no such thing as a pure act, no possibility that human action can be free of the influence of a perverse will, leads him to despair of achieving happiness itself. His sense of the wretchedness of the human condition is then all the more apparent in that he also acknowledges the need for moral rules and action guides. Without them, restraint would be impossible and human subjects could not become conscious of wrongdoing. Yet these action guides also incite persons to wrongdoing (Gal. 3.23; Rom. 7.7ff). The remorse expressed by St. Paul on behalf of moral self-consciousness reflects a sobering insight--that the ethical resource itself can be weighed and found wanting. Ethics itself is found to be an inadequate means for reconciling a person in actuality to the ideal of moral perfection. To realize the disparity between the goal of moral striving and the futility of all such striving is to realize despair itself. For pushed to the limit, ethical reflection posits a telos (summum bonum) that is ideal and to which one can relate oneself only by becoming--not by actualizing. The goal of moral perfection then becomes a fly in the ointment, for that goal announces to the moral striver that the goal itself is beyond human capacity. All becoming that is movement toward the goal of moral perfection and the "pure act" is necessarily a recognition that one seeks to be what one is not. One cannot simply will to be one's ideal self. To be self-conscious morally is to be conscious of an ideal self in relation to the actual self one is. And that actual self is necessarily imperfect, conscious of its imperfection, yet so constituted as to desire the perfection it cannot actually attain.[16]

It is clear from this analysis that moral consciousness entails not only duty (objectively) but guilt and remorse (subjectively); and awareness that

"The ethical always consists in the consciousness of wanting to do the good"[17] will, if reflection be pushed as far as St. Paul pushes it, occasion despair. The significance of akrasia, then, lies not only in the fact that the akrates can experience remorse and thereby effect self-reform and restoration to the moral community. The significance of akrasia, rather, lies in the fact that akrasia reflects a deeper problem of human disintegration, disunity, and insufficiency. This picture of broken and fragmented selfhood is apparent for one who would consider the disparity between one's actual and ideal self, both of which are metaphors for terms within one's own self-relations. Despair obtains as one considers one's actuality in the face of the most cherished of ideals, moral perfection.

Both the pastor and St. Paul are aware that they have failed to achieve moral perfection. St. Paul even goes so far as to say, "I do not understand my own actions" (Rom. 7.15). This does not mean that St. Paul is incapable of describing what he has done or that he is ignorant of the meaning of his actions vis-a-vis his declared desire to do the good. As I said, it is clear that in one sense he does understand his action, for he accurately describes a conflict situation in which he, as a morally self-conscious and reflective agent, realizes that he has not done the good he wants and wills to do. Rather, the fact that he is able to recognize that his own action does not conform to his own preferences brings him to a realization that as a self he is not unified but in conflict with himself. The conflict is made manifest in his awareness of a desire to do good as that is opposed by his awareness of having failed to do it. This describes the conflict, and the conflict expresses a depth of self-relatedness that eludes his own ability to grasp or correct. It is because St. Paul understands what he has done that he does not claim to understand how it occurs, how these actions which are his could be his own. He does not, however, like the self-deceiver, deny them as his own or rationalize them to mean something other than what they do, in fact, mean. Perhaps his analysis of motives and intentions reveals that when one acts in accordance with the letter of the law, one violates the spirit by impure motives or prudential considerations, which in turn reveals a lack of moral perfection. Whatever the particulars might be, it is clear that it is not a logical paradox he confronts, but a living opposition in the will. And it mystifies him. By confronting himself with his failure to do what he wants and wills to do, he perceives a deeper perversity, which befalls him even when he is otherwise blameless. His act of self-confrontation and self-recognition leads him to question himself as if he were his greatest enigma, as if he did not understand who he is.[18] The akrasia phenomenon leads him, as it undoubtedly leads the pastor, to consider the fundamental question of human being, "Who am I?"

In the akratic aftermath, in the reflective experience of remorse that attends his self-recognition, both St. Paul and the pastor encounter themselves as persons-in-conflict. They become reflectively aware that certain parties, terms, or interests constitutive of self-relatedness are in actual conflict. St. Paul <u>can</u> understand what he has done, but by understanding his actions in a descriptive sense, he is mystified by the strength of his understanding and the weakness of his resolve. He is mystified that his moral striving should end in remorse and occasion despair. The pathos of this realization is heightened by Paul's acknowledgment that in an external sense, he has observed the rules and regulations of the moral community and has kept the "law" in a way that marks a kind of perfection ("blameless"). Outward conformity and obedience to accepted social prescriptions, however, is finally insufficient to provide inward certainty that the ideal has been attained, and it is finally the law that serves to invite deeper reflection, the deeper realization of a more fundamental imperfection. As moral persons, both St. Paul and the pastor are left in despair. Both are aware of the wretchedness of their situations and await a solution that will either restore him to community, as in the case of the pastor, or free him from the guilt and despair that has been discovered to attend all ethical striving (St. Paul).[19]

These two examples of person's violating their own avowed preferences, are, in the <u>akrates'</u> own self-understanding, instances of voluntary wrongdoing. The psychic distress occasioned by the <u>akratic</u> action is not mitigated with excuses; neither is it "covered up" with rationalizations, denials, or evasive interpretive maneuvers. There is no self-deception here. In fact, analysis of the examples reveals that self-deception can be distinguished from <u>akrasia</u> simply on the basis of conceptual content. <u>Akrasia</u> does not require "unawareness," so, clearly, the concepts do not mean the same thing. Clearly, the two concepts are not interchangeable or translatable one into the other; neither are their meanings functionally equivalent. Despite the fact that both concepts refer to a simultaneous holding of opposing beliefs, a conceptual distinction obtains. And this holds even if in particular cases of self-conflict, the <u>akrasia</u> can be said to be functioning as a strategy toward self-deception. There are instances of "<u>akratic</u> belief" where a person reflectively ceases an inquiry realizing "deep down" that if that inquiry were to continue, his or her beliefs would have to be revised. It is this revision of beliefs that the person does not want to do. Even if "akrasia of belief and self-deception often go hand in hand," as suggested by Amelie O. Rorty,[20] there is no reason to equate the two concepts or otherwise blur a definite conceptual distinction.[21]

c. **Self-Deception and Akrasia: Related Concepts**

Having drawn a necessary conceptual distinction over the "unawareness" criterion, let me say a word or two about conceptual similarities. There are certain formal, structural congruities that self-deception and akrasia share. Certain of the the questions that have been asked about self-deception can also be asked about akrasia, and it is at this point that those formal similarities begin to emerge. Just as the question arose concerning a person's capacity for self-deception, a question arises whether a person is capable of voluntary wrongdoing, or, even more basically, whether there can even be such a thing as voluntary wrongdoing. Moral psychologists have debated this issue since Socrates, but the larger, more significant question is, of course, "Of what, then, is a person capable?" About self-deception one must ask, Does a person have a capacity to mislead his or her own beliefs? By the same token, Is a person able to act such that the act represents a voluntary violation of one's own preferences? And is such a preference violation necessarily immoral? As a concept that refers to the self-in-conflict, akrasia, like self-deception, invites us to consider the most basic issues of self-relatedness.

An analysis of akrasia in light of self-deception reveals that akrasia, too, is a reflexive concept. Akrasia, too, concerns a particular situation of self-conflict. The concept 'akrasia' is, like self-deception, governed by relations that are appropriately self-relations, and this holds even though akrasia is properly a moral term, a term, that is, relevant to the context of self-other relations. In moral discourse, akrasia not only describes, but evaluates a feature of action in the moral context of self-other relations or "other-regardingness." The akrates is an agent and capable of decision. The decision to act, however, is a judgment reached by the self in relation to itself. The decision, in other words, is to be described with reference to the context of the self-relatedness, for the akrates decides to act in the midst of self-conflict, in the midst of an awareness about what one wants to do as that desire conflicts with a belief about what one ought to do, which it is also one's desire to do. The self-deceiver's interpretive activity, as I have said, aims at creating a cognitive or epistemic split. In order to achieve an actual epistemic deficit, the self-deceiver acts to mislead belief, which is to create a cognitive split. The akrates creates a volitional split. Beset with possibilities for action, the akrates decides to act in accordance with the option that opposes his or her own avowed preferences. Even if one were to argue that akratic action is not necessarily immoral since it represents the "best" way to manage an intrapersonal conflict in a particular situation, there is no doubt that akratic actions occur, that preferences are violated, that such violation is voluntary, and that decisions to act are made in the midst of self-conflict. Self-relatedness is the context within which both self-deception and akrasia are to be rendered intelligible. Both are reflexive concepts, though each involves reflexivity in a different way, one cognitively, the other volitionally.

Akrasia, however, is not simply, or only, a reflexive concept. It is a term relevant to moral psychology, not simply to psychology or one's self-relations divorced from moral scrutiny. As I have said, it is a term that has been put to use in the context of moral discourse, particularly as a term of accusation or blame.

Akrasia is related to moral action in the sense that akratic action is morally wrong action that results form a weakness of will or from some lack of personal excellence (virtue). When describing akrasia, we often mean to refer to a sort of character deficiency. This was originally Aristotle's meaning for akrasia: a weakness that also specified a character deficiency for which the akrates was to held responsible. Consider the person who, as a result of morally wrong action that results from a weakness of will or from some lack of personal excellence (virtue). When describing akrasia, we often mean to refer to a sort of character deficiency. This was originally Aristotle's meaning for akrasia: a weakness that also specified a character deficiency for which the akrates was responsible. Consider the person who, as a result of losing his or her temper, harms another person. The immoral action that springs from this anger could be said to have arisen from a failure of personal virtue, (say) from intemperance, which is a lack of the virtue temperance. The intemperance refers to the inability of the person to master his or her passion. As a result the person fails to act virtuously, virtuous action in this instance being equivalent to acting temperately. This failure to act temperately, which issues in harm to another, is akratic action. It violates one's own desire to be a person of a certain sort, temperate and virtuous, a person capable of taking into one's relations with others the respect for persons that expresses moral concern. The failure to be other-regarding as a result of a failure in personal virtue refers to a flaw in character, the "weakness" of akrasia.

With certain exceptions (e.g., Hobbes, Sidgwick), moral philosophers have argued that other-regarding reasons for action are superior to personal preferences or reasons of self-interest and are therefore overriding.[22] Given this supremacy of moral reasons, reasons that concern what one ought to do in the other-regarding sphere of relations, over prudential or self-interested reasons, certain moral conclusions follow about the moral status of akrasia. The akrates wants to be moral, wants to do the good and right thing. This desire to be moral constitutes a first-order or prima facie preference, for it is in relation to this desire to be moral that akrasia obtains and remorse results. The akrates, however, violates his or her own first-order preference to be moral, opting to do the very thing that moral rules are designed to prevent. By violating his or her own first-order preference to be moral, the akrates allows prudential considerations to override the "better" or "stronger" reasons for action, which are those other-regarding reasons that moral rules are designed to uphold. The akrates, therefore, acts immorally to the extent that he or she follows self-interest in a situation where moral obligation would require the overriding of self-interest. The _akrates_ displays a weakness to the extent that he or she chooses to let some prudential preference that is in conflict with one's moral responsibilities override that moral claim. The _akrates_ who experiences remorse does so because he or she has acted to override moral reasons with self-interested reasons. To permit such an overriding of moral by prudential can mean that the _akrates_ will harm someone in the moral community, or, in some other way, come to realize that he or she is unworthy of happiness.

It is on the basis of this understanding of the disjunction between moral and prudential reasons for action that _akrasia_ has come to be used as a term of moral evaluation. The _akrates_ is, after all, thought to be one who fails to do the right thing, fails to perform up to the expectations of the moral community. The _akrates_ lacks the ability to do the morally right thing due to some deficiency of personal virtue, some character impediment or weakness with respect to _doing_ what one believes one _ought_.[23] That persons are capable of splitting their wills this way is an idea that appeals to "self-relatedness" for conceptual coherence, and this particular understanding of volitional capacity coincides with the view of J. W. N. Watkins, who has written about _akrasia_, rightly, that "[it] is perfectly possible that someone would personally _prefer_ to do one thing but decides, more or less regretfully after taking other persons' preferences into account, that he _ought_ to do another."[24] That the _akrates_ fails to do the very thing that he or she believes ought to be done, thereby denying the supremacy of moral over prudential reasons, explains why _akrasia_ has entered our moral discourse as a concept of moral assessment bespeaking a moral failure. John King-Farlow captures this typical sense of _akrasia_ when he remarks, "'Akrasia' is a term of blame that I have no wish to turn into one of praise."[25] _Akrasia_, being a term that is meaningful with respect to a volitional split, can then be said to carry a normative moral meaning, even thought there may be non-moral satellite meanings (e.g., prudential _akrasia_). It remains to be seen what normative moral evaluation will attend 'self-deception.'

This analysis of _akrasia_ has disclosed that _akrasia_ is a problem in self-relations. Because it is primarily volitional in nature and refers to a conflict that issues n action, the concept itself is relevant to the moral sphere and is therefore a term appropriate to moral discourse. It refers to action that is, by the person's own lights, action to be regretted, action that falls short, misses the mark, and violates moral preferences. It refers to action that either winds up harming another or to action that so violates one's own preference not to act prudentially that one is forced to despair of _ever_ achieving the ideal of moral perfection and pure action. The pastor and St. Paul illustrate persons who experience this conflict and reflect on it. Both realize that we can act against our own preferences for moral action. The regret we experience as a result of our _akratic_ actions is subjective confirmation of our moral failures. We are capable of recognizing these failures; we are capable of realizing that our actions can violate our preferences, that we can do wrong knowing that what we do is wrong, that such action reflects our lack of personal virtue and moral purity.

Akrasia is conceptually distinct from self-deception, yet, like self-deception, akrasia has been subject to various interpretations. It presents a conceptual difficulty in moral psychology not unlike the one we have already considered in examining self-deception. The nature of akrasia has sometimes been obscured because of philosophical debates that center not on the idea of persons violating their own preferences, but on the idea of "voluntary ignorance."[26] Akrasia, however, does not mean "voluntary ignorance." In fact, to equate "voluntary ignorance" with akrasia is to make a conceptual blunder, for to do so is to confuse akrasia with self-deception. We cannot collapse these two concepts, for such a move mistakes a problem in philosophical psychology with a problem in moral psychology. Although such confusion has occurred and we would do well to be alerted to the possibility of confusion as we come to consider the relation of "voluntary ignorance" to "voluntary wrongdoing," there is a more fundamental issue at stake.

The more fundamental issue at stake concerns how one is to conceive of human nature, or the nature of human being. Every interpretation of self-deception and akrasia is underwritten by a normative view of human capability. By appealing to the different theories of human nature and capacities upon which various and often incompatible perspectives on self-deception and akrasia themselves depend, we can come to understand how differing foundations give rise to the manifold conceptual analyses. Recall the argument about self-deception that because it is literally a paradox it "cannot happen." In Chapter Two ("Translation Model"), I argued that the logic that claimed that self-deception could not happen assumed as fact what in fact was not fact: that consciousness was incapable of being opaque to itself, unable to hide some matter of content from itself or make itself obscure to itself. Were that picture of consciousness to hold, it would not be possible to say that a person could hold opposing beliefs simultaneously. I argued that this particular approach was wrongheaded, for if 'self-deception' were an unresolvable paradox and literally contradictory, there could be no facts to be discovered, thereby rendering M. R. Haight's project aimed at "getting at the facts" otiose.[27] At present, the point to reiterate is that in the philosophical and psychological literature, 'self-deception' has been analyzed such that a paradox obtains. That conclusion, while logical, rested on unexamined assumptions about consciousness. That conclusion, while logical, appealed to a normative picture of human capability not based on empirical appeal, a picture that denied that one person could be both agent and victim, a simultaneous believer and unbeliever with respect to p.

I mention the Haight study once again because akrasia as "voluntary wrongdoing" has been similarly analyzed. There are two related views to be considered, each of which has parallels in the philosophical literature on self-deception. One is that akrasia cannot happen, for the idea of "voluntary wrongdoing" is contradictory. The other is that it can happen, but it cannot be rationally explained. Akrasia has been a problem in moral psychology for the same reason that self-deception has been a problem in philosophical psychology, namely, because of unexamined assumptions about human nature and capacity that inform and shape the particular theory of self-deception or akrasia. The normative picture of human capability underwriting those theories has either been left unexamined, or the operative assumption has led to one of two necessary logical conclusions: either it cannot happen, or it is irrational.

d. Voluntary Wrongdoing and Voluntary Ignorance

No less a philosopher than Socrates considered the idea of voluntary wrongdoing to be contradictory. Socrates assumed virtuous action to be a form of knowledge--knowledge of the Good. Socrates conceived of the Good as the most rational object of human striving and as the true desire of rational human beings. His position was that it is not only rational to seek virtue, but virtue is our true desire as rational persons. As Socrates conceived the matter, in order to do the Good, in order to act virtuously, one need only to know the Good. That is, virtue arises from the conjunction of true knowledge and true desire. The assumption, then, was that the human person is disposed to rationality by a desire for the Good, from which it followed that to know the Good was to do it--irresistibly. Knowledge not only affected action, but was action: to know was to do.

If, as Socrates thought, virtue be the true human desire, how could we conceive of an individual who would not do what he or she desires? How could persons act as free agents to frustrate their own true desire if they knew what that desire was? Socrates' answer was simple: they can't. The idea that persons could knowingly pursue evil or act against their own best judgment about the Good is, on Socrates' account, a contradictory notion, the Socratic paradox so familiar in moral philosophy. For Socrates, that we could desire to act against our own true desire, especially in light of the assumption that our true desire conforms to the requirements of reason itself, was inexplicable. On Socrates account, the idea of "voluntary wrongdoing" is a contradiction and the idea of "weakness of will" a paradox.[28]

"For Socrates," then, wrote Aristotle, an opponent of this view, "there was no such thing as incontinence; no one, he said, when he judges acts against what he judges best--people act so only by reason of ignorance."[29] Given Socrates' assumption that knowledge is virtue, the conclusion that evil is ignorance is irresistible since, by definition, to act wrongly is to lack knowledge of what is right. Wrongdoing, then, is possible, but only because an individual lacks the knowledge that is a necessary precondition and concomitant to virtuous action. Such ignorance is involuntary and therefore neither willful nor intentional, for it is not an expression of weakness of will. Socrates was not, of course, blind to the world around him. He did not deny the fact of evil or the fact of wrongdoing. His point, rather, was that evil cannot be explained by referring to a failure of will. Evil deeds are not accurately described in terms of "voluntary wrongdoing" but as the consequence of ignorance of the Good. When Socrates asked whether a rational person could knowingly pursue evil, he answers, in effect, "No," arguing that to so describe wrongdoing is non-sensical, paradoxical. Socrates concluded about akrasia what Haight concluded about self-deception: it cannot happen. As a paradox or contradictory notion, there are no facts that can be mustered to support this description; therefore it cannot happen. A person cannot knowingly pursue evil, for to know is to do. To know the Good is to act virtuously. To act otherwise is not to know the Good, for vice is ignorance.

The other track that could be taken--and it complements the Socratic equation of knowledge and virtue--is to consider akrasia a form of irrationality. On this view, one could say that akratic action is possible, but, as Donald Davidson has put the matter, "What is wrong is that the incontinent man acts, and judges, irrationally, for this is surely what we must say of a man who goes against his own best judgment."[30] Kierkegaard's Judge Wilhelm presaged this irrationality argument when he noted that the ethical individual is so constituted that he or she is of a piece with the universal person; and such an individual displays a confidence so overwhelming that after a while ethical requirements become broad, abstract, and universal principles, not specific guides that can be pressed into "every insignificant affair" where failures actually occur before the ethical ideal:

> The effort [to live up to the ethical ideal] always fails and is to be found only in those who do not possess courage to believe in the the ethical and who lack inward confidence in a deeper sense. There are men whose pusillanimity is recognizable precisely in the fact that they are never ready with the sum total because for them this is not single but manifold. But this, too, lies outside the ethical, and there is, of course, no other grounds for it but weakness of will, which like all other weakness of mind may be regarded as a sort of insanity.[31]

For Judge Wilhelm, akrasia exists; but it is irrational, a kind of insanity. Akratic action is incomprehensible.

Ethicality constitutes an arena of interest, concern, even passion, that focuses on our ability to understand ourself in relation to the universal, the comprehensible, the rational and knowable. As such, any violation of the universal action-guides accepted as normative though practical reason, any ethical violation, sin or wrongdoing, can be described as essentially a problem in knowing. To say this is to advance a particular kind of description of wrongdoing. As the viewpoints of Socrates, Davidson, and Kierkegaard's Judge Wilhelm indicate, moral action is rational action; it is action that expresses our desire to have the "sum total," to grasp what is understandable by all, what is accepted as universal, what is truly rational. When reason's grasp of the universal is subverted, when the universal is threatened by "insignificant affairs," then any action aimed at such subversion is not only lacking in virtue, but fundamentally unreasonable. In fact, for one to defy the universal by failing to do what one knows one ought is, to put it bluntly, cowardice. To act cowardly before the universal is to act as an akrates, and within the acceptable, rationally imposed limits of the universal akratic action is unintelligible. Any instance of akrasia, then, can be interpreted as a violation of the universally valid and reason-substantiated claims of the ethical sphere itself. In light of this conception of ethicality, in light of this view that right reason is an irresistible influence on human actions, any opposition to the universal through voluntary wrongdoing or vice constitutes a stand outside--and against--the universal. This is irrational, an opposition to reason itself. From this point of view, the idea of voluntary wrongdoing constitutes a "sort of insanity." It is something that cannot really happen, at least not under a description of voluntarily doing what one knows one shouldn't. In fact, when evil or vice or wrongdoing do occur, more adequate alternative descriptions may be found, e.g., "involuntary ignorance." One does what is wrong or immoral because one really does not know the Good.

By raising a question about the relation of knowing to doing, akrasia raises the more fundamental issue about human nature and capacity. Is there such a thing as "voluntary or intentional wrongdoing"? Socrates' view that akrasia is error or ignorance assumed that human beings are disposed to rationality and to the good. It is assumed that human beings are innately endowed with this disposition, from which it follows that any action that can be characterized as evil cannot be attributed to willful misconduct or to imperfections in the will, but to failures of knowing, comprehending, understanding. Evil, in other words, is ignorance. We must be attentive both to what this position is claiming and what is claimed in the name of this position. Consider A. E. Taylor's analysis of Socrates' ethical thought, keeping in mind that my interest here is in a particular way of conceiving the relation of knowing to doing, which in turn appeals to a certain conception of human being. What is at issue here is not Socrates' thought in particular, but a particular way of describing the fact of evil for which Socrates is an able spokesperson:

> We may most conveniently start with what appears to be the most violent paradox of all, the assertion that all wrongdoing is involuntary. 'Moral weakness,' the fact that men do what they themselves confess to be wrong, and that they do so without any forcing, is one of the most familiar facts of experience, and we are not to suppose that Socrates means to

deny this. He means to say that the popular phrase we have just used gives an inadequate analysis of the fact. A man often does evil in spite of the fact that it is evil; no man ever does evil simply because he sees it to be evil, as a man may do good simply because he sees it to be good. A man has temporarily to sophisticate himself into regarding evil as good before he will choose to do it. . . .To say that vice is involuntary means, therefore, that it never brings the vicious man that on which his heart, whether he knows it or not, like the heart of everyone else, is really set. . . . .Evil-doing always rests upon a false estimate of goods.^{32}

There are several things to be noted about this passage. First, Taylor describes akrasia as a familiar experience of the common life, a moral weakness that people are able to confront in themselves and acknowledge reflectively, with full awareness. This is an understanding we can heartily endorse. Secondly, Taylor's Socrates does not deny the fact of wrongdoing. The point, rather, is that Taylor's Socrates has a particular philosophical perspective that he believes best accounts for the facts. Thirdly, no one does evil because it is evil. Evil results, rather, from a mistaken conception about the Good. The vicious person persuades him- or herself that what is evil is really not evil, but consistent with the Good as the Good is (mis)understood. The evildoer acts to mislead his or her own beliefs, undertaking interpretive activity that obscures the evil and permits an interpretation of evil as good. What we must note is that this picture of a person being able to "sophisticate himself into regarding evil for good" appeals to the idea of a project to mislead belief. In other words, this description of akrasia appeals to self-deception for coherence. Lastly, a person can violate a preference that is the person's own, a real preference or disposition to do the good "whether he knows it or not."

We can agree with Taylor-on-Socrates that wrongdoing, evil, and moral weakness are all facts of human experience, and common ones at that. We can even agree that there are cases where an individual who has acted wrongfully would be ignorant of the evil of those acts due to an act of self-persuasion whereby evil has been mistaken for good. What I wish to point out is that by putting matters this way Taylor is interpreting Socrates' position in terms of self-deception, not akrasia. This is because wrongdoing can only be done if one deceives oneself that what is evil is good, for in order to do what is evil, one must first of all be persuaded that it is not evil, for no one voluntarily performs an evil act; and to know the good, even if one is actually mistaken about it, is to do the good. If this be the true interpretation of Socrates' evil is ignorance argument, then akrasia is not at issue and the will is not the problem. Evil, rather, is the result of an act of self-deception. Socrates' argument, then, takes evil out of the context of decision-making and free human action and puts it into a context of knowing and understanding, a cognitive and epistemological context. Evil action is action that is ignorant of the good, and this means that in order to do evil one must first believe it to be good so that one can, in fact, act on what (mistakenly) believes to be the good. Since this Socratic perspective located the source of wrongdoing in knowledge, it follows that evil results from persons deceiving themselves about the good. The good is "written on the heart" so to speak, but because of the human capacity for self-deception, the person may not have reflective or self-conscious access to the good, for the person may lack knowledge of the good (ignorance) or be actually unaware of the good (i.e., "whether he knows it or not").

We cannot simply accept this description of human wrongdoing, since something startling appears when we ask, "Is Socratic ignorance really self-deception?" If we permit an explanation of human evil in terms of self-deception, we are committing ourselves to the view that evil is really "voluntary ignorance" since our ordinary language idea of 'self-deception' refers to voluntary, willful ignorance. Akrasia, or voluntary wrongdoing, will not permit a shift in meaning to the idea of "voluntary ignorance." The evil as ignorance position holds that we do evil only because we do not know the good. In other words, we do evil involuntarily; it is an error or a blunder arising from ignorance. Aside from the problem that this position denies the freedom to abuse freedom, we must ask how one could be disposed to do the good and not do it. To say that one must "sophisticate oneself" into believing that one's evil actions are really good (self-deception) in the face of one's disposition to know the good simply begs a question about the nature of the ignorance being appealed to here. Is that ignorance really innocent error, or is that ignorance in some way willed and voluntary? If this "ignorance" be thought of as involuntary, non-volitional, or unintentional, it cannot be equated with, or even referred to, the concept 'self-deception,' for the concept 'self-deception' requires as a necessary feature of conceptual content purposeful action (interpretive activity) aimed a desired cognitive result, namely, the misleading of one's own beliefs.

Self-deception is a synthetic concept (Chapter Two, part C). If one argues that Socratic ignorance is really self-deception, which Taylor does on behalf of Socrates,[33] then one is also forced to conclude that the ignorance in question is not innocent but voluntary, purposeful, intentional, motivated. That is what 'self-deception' means. If one does not concede this point, then one is committed to the view that wrongdoing is involuntary ignorance, and, as Taylor presents it, that is what Socrates, in fact, does say. This is to say, however, that the logic of the "evil is ignorance" position is to affirm wrongdoing as error. Unless we are to equate error with the Freudian notion of parapraxis and thereby make error itself intentional, error means, generally speaking, an unintended mistake, like making a computational error in my checkbook. Then the quandary becomes, How do I distinguish a moral infraction from the kind of unintentional error I commit when I miscompute the additions and subtractions in my checkbook?

If individuals who do wrong cannot do what is wrong except by mistaking their evil action as good, an inescapable conclusion follows: that the interpretation that permits persons to "sophisticate" themselves into thinking that an evil action is really good is not like an error as we normally understand error, but purposeful activity. In order to mistake evil for good, one must engage in interpretive activity aimed at preserving one's self-image as good and moral, and it follows that anything can be done--good or evil--so long as the agent believes it to be good. Socrates, of course, never denies that there is evil in the world. He even makes mention of "monsters of wickedness." But given the implications of the "evil as ignorance" position, it follows that any act of wickedness can be subsumed under the category of error, since wickedness by definition is not a failure of will but a failure of understanding. This failure of understanding can be described in two ways. First, the agent is ignorant of the good because he or she does not recognize the evil act as deviating from the good. Secondly, the agent is in error because he or she mistakenly believes the act is good when, in fact, it is not. This formulation preserves the "evil as ignorance" contention that there is no such thing as akrasia, but it raises serious questions about accountability and responsibility, about human freedom, about the context for decision-making, about what it means to choose. On the "evil as ignorance" view, evil is neither the failure of will, nor can it issue from an act of self-deception; for self-deception is not simple error, but motivated error, not simple ignorance, but willful ignorance. Again, it is the "evil as ignorance" view sometimes associated with Socrates that is my concern, not the conceptual particularities or history of philosophy issues that one interested in analyzing Socratic thought would have to take into account.

What are the moral consequences of the "evil as ignorance" position? If wrongdoing be the result of involuntary ignorance (error), then the ascription of moral accountability to acts of wrongdoing will entail the view that every error is intrinsically immoral. After all, the great sin is not the wrongdoing itself but the ignorance--"sin is ignorance."[34] Several points can be made to challenge this view, but we must not overlook the obvious. It is counter-intuitive to equate a mistake in my checkbook with a heinous moral infraction; but both are, on this view, "unintentional errors." In the common life, our language will not easily accommodate such an equation. We have not authorized ourselves to attach the full weight of moral censure to simple errors and inadvertent mistakes, for the rules that are violated by one who errs are not, strictly speaking, moral rules but rules that govern truth assessment. These violations may be trivial (checkbook error) or due to uncontrollable factors, to forgetfulness, inattention or even stupidity. To accuse a person of blundering, or to think him or her inattentive or forgetful, is to hold that person responsible for a particular error, even culpable for attending damages; but this is not equivalent to a charge that the person has acted viciously or malevolently. It is "voluntary wrongdoing" that invites our moral scrutiny; yet it is this kind of wrongdoing that Taylor's Socrates denies. Is a checkbook mistake equivalent to an act of torture. Of course not. Yet, if wrongdoing be a problem of knowledge and not of will, it is just such an equation to which one becomes logically committed.

It is arguable that by conceiving of *akrasia* as a contradiction that cannot happen, Socrates has really denied the facts of wrongdoing as they are understood in the common life. Clearly, Taylor's assertion that Socrates does not mean to deny the facts of evil is rendered controversial in light of the fact that certain persons do evil claiming to know that their actions are evil, even that they fly in the face of the good. As Taylor presents Socrates, the "evil as ignorance" appeals to self-deception for coherence; but like *akrasia* itself, self-deception is only coherent if related to a criterion of willfulness. Self-deception is a project intended to achieve a certain epistemic state of affairs. Without reference to action and volition, self-deception itself is emptied of any conceptual content that would allow one to distinguish it from error *simpliciter*. Because self-deception entails purposefulness as a feature of conceptual content, Socrates or his intepreters cannot, then, deny *akrasia* while appealing to 'self-deception' in order to describe more adequately the *facts* of evil. 'Self-deception' cannot provide a better description since 'self-deception' refers to an ignorance that is itself voluntary, purposeful and motivated; and this is true by definition. If *akrasia* cannot happen, neither can self-deception. Both concepts appeal to a feature of volition that cannot be denied in one instance without also denying it in the other.

Self-deception and *akrasia* are different concepts, yes; but both arise from a similar conception of human nature and capability. That view is that the human person is not, as a practical matter, ever wholly integrated; that the self, being a dialectical and reflexive concept, is a relation that is also a disrelationship. As such, it is capable of manifesting the actuality of self-conflict in manifold ways, not only in guilt, vacillation, ambivalence and the like, but in *akrasia* as well as self-deception. *Akrasia* and self-deception are concepts that refer to the actualities of human behavior, publicly observable events which themselves reflect the *fact* of self-relatedness. Any attempt to deny that either concept can really happen is to deny the self-relations that govern the concept and the self-relatedness that constitutes the dialectic of selfhood. I have already shown how this dialectic of selfhood has been denied by those who assert that because self-deception is literally a paradox it cannot happen, a view that itself rests on the assumption that the self is unified and consciousness transparent (e.g., Haight, Paluch, Howie). A denial of *akrasia* because it is a paradox and therefore cannot happen appeals to a similar picture of selfhood and a similar conception of consciousness.

The "evil as ignorance" argument rests on an assumption that greater linguistic precision will dispel the "contradiction" and internal opposition that obtain when speaking of "voluntary wrongdoing." The idea that rationality is the essence of human being, that it is irresistible on action, and that it coordinates without opposition all of human existence into a unity of thought and being, action and understanding, is, however, a highly questionable assumption. My own view is that these assumptions will not withstand scrutiny and that a bracing tonic is available to awaken us from uncritical acceptance: the study of human history. E. J. Lemmon has written,

> I suspect that behind this philosophical amazement that there should be such a phenomenon as acrasia lies the Aristotelian (or Socratic) picture of man as a rational animal. How this definition could survive the millions of counter-examples during the last two millenniums remains mysterious, unless it has simply flattered the race. (It would surely be better to define man as that tragic animal who is sometimes capable of thinking rationally but in general is incapable of acting so.) Perhaps acrasia is one of the best examples of a pseudo-problem in philosophical literature: in view of its existence, if you find a problem you have already made a philosophical mistake.[35]

The idea that rationality is the essence of human being and that it is irresistible on action issues in a formal requirement: one can only do what is consistent with the good. Failures to satisfy this requirement are material failures, which is to say that particular instances of wrongdoing do not undermine the formal requirement. On the "evil is ignorance" position, instances of wrongdoing are simply failures of knowing and understanding; and the wrongdoing therefore is to be described as paradoxical (Hare), or voluntary only as the result of an imprecise characterization (Socrates), or, as Davidson and Kierkegaard's Judge Wilhelm put it, so unintelligible as to be "insane" or "irrational." These are all "better descriptions" because they provide the linguistic precision that disambiguates psychic conflict and the opposition--so easily translated into logical contradiction--that attends the human reality of self-relatedness. But just as a paradox arises over self-deception because it is assumed that consciousness is thoroughly conscious of itself, akrasia becomes a paradox when it is assumed that to know the good is to do it. If evil is a problem of knowing and not willing, one cannot choose not to do the good. Evil occurs, but only because one has failed to understand what the good is; or one has "sophisticated" oneself into believing that one's wrongdoing is good. Evildoing is either simple error or the result of self-deception.

These assumptions and the pictures of selfhood developed through them interfere with clear-eyed observation. The philosophical solutions generated on these premises are, to be blunt, solutions that extend no further than to a very confined notion in the linguistic realm--to the idea of "better descriptions." The problem with these "solutions" is that they are linguistic adjustments and fine-tunings that fit normative models of human nature and capability, rational models that, as Lemmon said, "flatter the race." Furthermore, when we attempt to translate the dialectics of selfhood into a non-conflicted unitary and transparent context of human being, we almost casually dispose of human conflict as it is experienced in the common life. <u>Akrasia</u> and self-deception, in other words, are no longer experiences of conflict but imprecise linguistic formulations that philosophers can make more precise. Gregory Vlastos, a critic of the "evil as ignorance" position, has written that Socrates lacked empirical understanding. Vlastos has written that Socrates was led to a "'despotic logic'" "impossible to be borne:"[36]

> The knowledge he sought, and with such marked success, is that which consists in arranging whatever information one has in a luminous, perspicuous pattern, so one can see at a glance where run the right lines of implication and where the dark ones of contradiction. But the other way of knowing, the empirical way, Socrates had little understanding, and he paid for his ignorance by conceit of knowledge, failing to understand the limitations of his knowledge of fact generally, and of the fact of knowledge in particular, [There are facts] that do not square with Socrates' theory.[37]

As in self-deception, one must ultimately test the idea that <u>akrasia</u> cannot happen in light of experience and a knowledge of the human heart. These are the criteria of the common life, criteria that must not be lost sight of in our quest for better descriptions or theoretical formulations. "Better," after all, may mean nothing more than that they "flatter the race." We must always return to consider the facts, neither allowing the facts to be obscured by theory nor allowing ourselves to believe that facts speak for themselves. What are the facts about human persons and our capacity for wrongdoing; what facts are revealed by the history of the race? Does Socrates --or Hare, or Davidson, or Kierkegaard's Judge Wilhelm--have the best theory to account for the fact of wrongdoing? Can voluntary wrongdoing be denied? Can it only be made intelligible by explaining it as "irrationality" or "insanity"? Again, what is the view of human nature, what is the assumption about the human heart, that grounds such interpretations?

For a counterpoint to the "evil is ignorance" position, consider the following reflections by one of Edgar Allen Poe's narrators. This character claims to be doing exactly what Socrates denied could be done: evil that knows the good yet does not do it. This narrator actual <u>defies</u> the good. This is, I believe, a suggestive example because we are tempted to view this individual as "insane" rather than hearing his rather lucid explanation of his act. The narrator is about to kill a black cat, a metaphor for the wife who will shortly be axed to death and "walled up"--itself a metaphor for conscience. Consider the appeal made to the reader's own experience:

> And then came, as if to my final and irrevocable overthrow,
> the spirit of PERVERSENESS. Of this spirit philosophy takes
> no account. Yet I am not more sure that my soul lives, than I
> am that perverseness is one of the primitive impulses of the
> human heart--one of the indivisible primary faculties, or
> sentiments, which give direction to the character of Man. Who
> has not, a hundred times, found himself committing a vile or a
> stupid action, for no other reason than because he knows he
> should not? Have we not a perpetual inclination, in the teeth
> of our best judgment, to violate that which is Law, merely
> because we understand it to be such? The spirit of perverse-
> ness, I say, came to my final overthrow. It was this unfathom-
> able longing of the soul to vex itself--to offer violence to
> its own nature--to do wrong for the wrong's sake only--that
> urged me to continue and finally to consummate the injury I
> had inflicted upon the unoffending brute. One morning, in cold
> blood, I slipped a noose about its neck and hung it to the
> limb of a tree;--hung it with tears streaming from my eyes,
> and with the bitterest remorse at my heart;--hung it because I
> knew that it had loved me, and because I knew that in so doing
> I was committing a sin--a deadly sin that would so jeopardize
> my immortal soul as to place it--if such a thing were possi-
> ble--even beyond the reach of the infinite mercy of the Most
> Merciful and Most Terrible God.[38]

Poe's appeal here is to another kind of inclination in the human heart, the very one Socrates denies. That is the inclination to act in accordance with a desire harm oneself or voluntarily make oneself unhappy. The Socratic view cannot account for perversion or defiance of the good. Poe's narrator, however, explicitly states that the evil he does is done with full knowledge of the good and in direct, conscious violation of the good because it is good. Poe provides a deft reflection on perversity and defiance, and this Faustian view entails a different sort of understanding about human nature and capability. For Poe, as for St. Paul (Christianity) and a moral philosopher like Kant ("radical evil"), perversity is a fact of moral life: human persons are capable of knowing the good, but they do not always enlist the will in order to act in support of what they know to be the good. Kant's doctrine of radical evil confirms Poe's point. Radical evil is, according to Kant, a "natural propensity in man to evil," and it is universal. Radical evil is the capacity for evil, which assumes one of thee forms: fragilitas, impuritas (lack of singlemindedness or integrity), and perversitas.[39] It is perversity, the kind both St. Paul and Kant write about, the kind exhibited by Poe's narrator, that indicates a radical evil beyond the tame notion that evil is ignorance. St. Paul, Kant, and Poe all begin with different assumptions, which are: that wrongdoing, as a factual matter, is voluntary; that the will is the seat of wrongdoing, the fountainhead of sin; and that human persons are, as selves in conflict, capable of knowing the good and not doing it--even of violating the good because it is good.

With these assumptions made explicit, an alternative assessment of human nature and capability begins to emerge. To take perversity into account means that expressions of self-conflict like akrasia or self-deception cease to be problems of knowledge or understanding alone. A new foundation is called for, a new premise. In order to know the human person, it is necessary to discern that the conflicts of selfhood are very much conflicts of the will--and it is in the will where the new premise is located. Kierkegaard's Christian author, Anti-Climacus, wrote against the "evil as ignorance" position, observing

> that the Greek mind does not have the courage to declare that a person knowingly does wrong, knows what is right and does the wrong; so it manages by saying: If a person does what is wrong, he has not understood what is right.
> That is why Christianity begins in another way: man has to learn what sin is by a revelation from God; sin is not a matter of a person's not having understood what is right but of his being unwilling to understand it, of his not willing what is right.
> [Sin] has its roots in willing, not in knowing. . . .[40]

Christianity, then, supplanted the Socratic assumption about human nature with a more dialectical picture, a picture in which knowledge and will were involved in unceasing strife and enmity. Kierkegaard, a great friend of Socratic thought, has his Christian author, Anti-Climacus, deny Socrates' theory of human nature on the grounds that it is insufficiently dialectical: "It lacks dialectical determinant appropriate to the transition from having understood something to doing it."[41] Similarly, what St. Paul, Kant, and even Edgar Allen Poe provide is a dialectical understanding, a self-relatedness conception of self: one can know the good but fail to do it; one can know the good, will to do it, yet fail to do it.

Contrasting the Greek and Christian view of human nature and the relation of knowing to doing is a complex affair. For Christianity, in one sense, does not deny Socrates' claim. Because Christian theological tradition holds that the human person is created in the image of God, that it is in reason where the imago dei is located, a Christian can also agree with Socrates that human persons are endowed with an innate disposition to know the Good, thereby affirming reason as the faculty of such knowing. The point of contrast with the "evil as ignorance" view then comes down to this: that Christianity denies that this knowing or understanding of the good is irresistible on action. Christianity posits an opposition to this knowledge of the good (imago dei) in the will. The consequence of locating the will as the source of wrongdoing is that one revises the notion of ignorance itself. "Ignorance of the good," should one still opt to use the expression in a Christian context, indicates a willful refusal to understand. And given the premise of self-relatedness and intrapsychic conflict, ignorance of the good now means voluntary ignorance. The Christian understanding holds that the self is in conflict with itself.

Knowledge and will are not unified. Given the context of freedom, we can decide not to do the good and can oppose the good by refusing to choose the good. Given this available option, we allow for the fact of voluntary wrongdoing (akrasia) and have a relational context that also allows us to account for the the fact of voluntary ignorance (self-deception). Both concepts, both akrasia and self-deception, express dimensions of the self-in-conflict. In a remarkable passage, Kierkegaard's Anti-Climacus writes about the relation of akrasia to self-deception. This radical Christian differs with Socrates about how the self is constituted, and on that basis finds Socrates' description of the relation of knowledge to action inadequate:

> The defect in the Socratic definition is its ambiguity as to how the ignorance is to be more definitely understood in its origin etc. In other words, even if sin is ignorance (or what Christianity perhaps would rather call stupidity), which in one sense certainly cannot be denied--is this an original ignorance, is it therefore the state of someone who has not known and up to now has not been capable of knowing anything about truth, or is it a resultant, a later ignorance? If it is the latter, then sin must essentially lodge somewhere else than in ignorance. It must lodge in a person's efforts to obscure his knowing. Given this assumption, however, that obstinate and very tenacious ambiguity comes up again: the question whether a person was clearly aware of his action when he started to obscure his knowing. If he was not clearly aware of it, then his knowing was already somewhat obscured before he began doing it, and the question simply arises again and again. If however, it is assumed that he was clearly aware of what he was doing when he began to obscure his knowing, then the sin (even if it is ignorance, insofar as this is the result) is not in knowing but in the willing, and the inevitable question concerns the relation of knowing and willing to each other.[42]

It is precisely this question about the relation of knowing and willing, or knowing and doing, that has preoccupied the present discussion. My conclusion is that the "evil is ignorance" position must not mean, as is sometimes claimed, that evil is involuntary ignorance. It is willed ignorance, so that if one performs an evil act and claims to be ignorant of its nature as an evil deed, the ignorance in question is volitional and invokes the volitional concept 'self-deception.' Although this argues against the Socratic formulation, it does account for a fact of the common life: that evildoers may refuse to acknowledge their evil deeds as evil.

Self-deception may accompany akrasia, for wrongdoers may be so pained at the prospect of acknowledging their wrongdoing in a linguistically explicit way that they will seek to evade that recognition by taking refuge in the self-deception project. That self-deception and akrasia may join together we can certainly accept, but we must note that by saying so, we commit ourselves to a picture of the human self at odds with that which underwrites the classic "evil as ignorance" position.

That one can keep oneself from recognizing one's sin, akrasia, or intentional wrongdoing, would be, according to Anti-Climacus, due to "an effort to obscure one's knowing," which describes quite precisely self-deception. Anti-Climacus so construes matters that we may even venture to say: given the fact of wrongdoing and the gap which can be observed in the common life between knowing and doing, the best description of akrasia is not as ignorance. Were ignorance the heart of the matter, evil would be equivalent to unintended or involuntary error. The best description, the one most consonant with the facts of our experience of wrongdoing as those facts are available to us in the common life, is that which locates reasons for the ignorance, ignorance here being understood as the result of purposeful effort. The ignorance to which I refer is that which springs from a desire not to accept one's wrongdoing as evil. In a strictly moral sense, one could claim that with respect to this one point, if Christianity did not exist, it would have to be invented; else one would be unable to account for the fact that persons can defy the good and act perversely--knowing what is right but doing what is wrong.

The St. Paul who in Romans 7 expressed despair over the possibility of attaining moral perfection in one verse ("Who will deliver me from this body of death?") answers his own question in the next. He leaps to a faith that affirms the possibility of being recreated so that the fact of perverseness need not occasion despair. St. Paul makes a movement required by Christian faith. He finds a religious solution to his moral quandary; he finds a religious solution to the conflict between knowing and doing. His analysis of the human moral situation has provoked a kind of reflection--he discerns that moral striving leads to despair; and despair is overcome only by moving toward a deeper recognition. In Anti-Climacus' words, that recognition is that ". . . sin is indeed ignorance: it is ignorance of what sin is."[43] What distinguishes St. Paul from Socrates, the Apostle from the Genius, Jerusalem from Athens, Christianity from "paganism," is this very issue, which is theologically referred to as the doctrine of sin: "Christianity assumes that neither paganism nor the natural man knows what sin is."[44] And what sin is, according to the Christian perspective, is a problem of willing, not a problem of understanding. Sin is located in the will, even if "ignorance" can be said to be the result. Making this statement does not entail that the faith claims of Christianity be affirmed in order to agree with a particular way of conceiving human nature and capability. From our moral point of view, that Christianity can be associated with this view is incidental to the moral understanding itself. It is the purpose of the moral perspective to clarify moral issues in light of facts and the requirements of practical reasoning.

We must not equate the voluntary wrongdoing of akrasia with the voluntary ignorance of self-deception. St. Paul in Romans, the pastor who runs off with Gertrude, even Poe's narrator in "The Black Cat" have all confessed to wrongdoing and have experienced the regret that attends it. None, however, has actually deceived himself; none has undertaken "an effort to obscure his knowing."

Although Christianity provides a counterpoint to the Socratic understanding of human nature and capability, we need not adopt the Christian standpoint to oppose the Socratic assertion that voluntary ignorance cannot happen. We could simply latch onto the kind of empirical knowledge that disputes the Socratic assertion (Vlastos). Or we could appeal in a common sense mood to the history of the race, which is a tragic history inasmuch as it is the story of our failure to act consistently with rational thinking (E.J. Lemmon). How one settles this issue about the relation of thought to action will, as I have argued, reveal a more fundamental assumption about human being. That fundamental assumption will require a decision about certain questions: Should I adopt an ameliorative attitude toward human nature and capability? Should reason be posited as that which is worthy of our confidence and hope (Socrates)? Or should I be more tragically inclined due to the fact that the story of the race is a story of our failure to do what we know we ought to do? What is at stake in this debate between Athens and Jerusalem is whether wrongdoing is to be construed in a context of freedom, and whether wrongdoing is a problem of will or the result of ignorance. How one decides this issue will determine how one conceives the very givenness of human existence itself. Is the will a servant of knowledge, or, as Anti-Climacus might put it, is human being a conflict between reason (imago dei) and will?

I will note before concluding this section that the attempt to translate defiance or perversion into insanity (Judge Wilhelm) or irrationality (Davidson) expresses commitment to the ameliorative stance associated with "evil as ignorance." Adjusting the language this way does not resolve the difficulties, for this move toward linguistic precision modifies the concept akrasia such that "ignorance" becomes a condition of psychological disorder over which the person has no control. An evildoer whose wrongdoing is the result of insanity is outside the common life, outside the life of reason with respect to which one can, if one is an ameliorator, place one's confidence; and such an individual can be neither an agent nor the subject of strict moral scrutiny. The Hare-Davidson-Judge Wilhelm description of wrongdoing as the result of insanity or irrationality discounts the dialectical-reflexive concept of a self-in-conflict. It does so by creating a disambiguation of that conflict in the name of linguistic precision. This simplifies matters, but it does not clarify the issue about the relation of will to knowledge. For the investigator interested in the ethics of self-deception, this issue is clearly the pivotal problem. I conclude this discussion by once again drawing attention to the importance of the self concept that underwrites the ideas of both voluntary wrongdoing and voluntary ignorance. Against Davidson's "irrationality" picture, Raziel Abelson has written that psychic integrity, unfortunately, is not a simple function of linguistic precision. If anything, linguistic confusion is an effect, rather than a cause, of psychic conflict. The reason why descriptions of abnormal states, such as 'self-deception', 'weakness of will' and 'divided self', are paradoxical in form is that the states they describe are states of <u>conflict</u> that almost necessitate a paradoxical description. Surely the reason cannot be that we are so careless in our use of language as to employ needlessly ambiguous phraseology.

The trouble with Davidson's intellectualist approach is that unlike Plato and Aristotle, he attends to the phraseology with which the conflict tends to be described and so proposes an escape from the verbal paradox <u>via</u> the emergency exit of disambiguation. But the fire raging in the soul of the <u>akrates</u> stays within him. Freud and Sartre realized that it is the agent himself who ignites and feeds the fire and that it is up to him to quench it by means of resolute action. There is no linguistic fire escape from internal conflicts. To resolve them, one must <u>act,</u> 'and by opposing, end them'. To believe otherwise, as Sartre noted, is self-deception.[45]

e. Conclusion

<u>Akrasia</u> and self-deception are distinct concepts. Despite differences with respect to conceptual content (i.e. the awareness/unawareness criterion) and contexts of meaning (moral/psychological), they are both what one might term "self-relatedness" concepts. That is, each is coherent to the extent that it can be shown to reflect a conflict in one's relationship to one's own self. In self-deception, the conflict is described in terms of opposing beliefs. That one is able to "cover up" through cognitive activity what one has perceived to be threatening to one's identity; that one can engage in a project to achieve unawareness; that one can "disavow" an engagement as one's own; that one can act as if <u>ignorant</u> due to voluntary action--all of these things characterize the self-deceiver's project to mislead belief. Analysis reveals that self-deception obtains as the result of purposeful activity and for definite reasons. If self-deception be described in terms of ignorance, it must be described as a particular form of ignorance--<u>willful ignorance.</u>

Similarly, <u>akrasia</u> represents a form of the self in conflict with itself. That conflict involves opposing beliefs in the sense that opposition obtains between opposing desires, each of which the person believes has merit. One term of the <u>akratic</u> conflict concerns what the person wants to do and believes ought to be done. The other term of the conflict concerns what the person wants to do even though it conflicts with this "ought." One acts <u>akratically</u> when one decides to act contrary to one's own preference to do what one ought. <u>Akrasia</u> obtains when one settles the conflict by deciding to do what one understands to be the lesser or least preferable course of action.

The <u>akrates</u> freely and without compulsion violates his or her own understanding of the good--the right and best thing to do. This decision is guided by desires and the beliefs that attach to those desires, which is to say that there are reasons for the decision to act akratically. It may be that one's desire for a certain object, as in the case of the pastor and Gertrude, is so strong that one would risk self-censure rather than risk the prospect of life without the desired object. It may be that a person allows self-interest to conflict with one's "oughts" in a given situation, thereby indulging one's desires in violation of one's moral responsibilities to the community or even to one's own self. It may even be that one defies the good and acts akratically for perverse reasons. Whatever the particulars of a given akratic situation, the akratic act is not, as I have shown, equivalent to "ignorance of the good." Akrasia is not simple error, but willful action and reflective decision to act contrary to one's own preferences. Whatever the particulars of desire and belief that attend an akratic situation be, akrasia itself points to self-conflict involving the will, a conflict that involves a free decision to act contrary to one's own preferences. The akrates is never unaware of the akrasia; for if that were the case akrasia would not entail as a necessary feature of its description regret. The unawareness criterion of self-deception never becomes a feature of conceptual content in akrasia; and this holds even if one who acts akratically also deceives him- or herself in order to stay the regret. In a situation where both akrasia and self-deception obtain, it is possible to separate the two. The willful violation of one's own preferences (voluntary wrongdoing) identifies the akrasia; the willful ignorance about one's act--which is akratic--is attributable, according to separate criteria, to the concept 'self-deception.'

Akrasia and self-deception are harmonious concepts to the extent that each appeals to a conflict of desire and belief, and both are volitional concepts to greater or lesser degree. One can even find instances of behavior where self-deception and akrasia appear on stage together, for akrasia can occasion self-deception. But even so, one can distinguish the self-deception from the akrasia. These are two concepts that are coherent in the context of "self-relatedness," but they are distinct nonetheless. There has been some confusion on this point, particularly when those who have denied the phenomenon of "voluntary wrongdoing" appeal to "voluntary ignorance" to explain the fact of evil. This is, as I have demonstrated, a conceptual confusion warranted by neither the facts (empirical appeal) nor by the criteria of 'self-deception.' Our analysis is not complete at this point. We can further explore the relation of akrasia to self-deception by examining 'self-deception' as a term of moral evaluation.

2. The Ethics of Self-Deception

In this section, I shall discuss issues related to a particular employment of 'self-deception,' namely, use of the expression for purposes of moral assessment. We must ask as we consider the ethics of self-deception, Is self-deception immoral? Is it always immoral, sometimes, or never immoral? These questions require response, but we will preface our response by once again noting a "diversity of opinion." Even though Bela Szabados is of the opinion that this issue has been settled in the philosophical literature: "That it is <u>always</u> immoral to deceive oneself seems to have been the received opinion of philosophers",[46] M. W. Martin has successfully challenged the accuracy of this sweeping generalization by a deeper analysis of that literature. For instance, Martin criticizes Szabados for including Bishop Butler and Herbert Fingarette as proponents of the "always immoral" viewpoint.[47] Martin is right to criticize Szabados on this point; but we must acknowledge that there are philosophers who do seem to hold the "always" immoral position. Kant, for one, wrote in the <u>Metaphysical Principles of Virtue</u> (previously noted) that by an "inner lie" individuals make themselves contemptible; and in a recent essay that attends to the problem that self-deception presents to Kantian ethics, the problem of "inappropriate maxims," Onora Nell has written that Kant was himself committed to the formulation: "Self-deception in the pursuit of ends is a violation of duty; self-knowledge a duty."[48] The Plato who wrote in <u>Cratylus</u> that there is "nothing worse than self-deception" seems also to be an "always immoral" proponent. And R. G. Collingwood did not mince words when assessing the moral status of self-deception:

> The untruthful consciousness, in disarming certain features of its own experience, is not making a bona fide mistake, for its faith is not good; it is shirking something which its business is to face. . . . Paradoxically, we may say that it is deceiving itself; but this is only a clumsy attempt to explain what is happening within a single consciousness on the analogy of what may happen as between one intellect and another. . . . The condition of a corrupt consciousness [self-deception] is not only an example of untruth, it is an example of evil. . . . So far as that corruption masters him, he is a lost soul, concerning whom hell is no fable.[49]

The "always immoral" perspective has received a sympathetic hearing and has its advocates. But there are other voices to be heard, other kinds of analyses to be considered. Fingarette has argued that self-deceivers have been subject to those who would condemn the self-deceiver (Sartre and Kierkegaard) and those who would offer a non-judgmental and scientific evaluation (Freud). For Fingarette, it is the rational therapist, Freud, who, ". . . was the great exponent of the medical, non-judgmental attitude toward self-deception."[50] And Fingarette interprets the non-judgmental approach, saying "The self-deceiver appears before us as the neurotic, as the victim of the compulsive force of the unconscious, as a sufferer from mental illness."[51] If "always immoral" represents one extreme, "non-judgmentalism" represents the other.

Fingarette's division of attitudes toward the self-deceiver is clear though oversimplified. I would argue for instance, that Freud did not escape formulating a moral perspective on neurotics. If, for the moment, we can accept that morality is concerned with life in community--the common life-- what is a neurotic but one who has, in some sense, escaped the common life? The neurosis interferes with the person's ability to meet social obligations and to conduct him- or herself in accordance with accepted, reasonable and normative action guides. What was the goal of psychoanalytic therapy except to restore the neurotic to that community so that he or she could achieve personal happiness (love) and contribute to the common welfare (work)? Freud's theory of culture is germane at this point, for according to Freud, civilization and survival require that instinct be renounced. Neurotics, however, constitute a "class of people" who react to the inevitable frustration of being civilized by "asocial behavior."[52] As the theory was advanced in <u>Future of an Illusion</u>, the primary function of civilization was to provide defense against nature. The problem with neurosis, however, was that neurosis, by threatening to disarm that defense, threatened civilization itself. For Freud, this was a frightening and morally unacceptable prospect.

What is to be stressed here is that Freud's theory of civilization expresses value judgments not only about civilization but also about the threat posed to it by the neurotic. Freud expresses a personal moral opposition to "asocial behavior," and not just to the behavior but to that class of persons which threatens the social order. Neurotics are, by definition, asocially oriented because of their neurosis. If this be an accurate description of Freud's theory, it is clear that the cure of neurosis is morally required in order to preserve the common life. That Freud adopted a scientist's stance with respect to the phenomena and aberrations of human behavior should not obscure the fact that Freud often makes value judgments at odds with the impartial observer's commitments. Freud occasionally let slip his opinion that neurosis was a sort of moral befuddlement that required for its correction a courageous move by the patient toward acceptance of responsibility; and, as I noted earlier, this responsibility extended even to one's own dreams.[53] The appeal to courage (personal, moral virtue) and to responsibility are clearly moral appeals, not non-judgmental descriptions. Nor should we fail to observe that Freud believed, as did Kant, that self-knowledge was a duty. Freud wrote that the blame for neurosis "lies with yourself" and then issues a moral imperative: "Look into the depth of your own soul and learn first to know yourself."[54] The "ought" here implies "can." This is the "moralist" Philip Rieff has written about so ably,[55] the moralist who exhorts the "lazy and unintelligent masses" to reason beyond illusion,[56] the moralist seeking to educate humanity and transform society in accordance with a reality principle because "Men cannot remain children forever."[57] Freud, then, was not non-judgmental as Fingarette suggests. Having said that, however, one can still consider the merits of the therapeutic ideal, which is to address self-deceivers in the spirit of scientific non-judgmentalism. Even if Freud can be shown to fall short of that ideal, the "ideal therapist" of whom Fingarette writes would adopt precisely this attitude.[58] Fingarette upholds that idea while placing self-deception in a moral, rather than simply a psychological context. Fingarette himself holds that the self-deceiver is one who fails to accept responsibility, and Fingarette goes so far as to attribute that failure to a cowardice on the patient's part. That cowardice is accompanied by a loss of personal agency, which in turn interferes with the self-deceiver's capacity for accepting responsibility. In this complex situation, the self-deception is rendered morally ambiguous, for by disavowing responsibility, the self-deceiver becomes unable to assume responsibility.

a. The Moral Issues

No conceptual analysis of self-deception that claims to be thorough can overlook the moral issues provoked by this topic. Among the relevant issues to be considered at this stage of our inquiry are the moral context of self-deception, the problem of the loss of moral capacity, and the self-deceiver's lack of personal virtue. Also worthy of attention are the following positions, which I too shall discuss in passing: that self-deception need not be related to moral considerations (Patrick Gardiner); that self-deception can spring from what is good; that a blanket condemnation of self-deception as immoral may itself reflect moral insensitivity (Amelie O. Rorty).

In the ordinary language analysis of 'deception' I argued that 'deception' may be employed in contexts where no moral violation occurs. The moral status of 'deception,' therefore, is contingent, though, of course, it is used primarily (first-order use) for purposes of moral assessment. In the common life we ordinarily think of deceivers as agents who act immorally, for deceivers use other persons as means to some self-serving end. Deceivers are liars, seducers, defrauders, or some other kind of "voluntary wrongdoers." The issue now is whether 'self-deception' shares by analogy this morally contingent character. In order to address this issue, it must be remembered that deception can occur unintentionally. Self-deception that is unintentional, however, cannot be literal 'self-deception,' since an unintended self-deception is really an innocent error, mistake or blunder--no motive can be ascribed. In light of this difference over the action or purposefulness feature (motive) --contingent in deception but necessary in self-deception--it looks as if self-deception requires stricter criteria. And if this be the case, perhaps we should expect stricter criteria in the moral context as well. If stricter criteria do hold, could it be that self-deception is, from the moral point of view, always immoral? Or, if we resurrect the idea that a self-deceiver is both a responsible agent as well as an innocent victim, are we not forced to consider self-deception a "moral paradox"--the self-deceiver is worthy of censure at the very moment he or she is not? And if we say that, do we not thereby render the concept ambiguous from a moral point of view?

b. Analysis of an Example: The <u>Akrates</u> as Self-Deceiver

It is not necessary to generate a new example in order to launch into a discussion of the ethics of self-deception. William Clifford's infamous shipowner was originally selected in order to enable us to shift our discussion from the context of philosophical psychology to that of moral discourse. Further consideration of that example is now in order.

To reset the stage: Clifford's shipowner had reason to believe his ship was in need of repair. He engaged in a belief-misleading project aimed at persuading himself that the ship was seaworthy despite initial doubts and evidence to the contrary. Having successfully suppressed his misgivings about the ship's seaworthiness, he authorized the ship to set sail with a full complement of stores, crew and human cargo. The shipowner believed Providence, rather than the demonstrated seaworthiness of the vessel, would see the ship safely to its destination. The ship sets sail, a storm comes up and the ship sinks. The shipowner, who had watched the ship depart with a "sincere and comfortable conviction that his vessel was thoroughly safe and seaworthy" collected his insurance money, and the ship itself, as Clifford put it, "told no tales."

This example is relevant to the ethics of self-deception issue for two reasons. First, Clifford's shipowner does illustrate an example of self-deception, as I have already shown. Secondly, the action of the shipowner in this example can be described as immoral. The ascription of "immorality" to the act of sending an unseaworthy vessel to sea can be made without qualification, for it is inconceivable that this particular moral conclusion, given the facts of the story, would be a matter of dispute. Even those who would disagree with Clifford's particular understanding of the "ethics of belief" (e.g., William James, Roderick Chisholm)[59] would not challenge Clifford's own conclusion that the shipowner ". . .was verily guilty of the death of those men." The issue at hand concerns the relationship of the self-deception to the immoral act. The connection is not as simple or clear-cut as Clifford assumes. Clifford's own position is that the shipowner is self-deceived, and <u>because</u> he is self-deceived he acts immorally. Therefore, self-deception is itself immoral. The shipowner's belief in Providence, for which there is "insufficient evidence," provides the shipowner with his "cover story," and that cover story, Clifford argues, makes the immoral act possible. Because that <u>belief</u> in Providence permits the shipowner to use persons as means to an end, the belief in Providence itself is morally suspect, even immoral. Certain conclusions necessarily follow from this analysis. According to Clifford,

> It is never lawful to stifle a doubt; for it can be honestly answered by means of the inquiry already made, or else it proves that the inquiry was not complete.
> To sum up: it is wrong always, everywhere, and for everyone, to believe anything upon insufficient evidence.[60]

Clifford, in other words, given the fact that a self-deceiver would be one who "stifles a doubt" in order to believe p upon insufficient evidence or in the face of contrary evidence, holds that self-deception is always immoral.

Clifford's "always immoral" position arises from his moral conception of belief itself: "Belief, that sacred faculty which prompts the decisions of our will, and knits into harmonious working all the compacted energies of our being, is our not for ourselves, but for humanity."[61] Clifford argues that no person's belief is "in any case a private matter which concerns himself alone,"[62] which is to say that a belief held upon insufficient evidence is a "defiance of our duty to mankind" and that we have a "duty to guard ourselves from such beliefs as from a pestilence."[63] Every belief, therefore, is implicated in the social order, and because every belief affects one's fellows, every belief is implicated in the moral order as well. Every belief, then, is of moral interest; and every belief can be situated in a moral context.

There are several problems with Clifford's conception of belief, not least of which is that Clifford would make certitude a necessary feature of belief. This is a difficult position to hold in light of the fact that ordinarily certitude is contingent: belief may or may not imply certitude in the believer.[64] Were every belief to meet Clifford's test, 'belief' could be dispensed with and 'know' could be appropriately substituted. Furthermore, it seems clear that one must draw a distinction between the position I have advocated in these pages, which is that every free action entails as a necessary feature of its description a belief (even if it be held and acted upon unawares), from Clifford's notion that every belief must issue in action and affect one's fellows. This would deny a distinction between occurrent and dispositional belief, a distinction I endorse even though I have argued self-deception is a conflict between two opposing dispositional beliefs.

Self-deception is a particular concept and commands 'belief' in a certain way; but this does not exhaust what can be said about belief itself, for certain concepts related to self-deception involve different conceptions of belief. For instance, a "wishful thinker" entertaining a fantasy might, in an occurrent sense, believe that fantasy, just as I might believe I can win a jackpot if I put my quarter in the one-armed bandit. I might, however, through reflection and prudence, reassess that occurrent belief and find myself constrained from acting on it. I can, as a free agent, deny this occurrent belief dispositional status, withhold assent, and save my quarter. The occurrent belief does not issue in action. It will not prove to be the "measure of my belief," neither does it affect my fellows. If I do grant this occurrent belief dispositional status and play my quarter, then my action will reveal to my fellows my belief. My fellows will think that I believe I can win a jackpot, and my behavior will support that inference. (If I play my quarter and deny that I am doing so because I believe I can win a jackpot, then my behavior is subject to other kinds of analyses, including the possibility that I am deceiving myself.)

This analysis does not deny that there are occurrent beliefs. Neither does it deny the empirical rule-of-thumb that action is governed by belief. But it certainly does not support the idea that every belief <u>must</u> issue in action. Against Clifford, this must be said: Certainly persons do not act on every hypothesis that is accepted (believed), nor do persons decide to grant dispositional status to every occurrent belief. There are, as Chisholm says, "epistemically indifferent" propositions that are neither evident nor unreasonable, and it just such propositions that Clifford denies.[65] I hold, against Clifford, that the dispositional/occurrent distinction is relevant to our understanding of belief. Furthermore, I hold that Clifford's position that a belief necessarily issues in action is fallacious and unsound; and it is not equivalent to the Jamesian notion advanced in these pages: that every human action can be shown to be measured or governed by belief.

Although sustained criticism of Clifford's understanding of belief could gravely affect the validity of his ethical argument, Clifford nevertheless raises a legitimate question concerning the ethics of self-deception. The issue is whether Clifford is justified in attributing the shipowner's immorality to his self-deception (belief) or whether the immorality is more appropriately attributed to his decision to allow a ship he suspected of unseaworthiness to set sail. The distinction drawn previously between self-deception and <u>akrasia</u> (voluntary wrongdoing) is relevant at this point.

A moral analysis of the shipowner example will concentrate attention on the shipowner's decision to put a higher value on his money than on the human life entrusted to his care. This conclusion, simple as it is, follows from the decision to put an unseaworthy vessel to sea; and a moral assessment of blameworthiness attaches irrespective of any self-deception to be found in the example. Curiously enough--and this is the irony of self-deception from a moral point of view--the self-deception actually provides evidence that the shipowner is committed to <u>preserving</u> a <u>moral</u> self-image, which is to say, he believes himself a moral person. Undoubtedly, the shipowner would find the accusation that he were anything but moral unbelievable. More about this in a moment.

The shipowner, recall, upon first suspecting unseaworthiness, contemplates repair, and this forces him to contemplate expense. As subsequent actions make clear, the shipowner desires to avoid further financial expenditure on the old vessel; for when he faces the decision either to follow up his suspicion of unseaworthiness or to let a dangerous vessel depart for one more journey, he chooses the latter. He does have options, and he decides on one course of action in preference to another.

There is no doubt that the shipowner experiences intrapsychic conflict. Neither is there any doubt that this conflict could be avoided by appealing to established action guides. If money were of lesser concern to him than the safety of cargo and crew, he would simply fix the ship. There would be no problem about what to do--no conflict, no ambiguity. From a moral point of view, it is curious that a conflict emerges in the first place, since the shipowner, having suspected the true nature of the ship's condition, ought to have authorized needed repairs. After all, in the common life, the public safety and the common good require that those who are designated to fulfill responsibilities such as those assumed by the shipowner actually do so when circumstances warrant. And because this is a universal expectation inasmuch as anyone who boards a ship under promise of safe passage has a right to expect safe passage from those to whom a fare is paid, the shipowner is under a moral obligation apart from any legal contract that might be involved. So why is there a conflict?

The shipowner is torn because he knows what he ought to do, yet he is reluctant to do what he ought because of other, even stronger, considerations he is unwilling to dismiss. The heart of the conflict is that the shipowner does not want to spend the money. Being reluctant to make an investment with no financial return, he wishes to avoid the expense of repair "at any cost" and will entertain any solution that will enable him to do so. His final solution is proof of this contention. Although his reasons for not wanting to invest in repair are not spelled out in the example, his actual behavior supports this speculation: The shipowner possesses an acquisitive spirit and the maintenance expense will offer no immediate financial return. So his total wealth will be diminished. The conflict then, is that the shipowner does not want to take a financial loss, even though he knows that in this particular situation he ought to, this "ought" being a moral "ought." His desire to acquire more wealth is pitted against his responsibilities as a shipowner. That responsibility entails the moral maxim that no financial consideration should prevent him from taking reasonable precautions for safety when the seaworthiness of a vessel is in question and the welfare of its passengers is at stake. Morally speaking, the shipowner is not permitted to use persons as a means to an end; but this is what he does.

The shipowner is "guilty of the death of those men," as Clifford says, but there is more to the story than this. It is important to note that we have reason to believe that the shipowner is not morally obtuse: he is not simply evil, vicious or malevolent. It is possible that another shipowner would have willingly, even joyfully, taken a financial loss because the evidence for unseaworthiness was as clear as the duty to passenger safety; but this shipowner is troubled by the prospect of a financial loss. He clearly struggles with his options, and this is our clue that he takes his responsibilities seriously. He does entertain doubts about seaworthiness, lets those doubts prey upon his mind, and becomes "unhappy" thinking about them. It is possible that another shipowner--one we might term malevolent--would be so defiant of the good, so concerned to spare his fortune that he would seize any opportunity to advance his self-interest, even at the expense of innocent lives. An immoral shipowner can be imagined who would send the unseaworthy vessel off with the express hope that it would sink so that the insurance money might be collected, or for even more perverse reasons. This shipowner, however, is neither so moral or immoral as these ideal types suggest. He is neither thoroughly other-regarding nor thoroughly self-aggrandizing. He is, rather, a man in conflict, a man facing a decision.

It is important that we keep in mind the fact that the shipowner believes himself to be a moral man. There is evidence for this even if Clifford did not see it. If moral considerations did not hold the shipowner's attention and influence his decision making, it would be impossible to come up with any reason (motive) for his self-deception. The shipowner decides on a course of action that violates his own moral preference, for we can expect that he would himself normally condemn this course of action as immoral. How then can he deal with his act? The shipowner forces himself into a position where the "best" option is to deceive himself about the true (i.e., immoral) nature of his action. Were he not to deceive himself, he would face unpleasant realities. He could send the ship off and admit that to do so was an immoral act. This would occasion psychic distress, for we know from his subsequent interpretive activity that he does seek to avoid recognizing his act as immoral. The shipowner is unwilling to confront the true meaning of his act, and succeeds in avoiding that meaning through self-deception. He could also refuse to send the ship off and take the financial loss. This would be the moral thing to do, yet even here there are potential problems for the deeply reflective person. If the shipowner permits moral reasoning to guide his action while knowing that he does not really want to accept the consequences of that decision (i.e., financial loss), he will finally end up regretting his decision to do the right thing. If he regrets doing the right thing, how can his conscience be assuaged? If he regrets deciding for the moral course will his conscience not continue to gnaw at him despite his conformity to normative action guides? To regret the moral course is to acknowledge that one really preferred another course, and this realization could, for a deeply reflective person, occasion despair. In ideal terms, the choice facing the shipowner is either to do the moral thing with regret or to do the immoral thing and acknowledge that one is not the moral person one thinks one is.

The shipowner, of course, can do neither, for he is in conflict. He wants to do the moral thing because he believes himself to be a moral person. In this situation, however, the moral option will force an unwelcome financial loss. As a moral person, he will regret doing the immoral thing, yet as one who is willing to do the immoral thing in order to preserve his wealth, he will also regret doing the moral thing. When all is said and done, he does the immoral thing and as a result incurs the guilt of having sent innocent person to their deaths. In the end, the desire to avoid taking a financial loss proves to be the overriding reason for action, and Clifford is clear about this. How does the shipowner interpret his decision on behalf of the immoral option? It is at this point that self-deception becomes relevant to the story, for the shipowner cannot admit to himself that he opts for the immoral choice. Self-deception is the cognitive activity whereby the shipowner persuades himself that the ship is, in fact, seaworthy. This is his rationalization, his attempt to justify to himself a decision that violates his own preferences and his own self-image as a moral person.

One could, as I suggested, imagine an immoral shipowner not only willing to profit by the loss of human life but who could also admit that to himself--a shipowner defiant of the good. <u>This</u> shipowner is not of that ilk. He does not consider himself to be vicious or malevolent or so self-aggrandizing that he would permit financial considerations to override moral obligations. Yet, despite his own moral self-understanding and his commitment to the moral life, he makes a decision that is immoral and self-aggrandizing, for he decides to send an unseaworthy vessel to sea in violation of his responsibility as a shipowner. The fact that the shipowner deceives himself about the nature of his decision should not obscure the fact that the decision is, from the moral point of view, wrong. The shipowner's preference for an immoral course of action conflicts with his moral self-image, and it is this conflict, and the shipowner's failure to resolve it forthrightly, that occasions the self-deception.

The shipowner wants to have two incompatible things at once. He wants to avoid a financial loss and he want to preserve a moral self-image. In this particular situation, however, he cannot have both: he must either send the ship out and imperil innocent lives (immoral) or he must refuse to send it out and authorize repairs. He cannot have it both ways. He cannot send it out in a state of disrepair and also meet his obligation to his passengers. Since he cannot have it both ways, he finally makes a decision, even if his self-deception seems to obscure the fact that he has done so. From a moral point of view, however, the meaning of his act is clear. How it is to be evaluated is clear. The interpretive activity that obscures the nature of his decision as immoral is aimed at alleviating and postponing the pain of self-recognition. The self-deception permits the shipowner to do the impossible, to hold contradictory positions at once. He can both serve his self-interest through immoral action while also keeping conscience at bay, thereby preserving his self-image. This is an "ingenious solution," one that only self-deception can make possible.

The shipowner's deed is immoral, even if his particular moral community does not have access to all the relevant facts. Since publicly available evidence of unseaworthiness vanished with the ship, the shipowner may find himself exempt from external moral censure and public prosecution. Only his confession of wrongdoing will suffice to convict him of immoral action in that community, and due to the self-deception, that confession will not be forthcoming. Since the ship is lost and the moral community is unable to judge his action, only the shipowner's conscience is left to accuse him. Only conscience is left to betray him to moral judgment and to condition him for self-reform. It was to avoid the censure from that last seat of judgment, conscience, that the shipowner began the self-persuasion process in the first place. The shipowner is acting selfishly. He is seeking certain desired ends that conflict with moral duty, and he seeks to acquire those ends with impunity, even though his action leads to the deaths of innocents and violates his own standards of right conduct. The deed itself is immoral, even if the shipowner keeps conscience at bay, even if his self-deception deceives the moral community into thinking nothing untoward occasioned the loss of the ship. By having to go so far to justify his decision to himself, by having to distort the normal processes of evidential evaluation, the shipowner reveals that he is aware of the true nature of his deed: deep down he knows. He reacts as he does because deep down he knows.

The purpose of the self-deception, then, is to make it possible for this individual to continue to live with himself. The self-deception represents the continuing power of the moral life on a man who cannot live with the thought that he has violated his own preference to be moral, a preference he is unable to renounce even as he acts contrary to it. Ironically, the fact of self-deception speaks on behalf of the shipowner's commitment to the moral life; for clearly the fact that he does not want to be thought an immoral man, either by his community or by himself, demonstrates the continuing influence of moral considerations on his actions and the respect he has for principles of morality and moral reasoning. Rather than admitting his wrongdoing, which would occasion self-conscious guilt over the deaths and a sorrow too great to bear, the shipowner attempts an "ingenious solution." A shipowner with no respect for the moral law or for moral obligations would have no reason to mislead his own beliefs. This shipowner is guilty of the deaths of passengers, yes, but his self-deception reveals that he is a fallible moral person, a person who, despite acting immorally, has moral commitments. And so strong are those commitments, so integral are they to his self-understanding, that he would rather deceive himself to preserve that self-understanding than face the fact that his deed is morally unworthy of the man he believes himself to be.

This analysis is relevant to other examples of moral persons deceiving themselves. Bishop Butler's sermon, "Upon Self-Deceit," for instance, takes as its case study the story of David and Uriah. David sends Bathsheba's husband, Uriah, to the front lines of battle where his death is all but assured. David does so for adulterous reasons, and Butler accuses David of murder.[66] David, certainly a moral man, does not act like a man whose conscience is bothering him until Nathan, the prophet, tells a parable and accuses David of voluntary wrongdoing. His well-known remark, relevant to all self-deceivers, is, "Thou art the man" (2 Samuel 12.7). In light of the shipowner analysis, the point to be stressed is that David acted akratically, then deceived himself in order to postpone a day of reckoning with his own conscience. Nathan speaks with authority, with the authority of David's own conscience, and is able to penetrate the self-deception. He is able to show David what David already knows but will not acknowledge, namely, that he is a murderer. Nathan does not accuse David of self-deception, since to do so would be superfluous to his moral accusation. For David to concede that he has murdered Uriah, it is necessary that he penetrate his own self-deception; and to concede Nathan's point requires that David also recognize that he has been deceiving himself. Once David is able to see the truth of Nathan's accusation, he drops the cover story that Uriah was killed in an unfortunate accident of war. David admits--to himself--that Uriah died unjustly, that he died by David's own decision and at his own direction. David suffers the full brunt of this self-confrontation, which Nathan has occasioned. The full weight of earned and incurred guilt afflicts David the King, a moral person. David concedes the fact that he was responsible for Uriah's death. He is forced to face the fact that his act, for which he alone was responsible, was his own and that it was immoral. The deed, which he now avows as his own, is adjudged by the remorseful David to be unworthy of the person he believes himself to be.

It is for murder that the moral community, Nathan, and David's own conscience censure him. David's self-deception is purposeful interpretive activity designed to postpone a day of reckoning. Nathan's intervention, however, cracked the cover story, and Nathan delivers David into the seat of his own conscience where he suffers what any moral man who commits a voluntary wrongful (akratic) act will suffer: guilt, remorse, and self-recrimination--as well as commitment to self-reform. It is the akrasia, the murder of Uriah, that merits moral censure. The self-deception is not the specific object of moral scrutiny, though it does present an obstacle to the self-confrontation required by morality. The self-deception hinders the self-examination required of the moral person so that the regret that is necessarily entailed by akrasia is postponed. The self-deception functions to preserve a moral self-image amid the challenges put to it by one's own action; and that action provides the evidence that one has acted contrary to a self-professed commitment to the rules and deliberations of the moral life.

In these examples of akratic agents who are also self-deceivers, self-deception attends the akrasia and postpones self-confrontation. The Biblical story of David and Uriah is valuable because it follows the course of the akratic agent to its logical conclusion, regret. Clifford does us no service by leaving the shipowner with his self-deception still in place; for the best moral analysis, given the facts of the story, would lead a reasonable person to conclude that the shipowner's day of reckoning has merely been postponed. His Nathan awaits him. Clifford's shipowner has not fully realized that he has acted akratically. He has not yet experienced regret over his voluntary wrongdoing. All that stands between him and the full weight of moral censure is a cover story, and one can only wonder how long that will last. The shipowner's respect for the moral life, his attention to moral obligations and responsibilities, may eventually be his undoing. Were he a malevolent man, an evil person prone to acts of defiance, the psychological complexity involved in his "ingenious solution" would simply be irrelevant if not unintelligible. A malevolent person could simply defy the rules of the common life. Such an individual would require no self-deception poultice to put off an accusing conscience. Clifford's shipowner has need of it. And should he ever honestly confront the best, most reasonable interpretation of his action, there is no doubt that this shipowner will suffer to the full extent required by conscience. The motive for his self-deception, to be specific, is to avoid the regret that he could not avoid were he to consider his act without benefit of a fabricated cover story.

What, then, is to be said about an "ethics of self-deception"? These examples suggest that self-deception is not the specific object of moral scrutiny. Self-deception, rather, attends one's actions and is the person's attempt to distort the meaning of those actions for reason of psychological gain. Self-deception may accompany akrasia; then again it may not. Furthermore, the akrasia in question may be indicative of actual moral violations, as in first-order uses of the term, or the akrasia may lack specific moral relevance "Because," as Amelie O. Rorty has rightly said, "many cases of akrasia fall outside the moral domain."[67] There can be, after all, a violation of preferences that also subscribes to the meaning of "voluntary wrongdoing" without an actual moral violation taking place. That is, the meaning of those actions may be distorted for reason of psychological gain. Self-deception may accompany akrasia; then again it may not. Furthermore, the akrasia in question may be indicative of actual moral violations, as in first-order uses of the term, or the akrasia may lack specific moral relevance "Because," as Amelie O. Rorty has rightly said, "many cases of akrasia fall outside the moral domain."[67] There can be, after all, a violation of preferences that also subscribes to the meaning of "voluntary wrongdoing" without an actual moral violation taking place. That is, there can be a non-moral satellite meaning of akrasia in addition to the first order uses: the person who "weakly" eats a piece of chocolate when for reasons of diet it is not his or her preference to do so. In any event, the important point is that even in instances where akrasia does fit a moral description, the akrates is not without a moral frame of reference. The akrates is not evil or malevolent, for such persons would not experience conflict between the nobler (rational-moral) impulses and the bases desires or promptings of the human heart. The akrates, rather, experiences conflict because desire for self-gratification or self-aggrandizement flies in the face of moral obligation, and the akrates is unwilling to let moral obligation rule the day and override the baser desire.

If one were unable to experience conflict, hence unable to regret one's actual failings, one would have no reason to deceive oneself about one's own voluntary wrongdoing.

Again, the thoroughly immoral individual, as opposed to the akrates, will not opt for self-deception, for such an individual has no reason to deny that his or her deeds are anything but what they are. Such a person lacks the governing moral self-image that the akrates so wants to preserve. Such persons are, of course, rare, for true villains appear almost as infrequently as true saints. Neither the angel of heaven nor his fallen counter-part is a realistic specter of the common life. Only those who seek to become morally perfect and fall short, only those who seek to indulge their self-interest at the expense of moral obligation and find themselves peculiarly unsatisfied with their success--only such persons as these comprise the constituency of the common life. Only with such persons as these can we claim the familiarity of intimacy. Only those who experience fundamental conflict and psychic distress can be fit candidates for akrasia and self-deception, and such candidates are made fit, ironically, by their ethical development and moral achievements. To be moral is to have the capacity to experience regret at one's moral failures. The pain of such regret, once it has been experienced, once it has led to the desire for self-reform and become an experience to avoid, may occasion an instance of self-deception. In the common life, in the moral life, a self-directed belief-misleading project will have as its purpose the staving off of the self-confrontation demanded by conscience. Where akrasia is, there may self-deception be.

c. Three Conclusions

Three conclusions relevant to the "ethics of self-deception" issue can be drawn. The first and third of these conclusions are in essence alike, though I shall draw different lessons from each.

First: Although self-deception may attend instances of akrasia, it need not. The presence of self-deception, therefore, is not to be construed as a necessary condition for akrasia, for knowledge is not action. A moral agent faced with a conflict between moral and prudential reasons for action may override the moral course, doing so despite his or her avowal of the good, despite being aware that one undermines the moral supports for one's self-understanding by so doing. On the other hand, because a self-deceiver acts to cover up a true interpretation of his or her acts, doing so because one's acts do not square with one's own preference to act morally, akrasia does describe the occasion of self-deception. We can even go so far as to say that self-deception is always accompanied by akrasia, though of course, the akrasia involved may not constitute immoral action. By this last qualification I mean that a self-deceiver may violate a certain preference which does not explicitly or directly violate moral (other-regarding) action guides. A person can have, for instance, a purely prudential conflict. A person may decide to indulge a pleasure or self-interest at the expense of other, "better" prudential interests or with respect to a higher prudential wisdom. And self-deception may obtain nonetheless. One thinks of drivers who deceive themselves into believing that wearing a seatbelt will do more harm than good in case of an accident; or of persons who seem convinced, despite substantial evidence to the contrary, that cigarette smoking will not harm them; or of overweight persons who believe they are dieting when they keep up the same amount of caloric intake but alter their eating schedules. These are all instances of persons acknowledging the best preference while also acting contrary, and akratically, with respect to it. And the "best" preference is not moral and other-regarding, but a prudential, self-regarding preference.

Because self-deception and akrasia are not conceptual equivalents, the ways in which they lend themselves to use in moral discourse must be subject to scrutiny. Conceptual analysis reveals that it is the akrasia, not the self-deception, that invites and authorizes moral judgment. It is the akratic action that merits moral evaluation, and this holds irrespective of any self-deception that can be shown to attend particular cases. This moral distinction between self-deception and akrasia is made all the more clear when we consider an akrates whose akrasia falls outside the moral domain. In such instances, we find ourselves reluctant to call for moral censure solely on the basis of self-deception. In fact, ascribing 'self-deception' in such instances lessens the weight of moral censure rather than increases it. This is a fact of usage, a fact of the common life. And even in cases where the akrasia does pertain to a moral infraction and has provided a motive for self-deception, even in these cases the self-deception seems to temper the moral reaction, if not the assessment itself. Self-deceivers who seem to have lost the capacity to comprehend the best, most reasonable interpretation of their actions are more often pitied than condemned.

Second: Self-deception provides evidence for the continuing influence of the moral life. People who act immorally, deceive themselves about the true meaning of their action by erecting a cover story to keep their moral self-image in tact, reveal a depth of moral constitution. Self-deception is, literally, self-directed. Only a moral agent, one who is capable of experiencing regret, one who is capable of taking action to prevent a self-confrontation that one knows deep down would lead to regret, would undertake a project to mislead one's own beliefs about the meaning of that action. Only a moral agent anxiously facing the prospect of self-censure (conscience) would attempt to persuade one's own self that his or her own act was moral when the best, most reasonable interpretation would say otherwise. Freud's analysis of neurosis confirms this insight: The most likely candidate for neurosis is one whose super-ego (conscience) is, so to say, "too well" developed. The person whose conscience is prone to relentless self-accusation is the person likely to repress an awareness of those inclinations deemed morally unworthy or threatening to the super-ego's control of the instinct renunciation process. In terms of moral psychology, it is clear that _akratic_ action yields a disintegration of personality and a loss of self-mastery. Self-deception represents an ingenious attempt to preserve one's moral identity in the face of a threat to it posed by one's own decisions, preferences and actions. By attempting to maintain identity, the self-deceiver also attempts to preserve a high degree of self-mastery and personality integration when that high degree is, because of _akrasia_, no longer warranted. Yet the desire to maintain personality integrity, even if by means of a project to mislead belief, expresses a concern to preserve the foundations of one's self-understanding. And because the self-deceiver's interpretive activity reveals a commitment to the norms and conditions of "other-regardingness," that expression of concern can be judged morally relevant. The person who argues, therefore, that self-deception is always immoral cannot mean by that assertion that self-deception itself springs from base or immoral motives, or that it expresses a fundamental moral depravity of the agent, or that the self-deceiver is no longer an agent with abiding commitments to the moral life. What a claim about the "immorality of self-deception" might mean I shall discuss in a moment. Let me first state my third conclusion.

Third: 'Self-deception' is a term that can be used in a meaningful way within the context of moral discourse. It is a term relevant to moral psychology and to the behavior of moral agents. That is not to say that self-deception is intrinsically immoral. It is not, and that assessment holds despite the fact that self-deception is intimately linked to the capacity for moral agency and is often found as the too-willing handmaiden of _akrasia_. 'Self-deception,' however, is not to be used to assess a person's moral condition, as if to say "So-and-so is self-deceived" were functionally equivalent to saying "So-and-so is immoral or acting immorally." Rather, the claim that a person is self-deceived asserts that a person is in a condition of psychological conflict. That conflict may have been occasioned by an _akratic_ preference that constitutes an actual infraction of moral rules. In many cases, the smoke of self-deception betrays a smoldering fire of voluntary wrongdoing and that wrongdoing may be immoral. One can even say where self-deception is, there an _akratic_ act, possibly an immoral act, will be lurking.

A few clarifications on these conclusions and on the discussion in general are in order.

d. The "Immorality" of Self-Deception

Given these conclusions, why would one assert that self-deception is immoral? The claim that self-deception is immoral may be derived from two different paths of reasoning. One could mean by this claim that the consequences of self-deception are such that they lead inevitably to action of an immoral sort, actions that would not have occurred but for the self-deception. This perspective holds that the self-deceiver's false belief drives the will to action that necessarily yields immoral consequences. This consequentialist position represents Clifford's perspective and reflects aspects of Bishop Butler's argument: the consequences of self-deception are destructive of the moral life.

Another perspective would hold that self-deception obtains as the result of a failure of self-knowledge. Moral assessment would obtain in relation to the idea that every person is under an obligation to acquire self-knowledge and to achieve the excellence (virtue) of self-honesty; for these are self-regarding duties, but also moral duties. Without self-knowledge, one would be unable to fulfill or even acknowledge one's other-regarding duties. One could not accede to one's duty to act with a good will, which is to act from reasons of duty, or to act from principles of fairness or according to notions of universalizability (i.e., governing one's own behavior by standards that could reasonably be adopted by all). One could say that self-deception interferes with doing one's duty and is an impediment to the moral life. A self-deceiver is one who acts in accordance with inappropriate maxims, actually going so far as to treat one's own self as a means to an end rather than as an end in itself. Or one could argue that self-deception is a kind of vice that exhibits a lack of moral capacity. To view self-deception as either a failure of duty or as a failure of moral capacity (vice) is to authorize 'self-deception' for use in ordinary language as a term of moral assessment.

The consequentialist position can be refuted by pointing to examples of self-deception that do not lead inevitably to immoral action. A logical argument will suffice: Since *akrasia* may accompany self-deception, and because many cases of *akrasia* fall outside the moral domain, in those cases where the two concepts can be said to conjoin, the conflict that gives rise to both the self-deception and the *akrasia* leads to no result directly relevant to a judgment of evildoing, even if there is a violation of preferences. The result of the self-deception would be that the self-deceiver believes something to be true that is not true, but that belief does not adversely affect the moral community despite the fact that for some reason, perhaps idiosyncratic, the belief is not epistemically indifferent. In the face of evidence to the contrary, one would believe something that, from the moral point of view, did not lead to action that violates moral prescriptions or principles. The *akrasia* in question simply falls outside the moral domain, and the psychological conflict would have been restricted to a conflict over concerns without moral interest.

As another way of countering the "always immoral" position and clarifying the use to which 'self-deception' may be put for purposes of moral assessment, consider a person who enacts a self-directed belief-misleading project with respect to acts of beneficence, supererogation or kindness--acts "above and beyond" the call of duty. It is certainly conceivable that a person could mistakenly believe that a certain act was morally obligatory when morality itself would not require such an act. Even though such an individual would be self-deceived about his or her duties, the moral point of view would certainly see that this kind of other-regardingness leads to an increase in social well-being: the recipient of the beneficence. Such an instance indicates that self-deception could attend decisions to act that lead to morally positive consequences. The consequentialist position is best refuted, however, by considering examples where a person who has deceived him- or herself is able to implicate that self-deception in prudential action that leads to beneficial ends--where the result of the <u>akrasia</u> and self-deception leads to a consequence that is, from a moral point of view, good.

Consider a cancer patient who has been told that her case is terminal. Her doctors give her a year to live. Let us say that this is a person desperately frightened by this information. Let us say, furthermore, that this person is prone to despair and that honest self-confrontation and acceptance of this information would lead to self-pity, resentment and great misery. Let us also stipulate that this woman's prudential interest in the face of this information is to avoid wholehearted acceptance. In other words, it would be in the person's self-interest to avoid the pain and distress that this information occasions. Her psychological conflict, then, is between an honesty that would lead to misery and a denial that would lead to possible well-being, even happiness. What does she do?

<u>This</u> patient opts for self-deception. She decides to undergo treatment and therapy, thereby giving public testimony that she recognizes the seriousness of the claim about her condition advanced by her physicians. Her decision to undergo treatment is a response to the fact that the situation is grave and the diagnosis probably true. Yet, because the patient does not want to surrender to the illness and lose self-mastery, thereby spending her final days in misery, she continues to take the treatments while persuading herself that this is more precautionary than medically required. For prudential reasons, she deceives herself. Without being aware that she is dong so, she enables herself to believe something that "deep won" she knows is false. She deceives herself into believing that the evidence for her terminal status is insufficient and unconvincing despite her doctor's prognosis, and that there is good reason (divine intervention by Providence) to believe that the best scientific diagnosis is only opinion. She takes her treatments and seeks no opinions from other doctors. We must note, of course, that her belief in survival is, despite scientific implausibility, not an actual impossibility,

since this patient, like any self-deceiver, uses reason and rationality to defend an epistemic position; and she reasons that there have been instances of documented remissions and survivals that are both unexpected medically and seemingly miraculous. Despite her behavioral avowal of the prognosis, however, it can be safely said that her belief in survival is unsound and at odds with the best, most reasonable interpretation of the evidence.

This patient would meet all the criteria of self-deception. The point, however, is that in this case the consequences of this patient's self-deception do not fall into the moral domain--at least not on the side of immoral consequences. If, after the one year, the patient dies, which is to say that her belief in survival is empirically falsified, the moral question will be this: since this self-deceiver has done all that the shipowner has done on the epistemic level, even going so far as to invoke Providence, is one to condemn her just as one previously condemned the shipowner? On Clifford's account, we would be justified in censuring this patient on moral grounds, since she has deceived herself into believing she has more than a year to live and believes that on the basis of insufficient evidence, thereby reneging on her moral duty to confirm any doubts she might have as to the truth of her prognosis. Her belief is wrong, and not only wrong, but immoral. And if she relies on Providence to make her well, that simply restates Clifford's case against theistic belief, which, too, is immoral.

Unlike the shipowner, this case illustrates a self-deceiver whose "wrong" belief does not eventuate in harm to others or even to herself. In fact, the self-deceiver's position to respond to the best, most reasonable interpretation of the evidence expresses a prudential interest that is in no obvious conflict with moral interests or requirements: she wants to go on living, and she does not want the quality of her life adversely affected by what she knows deep down to be worthy of her belief. Her belief-misleading project constitutes a decision to believe upon insufficient evidence, but we must note that this is not her wont. Were it this person's usual preference to believe things on insufficient evidence, there would be no reason for her to deceive herself in this instance. Yet the fact that she takes the treatments and seeks no outside confirmation of her prognosis reveals that her denial is <u>akratic</u>, by which I mean that this is not her usual preference. She is self-deceived, not deluded.

We may assume that this patient is so constituted as a moral personality that given the choice, she would prefer to be honest with herself rather than not. If this be granted, her decision to act in accordance with a preference aimed at avoiding psychic distress overrides her usual preference for self-honesty. Since she acts this way for <u>self-interested</u> reasons, we may say she acted for <u>prudential</u> reasons. Were we to hold that this preference for self-honesty is a <u>moral</u> duty (self-regarding duty <u>qua</u> moral duty), then Clifford's position holds; but if her preference for self-honesty is really a prudential interest--and I believe it to be as I shall explain in a moment--then we can identify the conflict here as being a conflict between two prudential interests. What is happening is that certain prudential considerations override other prudential considerations. The patient acts akratically with respect to her usual preference to be honest with herself; but this is not immoral akrasia, akrasia in which moral considerations have been overridden by less compelling prudential considerations. This would be one way to describe the intuition that the cancer patient's akrasia does not merit the same kind of moral evaluation as the shipowner's.

The point I wish to make is that this particular decision to believe for prudential reasons what is countered by the weight of the evidence does not yield morally unacceptable consequences. Perhaps the contrary. Not every decision made on behalf of a prudential consideration is immoral, for not every prudential interest conflicts in an obvious way with a moral interest. That such was the case with the shipowner (moral versus prudential) does not mean that the same must hold true for the cancer patient. Her prudential decision to live with the belief that her doctors are in error or that a miraculous remission will occur (Providence again) is aimed at maintaining a quality of life and preserving a sense of well-being. The consequence of this unconscious decision to mislead her own beliefs for prudential reasons and the result of this belief-misleading project is that she actually contributes to her own flourishing and, as one might expect, to that of others as well.

The patient's decision to allay the distress caused by accepting the truth and to preserve a sense of well-being by misleading her own beliefs is a "cowardly" choice in light of a prima facie duty to be honest with oneself. She acts akratically in relation to this self-regarding duty, for she prefers a course of action that violates her own preference to be honest with herself. But because it yields no apparent harm to others and because it contributes to the patient's sense of well-being at no expense to others, it ultimately has consequences in the moral domain that are positive. Another way to describe this would be as follows: This is an instance where there is a legitimate exception to a prima facie duty to be honest with oneself, and one can override that duty with another self-regarding duty when it does not yield unacceptable consequences in the moral domain. For present purposes, let us hold that the cancer patient avows that self-honesty is her preference and that in relation to that preference any choice that subverts her desire to attain self-honesty would constitute an instance of akrasia.

Clifford's position reveals moral insensitivity in this instance. Certainly it is counter-intuitive from a moral point of view to claim that the cancer patient, who is self-deceived, is as morally reprehensible as the shipowner, who is also self-deceived. The difference between them lies in the nature of the akrasia appropriate to each, not in the fact that each happens to be self-deceived. In making this distinction, one could still condemn the shipowner, yet relieve the cancer patient of the moral censure that would condemn her for preferring well-being to self-honesty. And this assessment can be made while holding her accountable for her self-deception. The shipowner's immoral _akrasia_ subverts the moral order. The cancer patient's _akrasia_, her dishonesty with herself, does not. It may actually be a benefit to others. Those who love and care for this person will not have to accept the burden of a despairing, fearful, unhappy and desperate woman, who, because of her honesty, rages at what she would otherwise hold to be an unjust fate. From a consequentialist point of view, the self-deception is part and parcel of an _akratic_ decision from which actual good issues: her own sense of well-being is maintained, and that in itself contributes to more general human flourishing.

As my analysis of Clifford's shipowner showed, the consequentialist view collapses _akrasia_ and self-deception, thereby eliminating the moral contingent of _akrasia_ itself. A more precise analysis of these concepts, however, challenges this understanding. To say that a self-deceiver will lie to others does not mean that the self-deception is the cause of the lying. To say that a self-deceiver may have difficulty reforming him- or herself does not mean that reform is necessary because of self-deception. In both cases, in both lying and in the need for reform, it is _akrasia_, not the self-deception that happens to attend it, which is the proper target for moral analysis. The distinction, as well as the intimacies, that hold between self-deception and _akrasia_ can be sorted out; and to sort them out is to relieve 'self-deception' of certain moral stigmas. 'Self-deception,' then, does not indicate some psychological reality that is also "immoral," nor does our everyday use of the term mean that whenever we press this linguistic expression into service we mean to express moral obloquy.

1. Misconception: Moral Means Prudential

Two other misconceptions contribute to the idea that self-deception is intrinsically immoral. First is the idea that self-deception is immoral because it vitiates and opposes a self-regarding duty to know oneself. On this view the self-regarding duty to know oneself entails the prohibition that one ought not to deceive oneself, and the force of that "ought" is moral, for it entails an imperative concerning action guides and principles of action. The imperative prescribes a universal requirement that is also a value judgment, so that to say "Don't deceive yourself" means that it is always wrong, everywhere and for everyone (Clifford), to mislead one's own beliefs with the result that one believes something to be true upon insufficient evidence.

If one means by this what Clifford meant, that the duty not to deceive oneself is absolute and not even a _prima facie_ obligation for which exceptions might be made, then problems arise. The difficulty with this absolutist position is that self-regarding duties are assumed to be equivalent to moral duties. To equate the two is to so broaden the reach of moral discourse that one cannot speak with precision about relevant differences that might hold in specific instances, differences that can be clarified by appealing to the moral/prudential distinction. Differences can be shown between the two domains, however, even though analysis of individual cases reveals that a particular action is "immoral" because self-interest has been permitted to conflict with, then override, a moral duty. In such cases, the classic virtue of prudence, once held to be an excellence in the character of the moral person (virtue), is likely to appear as a culprit, a potential opponent of morality. For when self-interest conflicts with other-regarding interests, and one decides to yield to self-interest, a moral conclusion obtains: one's prudence has led one to act such that one violates the universal requirement that moral interests take precedence, and ought to override, self-interest.

For the sake of clarity, let me stipulate that the relations involved in these respective spheres of influence define them as either "moral" or "prudential." I hold that the moral domain is governed by social relations. The moral sphere of relations obtains with respect to the person in the interpersonal context. The prudential sphere, strictly speaking, concerns one's relations to oneself in the social context: it is self-regarding and self-interested. It is clear that an immorality obtains as the result of a failure to let moral reasons override self-interest; yet this result obtains only where moral reasons come into conflict with self-interest. When they do, it is necessary to decide what to do, how to act, which interests to follow, and the decision is attended by psychological conflict. As the shipowner demonstrates, one can suffer conflict and make the wrong decision for the wrong reasons. Fallen angels and angels still in good graces do not experience this conflict. And conceding this point does not entail the conclusion that self-interest and prudential reasoning are intrinsically immoral, neither does it serve to advance the view that self-interest is an illegitimate concern unworthy of our attention, or evident only when it does come into conflict with our moral obligations. In fact, the conflict between the two may not really be a conflict at all, but only the result of the ambiguity that necessarily attends the context of free human action and decision making. For clarity's sake, however, I shall continue to refer to a conflict between self-regarding and other-regarding reasons for action, for even in situations of ambiguity it can appear that these two are opposed and competing for primacy. These are points that qualify, as well as clarify, what is at stake in the "ethics of self-deception" debate.

Addressing the ethics of self-deception issue requires that we keep in mind the analysis of self-deception that describes the concept as a project to mislead one's own beliefs, which is to say it is both a project and self-directed. The deception takes place within the context of psychological conflict and in response to self-opposition. The "ingenious solution" to the conflict is enacted by the self and is directed back to the self. Self-deception is a reflexive concept: it refers us back to the grammatical subject who is seeking to mislead his or her own beliefs. If, therefore, we are to adjudge the morality of self-deception, subject it to moral scrutiny, we must do so on the premise that the concept refers us to a self-directed activity. If self-deception is wrong, why is it wrong? If self-deception be adjudged "immoral," not just consequentially, but intrinsically, what is it that is immoral?

If self-deception be intrinsically wrong, then we all have a duty not to deceive ourselves. That duty is not owed to others, like moral prescriptions that pertain to the context of other-regardingness, but to ourselves. The issue, then, is twofold: First, are there any kinds of obligations that obtain in the context of self-regardingness, any kinds of duties that one owes oneself? Secondly, if there be such duties, does the context of self-relatedness provide adequate conceptual and linguistic provision to authorize a description, characterization and interpretation of these duties as moral?

The case can be made that certain obligations are binding in our relations to ourselves. Kant, who examines "self-regarding duties" in The Metaphysical Principles of Virtue, includes on his list such items as self-preservation, a duty not to treat oneself as a means to an end, not to abuse oneself or seek servility, and, particularly relevant to self-deception, a duty to know oneself.[68] The duty to know oneself can be construed as a duty not to deceive oneself, and Kant himself seems to hold that this is not a prima facie obligation but an absolute duty required in the context of one's self-relations, since lying to oneself obliterates one's dignity as a person. Because Kant applies moral criteria to his evaluation of the "internal lie," the self-regarding duty to know oneself (not to deceive oneself) constitutes a moral duty even if qualified by a relational context. Self-regarding duties can be said to be obligatory, and because they are a necessary precondition to the moral life, Kant is able to include self-regarding duties in the bailiwick of "morality" itself. Formally speaking, Kant could be said to hold that self-deception is always, everywhere and for everyone wrong--wrong here meaning morally impermissible. In violating a duty to ourselves not to deceive ourselves, we make ourselves contemptible by robbing ourselves of the prerogative to act in accordance with principles. We destroy our dignity as moral persons, rendering ourselves "playthings of the inclinations" and "thingifying" ourselves.

It may be thought that the idea of a self-regarding duty is a conceptual confusion at best, or worse, a contradiction. The contradiction appears when we ask whether a person can assume the opposing roles of one who imposes obligations while also being the one who accepts them. Can one impose obligations on oneself without invoking the contradiction of being the one who actively imposes an obligation which one is then required to passively accept? Another angle on this contradiction begins with a consideration of duty, which is the heart of the moral life. Duties require no reason for their observance other than the fact that they are perceived to be duties. In other words, a duty is self-justifying according to principles of practical reason. If one accepts a duty as a reason for action, one requires no further justification.

The idea of self-regardingness or prudence, on the other hand, posits a contrary reason for action. Prudence dictates that self-interest is the motive for our action, and self-interest is, by definition, not a moral duty. Self-interest, rather, is a concern that may actually conflict with our moral duties. The idea of a "self-regarding duty" or, to capture more accurately the paradox, a "prudential duty," can therefore be construed as a contradiction in terms. Action may issue from reasons of self-interest or from observance of duties; but it is confusing, even contradictory, to suggest that one can have a moral duty (other-regarding) in the context of one's relations to oneself (self-regarding).

Kant, I believe, was right to hold that there are certain obligations that each of us owe ourselves simply by virtue of the fact that we are persons. These obligations are tied to the respect each of us owes ourselves and to the requirement that each of us ought, as individual self-determining agents, to cultivate the character that will enable such self-respect to obtain. The corollary expression of this obligation is that we should never act such that we obliterate our dignity as human persons. We must not treat ourselves as a means to an end or otherwise violate fundamental human goods by malfeasance in our conduct of self-relations. These ideas are not controversial. On the other hand, I take issue with Kant's formulation of these self-regarding duties as moral duties, since linguistic precision requires that these duties be set in their appropriate relational context, since it is from a relational context that the meaning and coherence of self-regarding duties becomes transparent. Linguistic precision--and analyticity--requires that duties that are defined as self-regarding not also be defined as other-regarding. Because of the relations which, by definition, govern them, these self-regarding (prudential) duties are distinct from other-regarding (moral) duties. If self-regarding duties are to be considered duties at all, they must be duties set within the relational context of self-relatedness. They must be defined as duties that obtain due to the integrity of the relational context, duties that are not simply to be deferred to the moral (other-regarding) domain for meaning, intelligibility, and coherence. As self-regarding or "prudential duties," they must be coherent as duties within the context of one's relations to one's own self.

In one sense, Kant's notion of a self-regarding duty is contradictory given his technical use of the term: duty involves recognition of and submission to the "moral law." The moral law expresses the supreme principle of morality as an imperative because the moral law prescribes certain maxims (concern for fairness, treating others with respect, non-malfeasance, universalizability) that, by definition, oppose one's self-regarding inclinations. Furthermore, any actions that are unconditionally good will conform to the requirement that one act from a good will; and only acting from a sense of duty can certify the good will. It is important to note that this picture of duty is technical and framed entirely within the relational context of free action, which is the domain of other-regardingness and human community. In this picture, duty, even self-regarding duty, is coherent as duty only because it derives from the relational context of other-regardingness. The problem, however, is that if one refers to a self-regarding duty only within an other-regarding relational context--for what one "owes" oneself one really owes to others--one sacrifices the integrity of a duty which one owes oneself simply by virtue of being a person. Since duty is analytic with respect to the relational context of other-regardingness, a self-regarding duty must be, in an ultimate way, other-regarding. Kant as much as says that, since he holds that self-regarding duties necessarily precondition one's ability to observe one's moral duties. Kant believed that the idea of a self-regarding duty was coherent because of the necessary connection to that which is an end in itself--morality. But if we say that we ought to be self-regarding for other-regarding reasons, are we not thereby denying that there is such a thing as a literal duty that obtains within the context of one's self-relatedness? Kant's view disallows this possibility, and because a literal duty in the sphere of self-relatedness is disallowed, the whole idea of a self-regarding <u>duty</u> seems question-begging and even incoherent. No wonder "Recent philosophers. . .tend to discard the idea of a duty to oneself as a conceptual confusion."[69]

I am suggesting that we distinguish "prudential" from "moral" on the basis of the relations governed by each sphere of interest, concern and reasoning. This is a linguistically precise distinction based on relational contexts within the "moral domain" itself. If we can hold to this distinction, then the idea of a self-regarding or prudential duty may be validated and rendered coherent. What is required is that one find a more adequate and less technical idea of "duty" than that advanced by Kant.[70] I propose one of Kant's less technical uses of "duty," which is that a duty is anything one ought to do. If we take as a definition of duty, not Kant's technical-moral notion that a duty is recognition of and submission to the moral law, but a more ordinary sense of the term, the following definition will suffice: A duty is something one is expected to do by virtue of having assumed an office of some sort, and it functions as a consideration which guides action and constrains rational choice.[71] Duty is conceived here broadly: it is <u>anything one ought to do</u>.

With this definition of duty in hand, we can proceed to develop a more complete picture of a "prudential duty." If there be such a thing as a self-regarding duty, it will be qualified by the relations of self-regardingness. That is to say, the duty will obtain with respect to intrapersonal relations and it shall be a duty even if it does not appeal to the interpersonal context of moral relations. A prudential duty, therefore, will be an obligation one owes oneself by virtue of the fact that one is a self in relation. It will be a duty constitutive of reflexivity. The "office" one assumes is that of self-hood, and assuming that office requires that one meet certain expectations.

It is one's duty as an "office holder" to meet those expectations and to execute compliance with the requirements of reflexivity and selfhood.

The particulars that belong to the class of self-regarding duties, such obligations as seeking self-knowledge or avoiding self-deception, reflect a principle of self-respect which must be observed if one is to treat oneself as an intrinsically valuable end. They ought to be observed because they are duties, because not to do so would violate the principles of prudential reasoning that governs one's self-relations. We ought to be self-regarding, in other words, for self-regardingness is nothing less than a duty one owes oneself, a duty that "resembles a principle of right" in that one has a right to expect this from oneself.[72] At no time, however, does this "resemblance" to moral duties ever permit the equation of self-regarding with other-regarding. Neither is the self-regarding duty legitimated solely on the basis of a connection to moral or other-regarding duty, even is such connections do obtain (e.g., a duty to prevent another from interfering with one's self-development). Either of these moves would lend credence to the idea that a duty to oneself is incoherent and contradictory.

A self-regarding duty is not a duty that conflicts with a moral duty, though, in the post-Kantian world, this assumption is often made. Josef Pieper has commented on this assumption by saying:

> To the contemporary mind, then, the concept of the good excludes rather than includes prudence. Modern man cannot conceive of a good which might not be imprudent, nor of a bad act which might not be prudent. He will often call lies and cowardice prudent, truthfulness and courageous sacrifice imprudent.[73]

Not everything that expresses the prudence of self-regardingness constitutes a duty of self-regard (e.g., avariciousness, selfishness, deception, cowardice). Neither is everything that is in some way other-regarding necessarily relevant to moral interest. If a poor man asks my help and I respond by giving him all my money, the fruits of my other-regardingness will not merit assessment as "immoral." In this case, I have met my other-regarding duty, though I have also exceeded it by an act of supererogation beyond what is required for other-regardingness. My act should not be considered "immoral." Such disregard for self, however, might occasion the prudential judgment that this supererogatory act does conflict with a self-regarding duty. One could say that my kindness toward the poor man, in that I do harm myself by responding to his need with excessive largess, reveals a lack of self-respect. In other words, I do not treat myself as a co-equal center of meaning and value, and I abuse myself in my relation to myself. The act in question can therefore be evaluated as imprudent. Imprudence invites evaluation from the perspective of prudence itself: my act merits prudential blame, but not the judgment that I have acted in a way that is morally impermissible. I have not failed by my imprudence to fulfill basic moral obligations.

My point in distinguishing moral from prudential, other-regarding from self-regarding, is that if one understands how these two types of duties differ, then one can also see that these duties do not really conflict. It is of course possible to override either prudential or moral duties, but taken as duties, a duty to show respect to myself will never--as a matter of formal analysis--conflict with a duty to show respect to others. Since the observance of moral and prudential duties are always, everywhere and for everyone obligatory at the same time, a person fulfills a moral and a prudential duty by doing good and acting prudently simultaneously. We can of course override a moral duty with self-interest (shipowner) or with supererogatory acts, but the notion of duty that is at issue here is an obligatory minimal performance. Failure to meet that standard of performance occasions censure. In the self-regarding sphere, we censure persons for imprudence; in the other-regarding sphere, we censure persons for immorality. A failure to seek or acquire self-knowledge, then, is blameworthy, but it is blameworthy in the sense of imprudence rather than "immoral." Linguistic precision authorizes, enables and even requires these distinctions. In sum there is no moral duty that would ever require as a condition of satisfying the minimal performance requirements of other-regardingness that one not seek self-knowledge, or that one kill oneself or volunteer to become a slave--or otherwise treat oneself disrespectfully. Similarly, no prudential duty entails the sacrifice of any other-regarding moral obligation. The respective duties that obtain in the moral and prudential domains do not conflict with one another but hold for the relations which govern the interest, concern, and reasoning appropriate to each sphere. One can have moral conflicts concerning such things as which promise to keep when one cannot keep both; and one can have prudential conflicts like the cancer patient: pain avoidance versus self-honesty. One can even override one's moral duties by permitting self-regard to rule the day or by acting in a supererogatory fashion. But neither of these instances of persons using their freedom to act in ways that violate minimal requirements entails the judgment that moral duties will necessarily conflict with a self-regarding duty or vice versa.

Let us consider the value of this moral/prudential distinction for the ethics of self-deception debate.

To observe a self-regarding duty, to know oneself or to be honest with oneself, is to exhibit a fundamental respect for the person capable of acknowledging that duty. Self-regarding action depends upon listening to the counsels of prudence, which, as Kant says, issue forth in an imperative, and obeying what is literally a non-moral ought. To act self-regardingly is to accede to the requirement that one treat the party with whom one is in relation with respect, as if that party were worthy of respect by virtue of the office held. The office of selfhood, of being a human person, is an office worthy of esteem. In the moral sphere, one treats this office of person with respect, and Kant's notion of "mutual respect" governs interpersonal relations. In the prudential domain, one owes this respect to oneself. To do what is required in order to show respect, to fulfill an obligation of self-regardingness, is to exhibit this fundamentally prudential attitude. A lack of self-respect will lead to self-abuse and to imprudence in one's self-relations. There is no doubt that persons can and do abuse themselves, that they can undo themselves as a result of failing to cultivate an adequate regard for self. More often than not, this failure is exhibited in acts of self-destructiveness, in attitudes, acts and decisions that lead to a loss of self-mastery and increased self-fragmentation. These results are unwelcome and injurious from a prudential point of view. It is neither in one's self-interest nor an expression of self-regardingness to countenance such injury or foster its increase. The failure of self-respect is fundamentally imprudent-- it violates a duty one owes oneself and defies the canons of prudential reasoning. From a prudential point of view, it is wrong to let such imprudent results obtain, for on any occasion when they do obtain, one has failed to observe a duty of self-regard, which is one's own preference according to principles of prudential reasoning. One abuses one's freedom thereby. One denies the fulfillment one seeks in freedom--to become an agent who assumes responsibility for freedom by acting in a manner that expresses self-determination and concomitantly, self-fulfillment. It is by a failure to observe a duty of self-regard, which is one's own preference, that prudential <u>akrasia</u> occurs: when a one confronts a conflict between opposing desires that appeal to one's self-interest, one fails to choose the right one, one fails to yield to one's own prudential preference.[74] Prudential <u>akrasia</u> is voluntary wrong-doing in the context of self-relations and self-regardingness.

Prudential <u>akrasia</u> will express itself in improvident decisions, personality vagueness, lack of character, inattentiveness to the virtues, actual vice and perhaps just plain silliness. Duty and prudence in this relational context come together to lead to this prudential maxim: one has a duty to oneself to so cultivate oneself (one's character) that results injurious to one's own well-being do not obtain. In the context of other-relations, a distinction can be drawn between what one ought to do for moral reasons (duty) and what one is inclined to do for reasons of self-interest. There is no such convenient distinction in the self-relatedness context, since one's duty is, by definition, prudential, self-regarding and concerned for personal well-being. Inclination and prudence can conflict (to smoke or not to smoke, personal habits), but there is no convenient way to separate a self-regarding duty from a self-interested inclination. There is no way to distinguish the fact that one has a duty to cultivate one's character in order to avoid imprudent actions from the idea that it is in one's self-interest to avoid them. In the context of one's self-relations, the prudential and the obligatory close ranks, so that ones's responsibilities to oneself cannot be divorced from the well-being and benefits that accrue to one by doing what one, prudentially speaking, ought.

In the prudential sphere, to do one's duty to oneself will simultaneously contribute to one's own well-being. By acting from a principle of self-respect and by seeking to fulfill prescribed prudential duties, certain benefits will accrue in terms of personality formation and character development. It is literally a "prudential duty" to seek these benefits, and it is this conjunction of duty and prudence that constitutes the essential content of the prudential imperative to be self-regarding and seek the benefits of personal well-being. For to seek them is to exhibit the self-respect one owes oneself by virtue of the fact that one is a self-in-relation. To acquire them is to benefit oneself not at the expense of others, but on that minimal level of performance which is necessary for personal well-being and human flourishing.

As we consider the relevance of these two types of duties to the topic of self-deception, we must note that there are duties one owes oneself and that these duties are prudential and self-regarding, not moral in the sense of being other-regarding. The shipowner, for instance, is morally akratic when he decides to put an unseaworthy vessel to sea, thereby endangering innocent human life. For that action he merits moral censure. Prudential akrasia, in the other hand, is what is exhibited by the person who acknowledges a duty to be honest with him- or herself, but who, for reasons of self-interest that are not the best, most preferable reasons, violates that duty by taking refuge in self-deception. From the ethical point of view and in light of the moral/prudential distinction, we can evaluate the self-deception as follows: self-deception arises from a prudential failure. It is an instance of prudential akrasia.

Self-deception is always motivated by self-regarding interests, for a self-deceiver always seeks the personal advantage of psychological gain. In Clifford's illustration of akrasia cum self-deception, we observed that the shipowner's project to mislead his own beliefs arose from a desire to avoid the distress of self-recognition: he wished to avoid seeing himself as a person willing to act immorally. The shipowner did have an illicit desire: to act in a way that was morally akratic; yet he also was "aware" that to act on that desire would lead to the unwanted consequence of psychic distress. Therefore, in order to preserve his sense of well-being as a moral person, he sought an ingenious solution to stave off the pain of conscience. His desire to maintain a morally upright self-image provided the impulse for the self-deception, yet the self-deception represented yet another kind of akrasia--prudential. In deceiving himself, he allows one prudential concern (pain avoidance) to override another (self-honesty); and by his weakness in choosing pain avoidance over self-honesty he violates his own preference to be honest with himself about the true meaning of his actions. Likewise, the cancer patient violates her prudential duty to be honest with herself by refusing to acknowledge the weight of the doctor's prognosis. Her conflict of self-regardingness, too, is settled on the side of pain avoidance.

Neither the cancer patient's nor the shipowner's self-deception constitutes the preferable response to intrapsychic conflict from a prudential point of view; for the self-deception exhibits that lack of self-respect that is even more integral to one's true well-being than avoiding the psychic distress of self-recognition. Both of these prudential *akrates* sacrifice a fundamental value of the common life, self-honesty, to another, lesser value, pain avoidance. The value of pain avoidance, while certainly prudential, is a lesser value in this conflict because persons in the common life are so constituted that they would prefer the truth about themselves with distress to a self-directed cover up without distress. On purely prudential grounds, the prospect that one would deceive oneself in order to avoid the distress of self-recognition would be judged by a reasonable person as having potentially disastrous consequences (e.g., not being able to trust oneself; not knowing one's own mind). Persons in the common life are so schooled that commitment to "self-honesty" is enshrined in our moral make-up and can be said to represent a value that is constitutive of a duty and an inclination to personal well-being. Prudence, we can say, will always *prefer* self-honesty to self-deceit. Accordingly, the patient may be "blamed" for what is, from a prudential point of view a weakness or imprudence. This judgment of imprudence, however, does not merit or imply "moral censure," for the harm done is only to the woman herself. The violation that occurs is a violation of the woman's own preference to be honest with herself. And because the violation of preferences that occurs is motivated by a regard for her own well-being and leads to no immoral action comparable to the shipowner's, the prudential *akrasia* that is identified here must be distinguished from the moral *akrasia* of the shipowner, who, like the cancer patient is also guilty of prudential *akrasia*. While formally the prudential *akrasia* cannot be condoned, in neither case can it be condemned as immoral. One can argue that by this "lie" the cancer patient contributed positively to her own well-being and to those around her. Her imprudent action (self-deception) is implicated in morally positive consequences while the shipowner's imprudent action accompanies moral crimes.

The prudential *akrates*, then, may be censured for a lack of personal virtue, for to violate one's self-regarding duties and thereby bring injury to oneself is to exhibit the lack of excellence that prudence requires in one's self-relations. Without such excellences present to orchestrate those relations, a person's capacity for meeting other-regarding duties may be impaired. The virtues are personality and character achievements. They reveal one's capacity for doing one's duty, for virtues are manifest by their exercise. A virtue is exercised with respect to the excellence which is it is one's duty to acquire, and it is in one's self-interest to cultivate that virtue since virtue also contributes to one's well-being. One's duties pertain to both self-regarding and other-regarding spheres, and, no doubt, society has an interest in promoting the idea that person's should acquire character, achieve virtue, and cultivate excellences. The question, however, is this: Does a self-deceiver exhibit a lack of moral capacity by a self-regarding failure to be honest with his or her own self?[75] Because one's duties pertain to the other-regarding sphere as well, a failure to be honest with oneself could testify to a more general failure of character, which would then entail a failure of moral, as well as prudential, capacity. And it may be the case that self-deceivers will also be persons prone to disregard obligations in the other-regarding domain. Although this case has been argued, the connection between the two is not a necessary one. And saying that must not obscure the fact that self-deceivers do, as it happens, also deceive others.

What is clear is that failure to do one's prudential duty does not mean that one will necessarily fail to do one's moral duty. Failures of moral capacity, which are not failures of virtue but failures related to meeting the minimal requirements of agency itself, will not actually lead to disregard of others. The connection is not causal. By the same token, virtuous men and women are not guaranteed by the assiduous cultivation of their moral capacities that those capacities will always be properly exercised in the moral sphere. Knowing is not doing, wanting is not having, and--to side with Kant over Aristotle on this issue--goodness is not precluded by the lack of virtue.[76] From a moral point of view, the relations of other-regardingness certify that legitimate sphere of interest, concern and reasoning appropriate to the task of moral assessment. The shipowner is an example of a moral man who acts <u>akratically</u> wit respect to <u>moral duty</u>, then postpones the regret occasioned by his wrongful act with a second <u>akratic</u> act, this time a <u>prudential akrasia</u>. This prudential and voluntary wrongdoing involves a different sphere of relations and is aimed at a different, though still self-interested result (psychological gain). The shipowner's immorality is not compounded by his prudential <u>akrasia</u>; rather, he has committed two <u>akratic</u> acts. He has postponed a day of reckoning with his conscience by the second but has earned that day of reckoning by the first. The cancer patient is "guilty" of prudential <u>akrasia</u>, but given the facts of her case and the nature of her interpersonal behavior, it can be said that her capacity as an agent committed to other-regardingness has not been diminished in any discernible way by having deceived herself. In fact, the moral sphere of relations has been enhanced. Her self-deception, in that it has helped to stave off resentment and self-pity, has enabled her to persevere in her interpersonal relations as a moral agent willing and able to act other-regardingly. The self-deception has not affected her moral capacity except to preserve it.

2. Misconception: Self-Deception is Mendacity

The second misconception that has led to the view that self-deception is immoral is that self-deception reflects a character deficiency. That is, it expresses a desire to satisfy one's own inclinations at the expense of truthfulness and shows flagrant disregard for commitments to truthfulness. In this picture, self-deception is not simply a lack of virtue but an actual vice, much like the vice of mendacity; and inasmuch as self-deception is motivated and seems to override commitments one ought to have to truthfulness, the intent to mislead belief is as morally unworthy of the self-deceiver as that same intent, arising from mendacity, is for the deceiver. Self-deception, then, arises from the vice of mendacity and deserves the censure of the moral community.

This mendacity view rests on the common sense assumption that self-deception is not a good of life to be commended: we do not "en-courage" persons to learn the fine art of self-deception. Persons are, rather, advised to be wary of it, urged to suspect it in themselves, cautioned to exercise vigilance lest they fall prey to it. It is deemed an enemy of the good life and a threat to one's well-being in the common life.

That self-deception is disapproved of is a fact of the common life. The idea that one ought not to sacrifice self-honesty for reasons of psychological gain is a prima facie ought. Furthermore, it is clear that the self-deceiver acts as the agent of self-deception, thereby revealing both a weakness of character and a lack of excellence in one's constitution--as would any instance of akrasia, prudential or moral. Moreover, self-deception strikes at the heart of rationality itself; for if one were to eliminate all the conditions that make self-deception possible, one would have to eliminate rationality itself, since self-deception is a destination arrived at by travelling through established channels of information processing and evidential evaluation. Self-deception is not a good, but an evil, at least with respect to the idea that it constitutes a way of perverting our systems of evaluation and rational procedure. In short, if self-honesty be an excellence of character worthy of being termed a "virtue," self-deception is clearly the opposing "vice."

One could concede all these points and yet the question would still need to be answered: Does all of this disapproval and censure of self-deception amount to a moral reproof such that any instance of self-deception will merit the ascription of actual "immorality." Is self-deception really an expression of a deeper flaw, mendacity, that so influences how one acts in the intrapersonal arena that one is prone to lie to oneself just as one is prone to lie to others? Is a self-deceiver "given to deception" (mendacity)? We are now ready to answer these questions, for we now have in hand certain distinctions about governing relations that will help us to describe the moral status of self-deception with precision. Self-deceivers may be mendacious, but they are not mendacious because they are self-deceived.

3. The Imprudence of Self-Deception

I have argued that self-deception can be shown to be imprudent, and under "imprudence" one can grant all of the above objections. Imprudence, however, is not immorality. Both imprudence and immorality represent descriptions of failures to apply right reason to action, but they are not therefore equivalent terms. Conceptual analysis and common discourse support the distinction that obtains in the more broadly conceived "moral sphere" of existence--a distinction that can be described in terms of governing relations. A self-deceiver is imprudent in that his or her self-deception violates a preference to act consistently with ideas of excellence that govern the intrapersonal sphere of relations. Yet a self-deceiver may act such that his or her behavior, as adjudged by other-regarding criteria, has permissible, even morally commendable results (cancer patient). By these same other-regarding criteria, another person may merit contempt; the shipowner, for instance, violates action guides operative in the interpersonal context of relations. The cancer patient and the shipowner qualify for different evaluations. In the self-regarding sphere of relations, however, both happen to be self-deceived and therefore merit a judgement of prudential blameworthiness. Both have fallen victim to prudential <u>akrasia</u>, and censure falls on each since each violates a preference to which both may reasonably be assumed to be committed--self-honesty.

The central question here is whether the fact that something is considered a "vice" is sufficient to warrant the conclusion that it is also "immoral." Linguistic precision based on relevant governing relations can settle this issue. "Vice" is ordinarily meant to point to faulty actions based on imperfections, lack of excellence and failures of character. The moral vices, like the moral virtues, have been considered "moral" because they express the interest and concern of practical reason itself: a moral vice is contrary to human nature inasmuch as human beings are rational creatures (Aristotle and Aquinas). A vice, therefore, for which there is a corresponding virtue, refers to a lack of achievement in becoming the person who will act virtuously, i.e., with justice, temperance, fortitude and prudence. Virtue is "moral" because it pertains to principles of right reason, because it conforms to what is good. Virtues are to be cultivated and possessed because perfection requires them, and they will be manifest as achieved excellences of character.

In one sense, this broad employment of "moral," in that it specifies how one should use one's freedom to achieve human fulfillment, delimits the sphere of practical reason itself. But within that sphere of interest, concern and reasoning, how are we to distinguish the action guides and principles of right conduct that are appropriate to self-regarding, as opposed to other-regarding, behavior? The issue of self-deception raises this issue and urges us to greater linguistic refinement. The ordinary language assessment of self-deception--that self-deception is not a good of life but neither is it "immoral"--has urged us to reconsider the relation of moral to prudential. A more precise use of "moral" is called for, even if tradition holds that "moral" is the appropriate term to be employed to describe all facets--and all relations--within the sphere of practical reason. A more qualified use of "moral" seems in order, for the relations involved in, and affected by, other-regarding and self-regarding behavior authorize certain linguistic employments that are, in the common life, not translatable one to the other. An imprudent person merits censure, but that censure is not the same as that which falls on the person who violates the rules of interpersonal relations, who, for instance, overrides other-regardingness with self-regardingness in a situation where, for some reason, they conflict. This description arises from observation of the common life, and it is expressed in an ordinary language intuition, which is that the two kinds of censure differ, for the relational contexts within which the "voluntary wrongdoing" occurs differ. To recognize this is to be urged to clarify how one kind of censure differs from another; and it is with respect to that issue that a more refined and precise use for moral can obtain within the broad realm of practical reason itself.

A precise description will resolve the disputes involved in the "ethics of self-deception" debate. My description is this: Whenever self-deception occurs, a self-regarding duty to be honest with oneself is violated. The self-deceiver is capable of acknowledging that self-honesty is a good of life, a prima facie obligation constitutive of the person's true preference; but whenever a person violates the preference for self-honesty, he or she, as a self-deceiver, exhibits an instance of prudential akrasia. Self-deception, therefore, represents a form akrasia; but it is not a form of moral akrasia deserving moral censure. Self-deceiver's violate the self-regarding duty to be honest with themselves; and this is a violation that always occurs in a specific relational context, the context of self-relations. That self-deception appears in instances of moral akrasia (shipowner) is to be noted, but because the governing relations differ between the moral and prudential forms of akrasia no necessary, causal connection can be established between the two. One can act malevolently without being self-deceived; and one can be self-deceived without acting malevolently.

A self-deceiver exhibits an imperfection in his or her relation to prudential requirements of self-knowledge and self-honesty and therefore violates a self-regarding ought. Recalling Aquinas' statement that that "It is requisite for man's perfection that he should know himself,"[77] we can even say that self-deception violates this particular requirement of perfection, though the failure of self-knowledge will not generally arouse contempt or invite moral censure. What the self-deceiver receives from the moral community is more likely to be pity--if, that is, the self-deceiver is not also a moral akrates. Recent studies of the "ethics of self-deception" have advanced such a position, for our common life assessment of self-deception is such that we want on the one hand to disapprove of self-deception while not conceding that the self-deception is itself intrinsically immoral. It has been argued, for instance, that self-deception is blameworthy action, but that to say it is "vicious and immoral" is itself a sign of moral insensitivity (Szabados).[78] It has also been argued that self-deception can cover certain actions worth praising, since self-deception expresses through a project to mislead belief an essentially moral drive toward personality integration (King-Farlow).[79] Other have said what I have said: that individual instances of self-deception can be beneficial, even rational and "canny," despite the fact that self-deception is not, as a rule, to be considered beneficial (Rorty).[80] And Patrick Gardiner has observed that there are instances in which one could argue ". . .that even at the simplest level occasions for self-deception arise which are quite unrelated to moral considerations."[81]

Self-deception is not a good we seek in the common life. There is, in fact, a kind of "wrongdoing" attached to the concept, though it is of a peculiar sort: it is wrongdoing that appeals to blameworthiness without also invoking moral condemnation. It is to be likened to the kind of reaction aroused by the phenomenon of the "victimless crime." The victim of a victimless crime is the perpetrator: the action is "wrong" and not to be encouraged; and the crime represents a failure of practical reason. The victimless crime is one in which a person performs an act of self-mutilation, cutting off freedom of self-determination by a failure of right reason in action. But the victimless crime is different from the crime against persons. The victimless crime is self-directed even though, like crimes against persons, it is also abusive of freedom. Our reaction to self-deception, as to victimless crimes, is not such that it provokes our moral indignation. This is because in the common life we draw moral distinctions appropriate to the phenomenon in question: A self-deceiver's self-deception is assessed within the realm of practical reason ("moral" in the broad sense); and there it is adjudged and found wanting. The self-deceiver is held responsible for having failed to use right reason in his or her action. The excuses and rationalizations that are produced are noted, and not countenanced, and they are actually discouraged. Yet, by virtue of the fact that the self-deceiver has become his or her own victim, the full brunt of moral censure is withheld. The failure of practical reason in this instance, because it is self-directed and not other-directed, does not infringe on the rights of others and therefore does not merit the ascription of actual "immorality."

Because self-deception is victimless wrongdoing in the moral domain, the domain of other-regardingness, the blameworthiness that attaches is that appropriate to a particular kind of failure of practical reason. We can say that the self-deceiver exhibits an instance of imprudence, for we clearly witness a violation of a self-regarding duty to seek perfection in one's character. We can say that the self-deceiver lacks virtue while hesitating to say that the self-deception arises as an obvious "vice." The self-deceiver, therefore, is not a fitting subject for moral outrage by virtue of the fact that he or she is self-deceived. The fact that a self-deceiver has voluntarily done wrong will not suffice for an equation of that prudential akrasia with the kind of moral akrasia that characterizes evil acts in the other-regarding sphere of relations. The failure of self-honesty that occurs in self-deception is not to be applauded, approved or condoned. Having said that, however, it is also necessary to distinguish this lack of approval from that which obtains when morally impermissible acts occur in the interpersonal sphere of relations. We must be attentive to the common life understanding in which "governing relations" affect not only the description but the moral assessment of the akratic act. Who acts and who is affected are relevant to moral evaluation and to the form of censure that will be appropriately directed to the akrates in question.

e. Conclusion: The Benefit of the Moral/Prudential Distinction

A study of self-deception leads one to consider what is meant by the term "moral." Although both self-regarding and other-regarding failures are failures of practical reason, a further distinction is authorized on the basis of relevant governing relations. The wrongdoing that is implied by "lack of virtue" is governed by a distinct set of criteria, and this we know because in the common life, in the language of everyday. We discriminate instances of "immoral" action from self-regarding failures, which we are reluctant to attribute to immorality even as we censure them. Acquiring this power of linguistic and conceptual discrimination reflects our desire to clarify the boundaries of the intrapersonal with the language of virtue and self-regarding duty. We can, in other words, invoke prudence and self-regarding duty while also maintaining that the boundaries of morality are similarly confined to a specific relational context--the interpersonal. In the common life, these distinctions are actually drawn, but because "moral" has been equated with all that pertains to the realm of practical reason, a certain imprecision in usage has resulted. We see that imprecision in Clifford's judgment that the shipowner's belief in God is the seat of his immoral behavior. We see that imprecision when those seeking clarity about the moral status of self-deception (Szabados, Rorty, Gardiner, King-Farlow) attempt to mitigate Clifford's conclusion. The confusion that surrounds the moral status of self-deception can be rectified by using "moral" with greater precision. We can stipulate that the appropriate use of "moral/ immoral" is restricted to the sphere governed by other-regarding relations.

To have this distinction in hand enables us to clarify the connection between lack of virtue and immorality. Lack of virtue, which expresses a self-regarding failure (prudential akrasia), does not necessarily lead to moral failure as well, since even a self-deceived person can continue to do good in the other-regarding context. As Kant would have it, even a stupid person can do good. On the other hand, not every moral failure expresses an actual disposition to moral wrongdoing. Not every moral failure shows an accomplished failure to develop personal excellences (vice). A person can lie, thereby meriting moral censure; but that lie can express something other than mendacity. A lie can result from kindheartedness toward another person, which is often the case with the "white lie." It is not the mendacity of a person--the vice of mendacity--that lies behind all forms of prevarication; and this can be held even though all forms of prevarication come under moral scrutiny and merit censure. All lies, from a moral point of view, express a failure of right reason in the context of other-regarding action. The connection between exhibiting a lack of virtue and being morally culpable, however, is not a causally necessary connection; or, if it be so described, then one is using "moral" to cover all aspects of practical reason. The concept 'moral' is certainly used in this broad way, but we can specify a more particular use for 'moral/prudential' in order to distinguish what we often mean to distinguish in our everyday discourse--self-regarding failures and other-regarding failures. There is certainly room to debate whether lack of virtue and vice mean the same thing as "immoral." James D. Wallace's cogent and cautionary remarks on this point are worth considering:

> It is a plausible thesis generally that the faulty actions philosophers lump together under the heading "morally wrong" are actions fully characteristic of some vice, and that excuses which mitigate or remove fault are factors which show that the action does not satisfy some condition for action fully characteristic of some vice. A corollary may be that there exist some vices for which we have no names. That is not to say that every action fully characteristic of vice is "morally wrong." There is a disagreement about the extension of the term 'moral,' and several issues of substance are involved in these differences.[82]

I have tried in this discussion to point out some of those issues of substance, my case being that an investigation of the ethics of self-deception requires that we do so. Analyzing self-deception from a moral point of view forces us to consider disagreements that arise over moral evaluation. The moral question presses us to resolve the difficulties that obtain with respect to governing relations. My own conclusion is that we have not, as a linguistic community, authorized ourselves to judge self-regarding failures according to criteria of assessment designed for the context of other-regardingness, so that the imprudent action of self-deception does not carry the weight of censure that an immoral action does. The shipowner's act of "murder" is distinguishable from his act of self-deception. Ethical analysis requires that we be able to describe that difference, and distinguishing moral from prudential <u>akrasia</u> provides the means for doing so.

Although there is indeed disagreement about the meaning and the reach of the term 'moral,' I have presented a case for setting boundaries according to governing relations. The distinction that has been drawn between the moral and prudential aspects of practical reason is meant to perform two services. First is to clarify the idea of a duty to oneself, especially in light of the observation that contemporary philosophers tend to discard that idea as a conceptual confusion. Although no incoherence obtains as a result of holding that a self-regarding duty is a feature of practical reason, a conceptual confusion can result if we hold that the duty one owes oneself is a duty because it is also a duty enmeshed in other-regarding duties. This denies integrity to the "self-regardingness" of the self-regarding duty. Accordingly, I have argued that a conceptual confusion arises if one holds that a duty to oneself is a <u>moral</u> duty; for there is good reason to distinguish a self-regarding duty from a moral duty. For one thing, "moral" can be shown to pertain in a linguistically precise way to the domain of interpersonal relations, so that a moral person is one who meets obligations as prescribed by the principles of right reasoning in the sphere of other-regardingness. If that point be conceded, this conclusion follows: In the common life, we are not, as a general rule, authorized to use language so imprecisely that we can expect other persons to understand that when we speak of "duties to oneself" we actually mean by that "duties to others." This equation is precluded because the relations governing the duties in question differ. But neither are we authorized to disregard the vitality and flexibility of language. That is, we are not authorized to use language so strictly that we can disregard the idea that "duties" do fall on us in our intrapersonal relations, as certain ordinary language employments suggest, e.g., one <u>ought</u> to seek self-knowledge, since self-knowledge is requisite for human perfection. If such self-regarding duties are violated, the constituents of character will suffer accordingly. The results, none of which can be said to be of benefit to the person or contribute to personal well-being, will include such imprudent achievements as personality vagueness, egoistic action arising from unbridled self-interest, or the folly--masochism--of unchecked disregard for self. Such results are contrary to the most rational aim of the common life, and because these developments reflect the imprudence that adversely affects our hope for happiness, they are to be shunned. Moral education, training in the virtues, is meant to check these unwanted and destructive developments.

The second benefit performed by the moral/prudential distinction is that the rationale for a common response to the fact of self-deception becomes intelligible. That response is the reluctance, and in psychotherapy the refusal, to censure a self-deceiver under the rubric of "immorality." This response occurs simultaneously with the concession that the individual in question is responsible for the condition of self-deception, for it is a self-directed activity; yet also recognized is the fact that the self-deceiver is exhibiting an unwanted weakness or flaw in character. On the analysis presented here it can be concluded that self-deception is "wrong," that it results from a form of akrasia, that it shows a lack of excellence expressing a duplicity of intent, even that it is a form of sin in that it exhibits a lack of constitutional perfection. But all of this does not add up to "immorality." The ascription of immorality is confined to a particular aspect of practical reason, namely, that which takes as its interests and concern right reason applied to action in the other-regarding, interpersonal sphere of relations. A failure of right reason in the context of self-relatedness yields a different evaluation, yet a severe censure given the terms of censure available to it: imprudence.

This discussion has aimed at justifying the somewhat contradictory notion that self-deception is not a good of the common life even though, by the same token, it does not seem to merit condemnation as "immoral" behavior. To condemn a self-deceiver in moral terms for akrasia, to equate a person's voluntary wrongdoing in the prudential sphere with the moral sphere, as if deception of self were morally equivalent to deception of others, as if neurosis were morally equivalent to perjury, is to confuse matters, as I believe most members of our linguistic community skilled in the language of morals and the rules for employing moral concepts would agree. Such an equation, even if purely formal, would exhibit not only linguistic imprecision and conceptual confusion, but even moral insensitivity on the part of the accuser.

What, then, can be said? Is self-deception altogether irrelevant to moral interest, concern and reasoning? To say so would likewise be to miss the point. The point after all is that self-deception does pertain to the realm of practical reasoning since self-deception is not considered a good of life, but an unwanted prospect that can adversely affect us if we are not vigilant, if we do not guard it with self-scrutiny, if we do not assume a duty to ourselves to be honest with ourselves even to the point of recognizing that we have desires at odds with our self-image. What can be said is that 'self-deception' describes a certain kind of episode in psychic life, that it represents an act we undertake and direct in violation of a preference not act this way. 'Self-deception' is term relevant to moral discourse and ethical evaluation, and the phenomenon is itself must be considered in any analysis of the practical reason that concerns itself with our self-relations. It can also be said that because self-deception is the result of intrapsychic distress and represents a voluntary response to that conflict, it is a particular topic of interest to moral psychology. Self-deception is an anodyne to that distress, and the distress may be occasioned by moral akrasia, thereby rendering the anodyne a remedy not without moral significance of its own.

Moral psychology concerns itself with the reasons for akratic action. It seeks to understand the process whereby individuals engage in a project to mislead their own beliefs for reasons of psychological gain. Analysis reveals that the gain being sought turns on the question of one's own self-understanding and moral commitments. The self-deception arises as the person's response to intrapsychic conflict, and moral psychology interests itself with the person's own assessment of motive and asks why he or she acted this way rather than that. From the perspective of moral psychology, the fact of self-deception reveals, albeit indirectly, that the anodyne of self-deception is meant to preserve the moral self-image that the agent has assaulted by his or her own akratic act. The self-deception reveals the strength of the akrates' moral commitments as well as the strength of the akrates' desire to integrate his or her identity with those moral commitments. Furthermore, self-deception holds open the possibility that when the self-deception is overcome, regret will ensue and self-reform commence. Such considerations are relevant to the sphere of practical reason and the language of morals.

Akrasia is manifest in action; and akratic action obtains as the result of a decision to act, to do one thing rather than another. Because akrasia is manifest, however, the decision to act one way and not another presupposes conflict about what to do; and because conscience is party to the conflict an akratic act will necessitate a day of reckoning, bringing remorse and regret in its wake. Regret and remorse are the painful reminders that one has decided and acted in violation of avowed preferences, and this pain, like all pain, is to be avoided if at all possible. Right action is of course the preferred way to avoid it, but akrasia is by its very nature wrong action, action reflecting a weakness to choose what is by the person's own lights preferred. So unpleasant and distressing is the prospect of experiencing this regret, of facing up to the nature of one's decision to do what one knows in one's heart is wrong, that the conflict of decision making, which in one sense is ended by what one actually does, is, in another sense, continued. The conflict is transferred to the psychological arena and to the dynamics of mental life. It is here where self-deception occurs. It is here where the conflict of morals and of reasons for action continues unabated. The conflict persists in the self-deception; it is not resolved by it. What can be said is that this conflict expresses one possibility for free action, for this conflict also reveals the complexities of the person who would attempt to be a responsible and integrated moral agent in the midst of self-related opposition. In sum, the dynamics of psychological conflict that attend the self-deceiver's project to mislead his or her own beliefs are relevant to ethical analysis and are of significant interest to moral thinking. That a self-deceiver reveals through his or her self-deception weakness, wrongdoing and imperfection is not to be gainsaid; but if the self-deceiver is also to be held accountable for "immoral" acts, that ascription can be shown to depend on something other than the self-deception. In light of the analysis I have offered, the self-deception is not intrinsically "immoral." It is, rather, psychological reaction that can be described as a prudentially akratic act, but one which may or may not accompany morally akratic acts.

B. The Religious Perspective

In this section my purpose is to consider the relevance of 'self-deception' to religious thought and religious discourse. This particular aspect of our conceptual investigation is necessary because religious thinkers have actually authorized 'self-deception' to be employed within the linguistic context governed by the interests, concerns, presuppositions and reasoning associated with theological inquiry and religious reflection.

Self-deception is a problem that has, in one form or another, preoccupied religious thinkers. And because religious thinkers have analyzed the concept in a religious context and have even claimed to find a remedy for self-deception in the religious resource, the concept has been deemed a fit accompaniment to theological reflection. In this section my aim is to investigate the way in which representatives of the religious perspective have employed 'self-deception' to perform meaning tasks in the religious domain, in light of the commitments and relations that govern concepts as they are put to use in the context of religious discourse. This investigation must, of necessity, be limited; so I offer the following qualifications in order to restrict the scope of this aspect of our investigation.

The first qualification is that the religious perspective under discussion will be confined to the tradition of Western religious thought and to Christianity in particular. There is ample room for an examination of what, say, Eastern religious traditions have to say on this topic; for self-deception has met with some peculiar social responses that would be of academic interest: the fact that that self-deception is recognized but treated as if it were a skeleton in the closet. Many of the proposed techniques for overcoming self-deception advanced by Western psychologists offer a striking parallel to the self-cultivation techniques developed in Eastern meditative traditions. The present investigation cannot pursue this line of inquiry though I recognize that investigators can find fertile ground in other religious traditions. To pursue this now, however, would take us too far afield of the religious perspective stipulated as we began this inquiry.

A second qualification concerns the normative view of religion to be utilized in this discussion, the presuppositions that are to be expected of one who takes the religious point of view. To be noted at the outset is the fact that if 'self-deception' is to be meaningful in the domain of religious thought and discourse, the expression must be used by criteria governed by, and constitutive of, the concept as it is ordinarily used. The criteria for ascribing self-deception will not formally change. We are changing the context for employing the linguistic expression rather than the rules that govern meaning. The meaning of self-deception as it is ordinarily understood in the common life must still hold. What a religious perspective brings to the concept is a new, perhaps "logically odd" context for certain meaning possibilities, possibilities not made available in the scientific-philosophical (psychology) or even the moral contexts.

The religious perspective provides a distinct basis for understanding human existence. It brings to bear on thought about human nature and human possibilities a new presupposition. The presupposition created by the religious perspective concerns a new and distinct possibility for relationship. Inasmuch as human persons seek in their existence, in their condition of finitude, an ultimate source of meaning and value, the quest for such ultimacy leads to a quest for a new relational possibility. By this I mean that religion is that universal phenomenon that sanctions the quest for meaning and value beyond what universal reason is able to provide (ethics). Another way to say this is that in the religious realm of understanding, the fundamental relationship is not simply intrapersonal (psychology), or interpersonal (moral), but human-divine (religious). It is the God-relationship that governs the religious sphere of meaning and value, a domain of concern that is by definition ultimate and infinite. It is the God-relationship that determines the meaning of religious discourse and that will, for the religious person, provide a basis for evaluating that form of self-deception that arises in this relational context. Other perspectives--philosophy, psychology, ethics--are directed elsewhere. They do not seek this relational possibility, for even if God is affirmed in a philosophical system (Descartes) or rendered psychologically valuable or posited as a guarantor for morality, none of these perspectives takes as its central focus the relationship that is the heart of religious interest. Self-deception, then, is a topic of concern in the religious context of meaning to the extent that it proves relevant to the human relationship to an ultimate source of meaning and value. I shall term that the "God-relationship" and will claim that this relational possibility provides the context for conducting a religious analysis of 'self-deception.'

A third qualification concerns the particular area of religious thought where one can say with certainty that 'self-deception' is relevant. The religious term that is relevant to self-deception is sin. The meaning of sin can be interpreted in two distinct ways. One of those ways concerns injustice. This use of 'sin' was referred to in the previous section of this chapter for sin as injustice refers to moral infraction or action that can be described as "immoral." The other way to interpret sin is in terms of the God-relationship. 'Sin,' in this specifically religious sense, refers to the human disrelationship to God. In this religious discussion, 'sin' will not be used to refer to the wrongdoing that obtains when viewed from the moral point of view. In the religious domain, the meaning of sin is focused solely on the relationship of human persons to a non-representable transcendent source of meaning and value--God. Sin, in other words, bears a "numinous" quality. It expresses a fundamental disrelationship between a finite person and his or her infinite interests. The issue to be considered is how sin is connected to self-deception--how disrelationship with God is connected to the disrelationship of a person to his or her own self.

I shall approach this problematic from two sides. First, I shall consider the specific sin of pride in order to clarify the relationship of sin to self-deception. Secondly, I shall consider Kierkegaard's suggestion that sin is despair, then ferret out the relationship of sin as despair to self-deception. I shall consider Kierkegaard's reflection on the topic of self-deception as it pertains to his assessment, Biblically inspired, that human persons are capable of "double-mindedness," a religiously conceived description of self-deception. I remind my reader that I am analyzing an employment of self-deception in a particular context of meaning and value. My aim is to show how rich this employment is, how truly relevant it is to religious thinkers of different historical contexts and traditions. I do not necessarily endorse the idea that many of those who stand within a particular religious tradition will term all outsiders self-deceivers; but I am interested in the logic at work here even as my project continues to be descriptive. In order to make my case, I shall draw on a variety of figures representing a variety of Christian commitments. If my point that there is a religious employment of self-deception be valid, then a sweeping and inclusive approach is to be preferred to an in-depth analysis of any particular figure or viewpoint; and I do not wish to be accused of violating my own preferences.

1. Self-Deception and Sin: The Sin of Pride

The concept 'pride' is a passional or emotional concept that can be examined from different points of view. From a psychological point of view, 'pride' refers to the ". . .pleasure taken in possession of some quality that one deems valuable."[83] From a moral point of view, a genuine and reasonable pride expresses the self-esteem to which one is entitled by virtue of one's status as a person, a self-esteem that ". . .depends on a comprehensive and just sense of values."[84]

Conceptual analysis reveals that 'pride' refers to self-directed delight, elation or pleasure. Pride can be said, moreover, to express a fundamental quality of self-relatedness, as does its opposite quality, humility. The concept 'pride' is employed to perform different meaning tasks, from description to evaluation, positive or negative; and analysis of the concept permits us to say, as Hume said, ". . .that all agreeable objects, related to ourselves, by an association of ideas and impressions, produce pride, and disagreeable ones humility."[85] Although 'pride' is often used to identify a quality of conceitedness, there are other, less negative connotations associated with pride. Even Karl Barth is able to entertain the notion that natural pride bespeaks a sort of virtue, for Barth held that pride is a necessary quality for the person seeking an authentic human existence. Pride, writes Barth, accompanies the effort to achieve self-containment. Pride enables a person to enjoy the use of freedom to which each individual is entitled as a person, and it manifests the desire of persons to choose themselves authentically, in the fullness of human being:

> May it not be that God Himself has created and ordained man to be himself, to control himself, to be sufficient to himself? When man desires the enjoyment and use of his freedom, is he desiring anything more or other than the most obvious and natural thing in the world? And in what does his freedom consist if not first and last in the capacity and the right to choose himself? Where is the wrong in this? [It looks] as though man is modestly doing that which is obvious and right, fulfilling his true humanity and in that way the will of God as rightly understood.[86]

Pride, therefore, can be considered a reasonable and justifiable expression of self-esteem. It is subject to psychological scrutiny inasmuch as it is a form of self-relatedness; and it is subject to ethical analysis in two respects. First, it seems to be necessary for human well-being; second, pride is a requisite expression of the kind of agreeableness we seek to achieve intrapsychically. In other words, we cultivate pride in order to appreciate our own dignity as human persons, for without it, we cannot fulfill the obligation of self-respect which we owe ourselves in virtue of being human.

Pride thus has a positive side. This positive quality has standing in the common life and in the language of everyday, for it indicates that the self-sufficiency associated with pride is a good to be valued, and it points to an excellence of self-relatedness commonly associated with personal well-being. "Pride comes from virtue," Aquinas wrote, and even if it is not a direct cause of virtue, pride does express the appetite for excellence that marks the character of the virtuous person. That appetite for excellence reflects a good of life that persons should seek to cultivate, and this holds even if 'pride' can also be used to refer to an appetite for excellence in excess of right reason.[87]

To understand pride in this approving manner is to understand it in a particular context of moral evaluation. In the religious sphere this approval is withdrawn. Pride as an excellence or a condition of excellence is, for the religious thinker, shattered. This result is intelligible if we keep in mind that in the religious sphere the God-relation governs all other concepts and overrides all other considerations. In theistic religion, God is eternal and unconditioned and exists as the unqualified "highest good"--that "than which nothing greater can be conceived" (Anselm). From the religious point of view, as the highest good, God is that to which persons ought to relate themselves; for this is, as religious thinkers never tire of saying, the proper use of freedom. We should freely enter into relationship with the highest good for this is the relation that most truly fulfills human being. That such a relation to an infinite object is possible stems from a particular religious analysis of human being itself, an analysis that upholds the grandeur of human being while also holding that human being is complex, even contradictory. A few remarks on this issue will enable us to consider more precisely the nature of sin and pride and how they are implicated in self-deception.

a. The Religious Perspective on Self-Relatedness and Sin

From a religious point of view, to be human means to exists as a creature of infinite possibility. But this is not all it means. To be human also means that human persons are creatures of infinite possibility amid the finite constraints that necessarily preclude actualizing those possibilities.[88] Relation to God, then, or acquiring a religious consciousness, is possible because human beings can be said, theologically, to have been created in God's image and endowed with a capacity for the infinite. A capacity for the infinite is the capacity for possibility itself, for freedom and spirit, for transcendence, for what Pascal called the grandeur de l'homme. But because this is not the whole story, the truth of human being must be grasped dialectically. That is, the grandeur can only be considered as a contrariété, in opposed relation to misère. Human beings, in other words, are bound by the relativities of existence, constrained by nature, necessity, temporality and mortality. They are limited by the condition of finitude which is the human condition. The religious perspective affirms both the infinite possibilities and the constraints of finitude, locating the greatness of human being in the ability of persons to touch both extremes, both the grandeur and the misère, simultaneously. Pascal said it best: the human chimera is both "the glory and the refuse of the universe."[89]

Given this religious understanding of human beings as contrary, chaotic and conflicted, it is clear that the religious perspective lends itself to the kind of thinking about human nature and capacity that makes 'self-deception' not only a reasonable possibility but a likely prospect. The religious perspective offers the view that the God-relationship can only obtain as a result of concern for ultimate things. It is, that is to say, the expression of an infinite interest in the infinite. The religious perspective is concerned with the possibility of a God-relationship, with the capacity of human beings to be infinitely open, upward. For God is by definition the object--the only object--of "ultimate concern" (Tillich) and "infinite interest" (Kierkegaard), and this qualification of ultimacy characterizes the attitude that is appropriately religious. It is in terms of "ultimacy," "infiniteness," "highest" or "supreme" good that we define that quality unique to religious consciousness. By these qualifications we circumscribe the conceptual boundaries of the religious domain itself. Tillich advocated with eloquence that "ultimate concern" be acknowledged as the distinctive marker of religious thought and experience.[90] And Karl Barth, a theologian of quite different temperament, found himself in essential agreement with this distinctively religious analysis. "A man's god," he wrote, "is that which is supreme for him."[91]

The religious impulse arises from our human wonder, our question about the meaning of human existence. That question is referred to the possibility of transcendent reality, to the relational context where reflection about ultimate concerns, infinite interests and the supreme or highest good is sanctioned. Although this relational emphasis by no means exhausts the meaning of religion, or directly explores the multitude of religious issues to be derived from this relationship, it is the raison d'être of religion. It is on the basis of the God-relationship that we are able to examine the relation of sin, pride and self-deception; for the God-relation is the context for our religious inquiry.

The connections we wish to consider have been discussed in the theological writings of Reinhold Niebuhr. According to Niebuhr, the Biblical understanding of sin has a two-fold character. There is a moral or social dimension to sin, which is injustice, and there is a distinctly religious interpretation to be derived solely from a supernatural relation: "The religious dimension of sin is man's rebellion against God, his effort to usurp the place of God."[92] This second definition speaks to the disrelationship of sin created by human action and volition, and it reflects the attempt by human beings to create their own "religious solution" to the contradiction of the human condition. Niebuhr's analysis is widely shared by religious thinkers regardless of historical context or particularities of affirmation. Even the 19th century liberal, Albrecht Ritschl, is in agreement with Niebuhr's observation. Every religion, Ritschl said, seeks a solution to ". . .the contradiction in which man finds himself, as both a part of the world of nature and a spiritual personality claiming to dominate nature. . .[for] as spirit he is moved by the impulse to maintain his independence" from the finitude of the natural order that claims him, subjects and confines him.[93] This contradiction between nature and spirit, freedom and necessity, is the occasion for sin, but it is not sin itself. The most precise description of sin is that sin is disrelationship with God.

From a different theological tradition, sin has been defined as a "negative reaction, a refusal and a resistance" by the human person "who shuts himself off and hardens himself when openness and self-donation are expected."[94] This "No" of the person is directed at God and at the whole order of creation with which God has freely and lovingly established a covenant of grace. A sinner, then, is one who refuses to accept his or her destiny as a recipient of God's grace. The Catholic theologian, Piet Schoonenberg, has discussed the supernatural relation involved in this negativity as follows:

> The person upon whom the life of grace has been bestowed may sin by rejecting it directly, by falling away from faith, by hardening his heart, and by a conscious resistance to God's invitation for a more intimate life with him. . . .Grace is proffered in some way to each man, since God wishes all men to be saved [and] everyman is assumed in the order of grace and determined to a supernatural end. Sin always possesses a

supernatural order. [It] remains supernatural, inasmuch as it is a negative answer to the bestowal of grace.⁹⁵

Although these two versions come at the concept 'sin' from different angles, emphasizing different features, a fundamental agreement binds them together. They both conceive of sin in terms of a brokenness in the God-relation. Both views assume that disrelationship results from some form of rebellion by human beings, and that, furthermore, resistance to finitude as well as denial of intimacy with God constitute tendencies of human behavior and attitude. In other words, there is evidence in such behavior and attitudes that human beings seek to transcend the limitations of finite existence. Ironically, this quest to escape finitude also provides evidence that human beings are more than finite. Both analyses assume that a possibility for transcendent relationship actually exists. 'Sin' expresses that actuality, though in the negative terms of resistance and refusal, in terms of brokenness and disrelationship.

From a theological point of view, from the point of view of the thinker whose religious commitments are the necessary condition for all understanding, the following holds true: Disrelationship with God can only be overcome, and relationship with God is only possible, because God has made this possibility actual. Finite humanity, even though it be "made for the infinite," cannot attain relation with God on the basis of its own finite resource, by its own reason or strength. The qualitative difference between humanity and God precludes the possibility of coming into relationship with the eternal, infinite God by unassisted human effort or by human striving to attain God-like perfection. Humanity cannot enter this relationship with God on the basis of equal partnership, for the divine-human relation is by definition unequal. Even though human beings can share in the life of God, the human side of the relation is inherently unworthy of partnership due to its finiteness over against God's infinity, due to human imperfection over against God's perfection. If relationship is possible, then, it is only because God acts to create a bridge for relation, a means of access from the finite to the infinite. According to the logic of theistic faith, the possibility for entering into relationship with God is made actual only by divine intervention, divine assistance--grace. Moreover, human reason cannot grasp that this possibility for relationship exists through any resource of reason, even though natural reason is capable of conceiving the eternal, the infinite, God. As religious thinkers in the Christian tradition have emphasized over and over again, the possibility for human relationship with God can only be known because God reveals it. The religious believer, then, is the person who trusts that this relational possibility exists for him or her, that the possibility is itself actual, and that God has actually, even historically revealed it so that it can be trusted.

The God-relation requires for its actualization two partners: God, who acts and reveals, and the human person, who responds in faith. For the religious understanding, it is clear that the person God encounters must be a self. That is, the person must be a synthesis of finite and infinite, flesh and spirit, freedom and necessity. This synthesis identifies human nature in its truest form, for it indicates that the terms of opposition are brought together in the relation of self-relatedness. We have seen this before in the "psycho-somatic" duality (Sartre's *en soi*) that relates itself to itself (Sartre's *pour soi*). In any event, the terms of opposition are also the terms of self-relatedness, and their synthesis in the context of self-relatedness is achieved only with effort. By this I mean that self-relatedness is not a given of nature. It is, rather, a task that falls to each individual because of his or her nature. To fail at achieving synthesis between the terms of opposition, between freedom and necessity, is to fail at becoming a self. It is a failure which allows one term of the opposition to dominate another, thereby creating a dislocation in the opposition, which in turn creates a disrelationship. If disrelationship occurs, the contraries of existence will not be properly related in the synthesis of self-relatedness. To fail in the task of self-synthesis is to fail to become the person one truly is, which is to say that one can find oneself alienated from one's true being. One's true being is nothing more than this: to be in nature and of nature (finite, limited and determined) while also being "more than" nature (free, transcendent and spiritual). A "psycho-somatic" and intrapsychic dislocation can, on this analysis, identify a person's disrelationship to his or her own self, and to be disrelated this way means that one is alienated from true being and thereby suffers a loss of selfhood. To experience this self-alienation is to live with a mistaken identity; for an individual who looses him- or herself through being disrelated to one's true self is one who does not "know oneself" as true self-understanding (religiously conceived) requires. In other words, the person who is not a self does not synthesize but denies. The "self-less" person chooses him- or herself in some way that is not true to the condition of self-opposition or contradictoriness that is the human condition. By choosing one term of the opposition over another, the self-less person denies that the task of synthesizing the terms of opposition is a task relevant to his or her existence.

In the religious perspective, it is ironic that individuals who fail to become selves do so because they have found other ways to express ultimate concern and infinite interest, ways other than those appropriate to the task of selfhood. This means that rather than trying to synthesize the terms of self-relatedness, they choose one term over its dialectically related opponent. According to the religious perspective, human beings are capable of achieving synthesis, but they are also capable of deviating from the synthetic ideal in either of two directions--the direction of the finite or the direction of the infinite. In finite terms, individuals may so conceive themselves that they resolve the finite/infinite conflict by unifying themselves according to principles of reason and nature, reducing themselves to the level of necessity and conceiving themselves as determined by nature and by the limitations of temporality and fate. In infinite terms, individuals may so reject finitude that they indulge their mysterious desire for grasping the infinite to the point that they conceive themselves, through imagination, as god-like, as beings who exist unchecked by finitude. Neither of these options represents the true being of human being. A word or two more about these options is in order.

To opt for finitude is to opt for a self-understanding that excludes self-transcendence. To opt for finitude is to deny to human being freedom and spirit. When persons opt for finitude, reason, which is itself finite, is entrusted with the authority to decide questions of meaning and value (according to the canons of reason established by reason itself); and reason, which ever seeks its own authority, authorizes itself to become the final arbiter of truth. The religious perspective, however, offers the criticism that left to its own devices, reason cannot enable one to enter the God-relationship with God, even if reason itself decides that belief in a supreme being or "highest good" is a rational necessity. God, for one thing, is not determined, even by reason. Moreover, there is only one "highest good," one object worthy of one's ultimate concern and infinite interest, and that must itself be an infinite and ultimate object. If one's ultimate trust is in reason, it cannot also be placed in God; for it is a conceptual (as well as an existential) confusion to mistake a finite object, reason, for the appropriate object of infinite interest, God. This would be one way for religious thought to critique the self disrelated to itself and to God in the direction of the finite.

To opt for the infinite, on the other hand, is to opt for a self-understanding that excludes natural and temporal determination. The mistake here, for the religious consciousness, is that such self-understanding denies the limitations that are, of necessity, imposed on human being. Human persons who make this mistake exercise their capacity for transcending the finite--a capacity that is a native human endowment--in such a way that it leads to what Kierkegaard's Christian author, Anti-Climacus, referred to as "infinitizing reflection." The attempt to actualize one's capacity for the infinite opens up the category of the fantastic, which is ". . .that which leads a person into the infinite in such a way that it only leads him away from himself and prevents him from coming back to himself."[96] To so abstract the self, to volitize the self in the possibility of the infinite, is to lose the self in the direction of the infinite just as a deterministic self-understanding, in that it denies freedom and spirit, loses the self in the direction of finitude. In neither extreme is the self concrete, and in either case one loses oneself to the degree one fails to synthesize the terms of the self-relation.

Whenever one attempts to dispel the opposition that is the true nature of selfhood, doing so because one is discomfited by the tensions of self-relatedness (anxiety), one exhibits a fundamental lack of self-understanding. This, in turn, casts one away from true being. The temptation is to opt for one term over another, to seek resolution in an "either/or," to choose oneself and take it upon oneself to resolve the contradictions of existence by affirming the finite at the expense of the infinite or the infinite at the expense of the finite. These are both "religious solutions" to the problems of existence, for both appeal to an individual's ultimate concern about human existence. They are both religious solutions, even though they result from the misuse of freedom and thereby negate the true being of the self-as-synthesis.

Attempts to resolve the conflict of self-relatedness are religious in character. This is because human persons empower themselves and appeal to their own authority to resolve the conflict, making of the human self an object of ultimate concern and infinite interest by so doing. Several points are relevant here. The decision to settle the conflict by a self-directed and self-referring act of faith in oneself reflects what is, for the religious perspective, a failure to adhere to the highest good. In other words, one violates what the religious perspective holds to be the highest good, the God-relation. The God-relation requires a self that exists in the conflictedness and ambiguity of its true being. And because conflictedness and opposition identify true human being, the human attempt to resolve the ambiguity, settle the opposition or stifle the conflictedness is only undertaken at the expense of true being. To lose a grasp of one's true being is to lose the capacity for the God-relationship, for one desires God by substituting some other object, which is by definition finite, for God. One thereby holds to a self-created version of the "highest good" rather than the true highest good--relationship with God. Despite missing the mark with respect to acquiring one's true highest good, one does, by substituting something other than God for God, still make what is a "religious" movement, for one still expresses one's ultimate concern and one's infinite interest--even if it be in relation to an object that is not infinite and ultimate.

From a religious point of view, the problem is that we can find ourselves placing faith not in that which is truly our highest good, the God-relation, but a psychological good, namely, coherence in our self-relations. As we experience anxiety and seek to rid ourselves of psychological distress, we are likely to seek resolution of our self-conflicts in ourselves. We are, that is, prone to trust our own ability to resolve the contradictions of existence, trusting ourselves because of a faith that we are sufficient to resolve the conflict and bring the satisfaction of "inner peace." This faith in self is manifest as self-reliance, which reflects our belief that we can determine our destiny, master our passions, and control the chaotic oppositions that characterize our lives as human persons. And as we seek reunion within the context of self-relatedness, we express a form of reflexive care that is manifest as an act of self-love. From the religious perspective, then, we seek to become the agents of our own care-filled unification. We desire to heal the fractures in our self-relations, and by relying on our own reason and strength, we express a desire for greater unity with respect to an object of reflexive care, which is the self itself.

To so position one's own self as the center of meaning and value, even to the point of making oneself the repository of one's trust and the object of one's love, is to create an ultimacy within the context of self-relatedness. From a religious point of view, this ultimacy of self negates God's ultimate claim on the person, so that this ultimacy of self actually usurps the place reserved for God alone. This then is the self-assertion, the egoism, the presumption to God-likeness that is sin. For Christian thinkers, this presumptuousness is endemic to the human condition. Human beings are so constituted, say the Christian theologians, that they evaluate themselves according to criteria that conflict with the demands of the God-relation. Those criteria are self-serving and presume to establish an object fit for ultimacy--the self--when it is God alone who is worthy of "ultimate concern." This mistaking of self for God signals the fall from relation with God. To fall from relation with God means that one usurps God's place--even if under pretense of "being religious"--thereby denying that relation with the true God is possible. This movement disrupts and negates relation with God, and this is what it means to sin.

b. The God-Relation

Although the idea of God is of interest to philosophers, psychologists and ethicians, and rational inquiry has led some thinkers to infer God's existence on the basis of rational necessity--as that which makes a philosophical system or ethical system cohere--the religious conception of God is qualitatively distinct from the God pictured in such inquiry. Religion is not the handmaiden of psychology or ethics, and from a religious perspective God is not inferred but revealed. The God who is posited as the object of ultimate concern, with whom relation is required for human well-being and personal fulfillment, is not the God of the philosophers, but the God who encounters human person as a God _pro me_--"the God of Abraham, the God of Isaac, the God of Jacob" as Pascal put it in his celebrated _Memorial_. In the religious sphere the God-relation is not a hypothesis to be considered and understood but a basis for understanding itself. The God-relation governs all concepts, alters the foundation of knowing, and influences the nature and meaning of linguistic performances undertaken with respect to God. The God-relation overrides all other considerations. This is the religious point of view, and to operate from this point of view is to operate in light of the God-relation. The religious domain locates a region of meaning and value where the governing relation requires infinite interest. There are four considerations relevant to the relational aspects of the religious sphere that have been touched upon, and even though each could be subjected to further analysis and extensive discussion, they may be summarized as follows:

First, the God-relation provides the theist with a possibility made actual by God. Although the possibility of infinite relation is conceivable in that human beings are capable of imagining it ("infinitizing reflection"), the premise of the God-relation is that God is God and human beings are not God. Human beings are qualified by spirit, for they have been created in the divine image and are therefore disposed to seek the highest good. Yet the glory of human being is also manifested in human finitude. Human being must be analyzed in light of the fact that human beings are alienated from themselves, from God, and lack the integrity of constitution they desire. This desire for wholeness calls forth a religious response, and this response acknowledges that human being is in need of God. Only God, only the object of infinite interest and ultimate concern, can respond to the human situation with a promise of integration and wholeness. Only God can make the human potential for infinite and perfect being actual. The Christian, in fact, holds that God was so concerned to restore relationship with fallen humanity that relationship with humanity was actually entered into historically: God acted through historical revelation to make relation with God possible. Human beings, therefore, can be expected to enter that relation for, as Schoonenberg put it, "every man" is assumed in the order of grace and the offer of relation is made by God to all.

Second, the theistic believer holds that entering the God-relation requires that human beings be what they are and accept themselves in their condition of conflictedness and self-opposition. That is the true being of human being. This true being is also cause for anxiety and dissatisfaction, for human beings are tempted to resolve the contradictions of existence by relying solely on their own efforts. What is singularly important is the idea that God can only be approached in truth. To approach God in truth requires that one accept oneself as one is in one's true being, which means that one become the self one is. One is required, therefore, to undertake the task of synthesizing the opposing terms that comprise the human constitution, for to do so is how one presents oneself "truthfully." Sometimes a "false picture" of self looks more appealing since it appears that one can by one's own reason or strength resolve the contradictoriness of existence, rid oneself of anxiety, and achieve coherence as a self. Attempts to resolve the contradictions of existence by self-effort, however, only create a coherence of self that is, from the religious point of view, a contradiction of true being and a denial of the truth of human being. In fact, it is this faith in self that occasions the loss of selfhood. To seek relationship with God having lost one's self is to approach God as a deceiver, for one is attempting to be before God what God knows one is not.

Third, human beings are prone to self-regard, self-aggrandizement and self-love, inclined that is to so value the self that the self is made a religious object, an object of infinite interest and ultimate concern. As the religious perspective sees the matter, it is human nature to desire to master the relativities and contingencies of existence by exerting the self's own power, by relying on one's own resource, by having faith in one's own ability to act as a united and coherent ego capable of fashioning its own destiny. To do these things, however, is to create disrelationship with God. This religious critique issues forth even though these positions of self-reliance and self-sufficiency are not without warrant or merit from other points of view. For instance, the desire to achieve greater unity within the context of one's self-relations (self-love), to become a person capable of directing and controlling one's behavior, thereby mastering one's environment, is admirable from a psychological point of view, for such ego unification and the achievement of personality coherence represent the ideals of psychological well-being. Similarly, these ideals of self-mastery, self-directedness and self-sufficiency exhibit the dignity of human being. They are therefore to be cultivated as manifestations of the pride which each person ought to have, or owes himself by virtue of being human. Morality recommends and prescribes such pride and ideals of self-sufficiency. It applauds such achievements of character, deeming them essential constituents and necessary conditions of agency. In the religious context, however, such achievements conflict with the requirement that one must surrender self--and its pretense of self-sufficiency--to God. Such pride is therefore held to be inimical to relation with God.

Fourth, human beings are made for the infinite. Yet, because they are also finite and susceptible to the temptation of inordinate self-regard, they are prone to satisfy the criteria for a God-relationship by substituting a finite object for God. They will, in other words, impose, then satisfy, self-regarding criteria rather than submit to those set down (revealed) by God. If such "idolatry" is to be avoided, it is the point of view of the religious consciousness that the human person must surrender to the requirements for a God-relationship. God requires simply that the gift of relationship be accepted in its actuality. Acceptance of this gift, however, requires that one recognize the God-relation as one's highest good, that one act on that recognition by renouncing one's desire to position oneself as the center of existence. In the religious domain, God is the center of existence and any claim otherwise is pretentious and deceitful.

The religious perspective holds that to become God-conscious is to become aware that God alone has a claim to "ultimacy" and to "infinite interest." Because all activities are subordinated to the God-relation, even the process of becoming self-conscious is to become aware of the misère of humanity without God and the grandeur of humanity with God. In other words, self-consciousness in the religious context is ultimately God-consciousness.

To become God-conscious is to become aware of the actuality of relationship with God as it is made possible through theistic faith. And because self-consciousness leads ineluctably to awareness of the despair of human being without God, the self-conscious person, the person who becomes a self, will accept the offer of relation with God, approaching the relation in thanksgiving, humility and self-surrender. God-consciousness leads a believer to accept as fact that "before God" one is always in the wrong and that no act or attitude of self-assertion will enable one to merit standing with God. Human being, in other words, is incapable of entering relation with God on its own initiative, for it is precluded from such relation by the finitude of its natural and temporal condition. The God-relation, then, is inherently unequal, and any "infinitizing reflection" to the contrary, any imaginings that one can approach God as an equal, are vain, being pretense and presumption. Only God's grace and the human response to that grace in the act of self-surrender (faith) makes it possible for one to become "right-wised" with God such that the possibility of a God-relationship is made actual. In theistic faith, one's nature is perfected and made whole; in faith, the individual can recognize that God's offer of relationship recreates fallen humanity; in faith one's condition of brokenness is transcended and God is encountered in the relationship "personally."

This then is how one might conceive the religious sphere of existence--how one might, on a relational model, conceive of human being in alienation from itself and from the Good of Being.

c. Sin and Pride

Because the religious sphere is shaped by the assumption that the God-relationship is made available by God through grace, faith becomes the appropriate response that enables finite individuals to transcend themselves and to encounter the transcendent God who becomes visible--imminent--to the "eyes of faith" (Augustine). It is a fact of the common life, however, that not all to whom this possibility of relationship is offered accept it; and from a religious point of view, the refusal of, denial, or resistance to the God-relation constitutes the "voluntary wrongdoing" of sin.

Sin is a religiously conceived form of <u>akrasia</u>. Sin is the perverse choosing whereby persons refuse the offer of relationship with God. It is what we do to prevent ourselves from adopting the attitude of faith. As the religious consciousness conceives matters, the context for this choosing is freedom; and human subjects are free to accept or reject the offer of relationship with God, though, to reject it is to fall subject to the religious critique that freedom is being misused and abused.

To be in sin, to lack faith, is to turn one's back on what is by definition one's "highest good." According to the religious perspective the God-relationship defines the highest good for human beings, and to refuse it, deny it or resist it is to err, to make oneself ignorant of the truth that the God-relationship is, in fact, the highest good. This error, which is the sin of "disbelief," can be, and often is, justified and intelligible; though it must be said that unbelievers, in determining what is and what is not the "highest good," appeal to criteria other than those set down in the religious sphere. Unbelievers can, even in the religious sphere, use finite criteria to establish what is of infinite value in one's existence. In the religious sphere, however, only criteria of infinite value can determine what good is "highest," and it follows from this that if the God-relation is the highest good of human being and if God has actually offered a means for acquiring it, then the failure to enter into the covenant of grace is a purely volitional matter. It is an act of refusal whereby one prefers to use <u>finite</u> criteria to assess one's <u>ultimate</u> good. It is a voluntary decision, which, from a religious perspective, constitutes a wrongful, perverse, even defiant resistance to a relational possibility offered by God to all. What would motivate an individual to resist accepting his or her own "highest good"; why would a person resist faith and opt for disrelationship with God (sin)?

It is at this point that we can appropriately return to our discussion about the sin of pride. Religious thinkers have held that the cause for disrelationship with God is directly attributable to human pride. Theological analysis holds that it is because of pride that we make ourselves rather than God the center of existence. It is because of pride that we deny God the place reserved for God alone--the place reserved for our ultimate concern and infinite interest. In one sense, pride is not sin, for sin refers to nothing but the willful disrelationship with God. In another sense pride is sin, for pride constitutes a motive for choosing oneself--not God--as one's highest good, thereby creating the conditions for disrelating ourselves to God. It is therefore appropriate to speak of the sin of pride, for pride is the occasion of sin. I shall briefly consider this sin, doing so in the interests of examining how the sin of pride is connected to, and even entails, what can best be described, from a religious point of view, as 'self-deception.'

The human act of disrelating oneself to God constitutes a negativity that can be said to stem from pride. From a religious point of view, "the beginning of pride is sin" (Sirach 10.13 RSV), "The beginning of man's pride is to depart from the Lord; his heart has forsaken his Maker" (Sirach 10.12 RSV). Augustine reiterates this understanding by writing that pride is a "turning away from him who supremely is" toward the self that ". . .does not exist in that supreme degree."[97] Pride, therefore, is not only implicated in a negation of God's position as the legitimate center of human existence--the governing assumption in the religious sphere--but it is also the motivation for self-assertion. Self-assertion here refers to the presumption by the self that the self is worthy of the position that legitimately belongs only to that which "supremely is"--God. In Reinhold Niebuhr's terms, such self-assertion is "rebellion against" as well as "usurpation of." Pride is a self-directed passional concept. It refers to the attitude of self-concern whereby one exalts oneself and derives pleasure from one's own desire for excellences. Although pride is not always and everywhere held in contempt, in the religious sphere it is held that pride is inimical to the God-relationship and the primary cause for disrelationship with God.

Aquinas wrote that pride is a mortal sin, a general sin "by a kind of influence, in so far as all sins may have their origin in pride."[98] It is a sin always contrary to the love of God ". . .inasmuch as the proud man does not subject himself to the Divine rule as he ought;"[99] and it is the most grievous of sins since it is not weakness or ignorance that pride denotes, but actual ". . .aversion from God simply through being unwilling to be subject to God and his rule."[100] Furthermore, pride is "the cause of gravity in other sins," therefore to be considered the first sin, the sin of Adam: "Now the first thing he coveted inordinately was his own excellence; and consequently his disobedience was the result of his pride. This agrees with the statement of Augustine, who says that <u>man puffed up with pride obeyed the serpent's prompting, and scorned God's commands.</u>"[101] Aquinas makes clear that the object of Adam's covetousness was "God-likeness," which Adam inordinately sought so that he might "rely on himself in contempt of divine rule."[102]

Augustine was the theologian who contributed the most to elucidating 'sin' in terms of pride. In his *Confessions,* Augustine meditated on the search for God, doing so from the point of view of one who was once lost but now is found. Augustine realized that his coming to rest in God had been prevented by an obstacle of his own making, his pride. Recalling his theft of the pears, Augustine noted that in sin there is a certain show of beauty, for "Pride wears the mask of loftiness of spirit, although You alone, O God, are high above all."[103] As a young intellectual seeking to solve the mysteries of existence, Augustine found his search for wisdom ever frustrated. From the vantage point of the *Confessions* this autobiographer of the soul reflected on that frustration, realizing that "You resist the proud. What could be worse than the incredible folly in which I asserted that I was by nature what You are? . . .I chose rather to think You mutable than to think I was not as You are. [But] You resisted my windy pride."[104] This pride in human excellence, in human glory, was what had caused Augustine to fail in his search for a God-relationship. Augustine goes on to describe his pride before God as an extreme form of perversity. This perverse pride is noted when he reflects on his now repudiated association with the Manichees, for he had held the view

> [that] it was not that we sinned, but some other nature sinning in us, and it pleased my pride to be beyond fault. I very much preferred to excuse myself and accuse some other thing that was in me but was not I. My sin was all the more incurable because I thought I was not a sinner.[105]

The theme of pride as the source of disrelationship with God pervades the *Confessions* and appears prominently elsewhere in the Augustinian corpus. Augustine attributes his reluctance to enter into a God-relationship to his love of prideful flesh, to his desire to seek answers to the mysteries of existence by considering only things that are "contained in space,"[106] and by rising up against God "in my pride."[107] The Confessions can be read as a prayer in which Augustine gives thanks to God that God resisted his pride. By teaching him humility, God opened his eyes, enabling him to discern the grace that God had already granted him (Book X, xxxvii). In the Anti-Pelagian writing, On Nature and Grace, Augustine again focused on pride, saying that "the sin of pride is quite distinguishable from all other sins," that it is a sin to be considered "apart from all others," for "only ask what every sin is, and see whether you can find any sin without the designation of pride."[108] And what is pride for Augustine but the temptation to God-likeness: "For the serpent, in fact only sought for the door of pride whereby to enter when he said, 'You shall be as Gods' (Gen. 3.5)."[109] It was the desire to be like God that appealed to human pride. And, for Augustine, it was pride that led to the great event of disrelationship with God--the Fall.

We should note that this Augustinian version of sin as pride was revived and given a contemporary accent in the writings of Reinhold Niebuhr. Niebuhr wrote in his "Gifford Lectures" that human being is inclined to pride--pride of power, pride of knowledge, pride of virtue and spirit--and to self-love. The result of these inclinations is that human being makes itself, rather than God, the center of existence. Human persons seek to become the unconditioned author of their own existence:

> Man is insecure and involved in natural contingency; he seeks to overcome his insecurity by a will-to-power which overreaches the limits of creatureliness. Man is ignorant and involved in the limitations of a finite mind; but he pretends that he is not limited. He assumes that he can gradually transcend finite limitations until his mind becomes identical with universal mind. All of his intellectual and cultural pursuits, therefore, become infected with the sin of pride. The ego which falsely makes itself the centre of existence in its pride and will-to-power inevitably subordinates other life to its will and thus does injustice to other life.[110]

The picture of sin offered by Augustine and up-dated by Niebuhr--that sin results from unchecked pride and produces disrelationship with God--strikes a familiar chord in the literature of Western theological thought. This perspective on pride, ego-centrism, and self-love echoed in the thought of various religious thinkers. Pascal's analysis of self-love, for instance, is a variation on this theme. For Pascal, the human ego learns to measure all things by the standard of self-interest. Because the self loves itself above all else, it learns to hate the truth about itself: "The self is hateful. . . In a word, the self has two characteristics. It is unjust in itself for making itself centre of everything: it is a nuisance (unjust) to others in that it tries to subjugate them, for each self (moi) is the enemy of all the others and would like to tyrannize them."[111] Pascal, then, analyzes the self in light of its desire to dominate and be the center of existence, and this desire identifies the source of human misère. Another theologian, Jonathan Edwards, from yet another time and tradition, considers the issue of sin in similar terms. Sin refers to Adam's rebellion, for according to Edwards, when Adam rebelled, he broke God's covenant. Even so, by this terrible act of rebellion Adam could not extirpate the "superior principles instilled by God" from his heart:

> The inferior principles of self-love, and natural appetite, which were given only to serve, being alone, and left to themselves, <u>of course</u> become reigning principles, having no superior principles to regulate or control them, they become absolute masters of the heart. Man did not immediately set up <u>himself</u>, and the objects of his private affections and appetites, as supreme; and so they took the place of <u>God</u>. And God, still continuing strictly to require supreme regard for himself, and forbidding all gratifications of these inferior passions, but only in perfect subordination to the ends, and agreeableness to the rules and limits, which his holiness, honor, and law prescribe, hence immediately arises <u>enmity</u> in the heart, now wholly under the power of self-love; and nothing but <u>war</u> ensues, in a constant course, against God.[112]

The conviction that sin is pride, that pride is the occasion of sin, that it issues in rebellion against God, that it expresses a desire to dominate and even usurp God's rightful place, is a theological-anthropological analysis well established in the Christian tradition. The most precise, yet the most devastating, critique of pride is this: that the willful expression of pride has as its end the exaltation of the self; and the theological translation of this desired exaltation of the self is nothing less than the desire to become God. This was Adam's temptation, the reason for his fall, the reason for his shame--his nakedness before God. Yet, according to Karl Barth, the desire to be as God is concealed and inexplicit: Only a revelation from God can expose this desire as it truly is. The desire to be as God expresses pride and human inauthenticity, for God-likeness expresses the desire of the person who has lost his or her true self. As Barth has written about this desire to be God-like (pride), "It contradicts the concept of man. Man ceases to be man when he wants this."[113] God-likeness, furthermore, exposes an anthropological datum about human conflict. That datum can be observed and described--Barth writes as a theological empiricist here--but finally, this datum mystifies:

> Man does not want to pass his limits, to be as God. His thoughts and attitudes and actions are the result of this desire, which is opposed to the will and work of God. He simply makes himself impossible. But he does do it. In this act of his loving and choosing he is the good creature of God who does that which is bad. This contradiction of his being is the fact for which he is responsible, responsible in his will to be as God, in his contradiction and opposition to the

God who becomes and is as he is. There is no explanation of this human will to be as God. We can only state it as a fact that it is our desire. We have to state it because obviously it is this fact which God confronts with his own superior opposition and contradiction when he becomes and is as we are. In taking pity on us and condescending to us God accuses us of being those who want to exalt themselves. The omnipotent act of His humility exposes us as proud men. We are summoned to see and confess ourselves as such. To deny it is to make God a liar. But we cannot explain how and why we are proud. The absurd act that we commit is as such inexplicable. We can only try to describe it.[114]

What must not be overlooked in an analysis of sin and pride is the fact that from a religious perspective, both concepts indicate <u>an untruthful form of relatedness to the true religious object</u> (God). Falsehood is one of the forms of sin,[115] and the sin of pride, as I have indicated, points to a disrelationship with God that obtains as the result of the effort by human being to be what it is not, namely, self-contained and self-sufficient. Disrelationship with God can be described as a form of falsehood, so that pride can be said to express a <u>false</u> relation to the religious object. The God-relation requires self-surrender, an attitude that itself requires humility. Pride, however, opposes humility, and even more seriously, it engenders a self-understanding that is inimical to being related to the religious object in truth. Pride thus confuses and falsifies the terms of the God-relation, making of the human subject a usurper, a false claimant to the position of ultimacy and supremacy appropriately held by God alone.

In theological terms, pride expresses a fundamentally false understanding of the self and its condition. Theologically speaking, pride obtains whenever one has misevaluated one's own identity "before God." A self-image based on pride, therefore, is a self-image based not on the truth about human being but on a desire to elevate and exalt the self. This religious analysis constitutes, for religious persons, a "truth by description," even if, as Barth said, the actual explanation for the phenomenon is elusive and mysterious. Moreover, the religious critique of this pride-based self-understanding is devastating: it is a sham, a pretense, a presumption, a falsehood parading as truth. From the religious point of view, the idea that persons are self-sufficient and able to control the contradictions of human existence is simply inconsistent with the content of a self-understanding based on a true God-relation. Such an understanding reeks of falsehood, for the falsehood is premised on the idea that one can be what one is not, that one can make oneself something one is not, that one can exist "as God" when human beings are, by definition, not God but creatures dependent upon God.

To analyze pride in light of the God-relation, then, is to expose falsehood. The human subject, in asserting him- or herself "before God" "as God" does so in the guise of a unified and coherent ego, self-determined and capable of self-help. Such a self, however, is fundamentally disintegrated and falsely constituted. Such a self is divided, and wishing will not make it otherwise, will not, that is, make it exist as it wishes to exist--free of conflict and transparent to its own reflection. Of course, persons may assert this false identity as true. To do this, however, is to make one's self-image a "cover story." Cover stories are asserted to be true in linguistically explicit ways; yet the cover story that one is self-sufficient is, from the religious persepctive, an indication that the true story is too painful to bear--and human pride makes it so. Persons who believe in their own self-sufficiency appear "before God" untruthfully, which is to say that they appear in the role of a deceiver or liar. And because one's self-image is contradicted by God, who knows the truth, the person who, from pride, avows his or her self-sufficiency "before God" can be said to be a person who actually attempts to deceive God. Put another way, such a person attempts to make of God a liar (Barth). The self that appears "before God" pretending to be something it is not is the self that is falsely constituted and disrelated to both itself and to God--and this analysis holds even if the person is unaware of the pretense.

d. Pride and Self-Deception

The sin of pride is falsehood before God. About this falsehood it must be said that it expresses a desire of the human subject to accept itself in falsehood, as that which it is not ("as God"). There is undoubtedly pain, anxiety and discomfort involved in choosing oneself in truth and accepting one's true being, just as there is clearly psychological advantage to be gained by assuming a self-image that relieves that discomfort and anxiety. One can, after all, conceive oneself according to one's own wishes, according to criteria that serve one's own desire to be indomitable--capable of self-mastery, self-determination and self-reliance, capable of resolving the contradictions of existence on the basis of the human resource (self-help).

Human persons are not content by nature to accept a situation of helplessness, but "before God" that situation of helplessness is the human situation; and this is the truth advanced by the religious perspective. Pride, then, is an enemy of religiously conceived existence, for pride resists the idea of self-surrender when "before God" self-surrender is what is required. Again, the ideals of self-mastery, self-determination, and self-reliance are valued ideals of personal existence in all spheres of existence except the religious. In the religious sphere, these universally valued ideals of well-being are thought to be--again "before God"--pretense and falsehood, presumptive manifestations of human pride detrimental to the highest good--relation with God. The God-relationship requires of persons humility not pride, self-surrender not self-aggrandizement. From the religious point of view, the greatest human achievement is simply to be self-conscious in light of one's true highest good. That requires an act of self-surrender to the God who reveals to the conscious individual who he or she is in truth "before God." The religious ideal is that one be able to understand one's own situation as it actually is "before God," honestly, without pretense or falsehood.

What is viewed from a religious point of view, then, is the attempt by human persons to be what they are not, to seek a falsehood that conforms to a desired self-image while the truth about human being is suppressed for reasons of psychological gain. This creates a situation where, "before God," a deception is being perpetrated. Since the God-relation governs all concerns in the religious domain, an attempt to deceive oneself about who one is "before God" is also an attempt to dupe God into thinking that one is not what one is. This is a falsehood that one convinces oneself is the truth. God, however, cannot be lied to. Even though the religious perspective will certify that this description, this assertion of a false identity, is aimed at God, it will also certify that the person who attempts this deception achieves nothing but self-deception. One who attempts this deception "before God" only succeeds in persuading oneself that the truth about human being is not true. The religious response is always: God is not duped. God is always on the side of truth--however painful that truth might be to human subjects.

The religious consciousness conceives God as having addressed humanity as Truth, as the ultimate contradiction to falsehood. The sin of pride that motivates human persons to believe that they are something they are not, the pride that aims to deceive an other (God) into sharing in the falsehood, only serves, in the end, to misrelate individuals to God. Since God is not deceived, one who creates an a false, self-serving identity before God only succeeds in duping one's own self. In the end, pride inspires the falsehood that obtains in the context of the God-relation. It identifies the false self-understanding that is theological self-deception. Kierkegaard asks, "Can a man deceive God?" His answer: "No, in relation to God a man can only deceive himself. For the God-relationship is the highest good in such a way that he who deceived God frightfully deceives himself."[116] As an addendum to these remarks, Kierkegaard reiterates that "true superiority can never be deceived," and because God is by definition and by faith that true superiority, ". . .only one deception is possible in the infinite sense--self-deception."[117]

In the religious context of meaning and value, the God-relation governs the use of concepts and authorizes their employment for specified meaning tasks. The concept 'self-deception' is no exception to this context-dependent rule. A religious employment of 'self-deception' refers to a "self-directed belief-misleading project" that obtains in the context of the God-relation. The criteria for ascribing the concept are no different from those obtained by ordinary language analysis. Only the context is different--the relational context that governs how the concept is put to work. The God-relation establishes the context within which the psychological concept 'self-deception' stakes a claim to meaningfulness, and this God-relation is not of <u>central</u>

importance in other spheres of interest, neither the philosophical-psychological (self-relatedness) nor the ethical (other-relatedness). I shall briefly consider the claim to meaning that is advanced by those who employ 'self-deception' to perform meaning-tasks in the religious context, from the religious point of view--"before God."

There are four criteria that must be met if one is to ascribe 'self-deception:' (a) contradictory beliefs; (b) simultaneously held; (c) one of the beliefs is held "unconsciously" in that the person is unaware of it, though this unconscious belief is manifest in action and behavior; and (d) the act which establishes which of the beliefs will be subject to awareness--and which not--is a voluntary, motivated act. In an instance of theological, God-related self-deception, these criteria can be met and the meaningfulness of the concept affirmed. The use of the concept, however, depends upon one's willingness to adopt the presupposition of the religious sphere itself, namely, that the possibility of a God-relation has, in fact, been made actual by God's own act. In the religious sphere, this presupposition is accepted and held as true: It is the "best, most reasonable interpretation" against which the truth of all other propositions is measured. It is in light of this presupposition that one can advance a claim about 'self-deception'--that it is a meaningful cipher of communication that has been authorized to perform meaning tasks in the religious context of meaning and value.

The religious understanding so analyzes the nature of human being that the idea of a person holding contradictory beliefs, contradictory dispositions to action, is anything but far-fetched. It is, rather, a sort of working premise: human persons are conflicted and at odds with themselves, neither unified as selves nor in possession of transparent consciousness. That is their condition: to be human is to be a contradiction. The religious understanding, therefore, simply accepts the contradictoriness of human existence as its starting point. There is ample evidence to support this contradictoriness, for it is behaviorally manifest, and asserting it as fact simply states the obvious--that it is the true being of human being. Religion, in other words, accepts as fact that human being is a conjunction of opposing terms (finite/infinite; flesh/spirit; body/soul; grandeur/misère), deeming all human efforts to resolve, thus deny, these oppositions of existence as blindness, folly, and untruthfulness.

The opposition at issue for the religious perspective, at least the one that pertains to self-deception, is whether one can accept on faith that the God-relation is a possibility made actual by God pro me (belief that p) or whether this possibility cannot be conceived or believed to be actual (belief that not-p). Two things must be said, both of which are assertions arising from the foundation of the religious domain itself. First: In faith, this conflict between p and not-p is resolved in favor of p. There is no conflict between p and not-p if one is in relation to God. If one is in relation to God, one is in faith, and because to be in faith is to be in the truth, to be in faith is to have eliminated the possibility for "theological self-deception." The conflict between p and not-p arises, then, only when one is <u>disrelated</u> to God, which is to be in the situation where one does not accept the truth of p, but avows as true <u>not-p</u>. Theological self-deception, then, afflicts anyone who is improperly related to God. The second point is this: The conflict between p and <u>not-p</u> arises only in situations of disbelief or disrelationship with God (sin), for it is only in the situation of disrelatedness to God that a conflict exists between trusting p to be be true and denying, resisting, or refusing to accept p as true. Avowing <u>not-p</u> to be true is held to be a <u>willful resistance to that which is true</u>, the truth affirmed by theistic faith. Furthermore, it is held that this resistance to the truth obtains as a matter of willful perversity. That is to say, one denies or resists or rejects p as true, but only because on some level "deep down" one recognizes p to be true but resists accepting it as true for certain reasons.

Faithlessness is the refusal to make this "deep seated" belief linguistically explicit as a truth <u>pro me</u>. Why? The answer advanced by the religious traditions is human perversity. Christianity holds that human persons are free to reject or deny what is asserted by Christianity as true. Christianity offers itself as a way of achieving the highest good of human being, yet it realizes that persons can refuse to accept their highest good. Why persons do this is not as clear as the fact that they do this. As Barth said, this is a mystery that can only be described, though a theological assumption that human nature is vitiated and fallen certainly contributes to our understanding. The point, however, is that the logic of the religious perspective enables one to perceive that a <u>conflict</u> obtains between p and <u>not-p</u> when one opts to hold that <u>not-p</u>, which is not true, is true. This is because in the religious perspective, p is always true, and <u>not-p</u> contradicts the truth that p is true. The religious perspective accepts as true that the God-relation is available to all, that in the human inclination to seek good--one's highest good--<u>all</u> are disposed toward the God-relation and are capable of entering into that relation. Because all persons are disposed to achieve their highest good, all persons know "deep down" that this highest good is there for them, and this accounts for the universal disposition to seek the highest good. On the other hand, refusing the offer of relation is deemed a willful resistance to the truth. Resisting that which one knows deep down to be the truth expresses itself as a desire not to enter the God-relation. This is considered a perverse desire which is itself the product of a perverse will, for the desire to deny God stems from a will that rejects its own highest good.

For the religious consciousness, sin is a problem of will, not knowledge. It is not that sinners are ignorant of the good--though in a qualified sense they are--that they refuse, deny and resist acknowledging as good what is truly the highest good. It is the perverse will that accounts for this rejection of the God-relation: if the resister be considered ignorant, it is a <u>willful ignorance</u> that is being referred to. The religious perspective holds that a refusal, denial, misunderstanding or misuse of p is a willful perversion in which one turns one's back--voluntarily, even if not consciously--on the true and highest good of human being. The other side of the case is this: If in faith one accepts p as true one thereby eliminates the contradiction between p and not-p. "Not-p" drops out, and the fragmented self is unified around faith that p is true pro me.[118] The contradiction between the two arises, however, when one assumes that not-p is true. In the religious domain, however, there can be no denial of p that is true, no instance of an affirmation that not-p is true that is not also an actual opponent of p. Not to be in relation with God, not to affirm the truth of p, is therefore a contradiction, for one is perversely affirming as true what is by virtue of the religious premise not true. To avow not-p as true is to contradict p, which is true, and contradictory beliefs (p and not-p) obtain simultaneously whenever a human subject, created in God's image and disposed to its own highest good, denies the truth of p yet manifests in his or her behavior an ultimate concern or infinite interest. That ultimate concern or infinite interest, in that it is behaviorally manifest, affirms that p is present, and not only present, but true in that each person is disposed--mysteriously--to seek the highest good. Those who disavow the truth of p do so in the name of the highest good, thereby avowing the truth of p in their denial of it.

The religious perspective acknowledges that individuals are free to avow not-p as true, as in "I deny the possibility of the God-relation because I do not believe it to be true that there is a God." This assertion, however, constitutes a willful refusal to acknowledge the truth that God exists and makes actual the possibility of entering the God-relation. On the religious analysis, the belief that not-p is true is contradicted by a belief that p, a belief that is held "unconsciously." That we unconsciously affirm the truth of p while professing not-p is a claim that can be made because we manifest our beliefs in action; and in seeking to resolve the contradictions of existence in an ultimate way we express the very ultimate concern that our profession of not-p disclaims.

From the religious point of view, every person seeks a religious solution to the contradictions of existence, even if those solutions are false, even if one relates oneself with infinite interest and ultimate concern to a "false god," be it oneself, reason, power, ideologies of one sort or another. The religious perspective assumes that every person seeks some ultimate repository for his or her ultimate concern and infinite interest, and denials point to the willful refusal of theological self-deception. Even an "unbeliever" exhibits behavioral evidence that confirms an "unconscious faith" that p is true, that there is a possibility for ultimate resolutions to the quandaries of existence. The possibility that an ultimate repository of faith exists pro me is an actuality for each person, but each person decides whether to find this possibility in truth (God) or in falsehood (something posing "as God" and usurping the place of God). In light of the religious premise, the denial of p necessarily pits not-p which is false against p which is true, so that contradictory beliefs, one of them "unconsciously" held, accompany any denial that p is true. The one belief, the linguistically explicit or professed belief is that not-p is true. The other belief, which is now suppressed but still acted upon, is that p is true. Though one denies this, one's very denial affirms the truth of p, since this "unconsciously" held belief manifests an individual's quest for a religious solution to the problem of existence.

Human subjects who deny God express themselves religiously when they affirm that there are criteria adequate to the task of addressing--and passing judgment on--the God question, the question about the actuality of the God-relation. The fact that the person who denies the existence of God claims no God-relation must not obscure the fact that in the quest for truth, in the desire to acquire criteria that can be trusted to be adequate to the task of setting what is--and what is not--of ultimate concern in one's life, there is manifest the essential presupposition of the God-relation, namely, that persons are inclined--mysteriously--to seek their highest good and to seek the truth. This inclination reflects the fact that every person is disposed to affirm the truth of p--that a God-(or god-)relation is sought by all: If this be so, and if the question of unbelief is not then a problem of knowledge but of will, then it is only human perversity that prevents this relational possibility from being actualized.

Kierkegaard wrote that

> [One] can be deceived in many ways; one can be deceived in believing in what is untrue, but on the other hand, one is also deceived in not believing what is true; one can be deceived by appearances, but one can also be deceived by the superficiality of shrewdness, by the flattering conceit which is absolutely certain that it cannot be deceived. Which deception is most dangerous?[119]

Kierkegaard's own response to this question was to locate the greater danger in the person who "sees but does not see," who "dreams that he is awake," whose "foolish conceit of not being deceived is ludicrous."[120] The truth of p, the truth that one is actually related to God, is a truth written on the human heart. It is a truth that is denied only by willfully resisting grace or by defying the eternal. The consequence is that "[the] person who has deceived himself has prevented himself from winning the eternal" by conceit and by the perfidy of self-love.[121] Yet the religious affirmation is that the eternal is available to all and is affirmed as persons seek their religious solutions to the problems of existence--even if those solutions are false and result in a disrelationship to God. To be disrelated is still to be related, and this Kierkegaard's, as well as many other religious thinkers' point. The grace of God is extended to all, but it can be rejected because freedom can be misused and other desires can usurp the desire for God, thus giving rise to the voluntary error of disbelief or un-faithfulness. Rejection of the God-relation is nothing but a willful ignorance, and we can misuse our freedom to serve a perverse desire to "cover up" our true relation to God. To put this religious position positively, every person knows "deep down" where his or her highest good is located. To deny, resist or refuse to accept one's highest good is to be deceived "in not believing what is true" (Kierkegaard), but this deception is perpetrated by the person's own perverse act of defiance to that which he or she has already avowed as true (p). It can be said, then, that persons who deny the truth that God has made the possibility of relation to God actual deceive themselves by the "flattering conceit that [they] cannot be deceived."

Were human persons endowed with an incorruptible will, no gap would obtain between knowing and doing. The religious (Christian) point of view holds that such a gap does exist, and because it does, the human disposition to acquire the highest good can be frustrated. The consequence of this frustration is sin, and sinners mislead themselves into believing that something other than the God-relation is the highest good. Even though the highest good continues to be sought, that search is prompted by a perverse desire since that highest good is sought where it is not to be found--apart from the God-relationship. Theological self-deception requires contradictory beliefs simultaneously held, a requirement that is satisfied when persons reveal their ultimate concern and infinite interest through professed resistance to the God-relation.

Theological self-deception also requires that one of the contradictory beliefs be held unconsciously. Clearly, the "unconscious belief" at issue here is the belief that p is true. That belief is not avowed in a linguistically explicit way, though it is present in the disposition to act in accordance with it. Behavior that is attributable to "ultimate concern" and "infinite interest" manifests the unconscious belief that p is true. Furthermore, the person who denies or resists or refuses to accept what is in truth one's highest good (the God-relation) will do so for certain reasons. LIke any other self-deceiver, this one does not want to accept the best, most reasonable interpretation because a "cover story" is more amenable to one's self-image and less threatening to the person one wants to be. The cover story of self-sufficiency enables the theological self-deceiver to disavow the belief that p is true pro me.

That persons are disposed to act in accordance with p, and the fact that persons so disposed can be unaware of the belief p, is a phenomenon that modern theology has taken into account elsewhere. The idea of "unconscious Christianity" (Bonhoeffer) and "anonymous Christianity" (Rahner) participates in this general insight, though neither of these notions implies the perversity of will that is entailed by theological self-deception. A theological self-deceiver is one who denies his or her constitution as a "theological self," what Kierkegaard called the "self directly before God."[122] The denial of theological selfhood is, according to Kierkegaard and the religious perspective in general, a voluntary and perverse refusal to accept what an individual knows deep down to be true. This act of defiance keeps the belief that p is true from becoming linguistically explicit pro me. A split occurs, and that split accounts for the difference between one's desire to seek a religious solution to the problem of existence and the opposing desire not to acknowledge the God-relation as the proper object of one's infinite interest and ultimate concern.

The belief that p is true is therefore resisted and denied despite the fact that it manifests itself in behavior that expresses ultimate concern. One can freely enter into a "god-relation" with some object other than the "Holy Other," and that relation is likely to be with one's own self, the ego-- as God; but this error springs from a perverse and conflicted will. By making one's own self a party to a religious relation that expresses one's religious interest (ultimate concern), an individual can resist making linguistically explicit, or accepting as true, the true object of this religious relation (God). The religious perspective has no difficulty acknowledging that persons can say with their whole being (in faith) that there is no God. It acknowledges the capacity and propensity of persons to deceive themselves on this point--warning against it at times[123]--and it affirms the contradictoriness of human persons and human consciousness, thereby providing a context within which to make intelligible the propensity of persons to keep the truth at bay--an "aversion to truth" Pascal called it.[124] In sum, the refusal to express one's faith with respect to the appropriate object of the God-relation constitutes a willful refusal that effectively keeps the belief that p is true "unconscious."

Like any other kind of self-deception, theological self-deception is motivated; for the suppression of the belief p occurs for certain reasons, discernible reasons, reasons relevant to our topic of discussion, pride. It is pride, the desire for self-exaltation, that spurs one to resist acknowledging the truth of p, for pride resists the theological requirement that one approach the God-relation in humility, with the attitude of one "whose criterion is God!"[125] Awareness of God fosters a consciousness of self whereby the self understands its insufficiency before God and approaches relation to God in a mood of self-surrender. Pride resists this movement, for pride works to center existence around the human ego, around a self-image of autonomy, power and self-sufficiency. Pride is affronted by the requirement that one renounce this self-image, and the prospect of losing that self-centeredness is a threatening and painful prospect indeed. The motive for theological self-deception is pain avoidance on the one hand, retention of self-directed ego-enhancing pleasures on the other. It is painful to recognize oneself in light of the God-criterion, for one recognizes oneself as "always in the wrong," as a self insufficient to help itself acquire relation to God, as one in need of

God. Human pride rejects the "God criterion" and obstructs the God-relation. Pride is the reason one acts to suppress one's own awareness of one's true highest good. Pride is therefore the cause of theological self-deception.

For the person who refuses the God-relation, a conflict brews between p and not-p; but then for reasons of psychological gain, that conflict is suppressed. One seeks through interpretive behavior to avoid the pain of self-recognition that is necessitated by the "God criterion," for the self desires to be what it is not: it seeks to be "as God." Because it is a human desire to accept oneself through a self-image qualified by self-exaltation and self-glorification, pride motivates one to mislead one's own beliefs about who one is "before God." Pride authorizes the self to engage in interpretive activity that buttresses a self-serving self-image at the expense of a true, but unwelcome interpretation. According to the religious perspective, human beings are averse to accepting the truth about themselves because of pride, and pride, which leads to disrelationship with God, also presents itself to a theological analysis as that which occasions the project (decision) to suppress one's belief that p is true.

Theological self-deception is a "belief-misleading project" that obtains with respect to self-understanding "before God." A theological self-deceiver denies his or her true being as a "theological self." A theological self-deceiver chooses to evaluate him- or herself according to criteria of self-relatedness, psychological criteria that serve a desire to achieve by human effort what human effort is inadequate to provide. The theological self-deceiver prefers the human resource to the God criterion. He or she seeks psychological harmony, inner peace, and the unity of self-relatedness, but is willing to rely on the resource of one's own self rather than on God to achieve these psychological ends. Given the governing relations of the religious sphere itself, this self-reliance constitutes an akratic choice. So great may be one's need to achieve these psychological ends that one may actually project a God to fulfill a wish for psychic unity (Feuerbach, Freud). But the theological self-deceiver will become enmeshed in what is, from the religious point of view, a deep and grave contradiction. At the very moment such a person denies God, at the very moment he or she expresses an inordinate desire to exalt self-image and avoid the pain of self-recognition before God, the theological self-deceiver will also exhibit his or her disposition to acquire an ultimate criterion with which to dispense with the God-question, thereby revealing an affinity for the very God-relation he or she so vigorously rejects.

The contradiction, then, emerges from the conflict that obtains between a disposition to seek respite in an ultimate source of meaning and value while willfully rejecting and unconsciously suppressing the one relation that can satisfy the human need for ultimacy. The theological self-deceiver creates a "cover story" of self-sufficiency because the "real story" is too painful to bear in relation to one's own pride and image of self-sufficiency. By so doing, he or she employs finite criteria to determine an infinite good. The finite criteria of psychological well-being, however, are inadequate for determining the truth about ultimate things. Ultimate things are to be evaluated according to the God-criterion and that alone. To use finite criteria is to miss the relationship imposed by the God-criterion: It is to end up with a God whose actuality is to be denied or whose meaning can be appreciated only in finite psychological terms according to the finite criteria of psychological conflict and wish-fulfillment. From a religious point of view, denial of God based on finite criteria is a self-deceptive posture that postpones a day of reckoning, the day of honest self-confrontation when one will be forced to assess one's ultimate concerns according to the criterion of ultimacy, the God-criterion.

e. Theological Self-Deception: Some Descriptions

Having surveyed the logic of theological self-deception, I would point to a few descriptions of this meaning complex as it has been employed in the context of religious meaning and discourse, I would point to a few examples where the meaning complex associated with 'self-deception' has been used religiously. All of the religious thinkers referred to thus far (Aquinas, Augustine, Pascal, Edwards, Barth, Niebuhr) support the connection I have drawn between pride and self-deception. Because this claim warrants further attention, I shall briefly examine two ways in which self-deception occurs in the religious domain. First is the denial that the actuality of the God-relation is real *pro me*. The second way refers to the disrelation that occurs for one who believes that he or she is properly related to God, but who, lacking a self, is not. This disrelationship obtains because of a failure to synthesize the self in faith, which is also a failure to approach the God-relation in an attitude of self-surrender and humility. I begin by considering Aquinas and "blindness of mind," a conceptual equivalent of theological self-deception.

In the *Summa Theologica*, Aquinas devotes Question 15 (II-II) to the issue "Of Vices Opposed to Knowledge and Understanding."[126] It is in this section that he discusses the question, "Whether Blindness of Mind Is a Sin?" After citing Augustine's claim that "every sin is voluntary," Aquinas writes that "To understand the truth is, in itself, beloved by all; and yet, accidentally it may be hateful to someone, in so far as a man is hindered thereby from having what he loves yet more." This refers to what might be considered an instance of religious *akrasia*--preferring something *as* ultimate to *that which is* ultimate, so that 'blindness of mind,' that which keeps one's mind on "corporeal things," is to be accounted a sin, a voluntary "neglect" of "the careful consideration of spiritual things."

Blindness of mind entails contradictory beliefs, namely, the truth loved by all (p) and that which is avowed as true in virtue of blindness of mind (not-p). The significant point, however, is that this blindness is a voluntary, motivated act even if the person who is blind is not aware of the blindness. 'Intellectual blindness' describes the mind that is ". . .more busy about things which it loves more," which are finite and corporeal things, than it is about that which it truly loves, the object of ultimate concern, which is "the truth. . .beloved by all." This blindness has a spiritual consequence--that one misrelates oneself to God; for the voluntary sin of intellectual blindness obtains as a result of valuing something finite according to infinite criteria ("loving more"). This akratic action expresses an inordinate desire (lust) to take pleasure in corporeal delights at the expense of spiritual relations wherein one's highest good is to be found. "Blindness of mind,' in other words, results from a person's preference for the self-centered, for choosing according to the standard of the finite when only the infinite will do. Such choice expresses an ego-centric desire to direct pleasure at oneself, to take delight in self-directed pleasures. One loses the God-relation by choosing against one's true preference, and this religiously conceived form of wrongdoing is motivated by pride. Pride is the cause of all gravity in sin, and in Aquinas' analysis it is to be conceived as of a piece with the specific motive for blindness of mind, which he identified as lust.

Although Aquinas cites as the specific motive for 'blindness of mind' not pride but lust, lust is entailed by pride. In his discussion of lust, Aquinas makes this connection explicit, for he writes that ". . .pride is the mother of all sins, so that even that capital vices originate therefrom"; and lust Aquinas had identified as a capital vice.[127] He thus forges a connection between lust and pride, with pride being the cause of gravity in the sin of lust as well as in blindness of mind.

It is through pride that Aquinas believed we express our aversion to God. Blindness of mind is a motivated imperfection in intellectual operations "opposed to the gifts of understanding" that persons receive from God. It is, furthermore, a sin whereby one willfully misrelates oneself to God and all things spiritual, for the proud person desires to promote his or her own well-being or pleasure in contempt of divine rule. Pride is aversion to divine rule, and it is made manifest as the cognitive-psychological phenomenon of 'blindness of mind.' In that this sin is related to a desire for pleasures that "exclude almost entirely the knowledge of spiritual things," 'blindness of mind' identifies an instance of voluntary ignorance. From a theological point of view, blindness of mind identifies a voluntary process that yields a cognitive result. There is indeed a belief-misleading project at issue here, for the person acts to create the condition of 'blindness.' An epistemic deficit obtains as a result of certain activities that have as their aim the creation of intellectual blindness, and one seeks this result because pride and lust are allowed to determine one's choices. The result, theologically speaking, is that one achieves a 'voluntary ignorance' that separates one from God. Aquinas' concept 'blindness of mind' subscribes to the criteria for ascribing self-deception in a relational context governed by the God-relation. It is therefore to be considered a conceptual equivalent to theological self-deception.

Turning to another figure of importance, Augustine, I would note that despite the fact that he occasionally makes explicit reference to the possibility of "deceiving himself" before God,[128] the concept 'self-deception' is to be drawn out from a broader consideration of his thought. Reflecting on his association with the Manichees, for instance, Augustine accuses himself in the Confessions of an "impiety that had divided me against myself," for he connects sin, pride and self-deception to his belief--now admitted to be in error--that he was not responsible for his own sin: "My sin was all the more incurable because I thought I was not a sinner. And it pleased my pride beyond fault. . ." to think himself sinless and equal with God, not to confess the evil he had done as his own, preferring "to excuse myself and accuse some other thing."[129]

In these reflections we see disrelationship with God (sin), motive (pride) and a certain cognitive-volitional state of affairs (self-deception) all at work together. Elsewhere he refers to the sin that is a "kind of perverse blindness attributing their own qualities to You--so that they load with their falsehoods." The "they" here refers to the followers of Manes. He associates the "blindness" with pride, for "the proud cannot find You," not in truth.[130] It is Augustine's own pride that prevents him from recognizing the truth that deep down he knows is there to be found, pride that leads him to deceive himself into thinking he is "as God" and not responsible for his sin. Just as Augustine accuses the Manicheans--and himself in hindsight--of self-deception, of believing an untruth about human being before God, of doing so because he proudly fancied himself "raised on high and shining with the stars,"[131] so, too, Augustine will later condemn the Pelagian heresy because it elevated humanity to a position it does not warrant "before God." Pelagianism is also a view motivated by pride, since the Pelagians could only avow their belief in human ability by deceiving themselves that they were something other than what, before God, they in fact were.

The Pelagians thought sin was a failure of execution and capacity, not, as Augustine believed, a corruption or vitiation ("wounding") of nature that required persons "to be helped not to sin" by grace, a point Pelagius "has nowhere admitted."[132] Augustine presents Pelagius as defending the view that sin is a problem of nature and that "it was in our power that they [sins] not be committed." Augustine accuses Pelagius of "flattering himself," of being "fatally mistaken--however unwittingly" into thinking that humanity could thus exalt itself and its own self-understanding to the point that the gracious act of salvation through Christ could be negated. Augustine held that human nature could never attain equality with God, even if perfected,[133] and throughout the Anti-Pelagian writings, Augustine sprinkles 1 John 1.8: "If we say that we have no sin, we deceive ourselves, and the truth is not in us."

Pelagius is, then, guilty of not having the truth in him. According to Augustine, Pelagius is a self-deceiver, just as Augustine was guilty of the same untruthfulness, the same self-deception, the same disrelation with God as a follower of the Manicheans. And it is pride, the desire for self-glorification and self-exaltation "before God" that afflicts the Pelagians with false notions, sinful and heretical pronouncements. Pride engenders the Pelagian deceit, which is also conceit; for the the Pelagian error stems from the perverse desire to exalt an image of self-sufficiency at the expense of recognizing the truth. Augustine found their ignorance of the truth to be the result of a project aimed at misleading belief; so Pelagianism constitutes a perspective that exhibits theological self-deception.

Self-deception is a topic often overlooked in Augustinian thought, but Augustine's theory of mind and memory, his general epistemology, lend themselves to that picture of understanding wherein self-deception can be rendered intelligible. Although the mind is mysteriously in search of that which is already known, Augustine takes note of the non-unitary and non-transparent consciousness that is not only in conflict with itself, but an active opponent to that which it knows "deep down." The following Augustinian remark suggests these insights:

> Thus, thus, even thus, does the human mind, blind and inert, vile and ill-behaved, desire to keep itself concealed, yet desire that nothing should be concealed from itself. But the contrary happens to it—it cannot lie hidden from the truth, but only truth from it. Even so, for all its worthlessness, the human mind would rather find its joy in truth than falsehood.[134]

This is the contradictory state of affairs that contributes to particular instances of self-deception. In the religious domain, Augustine implements this picture of a divided mind, a mind at odds with itself, to advance the view that those who fail to enter into relation with God are motivated by pride to enact a glorified self-understanding that necessarily excludes God. This, says Augustine, is a "perverse blindness," a self-deception, just as conversion and faith is a calling forth of the truth through memory against the mind's desire to avoid self-recognition and recognition of God. Self-recognition, in sum, brings one to "humility before God," for it is also a recognition that before God one is inherently unequal, disrelated and in need of grace. To have recognized that truth, which is "within one" and to which one comes as if returning home, is to put at rest the conflict of a troubled mind and to "find rest in Thee."

For Augustine, it is faith that puts to rest the conflict that is self-deception, self-deception being the willed refusal to recognize the truth in humility. Self-deception is false pride for it is pride that stands opposed to truth. The result of this analysis is that the whole question of truth, when put in the context of Augustine's theory of memory and recognition, can be interpreted as a dialectic in which the epistemological sin--self-deception --is described in relation to its epistemological remedy: the belief sustained and maintained by the "one true faith."

The Augustinian corpus investigates not only the relation of volition to knowledge, but also the relation of pride to our ability to construe and discern "as true" what is not true according to faith. It can therefore be said about that corpus that it is vitally concerned with investigating the phenomenon of unbelief as the voluntary act of misleading one's own belief. That corpus, in other words, is engaged in an ongoing discussion about the meaning of self-deception as that concept is put to work in a religious context to describe and evaluate the cognitive component of sin.

Self-deception was a concern of many of those thinkers who found themselves influenced by Augustine's thought. One of those thinkers, Pascal, was certainly referring to self-deception when he remarked "We run heedlessly into the abyss after putting something in front of us to stop us seeing it."[135] Pascal's analysis of self-love and his ability to identify the egoism that pressures humanity into taking "great pains to cover up its faults both from others and from itself,"[136] allows one to say of Pascal that self-deception provided a <u>cantus firmus</u> in his theological anthropology. One of Pascal's most sensitive interpreters has made precisely this point. After noting Pascal's picture of the human person as inveterately egoistic, an egoism that is a "self-deception caused by self-love," Roger Hazelton summarizes that anthropology as follows: "What he has left us. . .is an unsparing view of man's inherent tendency toward 'disguise, falsehood, hypocrisy'--in short, for self-deception. To cajole and butter us ourselves and others, from an overweening love of self, becomes the rule of life."[137] It is self-deception that stands at the center of Pascal's reflection on the human person, and, as Hazelton concludes, "Pascal is saying [about human nature] what Saint Paul and Saint Augustine said before him and Sigmund Freud and Reinhold Niebuhr said after him."[138]

This picture of human being as divided and conflicted is everywhere apparent in Pascal's work. In his most pessimistic voice, Pascal reflects on the desire of human persons to conceal the truth from themselves, to deceive themselves about themselves, saying, "This human life is noting but a perpetual illusion; there is nothing but mutual deception and flattery. Man is therefore nothing but a disguise, falsehood and hypocrisy, both in himself and with regard for others. He does not want to be told the truth," a tendency, Pascal claimed, that is "naturally rooted in his heart."[139]

This capacity for self-deception, Pascal claimed, is implicated in the illusion of self-sufficiency "before God." Pascal the theologian speaks as one who has learned a terrible truth about the human relation to the truth (the God-relation). Self-deception is a theological concern in the <u>Pensées</u> inasmuch as it is self-deception that describes the cognitive-psychological dimension of sin. The willful aversion to truth, which obtains in conjunction with a preferred "cover story" of self-flattery, lies at the heart of the Pascalian anthropology. That anthropology revolves around the capacity of human persons to avoid the truth about themselves in their condition. Pascal held that human persons lack self-consciousness, and that self-consciousness is necessarily ingredient in the lack of God-consciousness. To miss seeing the abyss that is the human condition--because we do not want to, because to do so is painful and even "terrifying"--is to miss seeing the remedy of grace, which is the solution to the question of existence. For Pascal, all things mask God; and though God be hidden, yet is God made visible to the eyes of faith amid the conflicts and ambiguities of existence. The contrary-mindedness of human persons, however, can create a blindness that is nothing but a willful refusal to see: "There is enough light for those who desire only to see, and enough darkness for those of a contrary disposition."[140] It is the Pascal who wrote of human persons that "anything can become of [their] true good," that "Man's true nature, his true good and virtue, and true religion are things which cannot be known separately,"[141] who wrote the following:

> Instead of complaining that God has hidden himself, you will give him thanks for revealing himself as much as he has, and you will thank him too for not revealing himself to wise men full of pride and unworthy of knowing so holy a God. Two sorts of persons know him: those who are humble of heart and love their lowly estate, whatever their degree of intelligence, high or low, and those who are intelligent enough to see the truth, however much they may be opposed to it.[142]

Because of his preoccupation with the desire of human persons to deceive themselves about themselves and their predicament "before God," Pascal can be said to have been preoccupied with the peculiar phenomenon of mental gymnastic that is self-deception. Human persons, preferring oblivion to self-recognition, refuse to face the terror of existence and the pain of honest self-confrontation. By choosing to forsake the God-relation that is humanity's only hope, human persons "miss the mark" and fail to recognize the truth about themselves and God, the truth only available through the God-relation. For Pascal, only relation with God can enable us to understand ourselves without resorting to flattery or self-deception. Pascal reiterates a typically Christian insight through his analysis of theological self-deception--that human persons willfully refuse the God-relation because they prefer the illusion of self-love and self-flattery to the painful reality that is the premise of faith: that we are fragmented selves who love illusion more than truth, that we are in need of God. St. Paul had put the matter this way, invoking the concept pride to make his point: "[If] anyone thinks he is something when he is nothing, he deceives himself" (Gal. 6.3. RSV).

As we saw in Augustine, a theological self-deceiver is one who does not acknowledge that he or she is a sinner. This insight appears over and over again in the literature of theological reflection. To take another example, consider Jonathan Edwards. In analyzing the position of one who argues that "there is no fault at all in sin," Edwards describes this person in terms of self-deception, as one who "confutes himself and shows his own insincerity in his objection." Moreover, Edwards makes an empirical appeal to expose the true belief of the self-deceiver, the belief held unconsciously deep down yet acted on, the belief that is explicitly denied:

> For at the same time that he objects, that men's acts are necessary, from God's decrees, and original sin, and that this kind of necessity is inconsistent with faultiness in the act, his own practice shows that he does not believe what he objects to be true: otherwise why does he at all blame men? Or why are such persons at all displeased with men, for abusive, injurious, and ungrateful acts towards them? Whatever they pretend, by this they show that indeed they do believe that there is no necessity in men's acts, from divine decrees, or corruption of nature, that is inconsistent with blame. [Their] practice shows, that at the same time they do not believe this, but fully believe the contrary: for when they are abused by men, they are displeased with men, and not with God only.[143]

The concept 'self-deception,' used by Edwards with power and sophistication, makes the phenomenon of holding contrary beliefs intelligible, and elsewhere he connects this self-deceit to pride.[144] In a similar vein, John Calvin is worthy of mention, since he devoted a section of the Institutes to self-deception and the sin of pride: "The severity of law takes away from us all self-deception."[145] In this section, he writes that "For man, blinded and drunk with self-love, must be compelled to know and to confess his own feebleness and impurity," it being arrogance and pride ("puffed up with insane confidence in his own mental powers') that blinds him. In the same spirit, Emil Brunner would later write eloquently about the truths of faith, one of which is that God, not humanity, is the measure of all things, even though it is common that reason

> arrogates to itself the right to define the whole range of truth from the standpoint of man. Hence the protest of 'intellectual honesty,' which the autonomous reason always makes, is--even if unconsciously--always a lie. The question is not one of 'intellectual honesty' at all, but of rationalistic, that is, positivistic arrogance and self-will. Faith does not come into conflict with reason itself but with the imperialism of the human reason.[146]

Brunner makes clear that this imperialism of reason reflects the self-assertion that springs from pride and produces self-deception. In Brunner's analysis, sin is defined as a negation of an original positive revelation, and humanity has derived this revelation from God: "That is why the sinner stands 'before' God; that is why he is guilty and 'without excuse.'"[147] Sin is the "negative relation to God" for "sin itself is a relation to God."[148] Sin is the revolt of the creature against the Creator, "the striving to be autonomous; the will of the tenant to be lord." And the root of all sin is the "false love of pleasure and the destruction of community by the setting up of the self as an idol."[149]

Brunner's analysis of human falsehood before God appeals to the concept 'self-deception.' Brunner contends that the sinner is ". . .without excuse because he could, and might, know God, and indeed still more, because he really does know something of God, but he continually denies this knowledge."[150] This denial invokes theological self-deception, for it refers to the falseness of sin and describes the consequence of human pride. A theological self-deceiver, therefore, denies the original revelation of God, the revelation that permits individuals to see themselves before God, to understand themselves in their true being. That revelation is available to all inasmuch as all are created in God's image, for "Revelation is not something that is added to man's being; it is there even when it is denied, rejected, and ignored."[151] Those who deny sin and deny the reality of the original revelation ". . .do not," Brunner says, "know what they are doing."[152]

The negation that is sin has also been discussed by the towering theologian of the twentieth century, Karl Barth. Barth discusses three forms of sin: pride, sloth, and falsehood. Each refers to a particular way of describing the doctrine of sin, and although each of the forms is treated separately, Barth argues that together they comprise the actuality of sin itself. Pride entails falsehood "before God," and Barth is able to connect the error of being proud to the loss of true being as follows: "The error of man concerning himself, his self-alienation, is that he thinks he can love and choose and will and assert and maintain himself--<u>sese propter sepsum</u>--in his being in himself, his self-hood, and that in doing so he will be truly man."[153] It is through pride, which is the "mad desire to be as God," that this error is committed, for "If he himself is supreme, then he is his own God."[154] "And as a pseudo-divinity he secretly worships himself, appearing as such even outside and deceiving others as he first deceived himself."[155] In choosing oneself as supreme, out of pride and before God, one effects a substitution of self for God: "When man tries to make this mad exchange his first and supreme error is in relation to God," and it is this "stupid and ridiculous notion that we can take our place at His side"[156] that Barth characterizes as self-deceptive. In other words, pride and arrogance and sin and self-deception all refer to the general position of being disrelated to God. And the reality of sin, in that it is both pride and falsehood, leads to the situation in which humanity claims to know "what is best" for itself, a proud and arrogant claim that is also self-deceptive.

> When God Himself is the pledge that He has done all this,
> [i.e., acted to reconcile humanity to Himself through Christ,
> who has not only shown the way but made it], man cannot pretend that he knows better. When a truth speaks for itself,
> man's knowing is only falsehood, a lie. And again, this is
> the sin of Adam. . . .We are all at times, incorrigibly, those
> who know better--and, therefore, because grace is the truth
> revealed and known to us, we are all incorrigible liars. The
> consequences follow. Falsehood is self-destruction. Because
> man and the world live under the dominion of sin, lying to God
> and deceiving themselves, they live in self-destruction.[157]

Because Barth connects the concept 'sin' to pride and falsehood, he also connects the sin of pride to theological self-deception. 'Self-deception,' therefore, plays a prominent role in Barth's analysis of sin. It is a "meaning complex" that Barth is able to put to work to describe and evaluate the great contradiction of human existence: life before God that is also life without God.

A similar analysis appears in Reinhold Niebuhr's picture of "Man as Sinner."[158] In his "Gifford Lectures," Niebuhr explicitly connects sin, which is essentially pride, to falsehood and self-deception. Pride drives the an individual to a sort of ignorance, though, as Niebuhr points out, "His sin is never the mere ignorance of his ignorance. It is always an effort to obscure his blindness by overstating the degree of his sight and to obscure his insecurity by stretching his power beyond its limit."[159] The ignorance, therefore, is willful, and Niebuhr appeals to Philip Leon's statement concerning self-deception: "The self-deceiver does not believe. . .what he says or he would not be a deceiver. He does not believe what he says or he would not be deceived. He both believes and does not believe. . .or he would not be self-deceived," and Niebuhr himself concludes that "The mechanism of deception is too complicated to fit into the category of either pure ignorance or pure dishonesty."[160]

Niebuhr appeals to the concept 'self-deception' in order to explicate sin, and he includes a section on "The Relation of Dishonesty to Pride" in order to complete his picture of "Man as Sinner." This is perhaps the finest, most explicit statement of the relation of the sin of pride to self-deception, and the discussion is carried on by employing the concept 'self-deception' in a theological context while respecting its ordinary language meaning. Niebuhr concludes that the self-love of pride involves an element of deceit, that the blindness of self-deception is a consequence of sin, not ignorance. Self-deception is, in other words, a concomitant of sin. The self, knowing that it does not deserve unconditioned devotion, deceives itself into believing a "pretension it cannot easily believe because it was itself the author of the deception."[161] Reinhold Niebuhr's discussion of self-deception and the sin of pride captures the conceptual complexity of 'self-deception,' and it stands as a model of clarity for the investigator who seeks to understand what a theologian would mean by employing 'self-deception' in a context of meaning and value governed by the God-relation.

The last point to be considered in this particular section is that self-deception can occur as a form of misrelation to God, a relation that is based on faith rather than on unbelief or disbelief. Kant, for instance, referred to types of "illusory faith" and "artificial modes of belief," arguing that "artificial self-deception in religious matters have a common basis. Among the three divine moral attributes, holiness, mercy, and justice, man habitually turns directly to the second in order to avoid the forbidding condition of conforming to the requirements of the first."[162] In his own way, Kant is echoing the association made in Scripture that virtue (right action) is a necessary ingredient of faith without which one is a hearer only: "But be doers of the word, and not hearers only, deceiving yourselves" (James 1.22). That there is a false Christian identity due to self-deception was also a concern of Luther's. Luther wrote of the person who reneges on Christian duty, who disregards spiritual requirements and thereby deceives him- or herself about the truth of what it means--what is required--to be a Christian, that

> whoso obeyeth the flesh, and continueth without fear or remorse in accomplishing the desires and lusts thereof, let him know that he pertaineth not unto Christ; and although he brag in the name of a Christian never so much, yet doth he but deceive himself. For they which are of Christ, do crucify their flesh with the affections and lusts thereof.[163]

Luther's writings are replete with references to the kind of self-deception implicated in false belief, sin, and spiritual misunderstanding.

And, finally, another theologian concerned to expose the kind of self-deception that can appear within the faith on the basis of faith, Jonathan Edwards, picks up this particular thread of argument. He wrote of the self-deception that infects the person who does not accomplish in the totality of one's being the reality of faith. The reality of faith requires that one _do_ what one believes--that one enact the faith. Edwards argues that "a man's actions are the proper trial what a man's heart prefers," saying that

> It is therefore exceedingly absurd, and even ridiculous, for any to pretend that they have a good heart, while they live a wicked life, or do not bring forth the fruit of universal holiness in their practice. For it is proved in fact that such men do not love God above all. It is foolish to dispute against plain fact and experience. Men that live in ways of sin, and yet flatter themselves that they shall go to heaven, or expect to be received hereafter as holy persons without a holy life and practice, act as though they expect to make a fool of their judge. . . . '<u>Do not deceive yourself with an expectation of reaping life everlasting hereafter, if you do</u>

> not sow the Spirit here; it is vain to think that God will be made a fool of by you, that he will be shammed and baffled with shadow instead of substances, and with vain pretense instead of that good fruit which he expects, when the contrary to what you pretend appears plainly in your life before His face.'164

Edwards thus appeals to the concept of self-deception to make his case, and he adds that the pretense, which attempts to baffle God, arises from "self-conceit" and "deluded hypocrisy," both of which are manifestations of human pride.165

f. Conclusion

These capsule statements have been presented merely to indicate the kind of use to which 'self-deception' has been put by various religious thinkers. In the religious context of meaning and value, 'self-deception' does not cease being a psychological concept. It is used, rather, to reveal the cognitive-psychological dynamics of the voluntary disrelatedness of human persons to God. It is a concept that describes the cognitive dimension of sin and is a form of sin. It indicates the inherent falsehood of the person who misrelates him- or herself to God due to the quite human desire to achieve self-mastery, mastery of the environment, and self-sufficiency. These desires spring from pride, and because in the religious context all concepts are governed by the God-relation, they express the sin of pride.

"Before God" all achievements in self-relatedness, all striving to excuse oneself from the requirements of relatedness to God, all efforts to become "as God," constitute falsehood, pretense, excuses and lies. Self-justification before God is, from the religious point of view, an attempt to deceive God, to fool or baffle God, when God cannot be deceived. The effort at deception, then, misses the mark. The effort to deceive God about who one is in one's true being before God, misses God and turns back on the self. The deception arises from the self seeking pleasure as it glorifies and exalts itself. This self-directed pleasure (pride) is a sin (disrelationship with God), and it is in one of its forms a self-directed and willed falsehood, an actual instance of 'self-deception' in the religious domain. Thus it is that the logic of disrelationship with God imposes on the disrelated the qualification not only that they are sinners, but that their sin, which is a fundamental expression of a desire to deny God (rebellion) as well as a desire to be "as God" (usurpation), is self-deception. 'Self-deception' is a meaningful concept in the religious sphere of interest and concern, and there is ample evidence to support this contention in the writings of those who, as religious thinkers committed to the religious assumption, concentrate on analyzing the whys and wherefores of sin and falsehood before God.

I would briefly consider one other author whose religious literature informs us about the meaning of 'self-deception' and the use to which the concept can be put, Søren Kierkegaard. A poet-dialectician, Kierkegaard approached the topic of self-deception from three different contexts of meaning--philosophy/psychology, ethics and religion--doing so through a literature that contributes significantly, and uniquely, to our understanding of self-deception.

2. Self-Deception and Sin: Kierkegaard and "Despair is Sin"

Although the sin of pride has been used to gain access to the religious understanding of self-deception, pride is not our only sesame. The concept of despair will also permit access. Despair is, of course, a major concern of existential philosophy, but its use as an access to theological self-deception has not been exploited except, perhaps, by the author who used despair in a religious way to elucidate the problem of existence: life without God. That author was Søren Kierkegaard.

Kierkegaard used the concept of despair to launch a religious inquiry into a wide range of issues, all of which pertain in one way or another to the problem of becoming a self. By asking about the meaning of being human, Kierkegaard was able to focus on particular problems of human existence; by asking about the possibilities that freedom makes available, he was, as a religious author, able to concern himself with the ultimate conception of selfhood: What does it mean to exist as a self, in freedom, "before God?"

As a psychological investigator into the dynamics of self-relatedness, Kierkegaard analyzed the concept 'self-deception' from different points of view, different stages of existence, different contexts of meaning. So widespread is his treatment of the topic that, in the end, the student of the Kierkegaard literature discerns that self-deception is a constant preoccupation. Kierkegaard scholars have noted this fact, as have certain students of self-deception,[166] and self-deception has served as the orienting principle of a recent introductory text on Kierkegaard's thought.[167]

Kierkegaard believed that his task as an author was to explore the possibilities and the pathologies of selfhood. From a religious point of view, this means that his task was to examine not only the disrelatedness of the self without God (sin as despair) but also the remedy or "antidote" to despair, which is theistic faith. Kierkegaard created a unique and aesthetically satisfying literature, a literature designed to occasion reflection in the reader; and he did so as one who was always a religious author even though a major portion of that literature does not profess a religious point of view. He was, as he said of himself, a poet-dialectician. Being a poet, he exemplified self-deception in concrete--though imagined--instances of personal existence. The literature then "deceives" the reader into considering a particular possibility for him- or herself. Being a dialectician, he addressed the problem of self-deception in terms of its manifestations in existence, in despair, and in relation to its true remedy, religious faith.

Self-deception is a problem of human self-relatedness that Kierkegaard is able to "characterize" in his literature. Beyond that, however, he is capable of providing more direct analysis. For instance, his volume, Purity of Heart is to Will One Thing, explicitly discusses self-deception in light of the God-relation. He presents 'self-deception' as a fundamental expression of the human psychological condition of a conflicted self, which he termed, borrowing the term from the New Testament, "double-mindedness."[168] Purity of Heart is Kierkegaard's direct communication on the topic of self-deception, for this is his explicit analysis of the self that is, before God, turned against itself, divided in will and at odds with its own desires. Elsewhere Kierkegaard illustrates the self-deception that commonly and pervasively afflicts any and all who despair by misrelating themselves to God. In Purity of Heart, however, he moves beyond characterization to discuss the dynamics of the self-deceiver's activity.

Kierkegaard's claim is that self-deceivers despair by not willing to be themselves. They fail, that is, to choose themselves in freedom ("as spirit") and thereby fail to become agents who can freely choose as unified and coherent selves. Such persons are divided in mind and in conflict with God, and as such, are self-deceived as well. According to Kierkegaard, each individual can choose to use the occasion of intrapsychic conflict to misrelate him- or herself to the Good, God. In the religious sphere of existence, the Good is an objective value that is recognized as objective through the action of choosing oneself. It is objective despite its non-public status, but its objectivity is made manifest nonetheless in the act of choosing. Choosing oneself requires the cultivation of "inwardness" and "subjectivity," and it is this cultivation of subjectivity--which refers to one's response to objective, non-public goods of human well-being--that provides the route of access to the Good. An individual, however, can ignore, deny, resist, rationalize away or refuse to accept the goods of subjectivity. In freedom, one can opt to evade the call of the Eternal (the Good, God), even though the individual hears the call. Being constituted with an eternal aspect, the self cannot help but hear its call, but not wanting to hear it, one can evade it, and this evasion identifies the theological self-deceiver's response.

As Kierkegaard's analysis unfolds, he argues that the self can respond to the call of the Eternal in faith, but only if the self is willing to relate itself to God with purity of heart, with singleness of purpose, a singleness of heart, mind, soul, and strength. That it does not do so indicates a misuse of freedom in the direction of "double-mindedness." "Double-mindedness" is how Kierkegaard characterizes the cognitive-psychological condition of the person who hears the call of the Eternal but resists it. Double-mindedness, therefore, refers to an affirmation of selfhood in which one loses oneself by denying God. It indicates a despair in which one fails to choose to be a self, in which one opts to use freedom in the service of a falsehood, a deception that obtains "before God." Since God cannot be deceived, denying God is a deception directed at God that affects not God but oneself. Such denial is equivalent to choosing a self-understanding grounded in error and falsehood. Given this logic, to deny God is to deceive oneself. To be in despair is to be doubleminded, and, "before God," double-mindedness identifies a willful ignorance of the one thing that is necessary for single-mindedness-- the God-relation. For Kierkegaard, the act whereby one refuses the Eternal is fundamentally deceptive; and it can be characterized as the religiously conceived phenomenon I have termed "theological self-deception."

I do not propose to investigate what Kierkegaard said about self-deception in any great detail. My aim, rather, is to indicate the connection Kierkegaard makes between sin, despair and self-deception, affirming that his presentation of the concept 'self-deception' is both methodologically and hermeneutically sophisticated--as well as being consistent with the general contour of this study. I would reiterate what I said in the "Introduction," namely, that Kierkegaard has inspired this study. By that I mean that this study has followed a method of analysis that conforms in the broad sweep to Kierkegaard's own, though without the indirection and poeticizing that was Kierkegaard's unique means of analysis by exemplification. Kierkegaard did understand the meaning of self-deception in a way that supports our ordinary language analysis; and, furthermore, he did employ the concept in different contexts of meaning to perform different meaning tasks. His method was to exemplify the existential condition of the self-deceiver who, in not willing to be the self he or she is, stands before God in falsehood, having willfully misplaced his or her passion.

For the remainder of this section, I shall indicate the ways in which the Kierkegaard literature contributes to our understanding of the concept 'self-deception.' My case is that Kierkegaard understood the concept in its complexity as a synthetic action-cognition concept; that he was able to employ the concept with respect to particular governing relations, be they psychological, moral or religious; and that those contexts of meaning correspond to different and distinct existential stations.

As a religious thinker, Kierkegaard analyzes self-deception as a problem in self-relations. The logical problem, the paradox of the concept, did not represent an actual logical contradiction, but an accurate description of the self-opposition that constitutes personhood. Kierkegaard understood the philosophical problems attending the concept and the ethical-evaluational uses for 'self-deception.' But, in the end, he deemed self-deception to be a problem that was most serious--ultimately serious--when brought into the context of religious meaning and value. It is therefore fitting that the present study should conclude by considering the viewpoint of an author who began with an inquiry into self-relatedness and eventually connected his psychological interest in the problems of psychological dynamics to issues of ultimate concern and infinite interest.

As a religious author preoccupied with the problem of becoming a self, Kierkegaard investigated the dynamics of self-relatedness in different existential contexts. One of those contexts, the religious, was premised on the idea that human subjects are free to choose themselves in the infinite possibility provided by the God-relation. As a psychologist--and as a psychologist Kierkegaard achieved a degree of insight into the dynamics of self-relatedness that has invited comparison with Freud, whom he presaged in many respects[169]-- Kierkegaard employed 'self-deception' to describe one of the possible ways of being misrelated to oneself. In the spiritual context--in the context of freedom for the infinite--Kierkegaard employed 'self-deception' to describe and evaluate one way in which we misuse our freedom as persons; and that analysis investigates how persons achieve a false self-understanding. The false self-understanding is achieved by persons who, in despair, flee from the truth about themselves as that truth is revealed through a self-consciousness which is itself derived from a higher Power, God. 'Self-deception,' in other words, refers to the condition of being cognitively misrelated to oneself through the act of misleading one's own beliefs. But because self-deception arises from a misuse of freedom with respect to the infinite possibility of the God-relation, it is also a willful evasion of one's highest good, a willful wrongdoing in terms of the God-relation, an akratic act "before God."

It is anxiety that is examined by Kierkegaard's pseudonymous author, Virgilius Haufniensis, in the psychological study, The Concept of Anxiety. Under the microscope in this volume is the phenomenon of human subjects who contrive and maneuver to escape their condition of freedom. Anxiety is related to despair and is, as Haufniensis put it, "the psychological state that precedes despair."[170] Anxiety is not itself a conceptual equivalent to despair, for despair is sin, and the concept 'despair' refers to a deeper consciousness, the consciousness that is acquired when one achieves some awareness--however faint or obscure it might be--of the eternal within one's own constitution as a self. Anxiety obtains as the result of a preliminary awareness that one is free, that a multitude of possibilities are open to one. To be aware of these possibilities is to be aware that one must do something with these possibilities; and to be free, to be aware of the freedom that is one's context for decision-making, is to realize that one's possibilities extend to the infinite. To be free means that one can desire certain of these possibilities--a fact that itself expresses the infinite in the self. At the same time, however, one also finds oneself limited and confined by finite existence. That finitude, even though it cuts off possibilities, is a necessary aspect of human existence, and as such, it becomes a valued aspect, even one that is desired. The self that is free, then, finds security in finitude, and even though it desires freedom, it fears freedom as well. As human subjects, we fear the infinite that would separate us from the finitude that we also desire. 'Anxiety' identifies this dialectic of fear and desire.

"Freedom's possibility announces itself in anxiety,"[171] writes Vigilius

Haufniensis. Anxiety is the psychological phenomenon that identifies the impatience and disquietude persons experience as they grow toward an awareness that the mind/body synthesis is, in and of itself, insufficient to constitute the actual or true self. Vigilius' understanding of the phenomenon not only subscribes to the notion that anxiety results from the effort of self-transcendence, that it is, in other words, a consequence of persons relating themselves to possibility within the finite; but he describes anxiety dialectically: the lure of possibility, the impulse to transcend the finite, attracts individuals at the very moment it inspires fear and repulses them.

The self, for Kierkegaard, is spirit. The self is the self-relatedness that obtains as a result of freedom and possibility. The true self is that self-relatedness that points beyond the finitude of body and calls one back from "infinitizing" imaginings, for a self requires the synthesis of finite and infinite, temporal and eternal, possibility and necessity. Without this synthesis, there is no true self to become aware of itself in freedom. Should this synthesis be achieved, however, the self can then acquire a "transparency" as it becomes aware that it is derived from God and is constituted by God in freedom as spirit, as a dialectically related self-relation.

In <u>The Sickness Unto Death</u>, another of Kierkegaard's authors announces that this freedom enables finite and infinite to be related in a synthetic self-relation. Ideally, the synthetic self will be conscious of itself as both finite and infinite, for according to Anti-Climacus one moves to synthesis and to authentic selfhood by achieving awareness of oneself as a self. This means nothing more than that one becomes aware of one's own desire to grasp the Eternal. Religious consciousness claims that the Eternal itself announces this possibility for relationship to the individual, and the individual is free to respond, either to renounce it or to accept it as a possibility <u>pro me</u>. And given the religious premise, this is a possibility of consciousness available to all.

Despair, on the other hand, is the disrelationship that obtains when one refuses the task of selfhood, when one is not willing to be oneself. Selfhood is conceived religiously. The self is conceived in the context of the God-relation, and its article of faith, as well as its foundation for analysis, is that to be a self is to be related to God. Anxiety, then, is a topic of interest because anxiety is the growing--and gnawing--awareness of the Eternal possibility as it announces itself in the finite. A person's response to this growing awareness, which has not yet led one to despair or to an awareness that one is disrelated to the Eternal possibility, is anxiety, and anxiety identifies the psychological state that is experienced as "a desire for what one fears," a "sympathetic antipathy" that is itself "the alien power which grips the individual, [from which] one cannot tear himself free. . .and does not want to, for one fears, but what he fears he desires."[172]

There are two ways to respond to this anxiety. The first is to let oneself be educated by it with the result that self-consciousness will so increase that one will realize that one is a synthesis. If one achieves an awareness of oneself as spirit and becomes aware that in freedom one is related to an Eternal possibility, one will emerge from the despair of honest self-recognition--that one is not actually eternal thought one desires relation to the Eternal--to make the movement of faith ("Anxiety as Saving Through Faith").[173] On the other hand, since anxiety is also a negativity that repels one, the individual can also choose to ignore or reject the possibility of the infinite by opting for a self-understanding tied to the finite concerns of the finite world. This amounts to a rejection of the Eternal call. If one rejects the call of the Eternal, one directs one's ultimate concern to a false god, a finite object that one deceives oneself into thinking is infinite.

According to this Kierkegaardian analysis, it is possible to have an infinite interest in the finite, but to do so is to be disrelated to both God and self. This is inauthentic existence, freely chosen but premised on a false commitment. Were the individual sufficiently conscious, he or she would realize that the object of infinite interest postures as something it is not, and one's commitment would be exposed as a misdirecting of passion, a faith that is unwarranted because the object is false and a pretense. However one responds to the possibility, the freedom that one has to choose establishes a context that induces anxiety, for anxiety is a concomitant of freedom and integral to the human condition. The possibility that anxiety announces in freedom is that one can relate oneself to the object of infinite interest, and the anxiety arises because one is free to choose how to relate oneself--either in truth or in falsity. Freedom serves to make possible the movement of faith, for to move in faith is to choose truly and thereby acquire in truth one's highest good, the God-relation. One can, of course, misuse that freedom and misrelate oneself to God by denying the true God-relation, and according to Vigilius, this misuse of freedom takes a variety of forms. He analyzes such forms of disrelatedness as shut-upness, hypocrisy, pride, superstition and unbelief.

That self-deception is relevant to this phenomenon of anxiety is due to the project to mislead belief that can result. One can contrive to shun one's condition of freedom not only by misusing it, but by willfully denying the truth that one is a self, that one is constituted in freedom by God as that which expresses spirit, as that which is made for the Eternal. A negative response to freedom's possibility takes the form of a denial that the self is constituted by God. One refuses to acknowledge that one has been made for the Eternal, one denies that the self is endowed with the capacity to acknowledge its own desire for a relation to the Eternal possibility, which, in truth, is relation with God. Haufniensis holds that to believe that one is not what one is, that one chooses oneself as one wants rather than as one is, is a deception. It is an attempt to mislead one's own beliefs about who one is, and this is self-deception since the effort to act as one's own agent in the movement toward synthesis denies the religious truth that the self is derived from the God who constitutes the self in freedom as spirit.

Haufniensis affirms, as does Anti-Climacus in The Sickness Unto Death, that the human subject is "a synthesis of psyche and body sustained by spirit," a synthesis of the "somatic, the psychic and the pneumatic."[174] The denial that one is spirit leads inevitably to a disrelationship that destroys the dialectical nature of selfhood itself. The problem is that in order to avoid the anxiety that inevitably accompanies the reach for the infinite from the imposed limitations of the finite, a person may decide to choose him- or herself in a way that enacts a spiritual self-deception. Anxiety leads to a desire to do away with the anxiety, so anxiety leads to a decision. According to this somewhat rarefied analysis, the human subject may choose to resolve the tension which is the dialectic of human selfhood--that one is body but more than body. But to resolve this tension is to deceive oneself into thinking that it can be resolved. This tension is not a disability but a statement of identity. This tension is who I am--it is what it means to be a self and obtains from the configurations of one's intrapersonal relations.

In the Kierkegaardian anthropology, to be human is to be free. Human persons can decide all sorts of things in freedom, including how they are to understand themselves, and they are even free to choose wrongly. A self-understanding can be chosen in which one decides against recognizing that one is derived from God. This yields a false interpretation about how one is constituted and one chooses thereby to remain in ignorance about one's self and what it means to accept oneself as one truly is. The person who neglects the requirement that one must be, to be a self, both finite and infinite (synthesis), refuses to acknowledge the truth that the synthesis of selfhood can only arise with reference to spirit, to freedom and possibility. As Anti-Climacus puts the matter in theological rather than psychological terms, only with God are all things possible. That includes the possibility that one can accept oneself as one truly is, which means that one can accept oneself as a contradiction in which one holds together simultaneously the finite/infinite, temporal/eternal, necessary/possible oppositions that are the self. From a theological point of view, it is only before God that one can exist without anxiety or despair, or become transparent to oneself. It is only through the movement of faith that one can come to accept oneself as the contradiction one is, and this is the finite impossibility that God makes possible in truth.

Although despair is the deeper expression of anxiety, Haufniensis mentions that the anxious person can seek to avoid the disquiet of the existential situation, the restlessness and distress of being a self in opposition, by evading self-confrontation and self-recognition. The evasions are willful and many. Laziness, busyness, enthusiasms for the temporal, procrastination, idle speculation, affectation, arrogance and haughtiness all constitute misuses of freedom preliminary to sin. And also on this list is self-deception: "Men are not willing to think eternity earnestly but are anxious about it, and anxiety can contrive a hundred evasions."[175]

Anxiety is the manifestation of the "emotional perception" that some part of the self is eternal, and it is recognition of this truth that the anxious person will attempt to evade. Anxious persons, who are afraid to be qualified by spirit yet yearn for it, can engage in all kinds of evasive interpretive maneuvers to prevent themselves from becoming conscious or making linguistically explicit the basis for the anxiety. And were persons to be conscious that the basis for the anxiety is freedom and the possibility for self-transcendence, this self-consciousness would lead to the deeper anxiety of despair. The attempt to achieve by one's own finite resource respite from the disquiet of "fearing what one desires" leads to the point where persons will refuse in despair to choose themselves as the selves they could be ("despair as not willing to be oneself"). What is contrived by an individual in anxiety will be enacted in the next stage, despair, where one actually maneuvers to evade the claim of the Infinite. Individuals will deny that they exist "before God," will deny that they are qualified by spirit. In short, despair will lead one to maneuver to evade the spiritual possibility of the God-relation itself.

Self-deception fits into this analysis since self-deception describes the self-directed project to mislead belief involved in the effort to avoid this deeper consciousness of self and God. Self-deception befalls the person who refuses to be educated by anxiety into the deeper realization that an infinite possibility exists pro me, who in despair rejects the call of the Eternal, the call to deeper self-consciousness.

As this Kierkegaardian position unfolds, it becomes clear that the first step in that deeper consciousness is to reposition oneself for despair. Even though one may not make linguistically explicit the realization that one exists before God, despair repositions one beyond psychological anxiety to an awareness that one is disrelated and that an infinite qualitative difference exists between the self one is and the self one would like to be. Despair is the deeper realization that is itself the expression of being qualified as spirit, and anxiety is the necessary precondition for despair. From a theological point of view, despair prepares one for another kind of awareness, namely, that associated with theistic faith. It is beyond despair and as a result of despair that the God-relation opens up as one's true hope for rest and integration. It is the dialectic of despair/faith, which is taken up in another work, that provides a deeper insight into the religious conception of self-deception--beyond psychological dynamics, beyond anxiety.

In The Sickness Unto Death, Anti-Climacus explicitly connects despair to self-deception. One section of this volume is entitled "Despair is Sin"[176]; and in these pages sin is defined as despair. Sin and despair are both analyzed so that they point to the problem of human disrelatedness from God. Sin is, after all, "severance from the good,"[177] and "sin itself is the struggle of despair."[178] Despair signifies the state of disequilibrium that obtains when one fails to become a self, when one refuses the task of becoming a self by not willing to be oneself. Despair can take different forms, but generally speaking, it results from one's refusal to meet the requirement of becoming what one truly is. This refusal takes place "before God" and is a voluntary act. This refusal constitutes the willful wrongdoing before God that is sin:

> If the person who despairs is, as he believes, aware of his despair, he no longer speaks senselessly about it as something which happens to him, and how with all his might he will fight against it, but if he is not aware that the sickness lies still deeper, that the misrelation in him also reflects itself infinitely in the misrelation to the power [God] which established him as a relation--then he is still in despair, and with all his supposed labor he only works himself into an even deeper despair; he loses himself in despair and is again guilty and responsible for it.[179]

Because as human subjects we are free to recognize a spiritual possibility in our own self-relatedness, we may come to recognize the truth about human being: that we are creatures whose freedom is itself derived from an Eternal possibility. In freedom, the relation between the psychical and the physical is not established by oneself but in relation to an Other, and "Only by the relation to this other can [a self] be in equilibrium. As soon as there is a misrelation in the relation there is despair, but as soon as he does not in the relation relate himself to the other, there is also despair."[180]

Despair signifies the condition of one who is misrelated to oneself and to God, for "Despair signifies the misrelationship between the eternal in man and his concrete existence."[181] The sinner is one who lacks transparency "before God," who chooses to be opaque to his or her own view by refusing to see the truth about human being--by defying that which one realizes "deep down" as one's highest good, by believing oneself too weak to make the movement of faith to God. The sinner is one who wills obscurity before God, wills, that is, not to become the true self that is related in truth to God. According to Anti-Climacus, the sinner who lacks transparency before God is able to avoid seeing through his or her pretensions to the God who has constituted the person as a self and from whom selfhood itself derives. This blindness to God marks the person who cannot, will not, see his or her need for God, who chooses not to grasp that the Eternal possibility exists pro me. The sinner who despairs refuses to hope that a genuine eternal qualification is possible. Despair arises from the fact that the self has become aware that it is more than finite and that it is not totally the product of unmediated responses to the contingencies of finite circumstance.[182]

The sinner despairs, and despair expresses the condition of the sinner. The sinner is the person misrelated to God, and misrelated because he or she has chosen not to be a self. It is because despair can be described as a person's "not being conscious of oneself as spirit"[183] that the sinner can be said to be one who wills what is false. Sinners want to be what they imagine themselves to be rather than willing to be what they are in light of the Eternal possibility. One who sins therefore wills to be ignorant of oneself as one is "before God" in truth. From the theological point of view, this is a willful ignorance that can be dispelled by acknowledging the truth that one is derived from God and that one can act to ground oneself transparently in God: "If a man in relating himself to himself relates himself absolutely to God, there is no despair at all; but at every moment when this is not the case, there is also some despair. Consequently when a man in relating himself to himself absolutely relates himself to God, then all despair is annihilated."[184]

To be absolutely related to God requires that one dispel one's ignorance of the God-relation by acknowledging that relation as a possibility that exists pro me. This acknowledgement is the cognitive assent that accompanies theistic faith, for this specifies a linguistically explicit confession of one's condition and its remedy as governed by the terms of the God-relation. Another way of putting this is to say that the sinner who despairs chooses not to understand him- or herself in light of the God-relation. Preferring blindness, preferring to avow a false identity, the sinner in despair acts to refuse a true self-understanding, doing so because the truth is psychologically distressing. The distress arises from an awareness that the eternal possibility would separate one from the security of the finite, thereby forcing one to live amid the contradictions of existence and in the face of a realization that human effort is inadequate to resolve those contradictions. The sinner who despairs by choosing not to understand him- or herself chooses ignorance and wills to be ignorant of the highest good. The sinner does so because he or she wants to secure an identity where human autonomy and self-mastery constitute the person's self-image, and this is to say that given the truth made available in the religious domain, the sinner prefers something more than the truth--a false self-image. To willfully ignore the proper object of ultimate concern and infinite interest is to position oneself such that despair obtains--and it will remain until one overcomes the ignorance one has chosen by realigning one's awareness to the truth through theistic faith. The sinner who despairs, in that the despair rests on a willful and motivated refusal to acknowledge the truth, enacts a deception. Because that deception does not affect God, it can only affect the deceiver. And in falling victim to his or her own making, the sinner who despairs is to be characterized as a self-deceiver "before God."

Individuals can be conscious of their despair, but according to Anti-Climacus, there are also individuals who are unconscious that they are, in fact, in despair.[185] This distinction is ultimately irrelevant to deciding who is and who is not a sinner, since, from a theistic point of view, "it makes no difference whether the person in despair is ignorant that his condition is despair--he is in despair just the same."[186] The person who is conscious of being in despair is in a position to realize that theistic faith is an antidote to the "sickness unto death," though the despairing individual is free to remain in despair and can actually defy one's own highest good (despair as defiance). But even defiant individuals, even though they are conscious of the good and inclined to acquire the good, act against their own inclinations, defying their own desire to become synthesized selves. The defiant one, in other words, is a person who wills not to be the person one is, preferring to constitute the self by the self's own power.

The defiant self refuses to understand itself as derived from an other, God. It prefers, falsely, to imagine itself as ". . .its own master, absolutely its own master."[187] The defiant sinner usurps the place of God, for "In despair the self want to enjoy the total satisfaction of making itself into itself, of developing itself, of being itself; it wants to have the honor of this poetic, masterly construction, the way it has understood itself."[188] The defiant sinner, however, is self-deceived. From the religious point of view, the belief that one is sufficient to constitute oneself as a self, the belief that one can evaluate and understand oneself as a self according to self-regarding criteria in preference to the God-criterion, is a false belief that one has willed to believe as true. Such a self "constantly relates itself to itself only by way of imaginary constructions," and its despair is that it is "always building castles in the air" and "shadowboxing"; and as Anti-Climacus says, "[The] self in despair is satisfied with paying attention to itself, which is supposed to bestow infinite interest and significance upon his enterprises, but it is precisely this that makes them imaginary constructions."[189]

The self in despair makes of itself an "imaginatively constructed god" and rather than becoming an actual or concrete self, the self in despair is like a king without a country, a "hypothetical self" that is constituted by the illusion of sovereignty.[190] The despairing self does not understand itself as it is, as it is derived from God, and this misunderstanding appears to be ignorance and error. It is true that the despairing self may be unaware of its despair, but even so, its condition of "sickness unto death" is to be traced not to ignorance per se but in the will-to-ignorance. Sin is a problem of the will even if ignorance is the apparent result; though according to Anti-Climacus, ignorance of one's condition of despair "can in fact be the most dangerous form of despair":

> An individual is furthest from being conscious of himself as spirit when he is ignorant of being in despair. But precisely this--not to be conscious of oneself as spirit--is despair, which is spiritlessness, whether the state is a thoroughgoing morbidity, a merely vegetative life, or an intense, energetic life, the secret of which is still despair. In the latter case, the individual in despair is like the consumptive: when the illness is most critical, he feels well, considers himself

to be in excellent health, and perhaps seems to others to radiate health.[191]

The problem, however, is that this individual who falls ill with the "sickness unto death" is gripped by despair even as he or she seeks to evade by various interpretive maneuvers awareness of that fact. The person is in despair yet unaware that it is a condition of despair. Such a person keeps the truth at bay and wills to keep him- or herself ignorant of the illness. That this ignorance is willed Anti-Climacus assumes, for he declares that "despair of the eternal is impossible without having a conception of the self, that there is something eternal in it," which one is free to misuse or even to lose.[192] But when an individual loses the eternal and therefore the self by rejecting the eternal possibility, the self ". . .does not wish, so to speak, to hear anything about itself, does not itself know anything to say," ". . . does not want to acknowledge itself. . . ."[193] Such despair is not an involuntary happening for which one can disavow in all honesty all responsibility. Such despair is not merely something one suffers--though suffer it one does; for this ignorance, this despair is an act[194] for which each individual is responsible.[195] No one loses one's self but that he or she perversely wants to. One loses one's self when one prefers something finite, something reassuring and apparently devoid of anxiety producing effects, to the task of becoming a self. The task of selfhood, after all, requires self-consciousness and the courage to accept oneself as one is "before God," in complete honesty, with no thought of trying to deceive God. <u>Despair is how one exists in freedom without God</u>. It is a willful misuse of freedom that leads to despair, and it is a willful ignorance that obtains from despair, since despair is a denial of one's true being. It is a refusal to be the self one could be.

Despair is thus an instance of theological self-deception, for in despair one refuses God and thereby chooses ignorance about oneself. It is an ignorance about oneself that obtains through a voluntary act of denial. This denial is a refusal to admit that help is available to overcome the despair from the God for whom all things are possible. Anti-Climacus writes of the theological self-deceiver, "every human existence that is not conscious of itself as spirit or conscious of itself before God as spirit. . .is despair."[196] And despair is the act whereby one makes oneself unconscious of who one is before God: "[All] despair. . .is conscious, but this does not mean that the person who may appropriately be said to be in despair is conscious of it himself."[197] Despair, then, which is "misrelation in the relation of a synthesis that relates itself to itself,"[198] the misrelation "between the temporal and the eternal, of which [human] nature is composed,"[199] is the misrelation, which, before God, identifies sin. The sin is despair, and the despair entails the description that permits one to say that the sinner is also a self-deceiver. The theological self-deceiver has deceived him- or herself into believing that the self can decide about the highest good of life, happiness and true well-being by criteria it establishes, by criteria it decides are superior to the God-criterion. A sinner despairs, that is, by choosing itself in preference to that which would dissipate despair, faith. Faith, not virtue, is the antidote to the "sickness unto death." It is faith that Anti-Climacus describes as the self-relation that wills to be itself in truth, that wills to be itself by accepting the help offered by God. In the end, the self that is able to accept itself in truth by choosing not to make of itself a god is a self capable of overcoming despair by choosing to rest transparently in the Power which established it, God.

From the theological perspective, the will to be oneself is a lie if God is not party to the self-relation, which is to say that the effort to constitute oneself without God is not only despair but deception. This deception is apparent in Anti-Climacus' assumption that persons are capable of making themselves opaque to their own consciousness and capable of despair; for not just anyone can achieve despair, but only those who have chosen themselves as qualified by spirit, which assumes a person's prior awareness of the eternal. Anti-Climacus holds that human persons are conflicted and capable of evading the truth. They can resist the offer of assistance offered by God. Accordingly, any resistance to the truth that with God all things are possible--even the overcoming of the disrelationship that is despair--is itself despair, and one feature of that despair is that persons who resist God also makes themselves ignorant of their eternal possibility--existence "before God" in truth. This ignorance is no simple error, but a willed and voluntary choosing that leads to error, and it is to be viewed as the act of theological self-deception.

Kierkegaard's edifying discourse, Purity of Heart, is a meditation on repentance and the office of confession. The purity of heart required to "will the one thing necessary" for relating oneself to the Good, is the solution to the problem of multiplicity--the divided mind, the two wills, and the double-mindedness that obstructs one's relation to the Eternal. This volume is a religious reflection that urges its readers to confront themselves honestly and thereby come into relation with the Eternal. One who would stand before God must "be at one with oneself,"[200] since ". . .one cannot confess without this at-oneness with oneself."[201] One cannot, in other words, stand before God in a condition of double-mindedness, which is the description of the psychological state that accompanies despair, the despair of being divided against oneself within oneself (intrapsychically). In Purity of Heart, Kierkegaard elucidates the condition of intrapsychic conflict as it pertains to and affects the God-relation. His analysis, in a nutshell, is that if one be double-minded one is in despair, and, being double-minded and in despair signifies the misrelationship that obtains with respect to one's self-relation and one's possible relation to God. For Kierkegaard, relation to God relies entirely on one's ability to be honest with oneself (i.e., ability to confess), and self-honesty itself expresses the singleness of mind, will, and purpose that is necessary for overcoming self-deception. This edifying discourse took confession as its theme because confession is a form of self-confrontation; and self-confrontation is required for any individual who would seek the single-mindedness that eliminates sin, despair and self-deception.

Kierkegaard's point, then, was that a lack of faith, which identifies the misrelation of despair, is double-mindedness, and double-mindedness is misrelationship to God. To be in despair is to lack the purity of heart to will the one thing necessary to save one from the despair that robs one not only of the God-relation but of the possibility of acquiring a true and actual self. This discourse argues that true selfhood is acquired "before God" and only by means of the faith that the possibility for a God-relation exists pro-me. Double-mindedness refers to the condition--and to the cognitive capacity as it is affected by will--of being in dynamic conflict with oneself. The opposition of a mind divided against itself, of two wills each seeking to satisfy opposing desires, is the Kierkegaardian picture of the fragmented self in conflict with itself yearning for reunion and of the opaque consciousness anxious to acquire the transparency that will permit it to ground itself in the truth. The picture of the self and consciousness so aptly portrayed in Purity of Heart--and this picture is consistent with that put forward by psychologists of the stature of Freud and Sartre, as well as the by all the other religious thinkers mentioned in this chapter--has served as the normative view throughout this study.

The double-minded person, according to Kierkegaard, is one who has the psychological capacity to maneuver an operative and willed self-understanding such that it conforms to a desired self-image, thereby making it possible for one to avoid making linguistically explicit a truth or belief one "unconsciously" avows. An epistemic deficit is exposed. That deficit obtains between an explicit avowal that expresses one's wishes and one's desired self-image, which is manifest in self-interpretive activity, and a contrary avowal that is enacted though explicitly denied ("unconscious"). To be double-minded, then, is to be willing to deceive oneself into believing that one is, in truth, before God, what one is not, for the self that deceives itself will, in despair, excuse itself from the requirement that it confront itself honestly. The self that deceives itself will opt for a self-understanding more in keeping with the self it wants to be. The self-deceiver lacks nerve as well as will, for he or she retreats in cowardice before the challenge of self-recognition. The double-minded self chooses "that deceptive ignorance about itself because. . .it has forgotten the Eternal."[202] To serve anything but the Good (the one thing) to which conscience inclines one, is to engage one's passion such that one serves not the truth but the "deluded master" of oneself. Theologically speaking, this "deluded master" refuses to be related to itself in truth, Kierkegaard's normative religious understanding being that one is only related to oneself in truth by virtue of being related to God whence the true self is derived. The double-minded person is misrelated to

God because he or she is distracted by the multiplicity of finitude and therefore does not will the Good single-mindedly. The result is the despair of concentrating on the temporal or of using the eternal for reason of intellectual interest (the idea of God). In either case, the double-minded person exhibits a lack of self-understanding and denies being qualified by the Eternal, and, since this is an "ignorance" which is chosen, it is self-deception that is being described:

> There is an ignorance about one's own life that is equally tragic for the learned and the simple, for both are bound by the same responsibility. This ignorance is called self-deceit. . .[and] there is only one thing that can remove that ignorance which is self-deception. And to be ignorant of the fact that there is one thing and only one thing, and that only one thing is necessary, is still to be in self-deception.[203]

Kierkegaard's theological self-deceiver holds contradictory beliefs simultaneously and suppresses one of those beliefs for reasons of psychological gain. And although he puts the concept to work in a context of religious meaning and value, Kierkegaard describes and evaluates the "volitional/cognitive" phenomenon of 'self-deception' as it appeals to the language of the common life. Self-deception, then, refers to the refusal of a person to acquire self-understanding before God, to grasp the human need for God, to perceive the God-relation as the highest good, the Good perceived by the eternal aspect of the self (conscience). Because the particular form of resistance, denial and excusing is analyzed within the context of the God-relation, what is described in <u>Purity of Heart</u> is theological self-deception.

Because theological self-deceivers act to evade the Eternal, they fail to walk the path of self-recognition before God, thereby evading the only way to true salvation.[204] The divided and conflicted state of double-mindedness obtains because something other than the Eternal is preferred, and that something is temporal and finite. Kierkegaard's case is that we deceive ourselves in the religious domain because we fail to exhibit the purity of heart that will not be distracted by the interests, busyness, pride and evasions of finitude: "All double-mindedness has its ground in and is marked by the double-minded one's unwillingness to let go of the things of this world."[205] The willful refusal to allow the Eternal to heal one's condition of fragmentation, contradiction and despair springs from a desire to resist the truth that God is the one thing necessary: "The double-minded one wishes to be healed and yet does not wish to be healed: eternally he does not wish to be healed."[206] The double-minded one does not want to submit to the cure of purity of heart, though the cure promises to unify the fragmented self and render one's consciousness transparent before God.

Being in despair, double-minded persons refuse the God-relation, deceiving themselves about what is necessary for self-synthesis and for true relation to the appropriate object of ultimate concern. The theological self-deceiver relies not on God but on the self--and so doing loses the self. Such a person believes what deep down he or she knows is not true and lacks the courage to face the truth of human being. Preferring not to see the self as it is, the self-deceiver maneuvers him- or herself in order not to see at all. The theological self-deceiver prefers a cover story of self-assertion to the real story--which is that one is not, in fact, what one would like to be.

On Kierkegaard's analysis, the double-minded person is unwilling to surrender the afflicted self to the cure of the God-relation either due to a weakness or a strength, both of which are despair. In either case, the sinner/self-deceiver exhibits the two wills of the double-minded, the two wills whereby one wants to follow, yet avoids following, the pathway to the Eternal. The Eternal is that to "which a man's life ought to be" related,[207] yet, because such a person is in despair, he or she does not do so, preferring to maintain the psychologically appeasing cover story that is, in weakness or strength, despair. Echoing Anti-Climacus, Kierkegaard writes that in despair are ". . .met the cowardly timorous ill-temper of self-love, and the proud defiant presumption of the mind," and before God these ". . .are met in equal impotence."[208]

'Double-mindedness' refers to the intrapsychic conflict that is willed by the individual and for which the individual is responsible. By appealing to double-mindedness, Kierkegaard is able to portray dynamic self-relatedness. His analysis of double-mindedness reveals that this is the condition of one who is without God by virtue of a decision not to enter relation with God. Double-mindedness is despair,[209] and the double-minded person is in a state of profound disrelation, both with God and with his or her own self. The double-minded person lacks equilibrium in the synthesis of selfhood; for the self is divided against itself and consciousness lacks transparency and wills its own obscurity. Double-mindedness permits Kierkegaard to portray the state of willful ignorance that obtains for the theological self--the self that stands "before God". His case is that the self that seeks one thing, but finds it elsewhere than in the God-relation is a self that only pretends to will the Good.[210] That something other than God, which induces one to deny God as one's highest good, constitutes "a horrible falsehood. Only through a lie is it one thing."[211] That lie aims at God, but because God cannot be lied to, it eventuates in the only kind of deception that can obtain in the religious sphere--self-deception.

Kierkegaard's analysis of self-deception is neither simple-minded in conception nor presented in its details lacking sophistication. There is, for example, an interesting correlation between certain of Kierkegaard's remarks about the phenomenon of self-deception and certain descriptions of the same concept as presented by modern psychologists, particularly with respect to the phenomenon of perceptual avoidance. This correlation can be seen by comparing Kierkegaard's account of "busyness" with Gardner Murphy's account of "busy work," the avoidance behavior that indicates a "seeing without really looking." In certain of Murphy's experiments, it was observed that subjects "see and don't see" simultaneously. That is, subjects avoid recognizing something they perceive in the perceptual field because recognition avoidance relieves psychic distress. Disturbing pictures were presented to experimental subjects with the result that ". . .people manage to carry out free scanning while actually avoiding what they do not want to see."[212] Murphy himself participated in some of these experiments. After viewing a gruesome painting of the martyrdom of St. Sebastian, he reported an experience of self-deception:

> What is important about my own self-deception is that I managed to see almost nothing of the stressful situation. My eye movements in other directions were quite free, with a good sweep, as long as I did not look at troubled areas. Later on, when I was asked to recall the picture, my eyes showed another curious device, which was to jig around; that is to say, to do a lot of "busy work" with my eyes, without really looking, introducing noise into the system.[213]

Kierkegaard, the psychologist, had discussed the same kind of phenomenon a century earlier in much the same language. Having noted the fact of sense deception, the kind in which one allows one's senses to deceive one, Kierkegaard wrote that

> the press of busyness into which one steadily slips further and further, and the noise in which the truth continually slips more and more into oblivion, and the mass of connections, stimuli, and hindrances, these make it even more impossible for one to win any deeper knowledge of himself.[214]

The format of a theological meditation proved no hindrance to Kierkegaard as he discussed self-deception in the same terms as a modern experimental psychologist. Yet his aim was to push the analysis of the phenomenon into other contexts of meaning--even into the religious context beyond the scientific, while not overlooking the need to observe and report accurately the behavior of human persons. The religious meaning of self-deception was different from the kind of sense deception referred to in Murphy's study, but only inasmuch as the <u>object</u> in relation to which the self-deception obtained was different. We can locate that difference not in the meaning of the literal expression, 'self-deception,' but in the context of meaning where the concept was put to work. The difference can be traced to the relational context that governs the concept's use. Whether those relations pertain to self-relatedness, other-relatedness, or God-relatedness, the concept at issue, 'self-deception,' refers to a phenomenon of human behavior, a phenomenon in which one simultaneously sees and does not see, believes and does not believe, for certain reasons. Whatever the relational context at issue, the concept 'self-deception' is put to work to refer to the phenomenon of behavior in which we say one is disposed to act--and does act--"without knowing what he is doing." The Kierkegaard literature provides a remarkable guide to the meaning of self-deception--not only because Kierkegaard uses the concept in a way that conforms to our ordinary language understanding of the term, but because he is able to employ the concept in different relational contexts, thereby elucidating the concept such that the "intimate acquaintance" we have been seeking can be acquired.

One last general point about Kierkegaard's method of presentation. Kierkegaard, as I have said, describes instances of self-deception in his literature by creating characters who exemplify the self-deceiver's art. No better place is available to see this "truth-by-description" borne out than in the volume Either/Or. Both the Aesthete and the Judge, each of whom represents a particular viewpoint on existence and each of whom is constituted by commitments made within a particular sphere of existence (aestheticism, ethicality), are self-deceived. Both the Aesthete and the Judge are concerned to constitute themselves according to ideals that cannot possibly be achieved in existence. The ideals of existence which each exemplifies lead ineluctably to despair--and betray the exemplar's self-deception.

The Aesthete, for example, holds up Don Juan as the ideal of aestheticism. Don Juan represents the pure immediacy of the non-reflective self, an ideal that could not possibly exist in human consciousness. Don Juan is only able to express himself musically, for his consciousness is so unreflective that even language is unavailable to him. The Aesthete admires Don Juan, but he attempts what Don Juan could not conceive of doing. The Aesthete attempts to achieve the aesthetic ideal through language and by reflection, and this contradicts the immediacy and the musicality of pure Don Juan aestheticism. In other words, the Aesthete attempts to create--and live--and existential impossibility. Reflection, which is the Aesthete's aesthetic medium, pushes the Aesthete toward ethicality. Reflection is that which makes ethicality possible, so that the Aesthete's continual striving to make of reflection a source of immediacy continually brings him up short. He continually contradicts himself by attempting to make reflection a means of access to immediacy. He despairs and tries to take delight in that. In the end, his aesthetic project consists of an effort to fashion a work of art out of his despair. By the end of the first volume, however, the Aesthete is mysteriously troubled. His reading of Diary of a Seducer provides an occasion for reflection, and he experiences a sort of self-confrontation wherein conscience urges him to constitute himself in the honesty of self-reflection. He is, in fact, urging himself to become an ethical self. We do not follow the Aesthete beyond his uneasiness. We leave him short of decision: he can either opt to reflect himself back into immediacy, which is a contradictory notion, or he can "leap" into ethicality. What he does, we do not know. What we know is that his ideal of immediacy is maintained only by extraordinary reflective and linguistic maneuvers, and we realize, as readers, that his immediacy is a deceitful ploy that exemplifies self-deception.

So skilled at befuddling himself is this Aesthete that he even toys with the idea of consciously deceiving himself. That is, he tries at one point to reflect himself into the dynamics of the self-deception process to observe it mechanics; for the idea of deceiving oneself presents an aesthetic challenge in that the Aesthete would have to control, in a linguistically explicit way, the process of forgetting. This is the "art of forgetting" that would constitute the highest artistic achievement for reflective immediacy. He writes:

> The unpleasant has a sting, as all admit. This, too can be removed by the art of forgetting. But if one attempts to dismiss the unpleasant absolutely from mind, as many do who dabble in the art of forgetting, one soon learns how little that helps. In an unguarded moment it pays a surprise visit, and it is then invested with all the forcibleness of the unexpected. This is absolutely contrary to every orderly arrangement in a reasonable mind. No misfortune or difficulty is so devoid of affability, so deaf to all appeals, but that it may be flattered a little; even Cerebrus accepted bribes of honey-cakes, and it is not only the lassies who are beguiled. The art in dealing with such experiences consists in talking them over, thereby depriving them of the bitterness; not forgetting them absolutely, but forgetting them for the sake of remembering them. Even in the case of memories such that one might suppose an eternal oblivion to be the only safeguard, one need permit oneself only a little trickery, and the deception will succeed for the skillful. Forgetting is the shears with which you cut away what you cannot use, doing it under the supreme direction of memory. Forgetting and remembering are thus identical arts, and the artistic achievement of this identity is the Archimedian point from which one lifts the whole world. When we say that we consign something to oblivion, we suggest simultaneously that it is to be forgotten and yet also remembered.²¹⁵

The Aesthete's analysis is astute, but his confidence in his own mnemonic ability to carry out such a project is certainly misplaced. He can entertain the notion of being in control of his own forgetting as one who is transparent to himself in immediacy; but this is only an aesthetic ideal--another source of reflective entertainment--and it cannot be realized through reflection. He cannot do this in existence. In Freudian terms, he cannot decide to undertake a project in which he consciously censors himself, as if he could control the repression process under the supreme control of memory, doing so because his consciousness is transparent to itself and nothing can really be hidden. In this passage, the Aesthete deceives himself about his ability to deceive himself, for he assumes a transparent consciousness--and it is precisely a transparent consciousness he lacks. Persons do not decide in a self-reflective way to act in bad faith; nor do they become neurotic by a conscious, linguistically explicit, decision. Self-deception obtains as the result of certain dynamics of selfhood, and it is only when persons act for reasons of psychological gains to keep themselves from awareness that there is present, properly speaking, self-deception.

Don Juan <u>cannot</u> deceive himself. Being pure immediacy, he lacks the reflective capability to mislead himself into believing what deep down he knows is not true. The Aesthete, on the other hand, deceives himself about his reflective capability. He analyzes brilliantly, and even finds in 'self-deception' a logical puzzle of enormous aesthetic challenge. His assumption, which is mistaken, is that one can acquire transparency of consciousness by thinking one's way to transparency. What he fails to realize, what is obscure to his own consciousness, is the fact that he cannot achieve in existence the transparency he imagines in thought. We cannot come to immediacy by reflection; neither can we reflect ourselves into pre-reflection. This is all borne out by the fact that by the end of the volume, conscience, which is the harbinger of the Eternal, has awakened in the Aesthete. He verges on realizing the contradiction of his own existence, for he experiences the anxiety of one about to confront the futility of pretending that immediacy can be acquired by reflection. He is anxiously aware of his despair in a new way--not as a source of pleasure or entertainment, but as a qualification of spirit. The Aesthete is left to consider his contradiction is left on the verge of madness. Should he decide to reflect himself back into aestheticism, his decision to do so will itself be an act inconsistent with trying to live pre-ethically. He will then involve himself in another instance of self-deception; for being on the verge of realizing that he, too, is a potential self, he confronts reflectively that he, too, is constituted as spirit and is free to misuse his freedom. He nears the realization that he is even free to choose despair, and has, in fact, chosen it.

The Judge, author of the second volume of <u>Either/Or</u>, is aware of this contradiction in the Aesthete's existential plight. That is why he is able to say to the Aesthete, ". . .you enjoy deluding yourself and others,"[216] and "you are always afraid of continuity, principally for the reason that it deprives you of the opportunity of deceiving yourself."[217] "Your intent perhaps, is to deceive others, and yet there is a moment when without being aware of it you deceive yourself."[218] From the Judge's ethical point of view, from the point of view of one who has chosen himself in light of the universal, the Aesthete's entire existence is an elaborate "cover story," a tissue of lies in which the Aesthete has become ensnared by his own reflection. The Judge sees that the Aesthete has trapped himself by seeking an ideal of immediacy that is forever the source of anxiety for the awakening individual. But just as the Aesthete cannot attain the aesthetic ideal, neither can the Judge attain the ethical ideal--moral perfection. He, too, is self-deceived. He, too, has engaged in a belief-misleading project directed by and at his own self. He, too, will fail to meet his ideal in existence, for he mistakenly believes that he can acquire "eternal validity" by assuming total, absolute responsibility for himself. The Judge, in other words, also imagines an ideal of existence and measures himself against it. Rather smugly, he assumes that he has realized that ideal--at least to the extent any responsible and conscientious person can realize it. There are cracks in his idealistic edifice for his existence reflects profound moral failure. He quarrels with his wife though he idealizes her, and he idealizes the ethical context of his marriage by saying of his wife, "She is never tired and yet never inactive, [my] absolute refuge."[219] Only a self-deceiver would idealize this way, claiming that the ethical ideal has been actually attained, that one has oneself attained it.

It is the sermon at the end of the volume, a sermon written by an old friend of the Judge's, that brings the Judge to a state of disquiet. The effect of the sermon is to disrupt his ethical self-confidence. Just as the editor of Either/Or, Victor Eremeta, has the first--and last--word on the possibility of an aesthetic existence: "A single, coherent aesthetic view of life can scarcely be carried out,"[220] so, too, the Priest writes in earnest that moral striving is bound to lead to despair. The Priest, who speaks on behalf of the religious possibility, declares in his sermon that all moral striving falls short of perfection, and that before God, who is the possibility of perfection made actual, "we are always in the wrong." For the Priest, the reality of moral perfection eludes human ability. One cannot acquire it, though through theistic faith, only because God is gracious enough to bestow forgiveness, a person can be right-wised with that which is morally perfect and not be condemned by it (God). Louis Mackey has written the following about this sermon:

> Kierkegaard's priest suggests that dogged persistence in an ethical way of life will bring a man to the point where he must either choose to acknowledge himself absolutely in the wrong or lose himself in a maze of casuistries. If he does not reach this point he deceives himself and shortchanges his principles.[221]

The Judge, therefore, is left standing in much the same place, though in a different context, as the Aesthete. He, too, must decide. He, too, must push his reflection to the point of self-confrontation, to the point of painful self-recognition. That he is sobered by the thought that before God we are <u>always in the wrong</u> is hinted at, but not explicitly stated. <u>Either/Or</u> was not written to make decisions, only to explore the possibilities and invite reflection. As we turn our attention from Kierkegaard, it is worth noting again that despair attends the aesthetic and ethical spheres of existence, that his despair is, in the context of the God-relation, not only sin, but sin that entails self-deception.

Can the person who makes the movement of faith be deceived by the act of faith? Kierkegaard is quite explicit about this. His answer is "No." For

Kierkegaard, faith is the basis for true self-understanding, and true self-understanding is the basis for faith. This is the Kierkegaard who accepts the premise of the religious sphere, who accepts the God-relation for all reflection and for whom the God-relation is the final criterion of Truth. In faith, we are, Kierkegaard says, able to acknowledge ourselves as being in need of God, and recognizing this need is the basis for considering the God-relation as a possibility pro me. The possibility of the God-relation is the condition necessary for making the movement of faith, relating oneself to oneself in such a way that one grounds oneself transparently in the Power whence one is, as a self, derived. By making this movement, one becomes a self, the spirit that one truly is before God. For Kierkegaard it is though faith that one becomes a unified self, a consciousness purified of clever evasions and rationalizations. In faith, one no longer retreats from self-confrontation or self-awareness. One acquires, rather, a consciousness that is transparent to itself. One is made able, by faith, to see through oneself to God. One's blindness is healed and sight is restored. One sees what has always been there to see, for one recognizes the truth about God in light of the truth about oneself. Faith is the highest form of self-consciousness, the true at-oneness of selfhood, which, as Kierkegaard will say in Works of Love, is the noblest expression of human being, the true pride of human being that obtains as the result of humility, self-surrender and openness to God: ". . .for humility before God is genuine pride."[222]

Faith, then, is the remedy for despair. It is the movement toward relationship and reunification that expresses one's passion for true relationship, true unity, true transparency. One can only stand before God in truth with God. One can only acquire truth by realizing that God will not be fooled by human pride, arrogance or by one's desire to be what one is not--God's equal. God is not deceived. Any attempt to create an epistemic deficit between oneself and God is doomed to failure, doomed to boomerang on oneself. Before God, one's deceptive acts are only self-evasions. Before God, one only deceives oneself.

Kierkegaard's last word on the topic of self-deception is a word of hope--that self-deception can be avoided and overcome. This too is a possibility for human subjects, a possibility that counteracts the tendency to cynicism or despair that is likely to befall one who considers the pervasiveness of self-deception, the fact of self-deception in the common life. Self-deception is a problem of disrelationship that can be overcome by becoming self-conscious to the point of becoming God-conscious. Self-deception can be overcome by acquiring the God-relation, by relating oneself to oneself in truth, before God. According to the fascinating logic of faith, the God-relation precludes the very possibility of self-deception. For Kierkegaard, the faith that enables one to enter into partnership with God by grace also offers the only sure strategy for avoiding self-deception. Unflinching in his effort to urge his readers into self-confrontation, Kierkegaard makes his claim that faith dispels self-deception with characteristic boldness:

> So, my listener, turn your attention now to the occasion, while consciousness of sin sharpens the need until it becomes the one thing necessary; while the earnestness of this holy place strengthens the will in holy determination, while the all-knowing One's presence makes self-deception impossible, consider your own life.²²³

CHAPTER THREE

[1] Even those philosophers who sort out methodological issues in philosophical psychology note that self-deception is a particularly difficult concept that may challenge broader schemes of interpretation. See, for example, Paul Grice, "Method in Philosophical Psychology (From the Banal to the Bizarre)," Proceedings and Addresses of the American Philosophical Association XLVIII (1974-75), p. 48.

[2] On Sartre's view of consciousness, there is no ego-logical structure ("I" or "me") except as a thingified pseudo-object and no self-knowledge; and this is a view I find counter-intuitive. For an argument against Sartre on this point, see Phyllis B. Kenevan, "Self-consciousness and the Ego," in ed. Paul A. Schlipp,, The Philosophy of Jean-Paul Sartre, pp. 197-210.

[3] Catherine Wilson, "Self-Deception and Psychological Realism," Philosophical Investigations 3, 4 (Fall 1980), p. 57.

[4] Abelson, Persons, pp. 106-109. See also, Wilson, ibid., p. 48; and Donald Davidson, "How is Weakness of the Will Possible?" in Essays on Actions and Events, p. 42; and the several writing of Amelie O. Rorty that deal with akrasia.

[5] Plato, Protagoras, trans. W. K. C. Guthrie, in Plato: The Complete Dialogues, eds. Hamilton and Cairnes, pp. 343-349.

[6] Gwynneth Matthews, "Weakness of Will," in Weakness of Will, ed. G. W. Mortimore, (London & Basingstoke: Macmillan & Co., 1971), pp. 162-65.

[7] Davidson, "How is Weakness of the Will Possible?", p. 21.

[8] Abelson, Persons, pp. 106-109.

[9] R. M. Hare, Freedom and Reason, p. 67-85. Hare, too, draws a distinction between self-deception and akrasia. See his discussion of "backsliding" in The Language of Morals (New York: Oxford University Press, 1973), pp. 19-20, 168-70; and Moral Thinking: Its Levels, Method and Point (Oxford University Press, 1981), pp. 157-60. Hare is discussed at length in Weakness of Will, ed. Mortimer, pp. 97-176.

[10] In arguing that every instance of akrasia is irrational, Davidson has also argued that not every instance is necessarily immoral. See Davidson, "How is Weakness of the Will Possible?", p. 41. Amelie Rorty has argued that the best course of action available to a person may not necessarily be morally best; neither is it necessarily "irrational" from a prudential point of view: "by the agent's criteria of prudential rationality--his criteria of benefit-- the akratic alternative need not itself be irrational: it can violate his conception of what is most important and best, without violating his conception of what is either morally of prudentially beneficial" in "Where Does the Akratic Break Take Place?", Australasian Journal of Philosophy 58, 94 (December 1980), p. 337. I would remind my reader that my aim here is simply to show that a conceptual distinction can be made between akrasia and self-deception.

[11] See annotations to Romans 7.14-23 in the New Oxford Annotated Bible (New York: Oxford University Press, 1973), p. 1368. R. M. Hare used this

passage to illustrate "backsliding" in Freedom and Reason, pp. 78-79.

[12] Amelie O. Rorty, "Self-deception, Akrasia, and Irrationality," p. 917: "[there] can be overwhelming behavioral evidence that he recognizes what he denies. Of course that evidence will not have the force of certainty; but ascriptions of behavioral self-deception are no more unsound than are attributions of psychological states in opaque contexts generally are."

[13] Ibid.

[14] Aristotle, Nicomachean Ethics, vii (1150b), p. 1049.

[15] Rorty, "Self-Deception, Akrasia, and Irrationality," p. 918. See also Rorty, "Where Does the Akratic Break Take Place?", pp. 333-46, for further developments.

[16] The "duplex character" of the ethical self--the ideal versus the actual self--is discussed at length in Kierkegaard's portrayal of ethical consciousness in the second volume of Either/Or, trans. Walter Lowrie (Princeton: Princeton University Press, 1944, 1971), pp. 263-70.

[17] Ibid, p. 269.

[18] Certain Biblical commentators see the significance of Paul's claim that he does not understand or know (gnosco) his own actions as issuing in a larger, more fundamental question. Gerald Cragg's exposition of this text considers the meaning of this "ignorance" claim to be that "Man is an enigma to himself" in The Interpreter's Bible, Vol. IX (Nashville: Abingdon, 1954), p. 501. And Karl Barth writes in The Epistle to the Romans, 6th ed., trans Edwyn C. Hoskins (Oxford: Oxford University Press, 1933), p. 265: "And so the question arises once again: Who then am I? I am he that wills and he that does not perform: I am intolerably both at once. When my will is most steadfast, it does but remind me that the good is--not in me."

[19] In Romans 7.25 and 8.1-4, St. Paul adopts a religious solution. The solution has to be religious because the ethical resource has exhausted itself with despair. Paul seeks a solution that changes one's fundamental ontological grounding from being non posse non peccare to a "new creation" where one is "in Christ" non posse peccare, which is what Christ has made possible. For the Christian believer, Christ, through grace, opens up the ontological possibility of our not sinning. See Augustine's On Nature and Grace, chapter 49 in Saint Augustine: Anti-Pelagian Writings, Vol. 5, in Nicene and Post-Nicene Fathers (Grand Rapids: Wm. B. Eerdemans Publishing, 1975), p. 138.

[20] See Rorty, "Where Does the Akratic Break Take Place?", pp. 339-40, for a discussion of "akratic belief."

[21] Certain philosophers who hold that akrasia is not equivalent to self-deception disagree with each other on particulars: See Davidson, "How is Weakness of the Will Possible?", p. 42, and his opponent, Abelson, Persons, pp. 108-109; and Hare, Freedom and Reason, p. 83, and his opponent, Steven Lukes, "Moral Weakness," in Weakness of Will, ed. Mortimore, p. 154.

[22] Kurt Baier, for instance, argues for the supremacy of moral reasons in The Moral Point of View: A Rational Basis of Ethics, abridged ed., (New York:

Random House, 1966), pp. 148 ff., even though David A. J. Richards points out in A Theory of Reasons for Action, pp. 77-78, that Baier's appeal is ultimately prudential. One could always argue that moral reasons are overriding for essentially prudential reasons, as Hobbes did.

[23]It is on the "character" issue that Aristotle's picture of akrasia differed from Socrates. For an illuminating discussion see Rorty, "Akrasia and Pleasure: Nicomachean Ethics Book 7," in ed. Rorty, Essays on Aristotle's Ethics, pp. 267-284.

[24]J. W. N. Watkins, "Comment: 'Self-Interest and Morality,'" in Practical Reason, ed. Stephan Korner, (New Haven: Yale University Press, 1974), p. 74.

[25]John King-Farlow, "Akrasia, Self-Mastery and the Master Self," Pacific Philosophical Quarterly 62 (January 1981), p. 58.

[26]See, for example, Roderick Chisholm, "Practical Reason and the Logic of Requirement," esp. p. 16; G. E. M. Anscombe's "Comment," esp. p. 20; Chisholm's rejoinder, "Reply to Comments," p. 42, in ed. Korner, Practical Reason.

[27]One could say of akrasia what D. W. Hamlyn has said of Haight's description of self-deception: ". . .if 'self-deception' is a contradictory notion there can be no facts about self-deception." See Hamlyn's "Review" in The Philosophical Quarterly 32, no. 127 (April 1982), p. 184.

[28]See the section on the "Socratic Paradox" in Weakness of Will, G.W. Mortimer, ed., esp, pp. 37-62. See also section 439A-441C in Plato's Republic; and for a helpful clarification of want and desire as they pertain to the motive for action in the Socratic context see Raphael Demos, "What is It that I Want?", Ethics 55, 3 (April 1945), pp. 182-95.

[29]Aristotle, Nicomachean Ethics (1145b 25-28), p. 1038.

[30]Davidson, "How is Weakness of the Will Possible?", p. 41.

[31]Kierkegaard, Either/Or, Vol. II, pp. 261-62.

[32]A. E. Taylor, Socrates: The Man and His Thought (New York: Doubleday Anchor Books, 1953), pp. 141-42, 143.

[33]Eduard Zeller also interprets this ignorance as self-deception in his Outlines of the History of Greek Philosophy, trans. R. L. Palmer (Cleveland: World Publishing Co., 1965), p. 119.

[34]See discussion, "The Socratic Definition of Sin," in Søren Kierkegaard, The Sickness Unto Death, ed. and trans. Howard V. and Edna H. Hong (Princeton: Princeton University Press, 1980), pp. 87-96.

[35]E. J. Lemmon, "Moral Dilemma," Philosophical Review LXXI, 2 (April 1962), pp. 144-45. Lemmon also writes that "there are not logical barriers to the existence of self-deception" (p. 148).

[36]Gregory Vlastos, "The Paradox of Socrates," in The Philosophy of Socrates: A Collection of Critical Essays, ed. Gregory Vlastos, (Garden City:

Doubleday & Co., Anchor Books, 1971), p. 1.

[37] Ibid., p. 16.

[38] Edgar Allen Poe, "The Black Cat," in The Complete Tales and Poems of Edgar Allen Poe (New York: Modern Library, 1938), 224-25.

[39] On "radical evil" see Immanuel Kant, Religion Within the Limits of Reason Alone, trans. Theodore M. Greene and Hoyt H. Hudson (New York: Harper & Row, Harper Torchbook, 1960), pp. 23-34.

[40] Kierkegaard, The Sickness Unto Death, pp. 94-95.

[41] Ibid., p. 93.

[42] Ibid., pp. 88-89.

[43] Ibid., p. 96.

[44] Ibid., p. 89.

[45] Abelson, Persons, pp. 108-109.

[46] Bela Szabados, "The Morality of Self-Deception," Dialogue (Canada) 13,1 (March 1974), p. 25.

[47] M. W. Martin, "Immorality and Self-Deception (A Reply to Bela Szabados)," Dialogue (Canada) 16, 2 (June 1977), pp. 274-280.

[48] Onora Nell, Acting on Principle: An Essay on Kantian Ethics (New York: Columbia University Press, 1975), p. 124. See Nell's discussion of "inappropriate maxims" of which self-deception provides the most problematic and prominent example.

[49] R. G. Collingwood, The Principles of Art (London: Oxford University Press, 1938, 1972), pp. 219-220. Collingwood is mentioned as an "always immoral" proponent by M. W. Martin, "Immorality and Self-Deception," p. 280.

[50] Fingarette, Self-Deception, p. 137.

[51] Ibid., p. 140.

[52] Sigmund Freud, The Future of an Illusion, trans. James Strachey (New York: W. W. Norton & Co., 1961), p. 10.

[53] Freud, "Moral Responsibility for the Content of Dreams," p. 223-226.

[54] Freud, "One of the Difficulties of Psychoanalysis," p. 188.

[55] Rieff, recall, subtitled his study, "The Mind of the Moralist."

[56] Freud, The Future of an Illusion, p. 7.

[57] Ibid., p. 49.

[58] Fingarette, Self-Deception, p. 143.

[59] It is significant that both James and Chisholm refrain from challenging Clifford's moral conclusion in this example. Each challenges a particular principle inferred from Clifford's discussion of the ethics or right to believe: for James, the question of religious faith; for Chisholm, the relation of evidence to action. See James, "The Will to Believe"; and Roderick M. Chisholm, Perceiving: A Philosophical Study (Ithaca: Cornell University Press, 1957), pp. 3-39, 100.

[60] Clifford, "The Ethics of Belief," p. 26.

[61] Ibid., p. 23.

[62] Ibid.

[63] Ibid. p. 24.

[64] See 'belief' in Webster's Seventh New Collegiate Dictionary.

[65] Chisholm, Perceiving, p. 11. A true skeptic would assert that all propositions are "epistemically indifferent."

[66] Butler, "Upon Self-Deceit," p. 114.

[67] Rorty, "Akrasia and Pleasure" p. 283, ft. 1.

[68] Kant, The Metaphysical Principles of Virtue, pp. 77-104, ff.

[69] Thomas E. Hill, Jr., "Servility and Self-Respect," in Rights, David Lyons, ed., (Belmont, CA: Wadsworth Publishing Co., 1979), p. 122.

[70] For Kant's different uses of 'duty,' see Mary Mothersill, "Duty," in The Encyclopedia of Philosophy, II, pp. 442, 444.

[71] Ibid. p. 443.

[72] John Rawls, A Theory of Justice (Cambridge: Harvard University Press, 1971), p. 423. Rawls mentions the resemblance as being relevant to the original position, which, like Kant's move, begs the question about the integrity of a self-regarding duty or right.

[73] Josef Pieper, The Four Cardinal Virtues (Notre Dame: University of Notre Dame Press, 1966), p. 5.

[74] Prudential akrasia is discussed by M. J. Scott-Taggert, "Kant, Conduct and Consistency," in Practical Reason, ed. Korner, p. 226. W. H. Walsh, "Kant's Concept of Practical Reason" in the same volume has a helpful discussion of prudential reason, esp. pp. 194, 196 ff.

[75] This is how I would read Fingarette on the idea that self-deception is a "genuine subversion of moral agency" and a "subversion of moral capacity": that the acceptance of responsibility required for the overcoming of self-deception relies on an ability to achieve self-acceptance, which points matters back to the prudential sphere. I have come at the issue in a different

way, but with similar effect. See Fingarette, Self-Deception, pp. 141 ff.

[76] Alasdair MacIntyre, After Virtue: A Study in Moral Theory (Notre Dame: University of Notre Dame Press, 1981), p. 145: "So for Kant one can be both good and stupid; but for Aristotle stupidity of a certain kind precludes goodness."

[77] Aquinas, Summa Theologica II-II, Q. 132, art. 1, p. 1732. This is the question of "Vainglory" in the treatise on virtues and vices.

[78] Szabados, "The Morality of Self-Deception," p. 34.

[79] King-Farlow, "Akrasia, Self-Mastery and the Master Self," p. 58.

[80] Rorty, "Belief and Self-Deception," p. 402.

[81] Gardiner, "Error, Faith, and Self-Deception," p. 37.

[82] James D. Wallace, Virtues and Vices (Ithaca: Cornell University Press, 1978), p. 59.

[83] Arnold Isenberg, "Natural Pride and Natural Shame," in Explaining Emotions, ed. Rorty, p. 358.

[84] Ibid. I would direct the reader to the discussion of self-deception to be found on this page.

[85] David Hume, A Treatise of Human Nature, ed. L. A. Selby-Bigge, (Oxford: Clarendon Press, 1968), Book 2, part I, section VI, p. 290. For further analysis and specific examination of Hume on pride, see Gabriele Taylor, "Pride," in Explaining Emotions, ed. Rorty, pp. 385-402.

[86] Karl Barth, Church Dogmatics, IV, pt. I, trans. G. W. Bromiley (Edinburg: T. & T. Clark, 1956, 1974), p. 420.

[87] Aquinas, Summa Theologica, Pt. II-II, Q. 162, Art. 5, p. 1859.

[88] Reinhold Niebuhr, The Nature and Destiny of Man, I (New York: Charles Scribner's Sons, 1941, 1964), p. 170: In the Christian view, "The individual is conceived of as a creature of infinite possibilities which cannot be fulfilled within terms of this temporal existence."

[89] Blaise Pascal, Pensées, trans. A. J. Krailsheimer (Baltimore: Penguin Books, 1966), no. 131, p. 64.

[90] Paul Tillich, Dynamics of Faith (New York: Harper Torchbooks, 1957), pp. 1 ff.

[91] Barth, Church Dogmatics, IV, i, p. 421.

[92] Niebuhr, The Nature and Destiny of Man, I, p. 179.

[93] Albrecht Ritschl, The Christian Doctrine of Justification and Reconciliation, trans. H. R. Mackintosh and A. B. Macaulay (Clifton, NJ: Reference Book Publishers, 1966), p. 199. See Niebuhr's critique, ibid., p. 178.

[94] Piet Schoonenberg, Man and Sin: A Theological View, trans. Joseph Donceel (Notre Dame: University of Notre Dame Press, 1965), p. 20.

[95] Ibid., p. 21.

[96] Kierkegaard, The Sickness Unto Death, p. 31.

[97] Augustine, City of God, trans. Henry Bettenson, ed. David Knowles, (Harmondsworth, Middlesex, England: Penguin Books, 1972, 1980), p. 477.

[98] Aquinas, Summa Theologica, Pt. II-II, Q. 162, art. 5, p. 1859.

[99] Ibid.

[100] Ibid., art. 6, p. 1860.

[101] Ibid., Q. 163, art. 1 (ff), p. 1862.

[102] Ibid.

[103] St. Augustine, The Confessions, trans. F. J. Sheed (New York: Sheed & Ward, 1942), p. 28.

[104] Ibid., pp. 65-66.

[105] Ibid., p. 79.

[106] Ibid., p. 106.

[107] Ibid.

[108] St. Augustine, On Nature and Grace, p. 132.

[109] Ibid.

[110] Niebuhr, The Nature and Destiny of Man, I, pp. 178-179. This statement is to be compared to Augustine's classic statement on pride in City of God, XIV, xiii, pp. 571-72, which Niebuhr miscites.

[111] Pascal, Pensées, no. 597, pp. 229-30.

[112] Jonathan Edwards, Doctrine of Original Sin Defended, in Jonathan Edwards: Representative Selections, eds. Clarence H. Faust and Thomas H. Johnson, (New York: Hill and Wang, 1962), p. 326.

[113] Barth, Church Dogmatics IV, i, p. 326.

[114] Ibid.

[115] See Barth's study of sin as falsehood in Church Dogmatics, IV, iii (first half), pp. 368-478.

[116] Søren Kierkegaard, Works of Love, trans. Howard and Edna Hong (New York: Harper & Row, Harper Torchbooks, 1962), p. 222.

[117] Ibid., pp. 222, 223.

[118] Faith, one can say, is the passionate response of the entire personality to the offer of the God-relation. In faith, one responds with one's heart, mind, soul and strength to God in love, love being the quest or yearning for unity with God on the basis of a self that has itself achieved synthesis.

[119] Kierkegaard, Works of Love, p. 23.

[120] Ibid.

[121] Ibid., pp. 24, 25.

[122] Kierkegaard, The Sickness Unto Death, p. 79.

[123] See, for example, the prescription against self-deception in I Cor. 3.18. See also Gal. 6.3; Obad. 3; I Jo. 1.8; Isa. 44.20.

[124] Pascal, Pensées, no. 978 ("On Self-Love"), p. 349.

[125] Kierkegaard, The Sickness Unto Death, p. 79.

[126] Aquinas, Summa Theologica II-II, Q. 15, pp. 1237-39. All uncited quotations are taken from these pages.

[127] Aquinas makes this statement in his discussion of lust. See Summa Theologica II-II, Q. 153, art. 4, "Of Lust," p. 1813.

[128] Augustine, The Confessions, p. 205.

[129] Ibid., p. 79.

[130] Ibid., p. 70.

[131] Ibid., p. 71.

[132] Augustine, Nature and Grace, p. 127.

[133] Ibid., p. 134. See discussion of self-deception on this page.

[134] Augustine, Confessions, p. 191.

[135] Pascal, Pensées, no. 166, p. 82.

[136] Ibid., no. 798, p. 349.

[137] Roger Hazelton, Pascal: The Genius of His Thought (Philadelphia: Westminster Press, 1974), p. 92.

[138] Ibid., p. 91.

[139] Pascal, Pensées, no. 978, pp. 350-51.

[140] Ibid., no. 149, p. 80.

[141]Ibid., nos. 397, 393, p. 145.

[142]Ibid., no. 394, p. 145.

[143]Jonathan Edwards, "The Justice of God," in eds. Faust and Johnson, Jonathan Edwards: Selections, p. 115.

[144]Ibid., "The Peace Which Christ Gives," p. 138. To be quoted shortly.

[145]John Calvin, Institutes of the Christian Religion, I, trans. Ford Lewis Battles, ed. John T. McNeill, (Philadelphia: Westminster Press, 1960), pp. 354, 355. Calvin uses the "blindness" metaphor in this section.

[146]Emil Brunner, Revelation and Reason: The Christian Doctrine of Faith and Knowledge, trans. Olive Wyon (Philadelphia: Westminster Press, 1946), p. 213.

[147]Ibid., p. 52.

[148]Ibid., p. 51.

[149]Ibid.

[150]Ibid., pp. 52-53.

[151]Ibid., p. 54.

[152]Ibid., p. 52.

[153]Barth, Church Dogmatics, IV, i, p. 421.

[154]Ibid.

[155]Ibid., p. 422.

[156]Ibid., pp. 422, 453.

[157]Ibid., pp. 143-44.

[158]Niebuhr, The Nature and Destiny of Man, I, pp. 178-203.

[159]Ibid., p. 181.

[160]Philip Leon, The Ethics of Power, p. 258; quoted in Niebuhr, The Nature and Destiny of Man, I, p. 204, ft. 2.

[161]Ibid., pp. 206-07.

[162]Kant, Religion Within the Limits of Reason Alone, p. 188.

[163]Martin Luther, Martin Luther: Selections, ed. John Dillenberger, (Garden City: Doubleday Anchor Books, 1961), p. 158.

[164]Jonathan Edwards, The Religious Affections (Grand Rapids: Sovereign Grace Publishers, 1971), pp. 182-83.

[165] Ibid., p. 138.

[166] See discussions in Fingarette, Self-Deception, pp. 104-110; Louis Mackey, Kierkegaard: A Kind of Poet, passim; Alastair Hannay, Kierkegaard (London: Routledge & Kegan Paul, 1982), passim.

[167] John Douglas Mullen, Kierkegaard's Philosophy: Self-Deception and Cowardice in the Present Age, (New York: New American Library, Mentor Books, 1981).

[168] Purity of Heart is discussed in Hannay, Kierkegaard, pp. 205-240; and Jeremy Walker, To Will One Thing: Reflections on Kierkegaard's "Purity of Heart," (Montreal: McGill-Queen's University Press, 1972). The best analysis of Purity of Heart, by far, is Louis Mackey, "An Analysis of the Good in Kierkegaard's Purity of Heart," in ed. I. C. Lieb, Experience, Existence and the Good (Carbondale: Southern Illinois University Press, 1961), pp. 260-274.

[169] See J. Preston Cole's study, The Problematic Self in Kierkegaard and Freud (New Haven: Yale University Press, 1971).

[170] Kierkegaard, The Concept of Anxiety, p. 92.

[171] Ibid., p. 74.

[172] Søren Kierkegaard's Journals and Papers, I, A-E, ed. and trans. Howard V. and Edna H. Hong (Bloomington: Indiana University Press, 1967), p. 39.

[173] Kierkegaard, The Concept of Anxiety, pp. 155-162.

[174] Ibid., p. 122.

[175] Ibid., p. 154.

[176] Kierkegaard, The Sickness Unto Death, pp. 75 ff.

[177] Ibid., p. 109.

[178] Ibid., p. 110.

[179] Kierkegaard, Journals and Papers, I, A-E, p. 349.

[180] Ibid.

[181] Ibid., p. 524, note by editors.

[182] Ibid., pp. 60-67.

[183] Ibid., p. 44.

[184] Kierkegaard, Journals and Papers, I, A-E, p. 348.

[185] Kierkegaard, The Sickness Unto Death, p. 44.

[186] Ibid.

[187] Ibid., p. 69.

[188] Ibid.

[189] Ibid.

[190] Ibid.

[191] Ibid., pp. 44-45.

[192] Ibid., p. 62.

[193] Ibid.

[194] Ibid.

[195] Ibid., pp. 16-17.

[196] Ibid., p. 46.

[197] Ibid, p. 29.

[198] Ibid., p. 15.

[199] Ibid., p. 143 (journal entry).

[200] Kierkegaard, Purity of Heart, p. 47.

[201] Ibid.

[202] Ibid., p. 31.

[203] Ibid., p. 52.

[204] Ibid., p. 168.

[205] Ibid.

[206] Ibid., p. 166.

[207] Ibid., p. 61.

[208] Ibid.

[209] Ibid., pp. 61, 81, 151.

[210] Ibid., pp. 73, 76.

[211] Ibid., p. 65.

[212] Murphy, "Experiments in Overcoming Self-Deception," p. 793.

[213] Ibid., pp. 793-94.

[214] Kierkegaard, Purity of Heart, pp. 107-08. Voluntary sense deception is

mentioned pp. 58, 73.

 [215]Kierkegaard, Either/Or, I, pp. 290-91.

 [216]Kierkegaard, Either/Or, II, p. 202.

 [217]Ibid., p. 203.

 [218]Ibid., p. 205.

 [219]Ibid., pp. 312, 313.

 [220]Kierkegaard, Either/Or, I, p. 13.

 [221]Mackey, Kierkegaard: A Kind of Poet, p. 88.

 [222]Kierkegaard, Works of Love, p. 253. See also footnote 25, Chapter Three.

 [223]Kierkegaard, Purity of Heart, p. 178.

CONCLUSION

Self-deception is a feature of the common life, a common feature. Despite its commonness, however, self-deception presents itself as deeply mysterious. It is, after all, perplexing to think that persons are capable of dynamically relating themselves to themselves in such a way that they bring about the phenomenon that has been the topic of inquiry throughout these pages. Self-deception is not mysterious in the sense that it presents conceptual obstacles that cannot be overcome. It is mysterious because even though we know about it and can detect it, we find ourselves unable to rule ourselves according to the measure of this knowledge. We seem unable, that is, to prevent it or avoid it. The mystery, in other words, is that we choose self-deception. Our analysis has shown that any instance of self-deception can be traced to the fact that as self-deceivers we literally want to be self-deceived: we prefer self-deception to facing a belief or truth too painful and threatening to accept. This "willful ignorance" is mysterious and unfathomable. Even theologians armed with explicitly paradoxical conceptions of human nature content themselves with merely describing it.

Self-deception is mysterious, but that mystery need not lead to despair or futility. We can describe self-deception, and "knowledge by description" is a tried and true epistemological principle that permits us to say that we can "know about" this phenomenon. The phenomenon can be described, the concept can be analyzed and elucidated. We can acquire competence in the use of the language of 'self-deception' and perform meaning tasks with that language. Thy mystery of self-deception, it must be said, does not lie where certain philosophers seem to think it does. Self-deception raises a logical problem, but self-deception is not fundamentally a problem in logic. It is a problem in existence. This point is overlooked by analysts who permit logical considerations to override the experiences of persons who, in the common life, observe contradictions in human behavior, who see that persons can misunderstand the true meaning of their own actions, who reflect on their own acquaintance with self-deception and who acquire competence in using the language of 'self-deception.'

This study has defended the proposition that 'self-deception' is meaningful language. It has defended the idea that the phenomenon pointed to by this linguistic expression can be observed and analyzed, and that our language-- ambiguous as it is at times--can be trusted. Self-deception exists--and is pervasive--as an actual 'deception' that is modified by the governing relations of the 'self-' prefix. It is, in other words, a deception directed by the self at the self, an apparent paradox that yields no actual logical contradiction, for the paradox can be rendered coherent by taking into account the dynamics of self-relatedness. These dynamics can be described; hence the concept can be elucidated. But for all that can be done to render the concept coherent and intelligible, it is still mysterious that the 'self'--a reflexive pronoun used as a noun to perform the work of an adverb (action modifier)--can do what it does. Although this mysteriousness is a sort of premise for theologians, even tough-minded analytic philosophers can attune themselves to the realities of selfhood, realities that expose the limitation of particular philosophical enterprises. It was the Wittgenstein of the <u>Tractatus</u> who could marvel, after all, at the mystery of being a human subject: "The I," he wrote, "the I is what is deeply mysterious!"[1] Philosophers who have been baffled by 'self-deception' go astray at precisely the point where the 'I' must be elucidated and its dynamic relations appreciated.

The dynamics of selfhood can be described, but this self which is closest to us cannot be explained. Beyond description, itself an arduous intellectual task, we can only theorize. Although the self is deeply mysterious--a great "deep" as Augustine said--we can ascertain what it does. We can observe and reflect on our observations. Shunning skepticism, we can refuse to persuade ourselves that the language of self-deception is so ambiguous that we cannot use that language meaningfully. We betray a truth about ourselves--a truth painful to admit, especially if we want to believe ourselves not only rational but capable of always doing what reason bids--if we create a logical loophole that permits us to argue that self-deception is a grand linguistic mistake that "cannot happen." Self-deception is a feature of the common life, and it is problem of existence before it is a problem in logic. The intellectual task is to find a logic and a language that will enable this problem of existence to be clarified, a language that will conform to the reality of the phenomenon itself. A logic that concludes "self-deception cannot happen" flies in the face of human experience and the history of our thought about human experience. Such a logic inadvertently reveals the poverty of thought that refuses to a accept a true premise about itself; and because it is inconsistent with the facts available to all in the common life, it is a defective logic that ought to be scrapped.

Self-deception is a feature of the common life. Although my examples of self-deceivers have included a public speaker, a Lutheran pastor, a political leader, a cancer patient, a businessman, and all who reject the possibility of a God-relation, it is necessary once again to indicate the pervasiveness of this phenomenon. It is necessary to remind ourselves that, as Socrates said, self-deception is always near by, that the deceiver who would deceive us is "always at home and always with [us]." This study, after validating the "ordinary language" meaning of the concept, examined the use to which self-deception has been put in three relational contexts: the self-relations of psychology, the self-other relations of the moral domain, the God-relation of the religious sphere. Now that I have concluded with the religious point of view, which allowed us to examine the religious meaning of self-deception, I would ask that we lower our sights in order to emphasize once again that self-deception is always about, always a threat. If God be too high, too abstract, if the Kierkegaardian exposition of theological self-deception miss its mark, begin again--consider again the examples from the common life. One cannot see the point of theological self-deception by looking to the heavens anyway. Theological self-deception is a form of self-deception that is properly understood only in the context of the ordinary language meaning of the term, only as an extrapolation of the concept from one set of governing relations to another, from self-relatedness considered from a psychological point of view to self-relatedness considered from a religious point of view. If Kierkegaard is right, we will acquire the ability to construe the deeper dimensions of self-deception by looking around rather than up, by getting clear about the everyday experience and the ordinary language concept. Only then can we look inward and consider different relational possibilities. Any instance of self-deception can serve to illustrate the dynamics of self-relatedness as they are implicated in, say, neurosis (psychology) or sin (theology). Any instance of self-deception can serve to illustrate the disrelatedness--the despair--that can mark the human relation of persons to their own selves, be it the defiant despair of a Faust or the observations of an astute though average citizen of the common life commonwealth. Consider John Updike's dentist, Freddy, who, in the novel, *Couples*, remarks:

> People come to me all the time with teeth past saving, with abscesses they've been telling themselves are neuralgia. The pain has clearly been terrific. They've been going around with it for months, unable to chew or even close their jaws, because subconsciously they don't want to loose a tooth. Loosing a tooth means death to people. . . .They're scared to death of me because I might tell the truth. When they get their dentures, I tell 'em it looks better than ever, and they fall all over me believing it. It's horseshit. You never get your smile back when you lose your teeth.²

Freddy is a cynical (and vulgar) fellow, but what he has observed is there to be observed. His cynicism has not prevented him from seeing the despair in others. Seeing it in others provides an opportunity for him to see it in himself. This example of self-deception could be analyzed from various points of view, within the context of different governing relations. But the real significance of Freddy's observations is that those observations are informative and intelligible and coherent. The appeal to truth is an appeal to the experience of persons in the common life, for in the common life, 'self-deception' is a meaningful concept. Freddy, like Kierkegaard, or Luther, or Samuel Johnson, or Freud or Sartre, understands the meaning of self-deception in the common life. He can use that linguistic expression to describe psychological disrelatedness in others, to evaluate the lack of self-honesty in his patients, to point to a misuse of freedom, to indicate a deep despair which he himself, thorough his own cynicism, exhibits. Freddy is what he says he is: a person fascinated by our ability to deceive ourselves: "The most wonderful thing I know is the human capacity for self-deception. It keeps everything else going."³

With Freddy we stumble on another difficulty--how to prevent cynicism and despair. If we clarify self-deception, if we come to understand what it is and how it is to be understood, will we not also become so suspicious of our knowing, so mistrustful of our own self-understanding that we will see every instance of sincere belief as an occasion for the self-deception we seek to avoid? Can we trust ourselves to be honest with ourselves, especially if we understand that self-deceivers do think themselves honest with themselves?

Having examined our topic from several perspectives, we have learned that self-interest and self-regardingness are necessary conditions for self-deception. What if one decides it is in one's self-interest to avoid self-deception? What if one decides to be vigilant, to adopt a policy of complete and total honesty with oneself in hopes of avoiding self-deception? Does one not thereby deceive oneself into believing that one is capable of actually doing what one knows is reasonable to do and in one's self-interest to do, namely, to relate oneself to oneself without masking the truth, without evading or rationalizing or resisting the truth? The problem with making the conscious, reflective decision to avoid self-deception is that by willing oneself to self-honesty one presumes a transparency of consciousness that does not yet exist in actuality, but only potentially or ideally. Who, then, can really avoid self-deception? Who would be so bold as to claim to have acquired that ability knowing what self-deception is and how we are to understand it? In fact, is not knowledge about self-deception simply another occasion for despair, skepticism and self-uncertainty?

There are two issues here. One is the question, does knowledge about self-deception have practical, even therapeutic, significance? Can the person who seeks to avoid self-deception really benefit from a study of the concept? Or is such a study, in that it arms one with knowledge about the problem, simply a means by which one acquires one more occasion for deceiving oneself? For the person who is aware of self-deception and its pervasiveness in the common life--perhaps even as a result of reading these pages--will a renewed commitment to self-honesty suffice to prevent self-deception no matter what the cost to one's psychic well-being, no matter what the pain and distress? The second issue is this: Is there anything one can do beyond skepticism and cynicism to prevent or overcome self-deception?

With respect to the first issue, let me say that there is danger in assuming that to know about self-deception is equivalent to doing something to prevent it. "Knowledge about" self-deception, after all, can occasion an unwarranted confidence in which the seeds of self-deception rapidly germinate. Knowing about self-deception is not equivalent to "knowing how" to deal with it in one's own life. Yet knowing about self-deception is the first step to deeper reflection, the kind of reflection from which strategies for avoiding self-deception emerge. But always we must remember that devising a strategy and implementing it are two different things, and because a strategy for avoiding self-deception reflects a component of self-image and expresses an aspect of reflexive care--I don't want to be a person who permits him- or herself to become self-deceived"--one has already postulated a motive for yet another instance. Kierkegaard's brilliant Aesthete fell into this trap, and it is no idle character development that put the Aesthete on the brink of madness at the end of the first volume of Either/Or. The Aesthete is on the verge of awakening to the truth that he is not--cannot be--what he thinks he is. He perceives that only a decision, an act of will, can enable him to "put the blinders on" again.

What must be said, and said soberly, is that we human beings are complex beyond our wildest imaginings, that we are "chimeras" as Pascal put it, that we are not the unified selves and transparent consciousnesses we think we are. We are so torn in our desires, so divided in mind and will, so unable to do what reason bids that those who have understood this--persons like St. Paul, Pascal, Kierkegaard, Freud, Sartre--stop remarking on it with exclamations. Were we actually in possession of the ability to ground ourselves transparently in our own consciousness, or unify ourselves so that all intrapsychic conflict would cease, it is clear that we would be unlike our present selves, for we would be something inconsistent with our being human persons. We are never, by our own act, in complete possession of ourselves or thoroughly consistent in our choices--we only deceive ourselves into thinking so. We are self-deceivers, and this capacity for self-deception expresses a fundamental capacity. Were we to lose this capacity, our very humanity would be at risk, for our ability to reflect on our own selves, to understand ourselves and to relate ourselves to ourselves is involved in this capacity. Self-deception is a flaw or negativity in the system of reflection. It is reflection that obscures itself mysteriously from itself, reflection that opts for an untruth or a disavowal for reasons of psychological gain. But that system of reflection is what permits us to be human. We are endowed with a capacity to reflect on our action, and this permits us to act morally and to correct ourselves, to express ourselves linguistically, to transcend ourselves by acts of creativity, to imagine possibilities, to conceive of ourselves as more than finite, to relate ourselves to ourselves in freedom. Our reflective capacity permits us to achieve self-awareness, moral awareness and awareness of God. That we are capable of self-deception is part of the glory and wonder of being human. This assessment holds even if self-deception expresses the negativity or despair of self-awareness, even if self-deception expresses the perversity of a will that does not want to know a (painful) truth or an already avowed belief, even if self-deception expresses the misere of resisting, refusing and denying what could be known were our will stronger, were we but more perfect. Were we to rid ourselves of our capacity for self-deception, we would rid ourselves of our very humanity, for we would also lose our capacity for reflection and self-relatedness.

For those who express confidence in human reason, who see in rationality alone a hope and a panacea for the world's ills, it is painful to admit that we are conflicted selves unable to do what we know we ought and that our consciousness is opaque even--especially--at the very moment we believe it to be lucid. "The human mind is an untidy place," writes Bela Szabados, "but it cannot be as untidy as some philosophers would have us believe."[4] On the contrary, extreme breakdowns in self-relatedness, the severe cases of schizophrenia and multiple-personality with which we are familiar, suggest that the human mind is more untidy than we can even imagine. There is little comfort in empirical appeal, for this untidiness of mind, this distress of disrelationship, is amply attested to by evidence from the common life, even if some of the examples are themselves uncommon. We are not what we think we are--but "deep down" even that we know.

Are we then doomed to self-deception? Have we led ourselves to the point of hopelessness and despair? I would be remiss if I did not say that there is reason for a certain pessimism, for in the thought that self-deception is pervasive is also the thought that one can never trust oneself absolutely: the one who would deceive you is always at home and always with you. But we must be dialectical about this, by which I mean that a dialectical approach is called for. If self-deception is the negative term in the reflexive capability that is also the glory of human being, then we must say, too, that an actual check on self-deception is also available--reflection. That being so, there are things one can do to prevent, avoid and overcome self-deception.

If, indeed, we tend to believe what we want because it is reassuring and comforting to do so, then we must note those strategies that can be devised to counter this tendency. Such strategies will be premised on a certain spiritual courage. That is, in order to avoid self-deception, we must reflect courageously, working through the struggles of self-confrontation in order to arrive at the goal of self-honesty. Self-honesty, being painful, brings no immediate psychological gain; though the deepening of self-consciousness that can result from one's commitment to self-honesty can raise the self-deception threshold. By becoming more and more self-conscious, a person can become more and more capable of detecting those objects that tempt one to self-deception. Knowing this can inspire us to vigilance. We can assume postures aimed at preventing ourselves from excusing ourselves or blaming others too quickly.

The difficulty, of course, is that we can never be certain that we have become sufficiently self-conscious to say with confidence, "I cannot deceive myself." That is an ideal always beyond the reach of the self's grasp. Practical options, however, are available. In fact, Gardner Murphy has identified twenty three specific "everyday ways of coping with self-deception"[5] in <u>Outgrowing Self-Deception</u>. Murphy's shopping list is suggestive. He recommends everything from sheer fiat to bio-feedback training, using the models of self-alerting advocated by such diverse figures and movements as Harry Stack Sullivan, Carl Rogers, Freud, Jung, Morene ("psychodrama"), Darwin and Zen Buddhism. In the end, however, the value of any particular recommendation is the extent to which it urges deeper reflection, a deeper commitment to self-honesty, and encourages the movement of self-transcendence.

From a psychological point of view, one can only overcome self-deception by learning to raise the self-deception threshold, and we do this by learning about our own propensities to mask the truth. What kinds of things do I perceive as threatening to me? In order to answer this, I must learn to confront myself, and whether I do this by self-cultivation techniques acquired by self-study (e.g., Kierkegaard, or Freud the advocate of self-analysis and "lay" analysis) or by working with professional therapists, a "psychotherapy" is called for, the kind that breaks down one's our resistances to self-recognition. In a therapeutic situation, one's goal is to be able to confess --ultimately to oneself--one's deep, dark, hidden secrets. One proceeds by learning to trust an "other" whose only aim is to facilitate the self-recognition process. From a psychological point of view, the psychoanalyst and even the priest to whom one confesses perform the same analytic function.[6] They urge one to deeper self-confrontation and to self-acceptance on the basis of honesty rather than wishes and willed distortions of truth. I would add that from a moral point of view, as I argued in the last chapter, we ought to seek self-honesty, for it is a violation of the respect one owes oneself in virtue of being a person to "cover up" the truth. It is a sign of moral health, as well as psychological health, to be able to confront oneself with the truth about oneself. Only by facing the truth about one's actions and attitudes can one proceed to work from remorse to self-reform. The idea of perfect virtue depends upon one's ability to confront oneself honestly, to hear the call of conscience and to respond by confessing one's failures before the moral ideal without excuse and rationalization. From the guilt and remorse which attend such self-recognition, one can deepen one's own self-consciousness and resolve to reform oneself, thereby coming ever closer to the ideal of moral perfection and fulfilling one's self-regarding duties.

Religiously conceived strategies for overcoming self-deception are all related to the idea of self-transcendence. In the West, in Christianity, self-transcendence is a possibility that stems from faith. The religious perspective would urge one to conceive oneself "as one is"--as finite yet more than finite, as a limited and determined creature who is, in freedom and spirit, made for the infinite. Self-transcendence is a movement of spirit in freedom. It is the creative movement whereby one chooses to exercise one's freedom for possibilities beyond the finite. In religious terms, a self in transcendence is a self that rejects the idolatrous claim of the finite world to its infinite interest. The "true self" (Kierkegaard) owes no ultimate allegiance to the finite, but only to God. Faith is the expression of self-transcendence, the creative act wherein one pushes one's self-understanding beyond the considerations of finite desire and finite self-image. Faith enables one to "to climb across" (<u>transcendere</u>) one's limited and determined existence to an ideal self, invoked by conscience. From this "beyond" perspective one is able, in faith, to see one's own limitations, one's own contradictions, one's own propensity to self-deception. In self-transcending experiences, one enlarges and opens oneself to the realm of spirit where one creatively distances oneself from the finitude of the finite so that one might exercise one's freedom to be finite but more than finite. Self-transcendence is the experience of openness and self-enlargement; it is a deepening of consciousness that is, from a religious point of view, only headed in one direction--to God, the object of infinite interest and ultimate concern.

The self-transcendence of faith leads to a remarkable and starling conclusion. Kierkegaard, as I noted in the last chapter, ultimately concludes that for the person grounded in God, self-deception is impossible. No psychological or moral strategy aimed at inoculating one against the harmful effects of self-deception can guarantee that by this technique or that remedy one can actually eliminate the possibility of self-deception. It is, after all, "always with one" and always a possibility. Religious thinkers, however, make a radical claim. They claim that faith is a movement in which one actually unifies the fragmented self, actually achieves a transparent consciousness. Faith is a way of uniting the whole personality in truth, for "In true faith the ultimate concern is a concern about the truly ultimate; while in idolatrous faith preliminary, finite realities are elevated to the rank of ultimacy."[7] Idolatrous faith leads to ". . .a loss of the center and to a disruption of the personality,"[8] a condition of self-fragmentation, of self-conflict and disrelation that only faith as ultimate concern about truly ultimate things can restore to wholeness and proper integrity. If one is properly and truly related to God, one surrenders oneself to God; and if one surrenders oneself to the Power whence one is derived, then one loses all motive for deceiving oneself. Self-deception is therefore impossible, given the religious logic of things, because faith restores the person to self-unity; because the self is no longer in conflict with itself but can accept itself as it is in truth "before God"; because consciousness is grounded transparently in God and not in self; because one has relinquished one's self-regardingness and desires for ego-domination to God so that no motive now exists for undertaking to mislead one's own beliefs. One has distanced oneself through the act of faith and through the attitude of self-transcendence from the finitude of the finite. One has refused to let finitude control one, refused to let a finite concern posture and pretend to ultimacy. Religious faith proposes that faith is itself the ultimate--and the only--strategy that can actually overcome self-deception. For when one is in faith, one cancels all those factors that conspire to elicit in one the self-directed belief-misleading project that identifies self-deception.

The "strategy of faith" can be observed. A person who acts to confront self-deception via theistic faith will be characterized by certain attitudes. Irony is one such attitude. Irony has long been associated with the religious life, for it is a characteristic marker of religious thought and attitude.

Irony is a critical stance: "It exposes falsehood and stupidity, recognizes foolishness and pretense. It mocks those who think they are something when they are actually nothing."[9] Irony is characterized by "understatement or a method of suggestion rather than of plain statement" and it is "a stance in truth from which the perception comes."[10] One who is ironic (consider the Jesus of the Gospels) always aim to correct by urging others to deeper reflection, to await direct statement until the hearers are ready and qualified to hear. The ironic one must both know the truth and distance him- or herself from those who would collapse that distance. Irony is a stance against pretense and self-approval.

Humor, likewise, can be considered a strategy for overcoming self-deception, and it, too, is a marker of the religious person.

> If all have sinned and none is good save God, then the human arrangement by which to accommodate to that, either socially or individually, is rather difficult, to say the least. Then the whole of existence is not only a kind of illness, it is also a comedy in a very special sense. It is a divine comedy, an extraordinary spectacle, but with a happy ending of God's own choosing.
> There is also permitted the laugh from within the effort and within the consciousness that without God one can do nothing. Then laughter gets a new ring to it--it becomes part of the joy that has no limit, that has no surcease and terminus at all. One can afford to laugh, for human efforts are not that important; though they are required of each man, it not as if God needs moral Atlases who will bear everything up for him.[11]

A self that is unified, a consciousness that is transparent, a self that recognizes itself in its freedom is a self that can laugh. Laughter is a means of self-transcendence, a creative and joyful response to the human predicament. Laughter is what is expressed when one takes on faith the possibility of the _paradiso_ at the end of the _commedia_. Faith urges this joy and humor. One needs to contrast this joy with the dark moodiness that ends Sartre's _Being and Nothingness_. If existence is a tragedy, if bad faith is so pervasive that even the God-relation is only a possibility construed by the imagination, then despair is in order and ought to attend the idea that to be human is to be a "useless passion." But from the religious point of view, there is a possibility beyond despair that attends becoming lucid about one's condition. To accept the possibility of the God-relation is to accept the possibility that one's own proclivities to self-deception may be cancelled, for one renounces in the act of faith all claim to the ego-centrism that infects the self with finite ultimates and occasions for self-deception. One surrenders oneself to God so that one's motives for deceiving oneself might be said to have been surrendered too. Faith is an attitude of hope; it is the other side of the self-scrutiny that leads to despair. It is marked by "humor; gentle, playful, loving and ironic. . .[for] there is a humor which warms our humanity and draws us out of ourselves, liberating us from the heavy seriousness of sullen self-absorption."[12] This is the humor of faith.

In the end, it is religious faith that makes the most radical claim concerning our ability to avoid or overcome self-deception; for religious faith posits itself as the one and only strategy that makes self-deception, as Kierkegaard said, "impossible."

* * * * * * * * * * * * *

The aim of this study has been to acquire an "intimate acquaintance" with the concept self-deception. That intimate acquaintance begins to be available to the person who is able to affirm what at first seems incongruous or even paradoxical--that there is a fallacy in the philosopher's notion that self-deception "cannot happen" and a truth in the theologian's notion that in faith self-deception is "impossible." This investigation has enabled us to know about self-deception. Having acquired a "knowledge about" self-deception, however is insufficient for claiming "intimate acquaintance." For our acquaintance with self-deception to become truly intimate, we must move from knowing about self-deception to knowing how the concept is meaningful--how it is to be employed, what skills are required for its proper use, how one is to put one's knowledge about self-deception to work in one's own life. For this acquaintance to become truly intimate, there is nothing to do but--as Kierkegaard said--"reflect on your own life."

CONCLUSION

[1] Ludwig Wittgenstein, Notebooks, 1914-1916, trans. and ed. G. E. M. Anscombe (New York: Harper & Row, Harper Torchbooks, 1961), p. 80e.

[2] John Updike, Couples (New York: Alfred A. Knopf, 1968), pp. 241-42.

[3] Ibid., p. 240.

[4] Szabados, "Rorty on Belief and Self-Deception," p. 471.

[5] Murphy, Outgrowing Self-Deception, pp. 101-111.

[6] For the comparison between psychotherapy and "pastoral work," see Freud, The Question of Lay Analysis, pp. 108, 109.

[7] Tillich, Dynamics of Faith, p. 12.

[8] Ibid.

[9] Edwin M. Good, Irony in the Old Testament (Sheffield: The Almond Press, 1981), p. 17.

[10] Ibid., p. 31.

[11] Paul L. Holmer, "Something About What Makes It Funny," Soundings LVII, 2 (Summer 1974), p. 172.

[12] Donald Evans, Struggle and Fulfillment: The Inner Dynamics of Religion and Morality (Cleveland: William Collins, 1979), pp. 82, 83.

SELECT BIBLIOGRAPHY

Abelson, Raziel. "Definition." Encyclopedia of Philosophy, II, pp. 314-24. Edited by Paul Edwards. New York: Macmillan Publishing Co. and the Free Press, 1967.

_____. Persons: A Study in Philosophical Psychology. London: Macmillan, 1977.

Alexander, Peter. "Wishes, Symptoms, and Action." Aristotelian Society, Supplementary Volume 48 (1974).

Alston, William. "Emotion and Feeling." Encyclopedia of Philosophy, II, pp. 479-486.

_____. "Meaning and Use." In The Theory of Meaning, pp. 141-165. Edited by G. H. R. Parkinson. Oxford: Oxford University Press, 1968, 1978.

_____. "Self-Intervention and the Structure of Motivation." In The Self: Psychological and Philosophical Issues, pp. 65-102. Edited by Theodore Mischel. Totowa, NJ: Rowman and Littlefield, 1977.

Angeles, Peter A. Dictionary of Philosophy. New York: Barnes & Noble, 1981.

Anscombe, G. E. M. Intention. Ithaca: Cornell University Press, 1976.

_____. "Pretending." In Philosophy of Mind, pp. 294-310. Edited by Stuart Hampshire. New York: Harper & Row, 1966.

Aquinas, St. Thomas. Summa Theologica. Translated by Fathers of the English Dominican Province. New York: Benziger Brothers, 1947.

Arendt, Hannah. Eichmann in Jerusalem: A Report on the Banality of Evil. New York: Penguin Books, 1963, 1980.

Aristotle. The Basic Works of Aristotle. Edited by Richard McKeon. Nicomachean Ethics. New York: Random House, 1941.

Audi, Robert. "The Epistemic Authority of the First Person." Personalist 56 (Winter 1975): 5-15.

_____. "Epistemic Disavowals and Self-Deception." Personalist 57 (Autumn 1976): 378-85.

St. Augustine. Concerning the City of God Against the Pagans. Translated by Henry Bettensen. Introduced by David Knowles. Harmondsworth, Middlesex: Penguin Books, 1972.

_____. The Confessions of St. Augustine, Books I-X. Translated by F. J. Sheed. New York: Sheed and Ward, 1942.

_____. On Nature and Grace. Edited by Philip Schaff. Nicene and Post-Nicene Fathers, Volume 5. Grand Rapids: Wm. B. Eerdemans, 1975.

Aune, Bruce. "Intention." Encyclopedia of Philosophy, IV, pp. 198-201.

Austin, J. L. Philosophical Papers, pp. 55-75. 2nd ed. Edited by J. O. Urmson and G. J. Warnock. Oxford: Oxford University Press, 1970.

Bach, Kent. "An Analysis of Self-deception." Philosophy and Phenomenological Research XLI, 3 (March 1981): 351-370.

Baier, Kurt. The Moral Point of View: A Rational Basis for Ethics. Abridged edition. New York: Random House, 1966.

Baker, John A. "Audi on Epistemic Disavowals." Personalist 57, 4 (Autumn 1976): 376-77.

Barth, Karl. Church Dogmatics, IV, 1/IV,3,i. Edited by G. W. Bromiley and T. F. Torrance. Translated by G. W. Bromiley. Edinburgh: T & T Clark, 1956, 1974/1961.

_____. The Epistle to the Romans. 6th ed. Translated by Edwyn C. Hoskins. Oxford: Oxford University Press, 1933.

Beck, Lewis White. "Conscious and Unconscious Motives." Mind LXXV, 298 (April 1966): 155-179.

Bell, Richard H. & Hustwit, Ronald E., eds. Essays on Kierkegaard & Wittgenstein: On Understanding the Self. Wooster: College of Wooster, 1978.

Berger, Peter A. The Sacred Canopy: Elements of a Sociological Theory of Religion. Garden City: Doubleday & Co., Anchor Books, 1969.

Bok, Sissela. Lying: Moral Choice in Public and Private Life. New York: Vintage Books, 1978.

_____. "The Self Deceived." Social Science Information 19, 6 (1980): 923-935.

Bonhoeffer, Dietrich. Ethics. Edited by Eberhard Bethge. New York: Macmillan, 1969.

Brown, Lee and Hausman, Alan. "Mechanism, Intentionality, and the Unconscious: A Comparison of Sartre and Freud." In The Philosophy of Jean-Paul Sartre. Edited by Paul A. Schlipp. La Salle: Open Court, 1981.

Brunner, Emil. Revelation and Reason: The Christian Doctrine of Faith and Knowledge. Philadelphia: Westminster Press, 1946.

Burgess, Andrew. Passion, "Knowing How," and Understanding: An Essay on the Concept of Faith. Missoula: Scholars Press, 1975.

Butler, Joseph. "Upon Self-Deceit." Fifteen Sermons Preached at Rolls Chapel. 4th ed. London: 1749.

Buytendijk, F. J. J. "The Phenomenological Approach to the Problem of Feelings and Emotions." In Psychoanalysis and Existential Philosophy: 155-178. Edited by Hendrik M. Ruitenbeek. New York: E.P. Dutton & Co., 1962.

Calvin, John. Institutes of the Christian Religion, I. Edited by John T. McNeill. Translated by Ford Lewis Battles. Philadelphia: Westminster

Press, 1960.

Canfield, John and Gustavson, Donald F. "Self-Deception." *Analysis* 23 (December 1962): 32-36.

Catalano, Joseph S. *A Commentary on Jean-Paul Sartre's "Being and Nothingness."* New York: Harper & Row, Harper Torchbook, 1974.

Caton, Charles, ed. *Philosophy and Ordinary Language.* Urbana: University of Illinois Press, 1963, 1970.

Champlin, T. S. "Double Deception." *Mind* 85 (January 1976): 100-102.

_____. "Self-Deception: A Problem about Autobiography." *Aristotelian Society, Supplementary Volume* 53 (1979): 77-94.

_____. "Self-Deception: A Reflexive Dilemma." *Philosophy* 52 (1977): 281-99.

Chisholm, Roderick M. *Perceiving: A Philosophical Study.* Ithaca: Cornell University Press, 1957.

Chisholm, Roderick and Feehan, Thomas D. "The Intent to Deceive." *The Journal of Philosophy* 74 (1977): 143-59.

Cioffi, Frank. "Wishes, Symptoms and Actions." *Aristotelian Society, Supplementary Volume* 48 (1974): 97-118.

Clifford, William K. "The Ethics of Belief." *Lectures and Essays.* In *Problems and Perspectives in the Philosophy of Religion:* 20-26. Edited by George I. Mavrodes and Stuart C. Hackett. Boston: Allyn & Bacon, 1967, 1969.

Cole, J. Preston. *The Problematic Self in Kierkegaard and Freud.* New Haven: Yale University Press, 1971.

Collingwood, R. G. *The Principles of Art.* London: Oxford University Press, 1938, 1972.

Cragg, Gerald R. "Exposition on Romans." *The Interpreter's Bible*, IX. Nashville: Abingdon, 1954.

Crites, Stephen. "The Aesthetics of Self-Deception." *Soundings* 62 (Summer 1979): 107-129.

Cumming, R. D. "To Understand a Man." In *The Philosophy of Jean-Paul Sartre.* Edited by Paul A. Schlipp. La Salle: Open Court, 1981.

Danto, Arthur C. *Jean-Paul Sartre.* New York: Viking Press, 1975.

Davidson, Donald. *Essays on Action and Events.* Oxford: Clarendon Press, 1980.

Davis, Stephen T. "Wishful Thinking and 'The Will to Believe.'" *Transactions of the Charles S. Pierce Society* 8, 4 (Fall, 1972): 231-45.

Demos, Raphael. "Lying to Oneself." Journal of Philosophy, 57,17 (August 18, 1960): 588-94.

_____. "What is It that I Want?" Ethics 5, 3 (April 1945): 182-95.

de Sousa, Ronald. "Rational Homunculi." In The Identities of Persons, pp. 217-38. Edited by Amelie O. Rorty. Berkeley: University of California Press, 1976.

_____. "Review of Self-Deception." Inquiry 13, 3 (Autumn 1970): 308-334.

_____. "Rationality of Emotion." Dialogue (Canada) 18 (1979): 41-63.

_____. "Self-Deceptive Emotions." In Explaining Emotions, pp 283-97. Edited by Amelie O. Rorty. Berkeley: University of California Press, 1980.

Dietrichson, Paul. "Kierkegaard's Concept of the Self." Inquiry 8 (1974): 1-32.

Dilman, Ilham. Studies in Language and Reason. Totowa: Barnes & Noble Books, 1981.

Dilman, Ilham, and Phillips, D. Z. Sense and Delusion. New York: Humanities Press, 1971.

Dillenberger, John, ed. Luther: Selections from His Writings. Garden City: Doubleday & Co., Anchor Books, 1961.

Donaldson, Thomas. "Psychoanalysis and the Practical Inference Model." Philosophy Research Archives IV (1978): 3-16.

Durandin, Guy. Les Fondements du Mensonge. Paris: Flammarion, 1972.

Drengson, Alan R. "Review of Fingarette's Self-Deception." Canadian Journal of Philosophy III, 3 (March 1974): 474-485.

Edwards, Jonathan. The Religious Affections. Grand Rapids: Sovereign Grace Publishers, 1971.

Eliot, George. Adam Bede. Edited by Stephen Gill. Harmondsworth: Penguin, 1980.

Erikson, Erik. Young Man Luther: A Study in Psychoanalysis and History. New York: W. W. Norton & Co., 1958, 1962.

Evans, Donald. "Moral Weakness." Philosophy 50 (July 1975): 295-310.

_____. Struggle and Fulfillment: The Inner Dynamics of Religion and Morality. Cleveland: William Collins, 1979.

Exdell, John and Hamilton, James. "The Incorrigibility of First Person Disavowals." Personalist 56 (Autumn 1975): 389-94.

Factor, R. Lance. "Self-Deception and the Functionalist Theory of Mental Processes." Personalist 58 (April 1977): 115-123.

Faust, Clarence H., and Johnson, Thomas H., eds. <u>Jonathan Edwards: Selections</u>. New York: Hill & Wang, 1935, 1962.

Fingarette, Herbert. <u>Self Deception</u>. Atlantic Highlands: Humanities Press, 1969.

_____. <u>The Self in Transformation: Psychoanalysis, Philosophy and the Life of the Spirit</u>. New York: Harper & Row, Harper Torchbooks, 1963, 1965.

Foss, Jeffery. "Rethinking Self-Deception." <u>American Philosophical Quarterly</u> 17, 3 (July 1980): 237-243.

Fox, Michael. "On Unconscious Emotions." <u>Philosophy and Phenomenological Research</u> 34 (December 1973): 151-170.

Frankfort, Harry. "Freedom of the Will and the Concept of a Person." <u>Journal of Philosophy</u> 68 (1971): 3-20.

Frenkel-Brunswik, Else. "Mechanisms of Self-Deception." <u>The Journal of Social Psychology</u> 10 (1939): 409-420.

Freud, Sigmund. <u>Beyond the Pleasure Principle</u>. Translated and edited by James Strachey. New York: W. W. Norton & Co., 1961.

_____. <u>Character and Culture</u>. Edited by Philip Rieff. New York: Collier Books, 1963.

_____. <u>Collected Papers</u>, II. Translated by Joan Rivieri. New York: Basic Books, 1959.

_____. <u>The Ego and the Id</u>. Translated by Joan Riviere. Edited by James Strachey. New York: W. W. Norton & Co., 1960, 1962.

_____. <u>Inhibitions, Symptoms and Anxiety</u>. Translated by Alix Strachey. Edited by James Strachey. New York: W. W. Norton & Co., 1959.

_____. <u>Introductory Lectures on Psychoanalysis</u>. Translated and edited by James Strachey. New York: W. W. Norton & Co., Liveright Book, 1977.

_____. <u>The Future of an Illusion</u>. Translated and edited by James Strachey. New York: W. W. Norton & Co., 1961.

_____. <u>General Psychological Theory</u>. Edited by Philip Rieff. New York: Collier Books, 1963.

_____. <u>The Question of Lay Analysis</u>. Translated by James Strachey. New York: W. W. Norton, 1959, 1960.

_____. <u>Sexuality and the Psychology of Love</u>. Edited by Philip Rieff. New York: Collier Books, 1963, 1974.

_____. <u>Therapy and Technique</u>. Edited by Philip Rieff. New York: Collier Books, 1963, 1967.

Frondizi, Risieri. <u>The Nature of the Self: A Functional Interpretation</u>. Carbondale: Southern Illinois University Press, 1953, 1971.

Gabel, Joseph. False Consciousness: An Essay on Reification. Translated by Margaret A. Thompson. New York: Harper Torchbooks, 1962, 1978.

Gardiner, Patrick L. "Error, Faith, and Self-Deception." In The Philosophy of Mind. Edited by Jonathan Glover. Oxford: Oxford University Press, 1976.

Geach, Peter. Mental Acts: Their Content and Their Objects. New York: Humanities Press 1957.

Gert, Bernard. The Moral Rules: A New Rational Foundation for Morality. New York: Harper Torchbook, 1966, 1973.

Gide, André. Madeline. Translated by Justin O'Brien. New York: Bantam Books, 1968.

_____. Two Symphonies (La Symphonie Pastorale). Translated by Dorothy Bussy. New York: Alfred A. Knopf, 1954.

Goldman, Alvin I. A Theory of Human Action. Princeton: Princeton University Press, 1970.

Good, Edwin M. Irony in the Old Testament. Sheffield: Almond Press, 1965, 1981.

Grice, Paul. "Method in Philosophical Psychology (From the Banal to the Bizarre)." Proceedings of the American Philosophical Association LXVIII (1974-75): 23-53.

Grube, G. M. A. Plato's Thought. Boston: Beacon Press, 1938, 1966.

Gur, Ruben C. and Sackeim, Harold A. "Self-Deception: A Concept in Search of a Phenomenon." Journal of Personality and Social Psychology 37,2 (February 1979): 147-69.

Gustavson, Donald F., ed. Essays in Philosophical Psychology. Garden City: Doubleday & Co., Anchor Books, 1964.

Guthrie, Jerry L. "Self-Deception and Emotional Response to Fiction." The British Journal of Aesthetics 21, 1 (Winter 1981): 65-75.

Haight, M. R. A Study of Self-Deception. Atlantic Highlands: Humanities Press, 1980.

Hamlyn, D. W. "Review: A Study of Self-Deception by M. R. Haight." Philosophical Quarterly 32, 127 (April 1982): 184-85.

_____. "Self-Deception." Aristotelian Society, Supplementary Volume 45 (1971): 45-60.

_____. "Unconscious Intentions." Philosophy XLVI, 175 (January 1975): 12-22.

Hampshire, Stuart. Thought and Action. New York: Viking Press, 1959.

Hare, R. M. The Language of Morals. New York: Oxford University Press, 1981.

_____. Freedom and Reason. New York: Oxford University Press, 1981.

_____. Moral Thinking: Its Levels, Method and Point. Oxford: Oxford University Press, 1981.

Hauerwas, Stanley (with David B. Burrell). "Self-Deception and Autobiography: Reflections on Speer's Inside the Third Reich." In Truthfulness and Tragedy: Further Investigations Into Christian Ethics. Notre Dame: University of Notre Dame Press, 1977.

Hawthorne, Nathaniel. The Scarlet Letter. Cambridge: The Riverside Press, 1883.

Hazelton, Roger. Pascal: The Genius of His Thought. Philadelphia: Westminster Press, 1974.

Hegel, G. W. F. The Phenomenology of Spirit. Translated by H. V. Miller. New York: Oxford University Press, 1977, 1979.

Hilgard, E. R. "Human Motives and the Concept of Self." American Psychologist 4, 9 (September 1949): 374-82.

_____. "A Neodissociation Interpretation of Pain Reduction in Hypnosis." Psychological Review 80, 5 (September 1973): 396-411.

Hill, Thomas E., Jr. "Servility and Self-Respect." In Rights. Edited by David Lyons. Belmont, CA: Wadsworth Publishing Co., 1979.

Holborow, L. C. "Blame, Praise and Credit." Proceedings of the Artistotelian Society. N. S. LXXII (1971-72): 85-100.

Holmer, Paul L. The Grammar of Faith. New York: Harper & Row, 1978.

_____. "Something about What Makes It Funny." Soundings LVII, 2 (Summer 1972): 157-74.

Holmes, D. S. "Investigations of Repression: Differential Recall of Material Experimentally or Naturally Associated With Ego Threat." Psychological Bulletin 81, 10 (October 1974): 632-53.

Hong, Howard V. & Hong, Edna H., eds. Søren Kierkegaard's Journals and Papers, Vol. 1, A-E. Bloomington: Indiana University Press, 1967.

Hook, Sidney, ed. Psychoanalysis, Scientific Method and Philosophy: A Symposium. New York: New York University Press, 1959.

Howie, Duncan. "Perceptual Defense." Psychological Review 59 (1952): 308-15.

Hume, David. A Treatise of Human Nature. Edited by L. A. Selby-Bigge. Oxford: Clarendon Press, 1968.

_____. "Of Self-Love." In An Inquiry Concerning the Principles of Morals. Edited by Charles W. Hindel. Indianapolis: The Bobbs-Merrill Co., 1957.

Irwin. F. W. Intentional Behavior and Motivation: A Cognitive Theory. Philadelphia: Lippincott, 1971.

James, Henry. The Princess Casamassima. New York: Harper & Row, 1968.

James, William. The Principles of Psychology, I. New York: Dover Publications, 1950.

_____. The Varieties of Religious Experience: A Study of Human Nature. New York: Modern Library, 1929.

_____. "The Will to Believe." The Will to Believe and Other Essays in Popular Psychology, pp. 1-31. New York: Dover Publications, 1956.

Johnson, Samuel. Selected Essays. Edited by W. J. Bate. New Haven: Yale University Press, 1968.

Kant, Immanuel. The Doctrine of Virtue, Part II of the Metaphysic of Morals. Translated by Mary J. Gregor. New York: Harper Torchbooks, 1964.

_____. Lectures on Ethics. Translated by Louis Infield. Preface by L.W. Beck. Indianapolis: Hackett Publishing Co., 1980.

_____. Religion Within the Limits of Reason Alone. Translated by Theodore M. Greene and Hoyt H. Hudson. New York: Harper & Row, Harper Torchbook, 1960.

Kaufmann, Walter. Existentialism from Dostoyevsky to Sartre. Cleveland: World Publishing Co., 1956.

Kellenberger, J. "The Death of God and the Death of Persons." Religious Studies 16, 3 (September 1980): 263-82.

Kenevan, Phyllis B. "Self-Consciousness and the Ego." In The Philosophy of Jean-Paul Sartre. Edited by Phillip A. Schlipp. La Salle: Open Court, 1981.

Kenney, Anthony. Action, Emotion and Will. London: Routledge & Kegan Paul, 1963.

Ketchum, Sara Ann. "Moral Redescription and Political Self-Deception." In Sexist Language, pp. 279-89. Edited by Mary Vetterling-Braggin. Totowa: Rowman & Littlefield, 1981.

Kierkegaard, Søren. Concluding Unscientific Postscript. Translated by David F. Swenson and Walter Lowrie. Princeton: Princeton University Press, 1941, 1968.

_____. The Concept of Anxiety. Translated and edited by Reidar Thomte, with Albert B. Anderson. Princeton: Princeton University Press, 1980.

_____. Either/Or, Vol. I. Translated by David F. Swenson and Lilian M. Swenson. Princeton: Princeton University Press, 1944, 1971.

_____. Either/Or, Vol. II. Translated by Walter Lowrie. Revised and foreword by Howard A. Johnson. Princeton: Princeton University Press, 1959, 1971.

_____. The Point of View for My Work as an Author. Translated by Walter Lowrie. Edited by Benjamin Nelson. New York: Harper & Row, Harper Torchbooks, 1962.

_____. Purity of Heart is to Will One Thing. Translated by Douglas V. Steere. New York: Harper & Row, Harper Torchbooks, 1938, 1956.

_____. The Sickness Unto Death. Translated and edited by Howard V. and Edna H. Hong. Princeton: Princeton University Press.

_____. Works of Love. Translated by Howard V. & Edna H. Hong. New York: Harper Torchbooks, 1962, 1964.

King-Farlow, John. "Akrasia, Self-Mastery and the Master Self." Pacific Philosophical Quarterly 62 (January 1981): 47-60.

_____. "Critical Notice." Metaphilosophy 4, 1 (1973): 502-14.

_____. "Deception? Assertion? Or Second-String Verbiage?" Philosophy 56, 215 (January 1981): 100-105.

_____. "Self-Deceivers and Sartrian Seducers." Analysis 23, 6 (June 1963): 131-36.

Kipp, David. "On Self-Deceivers." Philosophical Quarterly 30 (October 1980): 305-17.

Korner, Stephan, ed. Practical Reason. New Haven: Yale University Press, 1974.

Lemmon, E. J. "Moral Dilemmas." Philosophical Review 71 (April 1962): 139-58.

Lukes, Steven. "Moral Weakness." In Weakness of Will, pp. 147-59. Edited by G. W. Mortimore. London and Basingstoke: Macmillan & Co., St. Martins, 1971.

Lyons, William. "Emotions and Behavior." Philosophy and Phenomenological Research, 38, 3 (March 1978): 410-418.

MacIntyre, Alasdair. After Virtue: A Study in Moral Theory. Notre Dame: University of Notre Dame Press, 1981.

_____. The Unconscious: A Conceptual Analysis. Atlantic Highlands: Humanities Press, 1958.

Mackey, Louis. Kierkegaard: A Kind of Poet. Philadelphia: University of Pennsylvania Press, 1971, 1972.

Martin, Michael W. "Factor's Functionalist Account of Self-Deception." Personalist 60, 3 (July 1979): 336-42.

_____. "Immorality and Self-Deception." Dialogue (Canada) 16 (June 1977): 245-73.

_____. "Morality and Self-Deception: Paradox, Ambiguity or Vagueness." Man and World 12 (1979): 47-60.

_____. "Sartre on Lying to Oneself." Philosophical Research Archive 4, 1252 (1978): 27-54.

_____. "Self-Deception, Self-Pretense and Emotional Detachment." Mind 88 (July 1979): 441-46.

Meehl, P. E. and Hathaway, S. R. "The K Factor as a Suppressor Variable in the Minnesota Multiphasic Personality Inventory." Journal of Applied Psychology 30,5 (October 1946): 525-64.

Melden, A. I. Free Action. New York: Humanities Press, 1961.

Miri, Mrinal. "Self-Deception." Philosophy and Phenomenological Research 34, 4 (1974): 576-85.

Mischel, Theodore. "Understanding Neurotic Behavior: From Mechanism to Intentionality." In Understanding Other Persons, pp. 216-59. Edited by Theodore Mischel. Oxford: Basil Blackwell, 1974.

Morris, Phyllis S. "Self-Deception: Sartre's Resolution of the Paradox." In Jean-Paul Sartre, pp. 30-49. Edited by Hugh Silverman. Pittsburg: Duquense University Press, 1980.

Mortimore, G. W., ed. Weakness of Will. London and Basingstoke: Macmillan & Co., St. Martins, 1971.

Mounce, H. O. "Self-Deception." Aristotelian Society, Supplementary Volume 45 (1971): 61-72.

Murphy, Gardner. "Experiments in Overcoming Self-Deception." Psychophysiology 6 (1970): 790-99.

_____. Outgrowing Self-Deception. New York: Basic Books, 1975.

Niebuhr, Reinhold. "The Christian Conception of Sin." An Interpretation of Christian Ethics. Cleveland: World Publishing Co, 1935, 1975.

_____. The Nature and Destiny of Man, I. New York: Charles Scribner's Sons, 1941.

Norris, Frank. McTeague: A Story of San Francisco. New York: New American Library, 1964.

Palmer, Anthony. "Characterizing Self-Deception." Mind 88 (January 1979): 45-58.

_____. "Self-Deception: A Problem about Autobiography." Aristotelian Society, Supplementary Volume 53 (1979): 61-76.

Paluch, Stanley. "Self-Deception." Inquiry 10 (Fall 1967): 268-78.

Paskow, Alan. "Towards a Theory of Self-Deception." Man and World. 12 (1979): 178-91.

Pears, David. "The Paradoxes of Self-Deception." In Questions in the Philosophy of Mind, pp. 80-96. Edited by David Pears. London: Gerald Duckworth & Co., 1975.

_____. "When I Disagrees with Me." Times Literary Supplement 4073 (24 April 1981).

Pieper, Josef. The Four Cardinal Virtues. Notre Dame: University of Notre Dame Press, 1966.

Penelhum, Terence. "Pleasure and Falsity." In Philosophy of MInd, pp. 242-265. Edited by Stuart Hampshire. New York: Harper and Row, 1966.

Peters, R. S. The Concept of Motivation. Atlantic Highlands: Humanities Press, 1958.

Perry, John, ed. Personal Identity. Berkeley: University of California Press, 1975.

Phillips, D. Z. "Bad Faith and Sartre's Waiter." Philosophy 56, 215 (January 1981): 23-31.

Pierce, Charles Sanders. "The Fixation of Belief." In Pragmatism: The Classic Writings, pp. 61-78. Edited by H. S. Thayer. Indianapolis: Hackett Publishing Co., 1982.

Plato. The Collected Dialogues of Plato. Edited by Edith Hamilton and Huntington Cairnes. Princeton: Princeton University Press, 1961, 1971.

Poe, Edgar Allen. The Complete Tales and Poems of Edgar Allen Poe. New York: Modern Library, 1938.

Price, H. H. "Half Belief." Aristotelian Society, Supplementary Volume 38 (1964): 339-61.

Pugmire, David. "Strong Self-Deception." inquiry 12 (Fall 1969): 339-361.

Rawls, John. A Theory of Justice. Cambridge: Harvard University Press, 1971.

Reilly, Richard. "Self-Deceit: Resolving the Epistemological Paradox." Personalist 57 (Autumn 1976): 391-94.

Richards, David A. J. A Theory of Reasons for Action. Oxford: Clarendon Press, 1971.

Ricoeur, Paul. Freud and Philosophy: An Essay on Interpretation. Translated by Denis Savage. New Haven: Yale University Press, 1970.

Rieff, Philip. *Freud: The Mind of the Moralist*. 3rd ed. Chicago: University of Chicago Press, 1959, 1979.

Robinson, Jonathan. *Duty and Hypocrisy in Hegel's "Phenomenology of Mind": An Essay in the Real and the Ideal*. Toronto: Toronto University Press, 1977.

Rorty, Amelie Oskenberg. "Adaptability and Self-Knowledge." *Inquiry* 18, 1 (Spring 1975): 1-22.

_____. "Akrasia and Pleasure: Nicomachean Ethics Book 7." In *Essays on Aristotle's Ethics*, pp. 267-284. Edited by Amelie Oskenberg Rorty. Berkeley: University of California Press, 1980.

_____. "Belief and Self-Deception." *Inquiry* 15 (Winter 1972): 387-410.

_____. "Self-Deception, Akrasia and Irrationality." *Social Sciences Information* 19, 6 (1980): 905-922.

_____. "Where Does the Akratic Break Take Place?" *Australasian Journal of Philosophy* 58 (December 1980): 333-346.

Rudin, Josef. *Psychotherapy and Religion*. Translated by Elisabeth Reinecke and Paul C. Bailey. Notre Dame: University of Notre Dame Press, 1968.

Russell, J. Michael. "Saying, Feeling and Self-Deception." *Behaviorism* 6 (Spring 1978): 27-43.

Ryle, Gilbert. *The Concept of Mind*. New York: Barnes & Noble, 1949, 1970.

Sackeim, Harold A. and Gur, Ruben C. "Self-Deception, Other Deception, and Self-Reported Psychopathology." *Journal of Consulting and Clinical Psychology* 47 (1979): 213-215.

_____. "Self-Deception, Self-Confrontation, and Consciousness." In *Consciousness and Self-Regulation, Advances in Research and Theory*, Vol II, pp. 139-97. Edited by G. E. Schwartz and D. Shapiro. New York: Plenum Press, 1978.

Santoni, Ronald. "Bad Faith and 'Lying to Oneself.'" *Philosophy and Phenomenological Research* 38 (March 1978): 384-398.

Sartre, Jean-Paul. *Being and Nothingness: An Essay on Phenomenological Ontology*. Translated by Hazel E. Barnes. New York: Philosophical Library, n.d.

Saunders, John Turk. "The Paradox of Self-Deception." *Philosophy and Phenomenological Research* 35 (June 1975): 559-70.

Schafer, Roy. "Emotion in the Language of Action." *Psychological Issues*, Monograph 36. New York: International University Press, 1975.

_____. "The Idea of Resistance." *International Journal of Psychoanalysis* 54 (1973): 259-85.

_____. *A New Language for Psychoanalysis*. New Haven: Yale University Press,

1976.

Schoonenberg, Piet. Man and Sin: A Theological View. Translated by Joseph Donceel. Notre Dame: University of Notre Dame Press, 1965.

Scott-Taggart, M. J. "Socratic Irony and Self-Deceit." Ratio 14 (June 1972): 1-15.

Sidgwick, Henry. The Method of Ethics. 7th ed. Foreword by John Rawls. Indianapolis: Hackett Publishing Co., 1907, 1981.

Shope, Robert K. "Freud on Conscious and Unconscious Intentions." Inquiry 13, 1-2 (Summer 1970): 149-59.

Siegler, Frederick A. "An Analysis of Self-Deception." Nous 2 (May 1968): 147-64.

_____. "Demos on Lying to Oneself." Journal of Philosophy 59 (August 1962): 469-74.

_____. "Self-Deception." Australasian Journal of Philosophy 4 (May 1963): 29-43.

_____. "Self-Deception and Other-Deceptions." Journal of Philosophy LX, 22 (October 1963): 759-64.

_____. "Unconscious Intentions." Inquiry 10, 2 (1967): 251-67.

Simon, Bennet. "Plato and Freud: The Mind in Conflict and the Mind in Dialogue." Psychoanalytic Quarterly 42, 1 (1973): 91-122.

Skinner, B. F. About Behaviorism. New York: Alfred A. Knopf Co., 1974.

_____. Science and Human Behavior. New York: The Free Press, Macmillan, 1953, 1965.

Solomon, Robert. The Passions. Garden City: Doubleday & Co., Anchor Books, 1977.

Sperry, R. W. "Hemispheric Deconnection and Unity in Conscious Awareness." American Psychologist 23,10 (October 1968): 723-33.

Steffen, Lloyd H. "Toward a Christian Conception of Selfhood." Unpublished Master's Thesis, Newton Centre, MA: Andover Newton Theological School, 1978.

_____. "Self-Deception: A Conceptual Analysis in Three Relational Contexts." Ann Arbor: University Microfilms, 1984. Dissertation, Brown University.

Stone, Robert V. "Sartre on Bad Faith and Authenticity." In The Philosophy of Jean-Paul Sartre, pp. 246-56. Edited by Paul A. Schlipp. La Salle: Open Court, 1981.

Szabados, Bela. "Fingarette on Self-Deception." Philosophical Papers 6 (May 1977): 21-30.

_____. "Hypocrisy." <u>Canadian Journal of Philosophy</u> 9 (June 1979): 195-210.

_____. "The Morality of Self-Deception." <u>Dialogue</u> (Canada) 13 (March 1974): 25-34.

_____. "Rorty on Belief and Self-Deception." <u>Inquiry</u> 17 (Winter 1974): 464-73.

_____. "Self-Deception." <u>Canadian Journal of Philosophy</u> 4, 1 (September 1974): 51-68.

_____. "Wishful Thinking and Self-Deception." <u>Analysis</u> 33 (June 1973): 201-05.

Taylor, A. E. <u>Socrates: The Man and His Thought</u>. New York: Doubleday Anchor Books, 1953.

Taylor, C. C. W. "Plato, Hare and Davidson on Akrasia." <u>Mind</u> 89 (October 1980): 499-518.

Taylor, Mark C. "Humor and Humorist." In <u>Concepts and Alternatives in Kierkegaard</u>, pp. 220-28. Edited by Marie M. Thulstrup. Copenhagen: C. A. Reitzels Boghandel, 1980.

_____. "Kierkegaard on the Structure of Selfhood." <u>Kierkegaardiana</u> 9 (1974): 84-103.

_____. "Psychoanalytic Dimensions of Kierkegaard's View of Selfhood." <u>Philosophy Today</u> 19 (1975): 198-212.

Thomas, D. M. <u>The White Hotel</u>. New York: Pocket Books, 1981, 1982.

Tillich, Paul. <u>Dynamics of Faith</u>. New York: Harper Torchbooks, 1957.

Toulmin, Stephen. "Self-Knowledge and Knowledge of the Self." In <u>The Self: Psychological and Philosophical Issues</u>, pp. 291-317. Edited by Theodore Mischel. Totowa: Rowman and Littlefield, 1977.

Updike, John. <u>Couples</u>. New York: Alfred A. Knopf, 1968.

Ver Eecke, W. "Epistemological Consequences of Freud's Theory of Negation." <u>Man and World</u> 14, 2 (1981): 111-125.

Vlastos, Gregory. "The Paradox of Socrates." In <u>The Philosophy of Socrates: A Collection of Critical Essays</u>, pp. 1-21. Edited by Gregory Vlastos. Garden City: Doubleday & Co., Anchor Books, 1971.

Walker, Jeremy. "Kierkegaard's Concept of Truthfulness." <u>Inquiry</u> 12, 2 (Summer 1969): 209-224.

_____. <u>To Will One Thing: Reflections on Kierkegaard's "Purity of Heart."</u> Montreal: McGill-Queens University Press, 1972.

Wallace, James D. <u>Virtues and Vices</u>. Ithaca: Cornell University Press, 1978.

Walter, Edmond. "The Logic of Emotion." Southern Journal of Philosophy 10 (Spring 1972): 71-78.

Warnock, G. J. The Object of Morality. London: Methuen & Co., 1971.

Wheelwright, Philip. Metaphor and Reality. Bloomington: Indiana University Press, 1968, 1973.

Wilde, Fr.-Eb. "Concept." In Concepts and Alternatives in Kierkegaard, pp. 18-32. Edited by Marie M. Thulstrup. Copenhagen: C. A. Reitzels Boghandel, 1980.

Wilder, Amos N. The Language of the Gospel. New York: Harper & Row, 1964.

Williams, Bernard. Descartes: The Project of Pure Inquiry. Atlantic Highlands: Humanities Press, 1978.

_____. Problems of the Self: Philosophical Papers, 1965-1972. Cambridge: Cambridge University Press, 1973.

Wilshire, Bruce. "Self, Body and Self-Deception." Man and World 5 (November 1972): 422-47.

Wilson, Catherine. "Self-Deception and Psychological Realism." Philosophical Investigations 3, 4 (Fall 1980): 47-60.

Winch, Peter, "Meaning and Religious Language." In Reason and Religion, pp. 193-221. Edited by Stuart Brown. Ithaca: Cornell University Press, 1977.

Wisdom, John. "Gods." In Logic and Language, First Series, pp. 187-206. Edited A. G. N. Flew. Oxford: Basil Blackwell, 1963.

_____. "Psychoanalytic Theories of the Unconscious." In The Encyclopedia of Philosophy, VIII, pp. 189-94.

Wittgenstein, Ludwig. The Blue and Brown Books. New York: Harper & Row, Harper Torchbooks, 1958, 1965.

_____. Notebooks: 1914-1916. Translated by G. E. M. Anscombe. Edited by G. H. von Wright and G. E. M. Anscombe. New York: Harper Torchbooks, 1961-1968.

_____. Philosophical Investigations. 3rd edition. Translated by G. E. M. Anscombe. New York: Macmillan, 1958, 1968.

_____. Remarks on the Philosophy of Psychology. 2 vols. Translated by C. G. Luckhardt and A. E. Ave. Edited by G. E. M. Anscombe, G. H. von Wright and Heikki Nyman. Chicago: University of Chicago Press, 1980.

_____. Zettle. Translated by G. E. M. Anscombe. Edited by G. E. M. Anscombe and G. H. von Wright. Berkeley: University of California Press, 1970.

Wolf, Ernest S. "Irrationality in a Psychoanalytic Psychology of the Self." In The Self: Psychological and Philosophical Perspectives, pp. 203-223.

Edited by Theodore Mischel. Totowa: Rowman & Littlefield, 1977.

Wolheim, Richard. *Sigmund Freud*. Cambridge: Cambridge University Press, 1971, 1981.

_____. "Wish-fulfillment." In *Rational Action: Studies in Philosophy and Social Science*, pp. 47-60. Edited by Ross Harrison. Cambridge: Cambridge University Press, 1979.

Wundt, Wilhelm. *An Introduction to Psychology*. New York: Macmillan, 1912.

Zeller, Eduard. *Outlines of the History of Greek Philosophy*. Translated by L. R. Palmer. Cleveland: World Publishing Co., Meridian Books, 1965.

INDEX

Abelson, R. 17,165,169,170,221, 225,234,259,363,366
Alston, W. 17,57,60,108,220
Angeles, P. 17,117
Aquinas, T. 25,104,293,294,304, 316,329,330,368,368,369
Aristotle 234,238,243,246,291, 293,364,365
Audi, R. 105,131,216,217
Augustine, 199,227,314-17,331-34,364-369,370,376
Aune, B. 106
Austin, J. 18
Ayer, A. 5
Bach, K. 138-146,152, 218,219
Baier, K. 364-65
Barth, K. 303,305,317,329,336, 337,364,368,369,371
Beck, L. 114
Bell, R. 18
Berger, P. 215
Bok, S. 103
Bonhoeffer, D. 104,105,326
Brown, L. 115,222
Brunner, E. 335,336,371
Burgess, A. 18
Butler, J. 21,103,262,271,367
Calvin, J. 335,371,
Canfield, J. 79,80,85,114,115, 138,143,150,159,219
Champlin, T. 114,216
Chisholm, R. 103,199,265,365, 367
Clifford, W. 133-36,158,217, 265-70,272,273,277,279, 280,281,296,367
Collingwood, R.G. 262,366
Cragg, G. 364
Crites, S. 107,116,220
Daly, M. 176
Davidson, D. 106,234,247,253, 259,260,363-65
Day, W. 108
Demos, R. 79,91,98,103,114,138, 143,159,365
Descartes, R. 65,110,166-67,302
de Sousa, R. 155,220,221
Dilham, I. 18
Donovan, P. 118
Drengson, A. 119,161,162,215,221
Durandin, G. 17
Edwards,J. 313,329,335,338,339, 371

Eliot, G. 18,125,215
Erikson, E. 223
Evans, D. 385
Exdell, J. 105,131,216
Factor, R. L. 216,217
Fingarette, H. 52,66,67,91,107, 112-116,137,138,142,153-62, 169,178,179,193,200,219-22, 224,225,262-64,366-368,372
Foss, J. 80,87,103,115,116
Foucault, M. 18
Fox, M. 113
Frenkel-Brunswik, E. 97-99,113, 116
Freud, S. 37-40,44,46-48,66,67, 78,84,85,91,105,106,115,157, 163-77,182,192-97,199,200, 224,229,260,262,263,275, 333,358,366,377,380,381, 214,221-23
Frondizi, R. 108
Gardiner, P. 107,215,264,295, 296,368
Geach, P. 17
Gert, B. 104
Gide, A. 18,121,125,170,181,215, 216
Goldman, A. 218
Good, E. 385
Grube, G. 115
Gur, R. (See Sackeim, H.)
Gustavson, D. (See Canfield, J.)
Guthrie, J. 215
Hamlyn, D. 79,111,114,365
Haight, M. 19,34,105,110,114, 147-49,219,245,252
Hampshire, S. 114
Hare, R. 152,219,234,253,259,363 364
Hauerwas, S. 216
Hawthorne, N. 18,125,215
Hazelton, R. 333,370
Hegel, G. 21,103
Heidegger, M. 176
Hilgard, E. 116
Hobbes, T. 17,27,243
Holmer, P. 17,385
Howie, D. 110,111,252
Hume, D. 108,152,219,368
James, H. 18,123,215
James, W. 8,9,10,18,66,111, 125,130,133,199,227,265
Jung, C. 108,380

Kant, I. 27,30,78,104,105,114, 114,199,227,225,262,263, 283-85,288,337,366,367,371
Kaufmann, W. 225
Kenney, A. 107,220
Ketchum, S. 18
Kierkegaard, S. ix,12-14,18,90, 98,111,123,175,176,224,232, 247,253,256,257,262,303, 305,309,321,325,362,364-66, 369,370,372-74,377,379,381-84
King-Farlow, J. 85,86,104,116, 164,221,244,295,296,365,368
Kipp, D. 22,103,106,215
Kohut, H. 58,109
Lemmon, E. 253,259,365
Luther, M. 338,371,377
MacIntyre, A. 106,367
McNally, P. 114
Malcolm, N. 18
Martin, M. 224,262,366
Matthews, G. 234,363
Meehl, P. 116
Mischel, T. 46,106,108,170,173, 195,224
Morris, P. 115,221,222,224
Mounce, H. 81,111,115
Mullen, J. 18,372
Murphy, G. 90,91,97-99,116,356, 373,380,385
Nell, O. 262,366
Niebuhr, R. 105,306,315,317,329, 333,337,368,369,371
Norris, F. 61,109,176
Olsen, C. 114
Otto, R. 29,105
Palmer, A. 122,123,215,216
Paluch, S. 110,252
Pascal, B. 305,3311,317,327,329 333,334,368,369,370
Paskow, A. 82,115
Paul, St. 66,111,235,237,239-41,244,255,258,333,334,364
Pears, D. 82,103,114,115
Penelhum, T. 79,80,114,115, 138,139,143,159,
Phillips, D. 18
Pieper, J. 367
Plato, 21,66,98,103,134,262,363 365
Poe, E. 254,255-258,366
Pugmire, D. 110
Quine, W. 115
Rahner, K. 326

Rawls, J. 367
Reilly, R. 114
Rieff, P. 112,168,171,222,223, 366
Ritschl, A. 306,368
Rorty, A. 85,86,108,116,164,165, 179,220,221,225,241,264,273, 295,296,363-65,368
Ryle, G. 8,17,111,123,148,152, 219
Santoni, R. 224
Sackeim, H. 19,91-94,96-99,107, 112,116-18,147,198,199
Sartre, J.-P. 10,21,48,54,71,78-79,82-85,91,98,100,103,107, 107,112-15,137,157,163,166, 167,169,170,172,176-197, 199,200,214,220,222,224,225-227,229,260,262,308,363,377, 383,
Saunders, J. 114,115,197
Schafer, R. 170,223,224
Schoonenberg, P. 306,368
Self-Deception, examples: seasick, 41-43; employer, 67 ff.; public speaker, 71; homosexual, 71 ff.; fear of flying, 81; Gide's pastor, 125 ff; Lon Nol, 131 ff; Clifford's shipowner, 133; David and Nathan, 271-73; cancer patient, 278 ff; theological 326 ff.
Sidgwick, H. 102,243
Siegler, F. 81,103,105,115,143
Skinner, B. 58,108
Socrates 233,242,246-57,265, 376
Steffen, L. 18,108,111,221,222
Szabados, B. 80,107,115,116,138 142,150,152,215,217-19,262, 295,296,366,368,380,385
Taylor, A. 248-52,365
Thomas, D. 168,222
Tillich, P. 305,368,385
Tolstoy, L. 10,18
Toulmin, S. 57,108-110
Updike, J. 377,385
Urmson, J. 18
Vlastos, G. 254,259,365
Wallace, J. 297,368
Warnock, J. 18,104,105
Wheelwright, P. 221
Williams, B. 108,110
Wilson, C. 233,363

Wisdom, J.   74,81,113
Wittgenstein, L.   11,17,18,48
    106,376,385
Wolf, E.   58,109
Wolheim, R.   114,223
Zeller, E.   365

Michael J. Zimmerman

AN ESSAY ON HUMAN ACTION

American University Studies: Series V, Philosophy. Vol. 5
ISBN 0-8204-0122-6   335 pp.   pb./lam., US $ 31.—
Recommended prices – alterations reserved

An *Essay on Human Action* seeks to provide a comprehensive, detailed, enlightening, and (in its detail) original account of human action. This account presupposes a theory of events as abstract, proposition-like entities, a theory which is given in the first chapter of the book. The core-issues of action-theory are then treated: what acting in general is (a version of the traditional volitional theory is proposed and defended); how actions are to be individuated; how long actions last; what acting intentionally is; what doing one thing by doing another is; what basic action is; and what omitting to do something is. Attention is also given to the concepts of causation, intention, volition, deciding, choosing, and trying. Finally, a libertarian account of free action is tentatively proposed and defended.

Contents: Three theories: of events; of human action; of free action.

PETER LANG PUBLISHING, INC.
62 West 45th Street
USA – New York, NY 10036